HISTORY OF THE
REFORMATION IN GERMANY

LEOPOLD von RANKE

HISTORY
OF THE
REFORMATION
IN
GERMANY

VOLUME I

FREDERICK UNGAR PUBLISHING CO.
NEW YORK

Translated by Sarah Austin

Edited by Robert A. Johnson

Republished 1966

Reprinted from the edition of 1905

Printed in the United States of America

Library of Congress Catalog Card No. 66-26513

TRANSLATOR'S PREFACE

It is, perhaps, necessary to offer some apology for the space occupied by the notes, in consequence of the plan I have adopted in respect of a large portion of them. The German authorities cited are chiefly contemporaneous—many of them unprinted, and drawn from different parts of the vast empire through which the German tongue is spoken. They abound in obsolete and provincial forms—if indeed the word provincial can be applied to any of the varieties of a language, no one of which then claimed a metropolitan authority,—and present difficulties, which even a German, if unprepared by special studies, often finds, to say the least, extremely perplexing.

To secure the reader, therefore, against any errors I may have fallen into, and in order that, if important, they may be pointed out, I have placed the original within reach. I hope the translations may give some idea of the light these notes throw on individual as well as national character. We find in them one source of the vigour and animation of the portraits, and the dramatic vivacity of the scenes, with which this history abounds. We see that the author has lived with his heroes, and listened to their own homely and expressive language.

I have much greater need of the indulgent construction of the reader in behalf of some few notes which I have ventured to add. Nothing but my own belief, and the assurance of others, that they were absolutely necessary to the understanding of certain passages in the work, would have induced me to risk such a departure from my proper province. Names of institutions and of offices scarcely ever admit of a translation. Words analogous in form, or allied in origin, generally express a totally different set of acts or functions in different countries, and can therefore only mislead. And if such names convey false ideas, others again convey none at all. Being compelled to endeavour to affix some tolerably distinct notions to the words of this class which I had to interpret, I ventured to think that the little information I had gathered for myself might not be unacceptable to the less learned of my readers. The scanty nature of it will hardly surprise them, and will, I hope, be pardoned. I have at least sought it in the most authentic and unquestioned sources.

I may perhaps be allowed to say, in extenuation of any defects in the

v

translation, that I have found it by far more difficult and laborious than any I had before attempted : indeed, had I clearly foreseen all the difficulty and labour, it is probable I should not have undertaken it, especially when cut off from the assistance and the resources which England or Germany would have afforded me.   Those who are acquainted with the original will, I am sure, be disposed to regard my attempt to put it into English with indulgence ;—and of those who are not, I must ask it.   While the gravity and importance of the subject demanded an unusually scrupulous fidelity, the difficulty of combining that fidelity with a tolerable attention to form, has been far greater than I ever encountered.   If in translating the " History of the Popes," I was anxious not to discolour, in the slightest degree, the noble impartiality which distinguishes that work, I have felt it equally incumbent on me not to heighten or diminish by a shade the more decidedly protestant tone which the author has given to his " History of the Reformation."   Whatever, therefore, might be my desire to offer to the English public a book not altogether uncouth or repulsive in style, it has always been inferior to my anxiety not to misrepresent the author, as much as that has been subordinate to my sense of the reverence due to the subject, and to truth.

S. A.

AUTHOR'S PREFACE

FROM the first ten years of the fifteenth century to the beginning of the thirty years' war, the constitution and political condition of Germany were determined by the periodical diets and the measures there resolved on.

The time was long past in which the public affairs of the country were determined by one supreme will ; but its political life had not yet (as at a later period) retreated within the several boundaries of the constituent members of the empire. The imperial assemblies exercised rights and powers which, though not accurately defined, were yet the comprehensive and absolute powers of sovereignty. They made war and peace ; levied taxes ; exercised a supreme supervision, and were even invested with executive power. Together with the deputies from the cities, and the representatives of the counts and lords, appeared the emperor and the sovereign princes in person. It is true they discussed the most important affairs of their respective countries in their several colleges, or in committees chosen from the whole body, and the questions were decided by the majority of voices. The unity of the nation was represented by these assemblies. Within the wide borders of the empire nothing of importance could occur which did not here come under deliberation ; nothing new arise, which must not await its final decision and execution here.

In spite of all these considerations, the history of the diets of the empire has not yet received the attention it deserves. The Recesses[1] of the

---

[1] The Recess (*Abschied*—literally, Departure ; called by the jurists of the empire, Recessus, was the document wherewith the labours of the diet were closed, and in which they were summed up. All the resolutions of the assembly, or the decisions of the sovereign on their proposals or petitions, were collected into one whole, and the session, or, according to the German expression, day (*Tag*), was thus closed with the publication of the Recess. Each separate law, after having passed the two colleges, that of the electors and that of the princes, received the emperor's assent or ratification, and had then the force of law. It was called a Resolution of the Empire (*Reichsschluss* or *Reichsconclusum*). The sum of all the decisions or acts of a diet was called the *Reichsabschied*.

The correspondence of this with the English term Statute will be seen in the following extract : " For all the acts of one session of parliament taken together make properly but one statute ; and therefore when two sessions have been held in one year we usually mention stat. 1 or 2. Thus the Bill of Rights is cited as 1 W. & M. st. 2, c. 2 ; signifying that it is the second chapter or act of the second statute, or the laws made in the second session of parliament in the first year of King William and Queen Mary."—*Blackstone's Comment*, vol. i., p. 85, 15th ed.

The earliest Recesses of the empire are lost. Since the year 1663, as the diet remained constantly sitting down to 1806, no recess, properly so called, could be published.—TRANSL.

vii

diets are sufficiently well known ; but who would judge a deliberative assembly by the final results of its deliberations ? Projects of a systematic collection of its transactions have occasionally been entertained, and the work has even been taken in hand ; but all that has hitherto been done has remained in a fragmentary and incomplete state.

As it is the natural ambition of every man to leave behind him some useful record of his existence, I have long cherished the project of devoting my industry and my powers to this most important work. Not that I flattered myself that I was competent to supply so large a deficiency ; to exhaust the mass of materials in its manifold juridical bearings ; my idea was only to trace with accuracy the rise and development of the constitution of the empire, through a series (if possible unbroken) of the Acts of the Diets.

Fortune was so propitious to my wishes that, in the autumn of 1836, I found in the Archives of the city of Frankfurt a collection of the very kind I wanted, and was allowed access to these precious documents with all the facility I could desire.

The collection consists of ninety-six folio volumes, which contain the Acts of the Imperial Diets from 1414 to 1613. In the earlier part it is very imperfect, but step by step, in proportion as the constitution of the empire acquires form and development, the documents rise in interest. At the beginning of the sixteenth century, from which time the practice of reducing public proceedings to writing was introduced, it becomes so rich in new and important materials, that it lays the strongest hold on the attention. There are not only the Acts, but the reports of the deputies from the cities—the Rathsfreunde,—which generally charm by their frankness and simplicity, and often surprise by their sagacity. I profited by the opportunity to make myself master of the contents of the first sixty-four of these volumes, extending down to the year 1551. A collection of Imperial Rescripts occasionally afforded me valuable contributions.

But I could not stop here. A single town was not in a condition to know all that passed. It was evident that the labours of the electoral and princely colleges were not to be sought for in the records of a city.

In the beginning of the year 1837, I received permission to explore the Royal Archives of the kingdom of Prussia at Berlin, and, in the April of the same year, the State Archives of the kingdom of Saxony at Dresden, for the affairs of the empire during the times of Maximilian I. and Charles V. They were of great value to me ; the former as containing the records of an electorate ; the latter, down to the end of that epoch, those of a sovereign principality. It is true that I came upon many documents which I had already seen at Frankfurt ; but, at the same time, I found a great number of new ones, which gave me an insight into parts of the subject hitherto obscure. None of these collections is, indeed, complete, and many a question which suggests itself remains unanswered ; yet they are in a high degree instructive. They throw a completely new light on the character and conduct of such influential princes as Joachim II. of Brandenburg, and still more, Maurice of Saxony.

Let no one pity a man who devotes himself to studies apparently so dry, and neglects for them the delights of many a joyous day. It is true that the companions of his solitary hours are but lifeless paper, but they are the remnants of the life of past ages, which gradually assume form and substance to the eye occupied in the study of them. For me (in a preface an author is bound to speak of himself—a subject he elsewhere gladly avoids) they had a peculiar interest.

When I wrote the first part of my " History of the Popes," I designedly treated the origin and progress of the Reformation with as much brevity as the subject permitted. I cherished the hope of dedicating more extensive and profound research to this most important event of the history of my country.

This hope was now abundantly satisfied. Of the new matter which I found, the greater part related, directly or indirectly, to the epoch of the Reformation. At every step I acquired new information as to the circumstances which prepared the politico-religious movement of that time ; the phases of our national life by which it was accelerated ; the origin and working of the resistance it encountered.

It is impossible to approach a matter originating in such intense mental energy, and exercising so vast an influence on the destinies of the world, without being profoundly interested and absorbed by it. I was fully sensible that if I executed the work I proposed to myself, the Reformation would be the centre on which all other incidents and circumstances would turn.

But to accomplish this, more accurate information was necessary as to the progress of opinion in the evangelical[1] party (especially in a political point of view), antecedent to the crisis of the Reformation, than any that could be gathered from printed sources. The Archives common to the

[1] It is, perhaps, hardly necessary to remark, that I have retained this word throughout the following work in its original acceptation ; viz., as denoting the party which, at the time of the Reformation, adhered to the Confession of Augsburg ; the party which declared the Gospel the sole rule of faith. In our own age and country it has been assumed by a party which stands in nearly the same relation to the Church of England as the party called pietistical (*pietistisch*) to the Lutheran Church of Germany. But this did not seem to me a sufficient reason for removing it from its proper and authorized place in German history. The word *protestant* hardly occurs in the original volumes ; and as it suggests another train of ideas and sentiments, I have not introduced it.—TRANSL.

whole Ernestine line of Saxony, deposited at Weimar, which I visited in August, 1837, afforded me what I desired. Nor can any spot be more full of information on the marked epochs at which this house played so important a part, than the vault in which its archives are preserved. The walls and the whole interior space are covered with the rolls of documents relating to the deeds and events of that period. Every note, every draft of an answer, is here preserved. The correspondence between the Elector John Frederick and the Landgrave Philip of Hessen would alone fill a long series of printed volumes. I endeavoured, above all, to make myself master of the two registers, which include the affairs of the empire and of the League of Schmalkald. As to the former, I found, as was to be expected from the nature of the subject, many valuable details ; as to the latter, I hence first drew information which is, I hope, in some degree calculated to satisfy the curiosity of the public.

I feel bound here publicly to express my thanks to the authorities to whom the guardianship of these various archives is entrusted for the liberal aid—often not unattended with personal trouble—which I received from them all.

At length I conceived the project of undertaking a more extensive research into the Archives of Germany. I repaired to the Communal Archives of the house of Anhalt at Dessau, which at the epoch in question shared the opinions and followed the example of that of Saxony ; but I soon saw that I should here be in danger of encumbering myself with too much matter of a purely local character. I remembered how many other documents relating to this period had been explored and employed by the industry of German inquirers. The work of Buchholtz[1] on Ferdinand I. contains a most copious treasure of important matter from those of Austria, of which too little use is made in that state. The instructive writings of Stumpf and Winter[2] are founded on those of Bavaria. The Archives of Würtemberg were formerly explored by Sattler ;[3] those of Hessen, recently, by Rommel[4] and Neudecker. For the more exclusively ecclesiastical view of the period, the public is in possession of a rich mass of authentic documents in the collection of Walch, and the recent editions of Luther's Letters by De Wette ; and still more in those of Melanchthon by Bretschneider. The letters of the deputies from Strasburg and Nürem-

---

[1] Buchholtz, F. B., Geschichte der Regierung Ferdinands I., 9 vols. Vienna, 1831–38.

[2] Winter, V. A., Geschichte der evangelischen Lehre in Baiern, 2 parts. Munich, 1809–10.

[3] Sattler, C. F., Geschichte des Herzogthums Würtemberg, 5 parts. Ulm, 1764–68.

[4] Rommel, Ch. v., Geschichte von Hessen, 10 vols. Marburg and Cassel, 1820–58.

berg,[1] which have been published, throw light on the history of particular diets. It is hardly necessary for me to mention how much has lately been brought together by Förstemann respecting the Diet of Augsburg of 1530, so long the subject of earnest research and labour.

Recent publications, especially in Italy and England, lead us to hope for the possibility of a thorough and satisfactory explanation of the foreign relations of the empire.

I see the time approach in which we shall no longer have to found modern history on the reports even of contemporary historians, except in so far as they were in possession of personal and immediate knowledge of facts ; still less, on works yet more remote from the source ; but on the narratives of eye-witnesses, and the genuine and original documents. For the epoch treated in the following work, this prospect is no distant one. I myself have made use of a number of records which I had found when in the pursuit of another subject, in the Archives of Vienna, Venice, Rome, and especially Florence. Had I gone into further detail, I should have run the risk of losing sight of the subject as a whole ; or in the necessary lapse of time, of breaking the unity of the conception which had arisen before my mind in the course of my past researches.

And thus I proceeded boldly to the completion of this work ; persuaded that when an inquirer has made researches of some extent in authentic records, with an earnest spirit and a genuine ardour for truth, though later discoveries may throw clearer and more certain light on details, they can only strengthen his fundamental conceptions of the subject :— for truth can be but one.

[1] Recent works on this correspondence are : Virch, H., und Winckelmann, O., Politische Korresp. der Stadt Strasburg im Zeitalter der Reformation, 3 vols. Strasburg, 1879–98.

Lüdewig, S., Die Politik Nürnbergs im Zeitalter der Reformation. Göttingen, 1893.

ERRATA

Page 739, note 2, line 8, *for* " his Provisional Government "
read " the Provisional Government " ; line 9, *for* " Thurian
Dampier " *read* " Thurian Dangin."

CONTENTS

Volume I

BOOK V.

BOOK VI.

BIBLIOGRAPHY

THIS short bibliography is compiled for the use of the general reader. No contemporary authorities are given ; for these and for fuller lists of secondary authorities the elaborate bibliographies given in the following works may be consulted : The Cambridge Modern History, Vols. I. and II. (*ut infra*) ; Lavisse and Rambaud, Histoire Générale ; Dahlmann Waitz, Quellenkunde der deutschen Geschichte.

A. GENERAL.

JOHNSON (A. H.). Europe in the Sixteenth Century : 1495–1598 (Periods of European History). 7s. 6d. Rivington, 1897.

Cambridge Modern History, Vol. I., Chaps. ix., xvi., xvii., xviii. ; Vol. II., Chaps. ii.-viii., x., xi., xix. Each 16s. net. Cambridge Press, 1902-1904.

Containing some admirable monographs on various aspects of the period.

ZELLER (J.). Histoire d'Allemagne, Vol. V. : La Réformation. Paris, 1854.

GEIGER (L.). Renaissance und Humanismus in Italien und Deutschland (Oncken's Allgemeine Geschichte in Einzeldarstellungen). Berlin, 1882.

BEZOLD (F. VON). Geschichte der deutschen Reformation (Oncken's series). Berlin, 1890.

Both the above are excellent surveys of the whole period.

JANSSEN (J.). Geschichte des deutschen Volkes seit dem Ausgang des Mittelalters. Freiburg-i.-B., 1897.

—— The same, translated by M. A. Mitchell and A. M. Christie ; *sub tit.*, History of the German People at the close of the Middle Ages. 6 vols. 75s. Paul, 1896-1903.

CREIGHTON (Bp. M.). History of the Papacy, Vols. III.-V. Each 6s. Longman (1882–94), 1897.

By far the best book on the subject in English.

RANKE (LEOPOLD VON). Die römischen Päpste.

—— The same, translated by Mrs. S. Austin ; *sub tit.*, History of the Popes of Rome. 3 vols. 30s. Murray, 1866.

PASTOR (LUDWIG). Geschichte der Päpste.

—— The same, translated by F. J. Antrobus, 4 vols. 48s. net. Paul, 1891–95.

The best book from the Roman-Catholic point of view.

xv

GREGOROVIUS (F.).   Geschichte der Stadt Roma in Mittelalter, Vol. VIII.
—— The same, translated by Annie Hamilton.   9s.   Bell, 1902.
Allgemeine deutsche Biographie.
HERZOG's Realencyclopädie für protestantische Theologie und Kirche.
　　These can always be consulted with confidence on any individual characters.

B. SPECIAL.

ALMAN. Kaiser Maximilian I.
RANKE (LEOPOLD VON).   Deutsche Geschichte im Zeitalter der Reformation.
　　Leipzig, 1881-82.
　　The English translation cannot be recommended.

STRAUSS (D. F.).   Ulrich von Hutten.   Second edition.   2 vols.   Leipzig, 1874.
—— The same, translated by Mrs. George Sturge.   1874.
GEIGER (L.).   Johann Reuchlin : sein Leben und seine Werke.   Leipzig, 1871.
FROUDE (J. A.).   Life and Letters of Erasmus.   3s. 6d.   Longman (1894), 1899.
　　An interesting book, which, however, must be read with caution.

SEEBOHM (F.).   The Oxford Reformers of 1498.   Third edition.   14s.   Longman,
　　1896.
　　John Colet—Erasmus—Thomas More.

ARMSTRONG (E.).   The Emperor Charles V.   2 vols.   21s. net.   Macmillan, 1902.
　　The best English life of the Emperor.

BAUMGARTEN (H.).   Geschichte Karls V.   3 vols.   Stuttgart, 1885–92.
　　The best German life of the Emperor.

MIGNET (F. A. M.).   Rivalité de François I. et de Charles V.   Second edition.
　　2 vols.   Paris, 1875.
　　The best book on the military side.

MAURENBRECHER (W.).   Studien und Skizzen zur Geschichte der Reformationszeit.
　　Leipzig, 1874.
—— Karl V. und die deutschen Protestanten.   Düsseldorf, 1865.
—— Geschichte der katholischen Reformation.   Nördlingen, 1880.
STIRLING MAXWELL (Sir W.).   The Cloister Life of the Emperor Charles V.   1852.
LINDSAY (T. M.).   Luther and the German Reformation.   3s.   Clark, Edinburgh,
　　1900.
BEARD (CHARLES).   The Hibbert Lectures, 1883 : The Reformation in the Six-
　　teenth Century and Modern Thought.   4s. 6d.   Williams and Norgate (1883),
　　1885.
—— Martin Luther and the German Reformation.   16s.   Paul, 1889.
KÖSTLIN (J.).   Martin Luther : sein Leben und seine Schriften.   2 vols.
STAHELIN (R.).   Huldreich Zwingli und sein Reformationswerk.   Halle, 1883.
HENRY (P.).   Das Leben Calvins, 3 vols.   Hamburg, 1835–44.
—— The same, translated by Stebbing ; *sub tit.*, The Life and Times of Calvin.
　　2 vols.   1849.

GUIZOT (F. P. G.). La vie de Quatre grands Chrétiens. Paris, 1873.
—— The same, translated; *sub tit.*, Great Christians of France. 6s. Macmillan (1869), 1878.

Calvin.

KAMPSCHULTE (F. W.). Johann Calvin in Genf.
BAX (E. BELFORT). The Peasants' War in Germany. 6s. Sonnenschein, 1899.
LAMPRECHT (K.). Die Entwickelung des rheinischen Bauernstandes (Westdeutsche Zeitschrift für Geschichte, Bd. VI.).
BRANDENBURG (E.). Moritz von Sachsen. Leipzig, 1898.

C. HISTORICAL GEOGRAPHY.

Consult Clarendon Press Historical Atlas, Nos. 37, 38, 39, and 47. Also Spruner-Menke's Historical Atlas, Nos. 43, 73, and 74.

CHRONOLOGICAL TABLE OF LEADING EVENTS

1508. Luther goes to Wittenberg.
1512. Opening of the Fifth Lateran Council.
1513. Death of Julius II.   Accession of Leo X.
1515. Accession of Francis I.
      Battle of Marignano.
1516. French Concordat with Leo X.
      Death of Ferdinand of Aragon.
      Treaty of Noyon.
1517. Close of the Fifth Lateran Council.
      Publication of Luther's Theses.
1518. Luther before the Cardinal-Legate at Augsburg.
      Zwingli at Zurich.
1519. Death of the Emperor Maximilian.
      Election of Charles V. to the Empire.
1520. Luther excommunicated.
      Publication of Luther's " Appeal to the Christian Nobility."
      Coronation of Charles V. at Aachen.
1521. Diet of Worms.   Luther placed under the ban of the Empire.
      Outbreak of war.   Milan occupied by the imperial and papal forces.
      Death of Leo X.
1522. Election of Adrian VI.
      Luther returns to Wittenberg.
      Battle of Bicocca.
      The Knights' War in Germany.
      Capture of Rhodes by the Turks.
1523. First public Disputation at Zürich.
      Defection of the Constable of Bourbon.
      Bonnivet in Italy.
      Death of Adrian VI.   Succession of Clement VII.
1524. Retreat of Bonnivet.
      The Peasants' War in Germany.
      Francis I. crosses the Alps.
1525. Battle of Pavia.
      Prussia becomes a secular Duchy.
1526. Treaty of Madrid.
      Charles V. marries Isabella of Portugal.
      League of Cognac.

Recess of Spire.
Battle of Mohacz.
Raid of the Colonna on Rome.
Ferdinand elected King of Bohemia and Hungary.
1527. The sack of Rome.
Invasion of Italy by Lautrec.
1528. France and England declare war on the Emperor.
Siege of Naples by Lautrec. Defection of Andrea Doria.
1529. Diet of Spire. "The Protest."
Civil War in Switzerland. First Peace of Cappel.
Treaty of Barcelona.
Peace of Cambray.
Siege of Vienna by the Turks.
Conference of Marburg.
1530. Last imperial coronation by the Pope.
Diets of Augsburg. Confession of Augsburg.
Capture of Florence.
Revolt against the Bishop at Geneva.
1531. Ferdinand elected King of the Romans.
Henry VIII. "Supreme Head of the Church" in England.
Battle of Cappel and death of Zwingli.
League of Schmalkald.
1532. Inquisition established at Lisbon.
Annates abolished in England.
Religious Peace of Nüremburg.
Second conference at Bologna.
1533. English Acts in restraint of appeals to Rome.
Wullenweber Burgomaster of Lübeck.
Address of Cop. Flight of Calvin.
1534. Anabaptist rising at Münster.
Ulrich recovers Würtemburg.
Peace of Cadan.
The Grafenfehde.
Ignatius Loyala founds the Society of Jesus.
Death of Clement VII. Accession of Paul III.

HISTORY

OF THE

REFORMATION IN GERMANY

INTRODUCTION.

VIEW OF THE EARLY HISTORY OF GERMANY.

For purposes of discussion or of instruction, it may be possible to sever ecclesiastical from political history; in actual life, they are indissolubly connected, or rather fused into one indivisible whole.

As indeed there is nothing of real importance in the moral and intellectual business of human life, the source of which does not lie in a profound and more or less conscious relation of man and his concerns to God and divine things, it is impossible to conceive a nation worthy of the name, or entitled to be called, in any sense, great, whose political existence is not constantly elevated and guided by religious ideas. To cultivate, purify and exalt these,—to give them an expression intelligible to all and profitable to all,—to embody them in outward forms and public acts, is its necessary as well as its noblest task.

It is not to be denied that this process inevitably brings into action two great principles which seem to place a nation at variance with itself. Nationality (*i.e.* the sum of the peculiar qualities, habits, and sentiments of a nation) is necessarily restricted within the bounds marked out by neighbouring nationalities; whereas religion, ever since it was revealed to the world in a form which claims and deserves universality, constantly strives after sole and absolute supremacy.

In the foundation or constitution of a State, some particular moral or intellectual principle predominates; a principle prescribed by an inherent necessity, expressed in determinate forms and giving birth to a peculiar condition of society, or character of civilisation. But no sooner has a Church, with its forms of wider application, embracing different nations, arisen, than it grasps at the project of absorbing the State, and of reducing the principle on which civil society is founded to complete subjection: the original underived authority of that principle is, indeed, rarely acknowledged by the Church.

At length the universal religion appears, and, after it has incorporated itself with the consciousness of mankind, assumes the character of a great and growing tradition, handed down from people to people, and communicated in rigid dogmas. But nations cannot suffer themselves to be debarred from exercising the understanding bestowed on them by nature, or the knowledge acquired by study, on an investigation of its truth. In every age, therefore, we see diversities in the views of religion arise in different nations, and these again react in various ways on the character and condition of the State. It is evident, from the nature of this struggle, how mighty is the crisis which it involves for the destinies of the human race. Religious truth must have an outward and visible representation, in order that the State may be perpetually reminded of the origin and the end of our earthly existence; of the rights of our neighbours, and the kindred of all the nations of the earth ; it would otherwise be in danger of degenerating into tyranny, or of hardening into inveterate prejudice,— into intolerant conceit of self, and hatred of all that is foreign. On the other hand, a free development of the national character and culture is necessary to the interests of religion. Without this, its doctrines can never be truly understood nor profoundly accepted : without incessant alternations of doubt and conviction, of assent and dissent, of seeking and finding, no error could be removed, no deeper understanding of truth attained. Thus, then, independence of thought and political freedom are indispensable to the Church herself ; she needs them to remind her of the varying intellectual wants of men, of the changing nature of her own forms ; she needs them to preserve her from the lifeless iteration of misunderstood doctrines and rites, which kill the soul.

It has been said, the State is itself the Church, but the Church has thought herself authorised to usurp the place of the State. The truth is, that the spiritual or intellectual life of man—in its intensest depth and energy unquestionably one—yet manifests itself in these two institutions, which come into contact under the most varied forms ; which are continually striving to pervade each other, yet never entirely coincide ; to exclude each other, yet neither has ever been permanently victor or vanquished. In the nations of the West, at least, such a result has never been obtained. The Califate may unite ecclesiastical and political power in one hand ; but the whole life and character of western Christendom consists of the incessant action and counter-action of Church and State ; hence arises the freer, more comprehensive, more profound activity of mind, which must, on the whole, be admitted to characterise that portion of the globe. The aspect of the public life of Europe is always determined by the mutual relations of these two great principles.

Hence it happens that ecclesiastical history is not to be understood without political, nor the latter without the former. The combination of both is necessary to present either in its true light ; and if ever we are able to fathom the depths of that profounder life where both have their common source and origin, it must be by a complete knowledge of this combination.

But if this is the case with all nations, it is most pre-eminently so with the German, which has bestowed more persevering and original thought on ecclesiastical and religious subjects than any other. The events of ten centuries turn upon the struggles between the Empire and the Papacy, between Catholicism and Protestantism. We, in our days, stand midway between them.

My design is to relate the history of an epoch in which the politico-religious energy of the German nation was most conspicuous for its growth and most prolific in its results. I do not conceal from myself the great difficulty of this undertaking ; but, with God's help, I will endeavour to accomplish it. I shall first attempt to trace my way through a retrospect of earlier times.

CAROLINGIAN TIMES.

ONE of the most important epochs in the history of the world was the commencement of the eighth century ; when, on the one side, Mahommedanism threatened to overspread Italy and Gaul, and on the other, the ancient idolatry of Saxony and Friesland once more forced its way across the Rhine. In this peril of Christian institutions a youthful prince of Germanic race, Karl Martell, arose as their champion ; maintained them with all the energy which the necessity for self-defence calls forth, and finally extended them into new regions. For, as the possessor of the sole power which still remained erect in the nations of Roman origin— the Pope of Rome—allied himself with this prince and his successors ; as he received assistance from them, and bestowed in return the favour and protection of the spiritual authority, the compound of military and sacerdotal government which forms the basis of all European civilisation from that moment arose into being. From that time conquest and conversion went hand in hand. " As soon," says the author of the life of St. Boniface, " as the authority of the glorious Prince Charles over the Frisians was confirmed, the trumpet of the sacred word was heard." It would be difficult to say whether the Frankish domination contributed more to the conversion of the Hessians and Thuringians, or Christianity to the incorporation of those races with the Frankish empire. The war of Charlemagne against the Saxons was a war not only of conquest but of religion. Charlemagne opened it with an attack on the old Saxon sanctuary, the Irminsul ;[1] the Saxons retorted by the destruction of the church at Fritzlar. Charlemagne marched to battle bearing the relics of saints ; missionaries accompanied the divisions of his army ; his victories were celebrated by the establishment of bishoprics ; baptism was the seal of subjection and allegiance ; relapse into heathenism was also a crime against the state. The consummation of all these incidents is to be found in the investiture of the aged conqueror with the imperial crown. A German, in the natural course of events and in the exercise of regular legitimate power, occupied the place of the Cæsars as chief of a great part of the Romance world ; he also assumed a lofty station at the side of the Roman pontiff in spiritual affairs ; a Frankish synod saluted him, as " Regent of the true religion." The entire state of which he was the chief now assumed a colour and form wherein the spiritual and temporal elements were completely blended. The union between emperor and pope served as a model for that between count and bishop. The archdeaconries into which the bishoprics were divided, generally, if not universally, coincided with the Gauen, or political divisions of the country. As the counties were divided into hundreds, so were the archdeaconries into deaneries. The seat of them was different ; but, in respect of the territory over which their jurisdiction extended, there was a striking correspondence.[2] According to the view of the lord and ruler, not only was the secular power to lend its arm to the spiritual, but the spiritual to aid the temporal by its excommunications. The great empire reminds us of a vast neutral ground in the midst of a world filled with carnage and devastation ; where an iron will imposes peace on forces generally in a state of mutual hostility and destruction, and fosters and shelters the germ of civilisation ; so guarded was it on all sides by impregnable marches.

[1] The Saxon idol, identified in later Germanic mythology with the Teutonic hero Hermann, the conqueror of Varus. Cf. Milman, History of Latin Christianity, Bk. v. c. i.

[2] See Wenck, Hessische Landesgeschichte, ii. 469.

But every age could not produce a man so formed to subdue and to command ; and for the development of the world which Charlemagne founded, it remained to be seen what would be the mutual bearing of the different elements of which it was composed ; whether they would blend with or repel each other, agree or conflict : for there can be no true and enduring vitality without the free motion of natural and innate powers and propensities.

It was inevitable that the clergy would first feel its own strength. This body formed a corporation independent even of the emperor : originating and developed in the Romance nations, whose most remarkable product it had been in the preceding century, it now extended over those of Germanic race ; in which, through the medium of a common language, it continually made new proselytes and gained strength and consistency.

Even under Charlemagne the spiritual element was already bestirring itself with activity and vigour. One of the most remarkable of his capitularies is that wherein he expresses his astonishment that his spiritual and temporal officers so often thwart, instead of supporting each other, as it is their duty to do. He does not disguise that it was the clergy more especially who exceeded their powers : to them he addresses the question, fraught with reproach and displeasure, which has been so often repeated by succeeding ages—how far they are justified in interfering in purely secular affairs ? He tells them they must explain what is meant by renouncing the world ; whether that is consistent with large and costly retinues, with attempts to persuade the ignorant to make donations of their goods and to disinherit their children ; whether it were not better to foster good morals than to build churches, and the like.[1]

But the clergy soon evinced a much stronger propensity to ambitious encroachment.

We need not here inquire whether the pseudo-Isidorian decretals were invented as early as the reign of Charlemagne, or somewhat later ; in the Frankish church, or in Italy : at all events, they belong to that period, are connected with a most extensive project, and form a great epoch in our history. The project was to overthrow the existing constitution of the church, which, in every country, still essentially rested on the authority of the metropolitan ; to place the whole church in immediate subjection to the pope of Rome, and to establish a unity of the spiritual power, by means of which it must necessarily emancipate itself from the temporal. Such was the plan which the clergy had even then the boldness to avow. A series of names of the earlier popes were pressed into the service, in order to append to them forged documents, to which a colour of legality was thus given.[2]

And what was it not possible to effect in those times of profound historical ignorance, in which past ages were only beheld through the twilight of falsehood and fantastic error ? and under princes like the successors

[1] " Capitulare interrogationis de iis quæ Karolus M. pro communi omnium utilitate interroganda constituit Aquisgrani 811."—*Monum. Germaniæ Histor.* ed. *Pertz,* iii., p. 106.

[2] A passage from the spurious Acts of the Synods of Pope Silvester is found in a Capitulary of 806. See Eichhorn, Ueber die spanische Sammlung der Quellen des Kirchenrechts in den Abhandll. der Preuss. Akad. d. W. 1834. Philos. Hist. Klasse, p. 102.

of Charlemagne, whose minds, instead of being elevated or purified, were crushed by religious influences, so that they lost the power of distinguishing the spiritual from the temporal province of the clerical office ?

It is indisputable that the order of succession to the throne which Louis the Pious, in utter disregard of the warnings of his faithful adherents, and in opposition to all German modes of thinking, established in the year 817,[1] was principally brought about by the influence of the clergy. " The empire," says Agobardus, " must not be divided into three ; it must remain one and undivided." The division of the empire seemed to endanger the unity of the church : and, as the emperor was chiefly determined by spiritual motives, the regulations adopted were enforced with all the pomp of religious ceremonies,—by masses, fasts, and distributions of alms ; every one swore to them ; they were held to be inspired by God himself.

After this, no one, not even the emperor, could venture to depart from them. Great, at least, were the evils which he brought upon himself by his attempt to do so, out of love to a son born at a later period of his life. The irritated clergy made common cause with his elder sons, who were already dissatisfied with the administration of the empire. The supreme pontiff came in person from Rome and declared in their favour ; and a universal revolt was the consequence. Nor did this first manifestation of their power satisfy the clergy. In order to make snre of their advantage, they formed the daring scheme of depriving the born and anointed emperor, on whom they could now no longer place reliance, of his consecrated dignity—a dignity which, at any rate, he owed not to them,— and of bestowing it immediately on the successor to the throne who had been nominated in 817, and who was the natural representative of the unity of the empire. If, on the one hand, it is indisputable that, in the eighth century, the spiritual authority contributed greatly to the establishment of the principle of obedience to the temporal government, it is equally certain that, in the ninth, it made rapid strides towards the acquisition of power into its own hands. In the collection of capitularies of Benedictus Levita, it is treated as one of the leading principles, that no constitution in the world has any force or validity against the decisions of the popes of Rome ; in more than one canon, kings who act in opposition to this principle are threatened with divine punishment.[2] The monarchy of Charlemagne seemed to be about to be transformed into an ecclesiastical state.

I do not hesitate to affirm that it was mainly the people of Germany who resisted this tendency ; indeed, that it was precisely this resistance which first awakened Germany to a consciousness of its own importance as a nation. For it would be impossible to speak of a German nation, in the proper sense of the word, during the preceding ages. In the more remote, the several tribes had not even a common name by which they recognised each other : during the period of their migration, they fought

---

[1] Fauriel, Histoire de la Gaule Mérid., iv. 47, examines this point more in detail.

[2] Benedicti Capitularia, lib. ii., p. 322. " Velut prævaricator catholicæ fidei semper a Domino reus existat quicunque regum canonis hujus censuram permiserit violandam." Lib. iii. 346. " Constitutiones contradecreta præsulum Romanorum nullius sunt momenti."

with as much hostility among themselves as against the stranger, and allied themselves as readily with the latter as with those of common race. Under the Merovingian kings they were further divided by religious enmities ; the Saxons, in presence of Frankish Christianity, held the more pertinaciously to their forms of government and to their ancient gods. It was not till Charlemagne had united all the Germanic tribes, with the exception of those in England and Scandinavia, in one and the same temporal and spiritual allegiance, that the nation began to acquire form and consistency ; it was not till the beginning of the ninth century, that the German name appeared as contra-distinguished from the Romance portion of the empire.[1]

It is worthy of eternal remembrance, that the first act in which the Germans appear as one people, is the resistance to the attempt of the clergy to depose their emperor and lord.

The ideas of legitimacy which they had inherited from their past political life and history, as members of tribes, would never have led them to derive it from the pretended grace of God,—that is to say, from the declaration of the spiritual authorities. They were attached to Louis the Pious, who had rendered peculiar services to the Saxon chiefs ; their aversion to his deposition was easily fanned into a flame : at the call of Louis the Germanic, who kept his court in Bavaria, the other tribes, Saxons, Swabians, and Franks, on this side the Carbonaria,[2] gathered around his banner ; for the first time they were united in one great object. As they were aided by an analogous, though much feebler, movement in the south of France, the bishops soon found themselves compelled to absolve the emperor from the penance they had imposed, and to acknowledge him again as their lord. The first historical act of the united nation is this rising in favour of their born prince against the spiritual power. Nor were they any longer inclined to consent to such a deviation from their own law of succession, as was involved in the acknowledgment of a single heir to the whole monarchy. When, after the death of Louis the Pious, Lothair, in spite of all that had passed, made an attempt to seize the reins of the whole empire, he found in the Germans a resistance, at first doubtful, but every moment increasing, and finally victorious. From them his troops received their first important defeat on the Riess, which laid the foundation of the severance of Germany from the great monarchy.[3]

Lothair relied on his claims recognised by the clergy ; the Germans, combined with the southern French, challenged him to submit them to the judgment of heaven by battle. Then it was that the great array of the Frankish empire split into two hostile masses ; the one containing a preponderance of Romance, the other of Germanic elements. The former defended the unity of the Empire ; the latter demanded, according to their German ideas, its separation. There is a ballad extant on the battle of Fontenay, in which one of the combatants expresses his grief at this bloody war of fellow-citizens and brethren ; " on that bitter night

---

[1] Rühs Erläuterung der zehn ersten Capitel von Tacitus Germania, p. 103 ; Mone : Geschichte des Heidenthums im Nördlichen Europa, Th. ii., p. 6.

[2] A famous forest near Louvain in Hainault.

[3] In Retiense. (Annales Ruodolfi Fuldensis ; Monumenta Germaniæ Hist., i., p. 352.) According to Lang (Baierische Gauen, p. 78), belonging to the Swabian territory.

in which the brave fell, the skilful in fight." For the destiny of the West it was decisive.[1] The judgment of heaven was triumphantly pronounced against the claims of the clergy; three kingdoms were now actually established instead of one. The secular Germanic principles which, from the time of the great migration of tribes, had extended widely into the Romance world, remained in possession of the field : they were steadfastly maintained in the subsequent troubles.

On the extinction of one of the three lines in which the unity of the empire should have rested, dissensions broke out between the two others, a main feature of which was the conflict between the spiritual and secular principles.

The king of the French, Charles the Bald, had allied himself with the clergy; his armies were led to the field by bishops, and he abandoned the administration of his kingdom in a great measure to Hinkmar, archbishop of Rheims. Hence, when the throne of Lotharingia became vacant in the year 869, he experienced the warmest support from the bishops of that country. "After," say they, "they had called on God, who bestows kingdoms on whom He will, to point out to them a king after His own heart; after they had then, with God's help, perceived that the crown was of right his to whom they meant to confide it," they elected Charles the Bald to be their lord.[2] But the Germans were as far now as before from being convinced by this sort of public law. The elder brother thought his claims at least as valid as those of the younger; by force of arms he compelled Charles to consent to the treaty of Marsna, by which he first united transrhenane Germany with that on the right bank of the Rhine. This same course of events was repeated in the year 875, when the thrones of Italy and the Empire became vacant. At first, Charles the Bald, aided now by the pope, as heretofore by the bishops, took possession of the crown without difficulty.[3] But Carlmann, son of Louis the Germanic, resting his claim on the right of the elder line, and also on his nomination as heir by the last emperor, hastened with his Bavarians and high Germans to Italy; and in spite of the opposition of the pope, took possession of it as his unquestionable inheritance. If this were the case in Italy, still less could Charles the Bald succeed in his attempts on the German frontiers. He was defeated in both countries; the superiority of the Germans in arms was so decisive that, at length, they became masters of the whole Lotharingian territory. Even under the Carolingian sovereigns, they marked the boundaries of the mighty empire; the crown of Charlemagne, and two thirds of his dominions, fell into their hands : they maintained the independence of the secular power with dauntless energy and brilliant success.

SAXON AND FRANKISH EMPERORS.

THE question which next presents itself is, what course was to be pursued if the ruling house either became extinct, or proved itself incapable of

---

[1] Angilbertus de bella quæ fuit Fontaneto.

[2] " Caroli Secundi Coronatio in Regno Hlotharii, 869."—*Monum.*, iii. 512.

[3] " Papa invitante Romam perrexit. Beato Petro multa et pretiosa munera offerens, in imperatorem unctus est."—*Annales Hincmari Remensis*, 875 et 876 ; *Monum. Germ.*, i. 498.

conducting the government of so vast an empire, attacked on every side from without, and fermenting within.

In the years from 879 to 887, the several nations determined, one after another, to abandon the cause of Charles the Fat. The characteristic differences of the mode in which they accomplished this are well worthy of remark.

In the Romance part of Europe the clergy had a universal ascendancy. In Cisjurane Burgundy it was " the holy fathers assembled at Mantala, the holy synod, together with the nobles," who " under the inspiration of the Holy Spirit," elected Count Boso king.[1] We find from the decretal for the election of Guido of Spoleto, that " the humble bishops assembled together from various parts at Pavia chose him to be their lord and king,[2] principally because he had promised to exalt the holy Roman church, and to maintain the ecclesiastical rights and privileges." The conditions to which Odo of Paris gave his assent at his coronation are chiefly ·in favour of the clergy : he promises not only to defend the rights of the church, but to extend them to the utmost of his information and ability.[3] Totally different was the state of things in Germany. Here it was more especially the temporal lords, Saxons, Franks, and Bavarians, who, under the guidance of a disaffected minister of the emperor, assembled around Arnulf and transferred the crown to him. The bishops (even the bishop of Mainz) were rather opposed to the measure ; nor was it till some years afterwards that they entered into a formal negotiation[4] with the new ruler : they had not elected him ; they submitted to his authority.

The rights and privileges which were on every occasion claimed by the clergy, were as constantly and as resolutely ignored by the Germans. They held as close to the legitimate succession as possible ; even after the complete extinction of the Carolingian race, the degree of kindred with it was one of the most important considerations which determined the choice of the people, first to Conrad, and then to Henry I. of Saxony.

Conrad had, indeed, at one time, the idea of attaching himself to the clergy, who, even in Germany, were a very powerful body : Henry, on the contrary, was always opposed to them. They took no share in his election ; the consecration by the holy oil, upon which Pepin and Charlemagne had set so high a value, he declined ; as matters stood in Germany, it could be of no importance to him. On the contrary, we find that as in his own land of Saxony he kept his clergy within the strict bounds of obedience, so in other parts of his dominions he placed them in subjection to the dukes[5] ; so that their dependence on the civil power was more complete than ever. His only solicitude was to stand well with these

[1] " Nutu Dei, per suffragia sanctorum, ob instantem necessitatem."—*Electio Bosonis ; Monum.*, iii. 547.

[2] " Nos humiles episcopos ex diversis partibus Papiæ convenientibus pro ecclesiarum nostrarum ereptione et omnis Christianitatis salvatione," &c.— *Electio Widonis Regis, Monum.*, iii. 554.

[3] Capitulum Odonis Regis. Ibid.

[4] " De collegio sacerdotum gnaros direxerunt mediatores ad præfatum regem," &c.—*Arnulfi Concilium Triburience, Monum.*, iii. 560. He says, " Nos, quibus regni cura et solicitudo ecclesiarum commissa est."

[5] " Totius Bajoariæ pontifices tuæ subjaceant potestati," is the promise of Liutprand the king to Duke Arnulf. Buchner, Geschichte der Baiern, iii. 38, shows what use the latter made of it. See Waiz, Henry I., p. 49.

great feudatories, whose power was almost equal to his own, and to fulfil other duties imperatively demanded by the moment. As he succeeded in these objects,—as he obtained a decisive victory over his most dangerous enemies, re-established the Marches, which had been broken at all points, and suffered nothing on the other side the Rhine that bore the German name to be wrested from him,—the clergy were compelled by necessity to adhere to him : he bequeathed an undisputed sceptre to his house. It was by an agreement of the court and the secular nobles that Otho was selected from among Henry's sons as his successor to the throne. The ceremony of election was attended only by the dukes, princes, great officers of state, and warriors ; the elected monarch then received the assembled body of the clergy.[1] Otho could receive the unction without scruple ; the clergy could no longer imagine that they conferred a right upon him by that ceremony. Whether anointed or not, Otho would have been king, as his father had been before him. And so firmly was this sovereignty established, that Otho was now in a position to revive and carry through the claims founded by his Carolingian predecessors. He first completely realised the idea of a Germanic empire, which they had only conceived and prepared. He governed Lotharingia and administered Burgundy ; a short campaign sufficed to re-establish the rights of his Carolingian predecessors to the supreme power in Lombardy. Like Charlemagne, he was called to aid by a pope oppressed by the factions of Rome ; like him, he received in return for his succour the crown of the western empire (February 2, 962). The principle of the temporal government, the autocracy, which from the earliest times had held in check the usurpations of ecclesiastical ambition, thus attained its culminating point, and was triumphantly asserted and recognised in Europe.

At the first glance it would seem as if the relation in which Otho now stood to the pope was the same as that occupied by Charlemagne ; on a closer inspection, however, we find a wide difference.

Charlemagne's connexion with the see of Rome was produced by mutual need ; it was the result of long epochs of a political combination embracing the development of various nations ; their mutual understanding rested on an internal necessity, before which all opposing views and interests gave way. The sovereignty of Otho the Great, on the contrary, rested on a principle fundamentally opposed to the encroachment of spiritual influences. The alliance was momentary ; the disruption of it inevitable. But when, soon after, the same pope who had invoked his aid, John XII., placed himself at the head of a rebellious faction, Otho was compelled to cause him to be formally deposed, and to crush the faction that supported him by repeated exertions of force, before he could obtain perfect obedience ; he was obliged to raise to the papal chair a pope on whose co-operation he could rely. The popes have often asserted that they transferred the empire to the Germans ; and if they confined this assertion to the Carolingian race, they are not entirely wrong. The coronation of Charlemagne was the result of their free determination. But if they allude to the German emperors, properly so called, the contrary of their

[1] Widukiveli Annales, lib. ii. " Duces ac præfectorum principes cum cætera principum militumque manu—fecerunt eum regem ; dum ea geruntur a ducibus ac cætero magistratu, pontifex maximus cum universo sacerdotali ordine præstolabatur."

statement is just as true ; not only Carlmann and Otho the Great, but their successors, constantly had to conquer the imperial throne, and to defend it, when conquered, sword in hand.

It has been said that the Germans would have done more wisely if they had not meddled with the empire ; or at least, if they had first worked out their own internal political institutions, and then, with matured minds, taken part in the general affairs of Europe. But the things of this world are not wont to develop themselves so methodically. A nation is often compelled by circumstances to increase its territorial extent, before its internal growth is completed. For was it of slight importance to its inward progress, that Germany thus remained in unbroken connexion with Italy ?—the depository of all that remained of ancient civilisation, the source whence all the forms of Christianity had been derived. The mind of Germany has always unfolded itself by contact with the spirit of antiquity, and of the nations of Roman origin. It was from the contrasts which so continually presented themselves during this uninterrupted connexion, that Germany learned to distinguish ecclesiastical domination from Christianity.

For however signal had been the ascendancy of the secular power, the German people did not depart a hair's breadth either from the doctrines of Christianity, the ideas upon which a Christian church is founded, or even from the forms in which they had first received those doctrines and ideas. In them the nation had first risen to a consciousness of its existence as a united body ; its whole intellectual and moral life was bound up with them. The German imperial government revived the civilising and Christianising tendencies which had distinguished the reigns of Karl Martell and Charlemagne. Otho the Great, in following the course marked out by his illustrious predecessors, gave it a fresh national importance by planting German colonies in Slavonic countries, simultaneously with the diffusion of Christianity. He germanised as well as converted the population he had subdued. He confirmed his father's conquests on the Saale and the Elbe, by the establishment of the bishoprics of Meissen and Osterland. After having conquered the tribes on the other side the Elbe in those long and perilous campaigns where he commanded in person, he established there, too, three bishoprics, which for a time gave an extraordinary impulse to the progress of conversion.[1] In the midst of all his difficulties and perplexities in Italy he never lost sight of this grand object ; it was indeed while in that country that he founded the archbishopric of Magdeburg, whose jurisdiction extended over all those other foundations. And even where the project of Germanising the population was out of the question, the supremacy of the German name was firmly and actively maintained. In Bohemia and Poland bishoprics were erected under German metropolitans ; from Hamburg Christianity found its way into the north ; missionaries from Passau traversed Hungary, nor is it improbable that the influence of these vast and sublime efforts extended even to Russia. The German empire was the centre of the conquering religion ; as itself advanced, it extended the ecclesiastico-military State of which the Church was an integral part ; it was the chief representative of the unity of western Christendom, and hence arose the necessity under which it lay of acquiring a decided ascendancy over the papacy.

[1] Adami Brem. Histor. Ecclesiastica, lib. ii., c. 17.

This secular and Germanic principle long retained the predominancy it had triumphantly acquired. Otho the Second offered the papal chair to the abbot of Cluny ; and Otho the Third bestowed it first on one of his kinsmen, and then on his instructor Gerbert. All the factions which threatened to deprive the emperor of this right were overthrown ; under the patronage of Henry III., a German pope defeated three Roman candidates for the tiara. In the year 1048, when the see of Rome became vacant, ambassadors from the Romans, says a contemporaneous chronicler, proceeded to Saxony, found the emperor there, and entreated him to give them a new pope. He chose the Bishop of Toul, (afterwards Leo IX.), of the house of Egisheim, from which he himself was descended on the maternal side. What took place with regard to the head of the church was of course still more certain to befall the rest of the clergy. Since Otho the Great, in all the troubles of the early years of his reign, succeeded in breaking down the resistance which the duchies were enabled by their clan-like composition to offer him, the ecclesiastical appointments remained without dispute in the hand of the emperor.

How magnificent was the position now occupied by the German nation, represented in the persons of the mightiest princes of Europe and united under their sceptre ; at the head of an advancing civilisation, and of the whole of western Christendom ; in the fulness of youthful, aspiring strength !

We must here however remark and confess, that Germany did not wholly understand her position, nor fulfil her mission. Above all, she did not succeed in giving complete reality to the idea of a western empire, such as appeared about to be established under Otho I. Independent and often hostile, though Christian, powers arose through all the borders of Germany ; in Hungary, and in Poland, in the northern as well as in the southern possessions of the Normans ; England and France were snatched again from German influence. Spain laughed at the German claims to a universal supremacy ; her kings thought themselves emperors ; even the enterprises nearest home—those across the Elbe—were for a time stationary or retrograde.

If we seek for the causes of these unfavourable results, we need only turn our eyes on the internal condition of the empire, where we find an incessant and tempestuous struggle of all the forces of the nation. Unfortunately the establishment of a fixed rule of succession to the imperial crown was continually prevented by events. The son and grandson of Otho the Great died in the bloom of youth, and the nation was thus compelled to elect a chief. The very first election threw Germany and Italy into a universal ferment ; and this was shortly succeeded by a second still more stormy, since it was necessary to resort to a new line—the Franconian. How was it possible to expect implicit obedience from the powerful and refractory nobles, out of whose ranks, and by whose will, the emperor was raised to the throne ? Was it likely that the Saxon race, which had hitherto held the reins of government, would readily and quietly submit to a foreign family ? It followed that two factions arose, the one obedient, the other opposed, to the Franconian emperor, and filled the empire with their strife. The severe character of Henry III. excited universal discontent.[1] A vision, related to us by his own chan-

---

[1] Hermannus Contractus ad an. 1053. " Regni tam primores quam inferiores magis magisque mussitantes, regem se ipso deteriorem fore causabantur."

cellor, affords a lively picture of the state of things. He saw the emperor, seated on his throne, draw his sword, exclaiming aloud, that he trusted he should still avenge himself on all his enemies. How could the emperors, thus occupied during their whole lives with intestine dissensions, place themselves at the head of Europe in the important work of social improvement, or really merit the title of supreme Lords of the West ?

It is remarkable that the social element on which they propped their power was again principally the clergy. Even Otho the Great owed his triumph over intestine revolt and discord, in great measure to the support of the bishops ; for example, of his brother Bruno, whom he had created Archbishop of Cologne, and who, in return, held Lotharingia in allegiance to him : it was only by the aid of the clergy that Otho conquered the Pope.[1] The emperors found it expedient to govern by means of the bishops ; to make them the instruments of their will. The bishops were at once their chancellors and their counsellors ; the monasteries, imperial farms. The uncontrollable tendency, at that time, of all power and office to become hereditary would naturally render the heads of the church desirous of combining secular rights, which they could dispose of at pleasure, with their bishoprics. Hence it happened, that just at the time when the subjection of the clergy to the imperial authority was the most complete, their power acquired the greatest extension and solidity. Otho I. already began to unite the temporal powers of the count with the proper spiritual authority of the bishop. We see from the registers of Henry II. that he bestowed on many churches two and three countships ; on that of Gandersheim, the countship in seven Gauen or districts. As early as the eleventh century the bishops of Würzburg succeeded in totally supplanting the secular counts in their diocese, and in uniting the spiritual and temporal power ; a state of things which the other bishops now strove to emulate.

It is evident that the station of an emperor of Germany was no less perilous than august. The magnates by whom he was surrounded, the possessors of the secular power out of whose ranks he himself had arisen, he could hold in check only by an unceasing struggle, and not without force. He must find a prop in another quarter, and seek support from the very body who were in principle opposed to him. This rendered it impossible for him ever to attain to that predominant influence in the general affairs of Europe which the imperial dignity would naturally have given him. How strongly does this everlasting ebb and flow of contending parties, this continual upstarting of refractory powers, contrast with the tranquillity and self-sufficiency of the empire swayed by Charlemagne ! It required matchless vigour and fortitude in an emperor even to hold his seat.

In this posture of affairs, the prince who possessed the requisite vigour and fortitude, Henry III., died young (A.D. 1056), and a child, six years old, in whose name the government was carried on by a tottering regency, filled his place :—one of those incidents which turn the fortunes of a world.

---

[1] Rescriptum patrum in concilio, in Liutprand, lib. vi., contains the remarkable declaration : " Excommunicationem vestram parvipendemus, eam potius in vos retorquebimus."

EMANCIPATION OF THE PAPACY.

THE ideas which had been repressed in the ninth century now began to revive ; and with redoubled strength, since the clergy, from the highest to the lowest, were become so much more powerful.

Generally speaking, this was the age in which the various modifications of spiritual power throughout the world began to assume form and stability ; in which mankind found repose and satisfaction in these conditions of existence. In the eleventh century Buddhaism was re-established in Thibet ; and the hierarchy which, down to the present day, prevails over so large a portion of Eastern Asia, was founded by the Lama Dschu-Adhischa. The Califate of Bagdad, heretofore a vast empire, then took the character of a spiritual authority, and was greatly indebted to that change for the ready reception it met with. At the same period, in Africa and Syria arose the Fatimite Califate, founded on a doctrine of which its adherents said, that it was to the Koran what the kernel is to its shell.

In the West the idea of the unity of the Christian faith was the pervading one, and had taken strong hold on all minds (for the various conversions which awakened this or that more susceptible nation to fresh enthusiasm belong to a later period). This idea manifested itself in the general efforts to crush Mahommedanism : inadequately represented by the imperial authority, which commanded but a limited obedience, it now came in powerful aid of the projects and efforts of the hierarchy. For to whom could such an idea attach itself but to the bishop of the Roman Church, to which, as to a common source, all other churches traced back their foundation ; which all western Europeans regarded with a singular reverence ? Hitherto the Bishop of Rome had been thrown into the shade by the rise and development of the imperial power. But favouring circumstances and the main course of events now united to impel the papacy to claim universal and supreme dominion.

The minority of the infant emperor decided the result. At the court of Rome, the man who most loudly proclaimed the necessity of reform— the great champion of the independent existence of the church—the man ordained by destiny to make his opinion the law of ages,—Hildebrand, the son of a carpenter in Tuscany, acquired supreme influence over all affairs. He was the author and instigator of decrees, in virtue of which the papal elections were no longer to depend on the emperor, but on the clergy of the Church of Rome and the cardinals. He delayed not a moment to put them in force ; the very next election was conducted in accordance with them.

In Germany, on the contrary, people were at this time entirely occupied with the conflicts of the factions about the court ; the opposition which was spread over Italy and Germany (and to which Hildebrand also belonged) at length got a firm footing in the court itself : the adherents of the old Saxon and Salic principles, (for example, Chancellor Guibert) were defeated ; the court actually sanctioned an election which had taken place against its own most urgent interest ; the German rulers, plunged in the dissensions of the moment, abandoned to his fate an anti-pope who maintained himself with considerable success and who was the representative of the ancient maxims.

Affairs, however, changed their aspect when the youthful Salian, with all his spirit and talents, took the reins of government into his own hand. He knew his rights, and was determined to assert them at any price. But things had gone so far that he fell into the most perilous situation at the very outset of his career.

The accession to the throne of a young monarch, by nature despotic and violent, and hurried along by vehement passions, quickly brought the long-fermenting internal discords of Germany to an open breach. The German nobles aspired after the sort of independence which those of France had just acquired. In the year 1073 the Saxon princes revolted ; the whole of Saxony, says a contemporary, deserted the king like one man. Meanwhile at Rome the leader of the hostile party had himself gained possession of the tiara, and now advanced without delay to the great work of emancipating not only the papacy but the clergy from the control of the emperor. In the year 1074 he caused a law to be proclaimed by his synod, the purpose and effect of which was to wrest the nomination to spiritual offices from the laity ; that is, in the first place, from the emperor.

Scarcely was Henry IV. seated on his throne when he saw its best prerogatives, the crown and consummation of his power, attacked and threatened with annihilation. He seemed doomed to succumb without a contest. The discord between the Saxons and Upper Germans, which for a time had been of advantage to him, was allayed, and their swords, yet wet with each other's blood, were turned in concert against the emperor ; he was compelled to propitiate the pope who had excommunicated him, to travel in the depth of winter to do that penance at Canossa by which he so profoundly degraded the imperial name.

Yet from that very moment we may date his most strenuous resistance. We should fall into a complete error were we to represent him to ourselves as crossing the Alps in remorse and contrition, or as convinced of the rightfulness of the claims advanced by the pope. His only object was to wrest from his adversaries the support of the spiritual authority, the pretext under which they threatened his highest dignity. As he did not succeed in this,—as the absolution he received from Gregory was not so complete as to restrain the German princes from all further hostilities,[1]— as, on the contrary, they elected another sovereign in spite of it,—he plunged into the most determined struggle against the assumptions of his spiritual as well as of his temporal foes. Opposition and injury roused the man within him. Across those Alps which he had traversed in penitential lowliness, he hurried back burning with warlike ardour ; in Carinthia an invincible band of devoted followers gathered around him. It is interesting to follow him with our eye, subduing the spiritual power in Bavaria, the hostile aristocratical clans in Swabia ; to see him next marching upon Franconia and driving his rival before him ; then into Thuringia and the Meissen colonies, and at length forcing him to a battle on the banks of the Elster, in which he fell. Henry gained no great victories ; even on the Elster he did not so much as keep the field ; but he was continually advancing ; his party was continually gaining strength ; he held the banner of the empire aloft with a steady and vigorous grasp.

---

[1] Lambertus Schaffnaburgensis : (*Pistor.* i., p. 420.) " His conditionibus absolutus est ut . . . . accusationibus responderet et ad papæ sententiam vel retineret regnum . . . . vel æquo animo amitteret."

After a few years he was able to return to Italy (A.D. 1081). The empire had been so long and so intimately allied with the episcopal power that its chief could not be without adherents among the higher clergy : synods were held in the emperor's behalf, in which it was resolved to maintain the old order of things. The excommunications of the pope were met by counter-excommunications. Chancellor Guibert, who had suffered for his adherence to Salic principles, was nominated pope under the auspices of the emperor ; and after various alternations of success in war, was at length conducted in triumph to Rome. Henry, like so many of his predecessors, was crowned by a pope of his own creation. The second rival king whom the Saxons opposed to him could gain no substantial power, and held it expedient voluntarily to withdraw his pretensions.

We see that the emperor had attained to all that is attainable by war and policy, yet his triumph was far from being as complete and conclusive as we might thence infer ; for the result of a contest is not always decided on a field of battle. The ideas of which Gregory was the champion were intimately blended with the most powerful impulses of the general development of society ; while he was a fugitive from Rome, they gained possession of the world. No later than ten years after his death his second successor was able to take the initiative in the general affairs of the West—a power which was conclusive as to results. One of the greatest social movements recorded in history—the Crusades—was mainly the result of his policy ; and from that time he appeared as the natural head of the Romano-Germanic sacerdotal and military community of the West. To such weapons the emperor had nothing to oppose.

The life of Henry, from this time till its close, has something in it which reminds us of the antique tragedy, in which the hero sinks, in all the glory of manhood and the fulness of his powers, under an inevitable doom. For what can be more like an overwhelming fate than the power of opinion, which extends its invisible grasp on every side, takes complete possession of the minds of men, and suddenly appears in the field with a force beyond all control ? Henry saw the world go over, before his eyes, from the empire to the papacy. An army brought together by one of the blind popular impulses which led to the crusades, drove out of Rome the pope he had placed on the throne : nay, even in his own house he was encountered by hostile opinions. His elder son was infected with the zeal of the bigots by whom he was incited to revolt against his father ; the younger was swayed by the influence of the German aristocracy, and, by a union of cunning and violence, compelled his own father to abdicate. The aged warrior went broken-hearted to his grave.

I do not think it necessary to trace all the various alternations of the conflict respecting the rights of the church.

Even in Rome it was sometimes deemed impossible to force the emperor to renounce his claims. Pope Paschal at one time entertained the bold idea of giving back all that the emperors had ever granted to the church, in order to effect the radical separation of the latter from the state.[1]

As this proved to be impracticable, the affairs of the church were again

---

[1] Heinrici Encyclica de Controversia sua cum Papa.—*Monum.*, iv. 70. The emperor asked, most justly, what was to become of the imperial authority, if it were to lose the right of investiture after the emperors had transferred so large a share of their privileges to the bishops.

administered for a time by the imperial court under Henry V., as they had been under Henry IV.[1]

But this too was soon found to be intolerable ; new disputes arose, and after long contention, both parties agreed to the concordat of Worms,[2] according to which the preponderant influence was yielded to the emperor in Germany, and to the pope in Italy ; an agreement, however, which was not expressed with precision, and which contained the germ of new disputes.

But though these results were little calculated to determine the rights of the contending powers, the advantages which gradually accrued to the papacy from the course of events were incalculable. From a state of total dependence, it had now attained to a no less complete emancipation ; or rather to a preponderance, not indeed as yet absolute, or defined, but unquestionable, and every moment acquiring strength and consistency from favouring circumstances.

RELATION OF THE PAPACY TO THE PRINCES OF THE EMPIRE.

THE most important assistance which the papacy received in this work of self-emancipation and aggrandisement arose from the natural and tacit league subsisting between it and the princes of the Germanic empire.

The secular aristocracy of Germany had, at one time, made the strongest opposition, on behalf of their head, to the encroachments of the Church ; they had erected the imperial throne, and had invested it with all its power : but this power had at length become oppressive to them ; the supremacy of the imperial government over the clergy, which was employed to keep themselves in subjection, became their most intolerable grievance. It followed that they at length beheld their own advantage in the emancipation of the papacy.

It is to be observed that the power of the German princes and that of the popes rose in parallel steps.

Under Henry III., and during the minority of his successor, both had laid the foundation of their independence : they began their active career together. Scarcely had Gregory VII. established the first principles of his new system, when the princes also proclaimed theirs ;—the principle, that the empire should no longer be hereditary. Henry IV. maintained his power chiefly by admitting in detail the claims which he denied in the aggregate : his victories had as little effect in arresting the progress of the independence of the great nobles as of the hierarchy. Even as early as the reign of Henry V. these sentiments had gained such force that the unity of the empire was regarded as residing rather in the collective body of the princes than in the person of the emperor. For what else are we to understand from the declaration of that prince—that it was less dangerous to insult the head of the empire than to give offence to the princes ?[3]

---

[1] Epistola Friderici Coloniensis archiepiscopi : Codex Vdalrici Babenbergensis, n. 277. " Synodales episcoporum conventus, annua consilia, omnes denique ecclesiastici ordinis administrationes in regalem curiam translata sunt."

[2] The concordat of Worms settled the quarrel concerning investitures. The Pope retained the rights of investing with the ring and crozier, but acknowledged the freedom of election.

[3] " Unius capitis licet summi dejectio reparabile dampnum est, principum autem conculcatio ruina regni est." Fragmentum de Hoste facienda.—*Monum.*, iv. 63.

—an opinion which they themselves sometimes expressed. In Würzburg they agreed to adhere to their decrees, even if the king refused his assent to them. They took into their own hands the arrangement of the disputes with the pope which Henry found it impossible to terminate : they were the real authors of the concordat of Worms.

In the succeeding collisions of the papacy with the empire everything depended on the degree of support the emperor could, on each occasion, calculate on receiving from the princes.

I shall not here attempt to give a complete view of the times of the Guelphs and the Hohenstaufen ; it would not be possible, without entering into a more elaborate examination of particulars than is consistent with the object of this short survey : let us only direct our attention for a moment to the grandest and most imposing figure with which that epoch presents us—Frederick I.

So long as Frederick I. stood well with his princes he might reasonably entertain the project of reviving the prerogatives of the empire, such as they were conceived and laid down by the emperors and jurists of ancient Rome. He held himself entitled, like Justinian and Theodosius, to summon ecclesiastical assemblies ; he reminded the popes that their possessions were derived from the favour and bounty of the emperor, and admonished them to attend to their ecclesiastical duties. A disputed election furnished him with a favourable occasion of acquiring fresh influence in the choice of a pope.

His position was, however, very different after the fresh rupture with his powerful vassal, Henry the Lion. The claims of that prince to a little town in the north of Germany,—Goslar in the Harz,—which the emperor refused to admit, decided the affairs of Italy, and hence of the whole of western Christendom. In consequence of this, the emperor was first stripped of his wonted support ; he was beaten in the field ; and, lastly, he was compelled to violate his oath, and to recognise the pope he had rejected.

It is true that, having turned his arms against his rebellious vassal, he succeeded in breaking up Henry's collective power : but this very success again was advantageous to the princes of the second rank, by whose assistance he obtained it, and whom, in return, he enriched with the spoils of his rival ; while the advantage which the papacy thus gained was never afterwards to be counter-balanced.

The meeting of Frederick I. and Alexander III. at Venice is, in my opinion, far more important than the scene at Canossa. At Canossa,[1] a young and passionate prince sought only to hurry through the penance enjoined upon him : at Venice,[2] it was a mature man who renounced the ideas which he had earnestly and strenuously maintained for a quarter of a century; he was compelled to acknowledge that his conduct towards the church had been dictated rather by love of power than of justice.[3]

---

[1] At Canossa Henry IV. submitted to Gregory VII., 1077. Cf. Milman, *Hist. of Latin Christianity*, Bk. vii., c. 2.

[2] The Pacification of Venice. Reconciliation between Frederick I. and Alexander III. Cf. Milman, Bk. viii., c. ix.

[3] " Dum in facto ecclesiæ potius virtutem potentiæ quam rationem justitiæ volumus exercere, constat nos in errorem merito devenisse." Oratio Impera‧ toris in Conventu Veneto.—*Monum.*, iv. 154.

Canossa was the spot on which the combat began ; Venice beheld the triumph of the church fully established.

For whatever might be the indirect share which the Germans had in bringing about this result, both the glory and the chief profit of the victory fell entirely to the share of the papacy.   From this moment its domination began.

This became apparent on the first important incident that occurred ; viz., when, at the end of the twelfth century, a contest for the crown arose in Germany.

The papacy, represented by one of the most able, ambitious, and daring priests that ever lived, who regarded himself as the natural master of the world—Innocent III.—did not hesitate an instant to claim the right of deciding the question.

The German princes were not so blinded as not to understand what this claim meant.   They reminded Innocent that the empire, out of reverence for the see of Rome, had waived the right which it incontestably possessed to interfere in the election of the pope ; that it would be an unheard-of return for this moderation, for the pope to assume an influence over the election of the emperor, to which he had no right whatever. Unfortunately, however, they were in a position in which they could take no serious steps to prevent the encroachment they deprecated.   They must first have placed on the throne an emperor equally strong by nature and by external circumstances, have rallied round him, and have fought the papacy under his banners.   For such a course they had neither the inclination, nor, in the actual state of things, was it practicable.   They had no love for the papacy, for its own sake ; they hated the domination of the clergy ; but they had not courage to brave it.   Innocent's resolute spirit was again victorious.   In the struggle between the two rivals, the one a Guelph, the other a Hohenstaufe, he at first supported the Guelph[1] because that family was well inclined to the church ; but when, after the accession of this prince to power, and his appearance in Italy, he manifested the usual antipathy of the empire to the papacy, Innocent did not hesitate to set up a Hohenstaufe[2] in opposition to him.   He had contended against the Hohenstaufen with the resources of the Guelphic party : he now attacked the Guelphs with those of the Hohenstaufen. It was a struggle in which the agitations of the rest of Europe were mingled. Events, both near and remote, took a turn so favourable, that Innocent's candidate again remained master of the field.

From that time the papacy exercised a leading influence over all German elections.

When, after the lapse of many years, Frederick II., (the Hohenstaufe whom he had raised to power,) attempted in some particulars to restore the independence of the empire, the pope thought himself justified in again deposing him.   Rome now openly avowed her claim to hold the reins of secular as well as spiritual authority.

"We command you," writes Innocent IV. to the German princes in 1246, "since our beloved son, the Landgrave of Thuringia, is ready to take upon himself the office of emperor, that you proceed to elect him unanimously without delay."[3]

---

[1] The Guelph, *i.e.,* Otto IV.   [2] Frederick II., son of Henry VI.
[3] Ex Actis Innocentii.—*Monum.,* iv. 361.

He formally signifies his approbation of those who took part in the election of William of Holland ; he admonishes the cities to be faithful to the newly-elected emperor, that so they may merit the apostolical as well as the royal favour.

In a very short time no trace of any other order of things remained in Germany. Even at the ceremony of homage, Richard of Cornwall was compelled to dispense with the allegiance of the cities, until it should be seen whether or not the pope might choose to prefer another aspirant to the throne.

After Richard's death Gregory X. called upon the German princes to prepare for a new election : he threatened that if they delayed, he and his cardinals would nominate an emperor. The election being terminated, it was again the pope who induced the pretender, Alfonso of Castile, to abandon his claim and to give up the insignia of the empire ; and who caused the chosen candidate, Rudolph of Hapsburg, to be universally acknowledged.[1]

What trace of independence can a nation retain after submitting to receive its head from the hands of a foreign power ? It is manifest that the same influence which determines the elections, must be resistless in every other department of the state.

The power of the princes of Germany had, it is true, been meanwhile on the increase. In the thirteenth century, during the struggles between the several pretenders to the throne, and between the papacy and the empire, they had got possession of almost all the prerogatives of sovereignty ; they likewise took the most provident measures to prevent the imperial power from regaining its vast preponderance. At the end of the thirteenth and the beginning of the fourteenth century the emperors were chosen almost systematically out of different houses. Consciously or unconsciously, the princes acted on the maxim, that when power began to be consolidated in one quarter it must be counterbalanced by an increase of authority in another ; as, for example, they curbed the already considerable power of Bohemia by means of the house of Hapsburg, and this again, by those of Nassau, Luxemburg, or Bavaria. None of these could attain to more than transient superiority, and in consequence of this policy, no princely race rose to independence : the spiritual princes, who conducted the larger portion of the public business, were almost of more weight than the temporal.

This state of things tended greatly to increase the power of the papacy, on which the spiritual princes depended ; and to which the temporal became very subordinate and submissive. In the thirteenth century they even made the abject declaration that they were planted in Germany by the church of Rome, and had been fostered and exalted by her favour.[2] The pope was, at least, as much indebted to the German princes as they were to him ; but he took good care not to allude to his obligations, and nobody ventured to remind him of them. His successive victories over the empire had been gained by the assistance of many of the temporal powers. He now possessed, uncontested, the supreme sovereignty of Europe. Those plans of papal aggrandisement which were first avowed

[1] Gerbert, Introductio ad Cod. Epist. Rudolfi, c. iv., n. 30.

[2] Tractatus cum Nicolao III. Papa, 1279. " Romana ecclesia Germaniam decoravit plantans in ea principes tanquam arbores electas."—*Monum.* iv., 42.

in the ninth century, and afterwards revived in the eleventh, were, in the thirteenth, crowned with complete success.

During that long period a state of things had been evolved, the outlines of which may, I think, be traced in a few words.

The pretensions of the clergy to govern Europe according to their hierarchical views—pretensions which arose directly out of the ecclesiastical institutions of Charlemagne—were encountered and resisted by the united body of the German people, still thoroughly imbued with the national ideas of ancient Germania. On this combined resistance the imperial throne was founded. Unfortunately, however, it failed to acquire perfect security and stability; and the divisions which soon broke out between the domineering chief and his refractory vassals, had the effect of making both parties contribute to the aggrandisement of that spiritual power which they had previously sought to depress. At first the emperors beheld in a powerful clergy a means of holding their great vassals in check, and endowed the church with liberal grants of lands and lordships; but afterwards, when ideas of emancipation began to prevail, not only in the papacy but in all spiritual corporations, the temporal aristocracy thought it not inexpedient that the emperor should be stripped of the resource and assistance such a body afforded him: the enfeebling of the imperial authority was of great advantage, not only to the church, but to them. Thus it came to pass that the ecclesiastical element, strengthened by the divisions of its opponents, at length obtained a decided preponderance.

Unquestionably the result was far different in the twelfth and thirteenth centuries from what it would have been in the ninth. The secular power might be humbled, but could not be annihilated; a purely hierarchical government, such as might have been established at the earlier period, was now no longer within the region of possibility. The national development of Germany had been too deep and extensive to be stifled by the ecclesiastical spirit; while, on the other hand, the influence of ecclesiastical ideas and institutions unquestionably contributed largely to its extension. The period in question displayed a fulness of life and intelligence, an activity in every branch of human industry, a creative vigour, which we can hardly imagine to have arisen under any other course of events. Nevertheless, this was not a state which ought to satisfy a great nation. There could be no true political freedom so long as the most powerful impulse to all public activity emanated from a foreign head. The domain of mind, too, was enclosed within rigid and narrow boundaries. The immediate relation in which every intellectual being stands to the Divine Intelligence was veiled from the people in deep and abiding obscurity.

Those mighty developments of the human mind which extend over whole generations, must, of necessity, be accomplished slowly; nor is it always easy to follow them in their progress.

Circumstances at length occurred which awakened in the German nation a consciousness of the position for which nature designed it.

FIRST ATTEMPTS AT RESISTANCE TO THE ENCROACHMENTS OF THE PAPACY.

THE first important circumstance was, that the papacy, forgetting its high vocation in the pleasures of Avignon,[1] displayed all the qualities of a prodigal and rapacious court, centralising its power for the sake of immediate profit.

Pope John XXII. enforced his pecuniary claims with the coarsest avidity, and interfered in an unheard-of manner with the presentation to German benefices : he took care to express himself in very ambiguous terms as to the rights of the electoral princes ; while, on the contrary, he seriously claimed the privilege of examining into the merits of the emperor they had elected, and of rejecting him if he thought fit ; nay, in case of a disputed election, such as then occurred, of administering the government himself till the contest should be decided [2] : lastly, he actually entered into negotiations, the object of which was to raise a French prince to the imperial throne.

The German princes at length saw what they had to expect from such a course of policy. On this occasion they rallied round their emperor, and rendered him real and energetic assistance. In the year 1338 they unanimously came to the celebrated resolution, that whoever should be elected by the majority of the prince-electors should be regarded as the true and legitimate emperor. When Louis the Bavarian, wearied by the long conflict, wavered for a moment, they kept him firm ; they reproached him at the imperial diet in 1334 with having shown a disposition to accede to humiliating conditions. A change easily accounted for ; the pope having now encroached, not only on the rights of the emperor, but on the prescriptive rights of their own body—on the rights of the whole nation.

Nor were these sentiments confined to the princes. In the fourteenth century a plebeian power had grown up in Germany, as in the rest of Europe, by the side of the aristocratic families which had hitherto exercised almost despotic power : not only were the cities summoned to the imperial diets, but, in a great proportion of them, the guilds, or trades, had got the municipal government into their own hands. These plebeians embraced the cause of their emperor with even more ardour than most of the princes. The priests who asserted the power of the pope to excommunicate the emperor were frequently driven out of the cities ; these

---

[1] Cf. Creighton's Popes, vol. i., p. 31. From 1305–1370 the popes lived at Avignon and were the creatures of the French king. " The Babylonish captivity," as it was called, was followed, on the death of Gregory XI. in 1378, by the Great Schism.

[2] " Attendentes quod imperii Romani regimen, cura et administratio (another time he says, imperii Romani jurisdictio, regimen et administratio), tempore quo illud vacare contingit, ad nos pertineat, sicut dignoscitur pertinere."— *Literæ Johannis in Rainaldus*, 1319 ; and *Olenschlager, Geschichte des Rom.-Kaiserthums, &c., in der ersten Hälfte des 14ten Jahrhunderts*, p. 102. In the year 1323 he declares that he has instituted a suit against Lewis the Bavarian ; " super· eo quod electione sua *per quosdam qui vocem in electione hujusmodi habere dicuntur*, per sedem apostolicam, ad quam electionis hujusmodi et personæ electæ examinatio, approbatio, admissio ac etiam reprobatio et repulsio noscitur pertinere, non admissa," &c.—*Olenschlager, Urk.*, n. 36.

were then, in their turn, laid under excommunication; but they never would acknowledge its validity; they refused to accept absolution when it was offered them.[1]

Thus it happened that in the present instance the pope could not carry the election of his candidate, Charles of Luxemburg; nobles and commons adhered almost unanimously to Louis of Bavaria: nor was it till after his death, and then only after repeated election and coronation, that Charles IV. was gradually recognised.

Whatever he might previously have promised the pope, that sovereign could not make concessions injurious to the interests of his princes: on the contrary, he solemnly and firmly established the rights of the electors, even to the long-disputed vicariate (at least in all German states). A germ of resistance was thus formed.

This was fostered and developed by the disorders of the great schism, and by the dispositions evinced by the general councils.

It was now, for the first time, evident that the actual church no longer corresponded with the ideal that existed in men's minds. Nations assumed the attitude of independent members of it; popes were brought to trial and deposed; the aristocratico-republican spirit, which played so great a part in the temporal states of Europe, extended even to the papacy (the nature of which is so completely monarchical), and threatened to change its form and character.

The ecclesiastical assembly of Basle entertained the project of establishing at once the freedom of nations and the authority of councils; a project hailed with peculiar approbation by Germany. Its decretals of reformation were solemnly adopted by the assembly of the imperial diet:[2] the Germans determined to remain neutral during its controversies with Eugenius IV.; the immediate consequence of which was, that they were for a time emancipated from the court of Rome.[3] By threatening to go over to his adversary, they forced the pope, who had ventured to depose two spiritual electors, to revoke the sentence of deposition.

Had this course been persevered in with union and constancy, the German Catholic church, established in so many great principalities, and splendidly provided with the most munificent endowments in the world, would have acquired a perfectly independent position, in which she might have resisted the subsequent polemical storms with as much firmness as that of England.

Various circumstances conspired to prevent so desirable a result.

In the first place, it appears to me that the disputes between France and Burgundy reacted on this matter. France was in favour of the ideas of the council, which, indeed, she embodied in the pragmatic sanction; Burgundy was for the pope. Among the German princes, some were in the most intimate alliance with the king, others with the duke.

The pope employed by far the most dexterous and able negotiator. If we consider the character of the representative and organ of the German

[1] *e.g.* Basel. Albertus Argentinensis in Urstisius, 142.
[2] Johannes de Segovia: Koch, Sanctio pragmatica, p. 256.
[3] Declaration in Müller, Reichstagstheater, unter Fred. III., p. 31. "In sola ordinaria jurisdictione citra præfatorum tam papæ quam concilii supremam auctoritatem ecclesiasticæ politiæ gubernacula per dioceses et territoria nostra gubernabimus."

opposition, Gregory of Heimburg, who thought himself secure of victory, and, when sent to Rome, burst forth at the very foot of the Vatican into a thousand execrations on the Curia ;—if we follow him there, as he went about with neglected garb, bare neck, and uncovered head, bidding defiance to the court,—and then compare him with the polished and supple Æneas Sylvius, full of profound quiet ambition and gifted with the happiest talents for rising in the world ; the servant of so many masters, and the dexterous confidant of them all ; we shall be at no loss to divine which must be the successful party. Heimburg died a living death in exile, and dependent on foreign bounty ; Æneas Sylvius ended his career, wearing the triple crown he had so ably served. At the very time we are treating of, Æneas had found means to gain over some councillors, and through them their sovereigns, and thus to secure their defection from the great scheme of national emancipation. He relates this himself with great satisfaction and self-complacency ; nor did he disdain to employ bribery.[1]

The main thing, however, was, that the head of the empire, King Frederick III., adhered to the papal cause. The union of the princes, which, while it served as a barrier against the encroachments of the church, might have proved no less perilous to himself, was as hateful to him as to the pope. Æneas Sylvius conducted the negotiation in a manner no less agreeable to the interests and wishes of the emperor than to those of the pope : the imperial coffers furnished him with the means of corruption.

Hence it happened that on this occasion also the nation failed to attain its object.

At the first moment, indeed, the Basle decretals were accepted at Rome, but under the condition that the Holy See should receive compensation for its losses. This compensation, however, was not forthcoming ; and Frederick III., who treated on the part of the empire, at length conceded anew to Rome all her old privileges, which the nation had been endeavouring to wrest from her.[2] It would have been impossible to carry such a measure at the diet ; the expedient of obtaining the separate consent of the princes to this agreement was therefore resorted to.

The old state of things was thus perpetuated. Ordinances which the papal see had published in 1335, and which it had repeated in 1418, once more formed, in the year 1448, the basis of the German concordat. It is hardly necessary to say that the opposition was not crushed. It no

---

[1] Historia Friderici III. ap. Kollar, Analecta, ii., p. 127.

[2] In the second half of the foregoing century attention had been strongly drawn to the assertion, that all the decrees of the council of Basle, which had not been expressly altered by the concordat, acquired legal validity in virtue of the same. Against this, Spittler has made the objection, that the brief runs thus : "donec per legatum concordatum fuerit vel per legatum aliter fuerit ordinatum ;" and, assuming that an "aliter" is wanting in the first part of the sentence, has concluded that the whole of the decrees had only been suffered to hold good *till the* conclusion of the concordat. (Werke, viii., p. 473.) But in the relation of Æneas Sylvius in Koch, Sanctio pragmatica, p. 323, the "aliter" missed by Spittler stands expressly next to "concordatum ;" "usque quo cum legato aliter fuerit concordatum." (Vide Koch, ii., § 24.) The sense of these words cannot therefore be doubted. For in no case can it be supposed that "aliter" had been left out with any sinister design.

longer appeared on the surface of events ; but deep below it, it only
struck root faster and acquired greater strength.   The nation was exasperated by a constant sense of wrong and injustice.

ALTERED CHARACTER OF THE EMPIRE.

THE most remarkable fact now was, that the imperial throne was no longer
able to afford support and protection.   The empire had assumed a position
analogous to that of the papacy, but extremely subordinate in power
and authority.

It is important to remark, that for more than a century after Charles IV.
had fixed his seat in Bohemia, no emperor appeared, endowed with the
vigour necessary to uphold and govern the empire.   The bare fact that
Charles's successor, Wenceslas, was a prisoner in the hands of the
Bohemians, remained for a long time unknown in Germany : a simple
decree of the electors sufficed to dethrone him.   Rupert the Palatine only
escaped a similar fate by death.   When Sigismund of Luxemburg, (who
after many disputed elections, kept possession of the field,) four years
after his election, entered the territory of the empire of which he was to
be crowned sovereign, he found so little sympathy that he was for a
moment inclined to return to Hungary without accomplishing the object
of his journey.   The active part he took in the affairs of Bohemia, and
of Europe generally, has given him a name ; but in and for the empire,
he did nothing worthy of note.   Between the years 1422 and 1430 he
never made his appearance beyond Vienna ; from the autumn of 1431
to that of 1433 he was occupied with his coronation journey to Rome ;
and during the three years from 1434 to his death he never got beyond
Bohemia and Moravia : [1] nor did Albert II., who has been the subject
of such lavish eulogy, ever visit the dominions of the empire.   Frederick III.,
however, far outdid all his predecessors.   During seven-and-twenty years,
from 1444 to 1471, he was never seen within the boundaries of the empire.

Hence it happened that the central action and the visible manifestation
of sovereignty, inasfar as any such existed in the empire, fell to the share
of the princes, and more especially of the prince-electors.   In the reign
of Sigismund we find them convoking the diets, and leading the armies
into the field against the Hussites : the operations against the Bohemians
were attributed entirely to them.[2]

In this manner the empire became, like the papacy, a power which
acted from a distance, and rested chiefly upon opinion.   The throne,
founded on conquest and arms, had now a pacific character and a conservative tendency.   Nothing is so transient as the notions which are
handed down with a name, or associated with a title ; and yet, especially
in times when unwritten law has so much force, the whole influence of rank
or station depends on the nature of these notions.   Let us turn our attention for a moment to the ideas of Empire and Papacy entertained in the
fifteenth century.

[1] The acts of his reign are dated from Ofen, Stuhlweissenburg, from Cronstadt
" in Transylvanian Würzland," from the army before the castle of Taubenburg
in Sirfey (Servia).   Häberlin, Reichsgeschichte, v. 429, 439.

[2] Matthias Döring in Mencken, iii., p. 4.   " Eodem anno principes electores
exercitum grandem habentes contra Bohemos se transtulerunt ad Bohemiam."

The emperor was regarded, in the first place, as the supreme feudal lord, who conferred on property its highest and most sacred sanction ; as the supreme fountain of justice, from whom, as the expression was, all the compulsory force of law emanated. It is very curious to observe how the choice that had fallen upon him was announced to Frederick III.,— by no means the mightiest prince in the empire ; how immediately there-upon the natural relations of things are reversed, and " his royal high mightiness " promises confirmation in their rights and dignities to the very men who had just raised him to the throne.[1] All hastened to obtain his recognition of their privileges and possessions ; nor did the cities perform their act of homage till that had taken place. Upon his supreme guarantee rested that feeling of legitimacy, security and permanence, which is necessary to all men, and more especially dear to Germans. " Take away from us the rights of the emperor," says a law-book of that time, " and who can say, this house is mine, this village belongs to me ? " A remark of profound truth ; but it followed thence that the emperor could not arbitrarily exercise rights of which he was deemed the source. He might give them up ; but he himself must enforce them only within the narrow limits prescribed by traditional usage, and by the superior control of his subjects. Although he was regarded as the head and source of all temporal jurisdiction, yet no tribunal found more doubtful obedience than his own.

The fact that royalty existed in Germany had almost been suffered to fall into oblivion ; even the title had been lost. Henry VII. thought it an affront to be called King of Germany, and not, as he had a right to be called before any ceremony of coronation, King of the Romans.[2] In the fifteenth century the emperor was regarded pre-eminently as the successor of the ancient Roman Cæsars, whose rights and dignities had been trans-ferred, first to the Greeks, and then to the Germans in the persons of Charlemagne and Otho the Great ; as the true secular head of Christen-dom. Emperor Sigismund commanded that his corpse should be exposed to view for some days ; in order that everyone might see that " the Lord of all the world was dead and departed."[3]

" We have chosen your royal grace," say the electors to Frederick III (A. D. 1440), " to be the head, protector, and governor of all Christendom." They go on to express the hope that this choice may be profitable to the Roman church, to the whole of Christendom, to the holy empire, and the community of Christian people.[4] Even a foreign monarch, Wladislas of Poland, extols the felicity of the newly-elected emperor, in that he was about to receive the diadem of the monarchy of the world.[5] The opinion was confidently entertained in Germany that the other sovereigns of Christendom, especially those of England, Spain, and France, were legally subject to the crown of the empire : the only controversy was, whether

[1] Letter of the Frankfort Deputies, July 5, 1440. Frankfurter Arch.

[2] Henrici VII. Bannitio Florentiæ, Pertz, iv. 520, " supprimentes (it is there said) ipsius veri nominis (Regis Romanorum) dignitatem in ipsius opprobrium et despectum."

[3] Eberhard Windeck in Mencken, Scriptt. i. 1278.

[4] Letter of the Prince-Electors, Feb. 2, 1440, in Chmel's Materialien zur Oestreich, Gesch. No. ii., p. 70.

[5] Literæ Vladislai ap. Kollar, Anal., ii., p. 830.

their disobedience was venial, or ought to be regarded as sinful.[1] The English endeavoured to show that from the time of the introduction of Christianity they had never been subject to the empire.[2] The Germans, on the contrary, not only did what the other nations of the West were bound to do—they not only acknowledged the holy empire, but they had secured to themselves the faculty of giving it a head ; and the strange notion was current that the electoral princes had succeeded to the rights and dignities of the Roman senate and people. They themselves expressed this opinion in the thirteenth century. "We," say they, "who occupy the place of the Roman senate, who are the fathers and the lights of the empire."[3] . . . . In the fifteenth century they repeated the same opinion.[4] "The Germans," says the author of a scheme for diminishing the burthens of the empire, "who have possessed themselves of the dignities of the Roman empire, and thence of the sovereignty over all lands."[5] . . . . When the prince-electors proceeded to the vote, they swore that " according to the best of their understanding, they would choose the temporal head of all Christian people, *i.e.*, a Roman king and future emperor." Thereupon the elected sovereign was anointed and crowned by the Archbishop of Cologne, who enjoyed that right on this side the Alps. Even when seated on the coronation chair at Rheims, the King of France took an oath of fealty to the Roman empire.[6]

It is obvious in what a totally different relation the Germans stood to the emperor, who was elevated to this high dignity from amidst themselves, and by their own choice, from that of even the most puissant nobles of other countries to their natural hereditary lord and master. The imperial dignity, stripped of all direct executive power, had indeed no other significancy than that which results from opinion. It gave to law and order their living sanction ; to justice its highest authority ; to the sovereignties of Germany their position in the world. It had properties which, for that period, were indispensable and sacred. It had a manifest analogy with the papacy, and was bound to it by the most intimate connection.

The main difference between the two powers was, that the papal enjoyed

---

[1] Petrus de Andlo de Romano Imperio : an important book, not indeed with reference to the actual state of Germany, but to the ideas of the time in which it was written. It dates from between 1456, which year is expressly mentioned, and 1459, in which year happened the death of Diedrich of Mainz, of whom it speaks. The author says, ii. c. 8 : " Hodie plurimi reges *plus de facto quam de jure* imperatorem in superiorem non recognoscunt et suprema jura imperii usurpant."

[2] Cuthbert Tunstall to King Henry VIII., Feb. 12, 1517, in Ellis's Letters, series 1. vol. i., p. 136. " Your Grace is not nor never sithen the Christen faith the kings of England wer subgiet to th'Empire, but the crown of England is an Empire of hitself, mych bettyr than now the Empire of Rome : for which cause your Grace werith a close crown."

[3] Conradi IV. electio 1237 : Pertz, iv. 322.

[4] P. de Andlo ii., iii. " Isti principes electores successerunt, in locum senatus populique Romani."

[5] Intelligentia Principum super Gravaminibus Nationis Germanicæ. MS. at Coblenz. See Appendix.

[6] Æneas Sylvius (Historia Friderici III. in the Kollar's Anal. ii. 288.) tries to make a distinction between the three crowns, and to assign them to the different kingdoms ; but in this case we do not ask what is true, but what was commonly thought. The opinions which he disputes are exactly those of importance in our eyes ; namely, those generally entertained.

that universal recognition of the Romano-Germanic world which the imperial had not been able to obtain : but the holy Roman church and the holy Roman empire were indissolubly united in idea ; and the Germans thought they stood in a peculiarly intimate relation to the church as well as to the empire. There is extant a treaty of alliance of the Rhenish princes, the assigned object of which was to maintain their endowments, dioceses, chapters, and principalities, in dignity and honour with the holy Roman empire and the holy Roman church. The electors lay claim to a peculiar privilege in ecclesiastical affairs. In the year 1424, and again in 1446, they declare that the Almighty has appointed and authorised them, that they should endeavour, together with the Roman king, the princes, lords, knights, and cities of the empire, and with all faithful Christian people, to abate all crimes that arise in the holy church and Christian community, and in the holy empire.[1]

Hence we see that the German people thought themselves bound in allegiance to the papal, no less than to the imperial authority ; but as the former had, in all the long struggles of successive ages, invariably come off victorious, while the latter had so often succumbed, the pope exercised a far stronger and more wide-spread influence, even in temporal things, than the emperor. An act of arbitrary power, which no emperor could ever have so much as contemplated—the deposition of an electoral prince of the empire—was repeatedly attempted, and occasionally even accomplished, by the popes. They bestowed on Italian prelates bishoprics as remote as that of Camin. By their annates, pallia, and all the manifold dues exacted by the curia, they drew a far larger (Maximilian I. said, a hundred times larger) revenue from the empire, than the emperor : their vendors of indulgences incessantly traversed the several provinces of the empire. Spiritual and temporal principalities and jurisdictions were so closely interwoven as to afford them continual opportunities of interfering in the civil affairs of Germany. The dispute between Cleves and Cologne[2] about Soest, that between Utrecht and East Friesland about Gröningen, and a vast number of others, were evoked by the pope before his tribunal. In 1472 he confirmed a toll, levied in the electorate of Treves[3] : like the emperor, he granted *privilegia de non evocando*.[4]

Gregory VII.'s comparison of the papacy to the sun and the empire to the moon was now verified. The Germans regarded the papal power as in every respect the higher. When, for example, the town of Basle founded its high school, it was debated whether, after the receipt of the brief containing the pope's approbation, the confirmation of the emperor was still necessary ; and at length decided that it was not so, since the inferior power could not confirm the decisions of the superior, and the papal see was the well-head of Christendom.[5] The pretender to the Palatinate, Frederick the Victorious, whose electoral rank the emperor refused to acknowledge, held it sufficient to obtain the pope's sanction, and received no further molestation in the exercise of his privileges as member of the empire. The judge of the king's court having on some occasion pro-

---

[1] Müller Rtth. Fr. iii. 305. [2] Schüren, Chronik von Cleve, p. 288.

[3] Hontheim, Prodromus Historiæ Trevirensis, p. 320.

[4] The privilege of exemption from having causes evoked to the Court of the Emperor granted to the Electors and to some princes.

[5] Ochs, Geschichte von Basel, iv., p. 60.

nounced the ban of the empire on the council of Lübeck, the council obtained a cassation of this sentence from the pope.[1]

It was assuredly to be expected that the emperor would feel the humiliation of his position, and would resist the pope as often and as strenuously as possible.

However great was the devotion of the princes to the see of Rome, they felt the oppressiveness of its pecuniary exactions; and more than once the spirit of the Basle decrees, or the recollections of the proceedings at Constance, manifested themselves anew. We find draughts of a league to prevent the constitution of Constance, according to which a council should be held every ten years, from falling into utter desuetude.[2] After the death of Nicholas V. the princes urged the emperor to seize the favourable moment for asserting the freedom of the nation, and at least to take measures for the complete execution of the agreement entered into with Eugenius; but Frederick III. was deaf to their entreaties. Æneas Sylvius persuaded him that it was necessary for him to keep well with the pope. He brought forward a few common-places concerning the instability of the multitude, and their natural hatred of their chief;—just as if the princes of the empire were a sort of democracy: the emperor, said he, stands in need of the pope, and the pope of the emperor; it would be ridiculous to offend the man from whom we want assistance.[3] He himself was sent in 1456 to tender unconditional obedience to Pope Calixtus. This immediately revived the old spirit of resistance. An outline was drawn of a pragmatic sanction, in which not only all the charges against the papal see were recapitulated in detail, and redress of grievances proposed, but it was also determined what was to be done in case of a refusal; what appeal was to be made, and how the desired end was to be attained.[4] But what result could be anticipated while the emperor, far from taking part in this plan, did everything he could to thwart it? He sincerely regarded himself as the natural ally of the papacy.

The inevitable effect of this conduct on his part was, that the discontent of the electors, already excited by the inactivity and the absence of the emperor, occasionally burst out violently against him. As early as the year 1456 they required him to repair on a given day to Nürnberg, for that it was his office and duty to bear the burthen of the empire in an honourable manner: if he did not appear, they would, at any rate, meet, and do what was incumbent on them.[5] As he neither appeared then nor afterwards, in 1460 they sent him word that it was no longer consistent with their dignity and honour to remain without a head. They repeated their summons that he would appear on the Tuesday after Epiphany, and accompanied it with still more vehement threats. They began seriously to take measures for setting up a king of the Romans in opposition to him.

[1] Sartorius, Gesch. des Hanse, ii., p. 222.

[2] *e.g.* Resolution of the spiritual Electors, &c.: Properly, a report upon the means of restoring tranquillity to the empire, and upon the necessity of a council, of about the year 1453, in the archives of Coblenz.

[3] Gobellini Commentarii de Vita Pii, ii., p. 44.

[4] Æneæ Sylvii Apologia ad Martinum, Mayer, p. 710; and the above-cited Intelligentia.

[5] Frankfurt, Sep. 10., 1456; a hitherto unknown and very remarkable document. Frankf. Arch.

From the fact that George Podiebrad, king of Bohemia, was the man on whom they cast their eyes, it is evident that the opposition was directed against both emperor and pope jointly. What must have been the consequence of placing a Utraquist[1] at the head of the empire ? This increased the zeal and activity of Pope Pius II. (whom we have hitherto known as Æneas Sylvius), in consolidating the alliance of the see of Rome with the emperor, who, on his side, was scarcely less deeply interested in it. The independence of the prince-electors was odious to both. As one of the claims of the emperor had always been, that no electoral diet should be held without his consent, so Pius II., in like manner, now wanted to bind Diether, Elector of Mainz, to summon no such assembly without the approbation of the papal see. Diether's refusal to enter into any such engagement was the main cause of their quarrel. Pius did not conceal from the emperor that he thought his own power endangered by the agitations which prevailed in the empire. It was chiefly owing to his influence, and to the valour of Markgrave Albert Achilles of Brandenburg, that they ended in nothing.

From this time we find the imperial and the papal powers, which had come to a sense of their common interest and reciprocal utility, more closely united than ever.

The diets of the empire were held under their joint authority ; they were called royal and papal, papal and royal diets. In the reign of Frederick, as formerly in that of Sigismund, we find the papal legates present at the meetings of the empire, which were not opened till they appeared. The spiritual princes took their seats on the right, the temporal on the left, of the legates : it was not till a later period that the imperial commissioners were introduced, and proposed measures in concert with the papal functionaries.

It remains for us to inquire how far this very singular form of government was fitted to satisfy the wants of the empire.

STATE OF GERMANY IN THE MIDDLE OF THE FIFTEENTH CENTURY.

WE have seen what a mighty influence had, from the remotest times, been exercised by the princes of Germany.

First, the imperial power and dignity had arisen out of their body, and by their aid ; then, they had supported the emancipation of the papacy, which involved their own : now, they stood opposed to both. Although strongly attached to, and deeply imbued with, the ideas of Empire and Papacy, they were resolved to repel the encroachments of either : their power was already so independent, that the emperor and the pope deemed it necessary to combine against them.

If we proceed to inquire who were these magnates, and upon what their power rested, we shall find that the temporal hereditary sovereignty, the germ of which had long existed in secret and grown unperceived, shot up in full vigour in the fifteenth century ; and (if we may be allowed to continue the metaphor), after it had long struck its roots deep into the earth, it now began to rear its head into the free air, and to tower above all the surrounding plants.

[1] Utraquists, also called Calixtins. The moderate party among the Hussites, who demanded the participation by the laity of the cup in the sacrament.

All the puissant houses[1] which have since held sovereign sway date their establishment from this epoch.

In the eastern part of north Germany appeared the race of Hohenzollern ; and though the land its princes had to govern and to defend was in the last stage of distraction and ruin, they acted with such sedate vigour and cautious determination, that they soon succeeded in driving back their neighbours within their ancient bounds, pacifying and restoring the marches, and re-establishing the very peculiar bases of sovereign power which already existed in the country.

Near this remarkable family arose that of Wettin, and, by the acquisition of the electorate of Saxony, soon attained to the highest rank among the princes of the empire, and to the zenith of its power. It possessed the most extensive and at the same time the most flourishing of German principalities, as long as the brothers, Ernest and Albert, held their united court at Dresden and shared the government ; and even when they separated, both lines remained sufficiently considerable to play a part in the affairs of Germany, and indeed of Europe.

In the Palatinate we find Frederick the Victorious. It is necessary to read the long list of castles, jurisdictions, and lands which he won from all his neighbours, partly by conquest, partly by purchase or treaty, but which his superiority in arms rendered emphatically his own, to form a conception what a German prince could in that age achieve, and how widely he could extend his sway.

The conquests of Hessen were of a more peaceful nature. By the inheritance of Ziegenhain and Nidda, but more especially of Katzenelnbogen, a fertile, highly cultivated district, from which the old counts had never suffered a village or a farm to be taken, whether by force or purchase, it acquired an addition nearly equal to its original territory.

A similar spirit of extension and fusion was also at work in many other places. Julich and Berg formed a junction. Bavaria-Landshut was strengthened by its union with Ingolstadt ; in Bavaria-Munich, Albert the Wise maintained the unity of the land under the most difficult circumstances ; not without violence, but, at least in this case, with beneficial results. In Würtemberg, too, a multitude of separate estates were gradually incorporated into one district, and assumed the form of a German principality.

New territorial powers also arose. In East Friesland a chieftain at length appeared, before whom all the rest bowed ; Junker[2] Ulrich Cirksena, who, by his own conquests, extended and consolidated the power founded on those of his brother and his father. He also conciliated the adherents of the old Fokko Uken, who were opposed to him, by a marriage with Theta, the granddaughter of that chief. Hereupon he was solemnly proclaimed count at Emden, in the year 1463. But it was to Theta, who was left to rule the country alone during twenty-eight years, that the new sovereignty chiefly owed its strength and stability. This illustrious woman, whose pale, beautiful countenance, brilliant eyes and raven hair survive in her portrait, was endowed with a vast understanding and a singular capacity for governing, as all her conduct and actions prove.

[1] See Table opposite.

[2] Junker, literally, the younger son of a noble house, became the title of the lesser aristocracy of Germany. It corresponds pretty nearly to squire in its common English acceptation.—TRANSL.

"THE PUISSANT HOUSES OF GERMANY."

I. House of Wettin in Saxony.
Frederick I., 1381–1428.

PROTESTANT. | CATHOLIC.

(Ernestine, Electoral Branch at Wittenburg.)
Ernest, 1464–1486.

Frederick the Wise, 1486–1525 (defends Luther).
John (his brother), 1525–1532.

John Frederick, 1532–1554.

(Albertine, at Meissen.)
Albert, 1485-1500.

Duke George, 1500–1535.
Henry (his brother, becomes a Protestant), 1529–1541.

Maurice, 1541–1553 (secures the Electorate).

II. House of Hohenzollern.

Younger Branches.
A. Albert of Prussia, Grand Master of the Teutonic Order, 1512–1568. Secularises his Duchy, 1525.
B. Albert Alcibiades, Margrave of Culmbach, 1536–1557.
C. John of Austria, Margrave of Neumark, brother of Joachim II., ob. 1571.

Electoral Branch.
Descended from Frederick I., 1417-1440.
Albert Achilles, 1470–1486.

John Cicero, 1486–1499.

Joachim I., 1499–1535.

Joachim II., 1535–1571. (Becomes a Protestant in 1539, though he never breaks with the Emperor.)

III. The House of Wittelsbach.
1. Bavaria.
Albert II., 1460–1508.

William I., 1508–1550.

2. Palatinate.
Frederick the Victorious, 1451–1476.
Philip (his nephew), 1476–1508.

Lewis V., 1508–1544.
Frederick II. (his brother), 1544–1552. (becomes a Protestant).

There were two other branches :
    i. Ingoldstadt, united to Landshut, 1445.
    ii. Landshut, which became extinct on the death of George the Rich, 1503.

IV. House of Guelph.
Duke Ernest I. of Luneburg, 1532–1541.

Duke Henry IV. of Wolfenbüttel, 1541–1568.

V. House of Cleves-Julich.
William III. of Julich and Berg,
    ob. 1511.
Mary - - - - - = John III., Duke of Cleves, 1521–1539.

Anne   William,
=Henry VIII. of   1539–1592.
England.

VI. House of Hesse.
William II., 1500–1509.

Philip I., 1509–1567.

VII. House of Würtemburg.
Ulrich I., 1503–1550, became a Protestant, 1534.

Already had several German princes raised themselves to foreign thrones. In the year 1448, Christian I., Count of Oldenburg, signed the declaration or contract which made him king of Denmark : in 1450, he was invested with the crown of St. Olaf, at Drontheim ; in 1457, the Swedes acknowledged him as their sovereign ; in 1460, Holstein did homage to him, and was raised on his account to the rank of a German duchy. These acquisitions were not, it is true, of so stable and secure a character as they at first appeared ; but, at all events, they conferred upon a German princely house a completely new position both in Germany and in Europe.

The rise of the princely power and sovereignty was, as we see, not the mere result of the steady course of events ; the noiseless and progressive development of political institutions ; it was brought about mainly by adroit policy, successful war and the might of personal character.

Yet the secular princes by no means possessed absolute sovereignty ; they were still involved in an incessant struggle with the other powers of the empire.

These were, in the first place, the spiritual principalities (whose privileges and internal organisation were the same as those of the secular, but whose rank in the hierarchy of the empire was higher), in which nobles of the high or even the inferior aristocracy composed the chapter and filled the principal places. In the fifteenth century, indeed, the bishoprics began to be commonly conferred on the younger sons of sovereign princes : the court of Rome favoured this practice, from the conviction that the chapters could only be kept in order by the strong hand and the authority of sovereign power ;[1] but it was neither universal, nor was the fundamental principle of the spiritual principalities by any means abandoned in consequence of its adoption.

There was also a numerous body of nobles who received their investiture with the banner, like the princes, and had a right to sit in the same tribunal with them ; nay, there were even families or clans, which, from all time, claimed exemption from those general feudal relations that formed the bond of the state, and held their lands in fee from God and his blessed sun. They were overshadowed by the princely order ; but they enjoyed perfect independence notwithstanding.

Next to this class came the powerful body of knights of the Empire, whose castles crowned the hills on the Rhine, in Swabia and Franconia ; they lived in haughty loneliness amidst the wildest scenes ; girt round by an impregnable circle of deep fosses, and within walls four-and-twenty feet thick, where they could set all authority at defiance : the bond of fellowship among them was but the stricter for their isolation. Another portion of the nobility, especially in the eastern and colonised principalities in Pomerania and Mecklenburg, Meissen and the Marches, were, however, brought into undisputed subjection ; though this, as we see in the example of the Priegnitz, was not brought about without toil and combat.

There was also a third class who constantly refused to acknowledge any feudal lord. The Craichgauer and the Mortenauer would not acknow-

---

[1] " Si episcopum potentem sortiantur, virgam correctionis timent."—*Æneas Sylvius.*

ledge the sovereignty of the Palatine, nor the Bökler and Löwen-ritter,[1] that of Bavaria. We find that the Electors of Mainz and Treves, on occasion of some decision by arbitration, feared that their nobles would refuse to abide by it, and knew not what measure to resort to in this contingency, except to rid themselves of these refractory vassals and withdraw their protection from them.[2] It seems, in some cases, as if the relation of subject and ruler had become nothing more than a sort of alliance.

Still more completely independent was the attitude assumed by the cities. Opposed to all these different classes of nobles, which they regarded as but one body, they were founded on a totally different principle, and had struggled into importance in the midst of incessant hostility. A curious spectacle is afforded by this old enmity constantly pervading all the provinces of Germany, yet in each one taking a different form. In Prussia, the opposition of the cities gave rise to the great national league against the supreme power, which was here in the hands of the Teutonic Order. On the Wendish coasts was then the centre of the Hanse, by which the Scandinavian kings, and still more the surrounding German princes, were overpowered. The Duke of Pomerania himself was struck with terror, when, on coming to succour Henry the Elder of Brunswick, he perceived by what powerful and closely allied cities his friend was encompassed and enchained on every side. On the Rhine, we find an unceasing struggle for municipal independence, which the chief cities of the ecclesiastical principalities claimed, and the Electors refused to grant. In Franconia, Nürnberg set itself in opposition to the rising power of Brandenburg, which it rivalled in successful schemes of aggrandisement. Then followed in Swabia and the Upper Danube (the true arena of the struggles and the leagues of imperial free cities), the same groups of knights, lords, prelates and princes, who here approached most nearly to each other. Among the Alps, the confederacy formed against Austria had already grown into a regular constitutional government, and attained to almost complete independence. On every side we find different relations, different claims and disputes, different means of carrying on the conflict; but on all, men felt themselves surrounded by hostile passions which any moment might blow into a flame, and held themselves ready for battle. It seemed not impossible that the municipal principle might eventually get the upper hand in all these conflicts, and prove as destructive to the aristocratic, as that had been to the imperial, power.

In this universal shock of efforts and powers,—with a distant and feeble chief, and inevitable divisions even among those naturally connected and allied, a state of things arose which presents a somewhat chaotic aspect; it was the age of universal private warfare. The *Fehde*[3] is a middle term

---

[1] In 1488 Albert IV., of Bavaria, imposed a tax instead of personal service. The Order of Knights, having vainly protested against this, formed the association called the Lion League (Löwenbund), and entered into alliance with the Swabian League. The other associations were probably of a similar kind.—TRANSL.

[2] Jan. 12. 1458. Document in Hontheim, ii., p. 432. "So sall der von uns, des undersaiss he ist, siner missig gain und ime queine schirm, zulegunge oder handhabunge widder den anderen von uns doin."—"Then shall that one of us, whose vassal he is, abandon him and yield him no protection, support or defence against the rest of us."

[3] Some resemblance in sound probably led to the use of the word *feud* (feodum), as the equivalent of *Fehde* (faida), a confusion which, however sanctioned by

between duel and war. Every affront or injury led, after certain formalities, to the declaration, addressed to the offending party, that the aggrieved party would be his foe, and that of his helpers and helpers'-helpers. The imperial authorities felt themselves so little able to arrest this torrent, that they endeavoured only to direct its course ; and, while imposing limitations, or forbidding particular acts, they confirmed the general permission of the established practice.[1]

The right which the supreme, independent power had hitherto reserved to itself, of resorting to arms when no means of conciliation remained, had descended in Germany to the inferior classes, and was claimed by nobles and cities against each other ; by subjects against their lords, nay, by private persons, as far as their means and connections permitted, against each other.

In the middle of the fifteenth century this universal tempest of contending powers was arrested by a conflict of a higher and more important nature—the opposition of the princes to the emperor and the pope ; and it remained to be decided from whose hands the world could hope for any restoration to order.

Two princes appeared on the stage, each of them the hero of his nation, each at the head of a numerous party ; each possessed of personal qualities strikingly characteristic of the epoch—Frederick of the Palatinate, and Albert of Brandenburg. They took opposite courses. Frederick the Victorious, distinguished rather for address and agility of body than for size and strength, owed his fame and his success to the forethought and caution with which he prepared his battles and sieges. In time of peace he busied himself with the study of antiquity, or the mysteries of alchemy ; poets and minstrels found ready access to him, as in the spring-time of poetry ; he lived under the same roof with his friend and songstress, Clara Dettin of Augsburg, whose sweetness and sense not only captivated

---

custom, I have thought it better to avoid. Eichhorn (Deutsche Staats und Rechtsgeschichte, vol. i., p. 441) says :—" In case of robbery, murder, &c., the injured party, or his heirs, was not bound to pursue the injurer at law ; but private help or self-revenge (Privathülfe und Selbstrache)—*Fehde* (faida), was lawful ; and the *Befehdete* (faidosus) could only escape this by paying the appointed fine." For the earliest mention of this fine, he refers to Tacitus (Germ. 21). It is remarkable too that the authority from which he quotes these terms is, the laws of Friesland, a country where, as is well known, feudalism never existed. And indeed the parties by whom diffidations (*Fehdebriefe*) were often sent, were obviously subject to no feudal relations. Although we appear to have lost the English cognate of the Anglo-Saxon Fœhthe (*capitalis inimicitia*), it is found in the Scotch *feid, fede, feyde* (see Gawin Douglas, Jamieson's Dict., &c.), and in most of the Teutonic languages.—TRANSL.

[1] *e.g.* the " Reformation " of Frederick III. of 1442 orders, " dass nymand dem andern Schaden tun oder zufügen soll, er habe ihn denn zuvor—zu landläufigen Rechten erfordert."—" that none should do, or cause to be done, injury to another, unless he have previously challenged him, according to the customary laws of the land." The clause of the golden bull, de Diffidationibus, is then repeated.*

---

* The clause is as follows :—" Eos qui de cetero adversus aliquos justam diffidationis causam se habere fingentes, ipsos in locis, ubi domicilia non obtinent aut ea communiter non inhabitant, intempestive diffidant ; declaramus damna per incendia, spolia, vel rapinas, diffidatis ipsis, cum honore suo inferre non posse." *Bulla Aurea* cap. xvii.—TRANS.

the prince, but were the charm and delight of all around him. He had
expressly renounced the comforts of equal marriage and legitimate heirs ;
all that he accomplished or acquired was for the advantage of his nephew
Philip.

The towering and athletic frame of Markgrave Albert of Brandenburg
(surnamed Achilles), on the contrary, announced, at the first glance, his
gigantic strength : he had been victor in countless tournaments, and
stories of his courage and warlike prowess, bordering on the fabulous,
were current among the people ;—how, for example, at some siege he had
mounted the walls alone, and leaped down into the midst of the terrified
garrison ; how, hurried on by a slight success over an advanced party of
the enemy, he had rushed almost unattended into their main body of 800
horsemen, had forced his way up to their standard, snatched it from its
bearer, and after a momentary feeling of the desperateness of his position,
rallied his courage and defended it, till his people could come up and complete the victory. Æneas Sylvius declares that the Markgrave himself
assured him of the fact.[1] His letters breathe a passion for war. Even
after a defeat he had experienced, he relates to his friends with evident
pleasure, how long he and four others held out on the field of battle ; how
he then cut his way through with great labour and severe fighting, and how
he was determined to re-appear as soon as possible in the field. In time
of peace he busied himself with the affairs of the empire, in which he took
a more lively and efficient part than the emperor himself. We find him
sharing in all the proceedings of the diets ; or holding a magnificent and
hospitable court in his Franconian territories ; or directing his attention
to his possessions in the Mark, which were governed by his son with all
the vigilance dictated by the awe of a grave and austere father. Albert
is the worthy progenitor of the warlike house of Brandenburg. He bequeathed to it not only wise maxims, but, what is of more value, a great
example.

About the year 1461 these two princes embraced, as we have said,
different parties. Frederick, who as yet possessed no distinctly recognised
power, and in all things obeyed his personal impulses, put himself at the
head of the opposition. Albert, who always followed the trodden path of
existing relations, undertook the defence of the emperor and the pope :[2]

[1] Historia Friderici III., in the part first published by Kollar, Anal., ii., p. 166.
[2] In the collection of imperial documents in the Frankfurt Archives, vol. v.,
there is a very remarkable report by Johannes Brun of an audience which he
had of Albrecht Achilles in Oct. 1461. He had to entreat him for a remission of
the succours demanded. Markgrave Albrecht would not grant this : " Auch
erzalte er, was Furnemen gen unssen gn. Herrn den Keyser gewest wäre und wy
ein Gedenken nach dem Ryche sy, auch der Kunig von Behemen ganz Meynung
habe zu Mittensommer für Francfort zu sin und das Rych zu erobern, und
darnach wie u. g. H. der Keiser yne, sine Schweher von Baden und Wirtenberg
angerufen und yne des Ryches Banyer bevolhen habe, über Herzog Ludwig, um
der Geschicht willen mit dem Bischof von Eystett, den von Werde und Dinkelsböl und umb die Pene, darin er deshalben verfallen sy ;—in den Dingen
er uf niemant gebeitet oder gesehen, sondern zu Stund mit den sinen und des
von Wirtenberg mit des Rychs Banyer zu Feld gelegen und unsern Herrn den
Keyser gelediget und die Last uf sich genommen, darin angesehen sine Pflicht,
und was er habe das er das vom Ryche habe, und meyne Lip und Gut von u. H.
dem Keiser nit zu scheiden."—" He also recounted what manner of enterprise

fortune wavered for a time between them. But at last the Jörsika, as George Podiebrad was called, abandoned his daring plans. Diether of Isenburg was succeeded by his antagonist, Adolf of Nassau ; and Frederick the Palatine consented to give up his prisoners : victory leaned, in the main, to the side of Brandenburg. The ancient authorities of the Empire and the Church were once more upheld.

These authorities, too, now seemed seriously bent on introducing a better order of things. By the aid of the victorious party, the emperor found himself, for the first time, in a position to exercise a certain influence in the empire ; Pope Paul II. wished to fit out an expedition against the Turks : with united strength they proceeded to the work at the diet of Nürnberg (A.D. 1466.).[1]

It was an assembly which distinctly betrayed the state of parties under which it had been convoked. Frederick the Palatine appeared neither in person nor by deputy ; the ambassadors of Podiebrad, who had fallen into fresh disputes with the papal see, were not admitted : nevertheless, the resolutions passed there were of great importance. It was determined for the next five years to regard every breach of the Public Peace[2] as a

---

there had been against our gracious lord the emperor, and how there was a design upon the empire ; also how the king of Bohemia had the full intention of being at Frankfort at midsummer, and of getting possession of the empire ; and how, thereupon, our gracious lord the emperor had summoned him, his brothers-in-law of Baden and Wurtemberg, and committed the banner of the empire to him rather than to Duke Ludwig, by reason of the affair with the bishop of Eystett, those of Werde and Dinkelsböl, and of the punishment he had incurred on that account : in these things he had tarried or looked for no one, but forthwith taken the field with his men and those of him of Wurtemberg, with the banner of the empire, and relieved our lord the emperor and taken the burthen upon himself, and had therein beheld his duty : and that what he had, he had from the empire, and had no thought of separating his life and lands from the cause of the emperor." As to the prayer of the cities, he says :—" wywol yme das Geld nutzer wäre und er mer schicken wolle mit den die er in den Sold gewönne denn mit den die in von den Städten zugeschicket werden, ye doch so stehe es ime nit zu und habe nit Macht eynich Geld zu nehmen und des Keisers Gebote abzustellen." " Although money was needful to him, and he should spend more with troops he took into his pay than with those the cities should send him, still it would not become him, and he had not power anyhow to take money and to set aside the emperor's command." Dispositions such as befit a prince of the empire. It were much to be wished there were someone capable of giving a more full and accurate account of the life and deeds of this remarkable prince.

[1] Proceedings at the papal and imperial diet held at Nürnberg on account of the Turkish campaign, in the 4th vol. of the Frankfort Acts of the Diet of the Empire, as published by Schilter and Müller, with some small variations.

[2] *Landfriede*—Peace of the land. The expression, public peace, which, in deference to numerous and high authorities I have generally used in the text, is liable to important objections. *A breach of the public peace* means, in England, any open disorder or outrage. But the *Landfriede* (Pax publica) was a special act or provision directed against the abuse of an ancient and established institution,—the *Fehderecht* (jus diffidationis, or right of private warfare). The attempts to restrain this abuse were, for a long time, local and temporary ; as for example, in the year 1382, Markgrave Sigismund of Brandenburg, and some of the neighbouring princes concluded a Landfriede for six years. In such cases tribunals called Peace Courts (*Friedensgerichte*), for trying offences against the *Landfriede*, were instituted and expired together with the peace. The first energetic measure

crime against the majesty of the empire, and to punish it with the ban. It was found that the spiritual tribunals must come in aid of the temporal sword ; and accordingly the pope denounced the heaviest spiritual penalties against violators of the Public Peace. The emperor formally adopted these resolutions at an assembly at Neustadt, in the year 1467, and for the first time revoked the articles of the Golden Bull and the Reformation of 1442, in which private wars were, under certain conditions, permitted.[1] A peace was proclaimed, " enjoined by our most gracious lord the king of the Romans, and confirmed by our holy father the pope," as the electors express themselves.

Some time afterwards—at Regensburg, in the year 1471—the allied powers ventured on a second yet more important step, for the furtherance of the war against the Turks, which they declared themselves at length about to undertake : they attempted to impose a sort of property tax on the whole empire, called the Common Penny,[2] and actually obtained an edict in its favour. They named in concert the officers charged with the collection of it in the archiepiscopal and episcopal sees ; and the papal legate threatened the refractory with the sum of all spiritual punishments, exclusion from the community of the church.[3]

These measures undoubtedly embraced what was most immediately necessary to the internal and external interests of the empire. But how was it possible to imagine that they would be executed ? The combined powers were by no means strong enough to carry through such extensive and radical innovations. The diets had not been attended by nearly sufficient numbers, and people did not hold themselves bound by the resolutions of a party. The opposition to the emperor and the pope had not

---

of the general government to put down private wars was that of the diet of Nürnberg (1466).

Peace of the realm, internal or domestic peace (as distinguished from foreign or international), would come nearer to the meaning of *Landfriede*. It is suffi- cient, however, if the reader bears in mind that it is opposed not to chance disorder or tumult, but to a mode of voiding differences recognised by the law, and limited by certain forms and conditions ; as, e.g. that a *Befehdete* (faidosus) could not be attacked and killed in church or in his own house. See Eichhorn, Deutsche Staats-und-Rechtsgeschichte, vol. ii., p. 453.—Transl.

[1] The constitution of the 18th August, 1467, in Müller Rtth., ii. 293. The provisions for the maintenance of peace contained in those laws were not to be annulled, "dann allain in den Artickel der gülden Bull, der do inhellt von Wider- sagen, und in den ersten Artickel der Reformation, der da inhellt von Angreifen und Beschedigen ; dieselben Artickel sollen die obgemeldten funf Jar ruhen,— auf dass zu Vehde Krieg und Aufrur Anlass vermitten und der Fride Stracks gehalten werde." " Then alone in the article of the Golden Bull, concerning challenges, and the first article of the Reformation, concerning assaults and damages : these articles shall remain unaltered the above-mentioned five years, —that all occasion of challenge, war, and disorder be avoided, and peace be thoroughly maintained." Unluckily the worthy Müller read Milbenstadt for Neuenstadt in this important passage,—a mistake which has found its way into a number of the histories of the empire.

[2] *Das gemeine Pfennig.*—I have not been able to find in any French or English writer the literal translation of this name given to the first attempt at general taxation in the empire ; but I have retained it as characteristic of the age, and of the nature of the tax.—Transl.

[3] The Duke of Cleves was named executor for Bremen, Münster, and Utrecht ; Duke Ludwig of Bavaria, for Regensburg and Passau.

attained its object, but it still subsisted : Frederick the Victorious still lived, and had now an influence over the very cities which had formerly opposed him. The collection of the Common Penny was, in a short time, not even talked of ; it was treated as a project of Paul II., to whom it was not deemed expedient to grant such extensive powers.

The proclamation of the Public Peace had also produced little or no effect. After some time the cities declared that it had occasioned them more annoyance and damage than they had endured before.[1] It was contrary to their wishes that, in the year 1474, it was renewed with all its actual provisions. The private wars went on as before. Soon afterwards one of the most powerful imperial cities, Regensburg, the very place where the Public Peace was proclaimed, fell into the hands of the Bavarians. The combined powers gradually lost all their consideration. In the year 1479 the propositions of the emperor and the pope were rejected in a mass by the estates of the empire, and were answered with a number of complaints.

And yet never could stringent measures be more imperiously demanded.

I shall not go into an elaborate description of the evils attendant on the right of diffidation or private warfare (*Fehderecht*) : they were probably not so great as is commonly imagined. Even in the century we are treating of, there were Italians to whom the situation of Germany appeared happy and secure in comparison with that of their own country, where, in all parts, one faction drove out another.[2] It was only the level country and the high roads which were exposed to robbery and devastation. But even so, the state of things was disgraceful and insupportable to a great nation. It exhibited the strongest contrast to the ideas of law and of religion upon which the Empire was so peculiarly founded.

One consequence of it was, that as every man was exclusively occupied with the care of his own security and defence, or could at best not extend his view beyond the horizon immediately surrounding him, no one had any attention to bestow on the common weal ; not only were no more great enterprises achieved, but even the frontiers were hardly defended. In the East, the old conflict between the Germans and the Lettish and Slavonian tribes was decided in favour of the latter. As the King of Poland found allies in Prussia itself, he obtained an easy victory over the Order,[3] and compelled the knights to conclude the peace of Thorn (A.D. 1466),

[1] " Dass die erbb. Städte und die jren in Zeitten sollichs gemainen Friden und wider des Inhalt und Mainung mer Ungemachs Beschädigung verderblicher Rost Schaden und Unfrid an jren Leuten Leiben und Guten gelitten, dann sy vorher in vil Jaren und Zeytten je empfangen." " That the hereditary cities and their people, in times of such common peace, and contrary to the intent and meaning, had suffered under more inconvenience, damage, cost, mischief, and disturbance, to the persons and possessions of their inhabitants, than had been undergone before during many years and seasons."—*Proceedings at Regensburg,* 1474. *Frankfurter AA.,* vol. viii.

[2] Æneas Sylvius, Dialogi de Autoritate Concilii, introduces in the second of these dialogues a Novanese, who calls out to the Germans : " Bona vestra vere vestra sunt : pace omnes fruimini et libertate in communi, magisque ad naturam quam ad opinionem vivitis. Fugi ego illos Italiæ turbines."—*Kollar, Anal.,* ii. 704.

[3] For a history of this Teutonic Order cf. Lodge, The Close of the Middle Ages (Rivington), p. 454, or the excellent article in the Encyclopædia Britannica.

by which the greater part of the territories of the Order were ceded to him, and the rest were held of him in fee.   Neither emperor nor empire stirred to avert this incalculable loss.   In the West, the idea of obtaining the Rhine as a boundary first awoke in the minds of the French, and the attacks of the Dauphin and the Armagnacs were only foiled by local resistance. But what the one line of the house of Valois failed in, the other, that of Burgundy, accomplished with brilliant success.   As the wars between France and England were gradually terminated, and nothing more was to be gained in that field, this house, with all its ambition and all its good fortune, threw itself on the territory of Lower Germany.   In direct defiance of the imperial authority, it took possession of Brabant and Holland ; then Philip the Good took Luxemburg, placed his natural son in Utrecht, and his nephew on the episcopal throne of Liege ; after which an unfortunate quarrel between father and son gave Charles the Bold an opportunity to seize upon Guelders.   A power was formed such as had not arisen since the time of the great duchies, and the interests and tendencies of which were naturally opposed to those of the empire.   This state the restless Charles resolved to extend, on the one side, towards Friesland, on the other, along the Upper Rhine.   When at length he fell upon the archbishopric of Cologne and besieged Neuss, some opposition was made to him, but not in consequence of any concerted scheme or regular armament, but of a sudden levy in the presence of imminent danger.   The favourable moment for driving him back within his own frontiers had been neglected.   Shortly after, on his attacking Lotharingia, Alsatia, and Switzerland, those countries were left to defend themselves.   Meanwhile, Italy had in fact completely emancipated herself.   If the emperor desired to be crowned there, he must go unarmed like a mere traveller ; his ideal power could only be manifested in acts of grace and favour.   The King of Bohemia, who also possessed the two Lusatias and Silesia, and an extensive feudal dominion within the empire, insisted loudly on his rights, and would hear nothing of the corresponding obligations.

The life of the nation must have been already extinct, had it not, even in the midst of all these calamities, and with the prospect of further imminent peril before it, taken measures to establish its internal order and to restore its external power ;—objects, however, not to be attained without a revolution in both its spiritual and temporal affairs.

The tendency to development and progress in Europe is sometimes more active and powerful in one direction, sometimes in another.   At this moment temporal interests were most prominent ; and these, therefore, must first claim our attention.

BOOK I.

ATTEMPT TO REFORM THE CONSTITUTION OF THE EMPIRE
1486—1517

SIMILAR disorders, arising from kindred sources and an analogous train of events, existed in all the other nations of Europe. It may be said, that the offspring and products of the middle ages were engaged in a universal conflict which seemed likely to end in their common destruction.

The ideas upon which human society is based are but partially and imperfectly imbued with the divine and eternal Essence from which they emanate ; for a time they are beneficent and vivifying, and new creations spring up under their breath. But on earth nothing attains to a pure and perfect existence, and therefore nothing is immortal. When the times are accomplished, higher aspirations and more enlightened schemes spring up out of the tottering remains of former institutions, which they utterly overthrow and efface ; for so has God ordered the world.

If the disorders in question were universal, the efforts to put an end to them were not less so. Powers called into life by the necessity of a change, or growing up spontaneously, arose out of the general confusion, and with vigorous and unbidden hand imposed order on the chaos.

This is the great event of the fifteenth century. The names of the energetic princes of that time, whose task it was first to awaken the nations of Europe to a consciousness of their own existence and importance, are known to all. In France we find Charles VII. and Louis XI. The land was at length delivered from the enemy who had so long held divided sway in it, and was united under the standard of the Lilies ; the monarchy was founded on a military and financial basis ; crafty, calculating policy came in aid of the practical straightforward sense which attained its ends, because it aimed only at what was necessary ; all the daring and insolent powers that had bid defiance to the supreme authority were subdued or overthrown : the new order of things had already attained to sufficient strength to endure a long and stormy minority.

Henry VII. of England, without attempting to destroy the ancient liberties of the nation, laid the foundation of the power of the Tudors on the ruins of the two factions of the aristocracy, with a resolution nothing could shake and a vigour nothing could resist. The Norman times were over ;—modern England began. At the same time Isabella of Castile reduced her refractory vassals to submission, by her union with a powerful neighbour, by the share she had acquired in the spiritual power, and by the natural ascendancy of her own grand and womanly character, in which austere domestic virtue and a high chivalrous spirit were so singularly blended. She succeeded in completely driving out the Moors and pacifying the Peninsula. Even in Italy, some stronger governments were consolidated ; five considerable states were formed, united by a free alliance, and for a while capable of counteracting all foreign influence. At the same time Poland, doubly strong through her union with Lithuania, climbed to the highest pinnacle of power she ever possessed ; while in Hungary, a native king maintained the honour and the unity of his nation at the head of the powerful army he had assembled under his banner.

However various were the resources and the circumstances by which it was surrounded, Monarchy—the central power—was everywhere strong enough to put down the resisting independencies ; to exclude foreign influence ; to rally the people around its standard, by appealing to the national spirit under whose guidance it acted ; and thus to give them a feeling of unity.

In Germany, however, this was not possible. The two powers which might have effected the most were so far carried along by the general tendency of the age, that they endeavoured to introduce some degree of order ; we have seen with what small success. At the very time in which all the monarchies of Europe consolidated themselves, the emperor was driven out of his hereditary states, and wandered about the other parts of the empire as a fugitive.[1] He was dependent for his daily repast on the bounty of convents, or of the burghers of the imperial cities ; his other wants were supplied from the slender revenues of his chancery : he might sometimes be seen travelling along the roads of his own dominions in a carriage drawn by oxen ; never—and this he himself felt—was the majesty of the empire dragged about in meaner form : the possessor of a power which, according to the received idea, ruled the world, was become an object of contemptuous pity.

If anything was to be done in Germany, it must be by other means, upon other principles, with other objects, than any that had hitherto been contemplated or employed.

FOUNDATION OF A NEW CONSTITUTION.[2]

It is obvious at the first glance, that no attempt at reform could be successful which did not originate with the States themselves. Since they had taken up so strong a position against the two co-ordinate higher powers, they were bound to show how far that position was likely to prove beneficial to the public interests.

It was greatly in their favour that the emperor had sunk into so deplorable a situation.

Not that it was their intention to make use of this to his entire overthrow or destruction ; on the contrary, they were determined not to allow him to fall. What for centuries only one emperor had accomplished, and he, in the fulness of his power and by dispensing extraordinary favours (viz. to secure the succession to his son), Frederick III. achieved in the moment of the deepest humiliation and weakness. The prince-electors met in the year 1486, to choose his son Maximilian king of the Romans. In this measure, Albert Achilles of Brandenburg, took the most prominent and active part. Notwithstanding his advanced age, he came once more in person to Frankfurt : he caused himself to be carried into the electoral chapel on a litter, whence, at the close of the proceedings, he presented the sceptre ; he was in the act of performing his high function as archchamberlain of the empire, when he expired. It could not escape the electors, that the claims of the house of Austria to the support of the empire were greatly strengthened

---

[1] See Unrest, Chronicon Austriacum ; Hahn. 660–688. Kurz, Oestreich unter Friedrich III., vol. ii.

[2] For an outline of the Germanic Constitution cf. Cambridge Modern History, vol. i., p. 288. Johnson, Europe in the Sixteenth Century, p. 106. Wolf, Deutsche Geschichte im Zeitalter der Gegenreformation, p. 1–113 (more fully).

by this event.   Maximilian, the son-in-law of Charles the Bold, who had undertaken to uphold the rights of the house of Burgundy in the Netherlands, encountered there difficulties and misfortunes not much inferior to those which beset his father in Austria, and must, on no account, be abandoned.   His election could hardly be regarded as fully accomplished, until the countries which had hitherto maintained a hostile attitude were subjected to him, and thus restored to the empire.   It was precisely by determining to send succours in both directions, that the states acquired a two-fold right to discuss internal affairs according to their own judgment.   They had rendered fresh services to the reigning house, which could not defend its hereditary possessions without their aid, and their voices must now be heard.

At this moment, too, a coolness arose between the emperor and the pope.   There was a large party in Europe which had always regarded the rise of the Austrian power with dislike, and was now greatly offended at the election of Maximilian to the Roman throne.   To this party, in consequence of the turn Italian affairs had taken, Pope Innocent VII. belonged. He refused the emperor aid against the Hungarians, and even against the Turks.   The imperial ambassador found him, as Frederick complained to the diet, " very awkward to deal with " (*gar ungeschickt*),[1] and could do nothing with him.   There was also a difference with the pope about the nomination to the see of Passau, as well as about a newly-imposed tithe. In short, the intervention of the Roman see was, for a moment, suspended.   For the first time, during a long period, we find numerous assemblies of German princes without the presence of a papal legate.

Under these circumstances the deliberations of the States were opened with a better prospect of useful results.

It was evidently not necessary to begin from the beginning ; all the elements of a great commonwealth were at hand.   The diets had long been regarded as the focus of legislation and of the general government : peace (*Landfriede*) had been proclaimed throughout the realm ; an imperial court of justice existed ; as long ago as the Hussite war a census had been taken with a view to the general defence of the empire.   Nothing remained but to give to these institutions that steady and pervading action which they had hitherto entirely wanted.

To this effect deliberations were incessantly held from the year 1486 to 1489.   Ideas embracing the whole land of the German people, and directed to the restoration of its unity and strength, were in active circulation.   In order to obtain a more complete and accurate conception of the several important points, we will consider them, not in their historical connection either with each other or with contemporaneous events, but each separately.

The first was the Public Peace, which had again been broken on every side, and now, proclaimed anew in 1486, had been rendered clear by some more precise provisions annexed in 1487 ; yet it differed little from those which had gone before it.   The execution of it was now, as heretofore, left to the tumultuous levy of the neighbourhood within a circle of from six to ten miles (German) ; nay, the declaration of 1487 expressly declares that a party in whose favour sentence had been pronounced might use

---

[1] Müller, Rtth. unter Friedrich III. v. 122.

force to secure its execution.[1]   The only difference was that the co-operation of the pope was no longer invited.   There was no further mention of
sending papal conservators with peculiar powers of executing justice, in
order to the maintenance of the Public Peace.   This, however, rendered
it doubtful whether the clergy, to whom the pope and the church were
much more proximate and formidable than the emperor and the state,
would choose to regard themselves as bound by the peace.   No other
means could be found to obviate this evil than that the emperor should
declare, as the bishops had done in regard to their own nobility, that he
would put the disobedient out of the favour and protection of the law, and
would not defend them from any aggression or injury.

We see what a state of violence, insubordination, and mutual independence still prevailed, and even manifested itself in the laws ; and how
necessary it was to establish internal regulations, by the firmness and
energy of which arbitrary power might be held in check, and the encroachments of an authority which, at the very first meeting of the estates, was
regarded as foreign, might be repelled.

The most essential point was to give to the imperial diets more regular
forms and greater dignity ; and especially to put an end to the resistance
offered to their edicts by the cities.

The cities, which were so often hostilely treated by the other estates,
and which had interests of so peculiar a nature to defend, held themselves
from the earliest period studiously aloof.   During the Hussite war they
were even permitted to send into the field a separate municipal army
under a captain of their own appointment.[2]   In the year 1460 they declined going to council with the princes, or uniting in a common answer
to the emperor's proposals.[3]   In the year 1474 the deputies refused to
approve the Public Peace concluded by the emperor and princes, and
obstinately persisted that they would say nothing to it till they had consulted their friends.[4]   In 1486 the princes having granted some subsidies

[1] Müller, Rtth. Fr. VI., 115.   "Wo aber der, der gewaltige Tate fürneme und
übe, das thete uf behapte Urtheil, so solt darüber nyemant dem Bekriegten das
mahl Hilf zuzuschicken schuldig seyn."   "When, however, anyone, undertaking and exercising acts of violence, does so upon judgment received in
his favour, then shall no one be bound to send help thereupon to him who is
attacked."
[2] In the year 1431.   Datt de Pace Publica, 167.
[3] Protocol in Müller, i., p. 782 : with this addition, however, " Sie wolten
solch fründlich Fürbringen ihren Fründen berümen."   " They would commend
so friendly a proposition to their friends."
[4] The answer given by them in Müller, ii., p. 626, is vague and obscure.   In
the Frankfurt Archives (vol. viii.) it runs thus : " Als die des Friedens nothurftig
und begerlich sind, setzen sy (die Städte) in kein Zweifel, E. K. M. (werde)
gnediglich darob und daran seyn, dass der vestiglich gehandhabt und gehalten
werde : dazu sy aber irenthalb zu reden nit bedacht sind, auch kein Befel haben,
unterteniglich bittend, das S. K. M. das also in Gnaden und Guten von in versten
und sy als ir allergnedigster Herr bedenken wolle."—" As they have need, and
are desirous of peace, they (the cities) make no doubt, your Imperial Majesty
will graciously strive to bring about that it be firmly maintained and kept ; but
beyond this they have no thought of speaking on their own behalf, nor have
any command so to do, submissively entreating, that his Imperial Majesty will
therefore take this in good and gracious understanding from them, and think
of them like their most gracious master."   It is evident that their acceptance

to the emperor to which the cities were called upon to contribute, they resisted, and the more strenuously, since they had not even been summoned to the meeting at which the grant was made.   Frederick replied that this had not been done, because they would have done nothing without sending home for instructions.

It was evident that this state of things could not be maintained.   The imperial cities justly deemed it an intolerable grievance that they should be taxed according to an arbitrary assessment, and a contribution demanded of them as if it were a debt ; on the other hand, it was just as little to be endured that they should obstruct every definite decision, and send home to consult their constituents on every individual grant.

So powerful was the influence of the prevailing spirit of the times, that, in the year 1487, the cities came to a resolution to abandon the course they had hitherto pursued.

The emperor had summoned only a small number of them to the diet of this year ; they determined, however, this time to send the whole body of their deputies, and not to require them to send home for instructions. The Emperor Frederick received them at the castle at Nürnberg, sitting on his bed, " of a feeble countenance," as they express themselves,[1] and caused it to be said to them that he was glad to see them, and would graciously acknowledge their coming.   The princes, too, were well satisfied therewith, and allowed the cities to take part in their deliberations.   Committees were formed—a practice that afterwards became the prevailing one—in which the cities too were included.   The first which sat to deliberate on the Public Peace consisted of six electors, ten princes, and three burghers.   From the second,—to consider the measures to be adopted against the Hungarians,—the cities were at first excluded, but afterwards were summoned at the express desire of the emperor.   Our reporter, Dr. Paradies of Frankfurt, was one of the members of this committee. Nor was the share taken by the burgher delegates barren of substantial results ; of the general grant of 100,000 gulden, nearly the entire half, (49,390 gulden) was at first assessed to them : they struck off about a fifth from this estimate, and reduced it to 40,000 gulden, which they apportioned to each city at their own discretion.

At the next diet, in 1489, the forms of general deliberation were settled. For the first time, the three colleges, electors, princes, and burghers, separated as soon as a measure was proposed ; each party retired to its own room, the answer was drawn up by the electoral college, and then presented for acceptance to the others.   Thenceforth this continued to be the regular practice.   At this juncture there was a possibility of the constitution of the empire assuming a form like that which arose out of similar institutions in other countries, viz. that the commons, who regarded themselves (in Germany as elsewhere) as the emperor's lieges (Leute),— as in an especial manner his subjects,—might have made common cause with him against the aristocracy, and have formed a third estate, or

---

is only very general, and that they would not suffer the more essential resolutions to be pressed upon them ; the emperor at last concedes the point relating to the instructions.

[1] Dr. Ludwig zum Paradies of Frankfurt, Monday after Judica, April 2, 1487. With this diet of the empire begin the detailed reports of the Frankfurt deputies. The earlier ones were more fragmentary.—*Rs. A.*, vol. xii.

Commons' House. Sigismund was very fond of joining his complaints of the princely power with theirs ; he reminded them that the empire had nothing left but them, since everything else had fallen into the hands of the princes; he liked particularly to treat with them, and invited them to come to him with all their grievances.[1] But the imperial power was far too weak to foster these sympathies to any practical maturity, or to give a precise and consistent form to their union ; it was incapable of affording to the cities that protection which would have excited or justified a voluntary adherence to the head of the empire on their part. The German Estates generally assumed a very different form from all others. Elsewhere the lords spiritual and temporal used to meet separately : in Germany, on the contrary, the electors, who united the spiritual and temporal power in their own persons, had so thoroughly defined a position, such distinct common privileges, that it was not possible to divide them. Hence it happened that the princes formed a single college of spiritual and temporal members : the committees were generally composed of an equal number of each. The cities in Germany were not opposed, but allied to the magnates. These two estates together formed a compact corporation, against which no emperor could carry any measure, and which represented the aggregate power of the empire.

In the consciousness of their own strength and of the necessity of the case, they now made a proposal to the emperor, which, however moderate in its tone, opened the widest prospect of a radical change in the constitution.

It was obvious that if order and tranquillity were really restored, and all were compelled to acknowledge him as the supreme fountain of justice, the emperor would necessarily acquire an immense accession of power. This the estates were little inclined to concede to him ; the less, since justice was so arbitrarily administered in his tribunal, which was therefore extremely discredited throughout the empire. As early as the year 1467, at the moment of the first serious proclamation of the Public Peace, a proposal was made to the emperor to establish a supreme tribunal of a new kind for the enforcement of it, to which the several estates should nominate twenty-four inferior judges [2] from all parts of Germany, and the emperor only one as president.[3] To this Frederick paid no attention : he appointed his tribunal after, as he had before, alone ; caused it to follow his court, and even decided some causes in person ; revoked judgments that had been pronounced, and determined the amount of costs and fees at his pleasure. He of course excited universal discontent by these proceedings ; people saw clearly that if anything was to be done for the empire, the first step must be to establish a better administration of

[1] See Sigismund's Speech to the Friends of the Council at Frankfurt. Printed by Aschbach, Geschichte Kaiser Sigmunds, i. 453. He there says, he will discuss with them " was ir Brest (Gebrechen) sy,"—" what may be their wants."

[2] The passage, as Harpprecht, Archiv. i. par. 109. gives it, is quite unintelligible, for instead of urtailsprecher (utterer of a sentence), urthel sprechen (to pronounce sentence) is printed, just as if the states themselves were to sit in judgment. It is more exact and connected in König von Königsthal, ii. p. 13.

[3] The words in the text are *Urtheiler* and *Richter*. As *Urtheil* is *judgment* or *decision*, and *Recht*, *law* or *right*, these titles seem to imply some analogy with the offices of the English jury and judge.—Transl.

justice. The subsidies which they granted the emperor in the year 1486 were saddled with a condition to that effect. The estates were not so anxious to appoint the judges of the court, as to secure to it first a certain degree of independence ; they were even willing to grant the judge and his assessors a right of co-optation for the offices becoming vacant. The main thing, however, was, that the judge should have the faculty of sentencing the breakers of the Public Peace to the punishment upon which the penal force of the law for the preservation of that peace—the punishment of the ban—mainly rested, as well as the emperor himself ; and also that it should rest with him to take the necessary measures for its execution. So intolerable was the personal interference of the emperor esteemed, that people thought they should have gained everything if they could secure themselves from this evil. They then intended in some degree to limit the power of the tribunal, by referring it to the statutes of the particular part of the empire in which the particular case arose, and by having a fixed tax for the costs and fees.[1]

But the aged emperor had no mind to renounce one jot of his traditional power. He replied, that he should reserve to himself the right of proclaiming the ban, " in like manner as that had been done of old " (*immaassen das vor Alters gewesen*). The appointment of assessors also must in future take place only with his knowledge and consent. Local statutes and customs should only be recognised by the court in as far as they were consistent with the imperial written law, *i.e.* the Roman (a curious proof how much the Idea of the Empire contributed to the introduction of the Roman law) : with regard to taxing the costs and fees, he would be unrestrained, as other princes were, in their courts of justice and chanceries.[2] He regarded the supreme tribunal of the realm in the light of a patrimonial court. It was in vain that the electors observed to him that a reform of the supreme court was the condition attached to their grants ; in vain they actually stopped their payments, and proposed other and more moderate conditions : the aged monarch was inflexible.

Frederick III. had accustomed himself in the course of a long life to regard the affairs of the world with perfect serenity of mind. His contemporaries have painted him to us ;—one while weighing precious stones in a goldsmith's scales ; another, with a celestial globe in his hand, discoursing with learned men on the positions of the stars. He loved to mix metals, compound healing drugs, and in important crises, predicted the future himself from the aspects of the constellations : he read a man's destiny in his features or in the lines of his hand. He was a believer in the hidden powers that govern nature and fortune. In his youth his Portuguese wife, with the violent temper and the habitual opinions of a native of the South, urged him in terms of bitter scorn to take vengeance for some injury : he only answered, that everything was rewarded, and punished, and avenged in time.[3] Complaints of the abuses in his courts of justice made little impression on him : he said " things did not go quite right or smooth anywhere." On one occasion representations were made to him by the princes of the empire, against the influence which he allowed

[1] Essay on an Ordinance of the Imperial Chamber ; Müller, vi. 29.

[2] Moruta Cæsareanorum ; Müller, vi. 69.

[3] Grünbeck, Historia Friderici et Maximiliani in Chmel, Oestreichischer Geschichtsforscher, i., p. 69.

his councillor Prüschenk to exercise : he replied, " every one of them had his own Prüschenk at home." In all the perplexities of affairs he evinced the same calmness and equanimity. In 1449, when the cities and princes, on the eve of war, refused to accept him as a mediator, he was content : he said he would wait till they had burnt each other's houses and destroyed each other's crops ; then they would come to him of their own accord, and beg him to bring about a reconciliation between them ;—which shortly after happened. The violences and cruelties which his hereditary dominions of Austria suffered from King Matthias did not even excite his pity : he said they deserved it ; they would not obey him, and therefore they must have a stork as king, like the frogs in the fable. In his own affairs he was more like an observer than a a party interested ; in all events he saw the rule by which they are governed,—the universal, inflexible principle which, after short interruptions, invariably recovers its empire. From his youth he had been inured to trouble and adversity. When compelled to yield, he never gave up a point, and always gained the mastery in the end. The maintenance of his prerogatives was the governing principle of all his actions ; the more, because they acquired an ideal value from their connection with the imperial dignity. It cost him a long and severe struggle to allow his son to be crowned king of the Romans ; he wished to take the supreme authority undivided with him to the grave : in no case would he grant Maximilian any independent share in the administration of government, but kept him, even after he was king, still as " son of the house ;"[1] nor would he ever give him anything but the countship of Cilli : " for the rest, he would have time enough." His frugality bordered on avarice, his slowness on inertness, his stubbornness on the most determined selfishness : yet all these faults are rescued from vulgarity by high qualities. He had at bottom a sober depth of judgment, a sedate and inflexible honour ; the aged prince, even when a fugitive imploring succour, had a personal bearing which never allowed the majesty of the empire to sink. All his pleasures were characteristic. Once, when he was in Nürnberg, he had all the children in the city, even the infants who could but just walk, brought to him in the city ditches ; he feasted his eyes on the rising generation, the heirs of the future ; then he ordered cakes to be brought and distributed, that the children might remember their old master, whom they had seen, as long as they lived. Occasionally he gave the princes his friends a feast in his castle. In proportion to his usual extreme frugality was now the magnificence of the entertainment : he kept his guests with him till late in the night (always his most vivacious time), when even his wonted taciturnity ceased, and he began to relate the history of his past life, interspersed with strange incidents, decent jests and wise saws. He looked like a patriarch among the princes, who were all much younger than himself.

The Estates saw clearly that with this sort of character, with this resolute inflexible being, nothing was to be gained by negotiation or stipulation. If they wished to carry their point they must turn to the young king, who had indeed no power as yet, but who must shortly succeed to it. On his way from the Netherlands, whence he was hastening to rescue Austria from the Hungarians, for which end he had the most

[1] Letter from Maximilian to Albert of Saxony, 1492, in the Dresden Archives.

urgent need of the assistance of the empire, they laid their requests before him and made a compliance with these the conditions of their succours. Maximilian, reared in the constant sight of the troubles and calamities into which his father had fallen, had, as often happens, adopted contrary maxims of conduct ; he looked only to the consequences of the moment : he had all the buoyant confidence of youth ; nor did he think the safety of the empire involved in a tenacious adherence to certain privileges. His first appearance in public life was at the diet at Nürnberg, in 1439, where he requited the support granted him by the empire with ready concessions as to the administration of justice. He could indeed only promise to use every means to induce his father to have the Imperial Chamber (Kammergericht) established as soon as possible on the plan proposed. In this, as was to be expected, he did not succeed ; but he was at all events morally bound to fulfil the expectations he had raised : it was a first step, though the consequences of it lay at a distance. This promise was registered in the recess[1] of the diet.[2]

This was the most important point of the administration of the empire. All internal order depended on the supreme court of justice. It was of the highest moment that it should be shielded from the arbitrary will of the emperor, and that a considerable share in the constitution of it should be given to the States.

Maximilian too now received the succours he required for the restoration of the Austrian power. While one of the bravest of German princes, Albert of Saxony, called the Right Arm of the empire, gradually, to use his own expression, " brought the rebellious Netherlands to peace,"[3] Maximilian himself hastened to his ancestral domains. Shortly before, the aged Archduke Sigismund of Tyrol had allowed himself to be persuaded to give the emperor's daughter, who had been confided to him, in marriage to Duke Albert of Bavaria-Munich ; and had held out to that prince the hope that he would leave him Tyrol and the Vorlande as an inheritance. But the sight of Maximilian awakened in the kindhearted and childless old man a natural tenderness for the manly and blooming scion of his own race ; he now dwelt with joy on the thought that this was the rightful heir to the country, and instantly determined to bequeath it to him. At this moment King Matthias of Hungary, who was still in possession of Austria, died. The land breathed again, when the rightful young prince appeared in the field surrounded by the forces of the empire and by his own mercenaries ; drove the Hungarians before him, delivered Vienna from their hands, and pursued them over their own borders. We find this event recorded, even in the journals of private persons, as the happiest of their lives[4] :—a district that had been mortgaged raised the mortgage money itself, that it might belong once more to its ancient lords.

Such was the vast influence of the good understanding between Maxi-

---

[1] " Recess," cf. translator's note, Preface to vol. i.

[2] Müller, vi., p. 171. A register of this imperial diet in the Frankfurt Archives, vol. xiii.

[3] From a letter of Albrecht to his son, in Langenn, Duke Albert, p. 205.

[4] Diarium Joannis Tichtelii, in Rauch, Scriptt. Rer. Austriacarum, ii. 559. He writes the name of Maximilian four times, one after the other, as if unable to write it often enough for his own satisfaction.

milian and the States of the empire, on the re-establishment of the power of Austria. It had, at the same time, another great effect in conducing to the conciliation of one of the most eminent of the princes, and to the consolidation of all internal affairs.

The Dukes of Bavaria, in spite of the family alliance into which they had been forced with the emperor by the marriage above mentioned, adhered to the opponents of Austria—the Roman see, and King Matthias.[1] They would hear nothing of furnishing aids to the emperor against the king ; they refused to attend the diets, or to accept their edicts : on the contrary, they made encroachments on the domains of their neighbours, enlarged the jurisdiction of their own courts of justice, and threatened neighbouring imperial cities—for example, Memmingen and Bibrach. Regensburg had already fallen into the possession of Duke Albert of Munich.[2]

Immediately after the renewal of the Public Peace, in the year 1487, it became evident that there was no chance of its being observed if these partial and turbulent proceedings were not put an end to.

This was the immediate and pressing cause of the Swabian league,[3] concluded in February 1488, by the mediation of the emperor,[4] and some of the more powerful princes. The order of knights, who the year before had renewed their old company of St. George's shield, quickly joined the league, as did also the cities. They mutually promised to oppose a common resistance to all strangers who sought to impose foreign (*i.e.* not Swabian) laws upon them, or otherwise to injure or offend them. But in order to secure themselves from disputes or disorders among themselves, and at the same time to observe the Public Peace—for this general object was, from the very first, included among the more particular ones, and gave the whole union a legitimate character,—they determined to settle their mutual differences by the decision of arbitrators, and appointed a

---

[1] In Lent, 1482, Albert and George determined, " with their several states, that, without the countenance of the holy father, help should not be given to King Matthias against the emperor." " Mit ihr beder Landschaft dass man ohne Gunst des h. Vaters dem Kaiser wider König Matthias nit helfen sollte." Anonymous contemporary Chronicle in Freiberg's Collection of Historical Papers and Documents, i. 159. All these circumstances deserved a closer examination. For the modern relations and political system of these states did not begin so late as is believed. From Hagek, Böhmischer Chronik, p. 828, it appears that the Bohemians would not put up with their exclusion from the election of Maximilian. They entered into a league with Matthias, drawing Poland into it also. (Pelzel. Geschichte von Böhmen, i. 494.) The deputies of Matthias tried to set the Italian princes in motion. (Philippus Bergomas, Supplementum Chronicorum.) France likewise belonged to this party. The reason why Bavaria joined it is evident. The eyes of her dukes were always turned either towards Lombardy or the Netherlands. Freiberg : Geschichte der Baierischen Landstände, i. 655.

[2] Pfister, Geschichte von Schwaben, v., p. 272.

[3] A league of cities, princes, and knights, founded 1488, primarily with the object of maintaining order in Swabia.

[4] In his very first address the emperor declares the object of the league to be, that the states, " bei dem heiligen Reiche und ihren Freiheiten bleiben," " should remain in adherence to the holy empire, and in possession of their liberties."— *Datt, de Pace Pub.*, 272. Who could believe that for the history of this most important of all early leagues we have still to refer chiefly to Datt ?

council of the league, composed of an equal number of members chosen from each body.   In a very short time the league was joined by neighbouring princes, especially Würtenberg and Brandenburg, and formed, as contra-distinguished from the knights and the cities, a third body, taking equal share in its council, submitting to the decisions of the arbitrators, and promising, in case of a war, to send the contingent agreed upon into the field.   Here, in the very focus of the old quarrels, a firm and compact union of the several classes arose, affording a noble representation of the Ideas of the constitution of the empire, and of public order and security ; though its main and proximate object was resistance to the encroachments of Bavaria.   Nevertheless, Duke Albert held himself aloof in haughty defiance, while the emperor, relying on the league, would hear of no reconciliation till the pride of the Duke was humbled.   At length resort was had to arms.   In the spring of 1492 the troops of the league and of the empire assembled on the Lechfeld.   Frederick of Brandenburg, " whose doublet had long been hot against Bavaria," carried the banner of the empire ; Maximilian was there in person.   At this moment Albert, abandoned by his kinsmen, at strife with his knights, felt that he could not withstand such an overwhelming force ; he relinquished the opposition which he had hitherto maintained, consented to give up Regensburg, and to abandon all claims founded on the assignments made by Sigismund.   By degrees even the old emperor was appeased, and received his son-in-law and his grand-daughters with cordiality. After some time Albert himself found it expedient to join the Swabian league.

We see that the reign of Frederick III. was by no means so insignificant as is commonly believed.   His latter years especially, so full of difficulties and reverses, were rich in great results.   The house of Hapsburg, by the acquisition of Austria and the Netherlands, had acquired a high rank in Europe.   A short campaign of Maximilian's sufficed to establish its claims to Hungary.[1]   The intestine wars of Germany were almost entirely suppressed.   The Swabian league gave to the house of Austria a legitimate influence over Germany, such as it had not possessed since the time of Albert I.   The diets had acquired a regular form, the Public Peace was established and tolerably secured, and important steps were taken towards the formation of a general constitution.   What form and character this should assume, mainly depended on the conduct of Maximilian, on whom, at the death of his father (August 19, 1493), the administration of the empire now devolved.

DIET OF WORMS, 1495.

IDEAS had long been universally current, and schemes suggested, pregnant with far more extensive and important consequences than any we have yet contemplated.

Among the most remarkable were those put forth by Nicholas von Kus, whose capacious and prophetic mind was a storehouse of new and just

---

[1] The treaty of Oedenburg, 1463, July 29, had already secured the succession to the house of Austria, upon the extinction of the Hunniads.   The new treaty, 1491, Nov. 7, the Monday after the feast of St. Leonard, renewed this right in case of failure of male issue from Wladislas.

views on the most various subjects.   At the time of the council of Basle
he devoted himself with earnest zeal and perspicacious judgment to the
internal politics of the empire.   He began by observing that it was impossible to improve the church without reforming the empire ; since it was
impossible to sever them, even in thought.[1]   He therefore urgently recom-
mends, though an ecclesiastic, the emancipation of the secular authority.
He is entirely opposed to the right claimed by the papacy, of transferring
the empire to whom it will : he ascribes to the latter a mystical relation
to God and Christ, absolute independence, and even the right and the
duty of taking part in the government of the church.   He desires that
the confusion arising from the jurisdiction of the spiritual and temporal
courts be put an end to.   He proposes a plan for superior courts of justice,
each provided with three assessors, chosen from the nobles, clergy, and
citizens respectively,[2] and empowered not only to hear appeals from the
inferior courts, but to decide the differences between the princes in the
first instance : it was only by such means, he thought, that the legal
practice could be brought into greater harmony with the principles of
natural justice.   Above all, however, he looked to the establishment of
yearly diets for the revival of the authority, unity, and strength of the
empire (*Reich*) ; for he clearly perceived that no such results were to be
expected from the power of the emperor (*Kaiserthum*) alone.[3]   Either
in May or in September he would have a general meeting of the Estates
held at Frankfurt, or other convenient city, in order to arrange any
existing dissensions, and to pass general laws, to which every prince
should affix his signature and seal, and engage his honour to observe
them.   He strenuously contends that no ecclesiastic shall be exempted
from their operation ; otherwise he would want to have a share in the
secular power, which was to be exercised for the general good.   He goes

---

[1] Nicolai Cusani de Concordantia Catholica, lib. iii.   Schardius, Sylloge de
Jurisdictione Imperiali, f. 465.

[2] Lib. iii. c. xxxiii.: " Pronunciet et citet quisque judicum secundum condi-
tionem disceptantium personarum, nobilis inter nobiles, ecclesiasticus inter
ecclesiasticos, popularis inter populares : nulla tamen definitiva feratur nisi ex
communi deliberatione omnium trium.   Si vero unus duobus dissenserit, vincat
opinio majoris numeri."   It is not to be believed that the customs of German
law also had not given rise to many complaints.   It is here said : " Sæpe sim-
plices pauperes per cavillationes causidicorum extra causam ducuntur, et a tota
causa cadunt, quoniam qui cadit a syllaba, cadit a causa : ut sæpe vidi per
Treverensem diocesim accidere.   Tollantur consuetudines quæ admittunt jura-
mentum contra quoscunque et cujuscunque numeri testes."—iii. c. 36.

[3] This is one passage among many in which the want of two words corresponding to Reich and Kaiserthum, both Englished by *empire*, is grievously felt :
Reich, and its numerous derivatives and compounds, Reichstag, Reichsabschied, &c., always relate to the great Germanic body called the Empire.   Kaiserthum, the office and state of Kaiser, relates to the personal dignity, power,
functions, &c., of the individual occupying the imperial throne.   As it is impossible every time these words occur to resort to a long paraphrase, the meaning
is often lost or obscured.   Reich is also applied to a monarchical state, and then
stands in a like relation to Königthum (the kingly office or state) ; somewhat
as *realm* does to *royalty*.   The title of a former section presents a difficulty of
a somewhat similar nature,—it is, Papstthum and Fürstenthum—Popedom
and Princedom : for the former we have Papacy ; for the latter abstraction,
nothing.—TRANSL.

on to remark that, in order seriously to maintain order and law and to chastise the refractory, it is necessary to have a standing army ; for to what end is a law without the penal sanction ? He thinks that a part of the revenues of the numerous tolls granted to individuals might be kept back by the state, and a fund thus formed, the application of which should be every year determined at the diet. There would then be no more violence ; the bishops would devote themselves to their spiritual duties ; peace and prosperity and power would return.

It is clear that the reforms suggested by this remarkable man were precisely those which it was the most important to put in practice ; indeed the ideas which are destined to agitate the world are always first thrown out by some one original and luminous mind. In the course of time some approach was made, even on the part of the authorities of the empire, to the execution of these projects.

Even during their opposition to Frederick III. in 1450—1460, the Electors were of opinion that the most salutary measure for the empire would be, when they were with the emperor in person—for example, in an imperial city,—to form a sort of consistory around him, like that of the cardinals around the pope, and from this central point to take the government of the empire into their own hands, and to provide for the preservation of public order. It was their notion that a permanent court of justice should be established, like that of the parliament[1] of Paris, whose judgments should be executed by certain temporal princes in the several circles of the empire ; the ban should be pronounced by the emperor according to justice and conscience, and should then be duly executed and obeyed.[2]

Similar suggestions appeared from time to time. In the archives of Dresden there is a report of a consultation of the year 1491, in which dissatisfaction is expressed with the plan of a supreme court of justice, and a scheme of a general government and military constitution for the whole empire, not unlike that of Nicholas von Kus, is proposed ; an annual diet for the more important business of the general government, and a military force, ready for service at a moment's notice, proportioned to the six circles into which it was proposed to divide the empire, and under twelve captains or chiefs.

With the accession of a young and intelligent prince, a tendency to improvement and a leaning towards innovation took the place of the invincible apathy of the old emperor ; and these dispositions, both in the chief of the empire and the Estates, were strengthened by other circumstances attending the new reign.

Maximilian had received some offences of an entirely personal nature from the King of France. According to the terms of a treaty of peace, that prince was to marry Maximilian's daughter, and, till she reached years of maturity, she was confided to French guardianship : Charles now sent her back. On the other hand, Maximilian was betrothed to the princess and heiress of Brittany, an alliance on which the people of Germany founded various plans reaching far into the future, and hoped to draw that province under the same institutions as they intended to give to the empire. Charles VIII., however, got the young princess into

---

[1] Cf. Cheruel, Dictionnaire des Institutions de la France.
[2] Final Edict of the spiritual Electors. See p. 58., n. 1.

his power by violence, and forced her to accept his hand.[1] The rights of the empire were immediately affected by these hostile acts. Whilst Maximilian was preparing to go to Rome to be crowned, and cherished the hope of restoring the imperial dignity and consideration in Italy, the French, anticipating him, crossed the Alps, marched unchecked through the Peninsula from north to south, and conquered Naples. We cannot affirm that Charles VIII. had any positive design of seizing the imperial crown ; but it is undeniable that a power, such as he acquired throughout Italy by the nature and the success of his enterprise, was calculated to oppose a direct obstacle to the revival of the authority of the German empire.

Irritated by such reiterated wrongs, and deeply impressed with the necessity of making a stand against French aggression ; availing himself of his incontestable right to demand succours from the States for his journey to Rome ; urged likewise by his Italian allies, Maximilian now appeared at Worms, and on the 26th March opened his diet with a description of the political state of Europe. " If we continue," exclaimed he, " to look on passively at the proceedings of the French, the holy Roman Empire will be wrested from the German nation, and no man will be secure of his honour, his dignity, or his liberties." He wished to invoke the whole might and energy of the empire to take part in this struggle. Independent of a hasty levy to keep alive the resistance of Italy, he likewise demanded a permanent military establishment for the next ten or twelve years, in order that he might be able to defend himself, " wherever an attack was attempted against the Holy Empire." He pressed for it with impetuous earnestness ; he was in a position in which the interests of the public were identical with his own.

The Estates also, which had assembled in unusual numbers, were fully impressed with the necessity of resisting the French. But in the first place, they regarded affairs with more coolness than the young emperor ; and, secondly, they deemed the accession of a new sovereign who had already pledged himself to them and was now in need of considerable assistance, a moment well adapted for the prosecution of their schemes of reform and the introduction of order into their internal affairs. They met the warlike demands of the king with one of the most comprehensive schemes ever drawn up for the constitution of the empire.

They too assumed the necessity of a strong military organisation, but they found the feudal system, now in its decline, no longer available ; they deemed it better to impose a general tax, called the Common Penny. This tax was to be levied, not according to the territorial extent, but to the population of the several parts of the empire. The application of it was not to devolve on the king, but to be entrusted to a council of the empire composed of members of the States, the cities included. This

---

[1] The old emperor says in his proclamation of the 4th of June, 1492, " Rather would we depart in peace and blessedness from this world, than suffer so unchristianlike and foul a deed to remain unpunished, and the Holy Empire and German people to put up with this scandalous and irreparable injury under our rule." " Wir—lieber von dieser Welt seliglich scheiden, dann einen solchen unkristlichen snoden Handel ungestrafft beleiben und das heil Reich und deutsche Nation in diesen lesterlichen und unwiederpringlichen Vall bei unserer Regierung wachsen lassen wolten."

council was to be invested with large general powers. It was to execute the laws, to put down rebellion and tumult ; to provide for the reintegration of any domains that had been subtracted from the empire ; to conduct the defensive war against the Turks and other enemies of the Holy Empire and of the German nation ; in short, it is evident that it was to have the sum of the powers of government in its hands ;[1] and certainly a large share of independence was to be awarded to it for that purpose. The weightiest affairs it was bound to lay before the king and the electors, subject to the revision of the latter ; but in all other respects the members were to be freed from the oath whereby they were bound to the king and the Estates, and act only in conformity with the duties of their office.[2]

The ideas by which this project was dictated show a very strong public spirit ; for it was by no means the king alone whose power was limited. The general interests of the country were represented in a manner which would admit of no division or exclusion. How utterly, for example, is the idea of a general tax, to be collected by the parish priest, and delivered under his responsibility to the bishop, at variance with any further augmentation of the influence of the territorial lords ! Which among them would have been strong enough to resist a central national power, such as this must have become ?

The first result, however, would have been that the power of the monarch —not indeed that which he exercised in the usual troubled state of things, but that which he claimed for better times—would have been limited.

It remained now to be seen what he would say to this project. The fiefs which he granted out, the knightly festivities devised in his honour, or given by him in return, the manifold disputes between German princes which he had to accommodate, occupied him fully. It was not till the 22nd of June that he gave his answer, which he published as an amendment of the project. On closer examination, however, its effect was in fact entirely to annul it. He had said at the beginning that he would accept the project with reservation of his sovereign prerogatives ; now, he declared that he thought these assailed in every clause. I will give an example of the alterations he made. According to the project, the council of the empire was charged to see that no new tolls were erected without the previous knowledge of the electors ; a precaution suggested by the tolls continually granted by Frederick and Maximilian. The clause, in its altered state, set forth that the council of the empire should itself take care to erect no toll without the previous knowledge of the king.

Strange that such a complete reversal of an original scheme should be announced as an amendment ! but such were the manners, such the courtesy of that time. The opposition in temper and opinion was not the less violent on that account. A visible irritation and ill-humour prevailed

[1] See the first scheme which the elector of Mainz communicated first to the king, and then to the cities. Protocol in Datt, de Pace Pub., p. 830. The protocol is the same with that found in the Frankfurt Acts, vol. xv.

[2] The latter is a provision of the larger draft, p. 838, nr. 17. " Sollen dieselben President und Personen des vorgemeldten Rathes aller Gelübd und Aide—damit sie uns oder inen (denen von welchen sie gesetzt worden) verbunden oder verstrickt wären, genntzlich ledig seyn." " The same president and persons of the before-mentioned council shall be wholly freed from all promise and oath, having the effect of binding them to, or connecting them with, us or them " (those by whom they had been appointed).

at the diet.   The king one day summoned to his presence the princes on whose friendship he could most confidently rely,—Albert of Saxony, Frederick of Brandenburg, and Eberhard of Würtenberg, to consult them on the means of maintaining his sovereign dignity.[1]

So directly opposed were the views of the monarch and those of the States at the very commencement of this reign.   Both parties, however, made the discovery that they could not attain their ends in the way they had proposed to themselves.   Maximilian clearly perceived that he should obtain no subsidies without concessions.   The States saw that, at present at least, they would not be able to carry through their scheme of a general government.[2]   While trying, however, to hit upon some middle course, they came back to experiments attempted under Frederick III.

In the first place, they settled the basis of that Public Peace which has rendered this diet so celebrated.   On a more accurate examination, we find indeed that it is in detail rather less pacific than the former ones ; as, for example, it restores a right, lately abrogated, of the injured party to make forcible seizure of a mortgaged estate ; the only advantage was, that this peace was proclaimed, not as before for a term of years, but for ever. By this act the law, in fact, ceased to contemplate the possibility of any return to the old fist law (Faustrecht).

The question of the Imperial Chamber (*Kammergericht*), or supreme court of justice for the empire, was next discussed.   Maximilian had hitherto treated this tribunal exactly as his father had done : he made it follow his court ; in 1493 it accompanied him to Regensburg, in 1494 to Mechlin and Antwerp, in 1495 to Worms.   We have, however, seen that he was bound by the concessions he made in 1489 to reform the administration of justice.   When, therefore, the proposals formerly laid before his father were submitted to him, he felt himself compelled to accept them. Under what pretext, indeed, could he have rejected an institution, the establishment of which he had so solemnly undertaken to promote with all his might ?   This, however, was one of the most important events in the history of the empire.   Maximilian gave his assent to the maxim that the statute law should have force in the supreme court, and that no more than the regular fees should be exacted ; above all, he ceded to the judge the office of proclaiming the ban of the empire in his name ; nay, he bound himself not to remove the ban when pronounced, without the consent of the injured party.   When we reflect that the judicial power was the highest attribute of the imperial crown, we feel all the importance of this step. Nor was it only that the supreme court of the empire was secured from the

---

[1] Notice in the Archives of Berlin, which contains, however, only fragmentary remarks upon this imperial diet.

[2] Later Declaration of the Elector Berthold of Mainz in Datt, p. 871.   " Daruf wäre erst fürgenommen ain Ordnung im Reich aufzurichten und Sr. ko. Mt. furgehalten, darab S. M. etwas Beswärung und Missfallens gehabt, hetten die Stende davon gestanden."   " Thereupon it was first determined to establish a regular government in the empire and submitted to his Royal Majesty, so that if H.M. had any objection or dislike to it, the States would have desisted from it."   Whether Müller, Rtth. unter M. (i. 329), be right in maintaining that a second scheme of a similar kind had also been presented, whereupon Maximilian had offered to appoint, instead of the imperial council, a court council, I must leave undetermined.   It would, in fact, have been but another evasive proposition.

arbitrary interference which had hitherto been so injurious to it—its offices were also appointed by the Estates. The king nominated only the president (*Kammerrichter*) ; the assessors were appointed by the Estates ; and the cities, to their great joy, were invited to propose certain candidates for that office : a committee was then appointed to examine and decide on the presentations.[1] Later jurists have disputed whether the court derived its penal sanction solely from the emperor, or from the emperor and the princes : but this much is certain, that it changed its whole character ; and from a simply monarchical institution, became dependent on the whole body of the States. It followed, of course, that it was no longer an append-age to the court and a companion of the emperor's travels ; but held its stated sittings in one fixed spot in the empire.

This great concession was met by the States with a grant of the Com-mon Penny, on the produce of which they allowed the king, who seemed intensely desirous of it on account of the state of his affairs in Italy, to raise a loan. The tax itself is a combination of poll-tax and property-tax, not very different from that formerly levied by the kings of Jerusalem, and also occasionally proposed in Germany ; for example, in the year 1207, by King Philip. In the fifteenth century, frequent mention of such taxes is made as being applied sometimes to the maintenance of the Hussite, sometimes of the Turkish war. The Common Penny was levied on the following plan :—Half a gulden was levied on every five hundred, a whole one on every thousand, gulden ; among persons of small means, every four-and-twenty above fifteen years of age, without exception, men and women, priests and laymen, were to contribute one gulden ; the more wealthy were to pay according to their own estimate of their property. The idea of taxation was still in some degree mixed up with that of alms ;[2] the priests were to admonish the people from the pulpit to give something more than what was demanded. The whole plan was still extremely im-perfect. Its importance consisted only in its being (as the whole course of the transaction proved) a serious attempt at a general systematic taxa-tion of the empire, destined for purposes both of peace and war, for the maintenance of the supreme courts of justice, the payment of the Italian allies, and the equipment of an army against the Turks.

It was in accordance with this character of a general tax that the choice of the treasurer of the empire, whose office it was to receive the money from the commissioners or collectors stationed in all parts of the country, was also entrusted to the States. Maximilian engaged to levy the Common Penny in the Austrian and Burgundian dominions upon the same plan, and to set the example herein to all other sovereigns.

But if the collection of the money could not safely be entrusted to the king, still less could its application. After the proposal for a council of the empire had been suffered to drop, the idea of a yearly meeting of the Estates of the empire for the purpose of controlling the public expenditure, first suggested by Nicholas von Kus, and then proposed in the project of 1491, was revived. This assembly was to meet every year on the first of February, to deliberate on the most important affairs, internal and ex-

[1] Notice from a document of later date in Harpprecht, Staats-archiv. des Reichskammergerichts, ii., p. 249.

[2] So the taxes levied by the contemporary King of England, Henry VIII., were called ' benevolences.'—TRANSL.

ternal.   To this body the treasurer of the empire was to deliver the money
he had received from the taxes ; and in it was to be vested the exclusive
power of deciding on the application of the same : neither the king nor
his son was to declare war without its consent ; every conquest was to
accrue to the empire.[1]   To this body was also committed a peremptory
authority for the maintenance of the Public Peace.   The question was,
when this tribunal (thus rendered independent of the crown and emanating
from the Estates) should have pronounced the ban, to whom the execution
of it was to be entrusted.   The king of the Romans wished that it should
be left to him.   The States, true to the principle on which their legislation
was founded, committed it to the annual assembly of the empire.

It is obvious that the States, though they gave up their original plan,
kept constantly in view the idea on which it was founded.   In the conflict
of the interests of the monarch and those of the States, the balance clearly
inclined in favour of the latter.   Maximilian had cause to complain that
he was made to feel this personally ; that he had been forced to withdraw,
and to wait before the door, till the resolution was passed.   He was often
inclined to dissolve the diet ; and it was only the want of a fresh subsidy
(which he then obtained) that restrained him.[2]   On the 7th of August, he
accepted the project in the form last given to it.

There is a grand coherency in its provisions.   All Germans are once
more seriously and practically regarded as subjects of the empire ; and
the public burthens and public exertions were to be common to all.   If the
States thus lost something of their independence, they received in compensation (according to their ancient organisation and their respective
ranks) a legitimate share in the supreme administration of justice, as well
as of the government.   The king submitted himself to the same ordinances, and to the same community.   He retained undiminished the
supreme dignity, the prerogatives of a sovereign feudal lord ; but in the
conduct of public business, he was to be regarded only as president of the
college of the Estates of the empire.   The constitution proposed was a
mixture of monarchical and federal government, but with an obvious preponderance of the latter element ; a political union, preserving the forms
of the ancient hierarchy of the empire.   The question whether these projects could be carried into execution, was now of the highest importance
to the whole future destiny of Germany.

Resolutions of so comprehensive a kind can be regarded as views only ;
—as ideas, to which an assembly has expressed its assent, but to the execution of which there is a long way yet to be traversed.   It is the ground-
plan of a building which is intended to be built ; but the question remains
whether the power and the means will correspond with the intention.

[1] Maintenance of Peace and Law established at Worms.   Müller, Rtth.
Max., i., p. 454.

[2] This second grant amounted to 150,000 gulden.   " Damit S. Königl. Gnad
unserm h. Vater Papst und Italien, bis der gemein Pfennig einbracht werde,
dester stattlicher Hülfe thun möchte."   " In order that his Royal Grace may be
so much the more able to give more liberal help to our holy father the pope and
Italy, until the Common Penny be collected."   To collect the loan, the king
despatched emissaries to single states ; *e.g.* Prince Magnus of Anhalt and Dr.
Heinrich Friese to the following ; the Abbot of Fulda, contributing 300 gulden ;
the two Counts of Hanau, 500 ; the Count of Eisenberg, 300 ; the city of Freiberg,
400 ; and the city of Frankfort, 2,100.   Instruction in Comm. Archiv. at Dessau.

DIFFICULTIES.—DIET OF LINDAU, 1496.

A GREAT obstacle to the execution of the resolutions of the diet occurred at once in the defective nature of its composition. A large number of powerful Estates had not been present, and as the obligatory force of the resolutions of an assembly upon those not present was as yet far from being determined, it was necessary to open separate negotiations with the absent. Among others, the Elector of Cologne was commissioned to negotiate with the bishops in his neighbourhood, those of Utrecht, Münster, Osnabrück, Paderborn, and Bremen ; the Elector of Saxony with Lüneburg, Grubenhagen, and Denmark ; and it was by no means certain what would be their success. Here again we find the possibility assumed that someone might not choose to be included in, or to consent to, the Public Peace.[1]

A still more important organic defect was, that the knightly order had taken no part in the diet. It is manifest that the mighty development which a government composed of different estates (*eine ständische Verfassung*) had reached in England, mainly rests on the union of the lower nobility and the cities in the House of Commons. In Germany it was not the ancient usage to summon the nobility to the diet. The consequence of this was, that the nobles refused to conform to the resolutions passed at it, especially when (as in the present case) these related to a tax. The Franconian knights assembled in December at Schweinfurt, and declared that they were free Franconians, nobles of the empire, bound to shed their blood, and in every war to guard the emperor's crown and sceptre at the head of all their youth capable of bearing arms ; but not to pay taxes, which was contráry to their liberties, and would be an unheard of innovation. This declaration had the assent of all their compeers. Unions of the same kind were formed in the several circles.[2]

We observed how much stress was laid at an earlier period on the spiritual authorisation. The consequence of the want of it now was that the abbots of the empire refused to recognise the authority of so purely secular a tribunal as the Imperial Chamber.

There were yet other Estates whose obedience was very doubtful. The Duke of Lorraine declared that, beyond the jurisdiction of his own tribunals, he was amenable to no other authority than that of the king in person. The Swiss confederates did not indeed as yet dispute the sovereignty or the jurisdiction of the empire, but at the first exercise of it they were offended and irritated into resistance. The king of Poland declared that Dantzig and Elbing were Polish cities, and rejected all claims made upon them on the part of the empire. As the first effect of a vigorous medicine is to set the whole frame in agitation, so the attempts to organise the Germanic body had the immediate result of calling into activity the hostile principles hitherto in a state of repose.

But if so strong an element of resistance existed on the side of the States, to whom the resolutions were clearly advantageous, what was to be expected from the king, whose power they controlled, and on whom they had been forced ? In contriving the means for their execution, every-

---

[1] Recess and ordinances in Müller, 459.
[2] Müller, Rtth. 688, 689.

thing had been calculated on his sympathy and co-operation ; whereas he incessantly showed that he set about the task with repugnance.

He certainly organised the Imperial Chamber according to its new forms. It held its first sittings at the Grossbraunfels at Frankfurt-on-Main,[1] on the 3rd of November. On the 21st of February it exercised its right of pronouncing the ban for the first time : the judge and his assessors, doctors and nobles, appeared in the open air ; the proclamation of the ban, by which the condemned was deprived of the protection of the law,[2] and all and every man permitted to attack his body and goods, was publicly read and torn in pieces. Yet the king was far from allowing the court of justice to take its free course. On more than one occasion he commanded it to stop the proceedings in a cause ; he would not suffer his fiscal, when judgment was given against him, to pay the usual fine of the defeated party : he sent an assessor from the Netherlands whom his colleague refused to admit, because he had not been regularly appointed ; he made no provision for the pay of the assessors as he was bound at first to do : after appointing Count Eitelfriedrick of Zollern, against the will of the States, who preferred another,[3] he very soon removed him, because he wanted him for other business. Nor did he take any measures for collecting the Common Penny in his own dominions, as he had promised. The meeting had been, as we saw, fixed for the 1st of February, but he did not appear, and consequently it did not take place.[4]

It is a matter of astonishment that the reputation of founder of the constitution of the empire has so long and so universally been given to a sovereign, on whom the measures tending to that object were absolutely forced, and who did far more to obstruct than to promote their execution.

There is no doubt that all attempts at reform would have been utterly defeated, had not the king's designs been counteracted by a prince who had embraced most of the opinions on which it was founded ; who had been the chief agent in bringing it thus far, and was not inclined now to let it drop—Berthold, Elector of Mainz, born Count of Henneberg.[5] Even under Frederick III., whose service he entered at an early age, he had taken

[1] Excerpta ex Collectaneis Jobi de Rorbach ; Harpprecht, ii. 216. In the Frankfurt Imp. Archives, a letter is still extant from Arnold Schwartzenberg to the council of Frankfurt, dated on the Friday after the Feast of the Assumption (Aug. 21) : "Item uf Samstag U L F. Abend hat Graf Hug von Wernberg nach mir geschickt, und vorgehalten, das Kammergericht werde gelegt gen Frankfurt, wo man ein Huss dazu bekommen mocht und ein Stuben daneben zum Gespreche." "Also upon the evening of Saturday, the feast of Our Blessed Lady, Count Hugh of Wernberg sent to me and represented, that the Imperial Chamber was transferred to Frankfurt, where it might be possible to get a house, and a room close to it for conferences." The price of meat and fish was to be determined, and the citizens were to be admonished to behave in a seemly and discreet manner (" zimlich und glimpflich ") towards the members.

[2] "Ans dem Frieden in den Unfrieden gesetzt "—literally, put out of the peace into unpeace."—TRANSL.

[3] To the Prince Magnus of Anhalt, he says in one of his own notes, " Conventus me elegerunt, sed revocavit rex."

[4] In the Frankfurt Archives, we meet with several letters from Jülich, Cölln, Mainz, &c., bespeaking a lodging, but also a letter dated from Frankfurt itself on the Saturday after Invocavit, to the effect that no one had as yet appeared.

[5] Of the Römhilde line, born in 1442. Diplomatische Geschichte des Hauses Henneberg, p. 377.

an active share in all attempts to introduce better order into the affairs of the empire. In 1486, he became Elector of Mainz, and from that time might be regarded as the most eminent member of the States. There are men, whose whole existence is merged in their studies or their business : there we must seek them if we wish to know them ; their purely personal qualities or history attract no attention. To this class of men belonged Berthold of Mainz. Nobody, so far as I have been able to discover, has thought it worth while to give to posterity a description of his personal appearance or characteristics : but we see him distinctly and vividly in the administration of his diocese. At first people feared his severity ; for his administration of justice was as inexorable as it was impartial, and his economy was rigorous ; but in a short time everybody was convinced that his austere demeanour was not the result of temper or of caprice, but of profound necessity : it was tempered by genuine benevolence ; he lent a ready ear to the complaints of the poorest and the meanest.[1] He was peculiarly active in the affairs of the empire. He was one of the venerable men of that age, who earnestly strove to give to ancient institutions which had lost their original spirit and their connection with higher things, the new form adapted to the necessities of the times. He had already conducted the negotiations of 1486 ; he next procured for the towns the right of sitting in the committees ; it was mainly to him that Germany owed the promises made by Maximilian in the year 1489, and the projects of Worms were chiefly his work. In every circumstance he evinced that serene and manly spirit, which, while it keeps its end steadily in view, is not self-willed as to the means or manner of accomplishing it, or pertinacious on merely incidental points ; he was wearied or discouraged by no obstacles, and a stranger to any personal views : if ever a man bore his country in his inmost heart, it was he.

In the summer of 1496, at the diet of Lindau, this prince acquired a degree of independent power such as he had not enjoyed before.

In the midst of the troubles of that summer, Maximilian thought he discerned the favourable moment in which he needed only to show himself in Italy, in order, with the help of his allies there, to re-establish the supremacy of the imperial power. He summoned the States to repair to Lindau, whither they were to bring the amount of the Common Penny, together with as many troops as it would suffice to pay, and whence they were immediately to follow him ; at the same time declaring that he would not wait for them, but must cross the Alps without delay with what force God had given him.

While he put this in execution, and, equipped rather as for some romantic enterprise of knight-errantry than for a serious expedition, rushed on to Italy, the States of the empire gradually assembled in Lindau. They brought neither troops, money, nor arms ; their attention was directed exclusively to internal affairs. How greatly in acting thus they relied on Elector Berthold is shown (among other documents) by the instructions to the ambassador of Brandenburg, ordering him implicitly to follow the course pursued by that prince.[2]

---

[1] Serarius, Res Moguntinæ, p. 799.

[2] In the Berlin Archives there is a Convolute concerning this Diet of the Empire, which, along with the Instruction, contains 1st, the letters received up to the time of the arrival of the deputies, and the propositions made by the foreign

On the 31st of August, 1496, the princes, as many as were assembled, embarked in boats and fetched the king's son, Archduke Philip of Bregenz, across the river ; on the 7th of September, the first sitting was held.   The Elector of Mainz took his place in the centre ; on his right sat the princes, the archduke, for the first time, amongst them ; on his left, the ambassadors or delegates of those who did not appear in person ; in front of him stood the deputies of the cities.   In the middle was a bench for the king's councillors, Conrad Stürzel and Walter von Andlo.

The Elector conducted the proceedings with unquestioned authority. If he absented himself, which was never but for a short time, they were stopped ; when he returned, he was the chief speaker, whether in the assembly or the committee ; he brought forward the propositions, demanded the grants, and found means to keep the plenipotentiaries steady to them.   He did not conceal the grief he felt at seeing the empire in such a state of decline.   " Even in the time of Charles IV. and Sigismund," exclaimed he, " the sovereignty of the empire was acknowledged in Italy, which is now no longer the case.   The king of Bohemia is an elector of the empire, and what does he do for the empire ? has he not even wrested Moravia and Silesia from it ?   Prussia and Livonia are liable to incessant attacks and oppression, and no one troubles himself about them ; nay, even the little which remains to the empire is daily wrested from it, and given to one or the other.   The ordinances of Worms were made to preserve the empire from decay ; but the union and mutual confidence which alone could sustain it are wanting.   Whence comes it that the Confederation enjoys such universal respect ? that it is feared by Italians and French, by the pope, nay, by everybody ?   The only reason is that it is united and of one mind.   Germany ought to follow the example. The ordinances of Worms should be revived, not to prate about, but to execute them."[1]

Berthold's was that powerful eloquence which is the expression of convictions founded on actual experience.   The committee resolved to look into the matter, and to see that the empire was better ordered.   On the motion of the Brandenburg ambassador, the members examined their credentials, and found that they were sufficient for that purpose.   Such being the dispositions of the States, affairs now took a decisive turn.

The Imperial Chamber, which had closed its sittings in June, was induced to open them again in November.   It was determined to appropriate the tax which was to be levied on the Jews in Regensburg, Nürnberg, Worms, and Frankfurt, to the payment of the assessors.   The Elector insisted that the sentences of the court should be executed, that no sovereign should recall his assessor, and that the cities should have justice against the princes.   It was resolved to transfer the chamber to Worms : the

---

deputies ; 2nd, the protocol of the proceedings on the Friday after the feast of St. Dionysius, Oct. 14.   What is especially remarkable in this protocol is, that the most distinguished of the plenipotentiaries, Erasmus Brandenburg, parish priest of Cotbus, was a member of the committee, and is the reporter of its transactions.   The greater part is in his handwriting.

[1] These words were spoken by the Elector on the 28th Nov.   A similar effusion is cited in Scherer's extract, and in Fels, Erster Beitrag zur Reichsgesch. Preface, § 7.   In these contributions is to be found the protocol of Lindau, contained in the Frankf. A., A. vol. xvi.

reason assigned for which was, that it was easier from thence to reach the four universities of Heidelberg, Basle, Mainz, and Cologne, whenever it was necessary " to ask the law."

On the 23rd of December, the edict for levying the Common Penny was renewed in the most stringent form. The knights (*Ritterschaft*) who complained of the demand made upon them by the king, were reminded that it was not the king who imposed this tax, but the empire ; that it was the most equal and the least oppressive that could be devised, and would be of advantage to their Order, if they would only get to horse and endeavour to earn the pay for which this fund was in part raised.

Another meeting of the States was appointed to consider of the disbursement of the Common Penny.

Other points were discussed ;—the necessity of instant and effective succours for the attacked ; new regulations of the courts of justice and of the mint ; above all, the firmest determination was expressed to maintain unaltered the measures passed at Worms. Should any attempt be made to thwart or oppose them or those of the diet of Lindau, the matter was to be referred to the Archbishop of Mainz, who should be authorised thereupon to convoke other members, in order that an answer from the whole body of the States might be given, and public order and tranquillity be defended by them in concert.[1]

All these resolutions the Archbishop carried without much difficulty. If there was occasionally some attempt at opposition on the part of the envoys of the princes, those of the electors and of the cities always supported him and compelled the former to give way. They were, therefore, incorporated in the Recess ; the usual practice as to which was, that each member should first write out for himself the resolutions which had been passed : these were then compared in the assembly, a fixed formula was determined on, and signed by the whole body.

On the 10th of February 1497, the diet of Lindau was closed. The States thanked the Archbishop for the trouble he had taken, and entreated his pardon for their negligences. The Elector, on the other hand, excused himself for having, perhaps, sometimes addressed them with too great earnestness, and exhorted them faithfully to enforce the resolutions that had been passed, each in his own territory or sphere, that so the empire might be profited.

DIET OF WORMS AND FREIBURG, 1497, 1498.

THE matter was, however, but half settled ; the difficulties which had arisen among the States had been removed, but as yet no influence had been obtained over the king, whose co-operation and executive power were indispensable.

Maximilian's romantic enterprise had ended as was to be expected : the same excitable fancy which had flattered him with exaggerated hopes,

[1] In order to avoid the appearance of a conspiracy, it had been previously resolved, " Die Handhabung, zu Worms versigelt, vorzunehmen und aus derselben ain Grund und Einung und Verstendtniss zu nehmen und was des zu wenig seyn will zu erweitern." " To take the declaration sealed at Worms, and from it to construct a groundwork, union, and agreement, and in those respects where it may come short, to enlarge it."—*Brandenburg Protocol.*

had prevented him from perceiving the true state of affairs.   After a short time the allies, whose assistance was all he had to rely on, had quarrelled among themselves ; he had returned to Germany filled with shame, disgust and vexation.   Here he found the finances of his hereditary domains exhausted and in the utmost disorder ; the empire in an attitude of defiance and sullen reserve, and disastrous tidings following each other in quick succession.   When Louis XII. ascended the throne in 1498, Maximilian hoped that troubles would arise in France, and that his allies would support him in a fresh attack upon that power.   The very contrary took place : Louis, by pacific and prudent measures, won from his subjects a degree of consideration such as no king had ever before possessed ; the Italian league endeavoured to bring about an accommodation with him : but the most unexpected thing was, that Maximilian's own son, Archduke Philip, instigated by his Netherland councillors, without consulting his father, entered into a treaty with France, in which he promised not to agitate any of his claims on Burgundy so long as Louis XII. lived, and never to attempt to enforce them by arms, or otherwise than by amicable and legal means.   The only consideration in return for this vast concession was the surrender of a few strong places.   Maximilian learned this when he had already begun his preparations for war ; in June 1498, in a state of the most violent irritation, he summoned the assembly of the empire which he could no longer do without.

The assembly had opened its sittings, as had been determined, in Worms,[1] but had transferred them at the king's request to Freiburg. Although, in consequence of the proceedings at Lindau, affairs were in a much better state than before,—the Common Penny began to be really collected, the Imperial Chamber at Worms held its regular sittings for the administration of justice, and the diet itself exercised an uncontested jurisdiction as between the several Estates, in the more weighty and difficult cases ; yet it was daily felt that so long as the king remained in the equivocal and half hostile attitude he had assumed, nothing permanent would be accomplished.   Before the very eyes of the assembled States, Elector John of Treves, with the help of his secular neighbours, Baden, the Palatinate, Hessen and Juliich, invaded the town of Boppard, and forced it to submit and to do homage to him.   The Swiss resisted a sentence of the Imperial Chamber against St. Gall, held the most insolent language, and were very near issuing formal diffidations.   The States pointed out to the king, in remonstrances incessantly reiterated, that, without his presence, neither the Public Peace could be maintained, nor the law executed, nor the taxes duly collected.

At length, on the 8th June, 1498, he arrived in Freiburg, but neither

---

[1] Transactions of the States of the Holy Empire at the Royal Diet at Worms, Fr. A., vol. xvii.   We see by them, amongst other things, as a matter of complete certainty, that Maximilian did not appear at Worms.   As Häberlin (Reichs-geschichte, ix. 84), however, assumes that he did, he must have been deceived by certain documents which were only laid before the Imperial Diet in the King's name.   At Freiburg, July 3rd, the Tuesday after the Visitation of the Holy Virgin, Maximilian made excuses for not having appeared at Worms : " he had been obliged to establish an excellent government (Regiment) in his hereditary states," &c., " it had been commented on as folly in him," &c., " but now he was present." (Brand. Protocol.)

with the views, nor in the temper, that his subjects wished.   His soul was galled by the failure of all his plans ;—deeply wounded by the defection of the Netherlands, and ardently excited by the thought of a war with France ; the more, I think, from a feeling of the difficulty, nay, impracticability of it.   At the very first audience (28th June) he vented all this storm of passion upon the princes.   He said that he did not come to ask their advice, for he was resolved to make war upon France, and he knew that they would dissuade him : he only wished to hear whether they would support him as they were bound to do, and as they had promised at Worms.   It was possible that he might accomplish nothing decisive ; but, at any rate, he would give the king of France a slap in the face (*Backenstreich*), such as should be remembered for a hundred years. " I am betrayed by the Lombards," said he, " I am abandoned by the Germans : but I will not allow myself again to be bound hand and foot and hung upon a nail, as I did at Worms.   War I must make, and I will make, let people say what they may.   Rather than give it up, I would get a dispensation from the oath that I swore behind the altar at Frankfurt ; for I have duties not only to the empire, but to the House of Austria : I say this, and I must say it, though I should be forced on that account to lay the crown at my feet and trample on it."

The princes listened to him with amazement.   " Your Majesty," replied the Elector of Mainz, " is pleased to speak to us in parables, as Christ did to his disciples !"   They begged him to bring his proposals before the assembly, which would then proceed to deliberate upon them.[1]   Strange meeting of this monarch with this assembly !   Maximilian lived in the interests of his House ; in the contemplation of the great political relations of Europe ; in the feeling that he was the bearer of the highest dignity of Christendom, which was now in jeopardy : he was ambitious, warlike, and needy.   The States, on the other hand, had their attention fixed on internal affairs ; what they desired above all things was a government of order and law ; they were cautious, pacific, frugal : they wanted to check and control the king ; he to excite and hurry on the States.

Nothing less than the singular prudence, moderation, and sense which distinguished the Archbishop of Mainz were necessary to prevent a total breach between them.

He conciliated the king by placing before his eyes the prospect of the revenue likely to accrue from the Common Penny.   He prevailed on the assembly to offer the king immediate payment of the sum formerly promised at Worms ; on the understanding that Maximilian should himself contribute to the fuller and more exact collection of the tax by his own example and assistance.   This brought on a more distinct explanation. Every individual was called upon to state how much of the Common Penny he had collected.   A slight review of these statements will give us an insight into the situation of the German princes of that day.

Elector Berthold of Mainz has collected and paid in the tax ; but some persons in his dominions had resisted.   To these he has announced that they subjected themselves to the ban of the empire, from which he would

[1] The Brandenburg protocol, our chief source of information regarding the Diet of Freiburg, adds, the king spoke " with many marvellous words and gestures, so as to be completely obscure and incomprehensible."

not protect them.—Cologne and Treves have received only a part of their share of the tax : they have met with not less refractory subjects, who excused themselves with the delays of the Netherlands.—The Electors of Brandenburg and of Saxony have collected the greater part of the tax, and are ready to pay it in ; but there are certain lords in Saxony of whom the Elector says, he can do nothing with them ; he does not answer for them.[1]—The ambassador of the Elector Palatine, on the other hand, has not even instructions to give any distinct explanation ; George of Landshut, too, gave only an evasive answer.   Albert of Bavaria expressed himself better disposed, but he complained of the great number of recalcitrants he met with.   Nor was this to be regarded. as a pretext : the Bavarian states had, in fact, made great difficulties ;—they had enough to do with the wants of their own country ; they thought it strange that the empire, also, should make claims upon them.[2]   The resistance in Franconia was not less vehement ; the Margraves of Brandenburg were forced in some cases to resort to distraint.—The cities, already prepared for contributions of this kind, had a much easier task.   Only three out of the whole number were still in arrear—Cologne, Mühlhausen, and Nordhausen ; the others had paid in their whole contingent.

Although the matter was, as we see, far from being perfectly accomplished, it was put into a good train, and Maximilian was highly satisfied with the result.   He now condescended to give a report of what his own hereditary dominions had raised.   From Austria, Styria, and Tyrol he had collected 27,000 gulden ; in the Netherlands, on the contrary, great resistance had been made.   "Some," says the king's report, "those of the Welsch (i.e. foreign, not German) sort, said they were not under the empire.   Those who hold to the German nation, on the other hand, declared that they would wait and see what their neighbours on the Rhine did."

Unfortunately it is impossible, from the reports before us, to arrive at any statistical results.   The payments were too unequal, and the accounts are generally wanting.

It was, however, for the moment a great point gained, that the States could either pay the king the money he required immediately, or at least promise it with certainty.   He was thus induced, on his side, to devote his attention and interest to the affairs of the empire.

The Public Peace was guarded with fresh severe clauses, especially against the abettors of the breakers of it.   The president of the Imperial Chamber was empowered, in peculiarly weighty and dangerous cases, to call together princes of the empire at his own discretion, and to require their help.   A former proposition of the Imperial Chamber, viz. to confer the right of representation on the heir, was at length carried, in spite of the objection that a third part of the nation held to the rules of the Sachsenspiegel[3] (Mirror of Saxony), which were at direct variance with

[1] In the Instruction of the Elector of Brandenburg it was further said, " Scarcely half of the Common Penny had been got in, on account of the great mortality. His electoral Grace would either deliver up what had been hitherto received separately, or would be responsible for the whole together."

[2] Freiberg, Gesch. der Baier. Landst., i., 568, 663.

[3] A collection of old Saxon or Frisian Laws of the beginning of the thirteenth century.

that right.[1] A regular criminal procedure was taken into consideration, chiefly on account of the frequent illegal infliction of the punishment of death. In order to put a stop to the confusion in the currency, it was resolved to coin all gulden of the size and form of the gulden of the Rhenish electors. In short, this diet of Freiburg, which opened so stormily, gradually despatched more business of various kinds than any that had yet met.

The question now remained what view the States would take of European affairs. The French had made the proposal that Genoa and Naples should be ceded to them, in which case they would not disturb Milan, and would conclude a permanent peace on all other points ;—a proposal which, if sincere, had much to recommend it, and was especially agreeable to the German princes. They argued that Genoa was little to be depended upon in any case, and was seeking a new master every day ; and what had the empire to do with Naples and Sicily ? It would, in fact, be far more advantageous to them to have a powerful prince there, who could hold the Turks in check. The sovereignty of Italy was a matter of indifference to them ; they declared themselves generally opposed to all alliances with the Welsch (non-Germans). Such, however, was not the opinion of the electors, and least of all, the ecclesiastical. They reminded their opponents that Genoa had been called by Frederick I. a chamber of the empire ; that Naples was a fief of the papal see, and must therefore be held by the King of the Romans, the steward of the church. But above all, that they must not suffer the King of France to become too powerful, lest he should attempt to get possession of the empire. They would not abate a single iota of the idea of the Germanic empire, with which indeed their own importance was indissolubly associated. These sentiments, which rendered them at once partisans of the king, were at length triumphant : the negotiations which Frederick of Saxony had set on foot with Louis XII. fell to the ground : at the moment when the States had placed the institutions of the empire on something like a firm footing, they were forced into a war.

Two great conflicting tendencies had been at work from the beginning of this reign ; that of the king, to hurry the nation into warlike enterprises ; and that of the States, to establish its internal tranquillity. They now seemed resolved on concession, union, and concert. The king had confirmed and established the proceedings of Worms, which were disagreeable to him ; and the States acceded to his desire to defend the majesty of the empire by arms.

EVENTS OF THE WAR.

IT remained however to be asked, whether either party had distinctly conceived, or maturely weighed, what they were about to undertake.

There may be governments to which war is a source of strength ; but it can never be so to those which have a strong federative element, yet in

---

[1] A very important protocol, which serves to complete the others, in Harpprecht, ii., p. 341. In the Berlin Archives, we find the document, which Müller, ii. 442, gives under the title " An Explanation of the Imperial Chamber," with some additions, however ; e.g. " with respect to the article concerning the succession of daughters and grandchildren, this article has been deferred till the arrival of the king's majesty." The presence of the king himself was needful to bring the affair to a conclusion.

which the danger attendant on failure is not common to the whole body. For Germany, nothing was more necessary than peace, in order that institutions yet in their infancy might be allowed tranquil growth, and identify themselves with the habits of the people ; and the scarcely recognised principle of obedience have time to take root. The collection and expenditure of the Common Penny needed above all to become habitual. But the diet at which these measures had been concluded was hardly closed when the nation rushed forth to war.

Nor was this all. The power they were about to attack was the earliest and the most completely consolidated of any in Europe ; a new sovereign, who had long enjoyed universal consideration, had assumed the reins of government and commanded the entire and cordial obedience of his subjects. Such was the monarch, and such the kingdom, which Maximilian, in daring reliance on the assistance of the empire, now proceeded in person to attack. After having regained for his troops the advantages they had lost in Upper Burgundy,[1] he fell upon Champagne with a considerable army. A truce was now offered by the enemy, which he declined.

I do not doubt that the leading princes saw the danger of the course Maximilian was taking ; but they could not prevent it. The agreement they had come to at Freiburg was obtained solely by the consent of the States to assist him in his campaign :—they must let him try his fortune.

The great superiority of the political position which Louis XII. had contrived to acquire now manifested itself. He had gained over the old allies of Maximilian in Spain, Italy, and even the Netherlands. Milan and Naples, which he had resolved to attack, had no other allies than the King of the Romans himself.

But even in Germany itself, Louis found means to excite enmities sufficient to furnish Maximilian with occupation. The Palatinate had always maintained a good understanding with France ; active negotiations were set on foot with Switzerland and the Grisons. Duke Charles of Gueldres, (of the house of Egmont, deposed by Charles the Bold, but which had never renounced its claims,) was the first to take up arms.

Maximilian was driven out of Champagne by incessant rain and the overflow of the rivers. He turned his arms upon Gueldres, and, with the assistance of Juliers and Cleves, gained some advantages ; but they were not decisive : the country adhered faithfully to Duke Charles, who had secured its attachment by granting it new privileges. Hence it happened, that Maximilian could not attend the assembly of the empire fixed to be held on the eve of St. Catherine (November 21st) at Worms, indispensable as that was to the completion and execution of the ordinances agreed on : this meeting, where, if he had been present, resolutions of the utmost practical importance would probably have been passed, broke up without doing any thing.[2] But, besides this, the troubles in Switzer-

---

[1] The Fugger MS. relates at length that the Germans had kept the advantage in a skirmish, Sept. 22, 1498, and had reconquered castles they had previously lost. It is incredible that Maximilian, as Zurita asserts, should have had 25,000 infantry and 5,000 horse in the field.

[2] Letter from Maximilian to Bishop Henry of Bamberg : Harpprecht, ii. 399. The king invited the assembly to meet at Cologne, where, however, many of th members did not appear, as their instructions only spoke of Worms.

land now broke out in the form of regular war. The empire was as yet far from renouncing its sovereignty over the confederated cantons : it had cited them before the imperial chambers, nor had any objection been taken to the legality of such a proceeding ; the Common Penny had been levied in them ; so lately as at the diet of Freiburg, the resolution was passed, " to keep the powerful cities of the Confederation, which bear the imperial eagle in their arms, in their duty and allegiance to the empire, and to invite them again to attend the meetings of the States. But these invitations could have no effect in a country where the want of internal peace was not felt, because they had secured it for themselves and were already in possession of a tolerably well-ordered government. A party which had always been hostile to the King of the Romans, and which found it more expedient to earn French money than to adhere to the empire, gained the upper hand. In this state of things, the Grisons, who were threatened by Tyrol on account of the part they had taken, injurious to the peace of the empire, by sheltering persons under the king's ban, found immediate assistance from the confederates. In one moment the whole frontier, Tyrol and Grisons, Swabia and Switzerland, stood in hostile array.

Strange that the measures taken to introduce order into the empire should have had results so directly contrary to the views with which they were undertaken ! The demands of the diet and of the imperial chamber set the Swiss Confederation in a ferment ; the summoning of the Grisons to deliver up a fugitive under ban occasioned their defection. If, on the other side, the city of Constance, after long hesitation, joined the Swabian league, this act was regarded with the utmost disgust by the Swiss, because the city possessed the jurisdiction over the Thurgau, a district of which it had obtained possession some years before. Independently of this, there existed, ever since the formation of the league, a hatred between Swabia and Switzerland which had long vented itself in mutual insults and now broke out in a wild war of devastation.

The constitution of the empire was far from being strong enough— its unity was far from having sunk deeply enough into the mind and consciousness of the people—to allow it to put forward its full strength in the conflict with France : the States convened, or rather huddled together in the utmost hurry at Mainz, passed partial and infirm resolutions ; it was, in fact, only the members of the Swabian league who supported the king, and even these were not inclined to risk their lives in a battle with sturdy peasants.

Under these circumstances, the empire was in no condition to make a successful resistance to those designs of King Louis upon Italy which Maximilian had vainly desired to prevent. Whilst the Upper Rhine was torn by private wars, the French crossed the Alps and took Milan without difficulty. Maximilian was compelled to make a very disadvantageous peace with the Swiss, by which not only the jurisdiction of the Thurgau was lost, but their general independence was fixed on an immovable basis.

A successful war would have strengthened the constitution of the empire : the inevitable effect of these reverses was to overthrow or, at the least, to modify it.

DIET OF AUGSBURG, AND ITS CONSEQUENCES.

THE immediate result of this assembly was that the authority of the king was even more limited than before ; the principle of representative government (*ständische Princip*) gained another victory, by which it appeared to have secured a fresh and lasting ascendancy.[1]

At the diet which was opened at Augsburg on the 10th of April, 1500, it was agreed that the means which had been hitherto adopted for the establishment of a military organization and a more regular government were insufficient.   The prospect of collecting the Common Penny was too remote ; events succeeded each other too rapidly to allow of the possibility of the States constantly assembling first for the purpose of guiding or controlling them.   Adhering to the idea which had got possession of their minds, they now resolved to try other means to the same end.   They proposed to collect the forces they wanted by a sort of levy.   Every four hundred inhabitants, assembling according to their parishes, were to furnish and equip one foot soldier,—a method which had been tried some time before in France : the cavalry proportioned to this infantry was to be raised by the princes, counts, and lords, according to a certain scale.   A tax was to be laid on those who could not take an active share in the war,— clergy, Jews, and servants, and the amount was to form a fund for the war ; propositions which, as it will be seen, are immediately connected with the former ones, and which assume an equally complete and comprehensive unity of the empire.   Maximilian embraced them with joy ; he made his calculations, and gave the Spanish ambassador to understand that he would shortly have 30,000 men in the field.   On the other hand, he adopted a plan which he had rejected five years before, and which must have been odious to a man of his character ; he now acknowledged the necessity of having a permanent imperial council, which might relieve him and the States from incessant recurrence to the diets, and to whose vigilance and energy the execution of the ordinances when issued might be entrusted.[2] A committee was formed for a fresh discussion of this institution, and its suggestions were then submitted to the general assembly of the States. Every member had the right of proposing amendments in writing.

The business was treated with all the gravity it deserved.   There were two points to be considered ; the composition, and the rights and functions, of the proposed council.   In the first place, a position suited to their high

[1] *Ständische Princip* is not literally " representative principle," or rather, it is that and something more.   *Ständisch*, the adjective of Stand, (status, class, order), as applied to government, signifies representation of the several states or orders of the nation.   The English and the Swedish constitutions are *ständisch ;* the American, though representative, is not *ständisch* at all, since there are no *Stände* to represent.   I may here point out another difficulty arising out of the double and often equivocal use of the word state, which represents both *Staat* and *Stand*—two words of totally different meaning.   *Staat*, the state, is the whole civil and political body of the nation ; *Stand* (status) is a class or order of the 'nation.   The United States of America are *Staaten ;* the States of the Empire were *Stände*.—TRANSL.

[2] Protocol of the Imperial Diet of Augsburg, in the Frankfurt Archives, vol. xix., unfortunately not so circumstantial as might be wished ; *e.g.* the objections which the cities had made, contained in three bills or advertisements, are not inserted, " because every city deputy knew them."

rank, and to the influence they had hitherto possessed in the country, was
assigned to the electors.   Each of them was to send a delegate to the council ; one of them, according to regular rotation, to be always present.   The
much more numerous college of princes was less favourably treated.   The
intention had at first been to let the spiritual side be represented according
to the archbishoprics ; the temporal, according to the so-called countries,
Swabia, Franconia, Bavaria, and the Netherlands ;[1] but these divisions
neither corresponded with the idea of a compact and united empire, nor
with the existing state of things ; and the assembly now preferred to include spiritual and temporal princes together within certain circles or districts.   Six of these were marked out, and were at first called provinces of
the German nation, Franconia, Bavaria, Swabia, Upper Rhine, Westphalia, and Lower Saxony ; they were, however, not as yet called by these
names, but were distinguished according to the several states which inhabited them.[2]   The interests whose disseverance would, in any case,
have been absurd and purposeless, were thus more closely united.   Counts
and prelates and cities were all included within these circles.   It was also
determined that one temporal prince, one count and one prelate should
always have a seat in the council.   Austria and the Netherlands were to
send two delegates.   Little notice had at first been taken of the cities ;
nor, indeed, in spite of the original intention, had they at a later period
been admitted to a place in the imperial chamber ; but they thought this
extremely injurious to them, and the more unjust, since the burthen of
raising the funds for the expenses of the States must fall mainly upon them ;
and at length they succeeded in obtaining the right of sending two members
to the imperial council.   The cities which were to enjoy this privilege in
turn were immediately named : Cologne and Strasburg for the circle of
the Rhine ; Augsburg and Ulm for the Swabian ; Nürnberg and Frankfurt for the Franconian ; Lübeck and Gosslar for the Saxon : the delegates
were always to be sent by two of these districts.[3]   A curious illustration
of the old and fundamental principle of the Germanic empire,—that every
right should be attached as soon as created, in a certain form, to a certain
place ; so that the general right wears the air of a special privilege.

Thus the three colleges of which the diet consisted were also the com-
ponent parts of the imperial council, which may, indeed, be regarded as a
permanent committee of the States.   The king had no other right there
than to preside in person, or to send a representative (*Statthalter*).   The
preponderance was doubtless on the side of the States, and especially in
the hands of the electors, who were now so firmly united and so strongly
represented.

This council, the character of which was so decidedly that of class

[1] These are Salzburg, Magdeburg, Bremen, and Besançon ; the electorates
were of course excluded ; the Netherlands on the Maass were instead of Saxony.
Datt, de Pace Publica, p. 603.

[2] Order of the Regency (*Regiment*) established at Augsburg, in the collections of the Recesses of the Imperial Diets.

[3] Chiefly from the letter of Johann Reysse to the City of Frankfurt, Aug. 17,
1500.   " So die Fürsten kainen von Stetten zu Reichsraidt verordnet hatten,
so haben die Stette bedacht," &c.   " As the princes had appointed none of the
cities to the council of the empire, the cities had therefore bethought themselves," &c.   He further remarks, that the princes immediately caused three
candidates to be proposed to them from each city, out of whom they chose one.

representation (*ständisch*), was immediately invested with the most important powers. Everything that regarded the administration of justice and the maintenance of public tranquillity ; everything relating to the measures of defence to be taken against the infidels and other enemies ; foreign as well as internal affairs, lay within its domain ; it had power " to originate, to discuss, to determine." It is evident that the essential business of the government was transferred to it, and indeed it assumed the title of the government or regency of the empire[1] (*Reichsregiment*).[2]

It seemed now as if not only the judicial but the legislative and administrative parts of the government must assume a thoroughly representative (*ständisch*) character.

If Maximilian suffered himself to be persuaded to make such large concessions in Augsburg, it was, doubtless, only because the preparations for war depended upon them ; because he hoped by this means to obtain from the States a durable, voluntary, cordial and effective support in his foreign enterprises. On the 14th of August, after everything was concluded, he urged the States to take example from him, and to do something for the empire, as he had done. He worked himself up, as it were intentionally, to the expectation that this would take place ; he wished to believe it ; but his hopes alternated with secret fears that, after all, it would not take place, and that he should have surrendered his rights in vain. He betrayed the greatest agitation of mind ; a feeling of impending danger and of present wrong, as he himself expressed it. Whilst he reminded the assembly of the oaths and vows by which each of them was bound to the holy empire, he added that unless more and better was done than before, he would not wait till the crown was torn from his head, he would rather himself cast it down at his feet.[3]

Very little time elapsed before he got into various disputes with the States. He was obliged to consent to publish an edict against the disobedient, the penalties attached to which were of a less severe nature than he deemed necessary.

A Captain-general of the empire, Duke Albert of Bavaria, was appointed, with whom Maximilian speedily felt that he could never agree.

The armament of the succours agreed upon did not proceed, in spite of the new council of the empire, which assembled in the year 1500. In April, 1501, the lists of the population of the several parishes, which were the necessary basis of the whole levy, were not yet sent in.

---

[1] That this was regarded as a sort of abdication is shown by the expression of the Venetian ambassador. Relatione di S. Zaccaria Contarini, venuto orator del re di Romani 1502 : in Sanuto's Chronicle, Vienna Archives, vol. iv. " Fo terminato et fo opinion del re rinontiar il suo poter in 16, nominati il senato imperial, quali fossero quelli avesse (i quali avessero) a chiamar le diete e tuor le imprese."

[2] The translation commonly in use for *Reichsregiment* (council of regency) does not convey any definite or correct idea to the mind of the reader, nor does any better suggest itself. *Das Regimen t*is as nearly as possible *the government*, according to the common and inaccurate use of the word, but that is far too vague and general. What its powers and functions were we see in the text. Eichhorn (vol. iii., p. 127) says : " This institution was agreeable neither to the emperor nor to the States. For the former it was too independent, and for the latter, too active ; and hence it remained only two years assembled."—TRANSL.

[3] Letter from Reysse, Aug. 17.

Lastly, the imperial council assumed an attitude utterly disagreeable to the king. Negotiations were set on foot, and a truce concluded, with Louis XII. of France, whom Maximilian had thought to crush with the weight of the empire. The council was not averse to grant the king of France Milan as a fief of the empire, at his request.[1]

At this the whole storm of anger and disgust which Maximilian had so long with difficulty restrained burst forth. He saw himself thralled and fettered as to internal affairs, and as to external, not supported. His provincial Estates in Tyrol remarked to him how insignificant he was become in the empire.

He appeared for a moment at the Council of Regency in Nürnberg, but only to complain of the indignities offered him,[2] and of the increasing disorders of the empire. He remained but a few days.

It had been determined that the Council of Regency should be empowered to summon an assembly of the States in cases of urgency. The state of things now appeared to that body highly urgent, and it did not delay to use the right conferred upon it. The king did everything he could to thwart it.

Another ordinance bound the king not to grant the great fiefs without consulting the electors. As if to punish the States for their negotiations with Louis XII., he now granted, of his own sole authority, the fief of Milan to this his old enemy.[3]

But if the king had not power enough to enforce order in the empire, he had enough to trouble that which was as yet but imperfectly established. In the beginning of the year 1502, everything that had been begun in Augsburg had fallen into a state of utter dissolution. The Council of Regency and the assessors of the imperial chamber, who neither received their salaries nor were allowed to exercise their functions, dispersed and went home. To the king, this was rather agreeable than otherwise. He erected a court of justice exactly similar to that of his father, with assessors arbitrarily appointed, over which he presided himself. It is evident from one of his proclamations that he meditated establishing in like manner a government (*Regiment*) nominated solely by himself, and, by its means, carrying into execution the plan of a military organisation determined on in Augsburg.

This conduct necessarily excited a universal ferment. A Venetian ambassador, Zaccharia Contarini, who was in Germany in the year 1502,

---

[1] Müller Reichstagsstaat, p. 63.

[2] In this Maximilian was not entirely wrong. It is not to be believed to what lengths the French Ambassador went. He said without reserve, that the reason why Maximilian took the part of Naples so warmly was, that he had been paid 30,000 ducats, though the negotiator of the affair had pocketed one half of the sum, and the remainder only had come into the hands of the emperor. He said the King of France had no thought of injuring the empire. But if they made war on him, then the king would find his way into the enemies' quarters as readily as they into his.—And yet to this ambassador the council of the empire gave a testimonial to the effect that if he had not accomplished the king's object, the fault lay not in him but in circumstances. Recreditive, May 25, 1501 ; Müller, p. 110.

[3] Contarini alleges the following very peculiar motive :—" Lo episcopo di Magonza voleva per il sigillo 80ᵐ duc. onde parse al re di Romani d'acordarsi et aver lui questi danari."

was astonished at the great unpopularity of the king,—how ill people spoke of him, how little they respected or cared for him. Maximilian himself said, " He would he were Duke of Austria, then people would think something of him ; as King of the Romans he received nothing but indignities. '[1]

Once more did the electors resolve jointly and resolutely to oppose his will. On the 30th of June, 1502, at a solemn congress at Gelnhausen, they bound themselves to hold together in all important affairs ; to act as one man at the imperial diets, and always to defend the wishes of the majority ; to allow of no oppressive mandates, no innovations, no diminution of the empire ; and, lastly, to meet four times every year, for the purpose of deliberating on the public affairs and interests. It does not distinctly appear whether they really, as was reported, came to the resolution to dethrone the king ; but what they did was in fact the same thing. Without consulting him, they announced a meeting of the empire on the 1st of the November following ; every member communicated to the one seated next him the topics on which they were to deliberate. They were the same which had formed the subject of all former deliberations of the Germanic body : the Turkish war, the relations with the pope, the public expenditure, but, above all, the establishment of law, tranquillity and order ; with a view to the maintenance of which, some new ordinances were presently inserted, to come into force after the Imperial Chamber and Council of Regency should cease to exist.[2]

The Elector Palatine, who had rather opposed the former measures of the diet, now that it had come to a breach with the king, distinguished himself by his active and zealous co-operation.

Maximilian was in the greatest perplexity. While he complained that attacks were made on the sovereignty which was his of right as crowned king of the Romans,—while he sought to take credit for having of his own accord established the Council of Regency and the Chamber,[3] he did not feel himself strong enough to forbid the proposed assembly of the empire ; he therefore took the course of proclaiming it himself ; announcing that he would be present at it, and would take counsel with the princes and electors on an expedition against the Turks ; the necessity for which daily became more urgent. This was, in truth, not very unlike the conduct of King Rupert, or the manner in which, at a later period, the kings of France put themselves at the head of factions which they could not subdue. But the electoral princes of Germany would not even make this concession. Some had already arrived at Gelnhausen for the proposed diet ; among them a papal legate ; and many others had bespoken dwellings, when a proclamation of the Elector Palatine of the 18th of October was circulated, putting off the diet.[4]

[1] Relatione, l. c. of 1502. " Il re è assai odiato, a poca obedientia in li tre stadi : questi senatori electi è venuti nimici del re : adeo il re dice mal di loro e loro del re. Il re a ditto più volte vorria esser duca d'Austria, perche saria stimato duca, che imperator è vituperato."

[2] I found them in the Archives of Berlin and Dresden ; to the Duke of Saxony they had sent the united electors of Brandenburg and Saxony. Müller has but a very unsatisfactory notice of the subject.

[3] Letter from Schwäbischwerd, Nov. 2, Frankf. R.A., tom. xx.

[4] Hinsburg, near Frankfurt, Oct. 20. (Thursday after Galli.) Gelnhausen sent to Frankfurt the letter of the elector Berthold, which arrived on the 19th, wherein the latter also declared " the diet appointed at Gelnhausen was delayed from special causes, and removed to another place."

To compensate for this they held an extraordinary meeting in Würzburg, at which they renewed their opposition, and announced a general assembly of the empire for the next Whitsuntide.

Maximilian, who was about to set out on a journey to the Netherlands, issued a proclamation, in which he invited the States to repair to his court, and to consult with him concerning the Turkish war and Council of Regency.[1]

Of the meeting summoned by the king there exists not a trace ; that appointed by the electors, however, certainly took place in June, 1503, at Mainz, though we are unable to discover whether it was numerously attended.   Maximilian's measures were here opposed, on the ground that they were injurious to the empire.   As there was nothing to be feared from his Council of Regency (since he was obliged to confess that he had been unable to find fitting members), the meeting contented itself with attacking his tribunal.   They declared to him that no prince of the empire would consent to submit to its decisions.   They reminded him of the ordinances passed at Worms and Augsburg, and urged him to adhere to them.

Such was the result of the attempts made in the year 1503 to constitute the Germanic body.

The authority of the empire was restored neither in Italy, nor in the Swiss Confederation, nor on the eastern frontier, where the Teutonic knights were incessantly pressed upon by the Poles and Russians.   At home, the old disorders had broken out new.   Not only had the attempt to establish a firm and durable constitution for war and peace utterly failed, but there was no longer any tribunal of universally recognised authority.

The highest powers in the nation, the king and his electors, had fallen into irreconcilable discord.   In Elector Berthold, especially, Maximilian beheld a dangerous and determined foe.   It had already been reported to him from Augsburg that Mainz had spoken contemptuously of him to the other princes ; and obsequious people had given him a list of not less than twenty-two charges which the Elector brought against him.   Maximilian had stifled his anger, and had said nothing ; but the impression now made upon him by every opposition he encountered, by every consequence of the Augsburg constitution that he had not anticipated, was the more profound ; he ascribed everything to the crafty schemes of the sagacious old man.   A hostile and bitter correspondence took place between the king and the arch-chancellor.[2]   Maximilian retorted upon his adversary a list of charges, twenty-three in number ;—one more than those brought against himself by Mainz, which he still kept concealed, but with whose contents he only fed his resentment the more constantly in secret.[3]

A state of things most perilous to himself.

[1] Antorf, April 7, Fr. A. " Des Reichsregiments wegen der Personen so daran geordnet seyen wir dann nit so pald erlangen haben mügen und dadurch wiederum in Anstand kommen ist."—" As to the Council of Regency, on account of the persons fitted for it, we have not been able to create it so quickly, and accordingly it is again delayed."

[2] Gudenus IV., 547, 551.

[3] " Königl Maj Anzeigen, item die Ursach darumb des Reichs Regiment und Wolfart zu Augspurg aufgericht stocken beliben ist."—" Declarations of his Royal Majesty, also the cause why the government and welfare of the empire established at Augsburg have stood stock-still."—*Frankf. A.A.*

The other Electors adhered firmly to Berthold, who, in the midst of all these troubles, had formed a fresh and strict alliance with the Palatinate. The cities clung to him as closely as ever.   There was a general feeling through the nation that the fate of Wenceslas was impending over Maximilian ;—that he would be deposed.   It is said that the Elector Palatine had formally proposed this measure in the electoral council ; that shortly after, the king arrived one day unexpectedly at a castle belonging to that prince where his wife was residing, and that during their morning's repast, he gave her to understand that he was perfectly acquainted with her husband's designs.   Such, however, was the grace and charm of his manner and the imposing dignity of his person and bearing, that the project was abandoned.[1]   However this may be, his affairs were in as bad a situation as possible.   The European opposition to Austria once more obtained that influence on the interior of Germany, formerly acquired through Bavaria, and now through the Palatinate, which maintained a close connection with France and Bohemia.

Yet Maximilian had still powers and resources in store ; and it was the Palatinate which soon afforded him an opportunity to rally and to apply them.

IMPROVED FORTUNES OF MAXIMILIAN.   DIET OF COLOGNE AND CONSTANCE ;
1505 AND 1507.

IN the first place Maximilian had connected himself with one of the most powerful houses of Europe.[2]   The marriage of his son Philip with the Infanta Johanna of Spain not only directly opened very brilliant prospects to his family, but indirectly afforded it a defence against the aggressions of France, in the claims, the policy, and the arms of Spain.   After a momentary good understanding in Naples, a war had just broken out between these two powers, the results of which inclined in favour of Spain ; so that the consideration of France began to decline in Germany, and the public confidence in the fortunes of Austria to revive.

Moreover, Maximilian had (which was much more important) a party at home among the States.   If the electors and the cities in alliance with Mainz were hostile to him, he had won over devoted friends and adherents among the princes, both spiritual and temporal.

For the name and state of King of the Romans was not an empty sound. In the general affairs of the realm his power might be controlled ; but the functions and the sacred dignity of sovereign head of the empire still gave him considerable influence over individual families, districts and towns. He was exactly the man to turn this influence to advantage.

By means of unremitting attention and timely interference he gradually succeeded in getting a certain number of bishoprics filled according to his wishes.   We find among them the names of Salzburg, Freisingen, Trent, Eichstädt, Augsburg, Strasburg, Constance, Bamberg : all these sees were

---

[1] Anecdote in Fugger, the truth of which, however, I will not warrant.
[2] The marriage that gave Spain to the Hapsburgs :
Maximilian—Mary of Burgundy.
|
Archduke Philip＝Juana, d. of Ferdinand and Isabella
|
Charles V.

now, as far as their chapters would permit, partisans of Maximilian, and favourers of his projects.[1] In these ecclesiastical affairs his connection with the pope was especially useful to him. For example, when a prebend of the cathedral of Augsburg became vacant in 1500, it was the papal legate who conferred it on the king's chancellor, Matthew Lang (the vacancy having occurred in a papal month). The chapter raised a thousand objections; it would admit no man of the burgher class, and, least of all, a son of a burgher of Augsburg: but Maximilian said, one who was good enough to be his councillor and chancellor was good enough to be an Augsburg canon. At a solemn mass Matthew Lang was unexpectedly placed among the princes, and afterwards seated within the altar. At length the canons were satisfied, upon Lang's promising them that if he delegated to another the business of the provostship, he would appoint no one whom the chapter did not approve.

Still more direct was the influence which Maximilian gained over the secular princes. In most cases he attached them to his cause, partly by military service, partly by the favours which he had to dispense as head of the empire. Thus the sons of Duke Albert of Saxony were indissolubly bound to the Netherland policy of Austria by the possession of Friesland, which Maximilian granted to their father as a reward of his services. Albert's son-in-law, too, Erich of Calenberg, connected through him with the house of Austria, gained fame in the Austrian wars: the whole house of Guelph was attached to Austria. Henry der Mittlere[2] of Lüneburg, as well as his cousins, won new privileges and reversions of estates in the service of the king. In the same position stood Henry IV. of Mecklenburg.[3] Bogislaw X. of Pomerania did not indeed accept the service offered him at his return from the East; nevertheless Maximilian thought it expedient to conciliate him by the grant of the tolls of Wolgast and other favours.[4] The granting of tolls was, indeed, with Maximilian, as with his father, one means of carrying on the government: Julich, Treves, Hessen, Würtenberg, Lüneburg, Mecklenburg, the Palatinate even, and many others, acquired at different times new rights of toll. Other houses transferred to Austria their ancient alliances with Burgundy. Count John XIV. of Oldenburg alleged that a secret treaty had existed between his ancestors and Charles the Bold, in consideration of which the king promised to support him in his claims on Delmenhorst.[5] Count Engilbert of Nassau fought by the side of Charles at Nancy, and of Maximilian at Guinegat, for which he was made Stadtholder-General of the Netherlands in 1501. From this moment we may date the firm establishment of the power of that house (which shortly after gained possession of Orange) in the Low Countries.[6] Hessen and Würtenberg were won over by Maximilian himself. He at length determined to grant the Landgrave of Hessen the investiture which he had always refused his father. At the diet of 1495 he presented himself

---

[1] Pasqualigo, Relatione di Germania (MS. in the Court Library at Vienna), to whom I am indebted for this remark, says of the bishops: " Li quali tutti dependono dal re come sue fatture, e seguono le voglie sue."

[2] Der Mittlere—the mid-brother of three.—Transl.

[3] Lützow, Geschichte von Meklenburg, ii., p. 458.

[4] Kanzow, Pomerania, ii., p. 260. Barthold im Berlin Kal. 1838, p. 41.

[5] Hamelmann, Oldenb. Chronik., p. 309.

[6] Arnoldi, Gesch. v. Oranien, ii. 202.

in front of the throne with the great red banner, upon which, round the
arms of Hessen, were displayed not only the bearings of Waldeck, but of
Katzenelnbogen, Diez, Ziegenhain, and Nidda : the banner was so splendid
that it was not torn up, as was usual on such occasions, but was borne in
solemn procession and consecrated to the Virgin Mary.[1]   Such was the
investiture of the house of Hessen ; and we find that William der Mittlere
took an ardent share in Maximilian's campaigns.

Still more intimate was the connection of Würtenberg with Austria.
Maximilian put the seal to the acquisitions of centuries made by the
counts of that house by consolidating them into a duchy ; from that time
he took a warmer interest in the affairs of that state than of any other : in
the year 1503, in defiance of the law, he declared the young Duke Ulrich
of age when only in his sixteenth year, and thus secured his entire devotion.
The Markgraves of Brandenburg were still true to the ancient allegiance
of their founder.[2]   Later historians complain bitterly of the costly journeys and the frequent campaigns of Markgrave Frederick, whose succours
always far exceeded his contingent.   We find his sons also, from the year
1500, commanding small bodies of men in the Austrian service.

These princes were, for the most part, young men who delighted in war
and feats of arms, and at the same time sought profit and advancement in
the king's service.   The gay and high-spirited Maximilian, eternally in
motion and busied with ever-new enterprises, good-natured, bountiful,
most popular in his manners and address, a master of arms and all knightly
exercises, a good soldier, matchless in talents and inventive genius, was
formed to captivate the hearts and to secure the ardent devotion of his
youthful followers.

How great was the advantage this gave him was seen in the year 1504,
when the Landshut troubles broke out in Bavaria.   Duke George the Rich
of Landshut, who died on the 1st of December, 1503, in defiance of the
feudal laws of the empire and the domestic treaties of the house of Bavaria,
made a will, in virtue of which both his extensive and fertile domains, and
the long-hoarded treasures of his house, would fall, not to his next agnates,
Albert and Wolfgang of Bavaria-Munich, but to his more distant cousin,
nephew, and son-in-law, Rupert of the Palatinate, second son of the
elector, to whom, even during his lifetime, he had ceded his most important
castles.

Had the Council of Regency continued to exist, it would have been
empowered to prevent the quarrel between the Palatinate and Bavaria
which this incident rekindled with great violence ; or had the imperial
Chamber still been constituted according to the decrees of Worms and
Augsburg, members of the States of the empire would have had a voice in
the decision of the question of law : but the Regency had fallen to nothing,
and the court of justice was constituted by the king alone, according to his
own views ; he himself was once more regarded as " the living spring of
the law,"[3] and everything was referred to his decision.

---

[1] The ballad on this subject, which Müller, Rtth. unter Max. I., 538, has
inserted, is of later date ; the thing itself is correct.
[2] Frederick of Hohenzollern, Margrave of Nuremburg.   Given the Electorate
of Brandenburg by the Emperor Sigismund, 1417.
[3] Expression of Lamparter in his address to the States at Landshut ; Freiberg, ii., p. 178.   Gesch. der baier. Landstände, ii., p. 38.

His conduct in this case was extremely characteristic. He insisted
upon the preservation of peace : he then appeared in person, and presided
at long sittings of the diet, in order to preserve a good temper and understanding : he did not shrink from the labour of hearing both parties, even
to the fifth statement of each ; and, lastly, he summoned the judge and
assessors of his chamber to assist him in forming a just and lawful decision.[1]
But in all these laudable efforts he had chiefly his own interest (he calls it
himself by that name) in view.

He now called to mind all the losses he had sustained on account of
Bavaria ;—for example, how the expedition to the Lechfeld had caused him
to neglect the defence of his rights in Brittany and Hungary. He found,
on the one side, that Duke George had incurred heavy penalties by his
illegal will; on the other, that Albert's claims, founded on family contracts, were not incontestably valid, since those contracts had never
been confirmed by the emperor or the empire. Hereupon he set
himself up a claim to one part of the land in dispute, and a not inconsiderable one.

Duke Albert, the King's brother - in - law, was quickly persuaded to
acquiesce, and at length published a formal renunciation of the disputed
districts. This was not surprising ; he was not yet in actual possession
of them, and he hoped by this compliance to establish a claim to still
larger acquisitions. On the other hand, the Count Palatine Rupert was
utterly inflexible. Whether it were that he reckoned on his father's
foreign alliances, or that the hostile spirit of the electoral college towards
the king gave him courage,—he rejected all these proposals of partition.
Maximilian had an interview with him one night, and told him that his
father would bring ruin on himself and his house : but it was all in vain ;
Rupert immediately afterwards had the audacity to take possession in
defiance of the king.

Upon this Maximilian lost all forbearance. The lands and securities
left by Duke George were awarded by a sentence of the Chamber to the
Duke of Bavaria-Munich ; the crown fiscal demanded the proclamation
of the ban, and on the same day (23d April, 1504) the King of the Romans
uttered it in person in the open air.[2]

The neighbours of the Palatine attached to the king's party only waited
for this proclamation to break loose upon him from all sides. The recollection of all the injuries they had been compelled to endure from " that
wicked Fritz " (so they called Frederick the Victorious), and the desire to
avenge themselves and redress their wrongs, was aroused within them.
Duke Alexander the Black of Veldenz, Duke Ulrich of Würtenberg, Landgrave William of Hessen, who led the Mecklenburg and Brunswick auxiliaries, fell with devastating bands upon the Rhenish Palatinate.[3] In the
territory on the Danube, the troops of Brandenburg, Saxony, and Calenberg joined the magnificent army which Albert of Munich had collected.
The Swabian league, once so dangerous an enemy, was now his most
determined partisan ; Nürnberg, which indeed wished to make conquests

---

[1] Harpprecht, Archiv. des Kammergerichts, ii., p. 178.
[2] Freiberg, *passim*, ii., p. 52.
[3] Trithemius, Zayner, and others, describe this devastation minutely. See
Ranke, Gesch. der romanisch-german. Völker, p. 231.

for itself. sent succours to the field four times as great as had originally been required of it.[1]   The King of the Romans first appeared on the Danube. It added not a little to his glory, that it was he who had gone in quest of a body of Bohemian troops—the only allies who had remained faithful to the Count Palatine—and had completely defeated them behind his own Wagenburg, near Regensburg.   He then marched on the Rhine ; the bailiwick of Hagenau fell into his hands without resistance.   Here, as on the Danube, his first care was to take possession of the places to which he himself had claims.   The Palatinate, in any case little able to withstand so superior and general an assault, was now totally incapacitated by the death of the young and war-like Count Palatine, the author of the whole disturbance, who fell in battle.   The old elector was obliged to employ another son (whom he had sent to be educated at the court of Burgundy) as his mediator with Maximilian.   An assembly of the empire, which had been talked of in the summer of 1504, had at that time been evaded by the king.   It was not till the superiority of his arms was fully established in February, 1505, that he concluded a general truce, and summoned a diet at Cologne (which assembled in the June of that year), for the settlement of all the important questions arising out of this affair, and now once more referred to his decision.[2]

How different was his present from his former meeting with the States ! He now appeared among them at the close of a war successfully terminated, with added renown of personal valour, surrounded by a band of devoted adherents, who hoped to retain by his favour the conquests they owed to their own prowess ; respected even by the conquered, who surrendered their destiny into his hands.   Nor was this all.   The affairs of Europe were propitious.   Maximilian's son Philip was become King of Castile, upon the death of his mother-in-law.   Many a good German cherished the hope that his mighty and glorious chief was destined to chase the Turks from Europe, and to add the crown of the Eastern empire to that of the West.   They thought that the united force of the empire was so great, that neither Bohemians, Swiss, nor Turks could withstand it.[3]

The first matter discussed at Cologne was the decision of the Landshut differences.   The king had the power of determining the fate of a large German territory.   He recurred to the proposals which he had made

---

[1] In the true historical accounts of the cities usurped by Nürnberg, etc., 1791, par. 15, this reproach is again brought against that city.

[2] One of the strangest reports of these occurrences is to be found in the Viaggio in Alemagna di Francesco Vettori, Paris, 1837, p. 95, from the mouth of a goldsmith at Ueberlingen.   First, the Count Palatine is in league with the Swiss and the French ; even the Swiss war is brought about by him : hereupon Maximilian concludes a treaty with France at Hagenau, in 1502 (it took place, as we know, in 1505), and forthwith attacks the Count Palatine, who calls upon the Bohemians for help, but then leaves them himself in the lurch, so that they get beaten.   This is another example how rapidly history turns into myth ; every detail is incorrect, while the whole is not entirely devoid of truth.   Vettori himself finds the statements of the goldsmith wanting in order, and not to be depended on ; but he readily admits them into his book, which has more the air of the Decameron than of a Diary of a Journey.

[3] The sentiment of the admirable song, " die behemsch Schlacht " (the Bohemian Fight), 1504, by Hormayr, from some publication of the day, and repeated by Soltau, p. 198.

before the beginning of the war : for the issue of the Count Palatine Rupert, he founded the new Palatinate on the other side the Danube, which was to yield a rent of 24,000 gulden ; the constituent parts of it were calculated to produce that amount. Landshut now, indeed, devolved on the Munich line, but not without considerable diminution : the dukes themselves had been compelled to pay by cessions of lands for the succours they had received ; the king kept back what he had advanced to others before the sentence was pronounced : not only did he not sacrifice, he promoted, his own interests. The Palatinate sustained still greater losses , the loans, the claims to ceded lands, and the king's claims, were more considerable in that territory than in any other. It availed little that the old elector could not bring himself to accept the terms offered him ; he was only the more entirely excluded from the royal favour : some time later his son was obliged to conform to them. If the possessions of the two houses of Wittelsbach were regarded as a whole, it had suffered such losses by this affair as no house in Germany had for ages sustained ; and it left so deep and lasting a resentment as might have proved dangerous to the empire, had not their mutual animosity been enkindled anew by the war, and rendered all concert between them impossible.

The position of Maximilian was, however, necessarily changed, even as to the general policy of the empire, by the course things had taken.

The union of the electors was broken up. The humiliation of the Palatinate was followed by the death of the Elector of Treves in the year 1503, to whose place Maximilian, strengthened by his alliance with the court of Rome, succeeded in promoting one of his nearest kinsmen, the young Markgrave James of Baden ;[1] and, on the 21st December, 1504, by the death of the leader of the electoral opposition, Berthold of Mainz. How rarely does life satisfy even the noblest ambition ! It was the lot of this excellent man to live to see the overthrow of the institutions which he had laboured so earnestly to establish, and the absolute supremacy of the monarch on whom he had sought to impose legal and constitutional restraints.

Maximilian had now a clear field for his own enterprises. It seemed to him possible to use the ascendancy which he felt he had acquired, for the establishment of organic institutions.   Whilst he endeavoured to ascertain why the measures taken at Augsburg had failed (the blame of which he mainly attributed to Berthold of Mainz), he published a plan for carrying them into execution, with certain modifications.[2]

His idea was, at all events, to form a government (*Regiment*) composed of a viceroy, chancellor, and twelve counsellors of the empire ; and for their assistance, and under their supervision, to appoint four marshals, each with twenty-five knights, for the administration of the executive power in the districts of the Upper and Lower Rhine, the Danube, and the Elbe. The imposition of the Common Penny was again expressly mentioned.

But a glance is sufficient to show the wide difference between this scheme

[1] Browerus, p. 320. He saw the Brief by which the Pope recommended the candidate of the King of the Romans.

[2] Protocol of the Imperial Diet in the Frankfurt Acts, which adds considerably to the particulars found in Müller's Reichstagsstaat.

and the former.   The king insisted on having the right of summoning this governing body to attend his person and court ;   it was only to be empowered to decide in the more insignificant cases ;   in all matters of importance it was to recur to him.   He would himself nominate a captain-general of the empire, if he could not come to an understanding with Albert of Bavaria.

In short, it is clear that the obligations and burdens of government would have remained with the states ; the power would have fallen to the lot of the king.

His ascendancy was, however, not yet so great as to induce, or to compel, the empire to accept such a scheme as this at his hands.

Was it indeed possible to revert to institutions which had already proved so impracticable ?   Was not the sovereignty of the lords of the soil far too firmly and fully developed to render it probable that they would lend or even submit themselves to such extensive and radical changes ? The only condition under which this could have been imagined possible was, that a committee chosen from the body of the princes should be invested with the sovereign power ; but that they would voluntarily abandon their high position in favour of the king, it would have been absurd to expect.

The diet of Cologne is remarkable for this—that people began to cease to deceive themselves as to the real state of things.   The opinions which prevailed during the last years of Frederick's and the first of Maximilian's reign ;   the attempts made to establish an all-embracing unity of the nation,—a combined action of all its powers,—a form of government which might satisfy all minds and supply all wants, are to be held in eternal and honourable remembrance ; but they were directed towards an unattainable Ideal.   The estates were no longer to be reduced to the condition of subjects properly so called : the king was not contented to be nothing more than a president of the estates.   It was therefore necessary to abandon such projects.

The estates assembled at Cologne did not refuse to afford succours to the king, but neither by a general tax (Common Penny) nor by an assessment of all the parishes in the empire, but by a matricula.[1]   The difference is immeasurable.   The former plans were founded on the idea of unity, and regarded the whole body of the people as common subjects of the empire ; the matricula, in which the States were rated severally, according to their resources, was, in its very origin, based on the idea of the separateness of the territorial power of the several sovereigns.

They declined taking any share in a central or general government (*Reichsregiment*) of the empire.   They said his majesty had hitherto ruled wisely and well ; they were not disposed to impose restraints upon him.

Public opinion took a direction far less ideal, far less satisfactory to those who had cherished aspirations after a common fatherland, but one more practical and feasible.

Maximilian demanded succours for an expedition against Hungary ; not against the king, with whom, on the contrary, he was on a good footing,

[1] The Matricula partook of the nature both of census and rate or assessment. It was the list of the contingents, in men and money, which the several States were bound to furnish to the empire, and was founded on their population and pecuniary resources respectively.—TRANSL.

but against a portion of the Hungarian nobles. The last treaty, by which his hereditary rights were recognised, had been agreed to only by a few of them individually ; it was not confirmed at the diet. The Hungarians now began to declare that they would never again raise a foreigner to the throne, alleging that none had consulted the interests of the nation. A resolution to this effect, which was as offensive to their monarch as it was injurious to the rights of Austria, was solemnly passed and sent into all the counties.[1] This Maximilian now resolved to oppose. He observed that the maintenance of his rights was important not only to himself but to the Holy Empire, for which Bohemia had been recovered, and with which Hungary was, through him, connected.

In a proclamation, in which the edicts concerning the Council of Regency (*Regiment*) and the Common Penny were expressly repealed, Maximilian asked for succours of four or five thousand men for one year. He expressed a hope that this might perhaps also suffice for his expedition to Rome. The States assented without difficulty : they granted him four thousand men for a year, raised according to a matricula. The levy was to consist of 1058 horse, and 3038 foot. Of these, the secular princes were to furnish the larger proportion of horse, namely, 422 ; the cities the larger of foot,—1106 : on the whole, the electors had to bear about a seventh, the archbishops and bishops a half, the prelates and counts not quite a third ; of the remaining seven parts, about one half was borne by the secular princes, the other half by the States.

These more moderate levies had at least one good result—they were really executed. The troops which had been granted, were, if not entirely (which the defective state of the census rendered impossible), yet, in great measure, furnished to the king, and did him good service. His appearance on the frontier at the head of forces armed and equipped by the empire, made no slight impression in Hungary ; some magnates and cities were quickly reduced to obedience. As a son was just then born to King Wladislas, whereby the prospect of a change of dynasty became more remote, the Hungarian nobles determined not exactly to revoke their decree, but not to enforce it. A committee of the States received unconditional powers to conclude a peace, which was accordingly concluded in July 1506 at Vienna ; Maximilian having again reserved to himself his hereditary right. Although the recognition of the states of Hungary expressed by accepting this treaty is only indirect, Maximilian thought his own rights and those of the German nation sufficiently guaranteed by this treaty.

He now directed his attention and his forces upon Italy. Till he was in possession of the crown and title of emperor he did not think he had attained to his full dignity.[2]

It was evident, however, that he would not be able to accomplish his purpose with the small body of men that followed him from Hungary.

---

[1] Istuanffy, Historia Regni Hungarici, p. 32.

[2] In his declaraton to the states, Maximilian designates the convention of Vienna as a treaty " whereby his Imperial Majesty and the German nation, God willing, might suffer no loss of their rights in the kingdom of Hungary, when the crown becomes vacant :"—" dadurch I. K. Mt. und deutsche Nation, ob Gott will, an ihrer erblichen und andern Gerechtigkeit des Königreichs Ungern, wenn es zu Fällen kommt, nicht Mangel haben werde."

Louis XII., with whom he had shortly before concerted the most intimate union of their respective houses, was led into other views by his
States.   He no longer thought it advisable to permit the ambitious,
restless Maximilian, sustained by the power of a warlike nation, to get a
footing in Italy.   In this the Venetians agreed.   At the moment when
Maximilian approached their frontiers, they hastened (favoured by a
revolt among the Landsknechts, which gave them time) to organise a very
strong defence.   Maximilian saw that, if he would obtain the crown, he
must conquer it by force of arms and in strenuous warfare.   He hastened
to summon a new diet.

Once more, in the spring of 1507, the States assembled, in the plenitude
of their loyalty and devotion to the king.   They were still under the
influence of recent events ; strangers were astonished at their unanimity,
and at the high consideration the king of the Romans enjoyed among
them.   A remark made by the Italians is not without foundation—that a
calamity which had befallen the king had been of advantage to him in the
affairs of Germany.[1]   His son Philip had hardly ascended the throne of
Castile when he died unexpectedly in September, 1506.   The German
princes had always regarded the rising greatness of this young monarch
with distrust.   They had feared that his father would endeavour to make
him elector, or vicar of the empire, and, after his own coronation, king of
the Romans ; and this first idea of a union of the imperial authority with
the power of Burgundy and of Castile had filled them with no little alarm.
The death of Philip freed them from this fear ; the sons he left were too
young to inspire anxiety.   The princes felt disposed to attach themselves
the more cordially to their king ; the more youthful hoped to conquer new
and large fiefs in his service.

On the 27th of April, 1507,[2] Maximilian opened the diet at Constance, in
the immediate neighbourhood of Italy.   Never was he more impressed
with the dignity of his station than at this moment.   He declared, with a
sort of shame, that he would no longer be a little trooper (*kein kleiner Reiter*),
he would get rid of all trifling business, and devote his attention only to
the great affairs.   He gave the assembly to understand that he would not
only force his way through Italy, but would engage in a decisive struggle
for the sovereignty of Italy.   Germany, he said, was so mighty that it
ought to receive the law from no one ; it had countless foot soldiers, and
at least sixty thousand horses fit for service ; they must now make an
effort to secure the empire for ever.   It would all depend on the heavy
fire-arms ; the true knights would show themselves on the bridge over the
Tiber.   He uttered all this with animated and confiding eloquence.   " I
wish," writes Eitelwolf von Stein to the elector of Brandenburg, " that
your grace had heard him."

[1] Somaria di la Relatione di Vic. Querini, Doctor, ritornato dal Re di Romani,
1507, Nov. Sanuto's Chronicle, Vienna Archives, tom. vii.   He is of opinion,
that the Elector of Saxony indulged the hope of one day getting possession of
the crown.   " Il re a gran poder in Alemagna," he also says, " è molto amato.
perche quelli non l' ubediva è morti."

[2] Tuesday after the feast of St. Mark.   Letter from Eitelwolf von Stein to
the elector of Brandenburg, April 6, 1507, in the Berlin Archives.   The previous
accounts are incorrect.

The States replied, that they were determined to aid him, according to their several means, to gain possession of the imperial crown.[1]

There remained, indeed, some differences of opinion between them. When the king expressed his determination of driving the French out of Milan, the States dissented.   They were only disposed to force a passage through the country in defiance of them, for a regular war with France was not to be engaged in without negotiations.   Nor would they grant the whole of the supplies the king at first demanded.   Nevertheless, the subsidy which they assented to, in compliance with a second proposal of his, was unusually large.   It amounted to three thousand horse, and nine thousand foot.

Maximilian, who doubted not that he should accomplish some decisive stroke with this force, now promised, on his side, to govern any conquest he might make according to the counsels of the States.   He hinted that the revenue she might derive from these new acquisitions would perhaps suffice to defray the charges of the empire.[2]

The States accepted this offer with great satisfaction.   Whatever, whether land or people, cities or castles, might be conquered, was to remain for ever incorporated with the empire.

This good understanding as to foreign affairs, was favourable to some progress in those of the nation.   The diet of Cologne, while it gave up all the projects of institutions founded upon a complete community of interests and of powers, had continued to regard a restoration of the Imperial Chamber as necessary.   This, however, they had never been able to accomplish : the Chamber which Maximilian had established by his own arbitrary act had held no sittings for three years ; the salaries of the procurators had even been stopped.[3]   Now, however, the diet assembled at Constance resolved to re-establish the Imperial Chamber according to

---

[1] Answer of the States, Frankf. A. A., tom. xxiii. : " They had appeared at this Imperial Diet, at his majesty's request, as his lieges fully inclined to advise, and according to their ability to aid in obtaining the imperial crown, and to offer resistance to the design of the King of France, which he is practising against the holy empire."—" Sie syen uf diesen Richstag uf irer Mt. Erfordern als die Gehorsame erschienen, ganz Gemüts zu raten und ires Vermögens die kaiserliche Krone helfen zu erlangen und des Königs von Frankreich Fürnemen, des er wider das h. Reich in Uebung steht, Widerstand zu tun."

[2] In the declaration in which he asks for 12,000 men, he adds : " And if the Sates now show themselves in such measure ready and prompt with help, then is his imperial majesty willing to act after their counsel, with respect to what money, goods, land and people will be requisite, how the same should be managed and applied, how also the conquered domains and people are to be treated and supported by the empire, so that the burdens in all future times may be taken off the Germans, and, according to what is reasonable, laid upon another nation ; also, how every king of the Romans may be supported honourably in due state without heavily burdening the German nation."—" Und wo sich die Stend des Reichs jetzo dermaassen dapferlich mit der Hilf erzaigen, so ist k. Mt. willig jetzo nach irem Rat zu handeln, was von Geld Gut Land und Lüten zuston wird, wie dasselb gehandelt und angelegt werden soll, wie auch die eroberte Herrschaften und Lut by dem Rich zu hanndhaben und zu erhalten syn, dadurch die Bürden in ewig Zeiten ab den Deutschen und der Billichait nach uf andre Nation gelegt, auch ein jeder romisch Konig eehrlich und statlich on sunder Beswerung deutscher Nation erhalten werden mög."

[3] Harpprecht, ii., § 240, § 253.

the edicts of Worms.   In the nomination of the members of it the electors
were to retain their privileges ; for the other estates, the division into
circles which had been determined on in Augsburg was adopted, so that
it was not entirely suffered to drop : no notice was taken of the cities.
The question now was, how this tribunal was to be maintained ?   Maximilian was of opinion that it would be best that each assessor should be at
the charge of the government which had appointed him : he would take
upon himself that of the judges and the chancery of the court.   Unquestionably however the States were right in desiring to avoid the predominancy
of private interests which this arrangement would have favoured :[1] they
offered to tax themselves to a small amount in order to pay the salaries
of the law officers.   They did not choose that the court should be stripped
of the character of a tribunal common to the whole body of the States,
which had originally been given to it.   With this view they determined
that every year two princes, one spiritual, the other temporal, should
investigate its proceedings, and report upon them to the States

If we pause a moment and reflect on what preceded the diet of Constance, and on what followed it, we perceive its great importance.   The
matricular assessment (or register of the resources of the empire) and the
Imperial Chamber were, during three centuries, the most eminent institutions by which the unity of the empire was represented ; their definitive
establishment and the connexion between them were the work of that
diet.   The ideas which had given birth to these two institutions were
originally founded on opposite principles ; but this was exactly what
now recommended them to favour ; the independence of the several
sovereignties was not infringed, while the idea of their community was
kept in view.

Another extremely important affair, that of Switzerland, was also
decided here.

Elector Berthold had been desirous of incorporating the Swiss in the
diet, and giving them a share in all the institutions he projected.   But
exactly the reverse ensued.   The Confederates had been victorious in a
great war with the King of the Romans.   In the politics of Europe they
generally adhered to France, and they continued to draw one city after
another into their league ; and yet they pretended to remain members and
subjects of the empire.   This was a state of things which became manifestly
intolerable when disputes with France arose.   Whenever war broke out
with France and Italy, a diversion was to be feared on the side of Switzerland, the more dangerous because it was impossible to be prepared for it.

The diet resolved to come to a clear understanding on this point.   An
embassy was sent by the States of the empire to Switzerland for that
purpose.

The members of it were, however, by no means confident of success.
" God send his Holy Spirit upon us," exclaims one of them : " if we
accomplish nothing, we shall bring down war upon the Swiss, and be
compelled to regard them as our Turks."

---

[1] " Es sy not, das Cammergerichte als ain versampt Wesen von ainem Wesen
unterhalten und derselbtige underhaltung nit zerteilt werden."—" It is needful
that the imperial chamber, as a collective body, be maintained by one body,
and that the maintenance of the same be not divided."—*Protocol of the Imperial
Diet in Harpprecht,* ii. 443.

But the Confederates had already, in the course of their service, fallen out with the French, so that the ambassadors found them more tractable than they had expected. They recalled all their troops still in Italy at the first admonition. They promised without the slightest hesitation to remain faithful to the empire. A deputation from them appeared at Constance, and was most graciously received by the king, who kept them there at his own expense and dismissed them with presents, after entering into an agreement to take into pay, in the next war, six thousand Swiss under the banners of the empire.

On the other hand, Maximilian made a most important concession to them. He formally emancipated them from the jurisdiction of the imperial courts ; declaring that neither in criminal nor in civil causes should the Confederation, or any member of it, be subject to be cited before the imperial chamber or any other royal tribunal.[1]

This measure decided the fate of Switzerland to all succeeding ages. At the very time when the empire agreed to subject itself to a general assessment and enrolment, and to the jurisdiction of the imperial chamber, it abandoned all claim to impose them on the Swiss : on the contrary, it took their troops into its pay and renounced its jurisdiction over them. They were, as Maximilian expressed himself, " dutiful kinsmen of the empire," who however must be kept in order when they were re- fractory.

Although it is not to be disputed that the real political grounds of these concessions was the increasing inclination of the Swiss to a separation from the empire, still it was the most fortunate arrangement for that moment. The quarrel was for a time appeased. Maximilian appeared more puissant, more magnificent than ever. Foreigners did not doubt that he would have, as they heard it affirmed, thirty thousand men to lead into the field : the warlike preparations which they encountered in some of the Swabian cities filled them with the idea that the empire was rousing all its energies.

Maximilian indulged the most ambitious and romantic hopes. He declared that with the noble and efficient aid granted to him, he hoped to reduce to obedience all those in Italy who did not acknowledge the sovereignty of the holy empire. But he would not stop there. When he had once reduced that country to order, he would confide it to one of his captains, and would himself march without delay against the infidels ; for he had vowed this to Almighty God.

The slow march of the imperial troops, the procrastination of the Swiss, the well-defended Venetian passes, doubly difficult to force in the approach- ing winter season, were indeed calculated to rouse him from these dreams of conquest, and turn his attention on what was really attainable. But his high spirit did not quail. On the second of February he caused a religious ceremony to be performed in Trent, as a consecration of his intended expedition to Rome. Nay, as if the very object for which he was going thither was already accomplished, he assumed, on the very same day, the title of elected emperor of the Romans.[2] Foreigners always called him so, and he well knew that the pope, at this moment his ally, would not oppose it. He was led to this act by different motives : on the one

[1] Fryheitsbull bei Anshelm, iii. 321.
[2] There is a closer examination of this point in the Excursus upon Fugger.

side, the sight of the formidable opposition he had to encounter, so that
he already feared he should not succeed in getting to Rome ; on the other,
the feeling of the might and independence of the empire, for which he
was anxious at all events to rescue the prerogative of giving a supreme
head to Christendom : the mere ceremony of coronation he did not regard
as so essential.   To Germany, too, his resolution was of the utmost importance : Maximilian's successors have always assumed the title of
Emperor immediately after their coronation at Aix-la-Chapelle ; though
only one of the whole line was crowned by the pope.[1] Although Pope
Julius appeared well pleased at this assumption, it was, in fact, a symptom
of the emancipation of the German crown from the papacy.   Intimately
connected with it, was the attempt of Maximilian at the same time to
revive the title of King of Germany, which had not been heard for centuries.   Both were founded on the idea of the unity and independence
of the German nation, whose chief was likewise the highest personage in
Europe.   They were expressions of that supremacy of the nation which
Maximilian still asserted : a supremacy, however, which rapidly declined.

VENETIAN WAR. DIET OF WORMS.

It had been debated at Constance whether the imperial forces should first
attack the French or the Venetian possessions in Italy.   Whatever conquests might be made, it was not the intention of the diet to grant them
out as fiefs (Milan had not even been restored to the Sforza), but to retain
them in the hands of the empire, as a source of public revenue.

Among the princes some were advocates for the Milanese, others, who
like the dukes of Bavaria had claims against Venice, for the Venetian,
expedition.   Even among the imperial councillors, difference of opinion
prevailed.   Paul von Lichtenstein, who was on good terms with Venice,
was for attacking Milan ; Matthew Lang and Eitelfritz of Zollern, on
the other hand, deemed it easier to make conquests from the Venetians
than from the French.[2]

The latter opinion at length prevailed.   The Venetians were not to be
brought to declare that they would not take part against the king of the
Romans : on the other hand, France held out hopes that if no attempt
was made upon Milan, she would offer no obstacle to the steps taken by

---

[1] The title of Emperor, though commonly given to Maximilian, belonged, of
right, only to those who had been crowned at Rome by the hands of the Pope,—
conditions which, as we shall see, Maximilian was never able to fulfil.   At the
head of the " Holy Roman Empire (Reich) of the German Nation," stands the
King, elected by the German estates of the empire, who, however, by his election
and his coronation in Germany (at Aachen) obtains only the rights and title of
King of the Romans (Römischen Königs), and acquires the rights and title of
Roman Emperor (Römischen Kaisers) only by his coronation at Rome ; to
which all the vassals of the empire must accompany him, and which the Pope,
if he be lawfully and duly elected, cannot refuse him.   His successor bears the
title of King of the Romans.   Eichhorn, Deutsche Staats-und Rechts-geschichte,
vol. ii., p. 365.—Transl.

[2] Relatione di Vicenzo Quirini.   He mentioned some of the council by name
as " nostri capitali inimici :" for a time, Maximilian said : " I Venetiani non
mi a fato dispiacer e Franza sì.   E su queste pratiche passa il tempo."

the empire for the assertion of its other claims in Italy.[1] Strongly as the Alps were defended, Maximilian was not to be deterred from trying his fortune there. At first he was successful. " The Venetians," he says, in a letter to the Elector of Saxony, dated the 10th of March, " paint their lion with two feet in the sea, one on the plain country, the fourth on the mountains ; we have nearly caught the foot on the Alps ; there is only one claw missing, which, with God's help, we will have in a week ; and then we hope to conquer the foot on the plain.[2]

But he had engaged in an enterprise which was destined to plunge his affairs in general, and those of Germany in particular, into inextricable difficulties.

In Switzerland, spite of all treaties, the French faction, especially supported by Lucerne, soon revived ;[3] the confederate troops hung back. This so greatly weakened the German forces (the emperor having intended to draw two thirds of the infantry from Switzerland), that the Venetians soon had the advantage of the imperialists. They did not rest satisfied with driving the Germans from their territory, they fell on the emperor's own dominions, just where he was least prepared for an attack. Görz, Wippach, Trieste, and forty-seven places, more or less strongly fortified, rapidly fell into their hands.

Germany was struck with astonishment and consternation. After subsidies which had appeared so considerable, after the exertions made by every individual for the empire, after such high-raised expectations, the result was shame and ignominy. It was in vain that the emperor alleged that the levies had not been furnished complete ; the fault of this was in part ascribed to himself. The Duke of Lüneburg, for example, had never received the estimate of his contingent. But, putting that aside :—To set out without having the least assurance of success !—to risk his whole fortunes on the levies of a Swiss diet ! The common lot— loss of reputation for one abortive undertaking—now fell with double and triple force on Maximilian, whose capacity and character had always been doubted by many.

Compelled to return immediately to Germany, Maximilian's first act was to call the electors together. The elector palatine he did not include with the rest ; Brandenburg was too far ; he contented himself with sending a messenger to him. But the others assembled in the beginning of May 1508, at Worms. Maximilian declared to them that he called on them first, on whom the empire rested as on its foundations, for their

---

[1] Pasqualigo, Relatione. " Non sarai molto difficil cosa che la (S. M.) dirizzasse la sua impresa contra questo stato, massime per il dubbio che li è firmato nell' animo che le Ecc^{ze} Vostre siano per torre l'arme in mano contra a lei quando la fusse sul bello di cacciar li Francesi d'Italia, et a questo ancora l' inclineria assai li onorati partiti che dal re di Francia li sono continuamente offerti ogni volta che la voglia lassar la impresa di Milano e ricuperar le altre jurisditioni imperiali che ha in Italia."

[2] Letter from Sterzing, March 1, accompanied by a letter from Hans Renner of the same date. He also has the best hopes.

[3] In the Relatione della Nazione delli Suizzeri 1508, Informm. politiche, tom. ix., the different persons who brought about this change are mentioned, but their names are difficult to decipher in our copy : " Amestaver at Zug, Nicolo Corator at Solothurn, Manforosini at Freiburg." Lucerne was the centre of the whole movement.

aid in his great peril : he craved their counsel how he might best obtain valiant, safe, and effective succours ; but, he added, without employing the Swabian league, whose help he should stand in need of elsewhere ; and without convoking a diet of the empire.[1]

Among the assembled princes, Frederick of Saxony was the most powerful. By his advice they declined the emperor's invitation to meet him in Frankfurt ; principally because they found it impossible to come to any resolution without a previous conference with the other states of the empire.[2] Maximilian replied that he was in the most perilous situation in the world ; if the troops of the empire, whose pay was in arrear, were now to withdraw, his country of Tyrol was inclined to join the French and the Venetians, out of resentment against the empire, by which it was not protected : he could in no case wait for a diet ; the loss of time would be too great ; the utmost that could be done would be hastily to call together the nearest princes.[3] The electors persisted in demanding a diet. They would not believe that the Swabian league entertained the thought of separating itself from the other states ; to grant any thing on their own responsibility and in the absence of the others, said they, would bring hostility upon them, and be useless to the king.[4] They were worked upon by the pressing and obvious exigency of the case, only so far as to facilitate a loan of the emperor's, by their intercession and guarantee.

The consequences of war must, in every age and country, have an immense influence on the current of internal affairs. We have seen how all the attempts to give to the empire a constitution agreeable to the wishes and opinions of the States were ultimately connected with the alliance by which Maximilian was elected king of the Romans, Austria and the Netherlands were defended, and Bavaria reduced to subjection. On the other hand, at the first great reverse—the unfortunate combat with Switzerland,—that constitution received a shock from which it never recovered. The position too which the king himself assumed, rested on the success of his arms in the Bavarian war. It was no wonder, therefore, that after the great reverses he had now sustained, the whole fabric of his power tottered, and the opposition which seemed nearly subdued arose in new strength. Success is a bond of union ; misfortune decomposes and scatters.

Nor was this state of the public mind changed by the circumstance that Maximilian, favoured by the disgust which the encroachments of the Venetians had excited in other quarters, now concluded the treaty of Cambrai, by which not only the pope and Ferdinand the Catholic, but the King of Bavaria, against whom he had just made war, combined with him

---

[1] The instruction for Matthias Lang, Bishop of Gurk ; Adolf, Count of Nassau ; Erasmus Dopler, prebendary of St. Sebaldus at Nürnberg ; and Dr. Ulrich von Schellenberg, is dated the last day of April, the feast of St. Wendel, 1508. (Weimar Archives.)

[2] The Archives at Weimar contain the advice of Frederick, and the answer. (May 8, Monday after Misericordia.)

[3] Letters of Maximilian from Linz, May 7, and from Siegburg, May 10. (Weimar Archives.)

[4] Answer, dated May 13, Saturday after Misericordia. (Weimar Archives.) In return for their guarantee, they desired some security from the emperor. The latter replied, " he could bind himself to nothing further, than to release them from their guarantee within a year's time, upon his good faith."

against Venice.[1] This hasty renunciation of the antipathy to France which he had so loudly professed, this sudden revolution in his policy, was not calculated to restore the confidence of the States.

Perhaps the present might really have been the moment in which, with the co-operation of such powerful allies, conquests might have been made in Italy ; but there was no longer sufficient concert among the powers of Germany for any such undertaking. On the 21st of April, 1509, the emperor made his warlike entry into the city of Worms (where after long delays, the States had assembled),[2] armed from head to foot, mounted on a mailed charger, and followed by a retinue of a thousand horsemen, among whom were Stradiotes and Albanians. He was destined to encounter such an opposition as never awaited him before.

He represented to the States the advantages which would accrue to the empire from the treaty just concluded, and exhorted them to come to his aid with a formidable levy of horse and foot as quickly as possible, at least for a year.[3] The States answered his appeal with complaints of his internal administration. A secret discontent, of which the fiery impetuous Maximilian seemed to have no suspicion, had taken possession of all minds.

The chief complaints arose from the cities ;—and indeed with good reason.

Under Elector Berthold they had risen to a very brilliant station, and had taken a large share in the general administration of affairs. All this was at end since the dissolution of the Council of Regency (*Regiment*). Nor were any municipal assessors admitted into the Imperial Chamber. Nevertheless, they were compelled to contribute not only to all the other taxes, as well as to the expenses of the administration of justice, but the rate imposed on them at Constance was disproportionately high. Even at Cologne they were not spared, as we saw ; they were compelled to furnish nearly two sevenths of the subsidies ; but at Constance a full third of the whole amount of foot soldiers and of money was levied upon

---

[1] Matthias von Gurk informs the elector Frederick, Sept. 24, that he was going with certain councillors and the daughter of the emperor to a place on the French frontier, in order to treat concerning the peace with the Cardinal de Rohan, who was also to come thither. " Frau Margareta handelt und muet sich mit allem Vleiss und Ernst umb ain Frid." " The Lady Margaret negotiates and exerts herself with all industry and earnestness for a peace."

[2] By a letter of summons, Cologne, May 31, 1508, after the above-mentioned meeting of the electors, " ein eilender Reichstag," " a speedy diet of the empire " was announced for July 16 ; deferred at Boppart, June 26, " bis wir des Reichs Nothdurft weiter bedenken,"—" till we have further considered the necessities of the empire," at Cologne, July 16., fixed for All Saints' day ; at Brussels Sept. 12, this term is once more resolved upon ; at Mechlin, Dec. 22, the reason of the fresh delay is explained, viz. the negotiations with France ; at last, March 15, 1509, the emperor renews his letter of summons, and fixes the term for Judica. Fr. Ar., vols. xxiv. and xxv.

[3] Verhandelung der Stennde des h. Reichs uff dem kaiserlichen Tage zu Worms ao dni 1509. Frankft. Ar. vol. xxiv. Address of his majesty, Sunday, April 22, at one o'clock. " Wo S. Heiligkeit nit gewest, hätte Kaiser. Mt. den Verstand und Practica nit angenommen." Had it not been for his holiness, his imperial majesty would not have accepted the treaty. Yet he remarks, the affair " werde sich liederlich und mit kleinen Kosten ausführen lassen,"—" might be executed easily and at little cost."

them.[1] Nay, as if this was not enough, immediately after the diet the emperor caused the plenipotentiaries of the cities to be cited before the fiscal of the empire, who called them to account for the continuance of the great merchants' company, which had been forbidden by previous imperial edicts, and demanded a fine of 90,000 gulden for carrying on unlawful traffic.   The merchants loudly protested against this sentence ; they said that they were treated like serfs ; it were better for them to quit their native country, and emigrate to Venice or Switzerland, or even France, where honourable trade and dealing was not restricted ; but they were forced at last to compound by means of a considerable sum.   The cities were not so weak, however, as to submit quietly to all this ; they had held town-meetings (*Städtetag*) and had determined to put themselves in an attitude of defence at the next imperial diet ;[2] the members of the Swabian league as well as the others.   They had not the slightest inclination to strain their resources against a republic with which they carried on the most advantageous commercial intercourse, and which they were accustomed to regard as the model and the natural head of all municipal communities.[3]

Among the princes, too, there was much bad blood.   The demands of the imperial chamber, the irregularities in the levies of men and money which we shall have occasion to notice again, had disgusted the most powerful among them.   The Palatinate was still unreconciled.   The old Count Palatine was dead ; his sons appeared at Worms, but they could not succeed in obtaining their fief.   The warlike zeal which had recently inflamed many for the emperor, had greatly subsided after the bad results of his first campaign.

But the circumstance which made a stronger impression than all the rest, was the conduct of Maximilian with regard to his last treaties.   At the diet of Constance, the States had proposed sending an embassy to France in order to renew negotiations with that power ; for they did not choose to commit the whole business of the empire implicitly to its chief. Maximilian had at that time rejected all these proposals, and professed

[1] Accounts in the genuine Fugger.   It appears to me that the sum amounted to 20,000 gulden.   See Jäger, Schwäbisches Städtewesen, 677.

[2] The resolutions of these municipal diets deserve much more accurate examination.   A letter from the Swabian league, Oct. 21, 1508, calls to mind, " welchermaass auf vergangen gemeinem Frei und Reichsstett-Tag zu Speier der Beschwerden halben, so den Stettboten uf dem Reichstag zu Costnitz begegnet sind, gerathschlagt und sunderlich verlassen ist, so die Röm. Königl. Mt. weiderum ein Reichstag fürnehmen wird, dass alsdann gemeine Frei und Reichsstette gen Speier beschrieben werden sollten."—" In what manner, at a former common diet of the free and imperial cities held at Spires by reason of complaints with regard to the treatment the deputies of the cities had met with at the imperial diet at Constance, it had been discussed and specially resolved on, in case his majesty, the King of the Romans, should again propose a diet of the empire, that then the free and imperial cities should be convened in common at Spires."

[3] Very curious indications of the light in which Venice was regarded by the trading towns of Germany are still to be found at Nürnberg.   That magnificent city endeavoured in all its institutions to imitate the queen of the Adriatic.   I have seen, in MS., an application from the council of Nürnberg to the senate of Venice for the rules of an orphan asylum, in which this sentiment is strongly expressed.—Transl.

an irreconciliable enmity to the French. Now, on the contrary, he had himself concluded a treaty with France, and without consulting the States ; nay, he did not even think himself called upon to communicate to them the treaty when ratified.[1] No wonder if these puissant princes, who had so lately entertained the project of uniting all the powers of the empire in a government constituted by themselves, were profoundly disgusted. They reminded the emperor, that they had told him at Constance that the grant he then received was the last ; and that he, on his side, had abandoned all claim to further aids. He was persuaded, they said, by his councillors, that the empire must help him as often as he chose to require help ; but this notion must not be allowed to take root in his mind, or they would have perpetually to suffer from it.

A very strong opposition thus arose on various grounds to the king's proposals. It made no change in public opinion, that the French obtained a brilliant victory over the Venetians, and that the latter for a moment doubted whether they should be able to retain their possessions on the main land. On the contrary, the first obstacle to the victorious career of the league of Cambrai was raised in Germany. At the same moment in which the Venetian cities in Apulia, Romagna and Lombardy fell into the hands of the allies after the battle of Aguadello, a committee of the States advised, and the whole body thereupon resolved, that an answer should be sent to the emperor, refusing all succours. They declared that they were neither able to support him in the present war, nor were they bound to do so. Unable, because the last subsidies had been announced to their subjects as final, and no fresh ones could be levied without great difficulties and discontents : not bound, since the treaty had not even been communicated to them, as was the custom from time immemorial in all cases of the kind.[2]

The emperor's commissioners (for he had quitted the diet again himself a few days after his arrival, in order to hasten the armaments on the Italian frontier,)[3] were in the utmost perplexity. What would the church, what would France, say if the holy empire alone did not fulfil its conditions?

[1] The Weimar Archives contain an opinion upon the necessity of refusing succours, in which persons are especially complained of, " so bei S. Kais. Mt. sein und sich allwege geflissen Ks. Mt. dahin zu bewegen Hilf bei den Stenden des Reiches zu suchen zu solchem Fürnemen, das doch ohne Rad und Bewusst der Stennde des h. Reichs beschehen ist : "—" who are about his imperial majesty, and in all ways strive to move his imperial majesty to seek help from the states of the empire, towards such undertaking, which, however, has been entered upon without the advice and knowledge of the states of the holy empire."

[2] Transactions, &c. " Dweile die Stende des Reichs davon kein gründliches Wissen tragen, so hab I. Ks. Mt. wohl zu ermessen, dass wo ichts darin begriffen oder verleipt das dem h. Reich jetzo oder in Zukunft zu Nachtheil thäte reichen, es were mit Herzogthum Mailand oder anderm, dem Reich zuständig, dass sie darin nit willigen können."—" Seeing that the states of the empire have no thorough knowledge thereof, his imperial majesty has to consider well that if any thing be therein contained or embodied which might tend now or hereafter to the injury of the holy empire, be it with regard to the duchy of Milan, or any other belonging to the empire, they cannot give their consent thereunto."

[3] Not out of anger, as has been commonly believed. He declared as early as the 22d of April, that he could not await the conclusion, and went away two days afterwards, before the diet had fully met : the real proposition of the

The States declined any further explanation on the matter ; if the commissioners had any proposition to make concerning law and order, concerning the administration of justice, or the coinage, the States were ready to entertain it. The commissioners asked whether this was the unanimous opinion of all the States ; the States replied, that was their unanimous resolution. The commissioners said, that nothing then remained for them but to report the matter to the emperor, and await his answer.

It may easily be imagined what a tempest of rage he fell into. From the frontiers of Italy—from Trent—he dispatched a violent answer, printed, though sealed. He began by justifying his own conduct ; especially the conclusion of the last treaty, for which he had power and authority, " as reigning Roman Emperor, according to the ordinance of the Almighty, and after high counsel and deliberation ; " he then threw the blame of his reverses back on the States, alleging, as the cause of them, the incompleteness of the subsidies. Their inability he could not admit. They should not try to amass treasure, but think of the oath they had sworn, and the allegiance they owed to him. Nor was that the cause of their refusal ; it was the resentment which some had conceived because their advice was not taken.

Before this answer arrived, the States had dispersed. No final Recess was drawn up.

DIET OF AUGSBURG, 1510 ; OF TREVES AND COLOGNE, 1512.

BEFORE I proceed further, I feel bound to make the confession that the interest with which I had followed the development of the constitution of the empire, began to decline from this point of my researches.

That at so important a moment, when the most desirable conquest was within their grasp—a conquest which would have more than freed them from the burdens they bore so reluctantly, and would have constituted an interest common to all the States—they came to no agreement, shows that all these efforts were doomed to end in nothing, and that the impossibility of reaching the proposed end lay in the nature of things.

Although the emperor by no means took the active, creative part which has been ascribed to him in the establishment of national institutions, he evinced a strong inclination towards them ; he had a lofty conception of the unity and dignity of the empire ; and occasionally he submitted to constitutional forms, the effect of which was to limit his power. Nor were there ever States so profoundly convinced of the necessity of founding settled coherent institutions, and so ready to engage in the work, as those over which he presided. Yet these two powers could not find the point of coincidence of their respective tendencies.

The States saw in themselves, and in their own union, the unity of the

---

diet took place only on May 16, Wednesday before the Feast of the Assumption, Casimir of Brandenburg acting as his Lieutenant (*Statthalter*), Adolf von Nassau and Frauenberg as his councillors. Frankf. Ar., vol. xxiv. The letters of the Frankfurt friend of the council (*Rathsfreund*), Johannes Frosch, repeat nearly what is contained in the Archives, with some additions. It appears from both that no final resolution was come to, although Müller and Fels seem to imply the contrary.

empire. They had in their minds a government composed of representatives of the several orders in the empire (*ständisches Regiment*) such as really existed in some of the separate territories of the empire ; by which they thought to maintain the dignity of the emperor, or, if occasion demanded, to set fixed bounds to his arbitrary rule ; and to introduce regularity and order into the establishments for war, finance, and law, even at the expense of the power of the territorial sovereigns. But the calamities of an ill-timed campaign, and the dissatisfaction of the emperor with the part they took in foreign affairs, had destroyed their work.

Maximilian then undertook to renovate the empire by means of similar institutions, only with a firmer maintenance of the monarchical principle ; resolutions to that effect were actually passed, not indeed of such a radical and vital character as those we have just mentioned, but more practicable in their details : but when these details came to be carried into execution, misunderstandings, reluctances without end appeared, and suddenly every thing was at a stand-still.

The States had been more intent on internal, Maximilian on external, affairs ; but neither would the king so far strip himself of his absolute power, nor the States part with so much of their influence, as the other party desired. The States had not power to keep the emperor within the circle they had drawn round him, while the emperor was unable to hurry them along in the path he had entered upon.

For such is the nature of human affairs, that little is to be accomplished by deliberation and a nice balance of things : solid and durable foundations can only be laid by superior strength and a firm will.

Maximilian always maintained, and not without a colour of probability, that the refusal of the empire to stand by him gave the Venetians fresh courage.[1] Padua, which was already invested, was lost again, and Maximilian besieged this powerful city in vain. In order to carry on the war, he was obliged to convoke the States anew. On the 6th of March, 1510, a fresh imperial diet was opened at Augsburg.[2] Maximilian represented the necessity of once more bringing an army against Venice. Already he had extended the empire over Burgundy and the Netherlands, and established an hereditary right to Hungary ; he would now annex to it these rich domains, on which the burdens of the state might fall, instead of resting wholly on Germany.

The prospect thus held out produced a certain impression on the States, yet they still remained very pacific. They wished to bring the affair to a conclusion by a negotiation with Venice. The Republic had already promised a payment of 100,000 gulden down, and 10,000 gulden yearly tax, and the diet was extremely inclined to treat on this basis. This will

[1] Rovereyt, Nov. 8, 1509. " Als uns der Stend Hilf und Beistand vorzigen und abgeschlagen, und den Venedigern das kund, wurden sy mehr gestärkt, suchten erst all ir Vermögen und bewegten daneben den gemein Popl in Stetten."
—" When the help and assistance of the states was withdrawn and refused us, and this became known to the Venetians, they felt further strengthened, examined into all their resources, and moreover stirred up the common people in the cities."—*Frankf. Ar.*

[2] Häberlin is uncertain whether the imperial diet had been summoned for the feast of the three kings, or for the 12th of Jan. The summons is addressed to the observers of the feast of the three kings, *i.e.* Jan. 13.

appear intelligible enough, when it is remembered with how much difficulty a grant of a few hundred thousand gulden was obtained. It would at least have relieved them from the small tax raised for the support of the Imperial Chamber, which was collected with great difficulty.[1]

To the emperor, however, these offers appeared almost insulting. He calculated that the war had cost him a million ; that Venice derived an annual profit of 500,000 gulden from Germany ; he declared that he would not suffer himself to be put off so.

The misfortune was now, as before, that he could not inspire the States with his own warlike ardour. All projects that recalled the Common Penny or the four-hundredth man, were rejected at the first mention. A grant was indeed at length agreed on ; they consented to raise succours according to the census and rate (*matricula*) fixed at Cologne (for they rejected that of Constance), and to keep them in the field for half a year :[2] but how could they hope to drive the Venetians from the terra firma by so slight an effort ? The papal nuncio spoke on the subject in private to some of the most influential princes. They answered him without reserve, that the emperor was so ill-supported because he had undertaken the war without their advice.

It followed by a natural reaction, that Maximilian felt himself bound by no considerations towards the empire. When he was requested at Augsburg not to give up his conquests at his own pleasure, he replied, that the empire did not support him in a manner that would make it possible to do otherwise ; he must be at liberty to conclude treaties, and to make cessions as he found occasion. So little advance was made at this dfet towards a good understanding and co-operation between the emperor and the States.

The emperor rejected even the most reasonable and necessary proposals. The States required that he should refrain from all interference with the proceedings of the Imperial Chamber. This had been the subject of continual discussion, and was at total variance with the idea upon which the whole institution was founded. Maximilian, however, did not scruple to reply, that the Chamber sometimes interfered in matters beyond its competence : that he could not allow his hands to be tied.

No wonder if the States refused to assent to a plan which he submitted to them for the execution of the sentences of the Imperial Chamber, notwithstanding its remarkable merits. Maximilian proposed to draw out a scheme of a permanent levy for the whole empire, calculated on the scale

[1] Proceedings at the Imperial Diet held at Augsburg in 1510. (Fr. Ar.) Answer of the States, second Wednesday after Judica. They advised the measure, in order neither to let the matter drop entirely for the future, " oder viel nachtheiliger und beschwerlicher Rachtigung annehmen zu müssen, als jetzt dem heiligen. Reich zu Ehr und Lob erlangt werden möge : "—" nor to be obliged to accede to a more disadvantageous and oppressive arrangement, than might now be got to the honour and praise of the holy empire."

[2] The emperor desired a free promise of " the grant made at Constance for as long as his majesty should have need of it." He was willing to give a secret promise in return, that he wanted them for one year only. The States proposed the levy of Cologne. The emperor replied that this shocked him ; that many of the States were able to contribute more than that singly. They persisted, however, and all they resolved on was, to grant the levy of Cologne for half, as they had before done for a whole, year.

of Cologne, of from one to fifty thousand men, so that, in any exigency, nothing would be needed but to determine the amount of the subsidy required. For, he said, a force was necessary to chastise the rebellious who break the Public Peace or disregard the ban of the Chamber, or otherwise refuse to perform the duties of subjects of the empire. The fame of such an organisation would also intimidate foreign enemies. A committee might then sit in the Imperial Chamber, charged with the duty of determining the employment of this force in the interior.[1] This was evidently a consistent mode of carrying out the matricular system. Maximilian, with the acuteness and sagacity peculiar to him, had once more touched and placed in a prominent light the exact thing needed. The States declared that this scheme was the offspring of great wisdom and reflection ; but they were not to be moved to assent to it—they would only engage to take it into consideration at the next diet. This was natural enough. The very first employment of the levy would have certainly been in Maximilian's foreign wars. The emperor's councillors, too, with whom the States were extremely dissatisfied, would have gained a new support in their demands.

It was not to be expected that affairs would turn out otherwise than they did.

No new disputes arose at Augsburg : to all appearance a tolerable harmony prevailed, but in essentials no approach was made to union.

Maximilian carried on the Venetian war for a few years longer, with various success, and involved in ever new complications of European policy. He interwove some threads in the great web of the history of that age, but all his attempts to draw the empire into a fuller participation in his views and actions were vain : neither the cities, nor even the Jews who inhabited them, gave ear to his demands for money ; the results of his levies were so inadequate that he was obliged to dismiss them as useless ; the utmost he could hope was, that the succours granted him in Augsburg would arrive at last. The surrender of one city after another, the loss of the hope of some alleviation of the public burthens, were partly the consequence, partly the cause, of all these misunder- standings.

In April, 1512, a diet again assembled at Treves, whence its sittings were afterwards transferred to Cologne.[2]

The emperor began by renewing his proposal for a permanent rate and census, and by praying for a favourable answer. The princes answered, that it was impossible to carry this measure through in their dominions,

---

[1] Commissioners for the maintenance of the law. " Also dass Kais. Mt. Jemand dazu verordnet, desgleichen auch das Reich von jedem Stand etliche, mit voller Gewalt, zu erkennen, ob man Jemand der sich beklagt dass ihm Unrecht geschehen, Hülfe schuldig sey und wie gross."—" So that his imperial majesty do appoint some one ; in the same manner, also, the empire, certain persons from each state, with full power to discover whether help, and to what extent, be due to any man complaining that wrong has been done him." In each quarter of the empire was to be a president, who would summon help upon such discovery. There was also to be a general captain for the empire.

[2] The acts of this diet are to be found tolerably complete in vol. xxxi. of the Frankfurt Collection. The letters of the Frankfurt deputy, Jacob Heller, from the 4th of May to the 29th of June, are dated from Treves ; one on the 12th of July from Cologne, in vol. xxix.

and with their subjects ; they begged him to propose to them other ways and means.   Maximilian replied, that he trusted they would then at least revert to the resolutions of the year 1500, and grant him the four-hundredth man that he might gain the victory over the enemy, and a Common Penny wherewith to maintain the victory when gained.   The States did not venture entirely to reject this proposal, feeling themselves, as they did, bound by the promises made at Augsburg.   The scheme of a Common Penny was now resumed, but with modifications which robbed it of all its importance : they lowered the rate extremely ; before, they had determined to levy a tax of one gulden on every thousand, capital ; now, it was to be only one on every four thousand.[1]   They likewise exempted themselves : before, princes and lords were to contribute according to their property ; now they alleged they had other charges for the empire, to defray out of their own exchequer.   Even the representations of the knights were immediately yielded to ; they were only to be bound to include their vassals and subjects within the assessment.   Maximilian made less objection to this, than to the insufficiency of the tax generally ; but the States answered that the common people were already overladen with burthens, and that it would be impossible to extort more from them. He then requested that at least the tax might be granted until so long as it should have produced a million of gulden.   The States replied that the bare mention of such a sum would fill the people with terror.

The emperor's other proposition, concerning the execution of the sentences of the Imperial Chamber, was received and discussed with greater cordiality.   Rejecting the division of the empire into four quarters, which Maximilian, like Albert II., had once thought of adopting, the States conceived the idea of employing the division into circles (hitherto used only for the elections for the Council of Regency and the Imperial Chamber) for that purpose, and of rendering it more generally applicable to public ends.   The electoral and imperial hereditary domains were also to be included among the circles.   Saxony and Brandenburg, with their several houses, were to form the seventh ; the four Rhenish electorates the eighth, Austria the ninth, Burgundy the tenth circle.   In each a captain or governor was to be appointed for the execution of the law.

But this subject also gave rise to the most important differences.   The emperor laid claim to the nomination of these captains, and demanded moreover a captain-general, whom he might employ in war, and a council of eight members who should reside at his court ; a sort of ministry (*Regiment*), from whose participation in affairs he promised himself peculiar influence in the empire.   The States, on the contrary, would hear nothing either of these councillors, or of the captain-general, and they insisted on reserving to themselves the nomination of the captains of their circles.

These points gave rise to fresh and violent disputes at Cologne, in August, 1512.   On one occasion the emperor refused to receive the answer sent by the States, which, he said, was no answer, and should not remain a moment in his hands.

[1] This was the principle :—Whoever possessed 50 gulden was to pay $\frac{1}{80}$ of a Rhenish gulden ; between 50 and 100, $\frac{1}{40}$; 100 and 400, $\frac{1}{20}$; 400 and 1000, $\frac{1}{10}$; 1000 and 1500, $\frac{1}{5}$; 2000 and 4000, $\frac{1}{2}$; 4000 and 10,000, 1 gulden.

It was only through the zealous endeavours of the Elector of Mainz, that the proposal for the eight councillors was at length accepted. Their chief office was to be that of putting an end to quarrels by conciliation. Of the captain-general, no further mention occurs. I do not find that there was any intention of limiting the circles in the nomination of the subordinate captains. The subsidy was granted in the way determined by the States, and the emperor abandoned his demand for a million.

At length, therefore, resolutions were passed, and finally embodied in a Recess of the empire.

When, however, we come to examine whether it was executed, we find not a trace of it. There was a numerous party which had never, from the first, assented to the resolutions, though they had not been able to prevent their adoption ; at the head of which was one of the most experienced and the most respected princes of the empire—Frederick, Elector of Saxony. The projected subsidy was never even called for, much less raised. The eight councillors were never appointed, nor the captains, whether supreme or subordinate. The division of the empire into ten circles did not assume any positive character till ten years later.

INTESTINE DISORDERS.

Had the attempts to give a constitution to the empire succeeded, a considerable internal agitation must necessarily have ensued, until an adaptation and subordination of the several parts to the newly-created central power had taken place. But that attempts had been made, and had not succeeded,—that existing institutions had been rudely shaken, and no real or vital unity been produced,—could result in nothing but a universal fermentation.

The reciprocal rights and duties of the head of the empire and the States, were now for the first time thrown into utter uncertainty and confusion. The States had demanded a share in the jurisdiction and the government ; the emperor had conceded some points and had held tenaciously to others ; no settled boundary of their respective powers had been traced. It was an incessant series of demands and refusals—extorted grants, inadequate supplies—without sincere practical efforts, without material results, and hence, without satisfaction on any side. Formerly the union of the electors had, at least, possessed a certain independence, and had represented the unity of the empire. Since 1504 this also was dissolved. Lastly, Mainz and Saxony had fallen into a bitter strife, which entirely broke up the college. The only institutions which had come to any real maturity were the Imperial Chamber and the matricula. But how carelessly was this constructed ! Princes who no longer existed, except in old registers, were entered in the list ; while no notice was taken of the class of mediate proprietors which had gradually arisen. Countless appeals were the consequence. The emperor himself named fifteen secular, and five spiritual lords, whose succours belonged to the contingent of his own dominions, and not to the matricula of the empire ; Saxony named fifteen secular lords and three bishops ;[1] Brandenburg, two bishops and two counts ;

[1] In the Archives at Dresden there is an instruction from Duke George for Dr. G. von Breyttenbach, according to which the latter was to declare at Worms (in 1509), " das wir uns nicht anders zu erinnern wissen, denn das alles, so wir

Cologne, four counts and lords ; every one of the greater States put forward mediate claims which had not been thought of.   A number of cities, too, were challenged.   Gelnhausen, by the Palatinate ; Göttingen, by the house of Brunswick ; Duisburg, Niederwesel, and Soest, by Juliers ; Hamburg, by Holstein.[1]   In the acts of the diets we find the memorial of an ambassador of Denmark-Holstein to the States of the empire, wherein he pleads that he has travelled two hundred miles (German) to the emperor, but could obtain no answer either from him or his councillors ; and now addressed himself to the States, to inform them that there was a city called Hamburg, lying in the land of Holstein, which had been assessed as an imperial city, but of which his gracious masters were the natural hereditary lords and sovereigns.[2]   There was no dispute about the principle.   It was always declared in the Recesses, that the States should retain their right over all the succours which belonged to them from remote times ; yet in every individual case the question and the conflicting claim were always revived.   Even the most powerful princes had to complain that the fiscal of the Imperial Chamber issued penal mandates against their vassals.

In short, the Imperial Chamber excited opposition from every side. The princes felt themselves controlled by it, the inferior States, not protected.   Saxony and Brandenburg reminded the diet that they had only subjected their sovereign franchises to the chamber under certain conditions.   Joachim I. of Brandenburg complained that this tribunal received appeals from the courts of his dominions ; which had never been done in his father's time.[3]   The knights of the empire, on the other hand, were discontented at the influence exercised by the powerful princes over the chamber ; when a prince, they said, saw that he would be defeated, he found means to stop the course of justice.   Maximilian, at least, did not think their complaints unfounded : " Either," says he, " the poor man can get no justice against the noble, or if he does, it is ' so sharp and fine pointed ' that it avails him nothing."   Nor were the cities backward with their complaints.   They thought it insufferable that the judge should receive the fiscal dues ; they prayed for the punishment of the abandoned men by whose practices many cities were, without any crime or offence,

---

uf dem Reychstage zu Costnitz zu Underhaltung des Kammergerichtes zu geben bewilligt, mit Protestation beschehen, also das dye Bischoffe und Stifte desgleichen Graven und Herrn die uns mit Lehen verwandt und auch in unsern Fürstenthumen sesshaftig seyn, welche auch an dem Kammergericht nie gestanden, ichtes dabei zu thun nicht schuldig, bei solcher Freiheit bleiben."— " That we have no other remembrance than that all which we consented to give at the diet at Constance for the maintenance of the Imperial Chamber, was accompanied with a protest ; that thus the bishops and chapters of such counts and lords as hold of us by feudal tenure and are vassals of our principalities, and who have never appeared before the Imperial Chamber and are under no obligation to do so, continue to be exempt."

[1] Proceedings concerning the Imperial Chamber, and such as claim exemption from its jurisdiction : Harpprecht, Staats Archiv, iii., p. 405.

[2] We know that he did not succeed.   The decision of the imperial diet of 1510 is the main foundation of the freedom of the empire possessed by Hamburg. Lünig, Reichsarch. Pars Spec. Cont., iv., p. 965.

[3] Letter from Frederick of Saxony to Renner, on the Wednesday after the feast of the Three Kings, 1509 (Weim. Ar.) ; Joachim I. die crps. Christi, 1510.

dragged before the court : in the year 1512 they again demanded that two assessors appointed by the cities should have seats in the chamber ;[1]—of course, all in vain.

The natural consequence of this inability of the supreme power either to enforce obedience or to conciliate approbation and respect, was an universal striving after separate and independent power—a universal reign of force, which singularly characterizes this period. It is worth while to try to bring before us the several States under this aspect.

I. In the principalities, the power of the territorial lord was much extended and increased. In particular ordinances we clearly trace the idea of a legislation for the whole territory, intended to supersede local unions or associations, traditional rules and customs ; and of an equally general supervision, embracing all the branches of administration. A remarkable example of this may be found in the ordinances issued by Elector Berthold for the government of his archbishopric.[2] In some places, a perfect union and agreement subsisted between the princes and their estates ; *e.g.* in the dominions of Brandenburg, both in the Mark and Franconia : the estates contract debts or vote taxes to pay the debts of the sovereign.[3] In other countries, individual administrators become conspicuous. We distinguish the names of such men as George Gossenbrod in Tyrol, created by Maximilian, Regimentsherr (master or chief of the government), and keeping strict watch over all the hereditary rights of the sovereign. In Styria, we find Wallner, the son of the sacristan of Altöttingen in Bavaria who accumulated the treasure of Landshut ; in Onolzbach, the general accountant Prucker, who for more than thirty years conducted the whole business of the privy chancery and the chamber of finance. It is remarkable too that these powerful officials seldom came to a good end. We often see them dragged before the tribunals and condemned to punishment : Wallner was hanged at the door of the very house in which he had entertained princes, counts, and doctors as his guests ; Gossenbrod was said to have ended his life by poison ; Wolfgang of Kolberg,[4] raised to the dignity of count, died in prison ; Prucker was forced to retreat to a prebend in Plassenburg.[5] In order to put an end to the arbitrary acts of the detested council of their duke, the Würtenbergers extorted the treaty of Tübingen in 1514. Here and there we see the princes proceeding to open war in order to extend their territory. In the year 1511 Brunswick, Lüneburg, Bremen, Minden, and Cleves fell with united forces on the country of Hoya, which could offer them no resistance. In 1514, Brunswick, Lüneburg, Calenberg, Oldenburg, and Duke George of Saxony, turned their arms against the remnant of the free Frieslanders in the marshes. The Butjadinger swore they would rather die than live exposed to the incessant vexations of the Brunswick officials,

---

[1] Jacob Heller to the city of Frankfurt, June 11. " Wir Stett sein der Meinung auch anzubringen zween Assessores daran zu setzen auch Gebrechen und Mangel der Versammlung fürzutragen."—" We cities are of the opinion that we should introduce two assessors to sit there (in the court), and to bring forward the abuses and defects of the assembly."

[2] Bodmann, Rheingauische Alterthümer, ii. 535.

[3] Buchholz, Geschichte der Mark, iii. 363. Lang, i., p. 111.

[4] Report in the Fugger MS.

[5] Lang, i., p. 147.

and flew to arms behind the impassable ramparts of their country; but a traitor showed the invading army a road by which it fell upon their rear; they were beaten, and their country partitioned among the conquerors, and the Worsaten and Hadeler compelled to learn the new duty of obedience to a master.[1]

In some cases the princes tried to convert the independence of a bishop into complete subjection; as, for example, Duke Magnus of Lauenburg demanded of the bishop of Ratzeburg the same aids[2] as were granted him by his States, perhaps with twofold violence, because that prelate had formerly served in his chancery; he encountered a stout resistance, and had to resort to open force.[3]   Or a spiritual prince sought to extort unwonted obedience from the knights of his dominions, who thereupon, with the aid of a secular neighbour, broke out in open revolt; as the dukes of Brunswick took the knights of Hildesheim, and the counts of Henneberg the chapter of Fulda and the nobility connected with it, under their protection.

II. For the increasing power of the princes was peculiarly oppressive to the knights.   In Swabia the associations of the knights of the empire (*Reichsritterschaft*) consolidated themselves under the shelter of the league.   In Franconia there were similar struggles for independence; occasionally (as, for instance, in 1511 and 1515), the six districts (*Orte*) of the Franconian knights assembled, mainly to take measures for subtracting their business under litigation from the tribunals of the sovereign: the results of these efforts, however, were not lasting; here and on the Rhine every thing remained in a very tumultuous state.   We still see the warlike knights and their mounted retainers, in helm and breastplate and with bent cross-bow before them—for as yet the horsemen had no fire-arms—riding up and down the well-known boundary line, marking the halting places, and lying in ambush day and night in the woods, till the enemy whom they are watching for appears; or till the train of merchants and their wares, coming from the city they are at war with, is seen winding along the road: their victory is generally an easy one, for their attack is sudden and unexpected; and they return surrounded by prisoners and laden with booty to their narrow stronghold on hill and rock, around which they cannot ride a league without descrying another enemy, or go out to the chase without harness on their back: squires, secret friends, and comrades in arms, incessantly come and go, craving succour or bringing warnings, and keep up an incessant alarm and turmoil.   The whole night long are heard the howlings of the wolves in the neighbouring forest. While the States of the empire were consulting at Treves as to the means of ensuring the execution of the laws, Berlichingen and Selbitz seized the train of Nürnberg merchants coming from the Leipzig fair, under the con-

---

[1] Rehtmeier, Braunschweigsche Chronik, ii., p. 861.

[2] *Bede*—precaria; (*beten*, to pray)—grants of money to the prince on extraordinary occasions, such as attendance on the emperor, the marriage of a daughter, &c.—Transl.

[3] Chytræus, Saxonia, p. 222.   By Masch, Gesch. von Ratzeburg, p. 421, we perceive that there were many other points of dispute.   On the 28th of March, 1507, bishop and chapter were obliged to promise, "that when the sovereign received a land-tax from his knights, it should be paid by the peasants on the church lands just as by the peasants of any other lords."

voy of Bamberg, and thus began the open war against the bishop and the
city.   The decrees of the diet were of little avail.[1]   Götz von Berlichingen
thought himself entitled to complain of the negotiations that were opened ;
for otherwise he would have overthrown the Nürnbergers and their Bur-
germeister " with his gold chain round his neck and his battle-mace in his
hand."[2]   At the same time another notorious band had collected under
the command of the Friedingers in Hohenkrähn (in the Hegau), originally
against Kaufbeuern, to avenge the affront offered to a nobleman who had
sued in vain to the fair daughter of a citizen : afterwards they became a
mere gang of robbers, who made the country unsafe ; so that the Swabian
league at length stirred itself against them, and the emperor himself sent
out his best men, the Weckauf (*Wake up*) of Austria, and the Burlebaus,
—at whose shots, as the historical ballad says, " the mountain tottered,
the rocks were rent, and the walls riven, till the knights fled, their people

---

[1] Emperor and States disputed as to the amount of the levy necessary.   The
emperor thought they wanted to put the affair off, and reminded them that
what had happened to-day to Bamberg, might happen to-morrow to another
city.   If the succours demanded appeared too considerable, he would ask
Bamberg to be content with a hundred horses fit for service.   This the States
agreed to ; but only under the condition that the ban must be first proclaimed
against outlaws or suspected persons before the troops were employed.   (Frankf.
A.)   The universal state of division extended even to this matter.

[2] Götzens von Berlichingen ritterliche Thaten.   Ausgabe von Pistorius,
p. 127.   Müllner's Chronicle (MS.) relates the whole affair, after the documents
in the Nürnberg Archives, in the following manner :—The attack was made
between Forchheim and Neusess, May 18, 1512, by a band of 130 horse ; 31
persons were carried off ; the damage done amounted to 8800 gulden ; the
horses were foddered and the booty divided in a wood near Schweinfurt.   The
prisoners were concealed by the knights of Thüngen, Eberstein, Buchenau.   The
council of Nürnberg hereupon took 500 foot soldiers into their pay, and announced
to the Great Council their determination to do every thing to bring the perpe-
trators to punishment.   Meanwhile, " solten sie ihre Kaufmannschaft so enge
es seyn könnte, einziehen, bis die Leufte etwas besser würden : "—" they must
draw in their dealings as much as possible till the ways became somewhat better."
And he actually produces a proclamation of ban of the 15th of July, accompanied, however, by a proposal for a commission before which the accused might
clear themselves.   Some did thus clear themselves ; others not.   Among the
last are mentioned, Caspar von Rabenstein, Balthasar and Reichart Steinrück,
Wilhelm von Schaumburg, Dietrich and Georg Fuchs, Conrad Schott.   Among
them are many Würzburg officials, who were jointly declared under ban by
the Imperial Chamber.   As in the mean time a number of fresh attacks had
taken place, at Vilseck, Ochsenfurt, Mergentheim (in which the Commander of
the Order at Mergentheim had drawn suspicion upon himself), the Swabian
league at last came forward with an armed force, to which the Nürnbergers
added 600 men on foot, a squadron of cavalry, and a small body of artillery.
Gangolf von Geroldseck led the troops of the league ; their first move was against
Frauenstein, belonging to Hans von Selbitz : several castles were carried, and
lands taken, and at last the way was opened to a treaty.   The emperor decreed
that the knights should pay 14,000 gulden as compensation.   Müller asserts that
of this sum the Bishop of Würzburg paid 7000 gulden, the Count Palatine
Ludwig 2000, the Duke of Würtenberg as much, the Master of Mergentheim
1000, and Götz himself 2000.   He infers that those princes, " dieser Fehd heimlich
verwandt gewesen,"—" had been privily concerned in this Feid."   On the
other hand, he speaks with praise of the bishop of Bamberg and Markgrave
Frederick of Brandenburg.

surrendered, and the castle was razed to the ground."[1]   But there was also many a castle in Bavaria, Swabia, and Franconia for which a similar fate was reserved.   The insecurity of the roads and highways was greater than ever ; even poor travelling scholars who begged their way along, were set upon and tortured to make them give up their miserable pittance.[2]   " Good luck to us, my dear comrades," cried Götz to a pack of wolves which he saw fall upon a flock of sheep, " good luck to us all and every where."   He took it for a good omen.

Sometimes this fierce and lawless chivalry assumed a more imposing aspect, and constituted a sort of tumultuary power in the state.   Franz von Sickingen had the audacity to take under his protection the enemies of the council which had just been re-established in Worms by the emperor ; he began the war with that city by seizing one of its vessels on the Rhine. He was immediately put under ban.   His answer to this was, instantly to appear before the walls of that city, to fire upon it with carronades and culverins, lay waste the fields, tear up the vineyards, and prevent all access to the town.   The Whitsuntide fair could not be held either in 1515 or 1516.   The States of the circle of the Rhine assembled, but dared not come to any resolution ; they thought that could only be done at an imperial diet.[3]   It is indisputable that some princes, out of opposition either to the emperor or to the Swabian league, favoured, or at least connived at, these acts of violence.   The knights were connected with the party among the princes which was inclined neither to the emperor nor to the league.

III. The cities were exposed to annoyance and injury from all sides ; from the imperial government, which continually imposed fresh burthens upon them ; from these lawless knights, and from the princes, who in 1512 agitated the old question of the Pfahlbürger.[4]   But they made a most gallant defence.   How many a robber noble did Lübeck drag from his stronghold !   Towards the end of the fifteenth century that city concluded a treaty with neighbouring mediate cities, the express object of which was to prevent the landed aristocracy from exceeding the powers they had hitherto exercised.   It availed nothing to King John of Denmark that the Emperor Maximilian for a time favoured his attempts.   In the year 1509, the Hanse towns or rather a part of them, attacked his islands, beat his ships at Helsingör, carried away his bells for their chapels, and remained absolute masters on the open sea.   A Lübeck vessel boarded by three Danish ones near Bornholm beat off two of them and captured the third : in the year 1511 the Lübeck fleet returned to the Trave with eighteen Dutch ships as prizes.[5]

[1] Anonymi Carmen de Obsidione et Expugnatione Arcis Hohenkrayen, 1512. Fugger, both MS. and printed.   Gassari Annales ad ann. 1512.

[2] Plater's Lebensbeschreibung.   The period he speaks of is about the year 1515, as he immediately afterwards mentions the battle of Marignano.

[3] Zorn's Wormser Chronik. in Münch's Sickingen, iii.

[4] Pfahlbürger (from *Pfahl*, pale or stake) were originally persons inhabiting a town, but not enjoying all the rights of citizenship.   (See Golden Bull, cap. 16.) They were often free peasants, subject to the sovereign lord's jurisdiction, but not his serfs.   It seems that they availed themselves of the protection and security afforded by the cities to the prejudice of the lord's feudal rights, and formed associations to resist him.   (See Eichhorn, ii. 162.)

[5] Becker, Geschichte von Lübek, vol. i., p. 488.

Nor did the inland cities make a less spirited resistance to those aggressions from which they were not protected by the Swabian league. How admirably did Nürnberg defend herself ! For every injury she sustained, she carried her vengeance home to the territory of the aggressor, and her mounted bands frequently made rich captures. Woe to the nobles who fell into their hands ! No intercession either of kinsmen or of neighbouring princes availed to save them ; the council was armed with the ever-ready excuse that the citizens absolutely demanded the punishment of the offender. In vain did he look out from the bars of his prison towards the forest, watching whether his friends and allies were not coming to his rescue : Berlichingen's story sufficiently shows us with how intense a dread even those of her neighbours who delighted the most in wild and daring exploits regarded the towers of Nürnberg. Noble blood was no security either from the horrors of the question or the axe of the executioner.[1]

Sometimes, indeed, commercial difficulties arose—for example, in the Venetian war—which could not be met with the same vigour by the inland towns as the Hanseats displayed at sea, but the effects of which they found other means to elude. All intercourse with Venice was in fact forbidden, and the Scala which had obtained the proclamation of the ban, often arrested the merchandise travelling along that road ; though this was done only in order to extort money from the owners for its redemption. I find that one merchant had to pay the emperor three thousand ducats transit duty, on three hundred horse-load of goods : the Tyrol government had formerly appointed a commissary in Augsburg, whose business it was to collect regular duties on those consignments of goods the safety of which it then guaranteed. The towns accommodated themselves to the times as they could ; thankful that their trade was not utterly destroyed. The connexion with the Netherlands, established by the house of Austria, had meanwhile opened a wide and magnificent field for commercial enterprise. Merchants of Nürnberg and Augsburg shared in the profits of the trade to the East and West Indies.[2] Their growing prosperity and indispensable assistance in all pecuniary business gave them influence in all courts, and especially that of the emperor. In defiance of all decrees of diets, they maintained " their friendly companies ;" associations to whose hands the smallest affairs as well as the largest were committed. There is sufficient ground for the belief that they gave occasion to many just complaints of the monopoly which was thus vested in few hands ; since the importers of wares had it in their power to regulate the price at will.[3] But they nevertheless maintained a strong position in the assemblies of the empire. The abortive results of the diets held from 1509 to 1513 were chiefly caused by their opposition. They found means to get the proposed measures concerning the Pfahlbürger, in virtue of which goods were to pay duty, not to the town in which the owner of them lived, but to the sovereign

---

[1] Müllner's Chronicle is full of anecdotes of this kind.

[2] Gassarus (Annales in Mencken, i. 1743) names those of the Welser, Gossenbrot, Fugger, Hochstetter, Foëlin ; the last are without doubt the Vehlin. He reckons the dividends from the first voyage to Calcutta at 175 per cent.

[3] Jäger, Schwäbisches Städtewesen, i. 669. As early as 1495, the plan was entertained of taxing the great companies. Datt., p. 844, nr. 16. Things remained in this state from one diet to another.

or lord in whose dominions that town was situated, indefinitely adjourned. (A.D. 1512.)[1]

It is evident that the peaceful security, the undisturbed prosperity, which are often ascribed to those times, had no existence but in imagination. The cities kept their ground only by dint of combination, and of unwearied activity, both in arms and in negotiation.

There was also a vehement and continual ferment in the interior of the towns. The old struggle between the town councils and the commons or people was continually revived by the increasing demands for money made by the former and resisted by the latter ; in some places it led to violence and bloodshed. In the year 1510 the Vierherr[2] Heinrich Kellner was executed in Erfurt for having, in the financial straits of the city, allowed the house of Saxony to redeem Capellendorf for a sum of money : all the following years were marked with violence and disorder. In Regensburg the aged and honest Lykircher, who had frequently held the offices of chamberlain, hansgrave, and judge of the peace, was brought to trial ; and, though the treasonable acts of which he was accused were never proved against him, was barbarously tortured in the Holy Week of 1513, and shortly afterwards put to death.[3] In Worms, first the old council, and afterwards its successor, was driven out. In Cologne the commons were furiously incensed against the new contributions with which they were vexed ; and still more against an association or company called the Garland, to which the most criminal designs were imputed.[4] Similar disturbances took place in Aix-la-Chapelle, Andernach, Speier, Hall in Swabia, Lübeck, Schweinfurt, and Nürnberg :[5] in every direction we meet with imprisonments, banishments, executions. Domestic grievances were often aggravated by the suspicion of a criminal understanding with neighbouring states. In Cologne it was Guelders ; in Worms and Regensburg, Austria ; in Erfurt Saxony, which was the object of their suspicions. The feeling of public insecurity burst forth in acts of the wildest violence.

IV. Nor was this excitement and agitation confined to the populations of towns ; throughout the whole breadth of the empire, the peasantry was in an equal state of ferment. The peasants of the Swiss mountains had completely changed their relation to the empire : from the condition of subjects, they had passed to that of free and independent allies : those of the marches of Friesland on the contrary had succumbed to the neigh-

---

[1] A counter representation from Wetzlar and Frankfurt " Es würde dem Reich und ihnen ein merklicher Abbruch seyn und wider ihre Privilegien laufen."— " It would be a signal injury to the empire and to them, and go against their privileges." (Fr. A.)

[2] Vierherr and Hansgraf are among the numerous titles of magistrates used in different parts of Germany. The former was probably the title of the four chief magistrates, like the four Syndics of Hamburg. The Hansgraf was a sort of president of the board of trade (if I may so apply the words) in the Hanse towns. There are still, I am told, two Hansgrafen in Lübeck.—TRANSL.

[3] Chronicle of Regensburg, vol. iv., part iii.

[4] Rhythmi de Seditione Coloniensi in Senkenberg, Selecta Juris et Hist., iv., nr. 6.

[5] Baselii Auctarium Naucleri, p. 1016. " Ea pestis pessimæ rebellionis adversus senatum in plerisque—civitatibus irrepsit. Trithemius (Chronic. Hirsaug., ii., p. 689) reckons them up, adding the remarks, " et in aliis quarum vocabula memoriæ non occurrunt."

bouring sovereigns; the Ditmarschers alone stood for a while after a glorious and successful battle, like a noble ruin amidst modern edifices. The antagonist principles which, in distant lands and from the furthest marches of the empire, gave rise to these conflicts, came into contact under a thousand different forms in the heart of the country. The subsidies for the empire and its growing necessities fell ultimately on the peasant; the demands of the sovereign, of the holders of church lands, and of the nobility, were all addressed to him.[1] On the other hand, in some countries the common people were made to bear arms; they formed the bands of landsknechts which acquired and maintained a name amongst European troops; they once more felt the strength that was in them. The example of the Swiss was very seducing to the south of Germany. In the country round Schletstadt, in Alsatia, a society of discontented citizens and peasants, the existence and proceedings of which were shrouded in the profoundest secrecy, was formed as early as the year 1493. Traversing almost impassable ways, they met at night on solitary mountains, and swore never in future to pay any tax which was not levied with their own free consent; to abolish tolls and duties, to curtail the privileges of the clergy, to put the Jews to death without ceremony, and to divide their possessions. They admitted new members with strange ceremonies, specially intended to appal traitors. Their intention was in the first place to seize on Schletstadt, immediately after to display the banner with the device of the peasant's shoe,[2] to take possession of Alsatia, and to call the Swiss to their aid.[3] But in spite of the fearful menaces which accompanied the admission to the society, they were betrayed, dispersed, and punished with the utmost severity. Had the Swiss in 1499 understood their own advantage and not excited the hatred of their neighbours by their cruel ravages, the people along their whole frontier would, as contemporaries affirm, have flocked to join their ranks. An incident shows the thoughts that were afloat among the people. During the negotiations preceding the peace of Basle, a peasant appeared in the clothes of the murdered Count of Fürstenberg. "We are the peasants," said he, "who punish the nobles." The discovery and dispersion of the conspiracy above-mentioned by no means put an end to the Bundschuh. In the year 1502 traces of this symbol were found at Bruchsal, from whence the confederates had already gained over the nearer places, and were extending their ramifications into the more remote. They declared that in answer to an inquiry addressed to the Swiss they received an assurance that the Confederation would help the right, and risk life and limb in their cause. There was a tinge of religious enthusiasm in their notions. They were to say five Pater nosters and Ave Marias daily. Their war-cry was to be,

---

[1] Rosenblüt complains that the noble draws his maintenance from the peasant, and yet does not insure him any peace; that he is constantly pushing his demands further, whereupon the peasant answers with abuse, and the noble rides down his cattle.

[2] The Bundschuh; the large rude shoe bound on the foot with thongs of leather, commonly worn by the Swabian peasantry and borne on their banner in the servile war to which they were driven by intolerable oppression. The *Bund* or league of the peasants was afterwards called the Bundschuh. —TRANSL.

[3] Herzog, Edelsasser Chronik, c. 71, p. 162.

" Our Lady !" They were to take Bruchsal, and then march forth and
onward, ever onward, never remaining more than twenty-four hours in
a place. The whole peasantry of the empire would join them, of that there
was no doubt ; all men must be brought into their covenant, that so the
righteousness of God might be brought upon earth.[1] But they were
quickly overpowered, scattered, and their leaders punished with death.

The imperial authorities had often contemplated the danger of such
commotions. Among the articles which the electors projected discussing
at their diet of Gelnhausen, one related to the necessity of alleviating the
condition of the common people.[2] It was always the conclusive argument
against taxes like the Common Penny, that there was reason to fear they
would cause a rebellion among the people. In the year 1513, the authorities hesitated to punish some deserters from the Landsknechts, because
they were afraid that they might enter into a combination with the
peasants, whose permanent conspiracy against the nobles and clergy had
been discovered from the confessions of some who had been arrested in
the Breisgau. In the year 1514, they rose in open and complete rebellion
in Würtenberg under the name of Poor Kunz (*der armer Kunz*): the
treaty of Tübingen did not satisfy the peasants ; it was necessary to put
them down by force of arms.[3] We hear the sullen mutterings of a fierce
untamed element, incessantly going on under the very earth on which we
stand.

While such was the state of Germany, the emperor was wholly occupied
with his Venetian war ;—at one time fighting with the French against the
Pope and the Venetians, at another with the Pope and the English against
the French : the Swiss, now in alliance with him, conquer Milan and
lose it again ; he himself, at the head of Swiss and Landsknechts, makes
an attempt to recover it, but in vain. We see him repeatedly travelling
from Tyrol to the Netherlands, from the sea-coast back to the Italian Alps ;
like the commander of a beleaguered fortress, hurrying incessantly from
bastion to bastion, and watching the propitious moment for a sortie.
But this exhausted his whole activity ; the interior of Germany was
abandoned to its own impulses.

A diet was appointed to be held at Worms again, in the year 1513 ; and
on the 1st June we find a certain number of the States actually assembled.
The emperor alone was wanting. At length he appeared, but his business
did not allow him to remain : under the pretext that he must treat in
person with the dilatory electors of Treves and Cologne, he hurried down
the Rhine, proposing to the States to follow him to Coblentz. They chose
rather to disperse altogether.[4]   " Of a truth," writes the Altbürgermeister

[1] Frankf. Acten, vol. xx. Baselii Auctarium, p. 997.

[2] " Der mit Fron Diensten Atzung Steure geistlichen Gerichten und andern
also merklich beschwert ist, dass es in die Harre nicht zu leiden feyn wird."—
" Who is so signally burthened with feudal services, taxes, ecclesiastical courts,
and other things, that in the long run it will not be to be borne."

[3] Wahraftig Unterrichtung der Ufrur bei Sattler Herzoge, i., App. no. 70.

[4] In the Frankfurt Acts, vol. xxx., there is a letter from Worms to Frankfurt,
according to which the States present, " prima Junii nechst verruckt einhelliglich
entschlossen und den kaiserlichen. Commissarien für endlich Antwort geben, dass
sie noch zehn Tag allhie bei einander verziehen und bleiben, und wo inen in mitler
Zeit nit weiter Geschefte oder Befel von Kais. Mt zukommen, wollen sie alsdann
sich alle wieder von dannen anheim thun."—" On the first of June just past,

of Cologne to the Frankfurters, " you have done wisely that you stayed
at home ; you have spared much cost, and earned equal thanks."

It was not till after an interval of five years (A.D. 1517), when not only
Sickingen's private wars threw the whole of Upper Germany into confusion,
but the universal disorder of the country had become intolerable, that a
diet was held again ;—this time at Mainz, in the chapter house of which
city it was opened on the 1st July.

The imperial commissioners demanded vast succours for the suppression
of the disturbances—not, as before, every four hundredth, but every fiftieth
man ; the States, however, did not deem it advisable to resort to arms.
The poor husbandman, already suffering under the torments of want and
famine, might, " in his furious temper," be still further exasperated ; the
rage which had long gnawed at his heart might burst forth ; a universal
rebellion was to be feared.   They desired rather to put down the prevailing disturbances by lenity and conciliation ; they entered into negotiations on all sides—even with Sickingen ; above all, they appointed a committee to inquire into the general state of the country, and into the causes
of the universal outbreak of disturbances.   The imperial commissioners
wanted to dissolve the assembly on the ground that they could do nothing
without ascertaining the opinion of his imperial majesty ; but the States
would not consent to be put off so : the sittings of the committee, two
members of which were nominated by the cities, were solemnly opened
by a mass for the invocation of the Holy Ghost (Missa Sancti Spiritus).
On the 7th August, 1517, they laid their report before the diet.

It is very remarkable that the States discover the main source of the
whole evil in the highest and most important institution that had been
founded in the empire—in the Imperial Chamber ; and in the defects in
its constitution and modes of procedure.   The eminent members of that
tribunal, they said, were gone, and incapable ones put in their places.
The procedure was protracted through years ; one great cause of which
was, that the court received so many appeals on trifling matters that
the important business could not be despatched.   Nor was this all.   The
court had not free course ; it was often ordered to stay all proceedings.   If,
after long delays and infinite trouble, a suitor succeeded in getting judgment pronounced, he could not get it executed ; his antagonist obtained
mandates to prevent its execution.   The consequence was, that the highest
penalties of the law, the ban and reban (*Acht und Aberacht*), had no longer
terrors for any one.   The criminal under ban found shelter and protection ;
and as the other courts of justice were in no better condition—in all,
incapable judges, impunity for misdoers, and abuses without end—disquiet
and tumult had broken out in all parts.   Neither by land nor by water
were the ways safe ; no safe-conduct, whether of the head or the members

---

unanimously resolved, and give this their final answer to the imperial commissioners, that they shall tarry and remain here together ten days longer, and if,
meantime, no further business or command reach them from his imperial majesty,
they shall all in that case betake themselves thence home."   In an address of
the 20th of August, Maximilian announces a new diet of the empire, " Die geringe
Anzahl der erschienenen Stände habe ihren Abschied genommen, da sie sich
keiner Handlung verfangen mögen."—" The small number of states which had
appeared, had taken their leave, as they were unwilling to meddle with any
business."

of the empire, was the least heeded ; there was no protection, whether
for subjects or for such foreigners as were entitled to it : the husbandman,
by whose labours all classes were fed, was ruined ; widows and orphans
were deserted ; not a pilgrim or a messenger or a tradesman could travel
along the roads, whether to fulfil his pious duty, or to deliver his message,
or to execute his business.   To these evils were added the boundless luxury
in clothing and food ; the wealth of the country all found its way into
foreign lands, especially to Rome, where new exactions were daily invented :
lastly, it was most mischievous to allow the men at arms, who had sometimes been fighting against the emperor and the empire, to return to their
homes, where they stirred up the peasantry to rebellion.

And while such was the statement of public grievances, the particular
petitions and remonstrances were countless.   The inhabitants of Worms
complained of " the inhuman private warfare (*Fehde*) which Franciscus
von Sickingen, in despite and disregard of his honour, carried on against
them ;" to which the deputies from Spires added, that Sickingen's troops
had the design to burn down the Spital of their city.   Mühlhausen complained in its own name, and those of Nordhausen and Goslar, that they
paid tribute for protection and were not protected : Lübeck enumerated
all the injuries it sustained from the King of Denmark, from nobles and
commons ; it could obtain no help from the empire, by which it was so
heavily burthened ; it must pay its money to the Imperial Chamber,
which always gave judgment against it, and never in its favour.   Other
towns said nothing of their grievances, because they saw it was of no
avail.   Meantime the knights held meetings at Friedberg, Gelnhausen,
Bingen, and Wimpfen, whither the emperor sent delegates to appease them.
Anna of Brunswick, the widowed Landgravine of Hessen, appeared in
person at the diet, and uttered the bitterest complaints : she said she
could obtain no justice in Hessen ; that she vainly followed the emperor
and the Imperial Chamber from place to place ; her dowry of Melsungen
was consumed ; she was reduced to travel about like a gipsy, with a
solitary maid-servant, and to pawn her jewels and even her clothes ; she
could not pay her debts, and must soon beg her bread.

" Summa Summarum," writes the delegate from Frankfurt, " here is
nothing but complaint and wrong ; it is greatly to be feared that no
remedy will be found."[1]   The States made the most urgent appeals to
the emperor : they conjured him for God's sake, for the sake of justice,
for his own, for that of the holy empire, of the German nation, nay of all
Christendom, to lay these things to heart ;—to remember how many
mighty states had fallen, through want of inward tranquillity and order ;
to look carefully into what was passing in the minds of the common
people, and to find a remedy for these great evils.

Such were the words addressed to him ; but they were but words.   A
remedy—a measure of the smallest practical utility—was not so much as

---

[1] Philip Fürstenberg, July 26.   In the 32d vol. of the Frankf. A., where
generally the transactions of this diet are to be found.   " Wo Kais. Mt.," he
says, on the 16th of Aug., of the representations which were made, " dieselbig
als billig und wol wäre verwilligen würde, hofft ich alle Dinge sollten noch gut
werden, wo nicht, so helf uns Gott."   " If his imperial majesty would comply
with the same, as were reasonable and right, I should hope that all things might
yet go well ; if not, then God help us."

suggested ; the diet was dissolved without having even proceeded to one resolution.

And already the excited mind of the nation was turned towards other evils and other abuses than those which affected its civil and political condition.

In consequence of the intimate union between Rome and Germany, in virtue of which the Pope was always a mighty power in the empire, a grave discussion on spiritual affairs had become inevitable. For a time, they had fallen into the back-ground, or been the subject only of chance and incidental mention : now, however, they attracted universal attention ; the vigorous and agitated spirit of the nation, weary and disgusted with the present and the past, and eagerly striving after the future, seized upon them with avidity. As a disposition was immediately manifested to go to the bottom of the subject, and to proceed from a consideration of the external interference of the church, to a general and thorough examination of its rights, this agitation speedily acquired an importance which extended far beyond the limits of the internal policy of Germany.

BOOK II.

EARLY HISTORY OF LUTHER AND OF CHARLES V.
1517—1521.

CHAPTER I.

ORIGIN OF THE RELIGIOUS OPPOSITION.

WHATEVER hopes we may entertain of the final accomplishment of the prophecies of an universal faith in one God and Father of all which have come down to us in the Hebrew and Christian Scriptures, it is certain that after the lapse of more than ten centuries that faith had by no means overspread the earth. The world was filled with manifold and widely differing modes and objects of worship.

Even in Europe, the attempts to root out paganism had been but partially successful; in Lithuania, for example, the ancient worship of the serpent endured through the whole of the 15th and 16th centuries, and was even invested with a political significance;[1] and if this was the case in Europe, how much more so in other portions of the globe. In every clime men continued to symbolise the powers of nature, and to endeavour to subdue them by enchantments or to propitiate them by sacrifices: throughout vast regions the memory of the dead was the terror of the living, and the rites of religion were especially designed to avert their destructive interference in human things; to worship only the sun and moon supposed a certain elevation of soul, and a considerable degree of civilisation.

Refined by philosophy, letters, and arts, represented by vast and powerful hierarchies, stood the mightiest antagonists of Christianity— the Indian religion and Islam; and it is remarkable how great an internal agitation prevailed within them at the epoch of which we are treating.

Although the Brahminical faith was, perhaps, originally founded on monotheistic ideas, it had clothed these in a multiform idolatry. But at the end of the 15th and beginning of the 16th century, we trace the progress of a reformer in Hindostan. Nanek, a native of Lahore, endeavoured to restore the primitive ideas of religion, and to show the advantages of a pure morality over a merely ceremonial worship: he projected the abolition of castes, nay, even a union of Hindoos and Moslem; he presents one of the most extraordinary examples of peaceful unfanatical piety the world ever beheld.[2] Unfortunately, his efforts were unsuccessful. The notions he combated were much too deeply rooted; even those who called themselves his disciples—the Sikhs—paid idolatrous honours to the man who laboured to destroy idolatry.

A new and very important development of the other branch of the religions of India—Buddhism—also took place in the fifteenth century.

---

[1] Æneas Silvius de Statu Europæ, c. 20. Alexander Guagninus in Resp. Poloniæ. Elz., p. 276.

[2] B'hai Guru the B'hale in Malcolm's Translation, Sketch of the Sikhs. Asiatic Researches, xvi. 271. That holy man made God the Supreme known to all—he restored to virtue her strength, blended the four castes into one—established one mode of salutation.

The first regenerated Lama appeared in the monastery of Brepung, and was universally acknowledged throughout Thibet ; the second incarnation of the same (from 1462 to 1542) had similiar success in the most remote Buddhist countries ;[1] from that time hundreds of millions revere in the Dalailama at Lhassa the living Buddha of the present,—the unity of the divine trinity,—and throng thither to receive his blessing. It cannot be denied that this religion had a beneficial influence on the manners of rude nations ; but, on the other hand, what fetters does such a fantastic deification of human nature impose on the mind ! Those nations possess the materials for forming a popular literature, a wide diffusion of the knowledge of the elements of science, and the art of printing ; but the literature itself—the independent exercise and free utterance of the mind, can never exist ;[2] nor are such controversies as those between the married and unmarried priests, or the yellow and the red professions which attach themselves to different chiefs, at all calculated to give birth to it. The rival Lamas make pilgrimages to each other, and reciprocally recognise each other's divine character.

The same antagonism which prevailed between Brama and Buddha, subsisted in the bosom of Islam, from its very foundation, between the three elder Chalifs and Ali ; in the beginning of the sixteenth century the contest between the two sects,[3] which had been dormant for awhile, broke out with redoubled violence. The sultan of the Osmans regarded himself (in his character of successor to Abubekr and the first Chalifs) as the religious head of all Sunnites, whether in his own or foreign countries, from Morocco to Bokhara. On the other hand, a race of mystic Sheiks of Erdebil, who traced their origin from Ali, gave birth to a successful warrior, Ismail Sophi, who founded the modern Persian monarchy, and secured once more to the Shiites a powerful representation and an illustrious place in history. Unfortunately, neither of these parties felt the duty or expediency of fostering the germ of civilisation which had lain in the soil since the better times of the early Chalifat. They only developed the tendency to despotic autocracy which Islam so peculiarly favours, and worked up political hostility to an incredible pitch of fury by the stimulants of fanaticism. The Turkish historians relate that the enemy who had fallen into Ismail's hands were roasted and eaten.[4] The Osman, Sultan Selim, on the other hand, opened the war against his rival by causing all the Shiites in his land, from the age of seven to seventy, to be hunted out and put to death in one day ; " forty thousand heads," says Seadeddin,

[1] Fr. Georgi Alphabetum Tibetanum, p. 326, says of it : " Pergit inter Tartaros ad amplificandam religionem Xacaicam in regno Kokonor cis murum magnum Sinorum : inde in Kang : multa erigit asceteria : redit in Brepung." He bears the name of So-nam-kiel vachiam-tzho, and is notwithstanding the old Reval-Kedun, who died in 1399.

[2] Hodgson, Notice sur la Langue, la Littérature, et la Religion des Boudhistes. " L'écriture des Tibétains n'est jamais employée à rien de plus utile que des notes des affaires ou de plus instructif que les rêves d'une mythologie absurde," &c. The objections of Klaproth, Nouv. Journ. Asiatique, p. 99, are not in my opinion of much weight, as the question is not concerning a literature, which may be old, or the existence of which may be unknown, but a living one of the present day.

[3] Sunnites and Shiites, the two great parties amongst the Mahommedans.

[4] Hammer, Osmanische Gesch., ii. 345.

" with base souls." The antagonists were, as we perceive, worthy of each other.

In Christendom, too, a division existed between the Græco-Oriental and the Latin Church, which, though it did not lead to acts of such savage violence, could not be healed. Even the near approach of the resistless torrent of Turkish power which threatened instant destruction, could not move the Greeks to accede to the condition under which the assistance of the West was offered them—the adoption of the distinguishing formulæ of confession—except for the moment, and ostensibly. The union which was brought about at Florence,[1] in the year 1439, with so much labour, met with little sympathy from some, and the most violent opposition from others : the patriarchs of Alexandria, Antioch, and Jerusalem, loudly protested against the departure from canonical and synodal tradition, which such an union implied ; they threatened the Greek emperor with a schism on their own part, on account of the indulgence he showed to the Latin heterodoxy.[2]

If we inquire which of these several religions had the greater external and political strength, we are led to the conclusion that Islam had unquestionably the advantage. By the conquests of the Osmans in the 15th century, it had extended to regions where it had been hitherto unknown, almost on the borders[3] of Europe ; combined too with political institutions which must inevitably lead to the unceasing progress of conversion. It reconquered that sovereignty over the Mediterranean which it had lost since the eleventh century. Its triumphs in India soon equalled those in the West. Sultan Baber was not content with overthrowing the Islamite princes who had hitherto held that land. Finding, as he expressed it, " that the banners of the heathen waved in two hundred cities of the faithful—that mosques were destroyed and the women and children of the Moslem carried into slavery," he proclaimed a holy war against the Hindoos, as the Osmans had done against the Christians. On the eve of a battle he resolved to abjure the use of wine ; he repealed taxes which were inconsistent with the Koran, and enkindled the ardour of his troops by a vow sworn upon this their sacred book ; his reports of his victories are conceived in the same spirit of religious enthusiasm, and he thus earned the title of Gazi.[4] The rise of so mighty a power, actuated by such ideas, necessarily gave a vast impulse to the propagation of Islam throughout the East.

But if, on the other hand, we endeavour to ascertain which of these different systems possessed the greatest internal force,—which was pregnant with the most important consequences to the destiny of the human

[1] For the Council of Florence brought about under Eugenius IV., 1439, *cf.* Creighton, vol. ii., p. 184. The well-known fresco in the Riccardi Palace commemorates this meeting of the Eastern and Western Churches.

[2] Passages from their letter of admonition in Gieseler Kirchengeschichte, ii. 4., p. 545.

[3] Borders of Europe, or more accurately, of Western Europe. The Turks' first conquest in Europe was that of Gallipoli, 1358. By the close of the fifteenth century they had taken Constantinople (1453) and most of the Balkan Peninsula. *Cf.* Cambridge Modern History, vol. i., c. iii., and Clarendon Press Historical Geography Series, No. viii.

[4] Baber's own Memoirs, translated into English by Leyden and Erskine, into German by Kaiser, 1828, p. 537, and the two firmans thereto annexed.

race,—we can as little fail to arrive at the conviction (whatever be our religious faith), that the superiority was on the side of Latin Christendom.

Its most important peculiarity lay in this—that a slow but sure and unbroken progress of intellectual culture had been going on within its bosom for a series of ages. While the East had been convulsed to its very centre by torrents of invasion like that of the Mongols, the West had indeed always been agitated by wars, in which the various powers of society were brought into motion and exercise ; but neither had foreign tribes overrun the land, nor had there been any of those intestine convulsions which shake the foundations of a society in an early and progressive stage of civilisation. Hence all the vital and productive elements of human culture were here united and mingled : the development of society had gone on naturally and gradually ; the innate passion and genius for science and for art constantly received fresh food and fresh inspiration, and were in their fullest bloom and vigour ; civil liberty was established upon firm foundations ; solid and symmetrical political structures arose in beneficent rivalry, and the necessities of civil life led to the combination and improvement of physical resources ; the laws which eternal Providence has impressed on human affairs were left to their free and tranquil operation ; what had decayed crumbled away and disappeared, while the germs of fresh life continually shot up and flourished : in Europe were found united the most intelligent, the bravest, and the most civilised nations, still in the freshness of youth.

Such was the world which now sought, like its eastern rival, to extend its limits and its influence. Four centuries had elapsed since, prompted by religious motives, it had made attempts at conquest in the East ; but after a momentary success these had failed—only a few[1] fragments of these acquisitions remained in its possession. But at the end of the fifteenth century, a new theatre for boundless activity was opened to the West. It was the time of the discovery of both Indies. All elements of European culture—the study of the half-effaced recollections of antiquity, technical improvements, the spirit of commercial and political enterprise, religious zeal—all conspired to render the newly-discovered countries tempting and profitable. All the existing relations of nations, however, necessarily underwent a change ; the people of the West acquired a new superiority, or at least became capable of acquiring it.

Above all, the relative situation of religions was altered. Christianity, especially in the forms it had assumed in the Latin Church, gained a fresh and unexpected ascendancy in the remotest regions. It was therefore doubly important to mankind, what might be the present or the future form and character of the Latin Church. The Pope instantly put forth a claim, which no one contested, to divide the countries that had been, or that yet might be found, between the two States by which they were discovered.

---

[1] *E.g.*, Crete and Cyprus, which were in the hands of Venice, and a few settlements on the Persian Gulf in the hands of the Portuguese.

POSITION OF THE PAPACY WITH REGARD TO RELIGION.

THE question, at what periods and under what circumstances the distinguishing doctrines and practices of the Romish Church were settled, and acquired an ascendancy, merits a minute and elaborate dissertation.

It is sufficient here to recall to the mind of the reader, that this took place at a comparatively late period, and precisely in the century of the great hierarchical struggles.

It is well known that the institution of the Seven Sacraments,[1] whose circle embraces all the important events of the life of man, and brings them into contact with the church, is ascribed to Peter Lombard, who lived in the twelfth century.[2] It appears upon inquiry that the notions regarding the most important of them, the Sacrament of the Altar, were by no means very distinct in the church itself, in the time of that great theologian. It is true that one of those synods which, under Gregory VII., had contributed so much to the establishment of the hierarchy, had added great weight to the doctrine of the real presence by the condemnation of Berengar : but Peter Lombard as yet did not venture to decide in its favour : the word transubstantiation first became current in his time ; nor was it until the beginning of the thirteenth century, that the idea and the word received the sanction of the church : this, as is well known, was first given by the Lateran confession of faith in the year 1215 ; and it was not till later that the objections which till then had been constantly suggested by a deeper view of religion, gradually disappeared.

It is obvious, however, of what infinite importance this doctrine became to the service of the church, which has crystallized (if I may use the expression) around the mystery it involves. The ideas of the mystical and sensible presence of Christ in the church were thus embodied in a living image ; the adoration of the Host was introduced ; festivals in honour of this greatest of all miracles, incessantly repeated, were solemnized. Intimately connected with this is the great importance attached to the worship of the Virgin Mary, the mother of Christ, in the latter part of the middle ages.

The prerogatives of the priesthood are also essentially connected with this article of faith. The theory and doctrine of the priestly character were developed ; that is, of the power communicated to the priest by ordination, " to make the body of Christ " (as they did not scruple to say) ; " to act in the person of Christ." It is a product of the thirteenth century, and is to be traced principally to Alexander of Hales and Thomas Aquinas.[3] This doctrine first gave to the separation of the priesthood from the laity,

---

[1] The Seven Sacraments, *e.g.* :
   1. Baptism.   2. Confirmation.   3. The Eucharist.   4. Penance.
   5. Extreme Unction. 6. Holy Orders.   7. Matrimony.

[2] It would amount to little, if what Schröckh (Kirchengeschichte, xxviii., p. 45,) assumes were true ; viz., that Otto of Bamberg had already preached this doctrine to the Pomeranians ; but it has been justly remarked, that the biography of Otto, in which this statement appears, was written at a later time.

[3] See the researches of Thomas Aquinas concerning the Birth of Christ, " Utrum de purissimis sanguinibus virginis formatus fuerit, &c." Summæ, pars iii. quæstio 31. It is evident what value was set upon the point.

which had indeed other and deeper causes, its full significancy. People began to see in the priest the mediator between God and man.[1]

This separation, regarded as a positive institution, is also, as is well known, an offspring of the same epoch. In the thirteenth century, in spite of all opposition, the celibacy of the priesthood became an inviolable law. At the same time the cup began to be withheld from the laity. It was not denied that the efficacy of the Eucharist in both kinds was more complete ; but it was said that the more worthy should be reserved for the more worthy—for those by whose instrumentality alone it was produced. " It is not in the participation of the faithful," says St. Thomas, " that the perfection of the sacrament lies, but solely in the consecration of the elements."[2]   And in fact the church appeared far less designed for instruction or for the preaching of the Gospel, than for the showing forth of the great mystery ; and the priesthood is, through the sacrament, the sole depository of the power to do this ; it is through the priest that sanctification is imparted to the multitude.

This very separation of the priesthood from the laity gave its members boundless influence over all other classes of the community.

It is a necessary part of the theory of the sacerdotal character above alluded to, that the priest has the exclusive power of removing the obstacles which stand in the way of a participation in the mysterious grace of God : in this not even a saint had power to supersede him.[3]   But the absolution which he is authorized to grant is charged with certain conditions, the most imperative of which is confession. In the beginning of the thirteenth century it was peremptorily enjoined on every believer as a duty, to confess all his sins, at least once in a year, to some particular priest.

It requires no elaborate argument to prove what an all-pervading influence auricular confession, and the official supervision and guidance of consciences, must give to the clergy. With this was connected a complete, organized system of penances.

Above all, a character and position almost divine was thus conferred on the high-priest, the pope of Rome ; of whom it was assumed that he occupied the place of Christ in the mystical body of the church, which embraced heaven and earth, the dead and the living. This conception of the functions and attributes of the pope was first filled out and perfected in the beginning of the thirteenth century ; then, too, was the doctrine of the treasures of the church, on which the system of indulgences rests, first promulgated. Innocent III. did not scruple to declare, that what he did, God did, through him. Glossators added, that the pope possessed the uncontrolled will of God ; that his sentence superseded all reasons : with perverse and extravagant dialectic, they propounded the question, whether it were possible to appeal from the pope to God,[4] and answered it in the negative ; seeing that God had the same tribunal as the pope, and that it was impossible to appeal from any being to himself.

[1] " Sacerdos," says Thomas, " constituitur medius inter Deum et populum. Sacerdos novæ legis in persona Christi operatur." Summæ, pars iii. quæstio 22, art. 4, concl.

[2] "Perfectio hujus sacramenti non est in usu fidelium sed in consecratione materiæ."—Pars iii. qu. 80, a. 12, c. 2^m.

[3] Summæ Suppl. Qu. 17, a. 2, c. 1^m.   " Character et potestas conficiendi et potestas clavium est unum et idem." But I refer to the entire question.

[4] Augustini Triumphi Summa in Gieseler, Kirchengeschichte, ii. iii. 95.

It is clear that the papacy must have already gained the victory over the empire,—that it could no longer have any thing to fear, either from master or rival,—before opinions and doctrines of this kind could be entertained or avowed. In the age of struggles and conquests, the theory of the hierarchy gained ground step by step with the fact of material power. Never were theory and practice more intimately connected.

Nor was it to be believed that any interruption or pause in this course of things took place in the fifteenth century. The denial of the right of the clergy to withhold the cup was first declared to be heresy at the council of Constance : Eugenius IV. first formally accepted the doctrine of the Seven Sacraments ; the extraordinary school interpretation of the miraculous conception was first approved by the councils, favoured by the popes, and accepted by the universities, in this age.[1]

It might appear that the worldly dispositions of the popes of those times, whose main object it was to enjoy life, to promote their dependents and to enlarge their secular dominions, would have prejudiced their spiritual pretensions. But, on the contrary, these were as vast and as arrogant as ever. The only effect of the respect inspired by the councils was, that the popes forbade any one to appeal to a council under pain of damnation.[2] With what ardour do the curalist writers labour to demonstrate the infallibility of the pope ! John of Torquemada is unwearied in heaping together analogies from Scripture, maxims of the fathers and passages out of the false decretals, for this end ; he goes so far as to maintain that, were there not a head of the church who could decide all controversies and remove all doubts, it might be possible to doubt of the Holy Scriptures themselves, which derived their authority only from the church ; which, again, could not be conceived as existing without the pope.[3] In the beginning of the sixteenth century, the well-known Dominican, Thomas of Gaeta, did not hesitate to declare the church a born slave, who could have no other remedy against a bad pope, than to pray for him without ceasing.[4]

Nor were any of the resources of physical force neglected or abandoned. The Dominicans, who taught the strictest doctrines in the universities and proclaimed them to the people from the pulpit, had the right to enforce them by means of fire and sword. Many victims to orthodoxy were offered up after John Huss[5] and Jerome of Prague. The contrast between the worldly-mindedness and sensuality of Alexander VI. and Leo X., and the additional stringency and rigour they gave to the powers of the Inquisition, is most glaring.[6] Under the authority of similarly

---

[1] Baselii Auctarium Naucleri, p. 993.

[2] Bull of Pius II. of the 18th of Jan., 1460. (XV. Kal. Febr., not X., as Rain. has it.) Bullar. Cocq. tom. iii. pars iii., p. 97.

[3] Johannes de Turrecremata de Potestate Papali (Roccaberti, tom. xiii.), c. 112. "Credendum est, quod Romanus pontifex in judicio eorum quæ fidei sunt, spiritu sancto regatur et per consequens in illis non erret : alias possit quis eadem facilitate dicere, quod erratum sit in electione quatuor evangeliorum et epistolarum canonis." He laments, however, over the "multa turba adversariorum et inimicorum Romanæ sedis," who will not believe this.

[4] De Autoritate Papæ et Concilii. Extracts in Rainaldus, 1512, nr. 18.

[5] For John Huss and his follower Jerome of Prague *cf.* Creighton's "Popes," vol. i., c. 4.

[6] Decretals in Rainaldus, 1498, nr. 25, 1516, nr. 34.

disposed predecessors, this institution had recently acquired in Spain a more fearful character and aspect than it had ever yet presented to the world ; and the example of Germany shows that similar tendencies were at work in other countries.   The strange distortion of the fancy which gave birth to the notion of a personal intercourse with Satan, served as the pretext for bloody executions ; the " Hexenhammer "[1] (Hammer for Witches) was the work of two German Dominicans.   The Spanish Inquisition had originated in a persecution of the Jews : in Germany, also, the Jews were universally persecuted in the beginning of the sixteenth century, and the Dominicans of Cologne proposed to the emperor to establish an Inquisition against them.   They had even the ingenuity to invent a legal authority for such a measure.   They declared that it was necessary to examine how far the Jews had deviated from the Old Testament, which the emperor was fully entitled to do, since their nation had formally acknowledged before the judgment-seat of Pilate the authority of the imperial majesty of Rome.[2]   If they had succeeded, they would certainly not have stopped at the Jews.

Meanwhile the whole intellectual energy of the age flowed in the channels marked out by the church.   Germany is a striking example to what an extent the popular mind of a nation of the West received its direction from ecclesiastical principles.

The great workshops of literature, the German universities, were all more or less colonies or branches of that of Paris—either directly sprung from it, like the earlier ; or indirectly, like the later.   Their statutes sometimes begin with a eulogy on the Alma Mater of Paris.[3]   From that most ancient seat of learning, too, had the whole system of schoolmen, the controversy between Nominalism and Realism, the preponderancy of the theological faculty,—" that brilliant star from which every thing received light and life,"—passed over to them.   In the theological faculty the Professor of Sentences [4] had the precedency, and the Baccalaureus who read the Bible was obliged to allow him to determine the hour of his lecture.   In some universities, none but a clerk who had received at least inferior ordination, could be chosen Rector.   The whole of education, from the first elements to the highest dignities of learning, was conducted in

---

[1] A court for the trial of Witchcraft.

[2] Report in Reuchlin's Augenspiegel (Mirror), printed by v. d. Hardt, Historia Liter. Reformationis, iii. 61.

[3] Principium Statutorum Facultatis Theologicæ Studii Viennensis ap. Kollar Analecta, i. 137, p. 240, n. 2.   Statute of Cologne in Bianco, Endowments for Students at Cologne, p. 451 : " Divinæ sapientiæ fluvius descendens a patre luminum—ab alveo Parisiens. studii tanquam cisterna conductu capto per canalia prorumpit Rheni partes ubertando."   University of Paris founded *circum* 1170.   *Cf.* Rashdall, History of the Universities in the Middle Ages, vol. i., pp. 273 ff.   The genealogy is as follows :—From the university of Paris issued those of Prague, Vienna, Heidelberg, and Cologne ; from Prague,—Leipzig, Rostock, Greifswald ; and for the greater part, Erfurt ; from Cologne,—Louvain and Treves ; from Vienna,—Freiburg, and, according to the Statutes, Ingolstadt. At Basle and Tübingen at first, deference was paid to Bologna also ; but even in Basle, the first Bursa was called the Parisian and in Tübingen the first teacher of Theology was a magister from Paris.

[4] Professor Sententiarum, the expositor of the " Sententiæ " of Peter Lombard. —Transl.

one and the same spirit. Dialectical distinctions intruded themselves into the very rudiments of grammar ;[1] and the elementary books of the eleventh and twelfth centuries were constantly retained as the ground-work of learning :[2] here, too, the same road was steadily pursued which had been marked out at the time of the foundation of the hierarchical power.

Art[3] was subject to the same influences. The minsters and cathedrals, in which the doctrines and ideas of the church are so curiously symbolised, rose on every side. In the year 1482, the towers of the church of St. Sebaldus at Nürnberg were raised to their present height ; in 1494, a new and exquisitely wrought gate was added to Strasburg minster ; in 1500, the king of the Romans laid the first stone of the choir of the Reichsgot-teshaus (Church of the Empire) St. Ulrich, in Augsburg, with silver trowel, rule, and hod ; he caused a magnificent block of stone to be brought from the mountains, out of which a monument was to be erected " to the well-beloved lord St. Ulrich, our kinsman of the house of Kyburg :" upon it was to stand a king of the Romans, sword in hand.[4] In 1513, the choir of the cathedral of Freiburg, in 1517, that of Bern, was finished ; the porch on the northern transept of the church of St. Lawrence in Nürnberg dates from 1520. The brotherhoods of the masons, and the secrets which arose in the workshops of German builders, spread wider and wider. It was not till a later period that the redundancy of foliage, the vegetable character, which so remarkably distinguishes the so-called gothic architecture became general. At the time we are speaking of, the interior of churches was principally adorned with countless figures, either exquisitely carved in wood, or cast in precious metals, or painted and enclosed in gold frames, which covered the altars or adorned the aisles and porches. It is not the province of the arts to produce ideas, but to give them a sensible form ; all the creative powers of the nation were now devoted to the task of repre-senting the traditional conceptions of the church. Those wondrous representations of the Mother of God, so full of sweet and innocent grace, which have immortalized Baldung, Schaffner, and especially Martin Schön, are not mere visions of an artist's fancy ; they are profoundly con-nected with that worship of the Virgin which was then peculiarly general and fervent. I venture to add that they cannot be understood without the rosary, which is designed to recall the several joys of the Holy Mary ;— the angelic salutation, the journey across the mountains, the child-bearing without pain, the finding of Jesus in the temple, and the ascension ; as the prayer-books of that time more fully set forth.

These prayer-books are altogether singular monuments of a simple and credulous devotion. There are prayers to which an indulgence for 146

---

[1] Geiler, Navicula : " In prima parte de subjecto attributionis et de habitibus intellectualibus, quod scire jam est magistrorum provectorum."

[2] Johannes de Garlandia, Alexander's Doctrinale. Dufresne, Præfatio ad Glossarium, 42, 43.

[3] For an account of German painters and engravers of the fifteenth century *cf.* Head, Schools of Painting in Germany, bk. iii. c. 1. For Architecture of the period, *cf.* Ferguson, History of Architecture, vol. ii. bk. iv. c. 5, or Dehis and Bezold, Die Kirkliche Baukunst des Abendlandes, vol. ii., pp. 249 ff.

[4] Account in the Fugger MS. We remember that St. Ulrich was the first saint canonised by a pope (Johannes, xv. 973) for the whole church.

days, others to which one for 7000 or 8000 years are attached : one morning benediction of peculiar efficacy was sent by a pope to a king of Cyprus ; whosoever repeats the prayer of the venerable Bede the requisite number of times, the Virgin Mary will be at hand to help him for thirty days before his death, and will not suffer him to depart unabsolved. The most extravagant expressions were uttered in praise of the Virgin : " The eternal Daughter of the eternal Father, the heart of the indivisible Trinity :" it was said, " Glory be to the Virgin, to the Father, and to the Son."[1]   Thus, too, were the saints invoked as meritorious servants of God, who, by their merits, could win our salvation, and could extend peculiar protection to those who believed in them ; as, for example, St. Sebaldus, " the most venerable and holy captain, helper and defender of the imperial city of Nürnberg."

Relics were collected with great zeal. Elector Frederick of Saxony gathered together in the church he endowed at Wittenberg, 5005 particles, all preserved in entire standing figures, or in exquisitely wrought reliquaries, which were shown to the devout people every year on the Monday after Misericordia.[2]   In the presence of the princes assembled at the diet, the high altar of the cathedral of Treves was opened, and " the seamless coat of our dear Lord Jesus Christ," found in it ; the little pamphlets in which this miracle was represented in wood-cuts, and announced to all the world, are to be found in the midst of the acts of the diet.[3]   Miraculous images of Our Lady were discovered ;—one, for example, in Eischel in the diocese of Constance ; at the Iphof boundary, by the road-side, a sitting figure of the Virgin, whose miracles gave great offence to the monks of Birklingen, who possessed a similar one ; and in Regensburg, the beautiful image, for which a magnificent church was built by the contributions of the faithful, out of the ruins of a synagogue belonging to the expelled Jews. Miracles were worked without ceasing at the tomb of Bishop Benno in Meissen ; madmen were restored to reason, the deformed became straight, those infected with the plague were healed ; nay, a fire at Merseburg was extinguished by Bishop Bose merely uttering the name of Benno ; while those who doubted his power and sanctity were assailed by misfortunes.[4] When Trithemius recommended this miracle-worker to the pope for canonization, he did not forget to remark that he had been a rigid and energetic supporter of the church party, and had resisted the tyrant Henry IV.[5]   So intimately were all these ideas connected. A confraternity formed for the purpose of the frequent repetition of the rosary (which is, in fact, nothing more than the devout and affectionate recollection of the joys of the Holy Virgin), was founded by Jacob Sprenger, the

---

[1] Extracts from the prayer-books : Hortulus Anime, Salus Animæ, Gilgengart, and others in Riederer, Nachrichten zur Büchergeschichte, ii. 157-411.

[2] The second Sunday after Easter, so called from the Introit for that Sunday in the Roman Missal, which begins, "Misericordia Domini plena est terra," and gives the key to the variable parts of the Mass. Zaygung des Hochlobwürdigsten Heiligthums, 1509. (The Showing of the most venerable Relics, 1509.) Extract in Heller's Lucas Kranach, i., p. 350.

[3] Chronicle of Limpurg in Hontheim, p. 1122. Browerus is again very solemn on this occasion.

[4] Miracula S. Bennonis ex impresso, Romæ 1521, in Mencken, Scriptores Rer. Germ. ii. p. 1887.

[5] His letter in Rainaldus, 1506, nr. 42.

violent and fanatical restorer of the Inquisition in Germany,—the author of the " Hexenhammer."

For it was one single and wondrous structure which had grown up out of the germs planted by former ages, wherein spiritual and temporal power, wild fancy and dry school-learning, the tenderest devotion and the rudest force, religion and superstition, were mingled and confounded, and were bound together by some mysterious quality common to them all ;— and, amidst all the attacks it sustained, and all the conquests it achieved —amidst those incessant conflicts, the decisions of which constantly assumed the character of laws,—not only asserted its claim to universal fitness for all ages and nations—for this world and the next—but to the regulation of the minutest particulars of human life.

I know not whether any man of sound understanding—any man, not led astray by some phantasm, can seriously wish that this state of things had remained unshaken and unchanged in Europe ; whether any man persuades himself that the will and the power to look the genuine, entire and unveiled truth steadily in the face—the manly piety acquainted with the grounds of its faith—could ever have been matured under such in-fluences.   Nor do I understand how any one could really regard the diffu-sion of this most singular condition of the human mind (which had been produced by circumstances wholly peculiar to the West) over the entire globe, as conducive to the welfare and happiness of the human race.   It is well known that one main ground of the disinclination of the Greeks to a union with the Roman church, lay in the multitude of rules which were introduced among the Latins, and in the oppressive autocracy which the See of Rome had arrogated to itself.[1]   Nay, was not the Gospel itself kept concealed by the Roman church ?   In the ages in which the scholastic dogmas were fixed, the Bible was forbidden to the laity altogether, and even to the priesthood, in the mother tongue.   It is impossible to deny that, without any serious reference to the source from which the whole system of faith had proceeded, men went on to construct doctrines and to enjoin practices, shaped upon the principle which had become the dominant one.   We must not confound the tendencies of the period now before us with those evinced in the doctrines and practices established at the Council of Trent ; at that time even the party which adhered to Catholicism had felt the influences of the epoch of the Reformation, and had begun to reform itself : the current was already arrested.[2]   And this was absolutely necessary.   It was necessary to clear the germ of religion from the thou-sand folds of accidental forms under which it lay concealed, and to place it unencumbered in the light of day.   Before the Gospel could be preached to all nations, it must appear again in its own lucid, unadulterated purity.

It is one of the greatest coincidences presented by the history of the world, that at the moment in which the prospect of exercising dominion over the other hemisphere opened on the Romano-Germanic nations of the

[1] Humbertus de Romania (in Petrus de Alliaco de Reform. Eccles. c. 2.) " dicit quod causa dispositiva schismatis Græcorum inter alias una fuit propter gravamina Romanæ ecclesiæ in exactionibus, excommunicationibus, et statutis."

[2] I hold it to be the fundamental error of Möhler's Symbolik, that he considers the dogma of the Council of Trent as the doctrine from which the Protestants seceded ; whilst it is much nearer the truth to say, that itself produced Pro-testantism by a reaction.

Latin church, a religious movement began, the object of which was to restore the purity of revelation.

Whilst other nations were busied in the conquest of distant lands, Germany, which had little share in those enterprises, undertook this mighty task. Various events concurred to give that direction to the mind of the country, and to incite it to a strenuous opposition to the See of Rome.

OPPOSITION RAISED BY THE SECULAR POWERS.

The efforts to obtain a regular and well compacted constitution, which for some years had occupied the German nation, were very much at variance with the interests of the papacy, hitherto exercising so great an influence over the government of the empire. The pope would very soon have been made sensible of the change, if that national government which was the object of such zealous and ardent endeavours had been organised.

The very earliest projects of such a constitution, in the year 1487, were accompanied with a warning to the pope to abolish a tithe which he had arbitrarily imposed on Germany, and which in some places he had actually levied.[1] In 1495, when it became necessary to form a council of the empire, the intention was expressed to authorize the president to take into consideration the complaints of the nation against the church of Rome.[2] Scarcely had the States met the king in 1498, when they resolved to require the pope to relinquish the Annates which he drew to so large an amount from Germany, in order to provide for a Turkish war. In like manner, as soon as the Council of Regency was formed, an embassy was sent to the pope to press this request earnestly upon him, and to make representations concerning various unlawful encroachments on the gift and employment of German benefices.[3] A papal legate, who shortly after arrived for the purpose of causing the jubilee to be preached, was admonished by no means to do anything without the advice and knowledge of the imperial government;[4] care was taken to prevent him from granting indulgences to breakers of the Public Peace : on the contrary, he was charged expressly to uphold it ; imperial commissioners were appointed to accompany him, without whose presence and permission he could not receive the money when collected.

We find the Emperor Maximilian occasionally following the same course. In the year 1510 he caused a more detailed and distinct statement of the grievances of the German nation to be drawn up, than had hitherto existed ; he even entertained the idea of introducing into Germany[5] the Pragmatic Sanction, which had proved so beneficial to France. In the year 1511 he took a lively interest in the convocation of a council at Pisa : we have an edict of his, dated in the January of that year, wherein he declares that, as the court of Rome delays, he will not delay ; as emperor,

[1] Letter, with the seals of Mainz, Saxony, and Brandenburg ; June 26. 1487, in Müller, Rtth. Fr. vi. 130.

[2] Datt, de Pace Publ., p. 840.

[3] Instructions of the Imperial Embassy. Müller, Reichstagsstaat, 117.

[4] Articuli tractati et conclusi inter Rev^{mam} Dominationem D^{num} Legatum ac senatum et conventum Imperii in Müller, Reichstagsstaat, p. 213.

[5] Avisamenta Germanicæ Nationis in Freher, ii. 678. Yet more remarkable is the Epitome pragmaticæ sanctionis in Goldast's Constitutt. Imp., ii. 123.

steward and protector of the Church, he convokes the council of which she is so greatly in need.   In a brief dated June, he promises to those assembled his protection and favour till the close of their sittings, " by which they will, as he hopes, secure to themselves the approbation of God and the praise of men."[1]   And, in fact, the long-cherished hope that a reform in the church would be the result of this council, was again ardently indulged. The articles were pointed out in which reforms were first anticipated. For example, the cumulation of benefices in the hands of the cardinals was to be prevented ; a law was demanded, in virtue of which a pope whose life was stained with notorious vice, might be summarily deposed.[2] But neither had the council authority enough to act upon ideas of this sort, nor was Maximilian the man to follow them out.   He was of too weak a nature ; and the same Wimpheling who drew up the statement of grievances, remarked to him how many former emperors had been deposed by an incensed pope leagued with the princes of the empire—certainly no motive to resolute perseverance in the course he had begun. Independent of this, every new turn in politics gave a fresh direction to his views on ecclesiastical affairs.[3]   After his reconciliation with Pope Julius II. in 1513, he demanded succours from the empire in order to take measures against the schism which was to be feared.   Had there really been reason to fear it, he himself would have been mainly to blame for the encouragement he had given to the Council of Pisa.

It is sufficiently clear that this opposition to Rome had no real practical force.   The want of a body in the state, armed with independent powers, crippled every attempt, every movement, at its very commencement.   But, in the public mind, that opposition still remained in full force ; loud complaints were incessantly heard.

Hemmerlin, whose books were in those times extensively circulated and eagerly read exhausted the vocabulary for expressions to paint the cheating and plunder of which the court of Rome was guilty.[4]

In the beginning of the sixteenth century there were the bitterest complaints of the ruinous nature of the Annates.[5]   It was probably in itself the most oppressive tax in the empire : occasionally a prelate in order to save his subjects from it, tried to mortgage some lordship of his see. Diether of Isenburg was deposed chiefly because he was unable to fulfil the engagements he had entered into concerning his Pallium.   The more frequent the vacancies, the more intolerable was the exaction.   In Passau, for example, these followed in 1482, 1486, 1490, 1500 : the last-appointed

---

[1] Triburgi XVI. mensis Januarii and Muldorf V. Junii in Goldast, i. 421, 429.

[2] In the Fugger MS. the decrees which were expected are noted down.

[3] Baselius, 1110.   " Admonitus prudentium virorum consilio—quem incaute pedem cum Gallis contra pontificem firmaverat, citius retraxit."

[4] Felix Malleolus, Recapitulatio de Anno Jubileo.   " Pro nunc de præsentis pontificis summi et aliorum statibus comparationis præparationem fecimus, et nunc facie ad faciem experientia videmus quod nunquam visus est execrabilioris exorbitationis direptionis deceptionis circumventionis derogationis decerptationis deprædationis expoliationis exactionis corrosionis et omnis si audemus dicere simoniacæ pravitatis adinventionis novæ et renovationis usus et exercitatio continua quam nunc est tempore pontificis moderni (Nicolas V.) et in dies dilatatur."

[5] The first-fruits in a year's revenue paid by bishops, abbots, and holders of benefices.

bishop repaired to Rome in the hope of obtaining some alleviation of the
burthens on his see ; but he accomplished nothing, and his long residence
at the papal court only increased his pecuniary difficulties.[1]   The cost of
a pallium[2] for Mainz amounted to 20,000 gulden ; the sum was assessed on
the several parts of the see : the Rheingau, for example, had to contribute 1000 gulden each time.[3]   In the beginning of the sixteenth century
vacancies occurred three times in quick succession—1505, 1508, 1513 ;
Jacob von Liebenstein said that his chief sorrow in dying was that his
country would so soon again be forced to pay the dues ; but all appeal to
the papal court was fruitless ; before the old tax was gathered in, the
order for a new one was issued.

We may imagine what was the impression made by the comparison of
the laborious negotiations usually necessary to extract even trifling
grants from the diet, and the great difficulty with which they were collected, with the sums which flowed without toil or trouble to Rome.   They
were calculated at 300,000 gulden yearly, exclusive of the costs of law proceedings, or the revenues of benefices which lapsed to the court of Rome.[4]
And for what purpose, men asked themselves, was all this ?   Christendom
had, nevertheless, lost two empires, fourteen kingdoms, and three hundred
towns within a short space of time : it was continually losing to the Turks ;
if the German nation were to keep these sums in its own hands and expend
them itself, it would meet its hereditary foe on other terms, under the
banners of its valiant commanders.

The financial relations to Rome, generally, excited the greatest attention.   It was calculated that the barefooted monks, who were not permitted by their rule to touch money, collected a yearly income of 200,000
gulden ; the whole body of mendicant friars, a million.

Another evil was the recurrence of collisions between the temporal and
spiritual jurisdictions, which gradually became the more frequent and
obvious, the more the territorial sovereignties tended towards separation
and political independence.   In this respect Saxony was pre-eminent.
In the different possessions of the two lines, not only the three Saxon
bishops, but the archbishops of Mainz and Prag, the bishops of Würzburg and Bamberg, Halberstadt, Havelberg, Brandenburg and Lebus,
had spiritual jurisdiction.   The confusion which must, at all events, have
arisen from this, was now enormously increased by the fact that all dis-

---

[1] Schreitwein, Episcopi Patavienses, in Rauch, Scriptt., ii. 527.

[2] The symbol of archiepiscopal authority.   A collar of white lamb's-wool with
two bands hanging in the front and back of the wearer, and decorated with six
black crosses.

[3] This is shown by the Articles of the inhabitants of the Rheingau in Schunck's
Beiträgen, i. p. 183.   Jacob of Treves also reckons in 1500, " Das Geld, so sich
an dem päpstlichen Hofe für die päpstlichen Bullen und Briefe, darüber Annaten,
Minuten, Servitien, und anders demselben anhangend, zu geben gebüret," " the
money, which it behoves to give to the papal court for the papal bulls and briefs,
moreover annats, minutes, services, and the rest belonging to the same," at
20,000 guldens.   Document in Hontheim, ii., ser. xv.

[4] This is, for instance, the calculation of the little book, Ein klägliche Klag
(A mournful Complaint) 1521, which, however, I am not for adopting.   It might
very likely be impossible to reckon the gains of the Romish court.   The tax of
the annates at Treves, for instance, legally amounted to 10,000 gulden, and yet
the actual charge was 20,000.

putes between laity and clergy could only be decided before spiritual tribunals, so that high and low were continually vexed with excommunication.   In the year 1454, we find Duke William complaining that the evil did not arise from his good lords and friends the bishops, but from the judges, officials, and procurators, who sought therein only their own profit. In concurrence with the counts, lords, and knights of his land, he issued certain ordinances to prevent this abuse,[1] in support of which, privileges granted by the popes were alleged ; but in 1490 the old complaints were revived, the administration of justice in the temporal courts was greatly obstructed and thwarted by the spiritual, and the people were impoverished by the consequent delays and expenses.[2]   In the year 1518, the princes of both lines, George and Frederick, combined to urge that the spiritual jurisdiction should be restricted to spiritual causes, and the temporal to temporal ; the diet to decide what was temporal and what was spiritual. Duke George was still more zealous in the matter than his cousin.[3]   But the grievances and complaints which fill the proceedings of the later diets were universal, and confined to no class or portion of the empire.

The cities felt the exemptions enjoyed by the clergy peculiarly burthensome.   It was impossible to devise any thing more annoying to a well-ordered civic community, than to have within their walls a corporate body which neither acknowledged the jurisdiction of the city, nor contributed to bear its burthens, nor deemed itself generally subject to its regulations.   The churches were asylums for criminals, the monasteries the resort of dissolute youth ; we find examples of monks who made use of their exemption from tolls, to import goods for sale, or to open a tavern for the sale of beer.   If any attempt was made to assail their privileges, they defended themselves with excommunication and interdict.   We find the municipal councils incessantly occupied in putting some check to this evil.   In urgent cases they arrest offenders even in sanctuary, and then take measures to be delivered from the inevitable interdict by the interposition of some powerful protector ; they are well inclined to pass over the bishops and to address themselves directly to the pope ; they try to effect reforms in their monasteries.   They thought it a very questionable arrangement that the parish priest should take part in the collection of the Common Penny ; the utmost that they would concede was that he should be present, but without taking any active share.[4]   The cities always vehemently opposed the emperor's intention of appointing a bishop to be judge in the Imperial Chamber.

The general disapprobation excited by the church on such weighty points, naturally led to a discussion of its other abuses.   Hemmerlin zealously contends against the incessant augmentation of ecclesiastical property, through which villages disappeared and districts became waste ; against the exorbitant number of holidays, which even the council of Basle had endeavoured to reduce ; against the celibacy of the clergy, to

---

[1] Ordinance of Duke William ; Gotha, Monday after Exaudi, 1454, in Müller, Rtth. Fr., i. 130.

[2] Words of an ordinance of Duke George in Langenn's Duke Albrecht, p. 319.

[3] Articles of the negotiations of the diet, as my gracious lord has caused them to be given in 1518.   In the Dresden Archives.

[4] Jäger, Schwäbisches Städtewesen : Müllner's Nürnberger Annalen, in several passages.

which the rules of the Eastern Church were much to be preferred ; against the reckless manner in which ordination was granted, as, for example, that two hundred priests were yearly ordained in Constance : he asks to what all this is to lead.[1]

Things had gone so far that the constitution of the clergy was offensive to public morals : a multitude of ceremonies and rules were attributed to the mere desire of making money ; the situation of priests living in a state of concubinage and burthened with illegitimate children, and often, in spite of all purchased absolutions, tormented in conscience and oppressed with the fear that in performing the sacrifice of the mass they committed a deadly sin, excited mingled pity and contempt : most of those who embraced the monastic profession had no other idea than that of leading a life of self-indulgence without labour.   People saw that the clergy took from every class and station only what was agreeable, and avoided what was laborious or painful.   From the knightly order, the prelate borrowed his brilliant company, his numerous retinue, the splendidly caparisoned horse, and the hawk upon his fist : with women, he shared the love of gorgeous chambers and trim gardens ; but the weight of the mailed coat, the troubles of the household, he had the dexterity to avoid.   If a man wishes to enjoy himself for once, says an old proverb, let him kill a fat fowl ; if for a year, let him take a wife ; but if he would live joyously all the days of his life, then let him turn priest.

Innumerable expressions of the same sentiment were current ; the pamphlets of that time are full of them.[2]

CHARACTER AND TENDENCIES OF THE POPULAR LITERATURE.

This state of the public mind acquired vast importance from its coincidence with the first dawnings of a popular literature which thus, at its very commencement, became deeply and thoroughly imbued with the prevalent sentiment of disapprobation and disgust towards the clergy.

It will be conceded on all sides that in naming Rosenblüt and Sebastian Brant, the Eulenspiegel (Owlglass) and the edition of Reineke Fuchs (Reynard the Fox) of the year 1498, we cite the most remarkable productions of the literature of that time.[3]   And if we inquire what characteristic they have in common, we find it to be that of hostility to the Church of Rome.   The Fastnachtspiele (Carnival Sports) of Hans Rosenblüt have fully and distinctly this character and intention ; he introduces the Emperor of Turkey, in order through his mouth to say the truth to all classes of the nation.[4]   The vast success of the Eulenspiegel was not to be attributed so much to its clownish coarseness and practical jokes, as

---

[1] The books De Institutione novorum Officiorum, and De Libertate Ecclesiasticâ, are especially remarkable with reference to this matter.

[2] Wimpheling also mentions, " scandalum odium murmur populi in omnem clerum."

[3] For a further account of these writings and writers, *cf.* Geiger, Renaissance und Humanismus in Deutschland, pp. 1344 ff., or Creighton, vol. v. c. i. ii., or Cambridge Modern History, vol. i. c. xvi. xvii.

[4] In the description also of the battle of Hembach in Reinhart's Beiträge zur Historie Frankenlandes, the nobles are mentioned " as a sharp scourge, which chastises us on account of our sins ; " " their hearts are harder than adamant."

to the irony which was poured over all classes ; the wit of the boor, " who scratches himself with a rogue's nails," put that of all others to shame. It was under this point of view alone that the German writer recast the fable of the fox ; he saw in it the symbolic representation of the defects and vices of human society, and he quickly detected its application to the several classes of men, and laboured to develop the lesson which the poet reads to each.   The same purpose is obvious to the first glance in Brant's Ship of Fools.   The ridicule is not directed against individual follies : on the one side is vice, nay crime, on the other, lofty aspirations and pursuits which rise far above vulgar ends, (as, for example, where the devotion of the whole mind to the task of describing cities and countries, the attempt to discover how broad is the earth, and how wide the sea,) are treated as folly.[1]   Glory and beauty are despised as transient ; " nothing is abiding but learning."

In this general opposition to the prevailing state of things, the defects in the ecclesiastical body are continually adverted to.   The Schnepperer declaims violently against the priests, " who ride high horses, but will not do battle with the heathen."   The most frequent subject of derision in the Eulenspiegel is the common priests, with their pretty ale-wives, well-groomed nags, and full larders ; they are represented as stupid and greedy.   In Reineke too the Papemeierschen—priests' households, peopled with little children—play a part.   The commentator is evidently quite in earnest ; he declares that the sins of the priests will be rated more highly than those of the laity on account of the evil example they set.   Doctor Brant expresses his indignation at the premature admission into the convent, before the age of reason ; so that religious duties are performed without the least sentiment of devotion : he leads us into the domestic life of the uncalled priests, who are at last in want of the means of subsistence, while their soul is heavy laden with sins ; " for God regardeth not the sacrifice which is offered in sin by sinful hands."[2]

This, however, is not the exclusive, nor, indeed, the principal matter of these books ; their significance is far more extensive and general.

While the poets of Italy were employed in moulding the romantic materials furnished by the middle ages into grand and brilliant works, these excited little interest in Germany : Titurel and Parcival, for example, were printed, but merely as antiquarian curiosities, and in a language even then unintelligible.

While, in Italy, the opposition which the institutions of the middle ages encountered in the advancing development of the public mind, took the form of satire, became an element of composition, and as it were the inseparable but mocking companion of the poetical Ideal ; in Germany that opposition took up independent ground, and directed its attacks immediately against the realities of life, not against their reproduction in fiction.

In the German literature of that period the whole existence and conduct of the several classes, ages and sexes were brought to the standard of the sober good sense, the homely morality, the simple rule of ordinary life ; which, however, asserted its claim to be that " whereby kings hold their crowns, princes their lands, and all powers and authorities their due value."

[1] Dr. Brant's Narrenschiff., 1506, f. 83.
[2] The 72nd Fool. fol. 94.

The universal confusion and ferment which is visible in the public affairs of that period, proves by inevitable contrast, that the sound common sense of mankind is awakened and busy in the mass of the nation ; and prosaic, homely, vulgar, but thoroughly true, as it is, constitutes itself judge of all the phenomena of the world around it.

We are filled with admiration at the spectacle afforded by Italy, where men of genius, reminded by the remains of antiquity around them of the significance of beautiful forms, strove to emulate their predecessors, and produced works which are the eternal delight of cultivated minds ; but their beauty does not blind us to the fact that the movement of the national mind of Germany was not less great, and that it was still more important to the progress of mankind. After centuries of secret growth it now became aware of its own existence, broke loose from tradition, and examined the affairs and the institutions of the world by the light of its own truth.

Nor did Germany entirely disregard the demands of form. In Reinecke Fuchs, it is curious to observe how the author rejects every thing appropriate to the style of romantic poetry ; how he seeks lighter transitions, works out scenes of common life to more complete and picturesque reality, and constantly strives to be more plain and vernacular (for example, uses all the familiar German names) : his main object evidently is to popularise his matter,—to bring it as much as possible home to the nation ; and his work has thus acquired the form in which it has attracted readers for more than three centuries. Sebastian Brant possesses an incomparable talent for turning apophthegms and proverbs ; he finds the most appropriate expression for simple thoughts ; his rhymes come unsought, and are singularly happy and harmonious. " Here," says Geiler von Keisersperg, " the agreeable and the useful are united ; his verses are goblets of the purest wine ; here we are presented with royal meats in finely wrought vessels."[1] But in these, as well as in many other works of that time, the matter is the chief thing ;—the expression of the opposition of the ordinary morality and working-day sense of mankind to the abuses in public life and the corruptions of the times.

At the same period another branch of literature,—the learned, took an analogous direction ; perhaps with even greater force and decision.

CONDITION AND CHARACTER OF LEARNED LITERATURE.

Upon this department of letters Italy exercised the strongest influence.

In that country neither the metaphysics of the schools, nor romantic poetry, nor Gothic architecture, had obtained complete dominion : recollections of antiquity survived, and at length in the fifteenth century, expanded into that splendid revival which took captive all minds and imparted a new life to literature.

---

[1] Geiler, Navicula Fatuorum, even more instructive as to the history of morals, than the original ; J, u. " Est hic," he continues, " in hoc speculo veritas moralis sub figuris sub vulgari et vernacula lingua nostra teutonica sub verbis similitudinibusque aptis et pulchris sub rhitmis quoque concinnis et instar cimbalorum concinentibus."

This reflorescence of Italy in time reacted on Germany, though at first only in regard to the mere external form of the Latin tongue.

In consequence of the uninterrupted intercourse with Italy occasioned by ecclesiastical relations, the Germans soon discovered the superiority of the Italians ; they saw themselves despised by the disciples of the grammarians and rhetoricians of that country, and began to be ashamed of the rudeness of their spoken, and the poverty of their written language. It was not surprising, therefore, that young aspiring spirits at length determined to learn their Latin in Italy. At first they were only a few opulent nobles—a Dalberg, a Langen,[1] a Spiegelberg, who not only acquired knowledge themselves, but had the merit of bringing back books, such as grammatical treatises and better editions of the classics, which they communicated to their friends. A man endowed with the peculiar talent necessary for appropriating to himself the classical learning of the age then arose—Rudolf Huesmann of Gröningen, called Agricola. His scholarship excited universal admiration ; he was applauded in the schools as a Roman, a second Virgil.[2] He had, indeed, no other object but his own advancement in learning ; the weary pedantries of the schools were disgusting to him, nor could he accommodate himself to the contracted sphere assigned to a learned man in Germany. Other careers which he entered upon did not satisfy his aspirations, so that he fell into a rapid decline and died prematurely. He had, however, friends who found it less difficult to adapt themselves to the necessities of German life, and to whom he was ever ready to afford counsel and help. A noble and intimate friendship was formed in Deventer, between Agricola and Hegius, who attached himself to him with all the humility and thirst for knowledge of a disciple ; he applied to him for instruction, and received not only assistance but cordial sympathy.[3] Another of his friends, Dringenberg, followed him to Schletstadt. The reform which took place in the Low German schools of Münster, Hervord, Dortmund, and Hamm, emanated from Deventer, which also furnished them with competent teachers. In Nürnberg, Ulm, Augsburg, Frankfurt, Memmingen, Hagenau, Pforzheim, &c., we find schools of poetry of more or less note.[4] Schletstadt at one time numbered as many as nine hundred students. It will not be imagined that these literati, who had to rule, and to instruct in the rudiments of learning, a rude undisciplined youth compelled to live mainly on alms, possessing no books, and wandering from town to town in strangely

---

[1] Hamelmann published in 1580 an Oratio de Rodolpho Langio, which has some merit, but which has also given rise to many errors.

[2] Erasmi Adagia. Ad. de Cane et Balneo.

[3] Adami, Vitæ Philosophorum, p. 12, mentions this correspondence " unde tum ardor proficiendi, tum candor in communicando elucet."

[4] They are so called, e.g. in the Chronicle of Regensburg. A list of the schools, very incomplete, however, is given by Erhard, Hist. of the Restoration of the Sciences, i. 427. Eberlin von Günzburg names in 1521, as pious schoolmasters, " deren trewe Unterweisung fast genützt," whose faithful instruction had been profitable," Crato and Sapidus at Schletstadt, Mich. Hilspach at Hagenau, Spinler and Gerbellius at Pforzheim, Brassicanus and Henrichmann at Tübingin, Egid. Krautwasser at Stuttgart and Horb, Joh. Schmidlin at Memmingen, also Coclens at Nürnberg, and Nisenus at Frankfurt. See Dr. Karl Hagen, Deutchlands literarische und religiöse Verhältnisse im Reformations Zeitalter, 1841, vol. i., pp. 164-237.

organized bands, called Bachantes and Schützen,[1] were very eminent scholars themselves, or made such ; nor was that the object : their merit, and a sufficient one, was that they not only kept the public mind steady to the important direction it had taken, but carried it onwards to the best of their ability, and founded the existence of an active literary public. The school-books hitherto in use gradually fell into neglect, and classical authors issued from the German press. As early as the end of the fifteenth century, Geiler of Keisersberg, who was not himself devoted to these pursuits, reproached the learned theologians with their Latin, which, he said, was rude, feeble, and barbarous—neither German nor Latin, but both and neither.[2]

For since the school learning of the universities, which had hitherto entirely given the tone to elementary instruction, adhered to its wonted forms of expression, a collision between the new and humanistic method, now rapidly gaining ground, and the old modes, was inevitable. Nor could their collision fail to extend from the universal element of language into other regions.

It was this crisis in the history of letters that produced an author whose whole life was devoted to the task of attacking the scholastic forms prevailing in universities and monasteries ; the first great author of the modern opposition, the champion of the modern views,—a low German, Erasmus of Rotterdam.

On a review of the first thirty years of the life of Erasmus, we find that he had grown up in ceaseless contradiction with the spirit and the systems which presided over the conventual life and directed the studies of that time ;—indeed that this had made him what he was. We might say that he was begotten and born in this contradiction, for his parents had not been able to marry, because his father was destined to the cloister. He had not been admitted to a university, as he wished, but had been kept at a very imperfect conventual school, from which he soon ceased to derive any profit or satisfaction ; and, at a later period, every art was practised to induce him to take the vows, and with success. It was not till he had actually taken them, that he felt all the burthen they imposed : he regarded it as a deliverance when he obtained a situation in a college at Paris : but here, too, he was not happy ; he was compelled to attend Scotist lectures and disputations ; and he complains that the unwholesome food and bad wine on which he was forced to live, had entirely destroyed his health. But in the meanwhile he had come to a consciousness of his own powers. While yet a boy, he had lighted upon the first trace of a new method of study,[3] and he now followed it up with slender aid from without, but with the infallible instinct of genuine talent ; he had constructed for himself a light, flowing style, formed on the model of the ancients, not by a servile imitation of particular expressions, but in native correctness

---

[1] Platter's Autobiography places this practice in a very lively manner before us. (Thomas Platter, after the autograph manuscript lately edited by Fechner, Basle, 1840.)

[2] Geiler, Introductorium, ii. c. " Quale est illud eorum Latinum, quo utuntur, etiam dum sederint in sede majestatis suæ, in doctoralis cathedra lecturæ !"

[3] He cannot, however, be properly considered as a scholar of Hegius. " Hegium," he says in the Compendium Vitæ, " testis diebus audivi." It was the exception.

and elegance far surpassing anything which Paris had to offer. He now
emancipated himself from the fetters which bound him to the convent
and the schools, and boldly trusted to the art of which he was master,
for the means of subsistence. He taught, and in that way formed connections which not only led to present success, but to security for the
future ; he published some essays which, as they were not less remarkable
for discreet choice of matter than for scholarly execution, gained him
admirers and patrons ; he gradually discovered the wants and the tastes
of the public, and devoted himself entirely to literature. He composed
school-books treating of method and form of instruction ; translated from
the Greek, which he learned in the process ; edited the classics of antiquity,
and imitated them, especially Lucian and Terence. His works abound with
marks of that acute and nice observation which at once instructs and
delights ; but great as these merits were, the grand secret of his popularity
lay in the spirit which pervades all he wrote. The bitter hostility to the
forms of the devotion and the theology of that time, which had been rendered his habitual frame of mind by the course and events of his life,
found vent in his writings ; not that this was the premeditated aim or
purpose of them, but it broke forth sometimes in the very middle of a
learned disquisition—in indirect and unexpected sallies of the most
felicitous and exhaustless humour. In one of his works, he adopts the
idea, rendered so popular by the fables of Brant and Geiler, of the element
of folly which mingles in all human affairs. He introduces Folly herself
as interlocutor. Moria, the daughter of Plutus, born in the Happy
Islands, nursed by Drunkenness and Rudeness, is mistress of a powerful
kingdom, which she describes and to which all classes of men belong.
She passes them all in review, but dwells longer and more earnestly on
none than on the clergy, who, though they refuse to acknowledge her
benefits, are under the greatest obligations to her. She turns into ridicule
the labyrinth of dialectic in which theologians have lost themselves,—
the syllogisms with which they labour to sustain the church as Atlas
does the heavens,—the intolerant zeal with which they persecute every
difference of opinion. She then comes to the ignorance, the dirt, the
strange and ludicrous pursuits of the monks, their barbarous and objur-
gatory style of preaching ; she attacks the bishops, who are more solicitous
for gold than for the safety of souls ; who think they do enough if they
dress themselves in theatrical costume, and under the name of the most
reverend, most holy, and most blessed fathers in God, pronounce a blessing
or a curse ; and lastly, she boldly assails the court of Rome and the pope
himself,[1] who, she says, takes only the pleasures of his station, and leaves
its duties to St. Peter and St. Paul. Amongst the curious woodcuts,
after the marginal drawings of Hans Holbein, with which the book was
adorned, the pope appears with his triple crown.

This little work brought together, with singular talent and brevity,
matter which had for some time been current and popular in the world,
gave it a form which satisfied all the demands of taste and criticism, and
fell in with the most decided tendency of the age. It produced an inde-

---

[1] Μωρίας ἐγκώμιον.   Opp. Erasmi, t. iii.   "Quasi sint ulli hostes ecclesiæ
perniciosiores quam impii pontifices, qui et silentio Christum sinunt abolescere
et quæstuariis legibus alligant et coactis interpretationibus adulterant et pesti-
lente vita jugulant."

scribable effect: twenty-seven editions appeared even during the lifetime
of Erasmus ; it was translated into all languages, and greatly contributed
to confirm the age in its anticlerical dispositions.

But Erasmus coupled with this popular warfare a more serious attack
on the state of learning. The study of Greek had arisen in Italy in the
fifteenth century ; it had found its way by the side of that of Latin into
Germany and France, and now opened a new and splendid vista, beyond
the narrow horizon of the ecclesiastical learning of the West. Erasmus
adopted the idea of the Italians,—that the sciences were to be learned
from the ancients ; geography from Strabo, natural history from Pliny,
mythology from Ovid, medicine from Hippocrates, philosophy from
Plato ; and not out of the barbarous and imperfect school-books then in
use : but he went a step further—he required that divinity should be
learned not out of Scotus and Thomas Aquinas, but out of the Greek
fathers, and, above all, the New Testament. Following in the track of
Laurentius Valla, whose example had great influence generally on his mind,
he showed that it was not safe to adhere to the Vulgate, wherein he pointed
out a multitude of errors ;[1] and he then himself set about the great work,—
the publication of the Greek text ; which was as yet imperfectly and
superficially known to the West. Thus he thought, as he expresses it,
to bring back that cold word-contender, Theology, to her primal sources ;
he showed the simplicity of the origin whence that wondrous and com-
plicated pile had sprung, and to which it must return. In all this he had
the sympathy and assent of the public for which he wrote. The prudence
wherewith he concealed from view an abyss in the distance, from which
that public would have shrunk with alarm, doubtless contributed to his
success. While pointing out abuses, he spoke only of reforms and improvements, which he represented as easy ; and was cautious not to offend
against certain opinions or principles to which the faith of the pious clung.[2]
But the main thing was his incomparable literary talent. He worked
incessantly in various branches, and completed his works with great
rapidity ; he had not the patience to revise and polish them, and accordingly most of them were printed exactly as he threw them out ; but this
very circumstance rendered them universally acceptable ; their great
charm was that they communicated the trains of thought which passed
through a rich, acute, witty, intrepid, and cultivated mind, just as they
arose, and without any reservations. Who remarked the many errors
which escaped him ? His manner of narrating, which still rivets the attention, then carried every one away. He gradually became the most
celebrated man in Europe ; public opinion, whose pioneer he had been,
adorned him with her fairest wreaths ; presents rained upon his house
at Basle ; visitors flocked thither, and invitations poured in from all

---

[1] In the edition of Alcala de Henares, on the other hand, the Greek text has
been changed according to the Vulgate ; e.g. 1 Joh. v. 7. Schröckh, KGsch.
xxxiv. 83. As to the rest, this adherence to the Vulgate was regarded at a later
period, and especially when his canonization was talked of, as the chief merit
of Ximenes, " ut hoc modo melius intelligeretur nostra vulgata in suo rigore et
puritate."—*Acta Toletana in Rainaldus*, 1517, nr. 107.

[2] A few years later he thus describes his situation : " Adnixus sum ut bonæ
literæ, quas scis hactenus apud Italos fere paganas fuisse, consuescerent de
Christo loqui." Epistola ad Cretium, 9 Sept., 1526. Opp. III. i., p. 953.

parts.[1] His person was small, with light hair, blue, half-closed eyes, ful of acute observation, and humour playing about the delicate mouth his air was so timorous that he looked as if a breath would overthrow him, and he trembled at the very name of death.[2]

If this single example sufficed to show how much the exclusive theology of the universities had to fear from the new tendency letters had acquired, it was evident that the danger would become measureless if the spirit of innovation should attempt to force its way into these fortresses of the established corporations of learning. The universities, therefore, defended themselves as well as they could. George Zingel, pro-chancellor of Ingolstadt, who had been dean of the theological faculty thirty times in three-and-thirty years, would hear nothing of the introduction of the study of heathen poets.   Of the ancients, he would admit only Prudentius ; of the moderns, the Carmelite Baptista of Mantua : these he thought were enough.   Cologne, which had from the very beginning opposed the introduction of new elementary books,[3] would not allow the adherents of the new opinions to settle in their town : Rhagius was banished for ten years by public proclamation ; Murmellius, a pupil of Hegius, was compelled to give way and to become teacher in a school ; Conrad Celtes of Leipzig was driven away almost by force ; Hermann von dem Busch could not maintain his ground either in Leipzig or Rostock ; his new edition ot Donatus was regarded almost as a heresy.[4]   This was not, however, universal.   According to the constitution of the universities, every man had, at least after taking his degree as Master of Arts, a right to teach, and it was not every one who afforded a reason or a pretext for getting rid of him.[5] In some places, too, the princes had reserved to themselves the right of appointing teachers.   In one way or another, teachers of grammar and of classical literature did, as we find, establish themselves ; in Tübingen, Heinrich Bebel, who formed a numerous school ; in Ingolstadt, Locher, who, after much molestation, succeeded in keeping his ground, and left a brilliant catalogue of princes, prelates, counts, and barons, who had been his pupils ;[6] Conrad Celtes in Vienna, where he actually succeeded in establishing a faculty of poetry in the year 1501 ; and in Prague, Hieronymo Balbi, an Italian, who gave instructions to the young princes, and

---

[1] He afterwards complains of the want of contradiction. "Longe plus attulissent utilitatis duo tresve fidi monitores quam multa laudantium millia Epp. III. i. 924.

[2] Compare this passage with Holbein's well-known portrait, by which it was doubtless inspired.

[3] According to Chyträus (Saxonia, p. 90). Conrad Ritberg, the bishop of Münster, was warned by the university of Cologne against the establishment of a school upon the new method, but he, who had himself been in Italy, was far more strongly worked on by the recommendations which Langen had brought with him thence ; e.g. even from Pope Sixtus.

[4] Hamelmann, Oratio de Buschio, nr. 49.

[5] Erasmi Epistolæ, i., p. 689. In the Epp. Obsc. Vir. ed. Münch, p. 102, a Socius from Moravia is complained of who wanted to lecture at Vienna without having taken a degree.

[6] "Qui nostri portarunt signa theatri."—*Catalogus Illustrium Auditorum Philomusi.* "Doctorum insignium magistrorum nobilium ac canonicorum infinitum pene numerum memorare nequeo, qui ore magnifico laudisonaque voce me præceptorem salutare gestiunt. Hæc citra omnem jactantiam apposuimus."—*Extract in Zapf. Jacob Locher, called Philomusus,* p. 27.

took some share in public affairs.   In Freiburg the new studies were connected with the Roman law ; Ulrich Zasius united the two professorships
in his own person with the most brilliant success ; Pietro Tommai of
Ravenna, and his son Vincenzo, were invited to Greifswald, and afterwards to Wittenberg in the same double capacity :[1] it was hoped that the
combined study of antiquity and law would raise that university.   Erfurt
felt the influence of Conrad Muth, who enjoyed his canonry at Gotha " in
blessed tranquillity " (" *in glückseliger Ruhe* ") as the inscription on his
house says : he was the Gleim of that age—the hospitable patron of
young men of poetical temperament and pursuits.   Thus, from the time
the new spirit and method found their way into the lower schools, societies
of grammarians and poets were gradually formed in most of the universities, completely opposed to the spirit of those establishments as handed
down from their fountain-head, Paris.   They read the ancients, and perhaps allowed something of the petulance of Martial, or the voluptuousness
of Ovid, to find its way into their lives ; they made Latin verses, which,
stiff and barbarous as they generally were, called forth an interchange of
admiration ; they corresponded in Latin, and took care to interlard it
with a few sentences of Greek ; they Latinised and Græcised their names.[2]
Genuine talent or accomplished scholarship were very rare ; but the life
and power of a generation does not manifest itself in mere tastes and
acquirements : for a few individuals these may be enough, but, for the
many the tendency is the important thing.   The character of the universities soon altered.   The scholars were no longer to be seen with their
books under their arms, walking decorously after their Magister ; the
scholarships were broken up, degrees were no longer sought after—that of
bachelor especially (which was unfrequent in Italy) was despised.   On
some occasions the champions of classical studies appeared as the pro-
moters of the disorders of the students ;[3] and ridicule of the dialectic
theologians, nominalists as well as realists, was hailed with delight by the
young men.

The world, and especially the learned world, must be other than it is
for such a change to be effected without a violent struggle.

The manner, however, in which this broke out is remarkable.   It was
not the necessity of warding off a dangerous attack or a declared enemy
that furnished the occasion : this was reserved for the most peaceful of
the converts to the new system, who had already fulfilled the active task
of life, and at that moment devoted himself to more abstruse studies,—
John Reuchlin.

Reuchlin, probably the son of a messenger at Pforzheim, was indebted
to his personal gifts for the success which attended him in his career.   A
fine voice procured him admittance to the court of Baden ; his beautiful
handwriting maintained him during his residence in France ; the pure
pronunciation of Latin which he had acquired by intercourse with

[1] Tiraboschi also mentions them, vi., p. 410.   Their catastrophe at Cologne
s not yet, however, thoroughly cleared up.

[2] Chrachenberger entreats Reuchlin to find some Greek name, " quo honestius
in Latinis literis quam hoc barbaro uti possim."   Lynz, Febr. 19, 1493.

[3] Acta Facultatis Artium Friburgensis in Riegger, Vita Zasii, i. 42.   " Con-
clusum, ut dicatur doctori Zasio, quod scholaribus adhæreat faciendo eos rebelles
in universitatis præjudicium."

foreigners, caused him to be appointed member of an embassy to Rome, and this led to an important post and considerable influence at the court of Würtemberg, and with the Swabian league generally.[1] His qualities, both external and internal, were very unlike those of Erasmus. He was tall and well made, and dignified in all his deportment and actions, while the mildness and serenity of his appearance and manner won instant confidence towards his intellectual superiority.[2] As an author, he could never have gained the applause of the large public of Latin scholars ; his style is not above mediocrity, nor does he evince any nice sense of elegance and form. On the other hand, he was inspired by a thirst for learning, and a zeal for communicating, which were without a parallel. He describes how he picked up his knowledge bit by bit,—crumbs that fell from the lord's table—at Paris and in the Vatican, at Florence, Milan, Basle, and at the Imperial Court ; how, like the bird of Apollonius, he left the corn for the other birds to eat.[3] He facilitated the study of Latin by a dictionary, which in great measure supplanted the old scholastic ones, and of Greek, by a small grammar ; he spared neither labour nor money to get copies of the classics brought across the Alps, either in manuscript, or as they issued from the Italian press. What no prince, no wealthy city or community thought of doing, was done by the son of a poor errand man ; it was under his roof that the most wondrous production of distant ages—the Homeric poems—first came in contact with the mind of Germany, which was destined in later times to render them more intelligible to the world. His Hebrew learning was still more highly esteemed by his contemporaries than all his other acquirements, and he himself regarded his labours in that field as his most peculiar claim to distinction. " There has been none before me," exclaims he with well-grounded self-gratulation, to one of his adversaries, " who has been able to collect the rules of the Hebrew language into a book , though his heart should burst with envy, still I am the first. Exegi monumentum ære perennius."[4] In this work he was chiefly indebted to the Jewish Rabbis whom he sought out in all directions, not suffering one to pass by without learning something from him : by them he was led to study not only the Old Testament, but other Hebrew books, and especially the Cabbala. Reuchlin's mind was not one of those to which the labours of a mere grammarian or lexicographer are sufficient for their own sake. After the fashion of his Jewish teachers, he applied himself to the study of the mystical value of words. In the name of the Deity as written in the Holy Scriptures, in its elementary composition, he discovers the deepest mystery of his being. For, he says, " God, who delights in intercourse with a holy soul, will transform it into himself, and will dwell in it : God is Spirit ; the Word is a breath ; Man breathes ;

---

[1] Schnurrer, Nachrichten von den Lehrern der Hebräischen Literatur, p. 11. A small essay of Michael Coccinius, De Imperii a Græcis ad Germanos Translatione, 1506, is dedicated to Reuchlin, together with his two colleagues in the court of the Swabian league, Streber and Winkelhofer (confœderatorum Suevorum judicibus consistorialibus et triumviris).

[2] Joannis Hiltebrandi Præfatio in Illustrium Virorum Epistolas ad Reuchlinum.

[3] Præfatio ad Rudimenta Linguæ Hebraicæ, lib. iii. *Cf.* Burkhard, de Fatis Linguæ Latinæ, p. 152.

[4] Reuchlini Consilium pro Libris Judæorum non abolendis in v. d. Hardt, Historia Ref., p. 49. This is moreover a fine specimen of German prose.

God is the Word. The names which He has given to Himself are an echo of eternity ; in them is the deep abyss of his mysterious working expressed ; the God-Man called himself the Word."[1] Thus, at its very outset, the study of language in Germany was directed towards its final end and aim— the knowledge of the mysterious connection of language with the Divine— of its identity with the spirit. Reuchlin is like his contemporaries, the discoverers of the New World, who sailed some north, some south, some right on to the west, found portions of coast which they described, and while at the beginning, often thought they had reached the end. Reuchlin was persuaded that he should find in the road he had taken, not only the Aristotelic and Platonic philosophies, which had already been brought to light, but that he should add to them the Pythagorean,—an offspring of Hebraism. He believed that by treading in the footsteps of the Cabbala, he should ascend from symbol to symbol, from form to form, till he should reach that last and purest form which rules the empire of mind, and in which human mutability approaches to the Immutable and Divine.[2]

But while living in this world of ideas and abstractions, it was his lot to be singled out by the enmity of the scholastic party : he unexpectedly found himself involved in the heat of a violent controversy.

We have already alluded to the inquisitorial attempts of the Dominicans of Cologne, and their hostility to the Jews. In the year 1508, a book was published by an old Rabbi, who at the age of fifty had abandoned his wife and child, and become a Christian priest. In this he accused his former co-religionists of the grossest errors ; for example, adoration of the sun and moon ; but, above all, of the most horrible blasphemies against the Christian faith, which he endeavoured to prove from the Talmud.[3] It was mainly on this ground that the theologians of Cologne urged the emperor to order the publication of the Talmud, and gave him, at his request, the opinion in which they affirmed his right to proceed against the Jews as heretics. The Imperial Council, however, deemed it expedient to consult another master of Hebrew literature. They referred the matter to the reviver of the cabbalistic philosophy—Reuchlin.

Reuchlin gave his opinion, as might be expected, in favour of the Judaical books. His report is a beautiful monument of pure dispassionate judgment and consummate sagacity. But these qualities were just those fitted to draw down the whole storm of fanatical rage upon himself.

The Cologne theologians, irritated to fury by the rejection of their proposition, which they ascribed, not without reason, to the adverse opinion of Reuchlin, incited one of their satellites to attack him ; he answered ; they condemned his answer ; he rejoined, upon which they appointed a court of inquisition to try him.

This was the first serious encounter of the two parties. The Dominicans hoped to establish their tottering credit by a great stroke of authority, and to intimidate the adversaries who threatened to become dangerous to them, by the terrors which were at their disposal. The innovators—the teachers and disciples of the schools of poetry whom we have mentioned—were fully sensible that Reuchlin's peril was their own ; but their efforts and

---

[1] Reuchlin de Verbo Mirifico, ii. 6, 15 ; iii. 3, 19.

[2] Reuchlin de Arte Cabbalistica, p. 614, 620, 696.

[3] Notices of this little Jewish book in Riederer's *Nachrichten*, I. i., p. 34. It appeared in Latin in 1509, as an " opus aureum ac novum."

aspirations were checked by the consciousness of opposition to existing authority, and of the dubious position which they occupied.

In October, 1513, a court of inquisition was formed at Mainz, composed of the doctors of the university and the officers of the archbishopric, under the presidency of the inquisitor of heretical wickedness—Jacob Hogstraten ; and it remained to be seen whether such a sentence as that pronounced some years before against John of Wesalia, would now be given.

But times were totally altered. That intensely Catholic spirit which had rendered it so easy for the Inquisition to take root in Spain, was very far from reigning in Germany. The Imperial Council must have been, from the outset, indisposed towards the demands of the Cologne divines, or they would not have appealed to such a man as Reuchlin for advice. The infection of the prevalent spirit of literature had already spread too widely, and had created a sort of public opinion. We have a whole list of members of the higher clergy who are cited as friends of the literary innovation—Gross and Wrisberg, canons of Augsburg, Nuenar of Cologne, Adelmann of Eichstadt, Andreas Fuchs dean of Bamberg, Lorenzo Truchsess of Mainz, Wolfgang Tanberg of Passau, Jacob de Bannissis of Trent. Cardinal Lang, the most influential of the emperor's councillors, shared these opinions. The superior clergy were not more disposed than the people to allow the Inquisition to regain its power.

Elector Diether had consented to the trial of Wesalia, against his will, and only because he feared the puissant Dominicans might a second time effect his deposition ;[1] now, however, the heads of the church were no longer so timorous, and after the tribunal had already taken its seat to pronounce judgment, Dean Lorenz Truchsess persuaded the Elector to command it to suspend its proceedings, and to forbid his own officers to take part in them.[2]

Nay, another tribunal, favourable to Reuchlin, was appointed to hold its sittings under the Bishop of Spires, in virtue of a commission obtained from Rome ; the sentence pronounced by this court on the 24th April, 1514, was, that the accusers of Reuchlin, having falsely calumniated him, were condemned to eternal silence and to the payment of the costs.[3]

So widely diffused and so powerful was the antipathy which the Dominicans had excited. So lively was the sympathy which the higher and educated classes testified in the efforts of the new school of literature. So powerful already was the opinion of men of learning. It was their first victory.

Persecuting orthodoxy found no favour either with the emperor or with the higher clergy of Germany. But its advocates did not give up the contest. At Cologne, Reuchlin's books were condemned to be burnt : unanimous sentences to the same effect were obtained from the faculties of Erfurt, Mainz, Louvain, and Paris ; thus fortified, they applied to the supreme tribunal at Rome ; the representatives of orthodox theology presented themselves before the pope, and urged him to give his infallible

---

[1] " Cogentibus Thomistis quibusdam, veritus ne denuo ab episcopatu ejiceretur jussu Romano pontificis."—*Examen Wesaliæ*, fasc. i. 327.

[2] Hutten's Preface to Livy, Opp. III., p. 334 ed. Münch proves the share of Lorenz Truchsess " quodam suo divino consilio."

[3] Acta judiciorum in v. d. Hardt, Hist. Lit. Reformationis, 114. The chief source of information respecting these events.

decision in aid of the ancient champions of the Holy See against innovators.

But even Rome was perplexed. Should she offend public opinion
represented by men so influential from their talents and learning ? Should
she act in opposition to her own opinions ? On the other hand, would it
be safe to set at nought the judgment of powerful universities ? to break
with the order which had so zealously contended for the prerogatives of
the Roman see, and had preached the doctrine and furthered the sale of
indulgences all over the world ?[1]

In the commission appointed by the pope at Rome, the majority was for
Reuchlin, but a considerable minority was against him, and the pope held
it expedient to defer his decision. He issued a *mandatum de supersedendo.*[2]

Reuchlin, conscious of a just cause, was not perfectly satisfied with this
result, especially after all that had gone before : he expected a formal and
complete acquittal ; nevertheless, even this was to be regarded as little
less than a victory. The fact that the party which assumed to represent
religion and to have exclusive possession of the true doctrines, had failed
to carry through their inquisitorial designs, and even, as secret reports
said, had only escaped a sentence of condemnation by means of gold and
favour,[3] was enough to encourage all their adversaries. Hitherto the latter
had only stood on the defensive ; they now assumed an attitude of open,
direct offence. Reuchlin's correspondence, which was published expressly to show the respect and admiration he enjoyed, shows how numerously and zealously they rallied round him. We find the spiritual lords we
have mentioned ; patricians of the most important cities, such as Pirkheimer of Nürnberg, who delighted in being considered as the leader of a
numerous band of Reuchlinists ; Peutinger of Augsburg, Stuss of Cologne ;
preachers like Capito and Œcolampadius ; the Austrian historians, Lazius
and Cuspinian ; doctors of medicine—all, in short, who had any tincture
of letters ; but chiefly those poets and orators in the schools and universities who beheld their own cause in that of Reuchlin, and now rushed in
throngs to the newly-opened arena ; at their head Busch, Jäger, Hess,
Hutten, and a long list of eminent names.[4]

The remarkable production in which the whole character and drift of
their labours is summed up, is, the Epistolæ Obscurorum Virorum. That
popular satire, already so rife in Germany, but hitherto confined to generals,
here found a particular subject exactly suited to it. We must not look for
the delicate apprehension and tact which can only be formed in a highly
polished state of society, nor for the indignation of insulted morality expressed by the ancients : it is altogether caricature,—not of finished
individual portraits, but of a single type ;—a clownish, sensual German
priest, his intellect narrowed by stupid wonder and fanatical hatred, who
relates with silly *naïveté* and gossiping confidence the various absurd and

[1] Erasmus ad Vergaram, Opp. III. ; 1015. " Quis enim magis timet monachos
quam Romani pontifices ?"

[2] Reuchlin de Arte Cabbalistica, p. 730. Acta Judiciorum, p. 130.

[3] In Hogstratus Ovans, 336, it is said, through the intercession of Nicolaus
von Schomberg.

[4] Even before the letters to Reuchlin, we find set down the Exercitus Reuchli-
nistarum. Pirkheimer, Epistola Apologetica, in Hardt, p. 136, has another list.
Later lists, *e.g.* in Mayerhoff, must, in several cases, be taken with restrictions.

scandalous situations into which he falls.   These letters are not the work
of a high poetical genius, but they have truth, coarse strong features of
resemblance, and vivid colouring.   As they originated in a widely-diffused
and powerful tendency of the public mind, they produced an immense
effect : the See of Rome deemed it necessary to prohibit them.

It may be affirmed generally that the genius of the literary opposition
was triumphant.   In the year 1518, Erasmus looked joyfully around him ;
his disciples and adherents had risen to eminence in every university—
even in Leipsig, which had so long resisted : they were all teachers of
ancient literature.[1]

Was it indeed possible that the great men of antiquity should have
lived in vain ?   That their works, produced in the youth-time of the human
race,—works with whose beauty and profound wisdom nothing that has
since arisen is to be compared, should not be restored to later ages in their
primitive form and perfection ?   It is an event of the greatest historical
importance, that after so many convulsions by which nations were overthrown and others constituted out of their ruins,—by which the old world
had been obliterated and all its elements replaced by other matter,—the
relics of its spirit, which could now exercise no other influence than that
of form, were sought with an avidity hitherto unknown, and widely
diffused, studied, and imitated.

The study of antiquity was implanted in Germany as early as the first
introduction of Christianity ; in the 10th and 11th centuries it had risen
to a considerable height, but at a later period it was stifled by the despotism of the hierarchy and the schools.   The latter now returned to their
original vocation.   It was not to be expected, that great works of literary
art could as yet be produced ; for that, circumstances were not ripe.
The first effect of the new studies showed itself in the nature and modes
of instruction—the more natural and rational training of the youthful
mind which has continued to be the basis of German erudition.   The
hierarchical system of opinions which, though it had been wrought up
to a high point of brilliancy and refinement, could not possibly endure,
was thus completely broken up.   A new life stirred in every department
of human intelligence.   " What an age ! " exclaims Hutten, " learning
flourishes, the minds of men awake ; it is a joy to be alive."   This was
peculiarly conspicuous in the domain of theology.   The highest ecclesiastic
of the nation, Archbishop Albert of Mainz, saluted Erasmus as the restorer
of theology.

But an intellectual movement of a totally different kind was now
about to take place.

EARLY CAREER OF LUTHER.

The authorities, or the opinions which rule the world, rarely encounter
their most dangerous enemies from without ; the hostilities by which they
are overthrown are usually generated and nurtured within their own sphere.

[1] In the Essay De Ratione conscribendi Epistolas, the dedication of which
belongs to the year 1522, he exclaims (ed. of 1534, p. 71.), " Videmus quantum
profectum sit paucis annis.   Ubi nunc est Michael Modista, ubi glossema Jacobi,
ubi citatur Catholicon brachylogus aut Mammætrectus, quos olim ceu rarum
thesaurum aureis literis descriptos habebant monachorum bibliothecæ."   It is
evident how much the method had changed.

In the bosom of theological philosophy itself, discords arose from which a new era in the history of life and thought may be dated.

We must not omit to notice the fact, that the doctrines of Wickliffe, which had spread from Oxford over the whole of Latin Christendom, and broke out with such menacing demonstrations in Bohemia, had not, in spite of all the barbarities of the Hussite wars, been extirpated in Germany. At a much later period we find traces of them in Bavaria, where the Böklerbund drew upon itself the suspicions of Hussite opinions ; in Swabia and Franconia, where the council of Bamberg at one time thought it necessary to compel all the men in that city to abjure the Hussites ; and even in Prussia, where the adherents of Wickliffite and Hussite doctrines at length submitted, though only in appearance.[1]   It was the more remarkable that after such measures, the society of the Bohemian brethren arose out of the fierce tempest of Hussite opinions and parties, and once more exhibited to the world a Christian community in all the purity and simplicity of the primitive church.   Their religion derived a new and singular character from the fundamental principle of their secession—that Christ himself was the rock on which the church was founded, and not Peter and his successors.[2]   Their settlements were in those districts where the Germanic and Slavonic elements are intermingled, and their emissaries went forth and traversed unnoticed the wide domain of either language, seeking those already allied to them in opinion, or endeavouring to gain over new proselytes.   Nicholas Kuss of Rostock, whom they visited several times, began at this time to preach openly against the pope (A.D. 1511.).[3]

The opposition to the despotism of the Dominican system still subsisted in the universities themselves.   Nominalism, connected at the very moment of its revival with the adversaries of the papacy, had found great acceptance in Germany, and was still by no means suppressed.   The most celebrated nominalist of that time, Gabriel Biel, the collector, is mainly an epitomizer of Occam.   This party was in the minority, and often exposed to the persecutions of its enemies who wielded the powers of the Inquisition ;[4] but it only struck deeper and firmer root.   Luther and Melanchthon are the offspring of nominalism.

And perhaps a still more important circumstance was, that in the 15th century the stricter Augustinian doctrines were revived in the persons of some theologians.

Johann de Wesalia taught election by grace ; he speaks of the Book in which the names of the elect are written from the beginning.   The tendency of his opinions is shown by the definition of the Sacrament which he opposes to that given by Peter Lombard : the former is that of St. Augustine in its original purity, while the latter is an extension of it ; the

---

[1] Zschokke, Baier. Gesch. ii., 429. Pfister, Gesch. von Schwaben, v. 378. Baczko, Gesch. von Preussen, i. 256.

[2] What it was which appeared dangerous in their doctrines is shown particularly in the Refutations of the Dominican Heinrich Institoris, from which Rainaldus (1498, nr. 25) gives copious extracts.

[3] Wolfii Lectiones memorabiles, ii. 27.

[4] In the Examen Magistrale Dris Joh. de Wesalia, the Concipient describes these disputes at the conclusion : " adeo ut si universalia quisquam realia negaverit, existimetur in spiritum sanctum peccavisse, immo—contra deum, contra Christianam religionem,—deliquisse."

general aim of his works is, the removal of the additions made in later times to the primitive doctrines of the church.[1] He denies the binding force of priestly rules, and the efficacy of indulgences ; he is filled with the idea of the invisible church.   He was a man of great intellectual powers, capable of playing a distinguished part at a university like that of Erfurt : he arrived at these convictions by degrees, and when convinced did not conceal them even in the pulpit ; nor did he shrink from a connexion with Bohemian emissaries.   At length, however, when advanced in age, he was dragged, leaning on his staff, before the Inquisition, and thrown into prison, where he died.

Johann Pupper of Goch, who founded a convent of nuns of the rule of St. Augustine at Mechlin about the year 1460–70, made himself remarkable by accusing the dominant party in the church of a leaning to Pelagianism.[2] He calls Thomas Aquinas the prince of error.   He attacked the devotion to ceremonies, and the Pharisaism of vows, upon Augustinian principles.

How often have the antagonists of the church of Rome made this the ground of their opposition !—from Claudius of Turin in the beginning of the ninth, to Bishop Janse[3] in the seventeenth century, and his followers in the 18th and 19th.   The deeper minds within her pale have always felt compelled to point back to those fundamental doctrines on which she was originally based.

The principles of the opposition now assumed the form of a scientific structure.   In the works of Johann Wessel, of Gröningen, we see a manly mind devoted to truth, working itself free from the bonds of the mighty tradition which could no longer satisfy a religious conscience.   Wessel lays down the maxim that prelates and doctors are to be believed only so far as their doctrines are in conformity with the Scriptures, the sole rule of faith, which is far above pope or church ;[4] he writes almost in the spirit of a theologian of later times.   It was perfectly intelligible that he was not permitted to set foot in the university of Heidelberg.

Nor were these efforts completely isolated.

At the time of the council of Basle, the German provincial society of the Augustin Eremites had formed themselves into a separate congregation, and had from that moment made it their chief endeavour to uphold the more rigorous doctrines of the patron of their order.   This was peculiarly the aim of the resolute and undaunted Andreas Proles, who for nearly half a century administered the Vicariate of that province.[5]   Another and a congenial tendency came in aid of this in the beginning of the 16th century.   The despotism of the schools had been constantly opposed by all those who were inclined to mystical contemplation : the sermons of Tauler, which had several times issued from the press, became extremely

[1] Joh. de Wesalia, Disputatio adversus indulgentias in Walch, Monimenta Medii Ævi, tom. i. fasc. i., p. 131.

[2] Dialogus de Quatuor Erroribus circa Legem Evangelicam in Walch, Monim. I. iv., p. 181.   " Hæc fuit insania Pelagii hæretici, a qua error Thomistarum non solum in hoc loco sed etiam in multis aliis non multum degenerare videtur." What impression this made, we perceive from Pantaleon's description.

[3] Bishop Janse : Bishop of Ypres, 1585—1638, and founder of the Jansenists, a sect which was finally condemned by the Bull Unigenitus in 1713.   *Cf.* article in Encyclopædia Britannica.

[4] Ullmann, Johann Wessel, p. 303.

[5] Joh. Pelz, Supplementum Aurifodinæ, 1504, in Kapp, Nachlese, iv., p. 460.

popular from their mild earnestness, their depth of thought and reason, and the tone of sincerity so satisfactory to the German mind and heart. The Book of German Theology, which appeared at that time, may be regarded as an offspring of Tauler's teaching. It chiefly insisted on the inability of the creature, of himself to comprehend the Infinite and the Perfect, to attain to inward peace, or to give himself up to that Eternal Good, which descends upon him of its own free motion. Johann Staupitz, the successor of Proles, adopted these ideas, and laboured to develop and to diffuse them.[1] If we examine his views of the subject,—as for example, the manner in which he treats of the love "which a man can neither learn of himself nor from others, nor even from the Holy Scriptures,— which he can only possess through the indwelling of the Holy Spirit,"— we are struck with their perfect connexion and accordance with the stricter ideas of grace, faith, and free-will; a connexion, indeed, without which these doctrines would not have been intelligible to the age. We must not assume that all Augustine convents, or even all the members of the one in question, were converted to these opinions; but it is certain that they first struck root among this order, whence they spread abroad and tended to foster the resistance to the prevailing doctrines of the schools.

It is manifest that all these agitations of opinion, from whatever source they proceeded, were allies of the literary opposition to the tyranny of the Dominican system. The fact that these various but converging tendencies at length found representatives within the circle of one university, must be regarded as in itself an important event for the whole nation.

In the year 1502, Elector Frederick of Saxony founded a new university at Wittenberg. He accomplished this object chiefly by obtaining the pope's consent to incorporate a number of parishes with the richly endowed church attached to the palace, and transforming the whole into a foundation, the revenues of which he then allotted to the new professors. The same course had been pursued in Treves and in Tübingen; the clerical dignities of the institution were connected with the offices in the university. The provost, dean, scholaster, and syndic formed the faculty of law; the archdeacon, cantor, and warden, that of theology; the lectures on philosophy and the exercises of the candidates for the degree of master of arts were attached to five canonries. The eminent Augustine convent in the town was to take part in the work.[2]

We must recollect that the universities were then regarded not only as establishments for education, but as supreme tribunals for the decision of scientific questions. In the charter of Wittenberg, Frederick declares[3] that he, as well as all the neighbouring states, would repair thither as to an oracle; "so that," says he, "when we have come full of doubt, we may, after receiving the sentence, depart in certainty."

Two men, both unquestionably belonging to the party hostile to the reigning theologico-philosophical system, had the greatest influence on

[1] Grimm de Joanne Staupitzio ejusque in sacrorum Christianorum restaurationem meritis, in Illgen Zeitschrift für die Hist. Theologie, N. F. i. ii. 78.

[2] The papal privilege in Grohmann, Geschichte der Universität Wittenberg, *cf.* p. 110.

[3] Confirmatio ducis Frederici, ib., p. 19.

the foundation and first organisation of this university. The one was Dr. Martin Pollich of Melrichstadt, physician to the elector, whose name stands at the head of the list of the rectors of the Leipzig university, where he was previously established. We know that he had contended against the fantastic exaggerations of scholastic learning, and the strange assertions to which they gave birth ; such as that the light created on the first day was theology ; that discursive theology was inherent in the angels. We know that he had already perceived the necessity of grounding that science on a study of letters generally.[1]

The other was Johann Staupitz, the mystical cast of whose opinions, borrowed from St. Augustine, we have just mentioned ; he was the first dean of the theological faculty, the first act of which was, the promotion of Martin Pollich to be doctor of theology :[2] as director of the Augustine convent, he likewise enjoyed peculiar influence. It was not an insignificant circumstance that the university had just then declared St. Augustine its patron. Notwithstanding his strong tendency to speculation, Staupitz was obviously an excellent man of business ; he conducted himself with address at court, and a homely vein of wit which he possessed, enabled him to make his part good with the prince ; he undertook an embassy, and conducted the negotiation with success ; but the deeper spring of all his conduct and actions is clearly a genuine feeling of true and heartfelt religion, and an expansive benevolence.

It is easy to imagine in what spirit these men laboured at the university. But a new star soon arose upon it. In the year 1508, Staupitz conducted thither the young Luther.

We must pause a moment to consider the early years of this remarkable man.

" I am a peasant's son," says he ; " my father, grandfather, and ancestors were genuine peasants ; afterwards, my father removed to Mansfeld, and became a miner ; that is my native place."[3] Luther's family was from Möhra, a village on the very summit of the Thuringian forest, not far from the spot celebrated for the first preaching of Christianity by Boniface ; it is probable that Luther's forefathers had for centuries been settled on their hide of land (*Hufe*) as was the custom with those Thuringian peasants, one brother among whom always inherited the estate, while the others sought a subsistence in other ways. Condemned by such a destiny to seek a home and hearth for himself, Hans Luther was led to the mines at Mansfeld, where he earned his bread by the sweat of his brow, while his wife, Margaret, often fetched wood from the forest on her back. Such were the parents of Martin Luther. He was born at Eisleben, whither his sturdy mother had walked to the yearly fair ; he grew up in the mountain air of Mansfeld.

The habits and manners of that time were generally harsh and rude, and so was his education. Luther relates that his mother once scourged him till the blood came, on account of one miserable nut ; that his father

[1] Löscher, in the unoffending accounts of 1716, and in the Acts of the Reformation, i. 88., has given extracts from his writings. In his epitaph in the parish church at Wittenberg, he is rightly called hujus gymnasii primus rector *et parens*.

[2] Liber decanorum facultatis theologorum Vitebergensis, ed. Foerstemann, p. 2.

Tischreden, p. 581.

had punished him so severely that it was with great difficulty that he could get over the child's terror and alienation ; at school he was flogged fifteen times in one forenoon.   He had to earn his bread by singing hymns before the doors of houses, and new year's carols in the villages.   Strange— that people should continually exalt and envy the happiness of childhood, in which the only certain foretaste of coming years is the feeling of the stern necessities of life ; in which existence is dependent on foreign help, and the will of another disposes of every day and hour with iron sway. In Luther's case, this period of life was full of terrors.

From his fifteenth year his condition was somewhat better.   In Eisenach, where he was sent to the high school, he found a home in the house of some relations of his mother ; thence he went to the university of Erfurt, where his father, whose industry, frugality and success had placed him in easier circumstances, made him a liberal allowance :[1] his hope was, that his son would be a lawyer, marry well and do him honour.

But in this weary life the restraints of childhood are soon succeeded by troubles and perplexities.   The spirit feels itself freed from the bonds of the school, and is not yet distracted by the wants and cares of daily life ; it boldly turns to the highest problems, such as the relation of man to God, and of God to the world, and while eagerly rushing on to the solution of them, it falls into the most distressing state of doubt.   We might be almost tempted to think that the Eternal Source of all life appeared to the youthful Luther only in the light of the inexorable judge and avenger, who punishes sin (of which Luther had from nature an awful and vivid feeling) with the torments of hell, and can only be propitiated by penance, mortification and painful service.   As he was returning from his father's house in Mansfeld to Erfurt, in the month of July, 1505, he was overtaken in a field near Stotternheim by one of those fearful tempests which slowly gather on the mountains and at length suddenly burst over the whole horizon.   Luther was already depressed by the unexpected death of an intimate friend.   There are moments in which the agitated desponding heart is completely crushed by one overwhelming incident, even of the natural world.   Luther, traversing his solitary path, saw in the tempest the God of wrath and vengeance ; the lightning struck some object near him ; in his terror he made a vow to St. Anne, that if he escaped, he would enter a convent.   He passed one more evening with his friends, enjoying the pleasures of wine, music, and song ; it was the last in which he indulged himself ; he hastened to fulfil his vow, and entered the Augustine Convent[2] at Erfurt.

But he was little likely to find serenity there ; imprisoned, in all the buoyant energy of youth, within the narrow gates and in the low and gloomy cell, with no prospect but a few feet of garden within the cloisters, and condemned to perform the lowest offices.   At first he devoted himself to the duties of a novice with all the ardour of a determined will.   " If ever a monk got to heaven by monkish life and practices (*durch Möncherei*),

---

[1] Luther's Erklärung der Genesis, c. 49, v. 15.   Attenb., tom. ix., p. 1525.

[2] The Augustinians (Austen Friars or Eremites) were not strictly monks but one of the four orders of Friars founded in the thirteenth century.   The others are—Dominicans or Black Friars, Franciscans or Grey Friars, Carmelites or White Friars.

I resolved that I would enter there," were his words.[1] But though he conformed to the hard duty of obedience, he was soon a prey to the most painful disquiet. Sometimes he studied day and night, to the neglect of his canonical hours, which he then passed his nights in retrieving with penitent zeal. Sometimes he went out into some neighbouring village, carrying with him his mid-day repast, preached to the shepherds and ploughmen, and then refreshed himself with their rustic music ; after which he went home, and shutting himself up for days in his cell, would see no one. All his former doubts and secret perplexities returned from time to time with redoubled force.

In the course of his study of the Scriptures, he fell upon texts which struck terror into his soul ; one of these was, " Save me in thy righteousness and thy truth." " I thought," said he, " that righteousness was the fierce wrath of God, wherewith he punishes sinners." Certain passages in the Epistles of St. Paul haunted him for days. The doctrine of grace was not indeed unknown to him, but the dogma that sin was at once taken away by it, produced upon him, who was but too conscious of his sins, rather a sense of rejection—a feeling of deep depression, than of hope. He says it made his heart bleed—it made him despair of God.[2] " Oh, my sins, my sins, my sins !" he writes to Staupitz, who was not a little astonished when he received the confession of so sorrowful a penitent, and found that he had no sinful acts to acknowledge. His anguish was the longing of the creature after the purity of the Creator, to whom it feels itself profoundly and intimately allied, yet from whom it is severed by an immeasurable gulph : a feeling which Luther nourished by incessant solitary brooding, and which had taken the more painful and complete possession of him because no penance had power to appease it ; no doctrine truly touched it, no confessor would hear of it. There were moments when this anxious melancholy arose with fearful might from the mysterious abysses of his soul, waved its dusky pinions over his head, and felled him to the earth. On one occasion when he had been invisible for several days, some friends broke into his cell and found him lying senseless on the ground. They knew their friend ; with tender precaution they struck some chords on a stringed instrument they had brought with them ; the inward strife of the perplexed spirit was allayed by the well-known remedy ; it was restored to harmony and awakened to healthful consciousness.

But the eternal laws of the universe seem to require that so deep and earnest a longing of the soul after God should at length be appeased with the fulness of conviction.

The first who, if he could not administer comfort to Luther in his desperate condition, at least, let fall a ray of light upon his thick darkness, was an old Augustine friar who with fatherly admonitions pointed his attention to the first and simplest truth of Christianity,—the forgiveness of sins through faith in the Redeemer ; and to the assertion of St. Paul (Rom. iii.), that man is justified without works, by faith alone :[3] doctrines

---

[1] Short answer to Duke George. Altenburg. t. vi., p. 22. Exposition of the eighth chapter of John, v. 770.

[2] He relates this in the Sermo die S. Joh. 1516, in Löscher, Reformations Acta, i., p. 258.

[3] Short notice by Melancthon on the Life of Luther. Works. Attenb. viii. 876. See Matthesius, Historien Dr. Luthers. First Sermon, p. 12. Bavarus in Seckendorf, Hist. Lutheranismi, p. 21.

which he might indeed have heard before, but obscured as they were by school subtleties, and a ceremonial worship, he had never rightly understood. They now first made a full and profound impression on him. He meditated especially on the saying " The just shall live by faith." He read St. Augustine's commentary on this passage. " Then was I glad," says he, " for I learned and saw that God's righteousness is his mercy, by which he accounts and holds us justified ; thus I reconciled justice with justification, and felt assured that I was in the true faith." This was exactly the conviction of which his mind stood in need : it was manifest to him that the same eternal grace whence the whole race of man is sprung, mercifully brings back erring souls to itself and enlightens them with the fulness of its own light ; that an example and irrefragable assurance of this is given us in the person of Christ : he gradually emerged from the gloomy idea of a divine justice only to be propitiated by the rigours of penance. He was like a man who after long wanderings has at length found the right path, and feeling more certain of it at every step, walks boldly and hopefully onward.

Such was Luther's state when he was removed to Wittenberg by his provincial (A.D. 1508). The philosophical lectures which he was obliged to deliver, sharpened his desire to penetrate the mysteries of theology, " the kernel of the nut," as he calls it, " the heart of the wheat." The books, which he studied were St. Paul's Epistles, St. Augustine against the Pelagians, and, lastly, Tauler's sermons : he troubled himself little with literature foreign to this subject ; he cared only to strengthen and work out the convictions he had gained.[1]

A few years later we find him in the most extraordinary frame of mind,

---

[1] In the " Histori, so zwen Augustinerordens gemartert seyn zu Bruxel in Probandt,"—" History, how two monks of the order of St. Augustine underwent martyrdom at Brussels in Brabant,"—there is in sheet B the following excellent and authentic passage upon Luther's studies. " In welchen Verstand (dass er die Schrift so klar und guadenreich erkläre) er kummen ist erst durch maniche Staupen dye er erlitten hat von Got, und mit vleissigen Bitten zu Got, steten Lesen, und nemlich Augustinus wider die Pelagianer hat ym grosse hilff gethan tzur erkenndnuss Pauli yn seyn Episteln. Sunderlich ein Predigbüchlin der Tawler genanndt yhm deutschen das hat er uns oft zu erkauffen ermant unter seym lesen yn der Schul, welches yn gefurt hat yn geist, els er offt uns bekannt : auch ist eyn Büchlyn genandt die deutsch Theologen, hat Er allzeyt hochgebrifft, als er den schreibtt yn der Vorrede gedachten Büchlyns.—Hat auch oft gesagt, das seyn Kunst mer yhm geben sey auserfaren denn lesen, und das vyll Bücher nit gelert machen. Darumb findt man (Später, 1523) yhn seiner Wonung nit vyll Bücher, den eyn Bibel und Concordanz der Bybel."—" To what understanding (enabling him to explain the Scriptures with such clearness and grace) he has arrived, first by manifold chastisements which he has suffered from God, and through diligent prayer to God, and constant reading ; and for instance, Augustine against the Pelagians has been of great help to him towards the comprehension of Paul in his Epistles. Especially a little book of sermons by Tauler, he has often admonished us to buy, in the middle of his teaching in the school, as what has guided him in spirit, as he has often acknowledged to us ; there is also a little book called the German Theology, which he has at all times highly praised, as he writes in the preface to the said little book. He has also often said, that his skill was given him more by experience than reading, and that many books do not make a man learned. Therefore many books are not to be found (this is later, in 1523) in his dwelling ; but one Bible and a Concordance of the Bible."

during a journey which he took for the affairs of his order to Rome.   As soon as he descried the towers of the city from a distance, he threw himself on the ground, raised his hands and exclaimed, " Hail to thee, O holy Rome !"   On his arrival, there was no exercise in use among the most pious pilgrims which he did not perform with earnest and deliberate devotion, undeterred by the levity of other priests ; he said he was almost tempted to wish that his parents were dead, that so he might have been able certainly to deliver them from the fire of purgatory by these privileged observances.[1]   Yet, at the same time, he felt how little such practices were in accordance with the consolatory doctrine which he had found in the Epistle to the Romans and in St. Augustine.   While climbing the Scala Santa on his knees in order to obtain the plenary indulgence attached to that painful and laborious work of piety, he heard a reproving voice continually crying within him, " The just shall live by faith."[2]

After his return in 1512, he became Doctor of the Holy Scripture, and from year to year enlarged his sphere of activity.   He lectured at the university on both the Old and New Testament ; he preached at the Augustine church, and performed the duties of the priest of the parochial church of the town during his illness ; in 1516, Staupitz appointed him administrator of the order during his absence on a journey, and we trace him visiting all the monasteries in the province, appointing or displacing priors, receiving or removing monks.   While labouring to introduce a profounder spirit of piety, he did not overlook the smallest economical details ; and besides all this, he had to manage his own crowded and extremely poor convent.   Some things, written in the years 1515 and 1516, enable us to understand the state and workings of his mind during that period.   Mystical and scholastic ideas had still great influence over him. In the first words of his on religious subjects in the German language which we possess,—a sketch of a sermon dated November, 1515,—he applies, in somewhat coarse terms, the symbolical language of the Song of Songs to the operations of the Holy Ghost, which acts on the spirit through the flesh ; and also to the inward harmony of the Holy Scriptures. In another, dated December of the same year, he endeavours to explain the mystery of the Trinity by the Aristotelic theory of being, motion, and rest.[3]   Meanwhile his thoughts were already turned to a grand and general reform of the church.   In a speech which appears to have been intended to be uttered by the provost of Lietzkau at the Lateran council, he sets forth that the corruption of the world was to be ascribed to the priests, who delivered to the people too many maxims and fables of human invention, and not the pure word of God.   For, he said, the word of life alone is able to work out the regeneration of man.   It is well worthy of remark, that, even then, Luther looked for the salvation of the world far less to an amendment of life, which was only secondary in his eyes, than to a revival of the true doctrines : and there was none with the importance of which he was so penetrated and filled as with that of justification by faith.   He continually insists on the absolute necessity of a man denying himself, and fleeing for refuge under the wings of Christ ; he seizes every

---

[1] Exposition of the 117th Psalm to Hans von Sternberg.   Luther's Werke, Altenb. v. 251.
[2] Story told by Luther in the Table Talk, p. 609.
   Sermo Lutheri in Nativitate Christi, 1515.

opportunity of repeating the saying of St. Augustine, that faith obtains what the law enjoins.[1]   We see that Luther was not yet completely at one with himself ; that he still cherished opinions fundamentally at variance with each other ; but all his writings breathe a powerful mind, a youthful courage, still restrained within the bounds of modesty and reverence for authority, though ready to overleap them ; a genius intent on essentials, tearing asunder the bonds of system, and pressing forward in the new path it has discovered.   In the year 1516, we find Luther busily occupied in defending and establishing his doctrine of justification.[2]   He was greatly encouraged by the discovery of the spuriousness of a book attributed to Augustine, on which the schoolmen had founded many doctrines extremely offensive to him, and which was quoted almost entire in Lombard's book, " De vera et falsa Penitentia ;" and he now took heart to attack the doctrine of the Scotists on love, and that of the Magister Sententiarum on hope ; he was already convinced that there was no such thing as a work in and for itself pleasing to God—such as prayer, fasts and vigils ; for as their whole efficacy depended on their being done in the fear of God, it followed that every other act or occupation was just as good in itself.

In opposition to some expressions of German theologians which appeared to him of a Pelagian tendency, he embraced with uncompromising firmness even the severer views of Augustine : one of his disciples held a solemn disputation in defence of the doctrine of the subjection of the will, and of the inability of man to fit himself for grace, much more to obtain it, by his own powers.[3]

If it be asked wherein he discovered the mediating power between divine perfection and human sinfulness, we find that it was solely in the mystery of the redemption, and the revealed word ; mercy on the one side, and faith on the other.   These opinions led him to doubt of many of the main dogmas of the church.   He did not yet deny the efficacy of absolution ; but no later than the year 1516, he was perplexed by the doubt how man could obtain grace by such means : the desire of the soul was not appeased by it, nor was love infused ; those effects could only be produced by the enlightenment of the mind, and the kindling of the will by the immediate operation of the Eternal Spirit ; for, he added, he could conceive of religion only as residing in the inmost depth of the heart.[4] He doubted whether all those outward succours for which it was usual to invoke the saints, ought to be ascribed to them.

Such were the doctrines, such the great general direction of mind immediately connected with the opinions implanted by Pollich and Staupitz, which Luther disseminated among the Augustine friars of his convent and his province, and, above all, among the members of the university. For a time Jodocus Trutvetter of Eisenach sustained the established opinions ; but after his death in the year 1513, Luther was the master spirit that ruled the schools.   His colleagues, Peter Lupinus and Andreas Carlstadt, who for a time withstood his influence, at length declared

[1] Fides impetrat quæ lex imperat.
[2] From the Sermo de propria Sapientia, it appears that he had already been attacked on this point.   " Efficitur mihi et errans et falsum dictum."
[3] Quæstio de viribus et voluntate hominis sine gratia, in Löscher, i. 328.
[4] Sermo x^{ma} post Trinitatis.   He still says himself occasionally, " Ego non satis intelligo hanc rem ; manet dubium," &c.—*Löscher*, p. 761.

themselves overcome and convinced by the arguments of Augustine and
the doctrines of the Holy Scripture which had made so deep an impression
on him ; they were almost more zealous than Luther himself.   A totally
different direction was thus given to the university of Wittenberg from
that in which the other seats of learning continued to move.   Theology
itself, mainly indeed in consequence of its own internal development,
made similar claims to those asserted by general literature.   In Wittenberg
arose the opposition to the theologians of the old and the new way, the
nominalists and the realists, and more especially to the reigning tho-
mistical doctrines of the Dominicans ; men turned to the scriptures and
the fathers of the church, as Erasmus (though rather as a conscientious
critic than an enthusiastic religionist) had recommended.   In a short
time there were no hearers for the lectures given in the old spirit.

Such was the state of things in Wittenberg when the preachers of papal
indulgences appeared in the country about the Elbe, armed with powers
such as had never been heard of before, but which Pope Leo X. did not
scruple, under the circumstances in which he found himself, to grant.

For no fear whatever was now entertained at Rome of any important
division in the church.

In the place of the council of Pisa, one had been convoked at the Lateran,
in which devotion to the see of Rome, and the doctrine of its omnipotence, reigned unalloyed and undisputed.

At an earlier period, the college of Cardinals had often made an attempt
to limit the powers of the papacy, and to adopt measures with regard to
it like those employed by the German chapters towards their bishoprics ;
they had elected Leo because they thought he would submit to these
restraints.   But the event proved how utterly they had miscalculated.
The men who had chiefly promoted Leo's election were precisely those
who now most severely felt his power.   Their rage knew no bounds.
Cardinal Alfonso Petrucci several times went to the college with a dagger
concealed beneath the purple ; he would have assassinated the pope
had he not been withheld by the consideration of the effect which the
murder of a pope by a cardinal would produce on the world.   He therefore held it to be more expedient to take another and less violent way to
the same end—to get rid of the pope by poison.   But this course required
friends and allies among the cardinals and assistants in the palace, and
thus it happened that he was betrayed.[1]

What stormy consistories followed this discovery !   The persons standing without, says the Master of the Ceremonies, heard loud clamours,—
the pope against some of the cardinals, the cardinals against each other,
and against the pope.   Whatever passed there, Leo did not allow such
an opportunity of establishing his power for ever, to escape him.   Not
only did he get rid of his formidable adversary, but he proceeded to create
at one stroke thirty-one cardinals, thus insuring to himself a majority in
all contingencies, and a complete supremacy.[2]

All doubts whatsoever in the reality of this conspiracy cease upon reading
the discourse held by Bandinelli upon receiving his pardon, in which he acknowledges, " qualiter ipse conspirarat cum Francisco Maria, . . . et cum Alfonso
Petrutio machinatus erat in mortem sanctitatis vestræ præparando venena,"
&c. &c.
[2] Paris de Grassis, in Rainaldus, 1517, 95.   Comp. Jovius, Vita Leonis, iv. 67.

The state, too, was convulsed by a violent storm. Francesco Maria, Duke of Urbino,[1] who had been driven out of his territory, had returned, and had set on foot a war, the result of which long kept the pope in a state of mingled exasperation and shame : gradually, however, he mastered this opposition also ; the war swallowed up streams of gold, but means were found to raise it.

The position which the pope, now absolute lord of Florence and master of Siena, occupied, the powerful alliances he had contracted with the other powers of Europe, and the views which his family entertained on the rest of Italy, rendered it absolutely indispensable for him, in spite of the prodigality of a government that knew no restraint, to be well supplied with money. He seized every occasion of extracting extraordinary revenues from the church.

The Lateran council was induced, immediately before its dissolution (15th of March, 1517), to grant the pope a tenth of all church property throughout Christendom. Three different commissions for the sale of indulgences traversed Germany and the northern states at the same moment.

These expedients were, it is true, resorted to under various pretexts. The tenths were, it was said, to be expended in a Turkish war, which was soon to be declared ; the produce of indulgences was for the building of St. Peter's Church, where the bones of the martyrs lay exposed to the inclemency of the elements. But people had ceased to believe in these pretences.

Devoted as the Lateran council was to the pope, the proposition was only carried by two or three votes : an extremely large minority objected to the tenths, that it was impossible to think of a Turkish war at present.[2] Who could be a more zealous catholic than Cardinal Ximenes, who then governed Spain ? Yet even in the year 1513, he had opposed the attempt to introduce the sale of indulgences into that country ;[3] he made vehement professions of devotion to the pope, but he added, as to the tenths, it must first be seen how they were to be applied.[4]

For there was not a doubt on the mind of any reasonable man, that all these demands were mere financial speculations. There is no positive proof that the assertion then so generally made—that the proceeds of the sale of indulgences in Germany was destined in part for the pope's sister Maddelena—was true. But the main fact is indisputable, that the ecclesiastical aids were applied to the uses of the pope's family. We have a receipt now lying before us, given by the pope's nephew Lorenzo to the king of France, for 100,000 livres which that monarch paid him for his services. Herein it is expressly said that the king was to receive this sum from the tenths which the council had granted to the pope for the Turkish war.[5] This was, therefore, precisely the same thing as if the pope had given the money to his nephew ; or, perhaps even worse, for he gave it him before it was raised.

The only means of resistance to these impositions were therefore to be

[1] Leoni, Vita di Francesco Maria d'Urbino, p. 205.
[2] Paris de Grassis, in Rainaldus, 1517, un. 16.
[3] Gomez, Vita Ximenis, in Schott, Hispania illustrata, i., p. 1065.
[4] Argensola, Anales de Aragon, p. 354.
[5] Molini, Documenti storici, t. i., p. 71.

sought in the powers of the state, which were just now gradually acquiring stability, as we see by the example of Ximenes in Spain ; or in England, where the decision of the Lateran council could not have reached the government, at the time when it forced the papal collectors to take an oath that they would send neither money nor bills of exchange to Rome.[1] But who was there capable of protecting the interests of Germany ?   The Council of Regency no longer existed ; the emperor was compelled by his uncertain political relations (especially to France) to keep up a good understanding with the pope.   One of the most considerable princes of the empire, the Archchancellor of Germany, Elector Albert of Mainz, born Markgrave of Brandenburg, had the same interests as the pope,—a part of the proceeds were to go into his own exchequer.

Of the three commissions into which Germany was divided, the one which was administered by Arimbold, a member of the Roman prelature, embraced the greater part of the dioceses of Upper and Lower Germany ; another, which included only Switzerland and Austria, fell to the charge of Cristofero Numai of Forli,[2] general of the Franciscans ; and the Elector of Mainz himself had undertaken the third in his own vast archiepiscopal provinces, Mainz and Magdeburg : and for the following reasons.

We remember what heavy charges had been brought upon the archbishopric of Mainz by the frequent recurrence of vacancies.   In the year 1514 the chapter elected Markgrave Albert for no other reason than that he promised not to press heavily on the diocese for the expenses of the pallium.   But neither was he able to defray them from his own resources.   The expedient devised was, that he should borrow 30,000 gulden of the house of Fugger of Augsburg, and detain one half of the money raised by indulgences to repay it.[3]   This financial operation was perfectly open and undisguised.   Agents of the house of Fugger travelled about with the preachers of indulgences.   Albert had authorized them to take half of all the money received on the spot, " in payment of the sum due to them."[4]   The tax for the plenary indulgence reminds us of the measures taken for the collection of the Common Penny.   We possess diaries in which the disbursements for spiritual benefits are entered and calculated together with secular purchases.[5]

[1] Oath of Silvester Darius, the papal collector (in curia cancellaria in aula palatii Westmonasteriensis) April 22, 1517, in Rymer's Fœdera, vi. i., p. 133.

[2] His deputy plenipotentiary was Samson, of whom it was said in a pamphlet of 1521 : er habe den Bauern " Bassporten geben in den Hymel durch ein Tollmetschen, von welchem Kaufmannschatz hatt er gut silberin Platten gefiret gen Mailand."—He had given the peasants " passports into Heaven through an interpreter, by means of which stock in trade he had taken good silver coin back to Milan."

[3] Notices from a manuscript essay, from which Rathmann Gesch. von Magdeburg, iii. p. 302., has made extracts.   In Erhard's Überlieferungen zur vaterländische Gesch., part iii., p. 12, is to be found a calculation addressed to Leo X., and a motuproprio by him referring to this point.   The money advanced by the Fuggers to the archiepiscopal oratores in Rome towards the payment for the pallium amounted to 21,000 ducats (100 ducats are equal to 140 gold gulden) ; the Fuggers received 500 Rhenish gulden over, as commission.

[4] Gudenus, Diplom. Moguntiac, iv. 587.

[5] *E.g.*, Johannis Tichtelii Diarium, in Rauch, ii. 558.   " Uxor imposuit pro se duas libras denariorum, pro parentibus dimidiam l. d , pro domino Bartholomæo dimidiam l. d."

And it is important to examine what were the advantages which were thus obtained.

The plenary indulgence for all, the alleged object of which was to contribute to the completion of the Vatican Basilica, restored the possessor to the grace of God, and completely exempted him from the punishment of purgatory. But there were three other favours to be obtained by further contributions : the right of choosing a father confessor who could grant absolution in reserved cases, and commute vows which had been taken into other good works ; participation in all prayers, fasts, pilgrimages, and whatever good works were performed in the church militant ; lastly, the release of the souls of the departed out of purgatory. In order to obtain plenary indulgence, it was necessary not only to confess, but to feel contrition ; the three others could be obtained without contrition or confession, by money alone.[1] It is in this point of view that Columbus extols the worth of money : " he who possesses it," says he seriously, " has the power of transporting souls into Paradise."

Never indeed were the union of secular objects with spiritual omnipotence more strikingly displayed than in the epoch we are now considering. There is a fantastic sublimity and grandeur in this conception of the church, as a community comprehending heaven and earth, the living and the dead ; in which all the penalties incurred by individuals were removed by the merit and the grace of the collective body. What a conception of the power and dignity of a human being is implied in the belief that the pope could employ this accumulated treasure of merits in behalf of one or another at his pleasure ![2] The doctrine that the power of the pope extended to that intermediate state between heaven and earth, called purgatory, was the growth of modern times. The pope appears in the character of the great dispenser of all punishment and all mercy. And this most poetical, sublime idea he now dragged in the dust for a miserable sum of money, which he applied to the political or domestic wants of the moment.   Mountebank itinerant commissioners, who were very fond of reckoning how much they had already raised for the papal court, while they retained a considerable portion of it for themselves, and lived a life of ease and luxury, outstripped their powers with blasphemous eloquence. They thought themselves armed against every attack, so long as they could menace their opponents with the tremendous punishments of the church.

But a man was now found who dared to confront them.

While Luther's whole soul was more and more profoundly embued with the doctrine of salvation by faith, which he zealously diffused not only in the cloister and the university, but in his character of parish priest of Wittenberg, there appeared in his neighbourhood an announcement of a totally opposite character, grounded on the merest external compromise

---

[1] Instructio summaria ad subcommissarios, in Gerdes, Historia Evangelii, i. App. n. ix., p. 83. For the most part agreeing word for word with the Avvisamenti of Arcimbold in Kapp's Nachlese.

[2] Summa divi Thomæ Suppl. Qu. 25. art. 1. concl. " Prædicta merita sunt communia totius ecclesiæ : ea autem quæ sunt alicujus multitudinis communia, distribuuntur singulis de multitudine secundum arbitrium ejus qui multitudini præest." Further : art. 2.   " Nec divinæ justitiæ derogatur, quia nihil de pœna dimittitur, sed unius pœna alteri computatur."

with conscience, and resting on those ecclesiastical theories which he, with his colleagues, disciples and friends, so strenuously combated. In the neighbouring town of Jüterbock, the multitude flocked together around the Dominican friar, John Tetzel, a man distinguished above all the other pope's commissioners for shamelessness of tongue. Memorials of the traffic in which he was engaged are preserved (as was fitting) in the ancient church of the town. Among the buyers of indulgences were also some people from Wittenberg ; Luther saw himself directly attacked in his cure of souls.

It was impossible that contradictions so absolute should approach so near without coming into open conflict.

On the vigil of All Saints, on which the parochial church was accustomed to distribute the treasure of indulgences attached to its relics,—on the 31st October, 1517,—Luther nailed on its gates ninety-five propositions ;— " a disputation for the purpose of explaining the power of indulgences."

We must recollect that the doctrine of the treasure of the church, on which that of indulgences rested, was from the very first regarded as at complete variance with the sacrament of the power of the keys. The dispensation of indulgences rested on the overflowing merits of the church : all that was required on the one side was sufficient authority : on the other a mark or token of connection with the church,—any act done for her honour or advantage. The sacrament of the keys, on the contrary, was exclusively derived from the merits of Christ ; for that, sacerdotal ordination was necessary on the one side, and, on the other, contrition and penance. In the former case the measure of grace was at the pleasure of the dispenser ; in the latter, it must be determined by the relation between the sin and the penitence. In this controversy, Thomas Aquinas had declared himself for the doctrine of the treasure of the church and the validity of the indulgences which she dispensed : he expressly teaches that no priest is necessary, a mere legate can dispense them ; even in return for temporal services, so far as these were subservient to a spiritual purpose. In this opinion he was followed by his school.[1]

The same controversy was revived, after the lapse of ages, by Luther ; but he espoused the contrary side. Not that he altogether denied the treasures of the church ; but he declared that this doctrine was not sufficiently clear, and, above all, he contested the right of the pope to dispense them. For he ascribed only an inward efficacy to this mysterious community of the church. He maintained that all her members had a share in her good works, even without a pope's brief ; that his power extended over purgatory only in so far as the intercessions of the church were in his hand ; but the question must first be determined whether God would hear these intercessions : he held that the granting of indulgences of any kind whatsoever without repentance, was directly contrary to the Christian doctrine. He denied, article by article, the authority given to the dealers in indulgences in their instructions. On the other hand, he traced the

[1] Scti Thomæ Summa, Supplementum tertiæ partis, Quæstio xxv., art. ii., expounds this doctrine very clearly. Its main ground, however, always remains the same, that the church says thus : for, " si in prædicatione ecclesiæ aliqua falsitas deprehenderetur, non essent documenta ecclesiæ alicujus autoritatis ad roborandam fidem."

doctrine of absolution to that of the authority of the keys.[1] In this authority, which Christ delegated to St. Peter, lay the power of the pope to remit sin.   It also extended to all penances and cases of conscience ; but of course to no punishments but those imposed for the purpose of satisfaction ; and even then, their whole efficacy depended on whether the sinner felt contrition, which he himself was not able to determine much less another for him.   If he had true contrition, complete forgiveness was granted him ; if he had it not, no brief of indulgence could avail him : for the pope's absolution had no value in and for itself, but only in so far as it was a mark of Divine favour.

It is evident that this attack did not originate in a scheme of faith new to the church, but in the very centre of the scholastic notions ; according to which the fundamental idea of the papacy—viz. that the priesthood, and more especially the successors of St. Peter, were representatives and vice-gerents of Christ,—was still firmly adhered to, though the doctrine of the union of all the powers of the church in the person of the pope was just as decidedly controverted.   It is impossible to read these propositions without seeing by what a daring, magnanimous, and constant spirit Luther was actuated.   The thoughts fly out from his mind like sparks from the iron under the stroke of the hammer.

Let us not forget to remark, however, that as the abuse complained of had a double character, religious and political, or financial, so also political events came in aid of the opposition emanating from religious ideas.

Frederick of Saxony had been present when the Council of Regency prescribed to Cardinal Raimund very strict conditions for the indulgence then proclaimed (A.D. 1501) : he had kept the money accruing from it in his own dominions in his possession, with the determination not to part with it, till an expedition against the infidels, which was then contemplated, should be actually undertaken ; the pope and, on the pope's concession, the emperor had demanded it of him in vain :[2] he held it for what it really was—a tax levied on his subjects ; and after all the projects of a war against the Turks had come to nothing, he had at length applied the money to his university.   Nor was he now inclined to consent to a similar scheme of taxation.   His neighbour, Elector Joachim of Brandenburg, readily submitted to it : he commanded his States to throw no obstacles in the way of Tetzel or his sub-commissioners ;[3] but his compliance was clearly only

[1] Just as the adversaries, whom Thomas Aquinas refutes, maintained : " indulgentiæ non habent effectum nisi ex vi clavium."

[2] At the Diet of Augsburg, 1510, the Saxon deputies declared to the papal nuncio, as appeared in one of their letters to Frederick the Wise : " es habe Pp. Heiligkeit leiden mögen, das E. Gn. das Geld so in iren Landen gefallen zu sich genommen, mit einer Verpflichtung wann es zum Streit wider die Ungläubigen komme es wyderum darzulegen : aus der Ursach hab E. Gn. wyewol mehrmal darum angesucht von Keys Mt. wegen, die auch gerne E. Gn. gemelte Summe um ihre Schuld geben hätt, dy Summa noch wy sy gefallen ist."—" His Papal Holiness has been obliged to allow that your Grace should take into your keeping the money collected in your States, under an obligation to produce it again whenever a war with the infidels should come about : from this cause, your Grace, although many times applied to for it, on behalf of his Imperial Majesty, who would gladly have given the before-mentioned sum to your Grace in payment of debts, still has the entire sum, as it was collected."

[3] Mandate of Joachim in Walch, Werke Luthers, xv. 415.

the result of the consideration that one half of the amount would go to his brother.   For this very reason, however, Elector Frederick made the stronger resistance : he was already irritated against the Elector of Mainz in consequence of the affairs of Erfurt, and he declared that Albert should not pay for his pallium out of the pockets of the Saxons.   The sale of indulgences at Jüterbock and the resort of his subjects thither, was not less offensive to him on financial grounds than to Luther on spiritual.

Not that the latter were in any degree excited by the former ; this it would be impossible to maintain after a careful examination of the facts ; on the contrary, the spiritual motives were more original, powerful, and independent than the temporal, though these were important, as having their proper source in the general condition of Germany.   The point whence the great events arose which were soon to agitate the world, was the coincidence of the two.

There was, as we have already observed, no one who represented the interests of Germany in the matter.   There were innumerable persons who saw through the abuse of religion, but no one who dared to call it by its right name and openly to denounce and resist it.   But the alliance between the monk of Wittenberg and the sovereign of Saxony was formed ; no treaty was negotiated ; they had never seen each other ; yet they were bound together by an instinctive mutual understanding.   The intrepid monk attacked the enemy ; the prince did not promise him his aid—he did not even encourage him ; he let things take their course.

Yet he must have felt very distinctly what was the tendency and the importance of these events, if we are to believe the story of the dream which he dreamt at his castle of Schweinitz, where he was then staying, on the night of All Saints, just after the theses were stuck up on the church door at Wittenberg.   He thought he saw the monk writing certain propositions on the chapel of the castle at Wittenberg, in so large a hand that it could be read in Schweinitz ; the pen grew longer and longer, till at last it reached to Rome, touched the pope's triple crown and made it totter ; he was stretching out his arm to catch it, when he woke.[1]

Luther's daring assault was the shock which awakened Germany from her slumber.   That a man should arise who had the courage to undertake the perilous struggle, was a source of universal satisfaction, and as it were tranquillised the public conscience.[2]   The most powerful interests were involved in it ;—that of sincere and profound piety, against the most purely external means of obtaining pardon of sins ; that of literature, against fanatical persecutors, of whom Tetzel was one ; the renovated theology against the dogmatic learning of the schools, which lent itself to all these abuses ; the temporal power against the spiritual, whose usurpations it sought to curb ; lastly, the nation against the rapacity of Rome.

But since each of these interests had its antagonist, the resistance could not be much less vehement than the support.   A numerous body of natural adversaries arose.

[1] A divine and scriptural dream from Caspar Rothen, Gloria Lutheri, in Tentzel's Histor. Bericht, p. 239.

[2] Erasmus to Duke George of Saxony, Dec. 12. 1524.   "Cum Lutherus aggrederetur hanc fabulam, totus mundus illi magno consensu applausit,— susceperat enim optimam causam adversus corruptissimos scholarum et ecclesiæ mores, qui eo progressi fuerant ut res jam nulli bono viro tolerabilis videretur."

The university of Frankfurt on the Oder, like that of Wittenberg, was an off-shoot of Leipzig, only founded at a later date, and belonging to the opposite party. Determined opponents to all innovation had found appointments there. Conrad Koch, surnamed Wimpina, an old enemy of Pollich, who had often had a literary skirmish with him, had acquired a similar influence there to that possessed by Pollich at Wittenberg. Johann Tetzel now addressed himself to Wimpina, and with his assistance (for he was ambitious of being a doctor as well as his Augustine adversary) published two theses, on one of which he intended to hold a disputation for the degree of licentiate, on the other, for that of doctor : both were directed against Luther. In the first he attempted to defend the doctrine of indulgences by means of a new distinction between expiatory and saving punishment. The pope, he said, could remit the former, though not the latter.[1] In the second thesis he extols most highly the power of the pope, who had the exclusive right of settling the interpretation of Scripture, and deciding on articles of faith ; he denounces Luther, not indeed by name, but with sufficient distinctness, as a heretic, nay a stiff-necked heretic. This now resounded from pulpit and chair. Hogstraten thundered out invectives, and clearly intimated that such a heretic was worthy of death ; while a manuscript confutation by an apparent friend, Johann Eck of Ingolstadt, was circulated, containing insinuations concerning the Bohemian poison.[2] Luther left none of these attacks unanswered : and in every one of his polemical writings he gained ground. Other questions soon found their way into the controversy ; *e.g.* that concerning the legend of St. Anne, the authenticity of which was disputed by a friend of Luther's at Zwickau, but obstinately maintained by the Leipzig theologians.[3] The Wittenberg views concerning the Aristotelian philosophy and the merit of works spread abroad : Luther himself defended them at a meeting of his order at Heidelberg ; and if he experienced opposition from the elder doctors, a number of the younger members of the university became his adherents. The whole theological world of Germany was thrown into the most violent agitation.

But already a voice from Rome was heard through the loud disputes of excited Germany. Silvester Mazolini of Prierio, master of the sacred palace, a Dominican, who had given out a very equivocal and cautious opinion concerning the necessity of repentance and the sinfulness of lying, but had defended the system of teaching practised by his order with inflexible zeal ;—who, in Reuchlin's controversy, had been the only member of the commission that had prevented it from coming to a decision favourable to that eminent scholar, now deemed himself called upon to take up arms against this new and far more formidable assailant. He rose, as he said, from the commentary in " Primam Secundæ " of St. Thomas, in the composition of which he was absorbed, and devoted a few days to throw himself like a buckler between the Augustine monk and the

---

[1] Disputatio prima, J. Tetzelii Thesis, 14. To this refers the passage in Luther's second sermon on Indulgences, in which he calls such a distinction mere talk.

[2] Obelisci Eckii, nr. 18 et 22.

[3] Joh. Sylvii Apologia contra Calumniatores suos, in qua Annam nupsisse Cleophæ et Salomæ evangelicis testimoniis refellitur. Reprinted in Rittershusii Commentarius de Gradibus Cognationum, 1674.

Roman See, against which he had dared to rear his head ;[1] he thought Luther sufficiently confuted by the mere citation of the opinions of his master, St. Thomas.   An attack emanating from Rome made some impression even upon Luther : feeble and easy to confute as Silvester's writing appeared to him, he now paused ; he did not wish to have the Curia his open and direct foe.   On the 30th May he sent an explanation of his propositions to the pope himself, and seized this occasion of endeavouring to render his opinions and conduct generally intelligible to the Holy Father.   He did not as yet go so far as to appeal purely and exclusively to the Scriptures ; on the contrary, he declared that he submitted to the authority of the fathers who were recognised by the church, and even to that of the papal decrees.   But he could not consider himself bound to accept the opinions of Thomas Aquinas as articles of faith, since his works were not yet sanctioned by the church.   " I may err," he exclaims, " but a heretic I will not be, let my enemies rage and rail as they will."

Affairs, however, already began to wear the most threatening aspect at Rome.

The papal fiscal, Mario Perusco,[2] the same who had rendered himself celebrated by the investigation of the conspiracy of cardinals, commenced criminal proceedings against Luther ; in the tribunal which was appointed the same Silvester who had thrown down the gauntlet to the accused on the literary ground was the only theologian.   There was not much mercy to be expected.

There is no question that German influences were also at work here. Elector Albert, who instantly felt that the attack from Wittenberg was directed in part against himself, had referred Tetzel to Wimpina ; the consequence of this was, that Frederick was attacked in Tetzel's theses (indirectly indeed, but with the utmost bitterness), as a prince who had the power to check the heretical wickedness, and did not—who shielded heretics from their rightful judge.[3]   Tetzel at least affirms, that the Elector had had an influence in the trial.   Personal differences, and the jealousies of neighbouring states, had influenced, from the very beginning, the course of these events.[4]

Such was the state of the spiritual power in Germany.   As yet, a secession or revolt from the pope was not thought of ; as yet, his power was universally acknowledged, but indignation and resistance rose up against him from all the depths of the national feeling and the national will. Already had his sworn defenders sustained a defeat ;—already some of the foundations of the edifice of dogma, on which his power rested, tottered ; the intense desire of the nation to consolidate itself into a certain unity, took a direction hostile to the authority of the Court of Rome.   An opposition had arisen which still appeared insignificant, but which found vigorous support in the temper of the nation and in the favour of a powerful prince of the empire.

[1] Dialogus rev[di] patris fratris Sylvestri Prieriatis—in præsumptuosas Martini Lutheri conclusiones, in Löscher, ii. 12.

[2] Guicciardini (xiii., p. 384) and Jovius mention him.

[3] Disputatio secunda, J. Tetzelii Thesis, 47, 48.

[4] Tetzel to Miltitz in Löscher, ii. 568. : " so doch hochbenannter Erzbischof inen bestellt hat zu citiren und nicht ich."—" Thus then the above-named archbishop has summoned him (Luther) and not I."

CHAPTER II

DESCENT OF THE IMPERIAL CROWN FROM MAXIMILIAN TO CHARLES V.

DIET OF AUGSBURG, 1518

HAD there been at this moment a powerful emperor, he might have turned these agitations to vast account. Supported by the nation, he would have been able to revive the ancient opposition to the papacy, and to inspire his people with a new life founded upon religious ideas.

Maximilian was by nature far from being inaccessible to such a project. Indeed, the expression he once let fall to Elector Frederick, that he wished " to take good care of the monk," for that it might be possible some time or other to make use of him, betrays what was passing in his mind ; but for the moment he was not in a condition to follow it out.

In the first place, he was old, and wished to secure to his grandson Charles the succession to the empire. He regarded this as the closing business of his life. He had laboured all his days, as he said, to aggrandize his house : all his trouble would, however, be lost, if he did not attain this his final aim.[1] But, for this, he especially required the support of the spiritual power ; for the minds of men were not yet so far emancipated from the ideas of the middle ages, as that they could be brought to recognise in him the full dignity of emperor, without the ceremony of coronation. While meditating the project of raising his grandson to the rank of king of the Romans, the first difficulty that occurred to Maximilian was, that he himself had not been crowned. He conceived the idea of causing himself to be crowned, if not in Rome, at least with the genuine crown of a Roman emperor, which he hoped to induce the papal court to send across the Alps, and opened negotiations with that view. It is evident how necessary it became for him, not only not to irritate, but to conciliate the pope.

On another point also, advances were made towards a good understanding between the emperor and the pope. We have mentioned the grant of a tenth for a Turkish war, which the Lateran council was induced to consent to, just before its close. It is a very significant fact, that while this excited amazement and resistance throughout Europe, Maximilian acquiesced in it. He, too, wished nothing more earnestly than once more to levy a large tax on the whole empire ; we know, however, what a mighty opposition he encountered, and that even the grants which he wrung from the States had been fruitless : he now hoped to obtain his end in conjunction with the pope. He therefore assented, without a question to the plan of the Court of Rome. It seems as if not only his self-interest was moved, but his imagination captivated. He exhorts the pope, in letters of the greatest ardour and vivacity, to undertake the campaign in person, surrounded by his cardinals, under the banner of the cross ; then he says, every one would hasten to his aid : he, at least, had from his youth had no higher ambition than to do battle against the Turks.[2] The victories of Selim I. over the Mamelukes revived his sense of the general danger. He convoked the States of the empire, in order at

[1] Letter of the 24th of May, 1518.
[2] Letter of Maximilian, Feb. 28. in Rainaldus, 1517, 2-5.

length to conclude on means of raising efficacious succour against the Turks, to whom already all Asia, as far as the domains of Prester John, belonged ; by whom Africa was occupied, and whom it would soon become utterly impossible to resist.[1] He hoped that the moment was come for realising his long-cherished project of establishing a permanent military constitution. Thus, after long interruption, the ancient union of the spiritual and temporal powers was once more beheld at the diet. Instead of opposing the pope, the emperor united with him ; while the pope sent a legate to assist the emperor in his negotiations with the States.

His choice fell on the Dominican, Thomas de Vio, the same who had so zealously defended the papal prerogatives ; this had opened to him the way to higher dignities, which had terminated in that of cardinal. The brilliant appointment of legate, now superadded, placed him at the summit of his ambition. He determined to appear with the greatest magnificence, and almost acted in earnest upon the pretension of the Curia, that a legate was greater than a king.[2] At his nomination he made special conditions as to the state and splendour of his equipments ; for example, that a white palfrey with bridle of crimson velvet, and hangings for his room of crimson satin, were to be provided for him : even his old master of the ceremonies could not refrain from laughing at the multiplicity of demands which he had to make. When at Augsburg he delighted beyond all things in magnificent ceremonies ; such as the high mass which he celebrated before all the princes, spiritual and temporal, in the cathedral, on the 1st of August ; when he placed the cardinal's hat on the head of the Archbishop of Mainz, kneeling at the altar, and delivered to the emperor himself the consecrated hat and sword—the marks of papal grace and favour. He indulged also in the most extravagant ideas. While exhorting the emperor to march forth against the hereditary enemy who thirsted for the blood of Christendom, he reminded him that this was not only the day on which Augustus had become master of the world at the battle of Actium, but also that it was sacred to St. Peter : the emperor might accept it as an augury of the conquest of Constantinople and Jerusalem, and the extension of the empire and the church to the farthest ends of the earth.[3] Such was the style of a discourse, framed according to all the rules of rhetoric, which he delivered to the assembly of the States.

It may easily be imagined, that it cost him no labour to persuade the emperor ; after a short deliberation they now made the joint proposal that in order to bring an army against the Turks into the field, every fifty householders should furnish one man, and the clergy should pay a tenth, the laity a twentieth, of their income for its maintenance.

It was extremely difficult, however, to carry this measure through the States. Whatever were the real designs of the emperor, people refused, whether in Germany or abroad, to believe that he was in earnest. Publications appeared, in which the intention of the See of Rome to make war on the infidels was flatly denied ; these were all Florentine arts, it was

---

[1] Address of the 9th February in the Frankf. A., vol. xxxiii. By a letter from Fürstenberg (July 3, 1518) it appears that the States had met by the beginning of July.

[2] " Legati debent esse supra reges quoscunque."—*Paris de Grassis* in *Hofmanni Scriptores novi*, p. 408.

[3] Jacobi Manlii Historiola duorum Actuum ; Freher, ii., p. 709.

affirmed, to cajole the Germans out of their money; the proceeds of indulgences were not even applied to the building which was represented as so urgently wanted; the materials destined for the building of St. Peter's wandered by night to the palace of Lorenzo de Medici;—the Turks whom they ought to make war upon were to be found in Italy.[1] As to the emperor, it was suggested that his object was to impose a tax on the empire under these pretexts.

The answer which the States returned on the 27th of August, therefore, was a decided negative. They observed, that it would be impossible to raise so considerable a tax, in the state to which the country had been reduced during the last years by war, scarcity, and intestine disorder. But that, independently of this, the common people complained of all the money that was sent out of Germany to no purpose; the nation had already frequently contributed funds for a Turkish war by means of indulgences and *cruciata*, but it had never yet heard that any expedition against the Turks had been attempted. The refusal thus assumed the character of an accusation. The States seized the opportunity afforded by the demand on the part of the See of Rome to retort upon it a multitude of grievances: *e.g.* the annates which were now exacted from abbeys, prebends, and parishes; the constantly increasing costs of the confirmation in spiritual offices caused by the creation of new officia; the apparently eternal burthens imposed by the rules of the Roman chancery; all the various encroachments on the right of patronage; the appointment of foreigners to spiritual posts in Upper and Lower Germany; and, generally, an incessant violation of the concordat with the German nation.[2] A memorial presented by the Bishop of Liege to the head and princes of the empire, served to give additional force to these complaints. It contained a complete catalogue of acts of injustice which the German church had to suffer from the courtiers of Rome; those mighty huntsmen, sons of Nimrod, as it said, sallied forth daily in chase of benefices; day and night they meditated on nothing but how to thwart the canonical elections; the German gold, formerly too heavy for an Atlas, had fled across the Alps.[3] Such a writing, " so full of boldness," said the Frankfurt envoy, had never been seen.

How greatly had the emperor deceived himself in imagining that he should more readily attain his end by the aid of the spiritual power!

Charges against the pope were now also advanced at the discussions on the grievances which had been brought forward a year before at Mainz; *e.g.* his encroachment on the right of collation; the conduct of the clergy generally; above all, the use of excommunication, to which the people had no mind to concede a validity equal to that of the sentence of the civil tribunals. But in urging these complaints, they did not lose sight

---

[1] Oratio Dissuasoria; Freher, ii. 701. The "conclusion of this discourse makes against the opinion that it is by Hutten. But how is the fact to be explained, that the dialogue, unquestionably Hutten's, 'Pasquillus Exul,' has so extraordinary a resemblance in many passages to this discourse, that it cannot possibly be accidental? It might, however, very well have had an influence upon the consultations, as it reached Wittenberg on the 2nd of September."— *Luther's Letters*, i., nr. 79.

[2] Answer of the States, Friday after the Feast of St. Bartholomew. Frankft. A.

[3] Erardus de Marca Sacra^mae Cæs^ae Majestati. Kapps Nachlese, ii., nr. 1.

of those against the emperor.   They again demanded a better composition
of the courts of justice, and a more perfect execution of the judgments of
the Imperial Chamber ; a commission was appointed in order to deliberate
on the code of criminal procedure.

Nor was this all ; the opposition to the imperial authority took a
perfectly new direction in the important discussions on the Turkish war.

The States did, indeed, after much debate, at length seem to come to
some agreement as to the nature and mode of a new tax ; it was actually
decreed in the Recess, that for three years every one who communicated
at the Lord's Supper should pay at least a tenth of a gulden, and that the
sum resulting from this collection should be kept by the government till
the commencement of a Turkish war ; but even a grant of so strange and
equivocal a kind was rendered nearly illusory by a condition attached to it.
The princes declared that they must first consult with their subjects upon
it.   The emperor's answer shows how astonished he was at this innovation.
He said, that was not the usage in the Holy Empire ; the princes were not
bound by the consent of their subjects ; it was the duty of the latter to
execute the decisions of their lords and rulers.[1]   The princes replied, that
they had often made promises without consulting their subjects, and the
consequence had been, that it had generally been found impossible to
execute them : continuance in such a course could end in nothing but
disgrace and contempt.   The Recess, accordingly, contained nothing more
than that the princes promised to treat with their subjects, and to report
the result at the next diet.

It is evident that the disposition which this betrays must have rendered
it impossible to come to any agreement on the other affairs of the empire.

A great deal was done about the Imperial Chamber, but without any
results.[2]   The Electors protested in a body that in virtue of their franchises
they were not subject to the Imperial Chamber : they could not agree
on the suggestions for a reform ; the old objections to the matricula for

---

[1] Declaration of the emperor on the 9th of Sept.   " Item, dass in dem allen
Churfürsten Fürsten und Stände kein Ausred noch Entschuldigung fürnemen,
noch solch Zusage thun mit eynicher Weigerung oder Condicion auf ihre Unterthanen, denn sollichs in bisher bewilligten Hülfen nie bedacht worden und daruf
gestellt ist, sondern Churff. FF. und Stend haben allezeit frei gehandelt und
bewilligt, nachdem sy Kaisr. Mt. und des Reichs Churf. belehnt seyen, auch
die Unterthanen schuldig seyn den Willen der Fürsten und Obern und nit die
Fürsten und Obern der Unterthanen Willen zu verfolgen und Gehorsam zu
beweisen."   " Also, that in all these things the electors, princes, and States take
upon themselves no evasion or excuse, nor make such promise with any hesitation
or condition having reference to their subjects, for none such had ever been
made, nor grounded thereon, on occasion of succours granted heretofore ; but
electors, princes, and estates have in all times freely acted and made grants, as
lieges of his Imperial Majesty and electors of the empire ; also the vassals are
bound to follow the wills of, and to show obedience to, princes and superiors, and
not princes and superiors to follow the will of, and to show obedience to, subjects."
—*Frankft. Acten.*

[2] The reason of the bad appointments lies in the bad pay.   Fürstenberg (Letter
of the 8th of Sept.) remarks that no better pay could be obtained,   " Daraus
folgt, dass es auch nit mit dem Inkommen, so jetzunder geben wird, mit gelehrt
fromm und verständig Leuten besetzt mag werden."   " Thence follows, that it
(the Imperial Chamber) cannot, with the income which is now given, be provided
with learned, pious and sensible men."

the contributions were urged again ; its operation was no longer felt, and in a short time it was entirely at a standstill.[1]

Disorder once more prevailed on all sides.   The same torrent of complaints poured in upon the diet at Augsburg, as the year before at Mainz.

The Count von Helfenstein invoked assistance against Würtemberg, Ludwig von Boyneburg against Hessen, the Archbishop of Bremen against the Worsats : all in vain.   The disputes between the city of Worms and their bishop, between the Elector Palatine and a company of merchants who were robbed when under his escort, were brought to no conclusion. The behaviour of the Elector Palatine in this affair, and the support which he appeared to find, raised the indignation of the city to the highest pitch.[2]   There was hardly a part of the country which was not either distracted by private warfare, or troubled by internal divisions, or terrified by the danger of an attack from some neighbouring power.   Those who wished for peace must take their own measures to secure it : it was in vain to reckon upon the government.

Such a state of anarchy necessarily led to a general conviction that things could not go on thus.   For a long time the emperor could come to no agreement with the Estates on any measure whatever, whether for tranquillity at home, or against the enemy abroad : what he had been unable to accomplish single-handed, he had tried to effect in conjunction with the pope—an attempt which had ended in more signal failure than before.   The highest authorities could no longer fulfil the prime duties of a government.

In so far it was of great importance that the States of the Empire made the innovation we have just mentioned ; viz. to render the grants dependent on the will of their subjects.   The life of the nation showed a tendency to fall off from what had hitherto been its centre, and to form itself into independent self-sufficing powers in the several territories.   This tendency was now greatly increased by the interests connected with the election of an emperor, which were already very active in Augsburg, and shortly afterwards began to occupy all minds.

In fact, we cannot advance a step further without some preliminary inquiry into the relations of the German principalities.

---

[1] Fürstenberg, Sep. 14.   "Somma Sommarum aller Handelung die uf diesem Reichstag gehandelt ist, dass von Friede und Recht nichts beschlossen wird, dass die Schatzung des Türkenzugs, wie K. Mt. dawider, bei den Unterthanen anbracht (wird).   "The sum total of all the affairs which have been transacted at this Imperial Diet is, that nothing is determined as to the peace and the laws, and that the taxation for the Turkish war, although his Imperial Majesty is opposed to it, is laid on the vassals."

[2] Fürstenberg, in transmitting the correspondence, expresses his dissatisfaction. "Hie ist nit anders : ein jeder sehe sich für.   Die Churf. Fürsten und Andre haben nit alle ob der Handlung Gefallens : es will aber diess Mal aus Ursachen nit anders seyn.   Gott erbarms."   "Here things are not otherwise : let each man look to himself.   The electors, princes, and others are not all content with the transaction : but this time there are causes why it cannot be otherwise. God have mercy on us."

MUTUAL RELATIONS OF THE GERMAN PRINCES

IT was impossible as yet to speak of German states, properly so called. The unity of even the larger principalities was not yet sufficiently cemented :—attempts were here and there made at a common government, which, however, seldom succeeded, so that people constantly returned to the principle of division ;—nor was there any settled system of representation. A vast number of independent powers and privileges still existed, incompatible with any form of government whatever. But, in the larger territories, there were efforts towards the establishment of unity and order ; in the smaller, local associations took the place of the princely power : in all directions the force of the local spirit struggled for ascendency with the imperial authorities, and, the more it succeeded, the more vain were the attempts of the latter at concentration and general efficient control.

It was unquestionably an important circumstance, that the head of the empire was less intent on the tranquil exercise of his legal sovereignty, than on acquiring influence by personal and irregular interference. It was only in moments of enthusiasm and excitement that Emperor Maximilian beheld his high station in its national aspect; in ordinary moments he regarded it rather as a fraction of his personal power. The nature of his administration was exactly calculated to excite agitations of every kind in the somewhat formless world around him.

In Upper Germany the emperor had naturally, after all that had passed, to encounter much opposition. The Elector Palatine could not yet forget the injuries he had sustained in the last war ; he was still unappeased, nor had he received his investiture. Although the emperor had then espoused the party of Bavaria, the people of that country were not the less sensible what the two branches of the sovereign house, viewed collectively, had lost. The young princes, William and Louis, had such a profound sense of this, that they arranged the disputes which had broken out between them as to their respective shares in the government, as quickly as possible, when they thought they detected, on the part of the emperor, a design of turning their disagreements to advantage in order to promote another interest, as in the year 1504.[1] They remembered what Bavaria had been stripped of ; and the first act of their combined government was to pledge themselves mutually to reconquer all that had been lost, as soon as the emperor, their uncle, was dead.[2]

It appeared that Maximilian might reckon more securely on Duke Ulrich of Würtemberg, whom he had declared of age before the legal term, who had accompanied him in his wars, had made conquests under his banner, and to whom he had given a consort : Ulrich seemed bound to him by every tie of gratitude. But this prince soon began to display a determined spirit of resistance to the emperor's designs, inspired by the most arrogant self-conceit. He was displeased that he was of so little importance in the Swabian league. He considered it an insufferable abridgment of his power, that of the one and twenty votes in the council of that body,

---

[1] From a letter of Duke Ludwig ; Freiberg, Landstände, ii. 149.
[2] The first document in the Urkundenbuch to Stumpf, Baierns Politischa Gesch., i.

fourteen belonged to the lower states,—prelates, counts, knights, and above all, cities ; and had the right of deciding on peace and war ; so that " his will and possession were in the hands of strangers."[1] In the year 1512, when the league was renewed, he obstinately refused to join it. He thus offended the league, began consequently to fear its hostility, and allied himself with its enemies, especially the Elector Palatine and the Bishop of Würzburg. He thus got into innumerable difficulties and quarrels with the emperor, with all his neighbours, and even with his own states and councils, which would rather have adhered to the emperor and the league. In all these affairs his behaviour became more and more violent, harsh, and overbearing. The peasants revolted against his taxes ; the estates of his dominions compelled him to sign a contract limiting his authority, which he showed an inclination to break : his councillors meditated setting a regency over him, which filled him with rage. At length the consummation of all these evils burst upon him in his own house.

Unhappily he had suffered himself to be carried away by an inclination for the wife of one of his courtiers, Hans von Hutten, his comrade in the field and the chase. Hutten at length seized an occasion to speak to his lord on this subject ; the duke threw himself at his feet, extended his arms imploringly to him, and conjured him to permit him to see and to love her ; he had tried in vain, he said, to conquer his passion—he could not.[2] It is reported, that in a short time they exchanged characters ; Hutten became the lover of the duchess Sabina. One day Ulrich thought he saw the betrothing ring which he had given his wife, on Hutten's finger, and fell into the most violent transports of jealousy. It is impossible, in the dearth of authentic accounts,[3] to say how much of the story is true. According to the legal documents, what peculiarly incensed the duke was, that Hutten had not kept the secret of his master's passion, and had given currency to reports by which he appeared at once vicious and ridiculous. It seemed that the servant was little alarmed at the anger which his lord gave vent to on this occasion ; he thought he should have to encounter some sharp words, to which he could return others as sharp and as proud. But Ulrich was now worked up to deeds of vengeance. They were riding together, and as they came into the Böblinger wood, the duke took the knight aside, upbraided him with his falsehood, called out to him to defend his life ; and, as Hutten was not armed, overpowered and killed him.[4] He then stuck his sword into the ground, and tied the lifeless body fast to it with a girdle twisted round the neck. He

[1] " Beswerung so wir Herzog Ulrich zu Wirtemperg haben, des Pundts Schwaben Erstreckung anzunemen." " Difficulty which we, Duke Ulrich of Würtemberg, have to consent to the extension of the Swabian League." Sattler, Herzoge, i. Appendix, nr. 56, p. 129.

[2] The printed address of the family of von Hutten in Sattler, a. a. O,. p. 213.

[3] See Heyd, Duke Ulrich, i., p. 394. It is not to be forgotten that a certain respect was observed in the statement in spite of all its violence. The Huttens would not have brought forward the connection with the wife of the murdered man, had not the Duke first mentioned it.

[4] Address of Duke Ulrich, a. a. O., p. 305. The relations maintained, that Hutten had been positively invited to join in the ride ; the Duke, that he had been warned, and yet had obstinately accompanied them. The account of the Duke seems to me to have greater moral probability.

said that as Freischöffe, as initiated member of the Fehme, he had the right and authority to do so. He carried home the bloody sword, and laid it by his wife's bedside. Alarmed for her freedom, and even for her life, she fled, first to her uncle the emperor, who was taking the diversion of hunting in the neighbourhood, and then to her brothers in Bavaria, between whom and Ulrich there was already much bad blood. Sabina accused her husband to the emperor, and demanded that her enemies should be delivered up. Ulrich, on the other hand, persecuted with vindictive fury her friends and all those whom he regarded as adherents of the emperor and the league. Attempts at reconciliation only served to bring the secret hostilities fully to light : a treaty was concluded, but immediately broken ; letters injurious to the honour of both parties were interchanged : never, in short, did a prince rend asunder all the ties that bound him to a party, as whose ally and associate he had risen to power, with greater violence than Duke Ulrich. At the diet of 1518 it was reported that he had arrested followers of the emperor, put them to horrible tortures, and threatened them with death. On the other hand, Maximilian intimated that he would appoint a criminal tribunal to try the duke, and would execute whatever sentence it might pronounce :[1] he immediately issued a special writ to the States, not only authorising, but summoning them to set at liberty their lord's prisoners.[2] This furnished an additional motive to the emperor for desiring a reconciliation with the Elector Palatine. This he accomplished so far that that prince appeared at the diet and received his investiture. It is clear that the emperor's policy acquired by this event, and by his influence over the league and Bavaria, the ascendency in Upper Germany ; nevertheless, affairs wore a very perilous aspect, and it was easy to foresee that, be the event what it might, differences could not be adjusted in an amicable manner. Their ramifications extended over the whole empire.

Another and far more formidable opposition to the emperor arose out of the affairs of Lower Germany connected with the house of Burgundy.

One of the earliest acts of Maximilian's government, in 1486, the year of his election, had been to grant the reversion of Julich and Berg to the house of Saxony, if those provinces should, " by reason of failure of lineal heirs male," become vacant.[3] In the year 1495 he confirmed this for himself and all his successors in the empire, " now as then, and then as now." The event in question seemed not far distant, since Duke William VII. had only a daughter ; this opened to the house of Saxony a prospect of a more commanding, indeed, of what might be called a European position, since Friesland had then been transferred to the younger line.

But difficulties soon arose. This assignment to so distant a master

[1] Fürstenberg, Sept. 9, calls it, " eine scharfe und übermessliche Antwort : " " a sharp and immoderate answer." " Wo er sich nicht füge, wolle ihm S. M. ein Halsgericht setzen, dass er daselbst in Schranken komme, und wess von anderen und Sr. Maj. Interessen wegen an ihn erlangt wird, dass dem auch Vollzug geschehe."—" In case he do not yield, his Majesty will sit in judgment on him, that he may be thereby brought within bounds, and whatever, by reason of his Majesty's and other interests may be decreed against him, that the same may also be executed."

[2] July 17, 1518. Sattler, i., App. 263.

[3] Document in Müller, Imp. Rtth. Fr., vi. 48.

was by no means popular in the country itself, which would have thought itself better provided for by a union with the neighbouring province of Cleves. Princes and states were unanimous in this opinion. In the year 1496 they already determined to marry the daughter of the Duke of Julich with the heir of Cleves, and to unite the two countries. A solemn treaty, which may be regarded as effecting a union of all these provinces, was entered into and signed by nobles and cities.[1] They prayed the emperor to confirm it, and to acknowledge the Princess of Julich as heiress of her father's possessions

The emperor, however, would have paid little attention to this petition, and would have adhered to the grant of reversion, had not certain political events occurred to change his designs.

From the time that Duke Charles, son of the Duke of Gueldres, formerly deposed by Charles the Bold, had returned to his hereditary dominions, and, in defiance of the unfavourable decrees of the empire, had found means, with the aid of his estates, to maintain himself, there had not been one moment's peace in those parts. He was closely allied with France ; all the enemies of Austria found in him an ever-ready protector. It was, therefore, a serious thing to make another powerful enemy in that neighbourhood. The Duke of Cleves threatened, in case his petition was refused, to enter into a matrimonial connexion and an indissoluble alliance with the Duke of Gueldres—a threat which filled the Netherlands with alarm.[2] The Governor Margaret, Maximilian's daughter, thought it would be impossible to wrest Julich and Berg from the Duke of Cleves ; the only effect would be to cause him to unite with Gueldres, Arenberg, and Liege, all foes of the house of Burgundy : this would furnish a power strong enough even to drive the emperor's posterity out of the Netherlands.

In Saxony it was believed that the emperor connected schemes of another kind with this design. Elector Frederick enjoyed singular consideration in the empire. He steadily adhered to the principles and sentiments of

[1] Treaty of Marriage and Agreement in Teschenmacher, Annales Cliviæ, Cod. dipl., nr. 98, 99, wherein the two princes promised one another—the Duke of Julich, that his daughter should bring the son of his brother of Cleves his principalities of Julich, Berg, his countship of Ravensburg, with all his other lordships,—the Duke of Cleves, that his son should bring the daughter of his brother of Julich his principality of Cleves, his countship of the Mark, and all his other lordships, now actually possessed, or still to be acquired.

[2] The emperor says to Cesar Pflug : " Die klevisch Tochter hindre I. M. Frau Tochter Margr." " The daughter of the Duke of Cleves stands in the way of the Lady Margaret, his Imperial Majesty's daughter." Renner states : " Clef lässt sich vernehmen, wolt man die Lehen nit thun, so musste sich Clef mit den Herrn verbinden, von denen es Trost und Hülf haben mecht das Sine zu erhalten." " Cleves says thus—if they will not bestow the fief, then Cleves must join the lords from whom she may have comfort, and help to hold her own."—*Weimar Acts.* Comp. Correspondance de l'Empereur Maximilien I. et de Marguerite d'Autriche, I., p. 390. Margaret further wrote in 1511 to the emperor, as is said in his answer : " Que se povons tant faire que nostre cousin le duc de Zaxssen voulsist quicter ou du moins mectre en délay la querelle qu'il prétend à la duché de Juillers, le jeusne duc de Clèves et son père se condescendroient facilement à eulx déclairer à la guerre et aydier à la réduction de nostre pays de Gheldres." The emperor hoped to conciliate the elector at the approaching imperial diet, but in this he did not succeed.

the old electors, and his power was constantly on the increase. His intellectual superiority checked the inclination which his cousin George now and then betrayed to oppose him ; so that the house of Saxony might still be regarded as one power. His brother Ernest had been Archbishop of Magdeburg up to the year 1513, and certainly one of the best that see had ever possessed ; his cousin Frederick was Grand Master in Prussia ; his sister Margaret, Duchess of Lüneburg, ancestress of that house. It is evident how extensive was the influence of this family ; an influence further augmented by the act of the States of Hessen, which, on the death of Landgrave William, in 1510, excluded his widow Anne from the guardianship of the minor, claimed by her, and committed it to the elector and house of Saxony, to which the regency thereupon appointed was subject. Boyneburg, the governor of the province, who was at the head of affairs, was entirely devoted to Frederick.[1] It appeared to the emperor highly inexpedient to throw Julich, and Berg also, which must soon be without a sovereign, into the hands of this powerful prince, who might thus become too mighty a vassal.

Under the influence of these considerations, Maximilian retracted the promise he had made at the time of his election (and doubtless with a view to that), and in various documents of the years 1508-9 revoked the contingent rights on Julich and Berg which had been conferred : he declared that the duke's daughter, Maria, was the worthy and competent successor of her father.[2] In the year 1511 William VII. died ; his son-in-law, John of Cleves, took possession of the country, without opposition. All attempts to recall the past, all persuasions and negotiations on the part of the house of Saxony, were vain.

The effect of this certainly was to induce Cleves to refuse the alliance with Gueldres, and to adhere faithfully to Austria. Saxony, on the contrary, declined in importance. The spiritual principalities which were occupied by members of that house passed into other hands on the death of their possessors. Boyneburg, by his somewhat tyrannical mode of governing, provoked the discontent of the States of Hessen, and especially of the cities (A.D. 1514). By a sort of revolution, the Princess Anne was restored to the guardianship of which she had been deprived ; Elector Frederick retaining nothing more than the name. Another proof of this anti-Saxon spirit was, that the emperor, at the suggestion of the order of knights, declared the young Landgrave Philip of age when only fourteen years old (March, 1518) ; alleging that he would be better off so, than under any guardianship or tutelage whatsoever. In these Hessian trans-actions, Duke George took part against the elector : so far from raising any cordial opposition to the designs of Anne, he betrothed his son with her daughter. Meanwhile he had already restored Friesland to Austria.

In this case, too, the policy of Austria was triumphant ; the dreaded coalition of the Netherland adversaries was prevented, and Saxony kept at a distance and depressed.[3] On the other hand, however, the hostility

---

[1] See Rommel, Philipp der Grossmüthige, vol. i., p. 26.

[2] The document in Teschenmacher, nr. 100, is inconclusive ; nr. 101 leaves no room for doubt.

[3] The Saxon councillors, as early as 1512, dreaded further disfavour : " Darum er (der Kaiser, nach jener Erklärung für Cleve) fort und fort auf Wege trachten mocht, Ewer Aller Fürstl. Gnaden zuzuschieben so viel ihm möglich, damit

of the most able and prudent of all the princes of the empire was provoked.   What the weight of that hostility was, soon appeared at the
diet of Cologne (A.D. 1512).   Frederick's resistance sufficed to defeat all
the emperor's plans ; at least, his biographer imputes to his opposition
the rejection of the project of a new tax.   This enmity affected even the
Netherlands through another channel.   The niece of the elector, a Lüneburg princess, married Charles of Gueldres (of whom we have already
spoken), who thus secured in two of the most powerful princely houses,
such a support as he had never before been able to obtain.

   While the house of Saxony was thus weakened by a contest with Austria,
Brandenburg rose upon her favour.   It was with the emperor's assistance
that Brandenburg princes succeeded to those of Saxony both in the grand
mastership of the Teutonic Order and the see of Magdeburg : he then
further favoured the elevation of the young archbishop, who was also
bishop of Halberstadt, to the Electorate of Mainz, which had formerly
been enjoyed by a brother of Elector Frederick : we have already seen
what was the nature of the relations which subsisted between these two
princes.   Maximilian also renewed his alliance with the Franconian line
of this house.   He confirmed the removal of the old Markgrave, who had
been declared idiotic, from the government ; and marrying the Markgrave's eldest son Casimir to his own niece, Susanna of Bavaria, he gave
that prince the whole support of his authority and an important advantage
over his brothers.   For this very reason, however, he did not win them
over completely ; with one of them, indeed, the Grand Master, he had a
serious difference.   The emperor had at first induced him to assume a
hostile attitude towards King Sigismund of Poland,[1] who was rendered
extremely formidable to the Austrian claims on the kingdom of Hungary,
by his connection with the House of Zapolya.   Maximilian wished to
hold him in check, on the one side by the Grand Duke of Moscow, on the
other by the Teutonic Order.   But the situation of things was now much
altered.   In the year 1515, Sigismund of Poland had formed very amicable

---

Ew. Aller Fürstl. Gn. in Dempfung und Abfall kämen."—" Lest he (the emperor,
after that declaration in behalf of Cleves) should more and more strive after
means of embarrassing your most Princely Grace as much as possible, so that
your most Princely Grace may fall into weakness and decline."—*Letter from
Cologne written Thursday after Jacobi*, 1512.   *Weimar Records.*

   [1] The Fugger MS. : " Deswegen die Kais. Maj. nach solchem Wege getrachtet,
dieweil S. M. erachtet, dass König Sigmund seinem Schwager Graf Hansen von
Trentschin Grossgrafen in Ungarn Rath und Hülfe erzeiget und denselben nach
Absterben des Königs Lasslew zu dem Reich Ungarn . . . befördern möcht, dass
er demselben etliche Könige und Fürsten zu Feinden machen wollt, und ward
durch S. Mt. so vil gehandelt, dass Markg. Albrecht von Brandenburg Hoch-
meister in Preussen den hochernannten König Sigmundt von Polen anfeindet."
" His Imperial Majesty on this account, because his Majesty considered that
King Sigismund had yielded counsel and aid to his brother-in-law, Count Hans
von Trentschin Grossgraf in Hungary, and after the decease of King Ladislas
might advance the same to the kingdom of Hungary, that he wished to render
sundry kings and princes enemies to the same ; and so much was done by his
Majesty, that Margrave Albert of Brandenburg, Grand Master in Prussia, opposes
the above-named King Sigismund of Poland."   The alliance with Russia was
concluded expressly for the reconquest of the lands of the Order seized on by
Poland.   This is the famous document in which Zar was translated into Kaiser
(emperor).—*Karamsin, Hist. of Russia*, vii. 45, 450.

relations with the emperor ; he now recognised the hereditary right of Austria to Hungary, and took a wife out of the Italian branch of that house. Maximilian, on his side, waived the claims of the empire : he granted Danzig and Thorn an exemption from the jurisdiction of the Imperial Chamber in 1515, as he had to Switzerland in 1507 ; a measure the more important in this case, since it substituted a Polish for a German jurisdiction ; it was, in fact, a sort of cession. It may readily be imagined how much less inclined he must now be to interpose earnestly on behalf of the Order ; and accordingly we find it stated in the preamble to the agreement, that the emperor recognised the peace of Thorn,—the very thing against which the Grand Master protested, and by which he had been made a vassal of the crown of Poland. Prussia was thus again alienated from the emperor, and this reacted on the other members of the house of Brandenburg. Elector Joachim, at least, was not disinclined to give the same support to the Grand Master as he did to his brothers in Franconia.

It may easily be imagined that the position of the other sovereign houses was affected in various ways by all these friendships and enmities.

Pomerania, forced to give way before the claims of Brandenburg to the supreme feudal lordship, was alienated from Austria by the support its rival received from that power. The Pomeranian historians ascribe it to the influence of Joachim I. that the projected marriage of a Pomeranian princess with King Christian II. of Denmark did not take place ; and on the contrary, that that monarch married a grand-daughter of Maximilian.[1] The result of this again was, that the uncle and rival of Christian Frederick of Holstein, who thought himself unjustly dealt with in the partition of the ducal inheritance, and, as king's son, believed himself to have claims even on Norway,[2] now sought to ally himself with the house of Pomerania ; whilst the third member of this house, the Count of Oldenburg, adhered firmly to the Austro-Burgundian alliance, and once more received a stipend from the Netherlands. Every event that occurred in the northern states immediately affected the dynastic houses of Germany through these various combinations.

It must not be imagined that open hostility broke out amongst them. There was a greater or lesser influence of the house of Austria ; a more or less visible favour shown by or inclination towards it ; but they remained on the footing of good neighbours, met at diets, interchanged visits at family festivals, endured what they could not alter, and kept their eye steadily on the point in view.

The discord was most fierce and undisguised in the house of the turbulent Guelfs. Calenberg and Wolfenbüttel held to the friendship of Austria ; indeed it was in her service that the duke of the former state had revived the ancient war-like renown of his house. Lüneburg sided with the opposition. There were a multitude of old disputes between them, mainly caused by an attempt of the Bishop of Minden, a Wolfenbüttler by birth, to appropriate to himself the countship of Diepholz, to

[1] Kanzow, Pomerania, ii. 313.
[2] Chief points of complaint, as set forth in the different publications on the dispute : Christiani, Neuere Gesch. von Schleswig-Holstein, i., p. 318. These complaints sufficiently refute the supposition of a good understanding, to which Christiani previously adheres.

which Lüneburg had ancient contingent claims.[1] Lauenburg was now drawn into these quarrels. During the absence of the Archbishop of Bremen—another Wolfenbüttler—the Worsats, who had recently been conquered, killed his officers ; Magnus of Lauenburg, to whom they appealed as the true Duke of Lower Saxony, lent them aid, and destroyed the fortress erected by the archbishop.[2] On his return, open war among all these princes appeared imminent, and was only prevented from breaking out by Mecklenburg, which stood in a tolerably impartial situation in the midst of all these disputes ; or rather, in that of an ally of both parties.

This example suffices to prove that there was but little distinction between temporal and spiritual princes.

For the highest posts in the church had long been distributed, not in consequence of spiritual merits, but in compliance with the wishes of some powerful prince, especially the emperor ; or of the interests of the neighbouring nobles, who had seats in the chapters : indeed it was, as we have seen, a maxim of the court of Rome, ever since the last century, to use its influence in promoting the younger sons of sovereign houses.[3] In the beginning of the sixteenth century this policy had been pursued with success in many sees. In Lower Germany, Brunswick, and Lauenburg in particular, rivalled each other in this respect. The house of Brunswick-Wolfenbüttel and Grubenhagen had got possession of the archbishopric of Bremen, the bishoprics of Minden, Verden, Osnabrück and Paderborn ; the house of Lauenburg, of Münster and Hildesheim. We have seen how richly Brandenburg was provided for. We find princes of Lorraine as bishops of Metz, Toul and Verdun. The palatinate possessed Freisingen, Regensburg, Speier, Naumburg, and afterwards Utrecht. Bavaria obtained Passau. In the year 1516, the chapter of Schwerin chose Prince Magnus of Mecklenburg, although not yet seven years old, its bishop.[4] It were impossible to enumerate all the prebends which came into the hands either of members of the less powerful houses, or favourites of the emperor. Melchior Pfinzing, his chaplain and secretary, was dean of St. Sebald, in Nürnberg, of St. Alban and St. Victor in Mainz ; and prebendary both in Trent and Bamberg. Hence it followed that the interests of the house to which a dignitary of the church belonged, or to which he owed his elevation, influenced the exercise of his functions : we find the spiritual principalities implicated in all the intrigues or dissensions of the temporal rulers.

These circumstances reacted on the other states of the empire, though perhaps less obviously. The cities of the Oberland, for example, whose strength was the main support of the Swabian league, belonged to the one party ; while the Franconian knights, who were at open war with the league, sided more with the other.

For imperfect and undefined as all relations were, the powers of Germany may be ranged under two great political parties. On the side of Austria were Bavaria, the League, Brandenburg (for the most part), Hessen, Cleves,

---

[1] Delius, Hildesheimische Stiftsfehde, p. 96.
[2] Chytræus, Saxoniæ Chronicon, lib. vii., p. 227.
[3] See p. 64. Æneas Sylvius, Epistola ad Martinum Maier, p. 679.
[4] Born July 4, 1509 ; elected June 21, 1516. Rudloff, Mecklenburgische Gesch., iii. 1, 37.

the Count of East Friesland (who had lately joined this party), Oldenburg, Denmark, Calenberg, Wolfenbüttel, and Albertine Saxony. On
that of the opposition, were Ernestine Saxony, Pomerania, Lauenburg,
Lüneburg, the Franconian knights, Würtemberg, and Gueldres. The
Duke of Gueldres was indeed in a state of open warfare. In the year 1517,
his troops devastated the whole of Holland ; he gave up Alkmaar to
pillage for eight days : in the year 1518, the Frisian corsair, Groote Pier,
appeared in the Zuyder Zee, and made himself complete master of it for
a considerable time. The duke employed all his influence to keep the
Frieslanders in a continual state of revolt. The palatinate and Mecklenburg occupied a sort of neutral or middle ground between these two
parties. The Elector palatine inclined to the house of Austria for a
singular reason. His brother Frederick, who had served for many years
at the court of Burgundy, had formed an attachment to the Princess
Leonora. One of his letters was found in her possession, and excited such
displeasure, that the unhappy prince was obliged to quit the court, with
the persuasion that he had thus thrown away all his well-earned claims
on the emperor's favour, unless he could re-establish them by still more
important services. But his brother was not disposed to forget what he
had suffered in the war of inheritance. On the contrary, the brave
knight who had risen to fame and honour in his service, Franz von Sickingen, now took revenge on Hessen for those very injuries.[1] While the
diet was sitting at Augsburg, he marched an army of 500 horse and 8,000
foot upon the fortified town of Darmstadt, and extorted from the inhabitants contributions to the amount of 45,000 gulden, on the hardest and
most oppressive terms. A deputation of the empire made representations to the emperor against this breach of the Public Peace ; but he did
not venture to do anything ; he had formerly taken Sickingen into his
own service, and he had no mind to alienate the palatinate again.

Such is the situation in which we find Maximilian towards the close of
his career.

The received opinion which recognises in him the creative founder of
the later constitution of the empire, must be abandoned. We saw above
that the ideas of organisation which first became current in the early
years of his reign experienced far more opposition than encouragement
from him ; and that he was incapable of carrying even his own projects
into execution. We now see that he had not the power of keeping the
princes of the empire together ; that, on the contrary, everything about
him split into parties. It followed of necessity that abroad he rather
lost than gained ground. In Italy nothing was achieved : Switzerland
acquired greater independence than she possessed before ; Prussia was
rather endangered than secured. The policy of France had obtained new
influence in the heart of Germany ; first Gueldres and then Würtemberg
openly declared for that power.

The glory which surrounds the memory of Maximilian, the high renown
which he enjoyed even among his contemporaries, were therefore not won
by the success of his enterprises, but by his personal qualities.

Every good gift of nature had been lavished upon him in profusion ;
health up to an advanced age, so robust that when it was deranged strong

[1] That this was the motive, is asserted in the Chronicle of Flersheim, by
Münch. iii. 210.

exercise and copious draughts of water were his sole and sufficient remedy ;[1] not beauty indeed, but so fine a person, so framed for strength and agility, that he outdid all his followers in knightly exercises, outwearied them in exertions and toils ; a memory to which everything that he had learnt or witnessed was ever present ; so singular a natural acuteness and justness of apprehension, that he was never deceived in his servants ; he employed them exactly in the services for which they were best fitted ; an imagination of unequalled richness and brilliancy ; everything that he touched came new out of his hands ; a mind, as we have already remarked, which always seized with unerring instinct on the necessary, though unfortunately the execution of it was so óften embarrassed by other conditions of his situation ! He was a man, in short, formed to excite admiration, and to inspire enthusiastic attachment ; formed to be the romantic hero, the exhaustless theme of the people.

What wondrous stories did they tell of his adventures in the chase ! How, in the land beyond the Ens, he had stood his ground alone against an enormous bear in the open coppice : how in a sunken way in Brabant he had killed a stag at the moment it rushed upon him : how, when surprised by a wild boar in the forest of Brussels, he had laid it dead at his feet with his boar-spear, without alighting from his horse. But above all, what perilous adventures did they recount of his chamois hunts in the high Alps, where it was he who sometimes saved the practised hunter that accompanied him, from danger or death. In all these scenes he showed the same prompt and gallant spirit, the same elastic presence of mind. Thus, too, he appeared in face of the enemy. Within range of the enemy's fire, we see him alight from his horse, form his order of battle, and win the victory : in the skirmish, attacking four or five enemies single-handed : on the field, defending himself in a sort of single combat against an enemy who selected him as his peculiar object ; for he was always to be found in the front of the battle, always in the hottest of the fight and the danger.[2] Proofs of valour which served not merely to amuse an idle hour, or to be celebrated in the romance of Theuerdank :[3] the Venetian ambassador cannot find words to express the confidence which the German soldiers of every class felt for the chief who never deserted them in the moment of peril. He cannot be regarded as a great general ; but he had a singular gift for the organisation of a particular body of troops, the improvement of the several arms, and the constitution of an army generally : the militia of the Landsknechts, by which the fame of the German foot soldiers was restored, was founded and organised by him. He also put the use of fire-arms on an entirely new footing, and his inventive genius displayed itself pre-eminently in this department ; he surpassed even the masters of the art, and his biographers ascribe to

---

[1] Pasquaglio, Relatione di 1507 : "Non molto bello di volto ma bene proportionato, robustissimo, di complessione sanguinea e collerica, e per l' età sua molto sano, nè altro il molesto che un poco di catarro che continuamente li discende, per rispetto del quale ha usato e usa sempre far nelle caccie gran esercitio."

[2] See the Geschichtbibel of Seb. Frank ; and particularly the Key to Theuerdank, reprinted in the edition of Theuerdank by Haltaus, p. 111.

[3] An allegory dealing with the adventures of Maximilian—partly written by Maximilian himself.

him a number of very successful improvements :[1] they add, that he brought even the Spaniards who served under him to the use of fire-arms. Wherever he was present he found means to allay the mutinous disorders which often arose in these bands of mercenaries, in consequence of the irregular state of his finances. We are told that once in extremity he appeased the discontent of his men by the jests and antics of a court fool, whom he sent among them. He had a matchless talent for managing men. The princes who were offended and injured by his policy could not withstand the charm of his personal intercourse. " Never," says the sagacious Frederick of Saxony, " did I behold a more courteous man." The wild turbulent knights against whom he raised the empire and the league, yet heard such expressions from his lips, that it was, as Götz von Berlichingen said, " a joy to their hearts ; and they could never bear to do anything against his Imperial Majesty or the house of Austria." He took part in the festivals and amusements of the citizens in their towns —their dances and their shooting matches, in which he was not unfrequently the best shot ; and offered prizes—damask for the arquebusiers, or a few ells of red velvet for the cross-bowmen : he delighted to be among them, and found in their company and diversions a relief from the arduous and weary business of the diet. At the camp before Padua he rode up to a suttler and asked for something to eat. John of Landau, who was with him, offered to taste the food ; the emperor inquired where the woman came from. From Augsburg, was the reply. " Ah !" exclaimed he, " then there is no need of a taster, for they of Augsburg are God-fearing people." In his hereditary dominions he often administered justice in person, and if he saw a bashful man who kept in the background, he called him forward to a more honourable place. He was little dazzled by the splendour of the supreme dignity. " My good fellow," said he to an admiring poet, " thou knowest not me nor other princes aright."[2] All that we read of him shows freshness and clearness of apprehension, an open and ingenuous spirit. He was a brave soldier and a kind-hearted man ; people loved and feared him.

And in his public life, we should do him injustice if we dwelt exclusively on his abortive attempts to reconstitute the empire. It is an almost inevitable defect of that form of government which excites a competition between the highest person in the state and a representative body or bodies, that the sovereign separates his personal interests from those of the community. Maximilian, at least, was far less intent on the pros-

---

[1] Grünbeck in Chmel, p. 96. " Bellicas machinas in minutas partes resolvere, parvis viribus bigis aptari et quocunque fert voluntas faciliter deduci primus invenit." The Fugger MS. : " Durch S. Mt. Erfindung sind die Poller und Mörser zu dem werfen, auch die langen Ror zu dem weitraichen, desgleichen die weiten kurzen Ror zu dem Haglschiessen in die Streichwehre darin auch etwa eisern Ketten und Schrot geladen werden, alsdann auch die grossen Karthaunen von neuen erfunden und zu gebrauchen aufbracht worden." " By his majesty's invention, mortars for throwing, also long tubes for distant range, likewise broad short tubes for firing canister shot from fortifications, and which may also be loaded with iron chains and balls ; moreover large carronades have been afresh discovered and brought into use."

[2] The Fugger MS. Cuspinian. Querini paints him, Nov. 1507, as " homo virtuoso, religioso, forte, liberal, quasi prodego. Adeo tutti l' ama : ma mancha di prudentia."—*Sanuto*, vol. vii.

perity of the empire than on the future fortunes of his house. When a youth of eighteen, he went to the Netherlands, and, by the union of Burgundy and Austria, founded a new European power. In States, as in the world of science, there are certain minds whose vocation it is to act as the pioneers of those gifted with the genius of construction. Incapable of bringing any thing new into existence, they are actively employed in preparing the materials and the instruments with which their more creative successors are to work. The force that was in embryo did not assume its complete form under Maximilian. But by maintaining the sovereign prerogatives in the Netherlands, as well as in Austria ; by defending the former against the French, the latter against the Hungarians ; by securing for his house the great Spanish inheritance ; by definitively founding that of Hungary and Bohemia, he exerted a vast and permanent influence on succeeding ages. How different was the position of his grandson from that of his father, an exile from his paternal land, or from his own, a prisoner in Bruges ! Never did a family enjoy more magnificent or more extensive prospects than those which now lay before that of Austria. This was the point of view from which Maximilian regarded the affairs of Germany. Until the latter half of the fifteenth century, Austria was almost shut out from Germany : she now interfered with a high hand in the affairs of every state and province, temporal or spiritual —territories of cities or of knights : nothing could stir, whether in an amicable or a hostile direction, by which she was not immediately affected. If it be undeniable that the empire, regarded as a whole, had sustained losses, it is not less true that it was the union of the house of Austria with Burgundy which restored the province of the Low Countries again to a conscious connection with Germany ; and that the remote prospects which were involved in the Hungarian, and still more in the Spanish family alliance, opened a new theatre of activity to the nation. The shadows of coming events continually flitted before the mind of Maximilian : it was this presentiment which influenced his whole conduct and actions, and produced all that was apparently unsteady, mysterious, and one-sided in his policy. It was not given to him to perfect or to found ; his mission was solely to prepare, to maintain, and to extend the views and the claims of his house, amidst the conflicting powers of the world.

The last decisive moment still remained ; and although he would never hear any thing on the subject at an earlier period of his reign, it is clear how earnestly he must have desired to secure his grandson's succession.

From the situation of things in Germany which we have just contemplated, it is easy to infer what was the support he might reckon upon, and what the obstacles he was likely to encounter. He had already made great progress in his negotiations at the diet of Augsburg. The renewal and confirmation of his good understanding with the Hohenzollern, and the large promises he made to that family, secured to him two electoral votes, those of Brandenburg and of Mainz, both of which had very recently been extremely dubious.[1] Hermann of Cologne, of

---

[1] Albert and Joachim had made preliminary promises in 1517 to the king of France, which they now retracted. The state of things appears from a memorandum which the emperor had drawn up for his grandson in Oct., 1518, wherein it is said : " Le mariage de dame Catherine avec le fils du Marquis Joachim n'im-

the family of Wied, who was intimately connected with Cleves, and hence well inclined to the emperor, was completely won by presents made to himself, and by pensions promised to his brothers and kinsmen :[1] lastly, the old misunderstandings with the palatinate were arranged by the mediation of the Count Palatine Frederick ; the elector received his investiture, entered into an agreement with Austria as to the inheritance, and gave his sanction to the order of succession.   After certain preliminary arrangements had taken place, these four electors had a meeting with the emperor, who was surrounded by his own council and that of his nephew, on the 27th August, 1518, and ratified their consent by a formal treaty. The ambassadors of Bohemia, who was now restored to her place in the Germanic body (as since the league of 1515, Austria was sure of her vote), gave their assent.

On the other hand, Frederick of Saxony, as may readily be believed, did not forget his numerous wrongs and affronts, and was not to be propitiated.   With him was Elector Richard of Treves, a Greifenklau by birth, who had already been opposed to the Prince of Baden, and had, at a more recent vacancy, obtained the electorate.   Their chief objections were, that it was an unheard-of thing to place a king of the Romans by the side of an uncrowned emperor, and that a papal constitution forbade the union of the kingdom of Naples, which Charles possessed, with the crown of Germany.

Maximilian laboured incessantly to remove these objections, as well as the deeper reasons for which they were only a cover.   Active negotiations were carried on with the court of Rome, both as to the sending of the crown across the Alps,[2] and the repeal of the above-mentioned constitution.   The strangest plans were suggested.   Maximilian once thought of abdicating and passing the rest of his life at Naples ; not, indeed, without receiving the crown of that country as compensation for the one which he renounced, so as to remove both of those obstacles at once.   Besides this, the physicians had told him he might recover his health in Naples. The German negotiations he thought he should conclude at a meeting

---

porte pas moins ; le marquis pour donner sa voix à Charles a dû renoncer à son mariage avec dame Renée de France et à une grande somme d'argent que le roi de France luy avoit promis."

[1] Argent Comptant et Pensions pour l'Archevesque de Coulongne ; Mone, Anzeiger für Kunde der teutschen Vorzeit, 1836, p. 409.   The records therein inserted from the Archives of Lille have all been of great use to me.   M. Mone had, however, left a great many untouched, from which M. Gachard of Brussels has lately given an extract in a " Rapport à Monsieur le Ministre de l'Intérieur sur les Archives de Lille," Annexé C., p. 146.   In addition to printed sources, I made use of a correspondence of the Venetian ambassador at Rome, who transmits home the news which reaches him, and paints admirably the varying dispositions of the court.

[2] Maximilian even demanded that the pope himself should come to Trent and crown him.   He alleged that the pontiff had gone to meet Francis I. at Bologna. But the master of the ceremonies held a coronation out of Rome to be thoroughly inadmissible.   Even were pope and emperor in one province, the pope might not, he said, then and there crown the emperor ; he must rather suffer him to proceed alone to Rome and be there crowned by a cardinal.—*Paris de Grassis, in Hoffmann*, p. 425.   Another idea was, that the cardinals, Giulio de Medici and Albert of Mainz, should perform the ceremony at Trent.

which was to take place in the following March at Frankfurt.　He begged
Elector Frederick in the most urgent manner not to fail to be present, and
added that he himself intended to set out soon after the new year.

But this was not permitted him.　He fell sick on the journey, at Wels,
within his own dominions.　His illness did not prevent him from carrying
on the negotiations concerning the succession : in his sleepless nights he
had the genealogical history of his early progenitors read to him ; he was
occupied with the past and the future fortunes of his race, when he expired,
on the 12th January, 1519.

His death suddenly plunged the issue of the pending negotiations into
fresh uncertainty.　The engagements already entered into related only to
the election of a king, as next in dignity and succession to the emperor ;
the affair altered its aspect now that the subject of them was an immediate
reigning king and emperor.　But so much more weighty was now the
decision, both as it regarded the distant future, and the present, pressing,
tempestuous moment.

Possibilities of every kind still presented themselves.

ELECTION OF EMPEROR IN 1511.

HAD the powers and functions of the head of the empire been defined by
a regular constitution, such as was once contemplated, the most illustrious
princes of the empire might have chosen one out of their own body to fill
that station.　But as the project had failed, who among them all would
have been powerful enough to allay the storm of hostilities that raged on
all sides, and to uphold the dignity of the empire among the powers of
Europe ?　It was a great question whether any one of them would venture
upon such a task.

Maximilian had entertained and declared various singular projects
before he would suffer it to be known that he had designs for his grandson.
He had offered the succession to the king of England : in one of the most
extraordinary documents existing, he at another time nominated the young
king Louis of Hungary and Bohemia, administrator of the empire during
his lifetime, and after his death, his successor ; and these two princes now
actually cherished some hopes of the imperial crown : but the one was at
too great a distance, the other not sufficiently powerful at home ; it was
impossible to entertain serious thoughts of either.

In declaring himself openly in favour of his grandson, Archduke Charles,
King of Spain and Naples, Maximilian now proposed a scheme which had
much to recommend it.　Charles was of German blood, heir to Austria,
and to many provinces of the German Netherlands, and sprung of the
house which had already acquired a sort of title to the imperial dignity.
There was, however, no want of objections to this young prince.　It was
observed that he did not even understand German, and had given no
proofs of personal valour or ability ; the multitude of his dominions
would leave him no time to devote to the empire ; lastly, he was expressly
excluded by the papal constitution.　His prospects, indeed, began to be
overclouded.　The electors, as we have observed, did not think themselves bound by their promises ; nor did Maximilian's daughter Margaret,
who now conducted the negotiations, deem it expedient to lay before them
the sealed copies of their several compacts, as she had been advised to do ;

she contented herself with reminding them in general terms of their expressions of good-will.   Added to this, disturbances of a very serious
nature had broken out in Austria after Maximilian's death, in which the
States established a government of their own[1] without troubling themselves about the young and absent princes ; " poor boys, of whom nobody
could tell whether they would ever be seen in Germany."   In Tyrol similar
troubles broke out.[2]   Louis, King of Hungary, thought it expedient to
recall his sister Anna from Austria, where she had already arrived in order
to conclude her marriage with one of the brothers.

Under these circumstances, a foreign monarch, already the natural rival
of the Austro-Burgundian power,—Francis I. of France,—determined to
grasp at the supreme dignity of Christendom.[3]

The fortune and fame of Francis were still in the ascendant.   The
battle of Marignano, by which he had reconquered Milan, and the personal valour which he had displayed there, had secured him a high station
in Europe, and a great name.   He was on an intimate footing with Leo X.
We find that this pope communicated the briefs which he intended to
address to the German princes, first to the court of France.   King Henry
of England, after a short hesitation, promised him his co-operation " by
word and deed."   A still more essential thing was, that he had gained an
influence over at least a portion of the German opposition.   We have
spoken of the Dukes of Gueldres and Würtemberg ; the existence of the
one, and all the hopes of the other, depended on France : old relations,
never entirely broken, united the palatinate to that country, and Duke
Henry der Mittlere of Lüneburg now also took part with the king.   " I
rejoice in his good fortune," says he in a letter, " I grieve at his bad fortune ; whether he be up or down I am his."   The king affirmed that he
was solicited by Germany to try to acquire the crown.   His adherents
insisted particularly on his bravery ; they urged that no other prince was
so well fitted to conduct the war against the Turks, which, sooner or later,
must be undertaken.

Kings of France, both before and after Francis, have entertained
similar projects—for example, Philip of Valois and Louis XIV. ; but none
ever had so much encouragement from the posture of affairs, none such
favourable prospects, as Francis I.

Two things were necessary to the success of his undertaking ; the
electors must be won over, and the anti-Austrian party must be supported and strengthened.   Francis was resolved to do every thing in his
power to accomplish both these ends, especially to spare no money ; he
gave out that he would spend three millions of kronthalers to become
emperor.   In the February of 1519, we find Germany again filled with

[1] Narratio de Dissensionibus Provincialium Austriæ. Pez. Scriptt., ii. 990.

[2] Zevenberghen to Margaret, March 28, Mone., p. 292.

[3] Il Cl. di Bibbiena al Cl. de' Medici, 13 Ott., 1518.   He gives an account of
an audience he had of the king relating to the elettion del Catholico (the grants
which had been made at Augsburg for Charles) : " sopra che in sustanza mi
disse, in grandissimo secreto, sua opinione et volontà essere, che per Nostro
Signore (the pope) e per sua Mtà si faccia ogni opera possibile, accioche ella non
vada innanzi et che si corrompano con danari et con promesse et con ogni possibil
mezzo gli elettori."—*Lettere di Principi*,, i., p. 47.   The whole correspondence,
which is printed in this collection, ought to be read ; it perfectly shews the
relations between Leo X. and Francis I.

his emissaries.   Somewhat later, his most confidential minister, Admiral Bonnivet, in whose talents the public had great confidence from his late successful conclusion of the peace with England and Spain, set out for the Rhine, largely provided with money ; whence he ventured, but in the profoundest secrecy, further into the interior of Germany.[1]

At one time it really appeared as if the king would attain his object with the electors.[2]

He had long had the most perfect understanding with Richard Greifen-klau, Elector of Treves.   Whatever were the cause,—whether ancient dis-sensions between Treves and the house of Burgundy concerning their claims on Luxemburg, or perhaps the hope which the Elector (who was already " Archchancellor through Gallia and the kingdom of Arles ") might entertain of an accession to his power and importance in case France were once more so closely united to the empire,—it is certain that Elector Richard had been equally deaf to the seductions of Maximilian and to the prayers of delegates from the Spanish Netherlands.   On the other hand, the terms of the credentials given him by Francis show the most implicit confidence in him.   " Convinced of his fidelity, his zeal, his honour and his prudence," the king nominated him his lawful and un-questioned procurator, envoy and commissary, with full powers to grant to the remaining electors and their confidential servants, or to any other princes of the empire, as much money as he thought fit, either in one sum, or in the form of yearly pension ; and to that intent, to mortgage the crown lands in the name of the king, and even in that of his successors : whatever he agreed to was to have the same force and validity as if concluded by the king in person.   While he declared himself ready to protect the rights and privileges of the princes, the nobles and the cities ; and, generally, to do every thing appertaining to an emperor,— especially to undertake the war against the Turks for the defence and extension of the faith,—he empowered the Elector of Treves, should the occasion present itself, to take the required oath on the salvation of his soul.

Nor were the king's negotiations fruitless in other quarters.   A com-plete outline of a treaty with the Elector Palatine was drawn up by his envoys,[3] and in the beginning of April that prince raised his pecuniary demands on Austria threefold, and revived his claim to the Stewardship (*Landvogtei*) of Hagenau.   Cologne received a warning from Austria not to allow herself to be seduced into the wrong way, while the French some-times thought themselves nearly sure of her support.

All these Rhenish electors feared the violence and vengeance of Francis I. in case they resisted him ; they were alarmed at perceiving no refuge or defence on the other side.   But the support of the See of Rome was still

[1] In Rome it was asserted, " che l' era in Augusta el dito Amirante," according to letters of the 1st of April ; but I find no further proof of it.

[2] The statements of Flassans, Histoire de la Diplom. Fr., i. 322, are not of importance.   But he there mentions a " liasse contenant des mémoires, lettres et instructions données par François I. à ses envoyés auprès des électeurs," in the Trésor des Chartes.   (I looked them over myself in the year 1839, and have extracted from them some remarkable notices.)   The accounts of the jeune aventureux (Mémoires de Fleuranges, Coll. univ., xvi. 227), though well worth reading, do no: go deep enough.

[3] In the extract in Stumpf, Baierns polit. Gesch., i., p. 24.

more advantageous to the king's cause, than the fears or the sense of weakness of these princes.   Pope Leo X. indeed sometimes expressed himself doubtfully, and it appeared as if he would not take part against Austria : but he was far too deeply versed in the policy of Italy, not to see the dangers that would impend over himself if Naples were united to the empire.   The Venetian ambassador, who enjoyed his confidence, affirms that Leo would on no account consent to that.[1]   Nor was the court of Spain deceived ; King Charles once ordered the pope's messengers to be arrested in Tyrol, in order to obtain proof of the illicit practices of the court of Rome in that country.[2]   He knew that the legate spoke ill of him ; one of his councillors was astonished when the Elector of Mainz showed him all the letters he had received from the papal court in the interest of the French.   Of all the electors he was the one whom it was the most important to gain ; and who had such ample means of gaining him as the pope ?   One of the favourite objects of the elector in Mainz was to get himself nominated legate of Germany, like Amboise of France and Wolsey in England.   It is well known how difficult it was to induce the See of Rome to grant that dignity to a native ; but at the present moment, and in favour of Francis I., it was disposed to do so. In a letter dated from St. Peter's, March 14, 1519, and bearing the seal of the fisherman's ring, Leo X. authorized the king, in the event of his obtaining the imperial crown by the vote and influence of the Elector of Mainz, to promise the same the dignity of legate in Germany : he, Leo X., binding himself, on the word of a true pope of Rome, to fulfil the engagement.   There seemed little reason to doubt that the elector would yield to such a temptation.

The bait which he held out to Joachim I., Elector of Brandenburg, brother of the Cardinal, was at least equally alluring.   Joachim, to whom Maximilian had promised his grand-daughter Catherine, the sister of Charles, in marriage to the hereditary prince, with a very large dowry, had conceived some suspicions that there was a design to disappoint him. The contract was indeed ratified, but only by Charles, not by the princess, without whose consent it could not be considered binding.   The Fuggers declared themselves not authorized to fulfil the pecuniary obligations contracted with the Elector.   Joachim, whether at home or in his foreign relations, was fiery, resolute, and suspicious ; in money matters, above all, he was not to be trifled with.   He was already mortified that the affair had not been terminated a year sooner, as he wished.   He therefore fixed a term within which the promises made him were to be fulfilled, and meanwhile gave audience to the French ambassador, de la Motte.   The French now in their turn promised him a princess of the blood for his son, —Madame Rénée, daughter of Louis XII. and Queen Anne,—with a still larger dowry, for the payment of which they offered greater security than their rival.   But they did not fail to accompany these promises with

---

[1] " Il papa dice vol far ogni cosa in favor del re christianissimo, et non vol sia il re cattolico per niuno partido per esserli troppo vicino, e poi S. Stᵃ è in liga col re christianissimo dicendo aver mandato al re cattolico il juramento ha fatto per il reame di Napoli accio si aricordi : poi pregò l'orator tenesse silentio." Roma, 12 April.

[2] " Pour dévoiler ses illicites poursuites." From the letter of the 31st of March in Gachard.

others of a far more extensive character.   In case Francis I. was really chosen, they declared themselves empowered to acknowledge the elector his lieutenant or viceroy ; but if that was found to be impracticable, they would use all their influence to raise Joachim himself to the throne. Joachim was not so free from ambition as not to be captivated by pro posals of such a kind.   The moment of Brandenburg's greatness seemed to him arrived.   It was something that he should be lieutenant of the future emperor ; his brother, legate of the pope ; the highest secular and spiritual honours would thus be united in his house.   Behind these, floated the far more splendid vision of the imperial crown.

While however the French became thus deeply implicated with the house of Brandenburg, they did not desist from attempts to gain over the elector of Saxony.[1]   We have no accurate knowledge of the negotiations carried on with him, but we have evidence that the French were perfectly well informed of the disgusts the elector had latterly had to endure re specting the Netherlands ; and presumed that he would not be very willing to recognize the sovereign of that province as his emperor.

During these negotiations, which awakened such lively hope, the oppo sition in the interests of France, so long kept down by the late emperor, broke out in acts of open violence.   Ulrich of Würtemberg, even on his way home from the obsequies of Maximilian, made an attack on Reut lingen, where one of his stewards was killed, took the town, and, with the aid of French money,[2] collected a numerous army, with which he thought to revenge himself on all his enemies, especially the Duke of Bavaria.   He negotiated with the Swiss, and hoped to excite them to take up arms against the Swabian league.   Somewhat later, the Bishop of Hildesheim also put himself at the head of his troops, and, during Passion week, under the invocation of the Blessed Virgin, inflicted the most fearful devastations on the territory of his Brunswick enemies. The Duke of Lüneburg, who had also received money from France, acted in concert with him, gained friends on all sides, and made magnificent preparations for war.   The Duke of Gueldres had promised to send him succours, and took troops into his service.

The French endeavoured to gain over other military chiefs, as for example, in Upper Germany, Sickingen ; in Lower, Henry of Mecklen burg.   The latter was to bind himself to appear with his troops at Coblentz in the territory of Treves, immediately after the election, in order to earn the pension promised him by the king.[3]   French money was offered to the Counts of the Harz, and to the nobles of Westphalia, through the mediation of Gueldres.[4]

The idea of the French doubtless was, that they should best attain their end by a union of negotiation and warlike demonstrations,—of persuasion

[1] Letter from the Venetian ambassador, dated Poisy, March 28 : " Del duca di Saxonia si confida : non vorrà il re catolico."

[2] Francis complained afterwards that Ulrich had declared the sum which he had received.   See Sattler, ii. 92.   A letter in Sanuto, dated April 27, 1519. " S. M. X^{ma} era quello che dava danari al duca de Virtenberg, accio tenesse la guerra in Germania."

[3] Rudloff, Neuere Gesch. von Mecklenburg, i., p. 50.

[4] The Count of Schwarzburg declared, according to a letter of Nassau, of the 20th of March, in Mone (p. 136.), that a pension of 600 livres for his life had been offered him, and that he had not accepted it.

and terror. The court already regarded the event as nearly certain. It
is said that the king's mother had ordered the jewels in which she meant to
appear at the coronation.[1] The ambition of her son took a higher flight.
When the English ambassador asked him whether it was his serious intention, if he became emperor, to take any active measures as to the long-
talked-of Turkish war, he solemnly assured him, laying his hand on his heart,
that in three years he would either not be alive, or be in Constantinople.[2]

But he was far from being so near the goal of his wishes as he and his
courtiers imagined. The attachment of Austria was not so weak in
Germany as to have lost all its force on the death of the emperor. The
electors might indeed vacillate, but they were not yet won by France.
Enemies of the House of Austria might arise, but it found friends who
adhered to it with constancy. Above all, too, that house possessed a
head determined to defend his claims, prepared to accept the challenge
of his French rival, and to sustain the combat to the last.

Some former councillors of Maximilian, Matthew Lang, Villinger,
Renner, and certain delegates from the court of the Netherlands, among
whom the most conspicuous was Maximilian of Zevenberghen, formed a
commission in Augsburg, which, under the presidency of Margaret,
watched over the interests of Austria. Able and devoted as these men
were, they sometimes took a very gloomy view of affairs and feared for
the event. At one time the thought passed through their minds, that it
would be better to put forward the Archduke Ferdinand, Charles's brother,
who was just arrived in the Netherlands from Spain : they were at all
events very desirous that he should come to Germany without loss of
time. But they little knew their master, King Charles, if they thought
this could be agreeable to him. He was not only displeased but incensed
at it. He declared to the Archduchess Margaret, that he was absolutely
determined to have the crown himself, by whatever means it was to be
obtained, and at whatever cost : he forbade his brother's journey.[3] He
who united in his person so many monarchies, felt that his ambition
would be unsatisfied till he had achieved the supreme dignity of Christendom. He had long reflected not only on the advantages likely to result
from it, but on the disadvantages he had to expect if he failed, and that
dignity was bestowed on another. He resorted without delay to every
form of canvass. To the electors he represented that his great-grand-
father, and his grandfather, the late Maximilian, when invested with the
imperial majesty, had governed the German nation long and well ; he
was resolved to tread in their footsteps, and to protect all franchises,
spiritual and temporal, particular and general ; and to abate every thing
which could be prejudicial to the liberties of Germany. He declared that
his sole object was to maintain peace throughout Christendom ; and,
after the pattern of his other grandfather, the King of Aragon, to make
war upon the unbelievers, and to reserve his whole force for the defence
and diffusion of the Catholic faith.[4] From this time Ferdinand was no

---

[1] Le Ferron, v. 118.

[2] Sir Thomas Boleyn to King Henry. Ellis Letters, i. 147.

[3] Margaret to Zevenberghen, May 15. " Absolument le roi est délibéré de
lui-mesme parvenir à l'empire, comment que ce soit et quoi que il luy doibve
couster."

[4] Papiers d'État du Cl. Granvelle, t. i., p. 112.

more thought of : the councillors reverted to their original project,—to raise their elder lord, the King of Spain, to the station of " Prince of princes," at whatever risk or sacrifice.

We must here examine a little in detail what were the means to which they resorted, what the circumstances which favoured them, and what the obstacles they encountered.

Their greatest advantage was precisely that from which their antagonist had hoped the most ;—the connection between Francis and the Pope.

At a meeting of the Rhenish electors at Wesel, in the beginning of April, the papal legate formally admonished them, in virtue of a prohibitory bull of Clement IV., not to elect the King of Naples, which country, he said, was the property of the Church of Rome. Though the negotiations between the French and the electors were at that moment peculiarly active, such a demand as this roused their spirit of independence. They replied that they were astonished that the pope should endeavour to throw a prohibition in the way of the election ;—a thing which the See of Rome had never done ; and expressed their hope that his holiness would desist from such an attempt. The legate answered with some bitterness ; he reminded them of their not altogether lawful transactions with Maximilian. A correspondence arose which betrayed great irritation, and was not much fitted to advance the cause the pope had espoused.[1]

The warlike movements of Francis and his allies were, if possible, yet more advantageous to his rival ; above all, the rising of the restless Würtemberger. Some few of the imperial council thought to settle the affair in good German fashion, by peaceful means ; but the more sagacious prevented this : they foresaw with certainty on whose side the superior strength lay, who would be victorious, and what an advantage would result to the interests of the election : they wished for war.[2] The Swabian league, irritated by former and by recent affronts, and now strengthened by considerable subsidies, was ready to take the field. Franz von Sickingen at length accepted a yearly pension from the house of Burgundy, broke off all negotiations with France, and promised to come to the aid of the league with his cavalry. It was, however, at the same time necessary to restrict the struggle within these limits, to prevent a general conflagration, and especially to keep the Swiss from siding with Würtemberg.

Duke Ulrich had already taken 16,000 Swiss into his pay ; and it was to be feared that the old hostility between the Confederation and the Swabian league might break out anew, as it had done twenty years before. This would have been as welcome a sight to Francis as it was to his predecessor Louis XII. It was all important not only that it should be avoided, but that contrary dispositions should be excited.

The election of emperor had already been discussed in the Swiss diet. French ambassadors had presented themselves to seek the support of the

[1] Correspondence in Bucholtz, iii. 670. Acta Legationis in Goldast, Political Imper., p. 102. This coincides with the fact of the electors demanding back so seriously and pressingly their circular letters from Augsburg.

[2] Letter from Zevenberghen, March 28. Mone. Matth. Schiner, Feb. 12 : " Que ce Duc de Wirtemberg estoit le plus grand ami du roi (Charles)—car à cause de sa folie la grande lighe feront de si grosses armées qui feront crainte aux François et autres qui veuillent empescher son election."

Confederation : the Swiss in Paris, among them Albert von Stein, advised their countrymen to declare for the king, were it only in order to enjoy the credit and the favour resulting from an event which was no longer to be averted.[1] The Confederation was not, however, so decidedly French as to follow this course. The Cardinal von Sitten, the old enemy of the French, well skilled in all the secret ways of diplomacy, was then in Zürich, and in the enjoyment of great consideration. In the middle of March, Zevenberghen came from Augsburg to his aid. They had, indeed, no easy task. Zevenberghen makes loud complaints of the bad words and threats he was obliged to endure from the pensionaries and speakers ; what it cost him to acknowledge " this low rabble as gentlemen, and to pay them respect ; he would rather carry stones ;" but he bore it all : he did among them, he said, as if at a fair—paid much, and promised more ; at length he succeeded. The main cause of his success was, indeed, the interests of Switzerland herself ; not only the recollection of the Swiss blood shed in the late wars, or of the numerous claims which still remained unsatisfied ; but above all, the consideration that France would, by the acquisition of the imperial dignity, become too mighty, would no longer need the assistance of the Swiss, and would consequently trouble herself no more about them,—still less, pay their pensions. On the 18th of March, the Swiss diet came to a formal resolution to oppose the election of the French king to the imperial crown, with body and soul (as they expressed it) ; and on the contrary to promote the election of a German prince, whether an elector or another. In pursuance of this they wrote to the electors, and to Francis himself ; they took the liberty to admonish the latter to content himself with his own kingdom. The Austrian ambassadors wished the Confederation to declare openly for King Charles, but this they could not accomplish. " Wherever they fall," said Zevenberghen, " there they abide."[2] Nevertheless much was effected. The ancient union with Austria was renewed. The diet determined to recall from the field those of their people who had joined the duke, and with such unanimous earnestness that they should not dare to resist.

This decided Duke Ulrich's ruin. Zevenberghen justly gloried in having persuaded the diet to pass such a resolution.

At the moment when letters of challenge (*Fehdebriefe*) poured in upon the duke from all sides—when even some of his own vassals renounced their allegiance, and the powerful troops of the league were preparing to fall upon his country—at that moment he was abandoned by those who alone could have defended him. His Würtemberg militia did not understand regular warfare ; his cavalry was no match whatever for that of the league. The league encountered no resistance. On the 21st of April they took Tübingen, where the duke's children were residing, and he himself was compelled to abandon his country.

So complete a victory—deciding the conquest of a considerable principality—turned the scale in favour of the Austrian interest through the whole of Upper Germany.

A similar change soon followed in Lower Germany. Towards the end

[1] Anshelm, Chronicle of Berne, v. 375.
[2] Mars 22. " Là où ils tombent, ils demeurent comme tels gens qu'ils sont." Gachard, 178. See Maroton to Margaret, April 10, Mone, 397.

of May the dukes of Calenberg and Wolfenbüttel had completed their preparations, and appeared in the field with their auxiliaries from Hessen and Meissen in undisputed superiority. They destroyed Waldenstein, stormed Peine, and plundered the Lüneburg territory. Fifty villages were seen in flames at once on their path, nor did they spare a single church ; they defaced the arms of their own house, the house of Guelf, on their cousin's castle, and carried off rich booty. "They were of a proud spirit," says a song of that day ; "they had silver and the red gold ; they went in velvet with golden chains ; they had two thousand chariots with them." They challenged the Duke of Lüneburg in mockery to do battle, while he was still waiting for the succour promised him from Gueldres.

But if the French thought to attain their end by the aid of the intestine wars of Germany, they soon found how completely they had deceived themselves. Exactly at the decisive moment, these private wars took a turn in favour of Austria.

Under the impressions produced by these events the plenipotentiaries of King Charles renewed their negotiations with the electors with the greatest diligence.

Towards the end of April a Spanish chargé-d'affaires arrived, bringing the archbishop of Mainz the assent to all his demands. Very remarkable concessions and promises were made to him ; full power over the chancery of the empire ; the protection of the emperor in the dispute of the arch-bishopric with Saxony about Erfurt, and in that with Hessen about a newly-erected toll ; the emperor's intercession with the pope that he would allow the archbishop to hold a fourth bishopric in Germany ; and, lastly, (for the example of France was to be followed in this) his appoint-ment as legate of the Apostolical See in the empire. Moreover, the pensions promised him were secured to him by special legal instruments from Mechlin and Antwerp.[1] From this time we find the archbishop, who had vacillated for a moment, unshaken in his attachment to Austria and doubly zealous in her cause. He threw the whole weight which the dignity of archchancellor gave him in Germany, into the scale of King Charles.

The elector palatine's support was secured by similar means. He had wavered, only because the publication of his new agreement with Austria as to the succession, and the promised compensation for the stewardship of Hagenau were delayed ; while, on the other hand, the Swabian league threatened to espouse the pecuniary claims urged against him by the Rhenish merchants. The Austrian plenipotentiaries hastened to allay these troubles ; they satisfied the demands of the merchants at their own cost. Count Palatine Frederick, moreover, exerted all his influence with his brother in favour of Austria, and considerable sums of money were granted to both.[2] Though the elector had said at first, that whatever wind blew, he would always be for Austria, he had not entirely kept his word ; but he gradually returned to his first intention, and remained constant to it.

---

[1] Carolus ad Albertum 12 Martii, in Gudenus, iv. 607. Jean de le Sauch à Marguer. 29th April ; Mone, p. 403.

[2] Correspondence in Mone, p. 34. See Hubert Thomas Leodius, Vita Friderici Palatini, iv., p. 100 sq.

The difficulties with Cologne were not so great.   The Count of Nassau, who conducted the negotiations in this part of the country, understood the means of conciliating the Rhenish counts generally, and the arch-bishop—who was by birth one of that body—in particular.   The con-cessions made to that prelate at Augsburg were now extended.   We have a letter of his, dated the 6th of June, in which he treats the affair of the election as settled, as soon as Bohemia shall be secured.[1]

The King of Bohemia had indeed at first contemplated availing himself of the engagements entered into with him by Maximilian, and had in consequence sent his ambassadors to Italy ; but he soon saw how little he had to expect.   The pope treated his documents with the greatest contempt, as some of the many *privilegia* which Maximilian had created in order to put money into the pockets of his clerks.   Upon this the government of Bohemia resolved to support the house of Austria, with which it was about to enter into so near a family alliance.   Perhaps the circumstance that John, brother of the Markgrave George of Brandenburg, who had great influence at that court, was just married to the widow of Ferdinand the Catholic and nominated Viceroy of Valencia,[2] contributed greatly to this result.

There remained, therefore, only Treves, Brandenburg, and Saxony ; and the Austrian plenipotentiaries showed no lack of zeal in their en-deavours to secure these important votes.

With Treves there was nothing to be done.   Although the dependents of the elector gave some hope, he himself declared he would keep his vote free, and from this resolution no representations could induce him to depart.   If, notwithstanding this, he had entered into the close connexion with France which we have already noticed, it must have been under some reservation which secured to him his freedom of voting at the decisive moment.   Such, at least, was the case with Brandenburg.

On the 20th of April the plenipotentiaries of King Charles, the Count of Nassau, M. de la Roche, and Nicholas Ziegler, who enjoyed the especial confidence of the archbishop of Mainz, arrived at Berlin.   They were commissioned to renew to Elector Joachim all the promises which had formerly been made to him, especially in relation to the marriage of his son with the archduchess and infanta Catherine.   They brought with them the infanta's ratification, and placed it in the hands of a kinsman of the elector, Markgrave Casimir.   But they found Joachim little dis-posed to listen to them.   The utmost that he would promise was, that he would vote for Charles, if the four electors who preceded him had done so ; and even for this very unsatisfactory engagement, he made greater demands than they were empowered to grant.   Nor had he given any promise to the King of France, but with the condition that two electors should have voted on that side before it came to his turn ; yet that sovereign had, in addition to various other concessions, agreed to these exorbitant demands.   According to the first proposal made by Margaret, her ambassadors certainly gave the elector reason to hope that he would have the lieutenancy of the empire, but I do not find whether this was confirmed by Charles or not.   The ambassadors did not accede to a sug-

[1] Bucholtz, iii. 671.
[2] Letter from Charles to Casimir on this subject, March 6, 1519 : Spiess, Brandenburgische Münzbelustigungen, i., p. 389.

gestion of Joachim's as to the vicariate of the empire for the Saxon provinces ; still less would they permit him to hope for the crown, in any case or under any condition.   As this was the prospect that first allured the elector, we need not wonder that they had no success with him.

It was the more important to obtain the vote of him whom Austria had lately so deeply offended, and whom the councillors regarded as their most formidable opponent—Frederick of Saxony.[1]   As the Bohemian vote did not carry great weight (and indeed the last election was concluded without Bohemia), the vote of Saxony was necessary to the formation of a majority that would be universally recognised.   The refusal of the elector to take part in the measures agreed on at Augsburg, which excited great discontent in the nation when they were known, had increased the already high consideration he enjoyed.   Moral authority and the consent of public opinion were attached to this vote ; every effort must be made to secure it.

The elector himself remained inaccessible.   He would hear of no promises ; he forbade his servants to receive presents, and referred all inquiries to the day of election, when it would be seen to whom he gave his vote ; till then he would keep it free.

But there is no position on earth so lofty or so impregnable, that it cannot be reached by some means or other.   The deputies determined to take a step which, if successful, would certainly put an end to all the animosities that had been accumulating between Saxony and Austria.   They now offered the Archduchess Catherine, sister of King Charles, who had just been the subject of their fruitless negotiations with Joachim I., to Duke John, brother of the elector, for his son, John Frederick, the future heir to the electorate.

To this proposal Duke John replied, that the king would be able to place his sister in a more exalted position.   The ambassadors answered, that the king only wished to renew the ancient alliance of the two houses. They overruled the objections raised by his modesty in the most dexterous and flattering manner, by reminding him that the sister of Emperor Frederick was the grandmother of the dukes of Saxony.[2]

The elector took no part in these negotiations, but he allowed them to go on.   The ambassadors thought they discovered that the whole business of the election depended on the success of them.   They wrote first from Lochau, and again on the 16th of May from Rudolstadt, to the king, in Spain, urging him to send them full powers to conclude this treaty of marriage as quickly as possible, if he would not have their endeavours prove fruitless : this was the only means of arriving at the desired end.[3] This was so obvious to the king that he did not hesitate an instant.   On the 30th of May he signed the act empowering his envoys to negotiate this marriage and every thing relating to it, in his name, and to arrange the terms with an authority equal to his own.[4]   Hereupon Duke John granted his council full powers to treat ; in the preamble to which he said that, " bearing in mind the dignity of the crown of Spain, and the name and

---

[1] Marnix to Margaret, March 16, traces the unfavourable disposition of Bohemia, amongst other sources, to Saxony : Mone, p. 131.

[2] Müller, Geschichte der Protestation, p. 689.

[3] Nassou et Peine, May 16, Mone, p. 406.

[4] Document in Arnoldi's Denkwürdigkeiten, p. 8.

race of the honourable house of Austria, he wished most especially to see his son, who was also well inclined thereto, advised to a friendly marriage with the most illustrious princess, the Lady Catherine." The Austrian ambassadors had now only to ascertain what effect this good understanding with the duke was likely to have on the elector, and to act accordingly.

At all events it is evident that they had successfully employed the interest of the house they served.

But the affair was not decided thus.

Austria had now unquestionably a majority of declared friends in the electoral college ; but the French, too, could reckon on more than one partisan, and did not relinquish the hope of gaining over one or two of the others. They had just made a vehement, and, as they believed, successful attempt on the elector of Cologne : they thought that even if they had only three votes, the pope would declare the election valid ; and his legate, at least, adhered firmly to their side up to the middle of June.

Austria was indeed victorious, and remained with arms in her hands ; but the partisans of France in Lower Germany were by no means crushed. We find traces of very extensive and unexpected plans ; *e.g.,* an original document, in which Francis promises to pay whatever troops the electors of Treves and Brandenburg should levy in Germany, under the extraordinary pretext that they were to maintain the peace of the country and the freedom of the roads for the meeting in Frankfurt. The Duke of Gueldres was already up in arms again. The French troops did not yet advance upon the German frontier, but they were prepared to do so.[1]

The two powers vied with each other in prodigal expenditure of money. It was a peculiar advantage on the side of Austria that the great mercantile house of Fugger, which conducted nearly the whole monetary business of Germany, refused its services to the French.[2] Admiral Bonnivet had, however, brought large sums in hard money to Germany, which many might think better than any bills of exchange whatsoever.

Had the event depended exclusively on pecuniary interests, its decision would have remained very doubtful.

But considerations of a totally different nature evidently had weight.

We must do the princes of Germany in old times the justice to admit that, spite of the many scandalous transactions they engaged in, the interests of the nation always prevailed at last.

To uphold the ancient privileges of the empire against all attacks or encroachments of the See of Rome, was the motive which led the Rhenish electors to reject the proposals and arguments of the legate.

But was not Francis also a foreigner ? Could the electoral college venture so lightly to alienate from the nation that imperial crown which, at every diet, they solemnly promised to maintain ? There were those

[1] Letter from France, May 26. " In Franza non è alcun motivo di arme, ma ben la zente preparata."

[2] Letter from Zevenberghen ; Mone, p. 36. In the Netherlands Margaret forbade business relating to French bills of exchange to be transacted. Ibid., p. 293. But we find the imperial agents not always on a good understanding with the Fuggers. The Welsers seem to have done business on lower terms.

who did not fail to remark that Francis was an absolute monarch, accustomed to implicit obedience and possessed of great power, under whose sceptre the maintenance of German liberties could hardly be expected. The violent acts of his partisans were not calculated to make quiet patriots his friends.

On the other hand, the young King of Spain was without question a German. He reminded the German princes that the true stem and the first blossom of his nobility were from Austria : were he not a German, had he not land and lordships in Germany, he would withdraw from the contest.

How profound an effect was produced by this difference in the pretensions of the rivals, is distinctly shown by a remark of the papal delegates. They say, everyone will, in the end, deem it infamous to receive money from France ; but to take it from King Charles, is thought nothing of.

Public opinion had also already declared itself on the matter. The electors had it in their power to choose one of their own body,—a German prince. Had they chosen the King of France, taking money too for their votes, the result might have been dangerous to themselves

All these things were gradually so distinctly felt, that, by the middle of June, Charles's superiority was decided, and no further doubt was entertained of the event.

Henry VIII. of England for a moment cherished the hope of placing the crown on his own head, during the contest of the other two sovereigns ; but his ambassador acted with great discretion and reserve. He looked at the affair like a man of business, and, on calculation, he found this crown too dear a purchase for its value and utility.[1] A letter of his, of the 12th of June, shows that he had then given up all hope.

At this conjuncture Carracciolo, one of the pope's chargés-d'affaires, caused himself to be carried, ill as he was, to the archbishop of Mainz, in order that he might once more recommend to that prelate the interests of the church and of the King of France. The archbishop answered, that he took upon his own head the affairs of the church, but that he would have nothing to do with the King of France. The envoy asked upon whom the choice of the electors would fall ? The cardinal said, on the King of Spain ; and if not upon him, then upon the Elector of Saxony. The envoy was perfectly astonished that the cardinal, notwithstanding such repeated misunderstandings, still preferred the Elector of Saxony to the King of France.[2] These words perhaps decided the conduct of the Roman see. When Pope Leo found what the dispositions of Germany were, he was heard to exclaim, that it would not do to run one's head against the wall ; an expression characteristic of his policy, which was always that of giving way before an obstinate resistance. After having so long held out, he at length yielded (June 24th), and announced to the electors his assent to the election of the King of Spain and Naples.

When the electors assembled in Frankfurt there was not the smallest

---

[1] Richard Pace ; Ellis, i. 156. See Herbert, Life of Henry VIII., p. 74.

[2] " Lż esso Moguntino habbi gran inimicitia con Saxonia, lo vol avanti che il re christianissimo."

hope left for Francis : the only remaining obstacle to Charles's success
was the wish which had existed among them, of having a native of the
soil of Germany for their emperor.[1] The elector Joachim, who now put
forward urgent claims,[2] was thought of ; but his own relations, above all
his brother of Mainz, were against him : they found that the maintenance
of the imperial dignity would necessitate exertions and expenses which
would consume the resources of the Mark, and those of their whole family ;
they knew, too, that the princes of the empire would not choose a head
of so harsh, severe and self-willed a character. Joachim would never
have conciliated a sufficient number of voices. A far more formidable
rival existed in the person of Frederick of Saxony, on whom the eyes of
the assembly were now turned. Richard of Treves went to him once by
night, and offered to take a part of the labour of the canvass on himself.
His own hopes being utterly at an end, the King of France determined
to use his influence in favour of Frederick. Considering the conduct of
that prince in the Lutheran affairs, and the national tendencies with
which these affairs were connected, this certainly opened one of the
grandest prospects for the destiny of Germany. The electors were, on
the whole, well disposed towards the measure ; indeed it was afterwards
said, in the way of reproach, that if there had been one among them
" capable of sustaining the empire," he would have been chosen. Had
Frederick only been inspired by a more daring ambition ! Had he not
been of so cautious a nature, rendered still less enterprising by age !
But he had too long and too profound an acquaintance with the history
of the empire, not to know that a vast preponderance of power was necessary to hold together in union and subordination these haughty, energetic
princes and states, all striving for independence.

Although his resolution was taken, he once asked his follower, Philip
of Solms, his opinion. Philip replied, that he feared his lord would not
be able to use his power of punishing with due severity. Frederick
answered, that he was of the same opinion ; and declined the proffered
support.[3] The time was come, too, when no more reserves could be
maintained : he declared himself openly for King Charles. This declaration decided those who had till then been wavering.

On the 28th of June, the tocsin was sounded, according to ancient
custom, and the electors assembled, clad in their scarlet robes of state,
in the small dark chapel in the choir of the church of St. Bartholomew,
which served them as conclave. They were already unanimous. Mainz
addressed himself first, according to ancient precedent, to Treves, who
replied that he voted for the Archduke Charles of Austria, Prince of

[1] The Italians, for instance, could not at all comprehend why such a one was
not chosen. " Li electori " says Lippomano, the Venetian ambassador at Rome,
" saranno pazzi a non si far uno di loro." On this ground they willingly believed
that the Elector of Brandenburg would be chosen. " Scrive il Cl. Sedunese, sarà
il Brandenburg, 5 Giugno." Hereon rests also Vettori's opinion, that Leo had
never wished to give his support to the king, in whose behalf, however, he had
expressed himself far too decisively.

[2] According to a letter from the admiral, of the 17th or 18th of June, " Il Tre-
verese havea rimosso il Marchese di Brandenburg qual volea esser electo lui ;"
but he concluded thence, that the king had fresh hope.

[3] Extract from Lucas Geierberg, Leben Philipsen, Grafen von Solms, after the
preface to Göbel's Beiträgen zur Staatsgeschichte von Europa, p. 19.

Burgundy, King of Spain.   So said they all ; the King of France had not a vote.[1]

The electors were however mindful, in choosing so puissant a prince, immediately to take measures for securing the rights of the empire. They laid before the elected King of the Romans a rigorous capitulation, constructed on the principles which had been established during the last negotiations with Maximilian.[2]   In this it was decided that the public offices should be filled exclusively by Germans, the public proceedings carried on exclusively in the German language, and the assemblies of the empire invariably held within the frontiers of the German nation.   Nor did the electors forget their own privileges.   They stipulated that they were to have seats in the Council of Regency ; that no war was to be declared, no alliance concluded, no diet convoked—it is hardly necessary to add, no tax imposed—without their consent ; whatever was acquired by the counsel and aid of the States in war, should remain for ever the property of the empire.[3]

And here another reflection suggests itself.   The princes, it is true, elected a puissant monarch as their chief.   But it may be asked, was not his position, which rendered inevitable his frequent absence, favourable to the development of their own power ?

Under a prince like this, who had to govern so many countries, to provide against so many wars, they could most easily obtain that representative constitution, that share in the government of the empire, which it had been the constant object of their endeavours to acquire under Maximilian.

How strange a mixture of the most heterogeneous motives combined to bring about the election of Charles V. !   Pecuniary bribes (it is not to be denied) to a large amount, both to the princes, among whom were even Treves and Duke John of Saxony, and to their dependents and councillors ; the concession of new privileges ; family alliances, near or remote, which either already existed, or were now concluded, or contracted for the future : on the other hand, some degree of dread of the army of the Swabian league which was still in the field and in the pay of Austria ;[4] and, lastly, antipathy to the stranger, in spite of his still more profuse offers of money ; attachment to the house which had already given several emperors to Germany and which enjoyed traditional respect ; the dangers atetnding every other course ; the expectation of good results from that pursued ;—in short, a mixture of purely personal considerations and of sincere regard for the public weal !   Among the various influences which determined the event, we must not omit to add that of luck.   On the very day, nay the very hour, of election, an event took place in Lower Saxony, which, had it occurred earlier, might easily have rendered the issue once more doubtful, and have revived the hopes of the French party.

[1] Protocollum Electionis in Goldast's Polit. Reichshändeln, p. 41.   The speeches said to have been delivered on this occasion are fictitious.   See Ranke, Zur Kritik neuerer Geschichtschreiber, p. 62.

[2] Revers in Bucholtz, iii. 668.

[3] Capitulation, amongst others, in Dumont, iv. 7.   Unfortunately I have not been able to examine the documents.

Richard Pace to Cardinal Wolsey, i. 157.   " Suerly they wold nott have electidde him yff fere of these persons hadde not dryven them thereunto "

The cavalry of Gueldres had at length joined Duke Henry of Lüne-burg, who had set out without delay to seek in the field the plunder-laden army of his cousins. He came up with this near Soltau on the Haide, and began the attack without waiting for his infantry. His strength lay in his cavalry, which rushed up to the enemy's artillery and took it, then broke the lines of the infantry, partly mercenaries, who took to flight and threw their arms into the sand : animated by this success, the conquering troop then made a violent attack on the squadron of Calenberg horse. Here they met with a gallant resistance ; Duke Eric of Calenberg, distinguishable by his white plume, forced his way into their ranks ; but, in spite of his bravery, the Lüneburgers overpowered him by their numbers, and gained a complete victory. Eric himself, his brother William, and a hundred and twenty knights, were made prisoners by the partisans of the King of France.[1]

But since, as we have observed, the election of the emperor was con-cluded on the same day, this victory was utterly fruitless. The victors were now compelled to avoid all connexion with France, while the van-quished found favour and assistance from the commissioners of Charles V. at Augsburg. In October, Henry the Younger of Wolfenbüttel took up arms anew, aided, as it was believed, by money from Augsburg, and committed devastations in Hildesheim, estimated at a hundred and fifty thousand gulden ; and it was with difficulty that he could be induced by the neighbouring princes to grant a truce. He would agree to no definitive terms proposed by the mediators. He quitted Zerbst, where they were assembled, by night, without bidding them farewell, and only leaving word that he must reserve the matter for the decision of his imperial majesty (May, 1520). If France had defended the Lüneburgers, Austria and her fortunes now lent more powerful support to their adver-saries.

The affairs of Upper Germany at the same moment took a still more decisive turn in the same direction. Würtemberg passed entirely into Austrian hands.

The cause of this was that Duke Ulrich, in this unexpected attack in August, had driven out the government of the league, taken the country again into his own possession, and was only expelled from it by renewed efforts of that body.[2] This conquest was now burdensome to the con-querors : the expenses of the former war, for which they earnestly desired some compensation, were now, on the contrary, increased by new ones. The members of the league, therefore, joyfully accepted the emperor's proposition to take into his charge and custody the country, together with the duke's children ; and, in consideration of this concession, he promised to accede to the demands of the States.[3] In February, 1520, the imperial commissioners took the administration into their own hands ; and by confirming the treaty of Tübingen, which Ulrich at his return had been imprudent enough to revoke, they secured a considerable party in the country.

[1] Chytræus, Saxonia, lib. viii., p. 207. Carmen prolixius, in Leibnitz, Scrip-tores Rer. Brunsv. iii. 257.

[2] Stumphart, Chronica gwaltiger Verjagung Herzog Ulrichs (Chronicle of the forcible Expulsion of Duke Ulrich) : Sattler, Herzoge, ii., Appendices, p. 43.

[3] Gwalt K. Karls V. auf seine Commissarien, ibid., p. 79.

This first act of Charles's government wore a very arbitrary aspect. For it was utterly unheard of that, as the Swiss expressed it, " a prince of the Holy Empire should be driven from his illustrious house, contrary to all law, and forcibly despoiled of the principality which was his by paternal inheritance and right." But the commissioners regarded the election as a triumph of the Austrian party, and were only anxious to turn it to their own advantage.

This had not been the intention of the electors,—least of all that of Frederick of Saxony; on the contrary, they had immediately considered how to introduce a uniform representative government, to convoke an imperial diet, and to appoint a Council of Regency. The court of Spain appeared to approve cordially of these measures ; a proclamation arrived, in which Elector Frederick was nominated lieutenant (*Statthalter*) of the Regency, and was also intreated to give his good counsel in public affairs. But the commissioners did not think fit to convoke a diet, still less to nominate a Council of Regency. They carefully avoided consulting the elector, and kept the diploma of his nomination to themselves. They were as fully determined now, as under Maximilian, to resist all interference on the part of the States ; they chose to retain the whole of the public business in their own hands.

This ought to excite no wonder. These imperial functionaries remained firmly attached to those views which had become current under Maximilian, and regarded the new government as a mere continuation of the old.

It therefore became a matter of double solicitude to ascertain in what light the young prince, on his arrival in Germany, and those around him, would regard affairs, or in what spirit he would undertake their management. His commanding station and wide sovereignty naturally led people to expect views proportionately grand and elevated ; and such indeed were displayed in all his letters. He wrote to Elector Frederick that he should find that he had given his vote to the most grateful of princes ; that he would shortly appear in person, hold a diet, and order the affairs of the empire with the counsel and approbation of his well-beloved, the Elector ; " for," said he, " we esteem marvellously the designs, the counsel, and the wisdom of thy rule."[1]

Before, however, Charles could arrive, the religious affairs of Germany had assumed a character which rendered the question, what course he would embrace, no less important to the church than to the empire.

CHAPTER III

First Defection from the Papacy, 1519-20.

CAJETAN AND MILTITZ.

During the interval we have been treating of, it had more than once appeared probable that the Lutheran controversy would be brought to a peaceful termination ; to this both sides were inclined.

---

[1] Instruction to Hieronymus Brunner, Barcelona, Sept. 25, 1519, in a register in the Weimar archives, which lays open the whole of the circumstances.

During the diet at Augsburg, Elector Frederick prevailed on himself to pay a visit to the papal legate, and to invite his mediation. I do not find that the latter had any special commission from Rome to this effect, but his general powers gave him full liberty to accept such an office. He promised the elector to listen to the monk whenever he should appear before him, and to dismiss him with paternal kindness.[1]

The business of the meeting was already ended, when Luther, well pleased at not being obliged to go to Rome, set out to present himself before the cardinal. He travelled indeed in a most lowly guise; the cowl he wore was borrowed, and he wandered on, craving hospitality from convent to convent, ill, and sometimes exhausted even to fainting.[2] He often said afterwards, that if the cardinal had treated him kindly, he might easily have induced him to keep silence. When he came into his presence he fell down at his feet.

Unhappily, however, this legate, Thomas de Vio of Gaeta (Cajetan), was not only a representative of the Curia, but a most zealous Thomist. His mother, it is said, dreamt when she was with child of him, that she saw St. Thomas in person teaching him, and afterwards bearing him to heaven.[3] In his sixteenth year, in spite of the great reluctance of his family, he was not to be withheld from entering a Dominican convent, where laying aside his original name of James, he took that of his saint, and exerted all his powers thoroughly to imbue his mind with the doctrines of St. Thomas, whom he esteemed the most perfect theologian that ever existed. He undertook to defend his great work, the Summa, step by step, against the objections of the Scotists.[4]

Luther, therefore, was already extremely odious to him as a nominalist, as an impugner of the theological despotism of St. Thomas, and as leader of an active opposition party in a newly-created university. At first he replied to Luther's humility with the official fatherly condescension of a spiritual superior. But the natural antagonism between them soon broke out. The cardinal was not disposed to be satisfied with mere silence, nor would he permit the matter to come to a disputation, as Luther proposed; he thought he had demonstrated the monk's error to him in a few words, and demanded a recantation. This awakened in Luther a feeling of that complete contrariety of opinions and systems, which acknowledges no subordination, whether spiritual or temporal. It appeared to him that the cardinal did not even understand his idea of faith, far less confute it: a conversation arose in which Luther displayed more reading, more distinctness and depth of view, than the legate had given him credit for; speculations of so extraordinary a kind had never come before him; the deep-set glittering eyes, fixed upon his, inspired him with a sort of

---

[1] Frederick's letter to Cajetan (Löscher, ii. 543): "Persuaseramus nobis, vestram pietatem audito Martino secundum vestram multiplicem promissionem eum paterne et benevole dimissuram esse." See Luther, wider Hans Worst Altenb. vii. 462. Letter to Lang in de Wette, i. 141.

[2] Luther to Spalatin, Oct. 10, 1518, in de W. 142.

[3] So says the Biography in Roccaberti, Bibl. Max. t. xix., p. 443.

[4] "Divi Thomæ Summa cum commentariis Thomæ de Vio, Lugduni, 1587. Præfatio: "Inter theologos quem divo Thomæ Aquinati præferre ausis, invenies neminem."

horror ; at length he exclaimed that Luther must either recant or never venture into his sight again.[1]

It was the dominican system which here, clad in purple, repulsed its antagonist.   Luther, though furnished with a safe-conduct from the emperor, thought himself no longer secure from violence ; he drew up an appeal to the pope, praying him to inquire into the matter, and took to flight.   His going corresponded with his coming.   Escaping through a secret gate which his Augsburg friends opened for him by night, mounted on a horse procured for him by his provincial, Staupitz, habited in his cowl, and without any proper riding garments, he rode, accompanied by a mounted guide, eight long German miles the first day ; on alighting, he fell half dead from fatigue by the side of his horse on the straw.   But he was happily out of the immediate jurisdiction of the legate.

Cajetan's accusations soon followed him to Saxony.   He conjured the elector not to stain the glory of his house for the sake of an heretical friar ; if he did not choose to send him to Rome, at least to get rid of him out of his country ; he declared that Rome would never suffer this affair to drop.   But he could no longer produce any impression ; his indiscreet and violent conduct had robbed him of all credit with Frederick.   The university wrote to their prince that they knew no otherwise than that Luther showed all due reverence for the church, and even for the pope ; were there wickedness in the man, they would be the first to notice it. This corporation was irritated that the legate should treat one of its members as a heretic, before any sentence had been pronounced.[2]   Thus seconded, Frederick replied to the legate, that it had not yet been shown by any of the numerous learned men in his own states, or those contiguous, that Luther was a heretic ; and refused to banish him.[3]

Luther however did not conceal from himself that the sentence pronounced by Rome might very probably be unfavourable to him.   He hastened to secure himself against this as far as possible by a fresh appeal to the general council which was just about to be called.

But the conduct of the cardinal did not obtain the approbation of Rome.   That court was not disposed to alienate so considerable and respected a sovereign as Frederick, who had just acquired twofold weight by his conduct at the election, and with whom it had probably rested to raise the King of France to the imperial throne, as the pope had desired. Leo therefore now made an attempt to bring the discussion concerning Luther to an amicable conclusion.   He determined to send the elector the golden rose, a mark of the apostolical favour, for which that prince had always been very anxious.   In order to draw the loosened ties closer between them, he likewise despatched a native of Saxony, and agent of the elector at Rome, to him as nuncio.

Karl von Miltitz unquestionably showed great address in the manner in which he set about the affair.

---

[1] Luther's report in the Acta Augustana, his letters, the addresses of the legate, finally a letter from Staupitz, in Grimm (passim, p. 123), give sufficient information about this interview.   It is to be regretted that the account sent by the legate to Rome has never come to light.

[2] With regard to the brief in which mention is made of a sentence already passed (in Löscher, ii. 438), I think I have shown in an Excursus, that it is not genuine.

[3] Correspondence in Löscher, 537–542.

On his arrival in Germany he abstained from visiting the legate, who indeed had lost all influence, and now showed a sullen resentment against the elector ; even on the journey, Miltitz contracted an intimacy with one of Frederick's privy councillors, Degenhard Pfeffinger. He did not scruple among friends, over the convivial table, or even in inns and taverns, to join in the complaints which were made in Germany of the Curia, and of the abuses of the church ; nay, to confirm them by anecdotes of what he had himself witnessed. But he assured his hearers that he knew the pope, and had influence with him, and that Leo did not approve these things. He pronounced the most entire and distinct disapprobation of the scandalous proceedings of the vendors of indulgences ; and in short the reputation which preceded him was such that Tetzel did not dare to present himself before him.[1]

On the other hand, the prince, towards whom he maintained the demeanour of a subject and servant, and Luther himself, whom he treated very indulgently, conceived great confidence in him. Without much trouble, he succeeded in bringing about that degree of approximation between himself and the anti-dominican party, which was absolutely necessary to the success of his negotiation.

On the 3rd January, 1519, he had an interview with Luther at Altenburg. The nuncio represented to the monk the evils which arose from his vehemence, and the great breach which he would thus make in the church : he implored him with tears to lay these things to heart. Luther promised to remedy, by a public explanation of his doctrine, whatever mischief he might have done. On the other hand, the nuncio gave up the idea of bringing Luther to a recantation. They came to an agreement that the matter should be referred to a German bishop, and that, meanwhile, both parties should be bound to observe silence.[2] So, thought Luther, the controversy would die away. They embraced and parted.

The explanation which Luther soon after published, in consequence of this conversation, is very remarkable. He touches on all the controverted points of the moment. Without abandoning the free attitude he had assumed, he shows that he considers himself as still within the pale of the Roman church ; for example, he maintains that the saints ought to be invoked for spiritual, rather than for temporal gifts, but he does not deny that God works miracles at their graves ; he still admits the doctrine of purgatory, and of indulgences in a certain sense ; he wishes for some relaxation of the commandments of the church, but is of opinion that this could only be granted by an ecclesiastical council ; although he ascribes salvation to the fear of God and the state of the thoughts and intentions, he does not entirely reject good works. It is evident that on every point he insists on inward, rather than outward influences and merits ; but he does so with great moderation, and endeavours to maintain external observances. In the same spirit he speaks of the church. He sees her essence in " inward unity and love " ; but he does not reject her constitution ; he acknowledges the supremacy of the church of Rome, " where St. Peter and St. Paul, forty-six popes, and hundreds of thou-

---

[1] His letter of apology, subscribed " Brother Tetzel, on the last day of Dec., 1519," (*i.e.* 1518), in Walch, xv., p. 860. The rest of Miltitz's Correspondence, first published by Cyprian, is also to be found in Walch.

[2] " In ir selbs vorgehn."—Luther to the Electors, in De Wette, i. 218.

sands of martyrs, poured out their blood, and overcame hell and the world " : no sin that can be committed in her can justify us in separating ourselves from her, or in resisting the commands of the pope.[1]

With this explanation the ecclesiastical authority might for the moment be content—and indeed was forced to be content. For, if Elector Frederick chose to accept it, there was no other power that could be turned against Luther : so great was the interest which the nation already took in his cause ; so strong the aversion which repelled all interference of the court of Rome.

In the early months of the year 1519, when the demands of the last diet in behoof of the Turkish war were made to the several States in all parts of Germany, the doubts expressed in that assembly as to the reality of the intention which served as pretext were now repeated in various circles, and were more and more widely diffused ; all the well-founded complaints which had there been more distinctly stated than ever, were now the topic of discourse through the whole nation.

Moreover, the interest which the papal legate had evinced in the views of Francis I. on the imperial crown, excited great disgust. It is a fact well worth notice, that the whole Austrian party thus naturally fell into a state of hostility to the Roman see. At the court of its leader, the Elector of Mainz, there appeared satires in which the pompous inanity of the legate, his personal peculiarities and the oppressive nature of his office, were ridiculed in the bitterest manner. In the spring of 1519,[2] it was with difficulty that he could find a boatman in Mainz who would consent to take him down the river to Niederwesel, where the Rhenish electors held a meeting : he was once told that he must renounce all his French schemes if he wished to get home in a whole skin.[3]

This universal unpopularity compelled the court of Rome to observe a discreet reserve, to which its interest in the election contributed, and thus it happened that Rome once more tried by every means in its power to be upon a footing of amity with Elector Frederick. Another plenipotentiary of the Curia besides Miltitz appeared in Saxony. The legate, although with obvious ill will, was at length prevailed upon to deliver to the elector the golden rose which had been entrusted to him, and which he had till now withheld. The prospect of putting an end to the controversy in Germany was desirable and commodious even to him. The Archbishop of Treves was selected as judge.[4]

ARRIVAL OF MELANCHTHON.

THE state of suspended controversy and preliminary calm that now arose was peculiarly advantageous to the university of Wittenberg. There was a general sentiment of an undertaking successfully begun, increasing in force of opposition, but yet not obnoxious to the condemnation of the

---

[1] D. M. L. Unterricht auf etliche Artikel so ihm von seinen Abgönnern aufgelegt worden : Walch, xv. 812.

[2] Hutten's Febris Prima (op. iii. 109) belongs to this period.

[3] Letter to Zürich in Anshelm, Berne Chronik, v. 373.

[4] Miltitz to the Electors : Walch, xv. 879 : he had seen the legate at Coblentz. The instruction to Miltitz, l. l., must likewise be assigned to the month of May, as it refers to his journey into Saxony, which he mentions in his letter, dated Wednesday after Misericordia, May 11.

church. The members of the university had time to carry forward the proper studies of the place in the spirit that had from the first presided over them. The most eminent teachers still held the same opinions on the main question. Besides this, in the summer of 1518, they had acquired a youthful assistant, whose labours from the first moment gave new life to their whole proceedings.

Philip Schwarzerd, surnamed Melanchthon, was, in the truest and most perfect sense, a disciple of Reuchlin. Reuchlin was one of his nearest relations, and had directed his education : the young man followed the precepts and the example of his master with intelligent docility ; the native powers which well-conducted studies never fail to develop, the sympathy he received from his fellow-students, and above all, a matchless capacity, certain, from the first, of its vocation, led him rapidly forwards. In his 17th or 18th year he had already begun to teach in Tübingen, and had published two or three little books on grammatical subjects.[1]

But the mind of the pupil, like that of the master, was not satisfied with philological studies. He attended lectures in all faculties; for the sciences were not as yet cultivated in such detail or in so special a manner, as to render that impossible ; they could still furnish nutriment to a large and liberal curiosity. Melanchthon felt peculiarly attracted towards the study of philosophy, in comparison with which all his other pursuits appeared to him mere waste of time. But the rigid, stationary spirit of the old universities still reigned in Tübingen ; and while his whole intellectual powers were stretching forward to unknown regions, his instructors sought to bind him down to a lifeless routine.

A circumstance, however, occurred which decided both his outward destiny and the direction of his mind. In the spring of 1518, Elector Frederick applied to Reuchlin to send him a teacher of the Greek language for his university. Without a moment's hesitation, Reuchlin recommended " his kinsman and friend," whom he himself had instructed.[2] This might be regarded as involving Melanchthon's decision ; for between master and disciple there was that noble relation which exists between a youth who beholds the world in the imperfect light shed over distant objects, and the admitted superiority of a matured judgment. " Whither thou wilt send me," writes Melanchthon to Reuchlin, " there will I go ; what thou wilt make of me, that will I become." " Get thee out," answered Reuchlin, " from thy country and from thy kindred." With the words once addressed to Abraham, he blessed him and bade him depart.

In August, 1518, Melanchthon came to Wittenberg. His first determination was, as he says, to devote himself entirely to the university, and to raise its fame in the classical studies which had as yet been cultivated with little success. With the high spirits of youth he reckoned up the labours he had before him, and hastened to enter upon them.[3] Before September was over, he dedicated to the elector the translation of one of

[1] Schnurrer de Phil. Melanchthonis rebus Tubingensibus : Orationes Academ. ed. Paulus, p. 52. Præfatio in primam editionem operum. Bretschneiders Corpus Reformatorum, iv. 715.
[2] Correspondence in the Corp. Ref. i. 28.
[3] To Spalatin, Sept., 1518. Corp. Ref. i. 43.

Lucian's works ; in October he printed the Epistle to Titus and a little dictionary ; in November he wrote the preface to a Hebrew Grammar. He immediately undertook a more elaborate work,—his Rhetoric, which appeared in three books, in January, 1519. In February followed another discourse ; in March and April editions of several of Plutarch's writings, with a preface—all during an equally varied and laborious course of teaching ; for the youthful stranger undertook to give instructions in Hebrew as well as Greek.[1]

Yet these immediate occupations led neither to the scope, nor to the results, of his laborious studies.

It was an important circumstance that a perfect master of Greek arose at this moment at a university, where the development of the Latin theology already led to a return to the first genuine documents of primitive Christianity. Luther now began to pursue this study with earnestness. His mind was relieved, and his confidence strengthened, when the sense of a Greek phrase threw a sudden light on his theological ideas ; when, for example, he learned that the idea of repentance (poenitentia), which, according to the language of the Latin church, signified expiation or satisfaction, in the original conception of the Founder and the apostles of Christianity signified nothing but a change in the state of mind :[2] it seemed as if a mist was suddenly withdrawn from before his eyes.

It was also of inestimable value to Melanchthon that he could here devote himself to subjects which filled his whole soul, and that he now found the substance of those forms to which his attention had hitherto been principally directed. He embraced with enthusiasm the theological views of Luther, and above all, his profound exposition of the doctrine of justification. But he was not formed to receive these opinions passively. He was one of those extraordinary spirits, appearing at rare intervals, who attain to the full possession and use of their powers at an early period of life. He was now but just twenty-one. With the precision which solid philological studies seldom fail to impart,—with the nice instinct natural to the frame of his mind, he seized the theological element which was offered to his grasp.

The somewhat unfavourable impression which the youthful and unpretending appearance of the new comer had at first made, was quickly effaced. The scholars caught the infection of their teacher's zeal. " They are as industrious as ants at the university," says Luther. Reforms in the method of instruction were proposed. With the approbation of the court, lectures were discontinued which had no value but for the scholastic system, and others were instituted, founded on classical studies ; the conditions upon which academical degrees were granted were rendered less severe. These measures unquestionably tended to place Wittenberg in stronger contrast to the other universities ; new views and ideas were introduced. Luther's letters show the ferment that was going on within him, but they equally show that neither he nor those associated with him were conscious of being involved in a general struggle with the church of Rome. We saw how carefully Luther kept within the bounds prescribed

---

[1] Luther to Spalatin, Jan. 25, in De Wette, i. 214. Upon these two correspondences, as may be imagined, my whole narrative is founded.

[2] μετάνοια.

by the church ; and Melanchthon, in one of his prefaces, extols the services rendered by his sovereign to monasteries.[1]   This, as well as the conduct pursued by Miltitz, and finally also by the legate, shows that every thing wore a peaceful aspect.

But at this very moment, when external peace at least was restored, and when, though vehement struggles were to be anticipated from differences of opinion and of education, it was possible they might be confined within the region of school learning, there arose a contest touching those important doctrines whereon the Church and the State are founded, and lighting up that war which has never since been extinguished.   It must be admitted that Luther was not the person who caused its outbreak.

DISPUTATION AT LEIPZIG.

DURING the diet of 1518, Eck had appeared in Augsburg, dissatisfied that his polemical writings had as yet procured him neither emolument nor honour :[2] he had called on Luther, and had agreed with him, in a perfectly amicable manner, publicly to fight out an old controversy which he had with Dr. Carlstadt in Wittenberg, concerning grace and free will. Luther had readily offered his mediation, in order, as he says, to give the lie to the opinion that theologians cannot differ without hostility.   Carlstadt consented to dispute with Eck in Erfurt or Leipzig ; upon which Eck immediately published a prospectus of the disputation, and made it known as widely as possible.

Luther's astonishment was extreme when he saw in this prospectus certain opinions announced as the subject of the debate, of which he was far more the champion than Carlstadt.   He held this for an act of faithlessness and duplicity which he was called upon openly to resist ; the agreement he had just concluded with Miltitz seemed to him broken ; he was determined to take up the gauntlet.[3]

It was of vast importance that Eck had annexed to the dogmatic controversy, a proposition as to the origin of the prerogatives of the papacy. At a moment when anti-papal opinions were so decidedly triumphant throughout the nation, he had the clumsy servility to stir a question, always of very difficult and dubious solution, yet from which the whole system of the Church and State depended, and, when once agitated, certain to occupy universal attention : he ventured to irritate an adversary who knew no reservations, who was accustomed to defend his opinions to the utmost, and who had already the voice of the nation on his side.   In reference to a former assertion of Luther's, which had attracted little attention, Eck propounded the maxim, that the primacy of the Pope of Rome was derived from Christ himself, and from the times of St. Peter ; not, as his opponent had hinted, from those of Constantine and Sylvester. The consequences of this gross imprudence were soon apparent.   Luther, who now began to study the original documents of the papal law—the decretals, and had often in the course of this study felt his Christian convictions wounded, answered with a much bolder assertion, namely, that the primacy of Rome had been first established by the decretals of the

---

[1] Dedication of Lucian in Calumniam.   C.R. i. 47.
[2] Bartholini Commentarius de comitiis Augustanis, p. 645.
[3] Luther's letters to Sylvius, Feb. 3 ; Spalatin, Feb. 7 ; Lang, April 13.

later popes in the last four centuries (he meant, perhaps, since Gregory VII.), and that the primitive church knew nothing of it.[1]

It is not surprising that the ecclesiastical authorities in Saxony, (for example, the bishop of Merseburg) and even the theologians of the university, were not much pleased that a disputation of the kind at last agreed upon between the parties, should be held in Leipzig. Even the elector hesitated for a moment whether he should allow Luther to go. But, as he had the firmest conviction that hidden truth would best be brought to light in this manner, he at length determined that it should take place, and endeavoured to obviate every objection that stood in its way. It was settled that, together with various other important points of doctrine on the mysteries of faith, the question, whether the papacy was established by God, or whether it was instituted by man, and consequently might be abolished by man (for that is in fact the point at issue in the two doctrines), was to be argued in a public disputation, at a great university, in the face of all Germany ; that this question, the very one in which all political and ecclesiastical interests met as in a point, was to be thus discussed in a period of ferment and of ardent innovation.

At the very moment when the electors assembled at Frankfurt to choose an emperor, (June, 1519,) the theologians met to perform an act of no less importance.

Eck arrived first from Ingolstadt. Johann Mayr von Eck was unquestionably one of the most eminent scholars of his time—a reputation which he had spared no pains to acquire. He had visited the most celebrated professors in various universities : the Thomist Süstern at Cologne, the Scotists Sumenhard and Scriptoris at Tübingen ; he had attended the law lectures of Zasius in Freiburg, those on Greek of Reuchlin, on Latin of Bebel, on cosmography of Reusch. In his twentieth year he began to write and to lecture at Ingolstadt upon Occam and Biel's canon law, on Aristotle's dialectics and physics, the most difficult doctrines of dogmatic theology, and the subtilties of nominalistic morality ; he then proceeded to the study of the mystics, whose most curious works had just fallen into his hands : he set himself, as he says, to establish the connexion between their doctrines and the Orphicoplatonic philosophy, the sources of which are to be sought in Egypt and Arabia, and to discuss the whole in five parts.[2] He was one of those learned men who held that the great questions which had occupied men's minds were essentially settled ; who worked exclusively with the analytical faculty and the memory ; who were always on the watch to appropriate to themselves a new subject with which to excite attention, to get advancement, and to secure a life of ease and enjoyment. His strongest taste was for disputation, in which he had made a brilliant figure in all the universities we have mentioned, as well as in Heidelberg, Mainz, and Basle : at Freiburg he had early presided over a class (the *Bursa zum Pfauen*) where the chief business was practice in disputation ; he then took long journeys,—for example, to Vienna and Bologna,—expressly to dispute there. It is most amusing

---

[1] Contra novos et veteres errores defendet D. Martinus Lutherus has sequentes positiones in studio Lipsensi. It is the thirteenth proposition. Opp. lat. Jen. i. 221.

[2] Eckii Epistola de ratione, studiorum suorum, in Strobel's Miscellaneen, iii., p. 97.

to see in his letters the satisfaction with which he speaks of his Italian journey : how he was encouraged to undertake it by a papal nuncio ; how, before his departure, he was visited by the young Markgrave of Brandenburg ; the very honourable reception he experienced on his way, in Italy as well as in Germany, from both spiritual and temporal lords, who invited him to their tables ; how, when certain young men had ventured to contradict him at one of these dinners, he had confuted them with the utmost ease, and left them filled with astonishment and admiration ; and lastly, how, in spite of manifold opposition, he had at last brought the most learned of the learned in Bologna to subscribe to his maxims.[1] He regarded a disputation with the eye of a practised fencer, as the arena of unfailing victory ; his only wish was to find new adversaries on whom to try his weapons. He therefore seized with avidity on an opportunity of extending his fame in North Germany. He was now seen in the midst of the Leipzig professors (who welcomed him as an ally against their neighbouring rival and enemy), taking part in the procession of the Corpus Christi, dressed in his priestly garments and with an air of great devotion. In his letters we find that he did not neglect to institute a nice comparison between the Saxon beer and that of Bavaria ; and also that the fair sinners of Leipzig did not escape his notice.[2]

On the 24th of June the Wittenbergers arrived ; the professers in low open waggons on rollers or solid wooden wheels (*Rollwagen*), Carlstadt first, then Luther and Melanchthon, and some young licentiates and bachelors ; with them was Duke Barnim of Pomerania, who was then studying in Wittenberg and held the dignity of rector ; around them, on foot, some hundreds of zealous students armed with halberds, battle-axes and spears. It was observed that the Leipzigers did not come out to meet them, as was the custom and the courtesy of those times.[3]

With the mediation of Duke George, the terms of the combat were next settled : Eck reluctantly acquiesced in the condition that the speeches and rejoinders should be written down by notaries ; while Luther was forced to concede that the decision was to be left to certain universities ; he himself proposed Paris and Erfurt. The duke insisted, with peculiar earnestness, on these things ; he treated the affair like a trial at law, and wanted to send the documents, as it were, to a court of appeal for its decision. Meanwhile he ordered a spacious hall in the castle to be got ready for the literary duel ; two pulpits were placed opposite to each other, covered with tapestry, on which were the figures of the warrior saints, St. George and St. Martin ; there was ample provision of tables for the notaries, and of benches for the audience. At length, on the 27th of June, the action was commenced with a mass and invocation of the Holy Ghost.

Carlstadt had insisted on his right of opening the debate, but he acquired little glory from it. He brought books, out of which he read passages, then hunted for others, then read again ; the objections which his opponent advanced one day, he answered the next.[4] How different a *dis-*

[1] Riederer, Nachrichten, &c., iii. 47.
[2] Eck to Haven and Burkard, July 1, in Walch, xv., p. 1456. In this respect he had the very worst reputation.
[3] Pfeifer's Beschreibung, ibid., p. 1435.
[4] Rubeus, in Walch, xv. 1491.

putator was Johann Eck ! His knowledge was all at his command, ready for use at the moment ; he required so little time for preparation, that immediately after his return from a ride he mounted the chair. He was tall, with large muscular limbs, and loud penetrating voice, and walked backwards and forwards while speaking ; he had an exception ready to take against every argument ; his memory and address dazzled his hearers. In the matter itself—the explanation of the doctrine of grace and free-will—no progress was, of course, made. Sometimes the combatants approximated so nearly in opinion, that each boasted he had brought over the other to his side, but they soon diverged again. With the exception of a distinction made by Eck, nothing new was produced ;[1] the most important points were scarcely touched upon ; and the whole affair was sometimes so tedious that the hall was emptied.

The interest was, therefore, the more intense, when at length, on Monday the 4th of July, at seven in the morning, Luther arose ; the antagonist whom Eck most ardently desired to meet, and whose rising fame he hoped to crush by a brilliant victory. Luther was of the middle size, at that time so thin as to be mere skin and bone ; he possessed neither the thundering organ, nor the ready memory stored with various knowledge, nor the skill and dexterity acquired in the gladiatorial exercises of the schools, that distinguished his opponent. But he, too, stood in the prime of manhood, and in the fulness of his strength : he was in his thirty-sixth year ; his voice was melodious and clear ; he was perfectly versed in the Bible, and its aptest sentences presented themselves unbidden to his mind : above all, he inspired an irresistible conviction that he sought the truth. He was always cheerful at home, and a joyous jocose companion at table ; he even, on this grave occasion, ascended the platform with a nosegay in his hand ; but when there, he displayed the intrepid and self-forgetting earnestness arising from the depths of a conviction till now unfathomed, even by himself. He drew forth new thoughts and placed them in the fire of battle, with a determination that knew no fear and no personal regards. His features bore the traces of the storms that had passed over his soul, and of the courage with which he was prepared to encounter those that yet awaited him ; his whole aspect breathed profound thought, joyousness of temper, and confidence in the future. The battle immediately commenced on the question of the authority of the papacy, which, at once intelligible and important, riveted universal attention. Two sons of German peasants (for Eck, too, was the son of a peasant,—Michel Mayr, who was for many years Ammann[2] of Eck, as Luther's father was Rathsherr[2] of Mansfeld) represented the two great tendencies of opinion which divided the world then, and divide it now ; the future condition of the Church and the State mainly hung on the issue of their conflict—on the success of the one in attack, and of the other in defence.

It was immediately obvious that Luther could not maintain his assertion, that the pope's primacy dated only from the last four centuries : he soon found himself forced from this position by ancient documents, and the rather, that no criticism had as yet shaken the authenticity of the false decretals. But his attack on the doctrine, that the primacy of the

[1] Rogatus largireturne totum opus bonum esse a deo respondit : totum quidem, non autem totaliter.—Melanchthon.
[2] Titles of local magistrates.—TRANSL.

pope (whom he still persisted in regarding as the ecumenical bishop) was
founded on Scripture and by divine right, was far more formidable.
Christ's words, " Thou art Peter, feed My sheep," which have always
been cited in this controversy, were brought forward :[1] Luther laboured
to support the already well-known explanation of them, at variance with
that of the Curia, by other passages which record similar commissions given
to the Apostles.   Eck quoted passages from the Fathers in support of his
opinions, to which Luther opposed others from the same source.   As soon
as they got into these more recondite regions, Luther's superiority became
incontestable.   One of his main arguments was, that the Greeks had never
acknowledged the pope, and yet had not been pronounced heretics ; the
Greek church had stood, was standing, and would stand, without the pope ;
it belonged to Christ as much as the Roman.   Eck did not hesitate at
once to declare that the Christian and the Roman church were one ; that
the churches of Greece and Asia had fallen away, not only from the pope,
but from the Christian faith—they were unquestionably heretics : in the
whole circuit of the Turkish empire, for example, there was not one soul
that could be saved, with the exception of the few who adhered to the
pope of Rome.   " How ?" said Luther, " would you pronounce damnation on the whole Greek church, which has produced the most eminent
fathers, and so many thousand saints, of whom not one had even heard
of a Roman primate ?   Would Gregory of Nazianzen, would the great
Basil, not be saved ? or would the pope and his satellites drive them out
of heaven ?"   These expressions prove how greatly the omnipotence and
exclusive validity of the forms of the Latin church, and the identity with
Christianity which she claimed, were shaken by the fact that, beyond her
pale, the ancient Greek church, which she had herself acknowledged,
stood in all the venerable authority of her great teachers.   It was now
Eck's turn to be hard pressed : he repeated that there had been many
heretics in the Greek church, and that he alluded to them, not to the
Fathers,—a miserable evasion, which did not in the least touch the assertion of his adversary.   Eck felt this, and hastened back to the domain
of the Latin church.   He particularly insisted that Luther's opinion,—
that the primacy of Rome was of human institution, and not of divine
right,—was an error of the poor brethren of Lyons, of Wickliffe and Huss,
but had been condemned by the popes and especially by the general
councils wherein dwelt the spirit of God, and recently at that of Constance.   This new fact was as indisputable as the former.   Eck was not
satisfied with Luther's declaration that he had nothing to do with the
Bohemians, nay, that he condemned their schism ; and that he would not
be answered out of the Collectanea of inquisitors, but out of the Scriptures.   The question had now arrived at its most critical and important
moment.   Did Luther acknowledge the direct influence of the Divine
Spirit over the Latin church, and the binding force of the decrees of her
councils, or did he not ?   Did he inwardly adhere to her, or did he not ?
We must recollect that we are here not far from the frontier of Bohemia ;

[1] In the exposition by Nicolaus von Lire (Lyranus) also, of which Luther
made the most use, there occurs this explanation, differing from that of the Curia,
of the passage in Matthew, chap. xvi. : " Quia tu es Petrus, *i.e.* confessor veræ
petræ, qui est Christus factus ;—et super hanc petram, quam confessus es,
i.e. super Christum, ædificabo ecclesiam meam."

in a land which, in consequence of the anathema pronounced in Constance, had experienced all the horrors of a long and desolating war, and had placed its glory in the resistance it had offered to the Hussites : at a university founded in opposition to the spirit and doctrine of John Huss : in the face of princes, lords, and commoners whose fathers had fallen in this struggle ; it was said, that delegates from the Bohemians, who had anticipated the turn which this conflict must take, were also present : Luther saw the danger of his position. Should he really reject the prevailing notion of the exclusive power of the Roman church to secure salvation ; oppose a council by which John Huss had been condemned to the flames, and perhaps draw down a like fate upon himself ? Or should he deny that higher and more comprehensive idea of a Christian church which he had conceived, and in which his whole soul lived and moved ? Luther did not waver for a moment. He had the boldness to affirm, that among the articles on which the council of Constance grounded its condemnation of John Huss, some were fundamentally Christian and evangelical. The assertion was received with universal astonishment. Duke George, who was present, put his hands to his sides, and shaking his head uttered aloud his wonted curse, " A plague upon it !"[1] Eck now gathered fresh courage. It was hardly possible, he said, that Luther could censure a council, since his Grace the Elector had expressly forbidden any attack upon councils. Luther reminded him that the council of Constance had not condemned all the articles of Huss as heretical, and specified some which were likewise to be found in St. Augustine. Eck replied that all were rejected ; the sense in which these particular articles were understood was to be deemed heretical ; for a council could not err. Luther answered that no council could create a new article of faith ; how then could it be maintained that no council whatever was subject to error ? " Reverend father," replied Eck, " if you believe that a council regularly convoked can err, you are to me as a heathen and a publican."

Such were the results of this disputation.[2] It was continued for a time, and opinions more or less conflicting on purgatory, indulgences, and penance were uttered. Eck renewed the interrupted contest with Carlstadt ; the reports were sent, after the solemn conclusion, to both universities ; but all these measures could lead to nothing further. The main result of the meeting was, that Luther no longer acknowledged the authority of the Roman church in matters of faith. At first, he had only attacked the instructions given to the preachers of indulgences, and the rules of the later schoolmen, but had expressly retained the decretals of the popes : then he had rejected these, but with appeal to the decision of a council ; he now emancipated himself from this last remaining human authority also ; he recognised none but that of the Scriptures.

PROGRESS OF THE THEOLOGICAL OPPOSITION.

At this period Luther conceived an idea of the Church different from any he had before entertained—deeper and more comprehensive. He recognised in the Oriental and Greek Christians true members of the

---

[1] " This I myself heard and saw."—*Froschel's Report in Walch*, xv. 1400.

[2] " Disputatio Excellentissimorum Theologorum Jodannis Eccii et D. Martini Lutehri Augustiniani quæ Lipsiæ cœpta fuit iv die Julii aō 1519. Opera Lutheri Jen., i. 231.

universal church : he no longer admitted the necessity of a visible head ; he acknowledged none but the Invisible, the ever-living Founder, whom he regarded as standing in a mystical relation to his faithful disciples of every nation and clime.   This was not only a dogmatic innovation, but at the same time the recognition of an incontestable fact—the validity of Christianity without the pale of the Latin church.   In asserting this opinion, Luther now took up a position which enabled him to appropriate all the various elements of opposition to the papacy that were afloat in the world.   He made himself better acquainted with the doctrines of the Greek church, and finding, for example, that it did not admit the doctrine of purgatory, of which he also found no mention in Scripture, he ceased to maintain it, as he had done even in Leipzig.[1]   A far stronger impression was made on him by the works of John Huss, which now reached him from Bohemia ; he was perfectly astonished at finding therein the doctrines expounded by St. Augustine, and derived from St. Paul, which he had adopted after such violent mental struggles.   " I taught Huss's opinions," says he, in February, 1520, " without knowing them, and so did Staupitz : we are all Hussites, without knowing it.   Paul and Augustine are Hussites : I do not know what to think for amazement."   He denounces woe to the earth, and predicts the fearful judgments of God, because evangelical truth had been known for a century, and had been condemned and burnt.[2]   It is evident that he not only receded in opinion from the church of Rome, but at the same time conceived a religious disgust, nay hatred, of her.   In the same month, the treatise of Laurentius Valla, on the donation of Constantine, first fell into his hands.   It was a discovery to him that this donation was a fiction : his German honesty was shocked and exasperated at finding that, as he says, " such shameless lies had been incorporated into the decretals, and almost made articles of faith."   "What darkness !" exclaims he ; " what wickedness !" All spirits and powers that had ever waged war against the papacy now gathered around him ; those which had never submitted from the beginning ; those which had emancipated themselves and never been reclaimed ; and all the tendencies of the opposition that existed in the bosom of Latin Christendom, whether theological or literary.   He had no sooner begun to study the papal laws, than he thought he perceived that tney were in contradiction to the Scriptures : he was now persuaded that the Scriptures and the papacy stood irreconcilably opposed.   It is quite in accordance with Luther's character that, while seeking a solution of the problem, how this could be permitted by Divine providence ; while struggling to recover the broken unity of his religious convictions, he fell, after violent contention and torture of mind, on the hypothesis that the pope was the antichrist whom the world was taught to expect.[3]

[1] Letter to Spalatin, Nov. 7.

[2] To Spalatin, in De Wette, nr. 208.

[3] To Spalatin, Feb. 23, (not 24) 1520, nr. 204.   " Ego sic angor ut prope non dubitem papam esse proprie antichristum."   This notion sprang from the old chiliastic notions still maintained in the West (see the passage of Commodian : " venturi sunt sub antichristo qui vincunt," in Giesler, Kirchengeschichte, i 271.), and was especially cherished in Germany.   One of the oldest German works in print, the first mentioned by Panzer in the Annal ender älteren deutschen Literatur, is, Das Buch vom Entkrist (The Book of Antichrist), or also : " Büchlin von des Endte Christs Leben und Regierung durch verhengiss Gottes, wie er

This mythical notion tended, no doubt, to obscure the historical view which might perhaps have been obtained of the subject ; but it had, in fact, no other meaning than that the doctrine of the church was corrupted, and must be restored to its original purity.

Melanchthon, meanwhile, who had taken the part of an ally and adviser in the Leipzig disputation, was occupied with a parallel, but peculiar train of speculation, and now devoted himself to theological studies with the quiet ardour natural to him ; with the enthusiasm which a successful and steady progress in a new path always excites.

The principles on which protestant theology rest are to be traced, at least as much to him as to Luther. One of the first that he enounced, referred immediately to the controversy in Leipzig.

Maxims of the Fathers of the church were appealed to by each side, and with equal justice. To extricate the matter from this contradiction, Melanchthon laid it down in a little treatise, published August, 1519, that the Scripture was not to be expounded according to the Fathers, but that these were to be understood according to the sense of Scripture.[1] He maintained that the expositions of the great pillars of the Latin church, Ambrose, Jerome and even Augustine, were often erroneous. This principle—that a Christian (or, as he expresses it, a Catholic) is not bound to receive any thing but what is contained in Scripture—he treated more at large in September, 1519. What he had said of the Fathers, he now repeated of councils—that their authority was of no account when compared to that of Scripture. Having reached this point, doubt on doubt inevitably presented itself to his mind, as to the entire system of authoritative dogmas. If Luther was resolute in action, Melanchthon was no less so in speculation. Even in September, 1519, he stated the polemical maxims in which he attacked the two most important fundamental doctrines of the whole system ; that of transubstantiation, and that of the sacerdotal character ; whereon the mystery of the visible church, as well as the sacramental ritual which governs the whole course of human life, rest.[2] The boldness of the attack, and the ingenuity with which it was carried on, filled everyone with surprise. " He has now appeared to all," says Luther, " as wonderful as he really is. He is the most powerful enemy of Satan and of the schoolmen ; he knows their folly and the rock

die Welt tuth verkeren mit seyner falschen Lere und Rat des Teufels, auch wie darnach die zween Propheten Enoch und Helyas die Christenheit wieder bekerne mit predigen den Christen Glauben." " Little Book concerning Antichrist's Life and Rule through God's Providence, how he doth pervert the World with his false Doctrine and Counsel of the Devil ; also how, thereafter, the two Prophets,, Enoch and Elias, again convert Christendom with preaching of Christ's faith." In 1516 this book was reprinted at Erfurt. We see how it came about that Luther was occasionally called Elias by his followers.

[1] Defensio contra J. Eckium : C. R. i., p. 113. " Patres judice Scriptura recipiantur."

[2] Unluckily these propositions, which play a chief part in the construction of the protestant system of belief, are no longer to be met with. From a letter of Melanchthon to John Hess, Feb., 1520 (C. R. i. 138), we get a knowledge of three of them, which are moreover the most important. According to Luther's letter to Staupitz in de Wette, i., nr. 162, they must date from the month of September. The propositions which appear in the C. R., p. 126, are, as Förstemann there remarks, of later origin ; seemingly of the date of July, 1520.

of Christ ; he has the power and the will to do the deed. Amen." Melanchthon now applied himself with fresh fervour to the study of the New Testament. He was enchanted by its simplicity. and found in it true and pure philosophy ; he refers the studious to it as the only refreshment to the soul, and the afflicted, as pouring peace and joy into the heart. In his course of study, too, he thought he perceived that much was contained in the doctrines of former theologians, which not only could not be deduced from Scripture, but was at variance with it, and could never be brought into accordance with its spirit. In a discourse on the doctrines of Paul, pronounced on the 18th of January, 1520, he first declared this without reserve. In the following month he remarked that his objections to transubstantiation and the sacerdotal character, were applicable to many other doctrines ; he finds traces of Jewish ceremonies in the seven sacraments, and esteems the doctrine of the pope's infallibility an arrogant pretension, repugnant to Holy Scripture and to common sense :—most pernicious opinions, he says, which we ought to combat with all our might ; more than one Hercules is needed for the work.[1]

Thus we perceive that Melanchthon arrives at the same point which Luther had already reached, though by a calmer and more philosophical path. It is remarkable how each expresses himself concerning the Scripture, in which both live. " It fills the soul," says Melanchthon : " it is heavenly ambrosia."[2] " The word of God," exclaims Luther, " is a sword, and war, and destruction : it meets the children of Ephraim like a lioness in the forest." The one views it in reference to the inward thoughts of man, with which it has so strong an affinity ; the other, in its relation to the corruptions of the world, against which it wars ; but they come to the same conclusion. They quitted each other no more. " That little Greek (*Griechlein*)," says Luther, " outdoes me even in theology." " He will make up to you," exclaims he, " for many Martins." All his solicitude is that any of those misfortunes should befall him which are incident to great minds. On the other hand, Melanchthon was deeply impressed and penetrated with the thorough comprehension of St. Paul, peculiar to Luther ; he prefers the latter to the fathers of the church ; he finds him more admirable every time he sees him ; even in ordinary intercourse, he will not admit the justice of the censures which his joyous and jocose humour brought upon him. It was truly a divine dispensation that these two men lived together and united at this crisis. They regarded each other as two of God's creatures endowed with different gifts, each worthy of the other, joined in one common object, and holding the same convictions ; a perfect picture of true friendship. Melanchthon is careful not to trouble Luther's mind.[3] Luther confesses that he abandons an opinion when Melanchthon does not approve it.

So immeasurable was the influence which the literary spirit had obtained over the new and growing theology ; an influence which we shall now see it exercising in another manner.

[1] Dedication to Bronner, C. R., p. 138. Letter to Hess.
[2] To Schwebel, Dec., 1519, 128.
[3] To John Lange, Aug., 1520. "Spiritum Martini nolim temere in hac causa, ad quam destinatus ὑπὸ προνοίας videtur, interpellare." (C. R., i. 221.)

HUTTEN.

The minds which took part in the poetical and philological movement of Germany of which we have treated, may be arranged under two distinct classes. Those of the one class, eager to acquire and apt to give instruction, sought by tranquil and laborious study to master the erudition they were afterwards to diffuse. The whole character of their labours, which from the first were directed to the Holy Scriptures, was represented by Melanchthon, and had formed in his person the most intimate union with the deeper theological tendencies which were exhibited in that of Luther, and had gained an ascendancy at the university of Wittenberg. We have seen what were the results of this union. The peaceful study of letters acquired solidity, depth, and intensity of purpose ; theology, scientific form and an erudite basis. But literature exhibited another phase : by the side of the tranquil students were to be seen the combative poets ;—well content with the ground they had gained, self-satisfied and arrogant ; incensed at the opposition they had experienced, they filled the world with the noise of their war. At the beginning of the Lutheran controversy, which they regarded as a mere dispute between two monastic orders, they had remained neutral. But now that this revealed a character of such vastness, and opened a vista so remote, now that it appealed to all their sympathies, they too took part in it. Luther appeared to them in the light of a successor of Reuchlin ; John Eck as another Ortwin Gratius, a hired adherent of the Dominicans, and in that character they attacked him. In March, 1520, a satire appeared with the title of " The Planed-off Angle," (*Der abgehobelte Eck*) which for fantastic invention, striking and crushing truth, and Aristophanic wit, far exceeded the " Literæ Obscurorum Virorum," which it somewhat resembled. And at this moment a leader of the band entered the lists, not nameless like the others, but with his visor up. It was Ulrich von Hutten, the temper of whose weapons and his skill in wielding them had long been well known.

The whole course of Hutten's life had, like that of Erasmus, been determined by his being very early condemned to the cloister ; but to him this constraint was far more intolerable : he was the first-born of one of the most distinguished equestrian families of the Buchen, which still laid claim to the freedom of the empire. On his friends earnestly pressing him to take the vows, he ran away, and sought his fortune, as Erasmus had done, in the newly opened career of literature.[1] He encountered every variety of suffering : plague and shipwreck ; the banishment of a teacher whom he followed ; robbery, and disease ; the scorn with which indigence and a mean garb are commonly regarded, especially in a strange land ; the utter neglect of his family, who acted as if he did not belong to them ; nay, his father even treated him with a sort of irony. But his courage remained buoyant, his mind free and unshackled ; he bid defiance to all his enemies, and a state of literary warfare became a second nature to him. Sometimes it was his own personal quarrels which he fought out on the field of literature ; for example, the ill-treatment he sustained

[1] Mohnike, Ulrich Huttens Jugendleben, p. 43. Hutten was born in 1488 ; in 1499 he entered the convent, and in 1504 deserted it.

from his hosts at Greifswald, who robbed him ; he called upon all his companions of the school of poets to take part against this act of injustice, which was, as it were, committed against them all.[1]   Another time he replied to the reproach which even in that age he had to encounter, that a man must *be* something, *i.e.*, must fill some office, or hold some title ; or some deed of violence, like the unjustifiable conduct of the Duke of Würtemberg to one of his cousins, moved him to vehement accusation. But his warlike muse was still more excited by the affairs of his country.

The study of Roman literature, in which the Germans have taken so eminent a part, has not unfrequently had the effect of awakening the patriotism of their descendants.   The ill success of the emperor in the Venetian war did not deter Hutten from eulogizing him, or from treating the Venetians, in their contest with him, as upstart fishermen ; he contrasts the treachery of the pope and the insolence of the French, with the achievements of the Landsknechts and the fame of Jacob von Ems.   He writes long poems to prove that the Germans have not degenerated, that they are still the ancient race.   Just as he returned from Italy, the contest between the Reuchlinists and the Dominicans had broken out, and he rushed to the side of his natural ally, armed with all the weapons of indignation and of ridicule ; he celebrated the triumph of his master in his best hexameters, which were embellished with an ingenious wood-cut. Hutten is not a great scholar, nor is he a very profound thinker ; his excellence lies more in the exhaustlessness of his vein, which gushes forth with equal impetuosity, equal freshness, in the most various forms,—in Latin and in German, in prose and in verse, in eloquent invective and in brilliant satirical dialogue.   Nor is he without the spirit of acute observation ; here and there (for example in the *Nemo*) he soars to the bright and clear regions of genuine poetry : his hostilities have not that cold malignant character which disgusts the reader ; they are always connected with a cordial devotion to the side he advocates : he leaves on the mind an impression of perfect veracity, of uncompromising frankness and honesty ; above all, he has always great and single purposes which command universal sympathy ; he has earnestness of mind, and a passion (to use his own words) " for godlike truth, for common liberty."   The victory of the Reuchlinists had turned to his advantage also : he had found an asylum at the court of the Elector Albert of Mainz, and formed an intimacy with the formidable Sickingen ; he was cured of his illness, and now thought of marrying and entering upon his paternal inheritance ; he thus hoped to enjoy the tranquillity of domestic life, while the brilliancy of the reputation he had already acquired secured to him an eminent station.   Under these circumstances the spirit which Luther had awakened in the nation breathed upon him ; a prospect opened, compared to which all previous results had been mere child's play ; it took possession of his whole convictions, of every impulse and energy of his mind.   For a moment Hutten deliberated.   The enemy to be attacked was the mightiest in existence, who had never been subdued, and who wielded power with a thousand hands ; whoever engaged in a conflict with him must be aware that he would never more find peace so long as he lived.   Hutten did not disguise

---

[1] Querelarum, lib. ii., eleg. x., " nostros, communia vulnera casus."

this from himself ; it was discussed in the family, who dreaded the losses and evils to which it would expose them. " My pious mother wept," said he. But he tore himself away, renounced his paternal inheritance, and once more took up arms.[1]

In the beginning of the year 1520, he wrote some dialogues, for which he could never hope to obtain pardon. In the one, called the Spectators (*Anschauenden*), the jests on the papal legate are no longer, as before, confined to certain externals ; all his spiritual faculties, his anathema and excommunication which he hurls against the sun, are treated with the bitterest scorn and derision. In another—Vadiscus, or the Roman Trinity—the abuses and pretensions of the Curia are described in striking triplets : in confirmation of the Wittenberg opinion, that the papacy was inconsistent with the Scriptures, Hutten drew a picture of the actual state of the court of Rome, in which he represented it as an abyss of moral and religious corruption, which the duty of Germans to God and their country equally called upon them to shun.[2] His ideas were profoundly national. An old apology for Henry IV. having accidentally fallen into his hands, he published it in March, 1520, with a view of reviving the recollection of the great struggle with Gregory VII., and the extinct sympathy of the nation with the empire, and of the empire with the nation.[3] He sent it to the young Archduke Ferdinand, who had just arrived in the Netherlands from Spain, with a dedication, in which he calls upon him to lend his aid to the restoration of the ancient independence of Germany, which had withstood the warlike and victorious Romans of old, and was now become tributary to the effeminate Romans of modern times.[4] It appeared as if the nation might reasonably look with hope to the two brothers of the house of Austria, whose elevation to the throne had been so earnestly opposed by the papal court. Most of their friends were indeed at this moment enemies of the papacy. We have already alluded to the disposition of the court of Mainz. In Switzerland all who had approved Luther's first book were adherents of Cardinal von Sitten, who had so successfully conducted the affairs of the house of Austria at the diet, partly by their assistance. Sickingen, who had contributed so much to the decision taken by Würtemberg, was likewise a partisan of Reuchlin, and found means to compel the Cologne Dominicans, although the process was still pending in Rome, to obey the sentence of the Bishop of Spires, and to pay the costs to which they had there been condemned. No one had contributed more to the election of Charles V. than Frederick of Saxony : by the protection which he had afforded to Luther and his university, he had rendered possible the national movement in that prince's favour. He now absolutely refused to allow Luther to be tried at Rome. On the day of the emperor's election the Archbishop of Treves had actually undertaken the office of umpire, and Elector Frederick declared that no steps should be taken against Luther till that prelate had pronounced his decision, by which

---

[1] Apology for Ulrich von Hutten in Meiner's Lebensbeschreibungen berühmter Männer, &c., iii. 479.

[2] Vadiscus, Dialogus qui et Trias Romana inscribitur. Inspicientes Dialogus Hutteni. Opera ed. Münch., iii. 427, 511.

[3] Waltramus de Unitate Ecclesiæ conservanda, etc., in Schardius, Sylloge, Part I.

[4] Præfatio ad Ferdinandum. Opp., iii. 551.

he would abide.[1] There was a secret connection between all these incidents, these various manifestations of opinion :—people were resolved to
get rid of the interference of Rome. Hutten preached in all parts, that
Germany must abandon Rome and return to her own bishops and primates.
" To your tents, O Israel !" exclaimed he ; and we perceive that sovereigns
and cities responded to his appeal.[2] He deemed himself destined to
accomplish this change, and hastened to the court of the archduke, in
order if possible to gain him over by personal intercourse, and to inspire
him with his own ardour. He felt the most confident assurance of success. In an essay written on the road, he predicted that the tyranny of
Rome would not long endure ; already the axe was laid to the root of the
tree. He exhorted the Germans only to have confidence in their brave
leaders, and not to faint in the midst of the fight ; for they must go on—
on, in this propitious state of things, with this good cause, with these
noble energies. " Liberty for ever—Jacta est alea," was his motto. The
die is cast ; I have ventured all upon the throw.[3]

Such was the turn which Luther's cause now took—not without great
faults on the side of the defenders of the See of Rome. The attack, which,
though only levelled at one side of the great system, would unquestionably have been very troublesome to the head of the Church, was now
directed against his entire position and functions,—against that idea of
his authority and prerogative which he had so successfully laboured to
establish. It was no longer confined to the domain of theology ; for the
first time, the literary and political elements of opposition existing in the
nation came into contact and mutual intelligence, if not into close union,
with the theological ; thus allied, they turned their united strength
against the prerogatives of the Pope of Rome.

This led to a similar combination on the other side ; and the See of
Rome, which had hitherto always maintained reserve, was now induced
to pronounce a definitive sentence.

BULL OF LEO X.

We must bear in mind that the advocates of the old opinions were not
satisfied with opposing Luther with all the authority they possessed (for
example, the Dominican universities of Louvain and Cologne pronounced
a solemn condemnation of his works), but sought to prove themselves the
strictest and most faithful allies of the Roman See. The attacks of the
Germans furnished them with an opportunity to exalt the omnipotence
of the papacy more extravagantly than ever. Silvestro Mazzolini, the
Master of the Sacred Palace, of whom we have spoken, published a pamphlet,[4] in which, indignant that Luther had dared to appeal from his judg-

---

[1] Transactions, Walch, xv. 916, 919. The chief reason why this did not come
to pass was, that Frederick wanted to bring Luther with him to the Imperial
Diet, which was to be held in Nov., 1519, but which the Imperial Commissioners
prevented.

[2] Agrippa a Nettesheim Johanni Rogerio Brennonio ex Colonia 16 Junii, 1520.
(Epp. Agrippæ, lib. ii., p. 99.) " Relinquat Romanos Germania et revertatur
ad primates et episcopos suos."

[3] Ad liberos in Germania omnes. Opp., iii. 563.

[4] De Juridica et Irrefragabili Veritate Romanæ Ecclesiæ Romanique Pontificis : Roccaberti, Bibl. Max., tom. xix., p. 264.

ment to the pope, and in the last resort to a council, he tries to demonstrate that there can be no judge superior to the pope ; that the Roman pontiff is the infallible arbiter of all controversies and of all doubts ; and further sets forth that the papal sovereignty is the only true monarchy, the fifth monarchy mentioned by Daniel ; that the pope is the prince of all spiritual, and the father of all temporal princes ; the head of the whole world, nay, that he is, virtually, the whole world.[1] In his former work, he had only said that the whole collective church was in the pope ; now he affected to prove that the pope was the world. In another place, too, he did not hesitate to declare that all the power of temporal sovereigns was a sub-delegation of the papal.[2] The pope, he says, is more superior to the emperor than gold to lead : a pope can appoint or depose an emperor ; appoint or depose electors ; make or abolish positive laws ; the emperor, he exclaims, together with all laws and all Christian peoples, could effect nothing contrary to his will.[3] The proofs that he adduces in support of his opinion are, indeed, strange enough, but it was not necessary to substantiate them ; it was enough that they were adduced by a man of so eminent a station, and that they emanated from the papal palace. German obsequiousness hastened to furnish Roman arrogance with a somewhat better groundwork for its pretensions. In February, 1520, Eck also completed a treatise on the primacy, in which he promises triumphantly and clearly to confute Luther's assertion, " that it is not of divine right," and also to set forth various other rare and notable things, collected with great labour, partly from manuscripts which he had most diligently collated. " Observe, reader," says he, " and thou shalt see that I keep my word."[4] Nor is his work by any means devoid of learning and talent ; it is an armoury of very various weapons ; but it affords the most distinct evidence of the importance of this controversy to science, independent of all theological considerations, and of the profound darkness in which all true and critical history still lay buried. Eck assumes, without the slightest hesitation, that Peter resided twenty-five years at Rome, and was a perfect prototype of all succeeding popes ; whereas, historical criticism has shown that it is a matter of doubt whether the apostle ever was at Rome at all : he finds cardinals, and even under that title, as early as the year 770, and assigns the rank and functions of cardinal to St. Jerome. In the second book, he adduces the testimony of

---

[1] C. iv. " Etsi ex jam dictis constat Romanum præsulem esse caput orbis universi, quippe qui primus hierarcha et princeps sit omnium spiritualium ac pater omnium temporalium principum, tamen quia adversarius negat eum esse ecclesiam catholicam virtualiter aut etiam ecclesiæ caput, eapropter ostendendum est quod sit caput orbis et consequenter orbis totus in virtute."

[2] De Papa et ejus Potestate, ibid., p. 369. " Tertia potestas (the first is that of the Pope, the second that of the prelates) est in ministerium data, ut ea quæ est imperatoris et etiam principum terrenorum, quæ respectu Papæ est sub-delegata subordinata."

[3] " Papa est imperatore major dignitate, plus quam aurum plumbo (371).— Potest eligere imperatorem per se immediate—ex quo sequitur quod etiam possit eligere electores imperatoris et mutare ex causa : ejus etiam est electum confirmare,— et dignum depositione deponere (372).—Nec imperator cum omnibus legibus et omnibus Christianis possent contra ejus voluntatem quicquam statuere."

[4] De Primatu Petri. In Eckii Opp. contra Lutherum, tom. i., f. iii,

the Fathers of the Church in support of the divine right of the pope, and places at their head Dionysius Areopagita, whose works are, unfortunately, spurious.   Among his favourite documents are the decretals of the elder popes, from which much certainly is derived that we should not other-wise be inclined to believe ; the only misfortune is, that they are alto-gether forgeries.   He reproaches Luther with understanding nothing whatever of the old councils ; the sixth canon of the council of Nice, from which Luther deduced the equality of the ancient patriarchate, he inter-prets in a totally different manner ; but here again he had the ill luck to rest his arguments on the spurious canon, which belongs not to the Nicene, but the Sardicene, synod.   And so on.

It is important to have a distinct idea of the actual state of things. With these claims of an absolute power, including all other earthly powers, were connected, not only dogmatic theology as elaborated in the schools, but this gigantic fiction, this falsification of history, resting on innumerable forged documents ; which, if not overthrown, as it subsequently was (and we must add chiefly by truly learned men of the Catholic church itself), would have made all authentic and well-founded history impossible : the human mind would never have arrived at the true knowledge of ancient times, or at the consciousness of the stages itself had passed through. The newly-awakened spirit of the German nation seized at once upon this entire system, and laboured energetically to open new paths in every direction of human thought and action—politics, religion, science, and letters.   Equal zeal was displayed on the other side in maintaining the old system entire.   As soon as Eck had finished his book, he hastened to Rome to present it himself to the pope, and to invoke the severest exercise of the ecclesiastical authority against his opponents.

It was asserted at that time that Eck was in fact sent to Rome by the house of Fugger, which was alarmed at the prospect of losing the profit arising from the money exchanges between Rome and Germany.   It is at least certain that the doctor had some intimate connection with those eminent merchants.   It was in their behalf that he defended usury in his disputation at Bologna.[1]

But his chief aid was derived from the judgment pronounced against the new opinions by Cologne and Louvain.   Cardinals Campeggi and Vio, who were well acquainted with Germany, gave him all the support in their power.   His book was fully calculated to place the imminence of the danger before their eyes.   A commission of seven or eight zealous theologians was appointed, of which Giovan Pietro Caraffa, Aleander, and probably also Silvestro Mazzolini and Eck himself, were members ; their judgment could not be, for one moment, doubtful ; already, in the beginning of May, the draft of the bull by which Luther was condemned was prepared.

In the trial of Reuchlin, it was matter of doubt how far the See of Rome made common cause with the Dominicans ; now, however, that order had completely succeeded in restoring the ancient alliance.   In the present case

---

[1] Literæ cujusdam e Roma.   From the Pirkheimer papers in Riederer, Nachrichten zur Kirchen Gelehrten und Büchergeschichte, i., p. 178.   As a letter, this document certainly inspires me with some suspicion ; at all events, however, it is of the same date, and expresses the opinion of a well-informed contemporary. Welser also says (Augspurgische Chroniken, ander theil, p. 275) that that dis-putation had been held " at the cost of Jacob Fugger and his partners."

the trial was hardly begun, when we hear that the monks at Cologne triumphed in a sentence which had been pronounced in their favour, and caused it to be affixed on their church doors.[1]

The Elector of Mainz was called to account for the protection he had afforded to Ulrich von Hutten, and exhorted to show severity against the author of so many libels. The main object, however, was the condemnation of Luther. The jurists of the Curia were of opinion that a citation and fresh hearing of the accused were necessary, adding, that " God had summoned even Cain once and again before him ;" but the theologians would accede to no further postponement. They at length came to a compromise, and determined that the propositions extracted from Luther's writings were to be judged without delay, but that an interval of sixty days was to be granted to him for recantation. The draft of the bull, framed by Cardinal Accolti, underwent many alterations. A consistory was held four times, to consider of each separate proposition ; Cardinal Vio, though suffering under a severe attack of illness, would on no account stay away ; he was carried to the meeting every time. A smaller conference met in the presence of the pope himself, at his country-house at Malliano, and in this Eck took part. At length on the 16th of June, the bull was completed. Forty-one propositions from Luther's writings were declared false, dangerous, scandalous, or absolutely heretical, and the damnatory decrees of the universities of Louvain and Cologne as learned, true, and even holy. Christ was invoked to protect his vineyard, the management of which he had, at his ascension, entrusted to St. Peter. St. Peter was besought to take the cause of the Church of Rome, the mistress of the faith, under his care. Luther, if he did not recant within the sixty days allowed him, was to be considered a stubborn heretic, and to be hewn off, as a sere and withered branch, from Christendom. All Christian authorities were exhorted to seize his person and to deliver him into the hands of the pope.[2]

It appears that no doubt of the complete success of this measure was entertained in Rome. Two vigorous champions who had a personal interest in the matter, Aleander and John Eck himself, were entrusted with its execution. In Germany there was no need of a royal *placet ;* the commissioners had their hands completely free.

How proud and elated was Eck on reappearing in Germany with the new title of papal prothonotary and nuncio. He instantly hastened to the

---

[1] Letter from Hedios to Zwinglius in Meiners, *passim*, p. 236. This matter deserved closer examination. That it had been really agitated again in Rome at that very time, is clear from the letters of the Elector Palatine and the Dominicans assembled at Frankfurt (Friedländer, Beiträge zur Reformations-geschichte, pp. 113, 116), May 10 and 20, 1520. But might not the letter of the Dominicans have been merely a consequence of the extorted agreement with Sickingen ? If so, no weight could be attached to it by the court of Rome. Even at Leipzig, Eck had drawn attention to the necessity of that reunion ; he blamed the pope for his leaning to the grammarians (grammaticelli), adding that he was not proceeding in the via regia: July 24, 1519 (not 1520): in Luther's Opp. Lat., ii., p. 469.

[2] Frequently printed in Luther's and Hutten's works. The authentic copy is in Bull. Cocq., III. iii., p. 487. It surprises me that Rainaldus, who gives it, should have taken it from Cochläus. On all these subjects he is very scanty. Pallavicini is somewhat better. A few notices are to be found in the Parnassus Boicus, iii., p. 205.

scene of the conflict, and in the month of September caused the bull to be-
fixed up in public places in Meissen, Merseburg and Brandenburg.   Meanwhile Aleander descended the Rhine for the same purpose.

It is said, and with perfect truth, that they did not everywhere meet
with the best reception ; but the arms they wielded were still extremely
terrible.   Eck had received the unheard of permission to denounce any of
the adherents of Luther at his pleasure, when he published the bull ; a
permission which, it will readily be believed, he did not allow to pass
unused.   Amongst others he had named Adelmann of Adelmannsfeld, his
brother canon at Eichstädt, with whom he had once nearly gone to blows
at dinner concerning the questions of the day.   In pursuance of the bull
the bishop of Augsburg now set on foot proceedings against Adelmann,
who was compelled to purge himself of the Lutheran heresy by oath and
vow.   Eck had not scrupled also to denounce two eminent and respected
members of the council or senate of Nürnberg—Spengler and Pirkheimer :
the intercessions of the city, of the Bishop of Bamberg, even of the Dukes
of Bavaria, were of no avail ; they were forced to bow before Eck, who
made them feel the whole weight of the authority of one commissioned by
the See of Rome.[1]   In October, 1520, Luther's books were seized in all the
bookseller's shops of Ingolstadt, and sealed.[2]   Moderate as was the Elector
of Mainz, he was obliged to exclude from his court Ulrich von Hutten,
who had been ill received in the Netherlands, and to throw the printer of his
writings into prison.   Luther's works were first burnt in Mainz.   Aleander's
exultation at this was raised to a pitch of insane insolence.   He let fall
expressions like those of Mazzolini,—that the pope could depose king and
emperor ; that he could say to the emperor, " Thou art a tanner ;" (*Du
bist ein Gerber*) he would soon, he said, settle the business of a few miserable
grammarians ; and even that Duke Frederick would be come at by some
means or other.[3]

But though this storm raged far and wide, it passed harmless over the
spot which it was destined to destroy.   Wittenberg was unscathed ; Eck
had indeed instructions, if Luther did not submit, to execute on him the
menaces of the bull, with the aid of the surrounding princes and bishops.[4]
He had been authorized to punish as a heretic the literary adversary whom
he was unable to overcome; a commission against which the natural instinct
of morality so strongly revolted, that it more than once endangered Eck's
personal safety, and which, moreover, it was found impossible to execute.
The Bishop of Brandenburg had not the power, even had he had the will,
to exercise the rights of an ordinary in Wittenberg ; the university was protected by its exemptions, and, on receiving the bull from Eck, he resolved
not to publish it.   The authorities assigned as a reason that his holiness
either knew nothing about it, or had been misled by the violent instigations
of Eck.   That Eck had, on his own authority, specified by name two other

---

[1] Riederer's little work, Beiträge, &c., is specially devoted to these events.
The privilege possessed by Eck appears from a paragraph of his Instructions,
quoted by him word for word, p. 79.

[2] Letter of Baumgartner to the Council of Nürnberg, Oct. 17.

[3] Erasmi Responsio ad Albertum Pium, in Hardt, Hist. Lit. Ref., i. 169.   For
the διπλωματοφόρος is no other than Aleander.

[4] Extract from the Breve Apostol. 15 Kal. Aug. Winter, Geschichte der
Evangel. Lehre, in Baiern, i., p. 53.

members of the university, Carlstadt and Johann Feldkirchen, as partisans of Luther, created universal indignation. Luther and Carlstadt were allowed to be present at the sittings in which the resolutions as to the bull were passed.[1] Already the university had greater authority in this part of Germany than the pope. Its decision served as a rule to the electoral government, and even to the official of the bishopric of Naumburg-Zeiz.

The only question now was, what the Elector of Saxony, who was just gone to meet the emperor on his arrival at the Rhine, would say. Aleander met him in Cologne and instantly delivered the bull to him. But he received a very ungracious answer. The elector was indignant that the pope, notwithstanding his request that the affair might be tried in Germany, notwithstanding the commission sent to the Archbishop of Treves, had pronounced sentence in Rome, at the instigation of a declared and personally irritated enemy, who had then come himself to publish, in the sovereign's absence, a bull, which, if executed, would ruin the university, and must inevitably cause the greatest disorder in the excited country. But, besides this, he was convinced that injustice was done to Luther. Erasmus had already said to him at Cologne, that Luther's sole crime was that he attacked the pope's crown and the monks' bellies.[2] This was likewise the prince's opinion ; it was easy to read in his face how much these words pleased him. His personal dignity was insulted, his sense of justice outraged ; he determined not to yield to the pope. He reiterated his old demand, that Luther should be heard by his equals, learned and pious judges, in a place of safety ; he would hear nothing of the bull.[3] This, too, was the opinion of his court, his brother, and his nephew,—the future successor to the throne—nay, of the whole country.[4]

For it was in the nature of things that the partial and ill-considered proceedings of the See of Rome should awaken all antipathies. We may safely affirm, that it was the bull which first occasioned the whole mass of public indignation to burst forth.

CRISIS OF SECESSION

During the early months of the year 1520, Luther had remained comparatively passive, and had only declared himself against auricular confession and against the administration of the Lord's Supper in one kind, or defended the propositions he had advanced at Leipzig ; but when the tidings of Eck's success at Rome, and of the impending excommunication, reached him, at first as a vague rumour, but daily acquiring consistency and strength, his ardour for spiritual combat awoke : the convictions which had meanwhile been ripening in him burst forth ; " at length," exclaimed he, " the mysteries of Antichrist must be unveiled :" in the course of June, just as the bull of excommunication had been issued at Rome, he wrote his Book to the Christian Nobility of the German Nation,

[1] Peter Burcard (Rector) to Spengler. Riederer, p. 69.

[2] Spalatin, Life of Frederic, p. 132. The " Axiomata Erasmi Roterodami pro causa Lutheri Spalatino tradita, 5 Nov., 1520, in Lutheri Opp. Lat., ii., p. 314,' are very remarkable, as throwing light upon the notions of Erasmus.

[3] Narrative of the proceedings at Cologne (W., xv. 1919) ; the idea that this is by Heinrich von Zütphen, is an error caused by the signature in the earlier edition, which, however, only refers to an annexed correspondence.

[4] Veit Warbeck ; Walch, xv. 1876.

which was, as his friends justly observed, the signal for a decisive attack. The two nuncios, with their bulls and instructions, were met by this book, which was published in August at Wittenberg.[1] It consists of a few sheets, the matter of which however was destined to affect the history of the world, and the development of the human mind ;—at once preparative and prophetic. How loud had been the complaints uttered in all countries at this time of the abuses of the Curia, and the misconduct of the clergy ! Had Luther done nothing more, it would have signified little ; but he brought into application a great principle which had taken firm hold on his mind since Melanchthon's disputation ; he denied the *character indelibilis* conferred by ordination, and thus shook the whole groundwork of the separation and privileges of the clergy. He came to the decision that in regard to spiritual capacity, all Christians are equal ; this is the meaning of his somewhat abrupt expression that " all Christians are priests." Hence followed two consequences ; first, that the priesthood can be nothing but a function ; " no otherwise separate or superior in dignity," says he, " than that the clergy must handle the Word of God and the Sacraments ; that is their work and office ;" but also that they must be subject to the sovereign power, which has another office to perform ; " which holds the sword and the rod in its hand wherewith to punish the wicked and to protect the good."[2] These few words run counter to the whole idea of the papacy as conceived in the middle ages ; on the other hand, they furnish a new basis to the secular power, for which they vindicate the scriptural idea of sovereignty ; and they include in themselves the sum of a new and grand social movement which was destined by its character to be prolonged through centuries. Yet Luther was not of opinion that the pope should be overthrown. He would have him remain, neither, of course, as lord paramount of the emperor, nor as possessor of all spiritual power ; but with well-defined limited functions, the most important of which would be to settle the differences between primates and archbishops and to urge them to the fulfilment of their duties. He would retain cardinals also, but only as many as should be necessary—about twelve—and they should not monopolise the best livings throughout the world. The national churches should be as independent as possible ; in Germany, especially, there should be a primate with his own jurisdiction and his chanceries of grace and justice, before which the appeals of the German bishops should be brought ; for the bishops, too, should enjoy greater independence. Luther strongly censured the interference which the See of Rome had recently been guilty of in the diocese of Strasburg. The bishops should be freed from the oppressive oaths with which they were bound to the pope : convents might still be suffered to exist, but in smaller number, and under certain strict limitations : the inferior clergy should be free to marry. It is not necessary to enumerate all the changes which were connected with these in his mind ; his meaning and purpose are clear. It could not be said that he wished to break up the unity of Latin Christendom, or completely destroy the constitution of the church. Within the bounds of their vocation, he acknow-

---

[1] Probably, however, in the beginning of August. On the third of August Luther writes to his brother Augustine, Voigt, " *jam edo* iibrum vulgarem contra-Papam de statu ecclesiæ emendando." (De V., i. 475.)

[2] An den christlichen Adel deutschen Nation ; von des christlichen Standes Besserung. Altenb. Augs. Werke, i. 483.

ledges the independence, nay, even the authority of the clergy;[1] but to this vocation he wishes to recall them, and at the same time to nationalise them and render them less dependent on the daily interference of Rome. This wish, indeed, he shared with every class of the community.

This was, however, only one point of his attack—the mere signal for the battle which soon after followed in all its violence. In October, 1520, appeared the treatise on the Babylonish captivity of the church;[2] for Luther regarded the gradual establishment of the Latin dogmas and usages, which had been effected by the co-operation of the schools and the hierarchy, in the light of a power conferred on the church. He attacked them in the very centre of their existence—in the doctrine of the sacraments— and, in the first place, in the most important of these, the Eucharist. We should do him injustice were we to look for a thoroughly elaborated theory on this subject ; he only points out the contradictions which subsisted between the original institution and the prevailing doctrine. He opposes the refusal of the cup, not because he did not believe that the bread contained the whole sacrament, but because nobody ought to attempt to make the smallest change in the original institutions of Christ. He does not, however, counsel the resumption of the cup by force ;[3] he only combats the arguments with which it had been attempted to justify the refusal of it from Scripture, and zealously traces out the vestiges of the pure and primitive practice. He then treats of the doctrine of transubstantiation. The reader will recollect that Peter Lombard had not ventured to maintain the transformation of the substance of the bread. Later theologians did not hesitate to do this ; they taught that the *accidens* alone remained ; a theory which they supported by a pretended Aristotelic definition of subject and accident.[4] This was the point taken up by Luther. The objections raised by Peter of Ailly to this hypothesis had, at a former period, made a great impression upon him ; but he now also thought it dishonest to introduce into Scripture any thing which was not found in it, and that its words were to be taken in their plainest and most precise meaning ; he no longer acknowledged the force of the argument, that the Church of Rome had sanctioned this hypothesis ; since she was that same thomist aristotelic church, with which he was engaged in a mortal struggle. Moreover, he believed himself able to prove that Aristotle had not even been understood on this point by St. Thomas.[5] But a yet more important doctrine, as affecting the practical views of Luther, was, that the celebration of the sacrament was a meritorious work—a sacrifice. This dogma was connected with the mysterious notion of the identity of Christ with the Church of Rome, which Luther now entirely rejected. He found nothing of it in the Scripture ; here he read only of the promise of redemp-

[1] " It does not beseem the pope to exalt himself above the temporal power, save only in spiritual offices, such as preaching and absolving " (p. 494).

[2] De Captivitate Babylonica Ecclesiæ Præludium M. L., ubi præcipue de natura, numero et usu sacramentorum agitur. Opp. ed. Jen., ii. 259.

[3] " Contra tam patentes potentes scripturas ; contra evidentes Dei scripturas," p. 262.

[4] One principal passage is in the Summa Divi Thomæ, pars iii., qu. 75., art. iv., c. lm. v. 4.

[5] Opiniones in rebus fidei non modo ex Aristotele tradere, sed et super eum, quem non intellexit, conatus est stabilire : infelicissimi fundamenti infelicissima structura (p. 263).

tion connected with the visible sign or token, and with the faith ; nor could he forgive the schoolmen for treating only of the sign, and passing over in silence the promise and the faith.[1]   How could any man maintain that it was a good work—a sacrifice—to remember a promise ?   That the performance of this act of remembrance could be profitable to another, and that other absent, was one of the most false and dangerous doctrines.   In combating these dogmas, he does not conceal from himself the consequences :—that the authority of countless writings must be overthrown ; the whole system of ceremonies and external practices altered : but he looks this necessity boldly in the face ; he regards himself as the advocate of the Scripture, which was of higher significance and deserved more careful reverence than all the thoughts of men or angels.   He said he only proclaimed the Word in order to save his own soul ; the world might then look to it whether it would follow that Word or not.   He would no longer adhere to the doctrine of the seven sacraments.   Thomas Aquinas delights to show how their order corresponds with the incidents of the natural and social life of man—baptism with his birth ; confirmation with his growth ; the eucharist with the nutriment of his body ; penance with the medicine of his diseases ; extreme unction with his entire cure :—how ordination sanctified public business ; marriage, natural procreation.[2]   But these images were not calculated to make any impression on Luther ; he only inquired what was to be clearly read in the Scriptures ; what was the immediate relation betweeen a rite, and faith and redemption : he rejected, almost with the same arguments as those to be found in the confession of the Moravian brethren, four of the sacraments, and adhered only to baptism, the Lord's Supper, and penance.   The others could not even be derived from the See of Rome ; they were the product of the schools, to which, indeed, Rome was indebted for all she possessed ;[3] and hence, there was a great difference between the papacy of a thousand years ago and that of the present day.

The hostile systems of opinion on the destiny and duties of man, and on the plan of the universe, now stood confronted in all their might.   Whilst the papal see proclaimed anew in every bull all the privileges which it had acquired during the gradual construction of its spirituo-temporal state in the middle ages, and the principles of faith connected with them, the idea of a new ecclesiastical constitution according to which the priesthood should be brought back to a merely spiritual office, and of a system of faith emancipated from all the doctrines of the schools and deduced from the original principles of its first apostles—an idea conceived by one or two teachers in a university, and emanating from a little town in Germany—arose and took up its station as antagonist of the time-hallowed authority.   This the pope

---

[1] If at a later period, Bellarmin, as Möhler, p. 255, relates, requires before all things " ex parte suscipientis voluntatem fidem et pœnitentiam," still it was exactly conclusions of this kind which Luther missed in the then prevailing thomistic writings ; and before we blame him, it must be shown that these doctrines had been really taught and inculcated in his time.   Their readmission into the Roman church is, as has been said, only the reaction of the spirit of reform.

[2] Tertia pars, qu. lxv. conclusio.

[3] " Neque enim staret tyrannis papistica tanta, nisi tantum accepisset ab universitatibus, cum vix fuerit inter celebres episcopatus alius quispiam qui minus habuerit eruditionem pontificum.

hoped to stifle in its birth.   What if he could have looked down that long vista of ages through which the conflict between them was destined to endure !

We have already observed that the pope's bull did not touch Wittenberg.   Luther had even the audacity to denounce the pope as a suppresser of the divine word, for which he substituted his own opinions ;—nay, even as a stubborn heretic.   Carlstadt also raised his voice against the fierce Florentine lion, who had never wished any good to Germany, and who now condemned the truest doctrines, contrary to laws divine and human, without even having granted the defenders of them a hearing.   The whole university rallied more and more firmly round its hero, who had in fact given it existence and importance.   When the intelligence arrived that in some places the authorities had begun to execute the bull, and to burn Luther's books, the monk felt himself sufficiently strong to revenge this arbitrary act on the pope's writings.   On the 10th of December, 1520, the academic youth,[1] summoned by a formal proclamation posted on a black board, assembled in unwonted numbers before the Elster Gate of Wittenberg ; a pile of wood was collected, to which a Master of Arts of the university set fire : in the full feeling of the orthodoxy of his secession, the mighty Augustine, clad in his cowl, advanced to the fire, holding in his hand the pope's bull and decretals: "Because thou hast vexed the Lord's saints," exclaimed he, " mayest thou be consumed in eternal fire !" and threw it into the flames.   Never was rebellion more resolutely proclaimed.   "Highly needful were it," said Luther another day, " that the pope (that is the papacy) with all his doctrines and abominations should be burnt."

The attention of the whole nation was now necessarily drawn to this open resistance.   What had first procured for Luther the general sympathy of the thinking and serious-minded among his contemporaries was his theological writings.   By the union of profound thought and sound common-sense which distinguishes them, the lofty earnestness which they breathe, their consolatory and elevating spirit, they had produced a universal effect.   " That know I," says Lazarus Spengler in the letter which was imputed to him as a crime, " that all my life long no doctrine or sermon has taken so strong hold on my reason.   Divers excellent and right learned persons of spiritual and temporal estate are thankful to God that they have lived to this hour, that they might hear Dr. Luther and his doctrine."[2]   The celebrated jurist Ulrich Zasius in the most explicit and animated terms proclaims his adoption of Luther's opinions as to absolution, confession, and penance ; his writings on the ten commandments and on the Epistle to the Galatians.[3]   The collections of letters of that time afford abundant proof of the interest which the religious publications—for example, the exposition of the Lord's Prayer, or the new edition of the German Theology—excited ; societies of friends were

---

[1] According to Sennert, Athenæ et Inscriptiones Viterbegenses, pp. 58, and 59, the names in the university books amounted in the year 1512 to 208 ; in 1513 to 151 ; in 1514 to 213 ; in 1515 to 218 ; in 1516 to 162 ; in 1517 to 232 ; in the year 1518 the number of the students entered already rose to 273 ; in 1519 to 458 ; in 1520 to 578.

[2] Speech in defence, Riederer, p. 202.

[3] Zasii Epp., p. 394.   I cannot possibly believe this letter to be spurious, as the same opinion reappears in so many others.

formed for the purpose of communicating them to each other, of getting
them reprinted and then distributed by messengers sent about with these
books, and no others, in order that the attention of the buyers might not
be diverted ; preachers recommended them from the pulpit.[1]

The boldness of this attack, so formidable and so immediately connected
with the deepest feelings of religion, was another cause of popular interest.   Some, and among them Zasius whom we have just quoted, disapproved the turn it had taken, but its temerity only served to heighten
the admiration and the sympathy of the majority ; all the elements of
opposition naturally congregated around a doctrine which afforded them
that of which they stood most in need—justification in their resistance
on religious grounds.   Even Aleander remarked that a great proportion
of jurists declared themselves against the ecclesiastical law ; but how
great was his error if he really thought what he asserted—that they only
wished to be rid of their canonical studies : he little knew the scholars of
Germany, who were actuated by a far different motive,—the vexatious
collisions, between the spiritual and temporal courts, complaints of which
had been laid before so many diets and assemblies of the empire.   The
very latest proceedings of the court of Rome had drawn down severe
criticism from the lawyers of Germany.   Jerome of Endorf, an imperial
councillor, declared that the mode taken by the pope of enforcing his bull
by the threat of " attainder for high treason, loss of inheritance and fief,"
was an encroachment of the spiritual power on the temporal, which he
exhorted the emperor not to endure.[2]   It was not, however, the jurists
alone, but even the clergy whom Aleander found wavering, especially the
inferior clergy who severely felt the pressure of the hierarchical power ;
he was of opinion that throughout Germany they approved Luther's doctrines.[3]   Nor did it escape him that the religious orders too were infected :
among the Augustines this arose from the influence of the later vicars, and
partiality for a brother of their own order ; with others, from hatred of
the tyranny of the Dominicans.   It was also inevitable, that in the heart
of many a reluctant inmate of a cloister, the events now passing would
awaken the wish and the hope of shaking off his fetters.   The schools of
the humanists belonged of course to this party ; no dissension had as yet
broken out among them, and the literary public regarded Luther's cause
as their own.   Already too attempts had been made to interest the un-
learned in the movement.   Hutten perfectly understood the advantage
he possessed in writing German : " I wrote Latin," he says, " formerly,
which not every one understands ; now I call upon my fatherland."   The
whole catalogue of the sins of the Roman Curia, which he had often insisted upon, he now exhibited to the nation in the new light thrown upon
it by Luther, in German verses.[4]   He indulged the hope that deliverance
was at hand, nor did he conceal that if things came to the worst, it was
to the swords and spears of brave men that he trusted ; by them would
the vengeance of God be executed.   The most remarkable projects began
to be broached ; some particularly regarding the relation of the German
church to Rome ; as that no man should for the future possess an ecclesi-

[1] Beatus Rhenanus to Zwinglius. Huldrici Zwinglii Opera, tom. vii., pp. 77, 81.
[2] To the Landeshauptmann of Styria, Siegm. v. Dietrichstein. Walch, xv. 1902.
[3] Extracts from the Report of Aleander in Pallavicini.
[4] Klage und Vermanung gegen die ungeistlichen Geistlichen.

astical dignity, who could not preach to the people in the German tongue ; that the prerogatives of the papal months, accesses, regresses, reservations, and of course, annates, should be abolished ; that no sentence of excommunication issued by Rome should have any validity in Germany : that no brief should have any force till a German council had pronounced whether it were to be obeyed or not ; the bishops of the country were always to hold in check the papal power.[1]   Others added proposals for a radical reform in details ; that the number of holy days should be diminished, the curates regularly paid, fit and decorous preachers appointed, fasts observed only on a few days in the year, and the peculiar habits of the several orders laid aside ; a yearly assembly of bishops should watch over the general affairs of the German church.   The idea even arose that a christian spirit and life would, by God's especial ordinance, spread from the German nation over the whole world, as once from out Judæa.   Thereunto, it was said, the seeds of all good had sprung up unobserved ;—" a subtle sense, acute thought, masterly skill in all handicrafts, knowledge of all writings and tongues, the useful art of printing, desire for evangelical doctrine, delight in truth and honesty."   To this end, too, had Germany remained obedient to the Roman emperor.[2]

All hopes now rested on Charles V., who was at this moment ascending the Rhine.   Those who opposed the new opinions wished him the wisdom of Solomon and of Daniel, " who at as early an age were enlightened by God ;" they even thought the state of things so desperate, that if not changed by a serious and thorough reformation, the last day must quickly come."[3]   The partisans of innovation approached him with the boldest suggestions.   He was asked to dismiss the grey friar his confessor, who boasted that he ruled him and the empire; to govern with the counsels of temporal electors and princes ; to entrust public business, not to clerks and financiers, but to the nobles, who now sent their sons to study ; to appoint Hutten and Erasmus members of his council, and to put an end to the abuses of Rome and to the mendicant orders in Germany. Then would he have the voice of the nation for him ; he would no longer stand in need of pope or cardinal, but, on the contrary, they would

---

[1] Etliche Artickel Gottes Lob und des heyligen Römischen Reichs und der ganzen Deutschen Nation ere und gemeinen nutz belangend."   " Divers articles touching God's praise, and the honour and the common profit of the holy Roman empire and of the whole German nation."   At the end, Printed at Hagenau by Thomas Anshelm, in Feb., 1521.

[2] " Ein Klägliche Klag an den Christlichen Röm. Kayser Carolum von wegen Doctor Luthers und Ulrich von Hutten," &c.—" A Doleful Complaint to the Christian Roman Emperor Charles, relating to Dr. Luther and Ulrich von Hutten," &c. ; the work known by the title of " The Fifteen Confederates." Panzer, Annals of the earlier German Literature, ii., p. 39, has shown that it is by Eberlin von Günzburg.   In the Epistola Vdelonis Cymbri Cusani de Exustione Librorum Lutheri, 1520, the contrast between the Romans and the Germans is described in the following manner : " Nos Christum, vos chrysum, nos publicum commodum, vos privatum luxum colitis, vos vestram avaritiam—et extremam libidinem, nostram nos innocentiam et libertatem tuentes pro suis quisque bonis animose pugnabimus."

[3] Verbatim, from Hieronymus Emser against the unchristian book of Martin Luther the Augustine, sheet iv.   He adds, all ranks are sinful, and " foremost, the clergy from the highest to the lowest."   He also applies to them the saying, " from the heel to the crown of the head there is no soundness."

receive confirmation from him ; " then," said one, " will the strong Germans arise with body and goods, and go with thee to Rome, and make all Italy subject to thee ; then wilt thou be a mighty king.   If thou wilt settle God's quarrel, he will settle thine."[1]

" Day and night," exclaims Hutten to him, " will I serve thee without fee or reward ; many a proud hero will I stir to help thee , thou shalt be the captain, the beginner, and the finisher ;—thy command alone is wanting."[2]

CHAPTER IV.

DIET OF WORMS.   A.D. 1521.

THE most important question for the intellectual and moral progress of the nation now unquestionably was, in what light Charles V. would regard exhortations of this kind ; what disposition he would evince towards the great movements of the national mind.

We have seen that as yet every thing was wavering and unsettled : no form had been found for the government ; no system of finance, no military organisation perfected ; there was no supreme court of justice ; the Public Peace was not maintained.   All classes in the empire were at strife—princes and nobles, knights and citizens, priests and laymen ; above all, the higher classes and the peasants.   In addition to all these sources of confusion, arose the religious movement, embracing every region of mind, originating in the depths of the national consciousness, and now bursting forth in open revolt against the head of the hierarchy. The existing generation was powerful, intelligent, inventive, earnest, thoughtful.   It had a presentiment that it contained the germ of a great moral and social revolution.

The want of a sovereign and chief, felt by all mankind, is in fact but the conscious necessity that their manifold purposes and endeavours should be collected and balanced in an individual mind ; that one will should be the universal will ; that the many-voiced debate should ripen into one resolve, admitting of no contradiction.   This, too, is the secret of power ; when all the energies of a nation give voluntary obedience to its commands, then, and then only, can it wield all its resources.

This was the important result which now hung upon the question, whether Charles would understand the sentiments and the wants of his nation, and thence be able to secure its full obedience.

In October, 1520, he proceeded from the Netherlands to Aix-la-Chapelle, where he was to be crowned.   The newly elected emperor was a young man of twenty, still imperfectly developed, who had just learned to sit his horse well and to break a lance ; but of feeble health, a pale and melancholy countenance, with a grave, though benevolent expression. He had as yet given few proofs of talent, and left the conduct of business to others ; it was principally in the hands of the high chamberlain, William of Croi, Lord of Chievres, who possessed, as it was said, absolute authority over finances, court and government.   The minister was as moderate as

[1] Ein Kläglicher Klag, sheet †† III.
[2] Compare Napoleon's expression of astonishment that Charles V. did not champion the Protestant cause, for had he done so he would have had all Germany at his feet.

his master, who had formed himself upon his model ; his manner of listening and answering satisfied everybody ; nothing was heard to fall from his lips but sentiments of peace and justice.[1]

On the 23rd October Charles was crowned ; he took the title of Roman Emperor Elect,[2] which his predecessor had borne in the latter years of his life.   No later than December we find him in Worms, where he had convoked his first diet, and whither the sovereigns and states of Germany now flocked together.   His whole soul was filled with the high significance of the imperial dignity.   He opened the diet on the 28th January, 1521, the day sacred to Charlemagne.   The reigning idea of his opening speech was, that no monarchy on earth was to be compared with the Roman empire, which the whole world had once obeyed, to which " God himself had paid honour and allegiance, and had left behind him."   Unhappily it was now but the shade of what it had been, but he hoped, with the help of the monarchies, the powerful countries and the alliances which God had granted him, to raise it again to its ancient glory.[3]

This seemed the echo of the common wish of Germany ; it remained to be seen how he would understand his work—how he would endeavour to perform it.

SECULAR AND INTERNAL AFFAIRS OF THE EMPIRE.

Charles's first care at the diet was to strengthen the advantageous relation in which, from the circumstances attending his election, he stood to the several German sovereigns.   The Elector of Mainz received an extension of his powers as arch-chancellor.   Whenever he was present in person at court, the despatch of all the internal business of the empire was to rest with him ; but in his absence, to be in the charge of a secretary appointed by himself, to act with the grand chancellor.[4]   The Elector of Saxony obtained the sanction of his nephew's marriage with the infanta Catherine. As the Saxon government wished, on account of the expense, to avoid a marriage by proxy, the emperor pledged himself to see that the infanta should arrive in Germany six months after his own return to Spain. Markgrave Casimir of Brandenburg had the reversion of the next considerable fief of the empire which might fall vacant in Italy.   The Count

[1] " Relatione di Francesco Corner venuto orator di la Ces^a e catolica M^ta 6 Zugno 1521.   Chievres : zentilhuomo per esser il secondo genito non di molta facoltà, ma adesso più non potria essere, per haver al governo suo non solum la persona del re, ma la caxa li stati li danari e tutto quello è sotto la S. M^ta.   E homo di bon ingegno, parla pocho, perho molto humanamente ascolta e benignamente risponde : non dimostra esser colerico, ma più presto pacifico e quieto che desideroso di guerra, et è molto sobrio nel suo viver, il che si ritrova in pochi Fiaminghi."

[2] A description of the place (in which the journey of Charlemagne to Jerusalem is still treated as an historical fact) and of the ceremonies, by an eye-witness, in Passero, Giornale Napol., p. 284.

[3] The Proposition, which is the first document in the Frankfurt and Berlin Archives relating to this Imperial Diet, was followed on the 14th of March, Monday after Oculi, by a special statement, which explains it ; this is given also by Olenschlager, Explanation of the Golden Bull.   Records, nr. vii., p. 15.   One of the best printed works of that time, but not however quite exact.   As to the rest, Charles's statement recalls strongly some passages in Peter von Andlo.

[4] Häberlin, Reichsgeschichte, x., p. 375.

Palatine Frederick, who had been promised the dignity of Viceroy of Naples, received as compensation the post of imperial lieutenant in the Council of Regency; Calenberg, and Wolfenbüttel, the old and devoted friends of Austria, were readily favoured in the matter of Hildesheim, upon which the Lüneburgers quitted the diet in disgust; they saw that they should have to pay severely for their inclination towards the French. Shortly after, a very ungracious decree was issued against them.[1] The proceedings of the Swabian league, on the other hand, met with a no less cordial approbation. The exiled Duke of Würtemberg, who had neglected to repair to the Netherlands, as he had promised, now declared himself ready to appear at the diet. He received for answer, that it was no longer convenient to his imperial majesty to give audience to the duke; nor would any intercession induce Charles to change this determination. Proceedings were instituted against him, which terminated as unfavourably as those of Lüneburg: both were shortly after placed under ban.[2] The affair of Würtemberg was the more important, since that country belonged to the territory which it was proposed to incorporate into the newly constituted state of Austria. Archduke Ferdinand, the emperor's brother, who was educated in Spain, but had been fortunately removed from that country,[3] where he might have become dangerous, received the five Austrian duchies, which Maximilian had once entertained the project of raising into a kingdom in his favour, as his portion of the inheritance of the German domains. The day on which this contract was ratified (28th April, 1521,)[4] is one of the most memorable in German history. It witnessed the foundation of the German line of the house of Burgundian Austria, which was destined to occupy so great and conspicuous a station not only in Germany but in the whole of western Europe. Emperor Maximilian's former plans were adopted; and those reciprocal engagements with the royal houses of Bohemia and Hungary which were pregnant with such vast and immediate results, were contracted. The emperor at first intended to keep Würtemberg and the upper hereditary domains for himself, and to appoint a government for the joint administration of them; but he did not carry this into execution; with great magnanimity he left first the government and then the possession of them to his brother, as his *alter ego*.[5] Many thought Ferdinand a man of greater talents than Charles; at all events he was evidently more animated, daring and warlike, and kept a vigilant eye on what occurred in every direction.

It cannot be said that in these transactions Charles showed a constant regard for the national feelings or interests. He suffered himself to be persuaded to strip the Bishop of Lübeck of the inferior feudal dominion of Holstein, to which he had a right, and to transfer it to the King of Denmark and his heirs: he forbade the duke, " under pain of his grievous displeasure and that of the empire," to oppose any obstacle. He had certainly no other motive for this measure than that the king was his

---

[1] In Delius Stiftsfehde, p. 175.
[2] Sattler, Herzöge, ii., p. 75.
[3] Corner: " Credo non si hanno fidato di lassarlo in Spagna nè al governo di Spagnoli dubitando di qualche novità."
[4] Bucholtz, Ferdinand, i., p. 155.
[5] Extracts from the Records, ib., 158.

brother-in-law, and forgot that that monarch would never be regarded in any other light than as a foreign prince.[1]   Nor was his conduct towards Prussia untainted by similar considerations : the emperor negotiated a truce between the Grand Master and the King of Poland for four years, within which time he promised, with the aid of his brother and the King of Hungary, to endeavour to adjust the difference.   The Grand Master would acknowledge no other allegiance than that he owed to the emperor and empire, and rejected every other demand.   The emperor took this occasion to institute an inquiry whether his vassal could, or could not, render feudal service to a foreign king.   He appointed the King of Hungary one of the umpires ; that prince being now related to the house of Austria through the Jagellon alliance, which, as we have observed, was the main cause of the change in the late emperor's policy with regard to Prussia.

It is evident that it was Charles's earnest purpose to maintain the position prepared by Maximilian, and occupied, even before his arrival, by his own commissioners.   Kinsmen and old partisans were favoured, and, as far as possible, promoted ; recently acquired friends, more closely attached ; the decision of difficult disputes, for example, those between Cleves and Saxony, Brandenburg and Pomerania, Hessen and Nassau, were, if possible, postponed, and rendered dependent on future favour : the old opposition was, for the moment, broken up and reduced to inactivity.

Such were the auspices under which the deliberations on the institutions of the empire now commenced.

We shall not examine what would have happened, or what course Charles's councillors would have entered on, if their hands had been perfectly free.   It is enough to say that this was not the case.

In the third article of the election capitulations, the emperor had promised to establish a government, or Council of Regency, " such as had formerly been devised and had been in course of formation, of pious, acceptable, brave, wise and honest persons of the German nation, together with certain electors and princes."   The purpose of this stipulation was not doubtful.   The nation wished now to establish, on a permanent basis, the representative form of government which had been under discussion in 1487, planned and proposed in 1495, and brought into operation in 1500, but abolished again by Maximilian.   The opinions and designs of Archbishop Berthold were now revived.

At Worms the electors renewed their ancient union, and interchanged their word to press for the performance of the promises contained in the capitulations.   In March a scheme of the Council of Regency was submitted to the emperor.   This scheme was no other than a repetition of the ordinance for the establishment of the Regency of the year 1500.   It was to be composed exactly in the same manner :—a lieutenant of the emperor as president, delegates from the electors and the six circles (for the division of the empire into ten circles was not yet carried into effect), and representatives of the different states in rotation : to remain in existence and in force when the emperor was present within the empire, as well as in his absence ; to have power to carry on negotiations, in urgent cases to contract alliances and to decide feudal questions.   In

---

[1] Copies of the Records, printed in Christiani, i., p. 541.

short, now, as at the former period, the greater part of the powers and functions of emperor were to be transferred to this representative body.

It was not in the nature of things that the emperor should assent to such a project. He was surrounded by the same school of German councillors who had been about his predecessor : the ideas of Elector Berthold were once more encountered by the views of Maximilian. The emperor declared, that his predecessor on the throne had found that the Council of Regency tended to the diminution of his own power and to the prejudice of the empire, and therefore had not established it ; that it could not be expected of him to attempt to repeat the experiment of an institution which could only lower his dignity in the eyes of foreign nations. He sent the States a scheme of a totally different nature for their consideration ; according to which the most important element of the Regency was six permanent imperial councillors ; the fourteen councillors named by the Estates, who were to be assessors to the former, were to be constantly changed. Although the interests of the emperor would thus be far more powerfully represented than before, yet the Council of Regency thus constituted was neither to make alliances, nor to decide important feudal questions ; nor to remain in existence, except during the emperor's residence out of the limits of the empire. The oath was to be pronounced, not to the emperor and the empire, but to the emperor alone. The imperial hereditary dominions, which it was one of the main objects of the States to render subject to the common duties and burdens of the empire, Charles insisted on keeping under a perfectly independent administration ; even Würtemberg was not included within the boundary he had assigned to the circles.

This led to a very animated encounter. The States considered the expressions about Maximilian as " more than highly vexatious." Had not that prince, they said, suffered himself to be persuaded by false friends to recede from the original plan, it would have been honourable, useful, and glorious for himself and the holy empire, and terrible to all adversaries. And this time they were immovably steadfast to their project. The emperor could obtain nothing but some mitigation of subordinate points.

The most vexatious thing to him was the mention of an administration of the empire which should continue its functions during his presence. He regarded this as a sort of tutelage—a stain upon his honour. On this point they yielded to him, and acceded to the title he proposed, " His Imperial Majesty's Regency in the Empire ;" also that it should at first be established only for the period of his absence. This was subject to the less difficulty, because its duration could not be fixed, and the emperor on his part promised to decide whether the existence of the institution should be prolonged or not, according to the situation of affairs at the time of his return.

Concessions were made to the emperor on some other matters of detail. The composition of the Council of Regency, which was the most important matter, was indeed to be precisely on the model of the former, but the number of assessors was increased from twenty to twenty-two, the two additional members to be nominated by the emperor. On the more important feudal questions, and in alliances with foreign powers, the approbation of the emperor was justly made a necessary condition ; but the initiative in affairs, and the negotiation of them, were to be left to the Regency. Würtemberg was restored to the Swabian circle. Austria and the Netherlands were to send deputies as before. The oath was unquestionably to be taken in the first place to the emperor, but a distinct pledge was given that the honour and welfare of the Holy Empire were to be mentioned immediately after in the formula of the oath.[1]

In a word, the emperor succeeded in maintaining his honour and authority—a point on which he showed great susceptibility ; but, at the same time, the States carried through their long-cherished idea, and obtained a share in the government of the empire, which Maximilian, after the first experiment, would never again grant them. The Electors of Saxony and of Treves were peculiarly satisfied with the result.

The Imperial Chamber, which had fallen into utter decay, was reconstituted upon the same principles. The original scheme was a very extensive one. As there were about three thousand causes undecided, it was proposed to name so many assessors that they might be divided into two senates ; the one of which should be entirely occupied in disposing of old causes. There was a project for reforming the procedure on the model of the Rota Romana and the parliament of France. But it was soon evident how little could be done. " I have as yet seen no doctor," writes the Frankfurt delegate home, " who has proposed any good scheme of reform. People say the judges' hearings should be increased, the holydays curtailed, and proceedings the only purpose of which is delay, abolished : any peasant might have advised that." " They are deliberating," says he, another time, " on the reform of the Imperial Chamber ; but that is like a wild beast, every body knows his strength, but nobody where to attack him ; one advises here, the other there." At last the States, with whom this proposal likewise originated, came to the conviction that nothing could be invented more expedient than the old ordinance of the year 1495, with the improvements it had afterwards undergone, and some new additions.[2]

---

[1] The documents exchanged in this contest are tolerably complete in Harpprecht. In the Frankfurt Archives there is, besides, an essay : " ungeverlich Anzeyg, was in Keys. Mt. übergebenem Regiment zugesetzt und umbgangen ist."—" a tolerably exact Account of what has been determined and done in the Regency appointed for his Imperial Majesty."

[2] The ordinance of the Imperial Chamber of 1521 is almost word for word the same as this project of the states. The beginning only is different. " Dienstag nach Lätare," lautet er, " ist auf Römisch. Ks. Mt. unsres Allergnädigsten Herrn Beger von Churfürsten Fürsten Stennden des heil. Röm. Reychs beratschlagt, da hievor auf erstgehalltenem Reychstag allhie zu Wormbs im xcv. I. ain Ordnung desselben Kaiserl. Cammergerichts aufgericht, welche nachmals zu vorgehalten Reychstagen zum Thail weiter declarirt und gebessert worden, das dieselbe als not-urfdeglich und hochlich ermessen und bedacht, im h. R zu hallten und zu vollziehen auch nachmals nit wol stattlicher zu machen oder zu ordnen seyn mocht dann wie hernach folgt ; darum Ir der Stennde getreuer Rate, das die kais. Mt. jetzo solich (Ordnung ?) wider allhie gegen und mit den Stennden des heyl. Reychs und herwiderumb sambt hernachgemeldten Enderungen Ratschlag und Zusatz genädigklich annem, approbir und wie bei S. K. Mt. Anherrn geschehen verpflicht und dieselben also zu halten und zu vollziehen als Römischer Keiser handhabe."—" On Thursday after Lætare," it proceeds, " at the desire of the Roman emperor, our most gracious lord, the electors, princes, and states of the Roman empire have debated on a new constitution of the Kammergericht having been, on a former diet here at Worms, in 1495,

The chief alteration was, that the emperor should be allowed to appoint two new assessors to the court of justice as well as to the Regency.   The constitution of the court was in other respects the same as that agreed to at Constance ; here, too, the division of the six circles was retained.   The three spiritual electors and the three first circles, Franconia, Swabia, and Bavaria, were to send assessors learned in the law ; the three temporal electors and the three last circles, Upper Rhine, Westphalia and Saxony, assessors of the knightly class.   Charles V. promised to send from his hereditary dominions two of the former and two of the latter description. He had also the joint nomination, with the States, of the judge or president of the court, and of the two assessors out of the class of counts and lords. The character of the tribunal, as we perceive, remained essentially that of class representation (*standisch*) ; and this was the more unequivocal, since it was to hold its sittings in the same place as the Council of Regency, which was so decidedly representative, and was to be subject to the supervision of that body.

What likewise contributed to impress this character on it was, that the States took upon themselves (as, indeed, they had from the first offered to do) the maintenance of all these authorities.   Many extensive plans were devised for that end : *e.g.* the keeping back the annates and the revenues of spiritual fiefs, which now went to Rome ; or a tax on the Jews ; or the imposition of an import duty throughout the empire, which had the most numerous and the warmest advocates ; at last, however, they came back to a matricula on the pattern of that proposed at Constance, only that the rate was much higher.   The cost of the courts of justice was estimated at 13,410 gulden ; that of the Council of Regency, the assessors of which must receive much higher salaries, at 28,508.[1]   But as it was foreseen that there would be many deficits, it was determined to make the estimates at 50,000 gulden.   The assessment of Constance was altered as follows : the principle was, to multiply the contributions then required by five, and this rule was generally adhered to, though not without many exceptions. Many of the counts and lords, who were always very intractable, were left at the old assessment ; others were raised, but only threefold at the highest.   On the other hand, some cities which had the reputation of being very flourishing and wealthy, were compelled to submit to a contribution above fivefold higher than the last.   Nürnberg and Ulm were raised from 100 to 600 gulden ; Danzig, from 70 to 400.   In this manner was the only permanent impost on the States of the empire, which, together with the supreme tribunal, had begun to fall into oblivion, revived.

Larger demands, with a view to a military organization, and also more

---

decreed, which constitution afterwards at other diets has been farther interpreted and amended ; that the same, as requisite and highly fitting and well-considered, should be kept and executed in the empire, since the same could not well be made or constituted more excellent than here follows.   Therefore it is the loyal advice of the said states, that his imperial majesty do now, in a common accord with the states of the empire, with the alterations, suggestions, and additions hereafter mentioned, graciously accept and approve of the said constitution, and, like his majesty's imperial predecessors, engage to keep and execute the same and uphold it as Roman emperor."

[1] Harpprecht, IV., iii. 35, has, it is true, only 27,508 gulden, but this is an error.   In the Frankfurt copy the sums are given more correctly than in Harpprecht.

immediately to the emperor's coronation journey to Rome, necessarily came under discussion.

It might have been thought that the projects of a general tax, and of a military training of the people in parishes, would have been revived in conjunction with that of the Council of Regency ; representative government and popular armament had always hitherto been kindred notions.   On this occasion, however, the latter was not suggested ; either because it had always been found to be impracticable, or because, since it was last entertained, the power of the princes had so greatly increased.   On the 21st of March Charles V. appeared in person in the assembly of the States, and, with much circumlocution, demanded through the mouth of Dr. Lamparter succours for his expedition to Rome, which he himself estimated at 4,000 horse and 20,000 foot, for a year,   He then promised to contribute 16,000 foot soldiers, 2,000 heavy horse, and a considerable body of light horse at his own cost.   Elector Joachim of Brandenberg answered in the name of the states, " his brothers, lords, and good friends,"[1] and prayed time for consideration.   To the demand itself, which was founded on the ancient customs of the empire, or to the number of troops specified, which was not unreasonable, there was no objection to be urged.   But again the States would promise nothing, till they were certain of the establishment of the supreme court and of the Council of Regency, which latter institution they more than ever felt bound in duty to insist on.   At length they granted the required number of troops, but only for half a year ; it was also agreed that they should furnish the men, and not money for raising them ; they would not give occasion a second time to all the disorders that had prevailed in this matter under Maximilian.[2]   Lastly, care was taken that the German troops should not be left to the command of foreigners : they were all to march under their own officers ; the emperor was only to have the appointment of the commander-in-chief, who also must be a German.   For every leader wished to see his own men in the field under his own banner.   A matricula was drawn out on the principles of that of Constance of 1507. As to the cavalry, it was almost exactly the same ; in addition to the 3,791 men then registered, there were now 240 from Austria and Burgundy, so that all the electors, and many others of the states, had only to furnish their old contingent.   For the infantry (to which Austria and Burgundy now contributed 600 men each) the former demand of 4,722 was generally quadrupled, though with many exceptions.[3]   Thus arose the matricula of 1521, which was the last, and formed the model for the military organisation of the German empire for ages.

Such were the most important measures proposed by the new emperor at this first diet.   It could not be said that they were fully adequate to the wants of the nation.   The resolutions adopted were chiefly to the advantage of the sovereign princes; the preliminary ordinances concerning the execution of the judgments of the Imperial Chamber—which was

[1] Letter from Fürstenberg to Frankfurt, March 24.   " S. Maj. sey auch willens gen Rom zu ziehen und dasjenige so dem Reich entwandt, wieder zu erlangen."—" His majesty purposes to go to Rome, and to regain possession of that which has been wrested from the empire."

[2] Fürstenberg, May 13 : " Damit kein Finantz in den gesucht werde."— " In order that it might not be turned into a matter of financial speculation."

[3] Neueste Sammlung der Reichsabschiede, ii., p. 211.

chiefly intrusted to them—were, for example, manifestly in their favour :
even in his capitulation, the emperor had proposed to forbid alliances or
leagues between the nobles and vassals ; and this might have the effect of
forming more compact local powers.   On the other hand, nothing was done
for the mass of the people, among whom such a ferment prevailed, though
it had been so much and so often talked of.   The nobility remained excluded from all share in the business of the empire ; counts, lords, and
nobles were in a constant state of excitement concerning the legal decision
of their disputes with princes and electors, which they wanted to have more
expeditious and equitable, and some rather acrimonious correspondences
on this subject passed at the diet.   The cities had vainly demanded a seat
in the Imperial Chamber for their deputies ; the great subsidies of the
empire were discussed and voted without consulting them ; many of them
were recently aggrieved by the new rate of contributions imposed on them ;
and, besides this, they were threatened with an import duty for the whole
empire, from which they feared a universal disturbance to commerce.
They made incessant complaints, and at last only agreed to the project
because they would not, as they said, be the only members of the empire
who resisted ; they would not have to bear the blame if peace and justice
were not established.[1]

Notwithstanding these defects, it was a great point gained that the disorders of the last years of Maximilian's reign were checked ; and that the
ideas of a representative government, which had never been realised under
him, were revived with such considerable success.   The constitution of
1521, like that of 1507, was founded on a combination of matricular with
representative forms ; but the latter were now far more comprehensive,
since they did not, as on the former occasion, regard the administration of
justice only, but, according to the propositions of 1495 and 1500, formed
the basis of a Council of Regency, enjoying considerable independence of
the emperor.   The attempt to revive an administration adapted to the
momentary interests of the policy of the house of Austria, such as that
constantly carried on by Maximilian, was met by a national institution,
which, if it could but acquire consistency and development, promised the
most important future results.

[1] Hans Bock and Dr. Peutinger, who had sat in the committee, got little
credit.   " Etlich geben," writes Fürstenberg on the 20th of May, " Hr. Hansen
Bock etwa spitz Wort, als ob er sich und die rheinischen Städte erhalten und
sie im Pfeffer habe stecken lassen.   Dazu verdriesst sie und uns alle, dass sie
die Grafen fast gelachert (erleichtert) und die Beschwerung auf uns getrieben
haben.   Dr. Peutinger der ist der aller onlustigst, er wolt gern dass man es
beim alten Anschlag liess, will nit ansehn dass Eine Stadt aufgeht die andre in
Abfall kommt."—" Some give Herr Hans Bock hard words, as if he had taken
care of himself and the Rhenish cities, and left them (the others) in the lurch.
Moreover, it vexes them and all of us that they have greatly relieved the counts,
and forced the burden upon us.   Dr. Peutinger is the most discontented of all ;
he would gladly have abided by the old assessment : he does not like to see that
whilst one city rises, another falls into decline."

FOREIGN RELATIONS.—LUTHER.

While these political arrangements were concluded, the spiritual interests of the empire were also frequently discussed : they opened another field to the emperor's policy.

On all the other questions which came before him, he had been able to keep in view Germany, his relation to the interior of the empire, and the interests of his family ; but the Lutheran agitation extended so widely that it affected even the most important foreign relations.

Charles V. was the child and nursling of that Burgundian court which had been mainly composed of French elements under Philip the Good and Charles the Bold, and had followed the peculiar line of policy dictated by the position of those princes. Even as opposed to Ferdinand the Catholic and the Emperor Maximilian, this court had maintained and acted on its own independent views, often in direct hostility to the former. The prospects which had been contemplated under Charles the Bold, and opened under Philip I., appeared to find a necessary fulfilment in the position and the rights of Charles V. The court of Brussels, which was not properly a sovereign court and wielded no extraordinary powers, was suddenly called, by the hereditary rights of its prince, to play the greatest part in Europe. To take possession of this pre-eminent station was of course its first care.

For the attainment of this end, the policy of the Netherlands was conducted with singular prudence and success by the Archduchess Margaret and the Lord of Chièvres. Friesland had been annexed to the Netherlands, which had also been strengthened by the appointment of a kinsman to the bishopric of Utrecht, and by the closest alliance with Liège and Cleves. The crowns of Castile and Aragon, with all their dependencies, had been taken possession of. Rebellious commotions had indeed been universal, even in Naples and Sicily, but they had all been put down : the national pride of the Castilians, offended by the dominion of a court composed of foreigners, burst forth in an insurrection of the communes; but the monarch possessed natural allies there in the clergy and the grandees, and needed not to fear the people.

The inheritance of Maximilian was now added to these vast territories. The Austrian hereditary dominions, with all their rights or expectancies in the east of Europe, which had been acquired by the late emperor, were now left to the younger scion of the house, who, however, was kept in constant dependence by his need of assistance : the empire Charles took into his own hands, and founded the ascendency of his house in Germany —with what care, we have just seen.

All this was carried into effect in the midst of continual irritations and collisions with France, originating in the disputes between former dukes and kings ; but matters were so skilfully conducted in Brussels, that peace was maintained under the most difficult circumstances. The successors of Louis XI. were compelled, however reluctantly, to allow the posterity of Charles the Bold to consolidate a power which infinitely exceeded all that could have been anticipated in his time.

Nothing now remained but for the Burgundian monarch to take possession of the imperial rights in Italy, which appeared the more practicable, since he already ruled Naples and Sicily, and since his expedition to Rome would be supported by the whole might of the Spanish monarchy ;

—a combination which had never existed before.   The Proposition[1] with which he opened the diet sufficiently showed that the young emperor was determined to avail himself of it.   During the proceedings, frequent allusion was made to the recovery of the imperial dominions that had been lost, and grants for that purpose were made by the diet ; negotiations were entered into with the Swiss, even at Worms.

The maintenance of peace with France, the country the most nearly interested, was no longer possible.   Francis I. held the duchy of Milan without having received or even sought the investiture ; the emperor's first efforts must be directed to this point.   Other plans, which gradually attained to maturity, lay in the background ; for example, that of recovering the duchy of Burgundy, taken by Louis XI., the loss of which the Netherlands had never learned to brook.   The consolidation of two great European powers completely opposed to each other, which had long been silently preparing, became at this moment fully manifest. France,—by her internal unity and her wide-spread connexions, both early in the 14th and (after the expulsion of the English) at the close of the 15th and beginning of the 16th centuries, unquestionably the most powerful country in Europe,—saw herself surrounded and overshadowed on all her frontiers by a vassal who had gradually risen to power, whom she thought she had crushed, but who, by a few easy and fortunate matrimonial alliances, had come into possession of a combination of crowns and dominions such as the world had never beheld.   Here we first perceive the hidden motives which rendered Francis so eager to obtain the imperial crown ; he could not endure that his ancient vassal should rise to a dignity superior to his own.   That this nevertheless had come to pass,—that his rival could now set up legitimate claims to the very country the possession of which was peculiarly dear to the king as the conquest of his own sword,—inflamed him with bitter and restless irritation.   Growing ill will was observable in all the negotiations, and it became evident that a breach was inevitable between these two great powers.[2]

This was the grand conjuncture destined to develop the political life of Europe ; the several states of which necessarily inclined to the one side or the other, according to their peculiar interests.   Its more immediate consequence was, to determine the position of the empire and the application of its forces.

For however highly Charles V. estimated the imperial dignity, it was natural that he should not look upon Germany as the central point of his policy.   The sum of all his opinions and feelings was, of necessity, the result of the aggregate of his various dominions and relations.   He ever felt himself the Burgundian prince who united the highest dignity of Christendom with the numerous crowns he had inherited from his ancestors ; and he thus, like his grandfather, necessarily regarded the rights he enjoyed as emperor as only a part of his power ; indeed the extent and variety of the countries subject to his sway rendered it even more impos-

[1] The Proposition was the speech with which the emperor opened the diet. It contained the topics proposed for discussion.—TRANSL.

[2] What were the mutual reproaches appears in the French Apologia Madritæ Conventionis Dissuasoria, and the Imperial Refutatio Apologiæ in Goldast, Politica Imperialia, pp. 863, 864.

sible for him to devote himself completely to the internal affairs of Germany, than it had been for Maximilian.

Of the workings of the German mind, he had not the faintest idea ; he understood neither the language nor the thoughts of Germany.

It was a singular destiny that the nation, in the moment of an internal agitation so mighty, so peculiar to itself, had called to its head a stranger to its character and spirit ; in whose policy, which embraced a much wider sphere, the wants and wishes of the German people could appear but as a subordinate incident.

Not that religious questions were indifferent to the emperor—they were very interesting to him ; but only in as far as they affected or threatened the pope, and afforded a new view of his own connexion with the court of Rome, or new weapons with which to encounter it.

Amidst all the various political relations of the emperor, this, however, was unquestionably now the most important.

For as a conflict with France was obviously inevitable—a conflict of which Italy must be the principal scene—the main question for the emperor was, whether he should have the pope with him or not. The two monarchs already rivalled each other in their efforts to gain Leo's favour. Both were lavish in their promises ; the king, in case he should conquer Naples, which he was resolved to attack ; the emperor, in the event of an attempt upon Milan, which he was about to make in favour of the pretender and the house of Sforza, and for the purpose of restoring the rights of the empire over that province.

This, however, was not the only close relation of the emperor to the see of Rome ; others of an ecclesiastical nature, but involving not less important results, existed in his other dominions, and especially in Spain.

It is matter of notoriety that the main prop of the government of that country, as constituted under Ferdinand the Catholic, was the Inquisition. But this institution was now the object of a simultaneous attack in Castile, Aragon, and Catalonia. That powerful body, the Cortes of Aragon, had applied to the pope, and had actually obtained from him some briefs, according to which the whole constitution of the Inquisition was to be altered and approximated to the forms of the common law.[1] In the spring of 1520, Charles sent an ambassador to Rome to effect a revocation of these briefs, which he foresaw must have important consequences in his other dominions, and endanger his whole government.

The negotiations were pending when Charles arrived in the Netherlands, and a loud and almost universal voice, expressing both a political and a religious opposition, called upon him to assume a bold attitude of resistance to the pope.

Charles's acute and able envoy, who arrived in Rome while Eck was there, and Luther's controversy gave rise to so many deliberations of the theologians and sittings of the consistory, immediately perceived all the advantage which might accrue from it to his master. " Your Majesty," he writes to the emperor on the 12th of May, 1520, " must go to Germany, and there confer some favour upon a certain Martin Luther, who is at the court of Saxony, and excites great anxiety in the court of Rome by the things he preaches."[2] This view of the case was actually adopted at the

Llorente, Hist. de l'Inquisition, i., p. 395, nr. x.

[2] Extract from Manuel's Despatches : Llorente, i., p. 398.

imperial court. When the papal nuncio arrived there with the bull against Luther, the prime minister let fall the expression, that the emperor would do what was agreeable to the pope, if his holiness would oblige him, and not support his enemies.[1] On another occasion, Chièvres said that if the pope embarrassed the affairs of the emperor (with France), other people would stir up embarrassments for him, out of which he would not easily extricate himself.

This, therefore, was the real point on which the affair, from the first moment, turned : not the objective truth of the opinions, nor the great interests of the nation connected with them,—of which the newly arrived sovereign was not conscious, and with which he could have no sympathy ; but the general situation of politics, the support which the pope was willing to grant the emperor, and the footing upon which the former intended to place himself with regard to him.

This was well known at Rome. Great pains were taken to gain over the emperor's confessor, Glapio, a Franciscan, who was not well disposed towards Rome, " by civilities." It was determined, after long hesitation, to nominate the Bishop of Liège, Eberhard of the Mark, who had gone over from the side of France to that of Austria, cardinal, offensive as this must be to the former power.[2] The same motives had dictated the mission of Aleander, who had been in the bishop's service before he came to Rome, and, from the influence which that prelate enjoyed over the government of the Netherlands, appeared there as the natural mediator between Rome and the empire. This bishop, Aleander thought, too, would be an active instrument in securing a favourable result to the negotiations with the empire, though his language was generally frank and audacious. All the measures which the nuncio suggested or employed were conceived in this spirit. The Bishop of Tuy, who had followed the emperor from Spain, and enjoyed great consideration with the prime minister, was to be conciliated by the gift of a benefice which had been already promised to one who had every possible claim to it. Aleander paid one of the imperial secretaries fifty gulden, for which sum the latter engaged to render him " secret and good service ;" and promised the same man a pension for some years, in consideration of his pledging himself to report to him all the deliberations of the Council of Regency hostile to the court of Rome. He expresses himself persuaded that most of these councillors and secretaries, although they hate the papacy, will " dance to Rome's piping," if they do but see her gold.[3] His bribes extended even to the door-keepers and beadles who were to seize Luther's works ; his sole and continual complaint is, that his employers send him too little money. By a similar course of " cunning and promptitude," as he boasts, he had carried into effect the mandate for the burning of Luther's books

---

[1] From Aleander's letters : Pallavicini, i., c. 24, p. 136.—To what does the emperor refer, when he afterwards reproaches the court of Rome with having tried to delay the coronation at Aix ? Caroli Rescr. Goldast, Const., p. 992.

[2] Molini, Documenti di Storia Italiana, i., p. 84.

[3] He asks on one occasion for " denari si per mio vivere come per donar a Segretarii et a sbirri, li quali ancorche siino infensissimi alla corte di Roma, tutta volta qualche danaro li farebbe saltar a nostro modo : quia aliter nihil fit et vix faciemus aliquid."—*Extracts from Aleander's Letters in Münter, Beiträge zur Kirchengeschichte*, p. 78.

in Flanders : " the emperor and his councillors saw the books burning, before they were fully aware that they had assented to the mandate." Aleander's letters present an odious and disgusting spectacle ; a most immoral mixture of cunning, cowardice, arrogance, affected devotion and mean ambition ; the vilest means employed in so great a cause. It is not probable that these were without influence, though of course others were needed to produce a decisive effect. But what had not been put in practice ? In the matter of the Inquisition, especially, the pope agreed to make the most important concessions. On the 21st of October, 1520, he declared to the grand inquisitor of Spain, that he would give no further encouragement to the demands of the Cortes of Aragon ; that he would not confirm the briefs he had issued, and that he would introduce no innovation in the affairs of the Inquisition, without the approbation of the emperor. Even this did not satisfy Charles ; he demanded the entire revocation of the briefs. On the 12th of December, the pope offered to declare all steps that had been taken against the Inquisition null and void. On the 16th of January, 1521, he at length actually permitted the emperor to suppress the briefs, and expressed the wish that they might be sent back to Rome in order that he might annul them.[1]

It is obvious that this state of things was little calculated to meet the wishes of the people of Germany. Charles's position and connexions required of him an alliance with the pope, instead of that opposition which the spirit of the nation would have dictated. How grievously were the hopes which such men as Hutten and Sickingen had placed on the young emperor disappointed ! The papal bull was executed without hesitation in the Low German hereditary dominions, where the higher clergy and confessors seemed to engross all the consideration of the court : in January, 1521, there was a general belief that the emperor was determined to destroy Luther, and, if possible, to exterminate his followers.[2] A brief arrived, probably together with the last concessions, wherein the pope exhorted the emperor to give the force of law to his bull by an imperial edict. " He had now an opportunity of showing that the unity of the church was as dear to him as to the emperors of old. Vainly would he be girded with the sword, if he did not use it, not only against the infidels, but against heretics, who were far worse than infidels."[3]

One day in the month of February, on which a tournament was to be held, the emperor's banner was already displayed, when the princes were summoned, not to the lists, but to the imperial quarters, where this brief was read to them, and at the same time an edict commanding the rigorous execution of the bull was laid before them.

Strange and unlooked for entanglement of events ! The Lutheran controversy led the pope to revoke that mitigation of the severities of the inquisition in Spain which he had already determined on at the request of the Cortes ; while in Germany, on the other hand, the emperor prepared to crush the monk who so audaciously incited the people to rebel against the authority of Rome. The resistance to the power of Dominican

---

[1] Extracts in Llorente, i., pp. 396 and 405.

[2] Spengler to Pirkheimer, Dec. 29, Jan. 10, in Riederer, pp. 113, 131.

[3] " Deus accinxit te terrenæ potestatis supremo gladio, quem frustra profecto gereres juxta Pauli apostoli sententiam, nisi eo uterere cum contra infideles tum contra infidelibus multo deteriores hæreticos."—*Fr. Arch.*

inquisitors was in both countries a national one.   This fully explains the fact that, among the Spaniards who accompanied the court, those at least of the middle classes took the liveliest interest in Luther and his writings.

In Germany however the emperor could accomplish nothing without the approbation of the empire ; and in submitting the draft of the mandate before alluded to to the States, he had added, " that if they knew of any thing better, he was ready to hear it."   This gave rise to very warm discussions in the imperial council.   " The monk," says the Frankfurt deputy, " makes plenty of work.   Some would gladly crucify him, and I fear he will hardly escape them ; only they must take care that he does not rise again on the third day."   The same doubt and fear, that condemnation by a party would produce no permanent effect, prevailed in the States.   The emperor had intended to publish the edict without further trial,[1] according to the advice of Aleander, who declared that the sentence of condemnation already pronounced was sufficient ; Doctor Eck, too, sent in a little memorial, full of flatteries and admonitions, to the same effect.[2]   It was the same question which had been discussed in the curia,[3] but the Estates of Germany were not so obsequious as the jurists of Rome.   They begged the emperor to reflect what an impression would be made on the common people, in whose minds Luther's preaching had awakened various thoughts, fantasies, and wishes, if he were sentenced by so severe a mandate, without being even called to take his trial.   They urged the necessity of granting him a safe-conduct, and summoning him to appear and defend himself.   But a new question arose.   On what basis was this trial to be conducted ?   The States distinguished between two branches of Luther's opinions ; the one relating to church government and discipline, which they were for handling indulgently, even if he refused to recant (and they seized this occasion of once more strongly impressing on the emperor the complaints of the nation against the See of Rome) ; the other, against the doctrine and the faith " which they, their fathers and fathers' fathers, had always held."   Should he

---

[1] In the draft it is said : " Und (weil) dann der gedacht Martin Luther alles das, so muglichen gewesen ist, offentlichen gebredigt, geschrieben und ausgebraitet, und yetzt am jungsten etlich Articul, so inn viel Orten in Behem gehalten werden und die von den hailigen Concilien für kätzerisch erkannt und erklärt seyn, angenommen, und ine darum die papstlich Heyligkeit für einen offenbaren Ketzer wie obstet erklärt und verdammt hat und deshalben inen weiter zu hören nit rat noch geburlich ist."—" And (since) then the said Martin Luther has openly preached, written, and spread all this as much as possible, and has now lately accepted certain articles which are maintained in many places in Bohemia, and which are recognised and declared by the holy councils to be heretical, and his papal holiness has, therefore, as beforesaid, declared and condemned him as an avowed heretic, and therefore it is neither advisable nor fitting to hear him further."

[2] " Ad Carolum V. de Ludderi causa : Ingoldstadt, 18 Feb. Saxones sub Carolo magno colla fidei et imperio dedere : absit ut sub Carolo maximo Ludder Saxo alios fidem veram et unicam deponere faciat."

[3] The Corte Romana in its wider sense, *i.e.*, the cardinals, bishops, and other officials in the Papal Court, making the Papal Government.   In its stricter sense the term would refer to the body of lawyers practising in the Papal Courts of Justice.

also persist in these, and refuse to recant, they declared themselves ready to assent to the imperial mandate, and to maintain the established faith without further disputation.[1]

Such were the views with which Luther was summoned to Worms. " We have determined," says the imperial citation, " we and the States of the Holy Roman empire, to receive information from thee concerning the doctrine and the books that have been uttered by thee." An imperial herald was sent to conduct him.

With regard to the opposition to the temporal interference of Rome, the States were essentially of the same opinion with Luther. As the emperor was bound even by his capitulation to restore and maintain the Concordat and the ecclesiastical liberties of the nation, which had been continually violated to an insufferable extent, the lesser committee was now employed in drawing up a complete statement of the grievances of the nation against the See of Rome. Their manner of proceeding was this ; each prince delivered in a list of the grievances of which he had more particularly to complain, and every charge alleged by more than one was received and recorded. Already it was feared that the spiritual princes would draw back ; but the councillors of the temporal were determined in that case to carry the matter on to the end alone. A statement of grievances was produced which reminds us of the writings of Hutten and the Book to the German Nobles ; so strong was the censure of the papal See generally, and above all, of the government of Pope Leo X.[2] It is filled with the cunning and malignant devices, the roguery and cheating, which prevailed at the court of Rome. The curia was also directly accused, in practice, of simony. If Luther had done nothing more than attack the abuses of the curia, he could never have been deserted by the States ; the opinion he had expressed on this subject was the general one, and was indeed their own. Probably the emperor himself would not have been able to withstand it ; his father confessor had threatened him with the chastisements of Heaven if he did not reform the church.

We feel almost tempted to wish that Luther had remained for the present satisfied with this. The nation, engaged under his conduct in a common struggle against the temporal sway of the church of Rome, would have become for the first time strongly united and completely

---

[1] " Der Stennd Antwurt auf keyserlicher Mt. Beger des Mandats."—" The answer of the States to the desire of his imperial majesty to the mandate." Without a date. Unfortunately, also, Fürstenberg has not dated his letters precisely. The one, for instance, which refers to this resolution, he has inscribed Saturday after Marthæ. Saturday after Matthiæ, March 2, is certainly meant. In which case this resolution of the States is of that date. For that their answer should have referred to a command of the emperor of the 7th of March, is impossible, since the letter of summons to Luther is dated the 6th of March.

[2] This document is republished from the old printed edition, in Walch, xv. 2058. The copy in the Frankfurt Archives, which agrees with the printed one, shows more plainly that the work consists of three parts ; the first reaching to E iiii., upon which follows an episode ; the second, with a fresh superscription, touching especially the usurpations of the spiritual courts of justice, reaching to G iii. ; finally, a third, containing chiefly the complaints of the clergy themselves, and of the ordinaries, against the court of Rome, which was presented on the Monday after Jubilate, April 22, Luther himself being by.

conscious of its own unity,   But the answer to this is, that the strength
of a mind like his would have been broken, had it been fettered by any
consideration not purely religious.   Luther had been incited not by the
wants of the nation, but by his own religious convictions, without which
he would never have done any thing, and which had indeed led him
further than would have been either necessary or expedient in a political
struggle.

Some still hoped, however, that he would recall one step ; that he
would at least not persist in his last most offensive expressions which
occurred in the Book of the Babylonish Captivity.   This was in particular the opinion of the emperor's confessor.   He did not regard the
papal anathema as an insuperable obstacle to an amicable adjustment.
Luther had not yet had a hearing ; a door remained open to the pope
for restoring him to the bosom of the church, if he would but consent to
retract this last book, which was full of the most untenable assertions
and not comparable to his other writings.   But by maintaining these
passages he laid a stumbling-block in his own path ; he would cause that
the precious wares which he might otherwise bring safely to port would
be shipwrecked.[1]   At first he proposed to the Elector of Saxony to nominate two or three councillors with whom he could consult as to the means
of arranging the affair.   The elector replied that he had not learned
councillors sufficient.   Glapio hereupon asked whether the parties would
submit the matter to chosen arbitrators, by whose decision the pope
himself would abide.   The elector did not believe it possible to induce
the pope to consent to this, especially since the emperor intended so soon
to leave Germany.   On hearing this, Glapio sighed.   The silent, reserved
prince, who repelled all attempts at intimacy or sympathy from others,
and who was in fact the only human being that had any influence over
Luther, was absolutely unapproachable : it was impossible to obtain from
him even a private audience.   The confessor, therefore, addressed himself to other friends of Luther.   He went to the Ebernburg to visit Sickingen, who had just then re-entered the emperor's service and was
esteemed one of Luther's most distinguished patrons, in the hope of
obtaining his mediation.   Here, too, Glapio expressed himself in such a
manner on some points, that he might have been supposed to be an
adherent of Luther.   I am not of opinion that this was a stratagem, as
so many have assumed ; Aleander, at least, was very uneasy about it,
and neglected no means of interrupting the course of the negotiations.
It is obvious that Luther's opposition to the pope promised to be a doubly
powerful instrument of the imperial policy, if the government did not find
itself compelled absolutely to condemn him on account of his open schism,
and could keep the matter pending before a court of arbitration.   Sickingen
sent an invitation to Luther to visit him in passing by.[2]

For Luther was already on his way from Wittenberg to Worms.   He
preached once on the road, and in the evening when he arrived at his inn,
amused himself with playing the lute ; he took no interest whatever in
politics, and his mind was elevated far above all subjects of mere personal
interest, whether regarding himself or others.   At various places on the
road he had to pass through, might be seen posted up the decretal con-

[1] Seckendorf, Comm. de Lutheranismo, i. 142.
[2] See Luther's Narrative.   Works, Altenb. Ed., t. i., p. 733.

demning his books, so that when they arrived at Weimar the herald asked him whether he would go on. He replied that he would rely on the emperor's safe-conduct. Then came Sickingen's invitation. He replied, if the emperor's confessor had any thing to say to him, he could say it in Worms. Even at the last station, a councillor of his sovereign sent him word that he had better not come, for that he might share the fate of Huss. "Huss," replied Luther, "was burnt, but not the truth with him : I will go, though as many devils took aim at me as there are tiles on the roofs of the houses."[1] Thus he reached Worms, on the 18th of April, 1521, one Tuesday, about noon, just as people sat at dinner. When the watchman on the church tower blew his trumpet, every body crowded into the streets to see the monk. He sat in the open waggon (*Rollwagen*) which the council of Wittenberg had lent him for the journey, in the cowl of his order ; before him rode the herald, with his tabard, embroidered with the imperial eagle, hung over his arm. Thus they passed through the wondering, gaping crowd, regarded by some with sympathy, by all with various and unquiet emotions. Luther looked down upon the assembled multitude, and his daring courage rose to the height of firm confidence : he said, "God will be with me." In this state of mind he alighted.

The very next day towards evening he was conducted into the assembly of the empire. The young emperor, the six electors (among whom was his own master), a body of spiritual and temporal princes before whom their subjects bowed the knee, numerous chiefs celebrated for deeds in war and peace, worshipful delegates of cities, friends and foes, were there, awaiting the entrance of the monk. The sight of this majestic and splendid assemblage seemed for a moment to dazzle him. He spoke in a feeble and almost inaudible voice. Many thought he was frightened. Being asked whether he would defend his books (the titles of which were read aloud) collectively, or consent to recant, he replied that he begged for time to consider : he claimed, as we have seen, the benefit of the forms and customs of the empire.

The following day he appeared again before the diet. It was late before he was admitted ; torches were already lighted ; the assembly was perhaps more numerous than the day before ; the press of people so great, that the princes hardly found seats ; the interest in the decisive moment, more intense. Luther now exhibited not a trace of embarrassment. The same question as before being repeated to him, he answered with a firm, distinct voice and with an air of joyful serenity. He divided his works into books of Christian doctrine, writings against the abuses of the See of Rome, and controversial writings. To be compelled to retract the first, he said, would be unheard of, since even the papal bull had acknowledged that they contained much that was good ; the second, would afford the Romanists a pretext for the entire subjugation of Germany ; the third, would only give his adversaries new courage to resist the truth :—an

---

[1] Müller, Staatscabinet, viii. 296. I retain the expression, which he himself makes use of in a subsequent letter : "Wenn ich hätte gewusst, dass so viel Teufel auf mich gehalten hätten, als Ziegel auf den Dächern sind, wäre ich dennoch mitten unter sie gesprungen mit Freuden."—"If I had known that as many devils would have set upon me as there are tiles on the roofs, I should still have sprung into the midst of them with joy."—*Letters*, ii. 139.

answer which was more directed against the erroneous form in which the
questions had been arranged, than against the views with which the
States had entered on the trial.   The official of Treves put the matter in
a more tangible shape, by advising Luther not to give a total and unqualified refusal to the proposal to retract.   Had Arius, he said, retracted
some points, his good books would not have been destroyed together with
the bad.   In his (Luther's) case, too, means would be found to rescue
some of his books from the flames, if he would recant what had been condemned by the Council of Constance, and what he had repeated in defiance
of that condemnation.   The official insisted more on the infallibility of
councils than on that of the pope.

But Luther now believed as little in the one as in the other ; he replied
that even a council might err.   This the official denied.   Luther repeated
that he would prove that this might happen, and that it had happened.
The official could not of course go into the inquiry in that assembly.   He
asked again definitively whether Luther meant to defend all his works as
orthodox, or to retract any part.   He announced to him that, if he utterly
refused to recant, the empire would know how to deal with a heretic.
Luther had expected that a disputation or confutation, or some attempt
at demonstrating his errors, awaited him in Worms ; when therefore he
found himself at once treated as a false teacher, there arose in his mind
during the conversation the full consciousness of a conviction dependent
on no act of the will, founded on God's word, regardless of and untroubled
by pope or council : threats alarmed him not ; the universal sympathy,
the warm breathings of which he felt around him, had first given him
strength and courage : his feeling was, as he said at going out, that had
he a thousand heads he would let them all be struck off sooner than
recant.   He repeated now, as he had done before, that, unless it were
demonstrated to him by texts from the Holy Scripture that he was in
error, he could not and would not recant, since his conscience was captive
to God's word.   " Here I stand," exclaimed he : " I can do no otherwise ; God help me.   Amen."[1]

It is remarkable how different was the impression which Luther made
upon those present.   The Spaniards of high rank, who had always spoken
of him with aversion and contempt, who had been seen to take a book of
Luther's or Hutten's from a book-stall, tear it in pieces and trample it in
the mire,[2] thought the monk imbecile.   A Venetian, who was otherwise
perfectly impartial, remarks, that Luther showed himself neither very
learned nor remarkably wise, nor even irreproachable in his life, and that
he had not answered to the expectations conceived of him.[3]   It is easy
to imagine what was Aleander's judgment of him.   But even the emperor
had received a similar impression : " That man," said he, " will never

---

[1] Acta, Rev[di] Patris Martini Lutheri coram Cæs[a] Majestate, etc., Opp. Lutheri,
lat. ii. p. 411.   The account which Pallavicini drew from the letters of Aleander
contains somewhat more : a good deal of the detail which he gives, as well as
different pieces of news, I found in the letters of the Frankfurt delegates, Fürstenberg and Holzhausen.

[2] Buschius ad Huttenum.   Opp. Hutt., iv., p. 237.

[3] Contarenus ad Matthæum Dandulum Vormatiæ, 26mo d. April, 1521, in
the Chronicle of Sanuto, tom. xxx.

make a heretic of me." The next day (19th of April) he announced to
the states of the empire in a declaration written in French and with his
own hand, his determination to maintain the faith which had been held
by his predecessors, orthodox emperors and catholic kings. In that word
he included all that had been established by councils, and especially that
of Constance. To this he would devote his whole power, body and soul.
After the expressions of obstinacy which they had yesterday heard from
Luther, he felt remorse that he had spared him so long, and would now
proceed against him as against an avowed heretic. He called upon the
princes to act in the same spirit, according to their duty and their promises.

Luther had, on the contrary, completely satisfied his own countrymen.[1]
The hardy warriors were delighted with his undaunted courage ; the
veteran George of Frundsberg clapped him on the shoulder, encourag-
ingly, as he went in ; the brave Erich of Brunswick sent him a silver
tankard of Eimbeck beer through all the press of the assembly. At
going out a voice was heard to exclaim, " Blessed is the mother of such
a man !" Even the cautious and thoughtful Frederick was satisfied with
his professor : " Oh," said he to Spalatin in the evening, in his own
chamber, " how well did Doctor Martinus speak before the emperor and
states !" He was particularly delighted at the ease and ability with
which Luther had repeated his German declaration in Latin. From this
time, the princes rivalled each other in the frequency of their visits to
him. " If you be right, Sir Doctor," said Landgrave Philip of Hessen,
after a few jocose words, which Luther gently rebuked with a smile, " may
God help you." Luther had already been told, that if his enemies burned
him, they must burn all the German princes with him. Their latent
sympathy was aroused and set in motion by the emperor's peremptory
manifesto, so foreign to all the forms of the empire. A paper was found
in his apartments on which were written the words, " Woe to the land
whose king is a child !" A declaration of open hostility was fixed on the
town-hall, on the part of four hundred allied knights against the Romanists,
and especially against the Archbishop of Mainz, for trampling under foot
honour and divine justice. They had sworn not to abandon the upright
Luther. " I am ill at writing," said the author of this proclamation ;
" but I mean a great mischief, with 8,000 foot soldiers at my back. Bundschuh, Bundschuh, Bundschuh !"[2] This seemed to announce a combination between the knights and the peasants to protect Luther against his
enemies. In fact, the courtiers did not feel perfectly at ease, when they
saw themselves thus unarmed and defenceless, in the midst of a warlike
nation in a state of violent excitement and agitated by conflicting passions.

For the moment, however, there was nothing to fear, since Sickingen
and many other knights and captains had entered Charles's service, in

---

[1] " Contarenus ad Tiepolum, 25ᵐᵒ d. Apr. Habet intentissimos inimicos et
maximos fautores : res agitur tanta contentione quantam nemo crederet."—
Letter of Tonstall from the Diet of Worms, in Fiddes' Life of Wolsey, p. 242. The
Germans every where are so addicted to Luther, that rather than he shall be
oppressed by the pope's authority, a hundred thousand of the people will sacrifice
their lives.

[2] The war-cry of the league of the peasants of the Upper Rhine in 1501-2.

the hope of soon reaping an ample harvest of glory and gain under his banners.

Before the States entered on the discussion of the emperor's proclamation, they proposed that an attempt should be made to induce Luther to renounce his most offensive opinions ; they intimated that there was danger of a rebellion, if the proceedings against him were of so hasty and violent a kind : for this purpose the emperor granted a delay of some days.

But it was easy to foresee that little could be accomplished by such means. Representations were made to Luther concerning his opinions on the councils ;—he persisted in affirming that Huss was unjustly condemned at Constance. He was again asked to acknowledge the emperor and states as judges of his doctrines ;—he declared that he would not allow men to be the judges of God's word.

Aleander maintains that Luther had really, at one moment, been advised to abandon some of the opinions he had last proclaimed, and to defend only those immediately directed against Rome. No trace of this is to be found in German authorities. It does not even appear that the question contained in the memorial of the States was very precisely put ; but all his declarations were so clear and explicit, so profoundly religious, that no personal considerations were to be expected from him : he had emancipated himself for ever from the forms of the church of Rome ; in rejecting the decision of one council, he rejected the whole idea on which it rested : a compromise was now impossible.

But as he quitted Worms without having consented to the smallest limitation of his opinions, the former resolution of the States, which had given occasion to his being summoned before them, was now put in force as an instrument of his condemnation. The emperor, at least, could not have contemplated a revision of this decree or a fresh debate upon it, since he had just formed the most intimate relations with the See of Rome.

The ill concealed hostile disposition in which Don Juan Manuel had found the court of Rome in the spring of 1520, had been converted into the strictest union by his efforts, within the space of a year. On the 8th of May, 1521, an alliance was concluded between Charles and Leo, in which they mutually promised " to have the same friends and the same enemies, without exception ; the same will in consent and denial, in attack and defence." They began by making common cause against France ; the pope having at length determined completely to take the side of the emperor, and to exert all his powers to drive the French out of Milan and Genoa. The immediate object, however, was the spiritual affairs of Germany.

In the 16th article of the treaty, the emperor promised that, " inasmuch as certain men had arisen, who fall off from the Catholic faith and wickedly slander the apostolic see, he would employ all his powers in punishing them and avenging the wrong they had committed against the apostolic see, in like manner as if it had been done against himself."[1]

It cannot be affirmed that the conduct of Charles V. in the affair of

---

[1] Tabulæ Fœderis, &c., in Dumont, t. iv., part iii., p. 98. " Quoniam sanctissimo domino nostro cura est aliquanto etiam major rerum spiritualium et pastoralis officii quam temporalium——"

Luther was dictated exclusively by political motives ; it is very probable
that a denial of the infallibility of councils and an attack on the sacraments, was as offensive as it was unintelligible to him ; but it is perfectly
clear that he was mainly determined by politics.   To what purposes
might not Luther havo been turned, if he had moderated his tone so as
to render it unnecessary to condemn him ?   But as this was not to be
avoided, it was made a condition of the great war which was about to be
declared.

There was, however, still a certain difficulty in adopting decisive
measures, arising from the universal sympathy which Luther had excited
during his presence.   The resolution passed by the States was now repugnant to a considerable number of them.   The question was, whether
they would acquiesce without contest in an edict founded upon this
resolution.

In order to obtain this result, the following course was adopted.

Nothing was said for some time ; meanwhile many quitted Worms, as
all the other business was ended.

On the 25th of May, when the emperor appeared at the town-hall to
go through the formalities of receiving the resolutions concerning the
Council of Regency, the courts of justice, and the matricula, in person,
he requested the States to adjourn their departure for three days, in order
to terminate some matters which were still undecided.[1]   According to
ancient usage, the members of the diet escorted him back to the bishop's
palace, where he resided ; the electors of Saxony and the Palatinate had
left Worms, but the four others were present.   On their arrival at the
palace, they found the papal nuncios awaiting them.   In consequence of
Aleander's urgent representations of the necessity of sending this mark
of honour, briefs had arrived from the pope to the electors, and were
presented to them by the nuncios.   A brief had also arrived addressed
to the emperor, the publication of which had been designedly delayed
till this moment.   Under the impressions made by these flattering communications, the emperor now declared that he had caused an edict on
the Lutheran affair to be drawn up, on the basis of the former resolution
of the States.   This document had even been composed—such was the
confidence now prevailing between emperor and pope—by one of the
nuncios ; the present was esteemed the favourable moment for communicating it to these members of the diet.   There was now no legitimate or
efficient line of opposition open to them, even had they been disposed to
pursue it ; and the Elector of Brandenburg, Joachim I., replied that the
opinion of the States was certainly conformable to the measure in question.
Aleander hastened to place this instantly on official record.[2]

We perceive that the edict was not laid before the States in assembly ;
it was not submitted to any new deliberation ; it was announced to them
unexpectedly, in the emperor's apartments, and after every artifice had
been employed to incline them to listen favourably to any proposal : their

[1] Letter of Fürstenberg, May 28, Frankf. Arch.

[2] Pallavicini, lib. i., c. 28, from Aleander's Letters.   It is evident what pleasure
the narrator takes in the success of so dexterous a proceeding : " Era ignoto il
misterio all' istesso Grancancelliere—crucciava forte i ministri di papa, veggendo
nel discioglimento della dieta rimanerse con le mani vacue : ma i principi se
vogliono adoperare prudentemente, conviene," &c., &c.

assent, which cannot even be called a formal one, was extorted by a sort of surprise.[1]

It was, however, as severe and peremptory as possible. Sentence of ban and re-ban was declared against Luther as a member lopped off from the church of God ; together with all his adherents, patrons and friends. His writings, and those of his followers, were prohibited and sentenced to be burnt.   And that no similar works might appear in future, a censorship was appointed to control the press.[2]

Aleander had thus attained the long-desired object of all his negotiations.   In the course of the day he had two fair copies made, the one in German, the other in Latin : the next morning—Sunday,—he hastened with them to the emperor ; he found him with the States and the court in the church, but even this did not prevent him from laying the paper before Charles on the spot ; in the church it received the imperial signature.   This was on the 26th of May ; but Aleander had thought it expedient to date it the 8th, at which time the assembly was still tolerably full.

By this act the temporal power, as well as the spiritual, declared open resistance to the spirit of religious innovation which was awakened in the nation.   The opposition had not succeeded, as they had hoped, in inspiring the emperor with their own hostility to the papacy ; on the contrary, he had drawn closer all the ties which bound him to the pope. The two representatives of the secular and ecclesiastical powers had united, in order to uphold the established constitution of the church.

Whether they would succeed was, indeed, another question.

[1] Dr. Caspar Riffel, in his Christl. Kirchengesch. der Neuesten Zeit, vol. i., p. 214, cannot, in fact, avoid admitting this.   But he rejoices, that " the emperor, by means of this ' surprise,' removed all opportunity for even one of them (the princes) to break his word at the decisive moment."   It could not well be said more plainly that a serious difference prevailed between the emperor and the princes.

[2] Edict of Worms in Walch, xv. 2264.   It is remarkable that in all other departments the censorship is conferred on the bishop alone ; but in that of theology, only in conjunction with " the faculty of the Holy Scriptures of the nearest situated university."—§ 36.

BOOK III.

ENDEAVOURS TO RENDER THE REFORMATION NATIONAL AND COMPLETE.

1521—1525.

THE peculiar character and form which the Latin church had gradually assumed gave rise, as we have already seen, to the necessity for its reform ; —a reform demanded by the state of the world, and prepared by the national tendencies of the German mind, the advancement of learning, and the divergencies of theological opinion. We have likewise remarked how the abuse of the traffic in indulgences, and the disputes to which it gave birth, led, without design or premeditation on the part of any concerned, to a violent outbreak of opposition.

While we regard this as inevitable, we cannot proceed further without pausing to make some observations on its extreme danger.

For every member and every interest of society is enlinked with the whole established order of things which forms at once its base and its shelter ; if once the vital powers which animate this mass are thrown into conflict, who can say where the victorious assailants will find a check, or whether every thing will not be overwhelmed in common ruin ?

No institution could be more exposed to this danger than the papacy, which had for centuries exercised so mighty an influence over the whole existence of the European nations.

The established order of things in Europe was, in fact, the same military-sacerdotal state which had arisen in the eighth and ninth centuries, and, notwithstanding all the changes that had been introduced, had always remained essentially the same—compounded of the same fundamental elements. Nay, even those very changes had generally been favourable to the sacerdotal element, whose commanding position had enabled it to pervade every form of public and private life, every vein of intellectual culture. How then would it have been possible to assail it without producing a universal shock ; to question it, without endangering the whole fabric of civilisation ?

It must not be supposed that so resistless a power of persuasion resided in a merely dogmatic faith, wrought out by the hierarchy and the schools. The establishment of this would, on the contrary, have excited incessant controversy, which, though generally confined within the region of received ideas, would sometimes have been carried beyond that limit. But the intimate connexion which the papacy maintained with all established authorities had defeated every attempt at opposition. How, for example, could an emperor have ventured to take under his protection religious opinions opposed to the dominant system of faith, not on particular and unimportant points, but profoundly and essentially ? Even as against a pope on whom he was making war, he could not have dared to do it ; he must have feared to undermine the spiritual basis on which his own rank and power were founded ; to be the first to break through the circle of ideas and associations by which the minds of men were bounded. The authorities felt, at every moment, the indissoluble nature of their connexion with the hierarchy, and generally made themselves the instruments of the persecution of all who dissented from the faith prescribed by the church.

It was now also to be considered that projects and attempts of the most dangerous kind had been connected with the more recent attacks on the doctrine and discipline of the church of Rome.

A century and a half had elapsed since John Wicliffe had engaged in a similar contest with the papacy in England (with nearly the same weapons, and supported by the same national impulses) to that which Luther now entered upon in Germany ; this was instantly accompanied by a tumultuous rising of the lowest classes of the people, who, not content with reforms in the creed, or an emancipation from the see of Rome, aimed at the abolition of the whole beneficed clergy,[1] and even at the equalisation of the nobleman and the peasant ; *i.e.* at a complete overthrow of Church and State. It is uncertain whether Wicliffe had any share in these proceedings or not. At all events, the resentment they excited fell upon him, and he was removed from Oxford, the scene of his labours, whence he might have exercised a singular influence over England and the world, to the narrow and obscure sphere of a country parish.

The disorders in Bohemia, which broke out in consequence of the teaching and the condemnation of Huss, at first related exclusively to the spiritual matters whence they arose ;[2] but the severity with which they were repressed soon excited an extremely dangerous fanaticism. The Taborites[3] not alone rejected the doctrines of the Fathers of the church equally with those of later times, but they demanded the destruction of all the books in which those doctrines were contained. They declared it vain and unevangelical, nay, sinful, to prosecute studies and to take degrees at the universities ;[4] they preached that God would destroy the world, and would only save the righteous men of five cities ;[5] their preachers deemed themselves the avenging angels of the Lord, sent to execute his sentence of annihilation. Had their power corresponded with their will, they would have transformed the earth into a desert in the name of the Lord.

For a thirst for destruction is inevitably excited by successful opposition, and is the more violent, the more powerful the enemy with whom it has to contend.

Was not then, we must now inquire, a similar storm to be feared in Germany, where the pope had hitherto wielded a portion of the imperial power ?

The nation was in a state of universal ferment ; a menacing revolt against the constituted authorities was already stirring in the depths of

[1] See Prioris et Capituli Cantuarensis Mandatum, Sept. 16, 1381, in Wilkins's Concilia Magnæ Britanniæ, iii., p. 133.

[2] One chief cause of this movement which is commonly overlooked, is mentioned by the well-informed Hemmerlin in his tract De Libertate Ecclesiastica. I will give this in his own words. " In regno Bohemiæ quasi omnes possessiones et terrarum portiones et portiones portionum quasi per singulos passus fuerunt occupatæ, intricatæ et aggravatæ per census, reditus et proventus clero debitos. Unde populares nimis exasperati—insultarunt in clerum et religiosos—et terram prius occupatam penitus liberarunt."

[3] The extreme party among the Hussites, in contradistinction to the Calixtines.

[4] Formula fidei Taboritarum apud Laur. Byzynium (Brzezina) : Ludewig Reliquiæ MSS., tom. vi., p. 191.

[5] Byzynii Diarium belli Hussitici, ib., p. 155 sq.

society; would not this be called into action by an attack on the highest of all acknowledged earthly authorities? Would not the destructive forces which every society harbours in its bosom, and which this sacerdotal-military state had certainly not been able to neutralise or destroy, now rear their heads?

The whole future destiny of the German nation was involved in the question whether it could withstand this danger or not; whether it would succeed in severing itself from the papacy, without imperilling the state and the slowly won treasures of civilisation in the process; and what form of constitution—for without political changes the separation was impossible—the nation would then assume. On the answer to these questions rested, at the same time, the possible influence of Germany on the rest of the world.

The immediate course of events assumed a most menacing and dangerous character.

CHAPTER I.

DISTURBANCES AT WITTENBERG—OCTOBER, 1521, TO MARCH, 1522.

ONCE more had the supreme temporal power in Germany allied itself with the papacy, and this at first could not fail to make a deep impression. The edict of Worms was published in all parts of the empire; and in some places the confessors were instructed by the bishops to refuse absolution to every one who should be guilty of avowing Lutheran tenets. Luther's own sovereign could only save him by seizing him on his way through the Thuringian forest, and carrying him, in feigned captivity, to the safe asylum of the Wartburg. A report was spread that an enemy of the elector had imprisoned and perhaps killed him.

It soon, however, became manifest how little had been effected by these severities.

In the towns of the Netherlands in which Charles happened to be residing, Luther's writings were collected and publicly burned; but the emperor might be seen to smile ironically as he passed these bonfires in the market-place, nor do we find any trace of such executions in the interior of Germany. On the contrary, the events of the diet and the new edict only gained fresh partisans for Luther's cause. It appeared a powerful argument for the truth of his doctrines, that when he publicly avowed his books at Worms, and declared that he was ready to retract them if any one could confute him, no one had ventured to accept the challenge.[1] "The more Luther's doctrine is pent up," says Zasius, "the more it spreads."[2] If this was the experience of the university of Freiburg, where the orthodox party was so strong, what must it have been elsewhere? The Elector of

---

[1] "Ein schoner dialogus und gesprech zwischen eim Pfarrer und eim Schulthayss, betreffend allen übelstand der Geystlichen," &c. "A fine dialogue and conversation between a parish priest and a sheriff touching the ill condition of the clergy," &c., doubtless written immediately after the meeting of the diet; in which are these words: "Warum hand ir dan nit Doctor Luther mit disputiren *yez zu Worms* überwunden." "Why did you not then overcome Doctor Luther in the disputation now held at Worms?" This is the argument with which the sheriff brings over the parish priest to his views.

[2] Epp., i. 50.

Mainz did not think it expedient to grant the Minorites the permission begged by their provincial, to preach against Luther in his diocese, fearing that it would but increase the agitation of the public mind.[1] In despite of the new regulations for the censorship contained in the edict, pamphlet after pamphlet appeared in favour of the new doctrines. These were mostly anonymous, but Hutten ventured to put his name to a direct attack on the pope's nuncio, Aleander, the author of the edict. In this he asks him whether he imagines that he can crush religion and freedom by means of a single little edict, artfully wrung from a youthful prince ; or that an imperial command had any power against the immutable word of God. Were not rather the opinions of a prince subject to change ? The emperor, he believed, " would learn to think very differently in time."[2] The agents of Rome themselves were astonished to find of how little avail was the edict they had obtained with so much difficulty. The ink, they said, was scarcely dry with which the emperor had signed it, when already it was violated on every side. They are said, however, to have consoled themselves with the reflection, that if it had no other results, it must lay the foundation for inevitable dissension among the Germans themselves.

It was a most significant circumstance that the university of Wittenberg was as little affected by the imperial edict as it had been by the papal bull. There the new doctrines had already taken root and flourished independently of Luther's personal influence, and thither the flower of the German youth flocked to receive and adopt them. It made indeed but little difference whether Luther was present or not ; the lecture rooms were always crowded, and his doctrines[3] were defended with the same enthusiasm, both orally and in writing. In short, this infant university now took the boldest ground. When the Sorbonne at last broke silence, and declared itself against Luther, Melanchthon thought himself not only bound to undertake the defence of his absent friend, but he even dared to fling back the accusation upon the university of Paris, the source of all theological learning, the parent stem of which the German universities were branches, the Alma Mater to whose decision the whole world had ever bowed, and to charge her herself with falling off from true Christianity. He did not hesitate to declare the whole of the doctrines current at the universities, especially the theology of the schools, false and heretical when tried by the standard of Scripture.[4] The highest powers in Christendom had spoken, the pope had issued an anathema, and his sentence had been confirmed by that of the great mother university, and, finally, the emperor had ordered it to be executed ; and yet, in the small town of Wittenberg, which a few years before was hardly known, a professor little more than twenty years of age, in whose slight figure and modest bearing no one could have detected any promise of heroism or

[1] Capito ad Zwinglium Hallis, iv., Aug., 1521. (Epp. Zw., i. 78.) He required sermons, " citra perturbationem vulgi, absque tam atrocibus affectibus."

[2] Invectiva in Aleandrum. Opera, iv., p. 240.

[3] Spalatini Annales, 1521, October. " Scholastici, quorum supra millia ibi tum fuerunt." Nevertheless, in the course of the winter, the electors of Brunswick and Brandenburg forbade their subjects to attend this University. Mencken, Script., ii. 611. The number of matriculations fell off considerably during the winter term. Sennert, p. 59.

[4] Adversus furiosum Parisiensium theologastrorum decretum Phil. Melanchthonis pro Luthero Apologia. Corp. Reformatorum, i. 398.

boldness, dared to oppose all these mighty powers, to defend the condemned doctrines, nay, to claim for them the exclusive glory of Christianity.

One cause of this singular phenomenon was, that it was well known
that the appearance was more formidable than the reality :—the motives
which had determined the course taken by the court of Rome (chiefly
Dominican influence), and the means by which the edict had been extorted
from the emperor, and the manner of its publication, were no secret.   The
three men from whom the condemnation in Paris originated were pointed
out, and called by the most opprobrious names.[1]   The reformers, on the
other hand, were conscious of pure motives, and a firm and impregnable
foundation for their opinions.   The influence of their prince, who afforded
them undoubted though unacknowledged protection, was a safeguard
against actual violence.

But those who ventured to take up so independent and imposing a
position, at variance with all established authorities, and supported only
by opinions which had not yet attained their full development nor acquired
a precise form, obviously incurred an enormous weight of responsibility.
In carrying out the principles professed, it was necessary to be the pioneers
of a numerous, susceptible, and expecting crowd of sympathising spirits.
Here, where all the elements of a state at once military and sacerdotal
were to be found as abundantly as elsewhere, the experiment was to be
tried, how far the authority of the priesthood might be destroyed without
endangering the safety of the state.

It had, however, become impossible to remain stationary. Men's
minds were too much excited to be content with doctrines alone. On
the faith which was now so profoundly shaken, were founded practices
that influenced every day and hour of common life ; and it was not to
be expected that an energetic generation, conscious of its own power, and
impelled by new and mighty ideas, should do violence to its own convictions
and submit to ordinances it had begun to condemn.

The first remarkable incident that occurred was of a purely personal
nature. Two priests in the neighbourhood, Jacob Seidler and Bartholomew Bernhardi, both professing the doctrines of Wittenberg, solemnly
renounced their vows of celibacy.   Of all the institutions of the hierarchy,
this, indeed, was the one which, from the strong taste for domestic life
inherent in the nation, had always been most repugnant to the German
clergy, and, in its consequences, most profoundly offensive to the moral
sense of the people.   The two priests declared their conviction that
neither pope nor synod were entitled to burden the church with an ordinance which endangered both the body and the soul.[2]   Hereupon they
were both claimed for trial by the spiritual authorities ; Seidler alone,
who resided in the territory of Duke George of Saxony, was given up to
them, and perished in prison ; the Elector Frederick refused to lend his
authority to the Bishop of Magdeburg against Bernhardi ; he refused,
as Spalatin expresses it, to let himself be employed as a constable.   Carl-

---

[1] Glareanus ad Zwinglium Lutetiæ 4 non. Julii, 1521.   Beda, Quercus, Chris-
tophorus : Bellua, Stercus, Christotomus.   Epp. Zw., p. 176.   The work of
Glareanus, p. 156, in which the death of Leo X. is mentioned, does not belong to
the year 1520, but to the following year.

[2] "Quid statuerint Pontificii canones, nihil refert Christianorum."—*Epistle
from the Theologians of Wittenberg to the Bishop of Meissen, Corp. Ref.*, i. 418.

stadt now took courage to attack the institution of celibacy in a work of considerable length.

As the vow of celibacy was originally confined to the monastic orders, and had subsequently been extended to the whole priesthood, its dissolution necessarily affected the whole idea of the monastic system. In the little Augustine church which had been the scene of Luther's first appearance, Gabriel Zwilling, one of his most able fellow-labourers, preached a series of fervent discourses, in which he attacked the very essence of monachism, declaring that it was not only lawful but necessary to renounce it ; for that " under the cowl there was no salvation." Thirteen Augustine monks left the convent at once, and took up their abode, part among the students and part among the townspeople. One of them who understood the trade of a cabinet-maker, applied for the right of citizenship and proclaimed his intention of marrying.[1] This was followed by a general disturbance : the Augustines who had stayed in the convent thought themselves no longer safe ; and the Carmelite convent in Wittenberg had to be protected every night by a strong guard.

Meanwhile Brother Gabriel made another still more formidable attack upon the Catholic church. He carried Luther's doctrines about the sacrament so far as to declare the adoration of it, and even the celebration of the mass without communicants, simply as a sacrifice (the so-called private mass), an abuse and a sin.[2] In a short time the prior of the convent was compelled by the general agitation to discontinue the celebration of private masses in his church, in order, as he said, to avoid still greater scandal. This of course produced a great sensation both in the town and university. On the 3d of December, 1521, when mass was going to be sung in the parish church, several of the students and younger burghers came with knives under their coats, snatched away the mass books and drove the priests from the altar. The town council summoned the offenders subject to its jurisdiction, and showed an intention of punishing them ; upon which the townspeople rose tumultuously and proposed terms to the council, in which they demanded the liberation of the prisoners in a tone almost amounting to open rebellion.[3]

All these were attempts made without plan or deliberation to overthrow the existing form of divine worship. The Elector, to whose decision such affairs were always referred, wished, as was usual with him, to take the opinion of some constituted authority.

[1] Report of Gregorius Bruck to the Elector, Oct. 11. Corp. Ref., i. 459.
[2] Report from Helt the prior of the Augustines to the Elector, Nov. 12. Corp. Ref., p. 483.
[3] The Council of Wittenberg to the Elector. Dec. 3 and 5. Corp. Ref., p. 487. The impression made by these innovations in distant countries is remarkably displayed by a passage in vol. xxxii. of the Venetian Chronicle of Sanuto, in the Archives of Vienna. " Novità di uno ordine over uso de la fede christiana comenzada in Vintibergia. Li frati heremitani di S. Augustino hanno trovato è provato per le St. Scripture che le messe secondo che se usano adesso si é gran peccato a dirle o a odirle (thus it appears that the whole innovation was looked upon as an invention of the Augustine order) e dapoi el zorno di S. Michiel, 1521, in qua ogni zorno questo hanno predichado e ditto, e stanno saldi in questa soa oppinione, e questo etiam con le opre observano e da poi la domeniga di S. Michiel non hanno ditto piu messe nella chiesia del suo monasterio, e per questo è seguito gran scandalo tra el popolo li cantori e canonici spirituali e temporali——"

His first step was to summon to Wittenberg a council of Augustines from the provinces of Meissen and Thuringia. These monks all more or less shared Luther's opinions and regarded his cause as their own. Their judgment, as he afterwards declared, coincided with his own, even during his absence ; they did not go so far as Brother Gabriel, who denounced the monastic vows as sinful, but they no longer acknowledged them to be binding. Their decision was as follows : " Every creature is subject to the word of God, and needs not allow himself to be oppressed by burdensome human institutions ; every man is at liberty to leave the convent or to remain in it ;[1] but he who leaves it must not abuse his freedom according to the lusts of the flesh ; he who prefers to stay, will do well to wear the cowl and render obedience to his superiors from choice and affection." They determined at the same time to desist from the practice of begging, and to abolish votive masses.

Meanwhile the prince had called upon the university to pronounce an opinion on the mass in general. A commission was accordingly chosen, of which Melanchthon was a member, and which decided for the entire abolition of the mass, not only in Wittenberg but throughout the country, be the consequences what they might.[2] When, however, the moment arrived for the whole corporation to confirm this sentence, they absolutely refused to do so ; several of the most influential members stayed away from the meeting, declaring that they were too insignificant to undertake to reform the church.[3]

Thus as neither the Augustine order nor the university declared themselves distinctly in favour of the innovators, the Elector refused to move any further in the matter, saying that if even in Wittenberg they could not agree, it was not probable that the rest of the world would think alike on the proposed change : they might go on reading, disputing, and preaching about it, but in the mean while they must adhere to established usages.[4]

The excitement was, however, already too great to be restrained by the command of a prince whose leniency was so well known ; and accordingly Dr. Carlstadt announced, in spite of it, that on the feast of the circumcision he should celebrate the mass according to a new rite, and administer the Lord's Supper in the words of the Founder. He had already attempted something of the kind in the month of October, but with only twelve communicants, in exact imitation of the example of Christ. As it seemed probable that difficulties would be thrown in his way, he determined not to wait till the day appointed, and on Christmas Day, 1521, he preached in the parish church on the necessity of abandoning the ancient rite and receiving the sacrament in both kinds. After the sermon he went up to the altar and said the mass, omitting the words which convey the idea of a sacrifice, and the ceremony of the elevation of the host, and then distributed first the bread and next the wine, with

[1] Decreta Augustinianorum. Corp. Ref., i. 456. This meeting is not to be placed in the month of October, but rather in December or the beginning of January, as is remarked by Seckendorf (Historia Luther., i., s. 54, § 129) on the authority of a contemporary letter. See Spalatini Ann., 610.

[2] Ernstlich Handlung der Universität, &c., Corp. Ref., i. 465.

[3] Report of Christian Beiers, Dec. 13, ib., 500.

[4] Instruction of the Elector, Lochau, Dec. 19, ib., 507.

the words, " This is the cup of my blood of the new and everlasting covenant." This act was so entirely in harmony with the feelings of the congregation that no one ventured to oppose it. On New Year's Day he repeated this ritual, and continued to do so every succeeding Sunday ; he also preached every Friday.[1]

Carlstadt belonged to a class of men not uncommon in Germany, who combine with a natural turn for deep speculation the boldness to reject all that has been established, or to maintain all that has been condemned ; yet without feeling the necessity of first arriving at any clear and precise ideas, or of resting those ideas upon arguments fitted to carry general conviction. Carlstadt had at first adopted the doctrines of the schoolmen ; he was afterwards urged by Luther to the study of the sacred writings, though he had not, like him, patience to acquire their original languages ; nor did he hesitate at the strangest and most arbitrary interpretations, in which he followed only the impulse of his own mind. This led him into strange aberrations ; even at the time he was preparing for the disputation at Leipzig, he used the most singular expressions with regard to the Holy Scriptures, applying to them as a whole that which has generally been understood of the law only ; viz. that they lead to transgression, sin, and death, and do not afford the true consolation the soul requires. In the year 1520 he entertained doubts whether Moses was really the author of the books which bear his name, and whether the Gospels have come down to us in their genuine form ; speculations which have since given so much occupation to learning and criticism, presented themselves at this early period to his mind.[2] At that time he was overawed by the presence and authority of Luther ; now, however, he was restrained by no one ; a wide arena for the display of his ambition lay before him, and he was surrounded by an enthusiastic public. Under these circumstances he was himself no longer the same ; the little swarthy sun-burnt man, who formerly expressed himself in indistinct and ambiguous language, now poured forth with the most vehement eloquence a torrent of mystical extravagant ideas, relating to a totally new order of things, which carried away all imaginations.

Towards the end of the year 1521 he was joined by allies who had entered on a similar career from another direction, and who pursued it with still greater audacity.

It is well known that at the beginning of the Hussite troubles, two strangers, Nicolas and Peter of Dresden, who had been banished by the Bishop of Meissen and found an asylum in Prague, were the persons who, during the absence of Huss and Jerome, instigated the populace to demand a change of the ritual, especially in the administration of the sacrament ; and that various other fanatical opinions were quickly combined with these.[3]

Whether it was that these opinions re-acted on the country in which they originated—or whether they had from the first taken deeper and

---

[1] Zeitung aus Wittenberg ; account of what took place in 1521, &c. ; in Strobel's Miscellanien, v. 121.

[2] See extracts from his works in Löscher's Historia Motuum, i. 15.

[3] The notice of this is very remarkable in Pelzel's Wenceslas, ii. (Urkunden, nr. 238, ex MS. coævo capituli.) They declared at the very beginning " quod papa sit antichristus cum clero sibi subjecto."

more lasting root there,—the same spirit which had formerly directed the movement at Prague, now revived at Zwickau (a town in the Erzgebirge, where Peter of Dresden had for some time resided), and appeared likely to guide the agitation now prevailing at Wittenberg.

This spirit was remarkably displayed in a sect which congregated round a fanatical weaver of the name of Claus Storch, of Zwickau, and professed the most extravagant doctrines. Luther did not go nearly far enough for these people. Very different men, they said, of a much more elevated spirit, were required; for what could such servile observance of the Bible avail? That book was insufficient for man's instruction; he could only be taught by the immediate inspiration of the Holy Ghost.[1] Their fanaticism soon rose to such a pitch as to convince them that this was actually granted to them; that God spoke to them in person, and dictated to them how to act and what to preach.[2] On the strength of this immediate inspiration from Heaven, they pressed for various alterations in the services of the church. Above all, they maintained that a sacrament had no meaning without faith, and therefore entirely rejected the baptism of infants, who are incapable of faith. But their imaginations took a much wilder flight. They asserted that the world was threatened with a general devastation, of which the Turks were perhaps to be the instruments; no priest was to remain alive, not even those who were now contracting marriage, nor any ungodly man; but after this bloody purification the kingdom of God would commence, and there would be one faith and one baptism.[3] They seemed well inclined to begin this work of violent convulsion themselves. Finding resistance from the moderate portion of the citizens and town council of Zwickau, they collected arms in the house of one of their party, with the design of falling suddenly on their opponents and putting them all to death. Fortunately they were anticipated by Wolf of Weissenbach, the chief magistrate of the place; he arrested a number of the misguided men, kept the peace and compelled the ring-leaders to quit the town.[4] The fanatics hoped to accomplish abroad what they had failed in at home. Some of them went to Prague with a view to reviving the old Taborite sect there,—an attempt which proved abortive. The others, of whom it is more especially our business to speak, came to Wittenberg, where they found the ground admirably prepared for the seed they had to sow, by the universal restlessness of minds craving for some unknown novelty, not only among the excitable class of students, but even among the townspeople. We accordingly find that after their arrival in Wittenberg the agitation assumed a bolder character.

[1] A report sent from Zwickau to the elector, of which he informs the university, gives this account of their opinions. Acta Einsiedelii cum Melanthonio, C. R., p. 536. The statements in Enoch Widemann Chronicon Curiæ, in Mencken, Scriptt. R. G., iii. 744, shows a somewhat later development of the fantasies of Storch. Tobias Schmidt's Cronica Cygnea, 1656, is not without its value for the events of the thirty years' war, but is insufficient for the times of the Reformation.

[2] Official Report of Melanchthon, Jan. 1, 1522, C. R., i. 533, from which it is evident that half a year before, these people had not begun to boast of this communion with God.

[3] Zeitung aus Wittenberg, p. 127.

[4] According to G. Fabricius, Vita Ricii, in Melchior Adam, Vitæ Philosophorum, p. 72.

Carlstadt, with whom they immediately allied themselves, introduced more striking innovations every day. The priestly garments were abolished and auricular confession disused. People went to receive the sacrament without preparation, and imagined that they had gained an important point, when they took the host with their own hands instead of receiving it from those of the priest. It was held to be the mark of a purer Christianity to eat eggs and meat on fast days especially. The pictures in the churches were now esteemed an abomination in the holy place. Carlstadt disregarded the distinction which had always been made between reverence and adoration, and applied all the texts in the Bible directed against idolatry to the worship of images. He insisted upon the fact that people bowed and knelt before them, and lighted tapers, and brought offerings ; that, for example, they contemplated the image of St. Christopher, in order that they might be preserved against sudden death ; he therefore exhorted his followers to attack and destroy " these painted gods, these idol logs." He would not even tolerate the crucifix, because he said men called it their God, whereas it could only remind them of the bodily sufferings of Christ. It had been determined that the images should be removed from the churches, but as this was not immediately executed, his zeal became more fiery ;[1] at his instigation an iconoclast riot now commenced, similar to those which half a century afterwards broke out in so many other countries. The images were torn from the altars, chopped in pieces and burnt. It is obvious that these acts of violence gave a most dangerous and menacing character to the whole controversy. Carlstadt not only quoted the Old Testament to show that the secular authorities had power to remove from the churches whatever could give scandal to the faithful, but added, that if the magistrates neglected this duty, the community was justified in carrying out the necessary changes. Accordingly the citizens of Wittenberg laid a petition before the council, in which they demanded the formal abolition of all unbiblical ceremonies, masses, vigils, and processions, and unlimited liberty for their preachers. The

---

[1] Von Abtuhung der Bylder. Und das keyn Betdler unther den Christen seyn soll. Carolstatt in der christlichen Statt Wittenberg. Bog. D. (Concerning the Abolition of Images. And that there should be no Worshipper among Christians. Carlstadt in the Christian Town of Wittenberg. Sheet D.) The decree was made on Friday after St. Sebastian, Jan. 24, 1522. The dedication to the paper on the first sheet, which also was first printed, is dated Monday after the conversion of St. Paul, 27th Jan. Carlstadt then had the greatest hopes. The date shows how zealous he was. When he came to the fourth sheet, he plainly saw that matters would not proceed so rapidly. " Ich hette auch gehofft, der lebendig got solt seine eingegeben werk das ist guten willen tzu abtuhung der bilder volzogen und yns eusserlich werk gefurt haben. Aber ess ist noch kein execution geschehen, vileicht derhalben, das got seinen tzorn vber vns lest treuffen yn meynung seynen gantzen tzorn ausszuschüden, wu wir alsso blind bleiben vnd fürchten vns vor dem dass vns nicht kan thun. Das weiss ich das die Obirsten deshalb gestrafft werden. Dan die schrifft leugt ye nit."—" I had also hoped that the living God would have carried into execution and openly brought to bear his appointed work, that is, good will towards the abolition of images. But no execution has yet taken place, perhaps because God lets his anger drip upon us, intending to pour out all his wrath, if we remain thus blind, and *fear not that which he is able to do. Thus much I know, that they in high places will be punished therefore. For the Scripture lieth not."

council was forced to concede these points one after the other ;[1] nor did
even these concessions satisfy the innovators. Their project was to realise
without delay their own conception of a strictly Christian community.
The council was called upon to close all places of public amusement, not
only those which the law prohibited, but those which it had sanctioned ;
to abolish the mendicant orders who, they said, ought not to exist in
Christendom, and to divide the funds of the religious communities, which
were pronounced to be altogether mischievous and corrupt, among the
poor. To these suggestions of a bigoted fanaticism, blind to the real
nature and interests of society, were added the most pernicious doctrines
of the Taborites. An old professor like Carlstadt suffered himself to be
carried away by the contagion to such a degree as to maintain that there
was no need of learned men, or of a course of academic study, and still
less of academic honours. In his lectures he advised his hearers to return
home and till the ground, for that man ought to eat his bread by the
sweat of his brow. One of his most zealous adherents was George Mohr,
the rector of the grammar school, who addressed the assembled citizens
from the window of the school-house, exhorting them to take away their
children. Of what use, said he, would learning be henceforth ? They
had now among them the divine prophets of Zwickau, Storch, Thomä,
and Stübner, who conversed with God, and were filled with grace and
knowledge without any study whatsoever. The common people were
of course easily convinced that a layman or an artisan was perfectly
qualified for the office of a priest and teacher.

Carlstadt himself went into the houses of the citizens and asked them
for an explanation of obscure passages in Scripture ; acting on the text
that God reveals to babes what he hides from wise men. Students left
the university and went home to learn a handicraft, saying that there
was no longer any need of study.[2]

The conservative ideas to which Luther had still clung were thus abandoned ; the idea of temporal sovereignty, on which he had taken his
stand to oppose the encroachments of the priesthood, was now rejected
with no less hostility than the spiritual domination. Luther had combated the reigning faith with the weapons of profound learning ; one of
the rudest theories of inspiration that has ever been broached now threatened to take its place. It is evident, however, that its success was impossible. All the powers of the civilised world would have risen against such
a wild, destructive attempt, and would either have utterly crushed it, or
at all events have driven it back within the narrowest limits. Had such
anarchical dreams ever become predominant, they must have destroyed
every hope of improvement which the world could attach to the reforming
party.

In Wittenberg there was no one capable of resisting the general frenzy.
Melanchthon was then too young and inexperienced, even had he possessed
sufficient firmness of character. He held some conferences with the
prophets of Zwickau ; and finding not only that they were men of talent,
but well grounded in the main articles of a faith which was likewise his
own ; being also unable to refute their arguments concerning infant

[1] Strobel, v. 128.

[2] Fröschel : Tractat vom Priesterthum (Appendix), 1565. Reprinted in the
Unschuldigen Nachrichten, 1731, p. 698.

baptism, he did not feel. himself competent to enter the lists against them. We find disciples and friends of Melanchthon among their adherents.[1]

The elector was equally incapable of offering any efficient resistance. We are already acquainted with the character of this prince,—his temporising policy, his reluctance to interfere in person, his habit of letting things take their own course. His was the most peaceful nature produced by this troubled and warlike age ; he never had recourse to arms ; when advised to seize Erfurt, on the plea that he might accomplish it with the loss of only five men, he replied, " One were too many."[2] Yet his quiet, observant, prudent, and enlightened policy had ever been crowned with ultimate success. His pleasure was to adorn his own territories, which he thought as beautiful as any on earth, with castles, like those of Lochau, Altenburg, Weimar and Coburg ; to decorate his churches with pictures from the admirable pencil of Lucas Kranach, whom he invited to his court ; to keep up the high renown of his chapel and choir, which was one of the best in the empire, and to improve the university he had founded.

Although not remarkable for popular and accessible manners, he had a sincere affection for the people. He once paid back the poll-tax which had been levied, when the purpose to which it was to be applied was abandoned. " Truly," said he of somebody, " he is a bad man, for he is unkind to the poor folk." Once, when on a journey, he gave money to the children who were playing by the roadside : " One day," said he, " they will tell how a duke of Saxony rode by and gave each of them something. " We read of his sending rare fruits to a sick professor.[3] The elector was now in years ; most of the older German princes with whom he had lived in habits of intimacy, " his good comrades and friends," as he called them, were dead, and he had many annoyances and vexations to bear. He was in doubt and perplexity as to the real inclinations of the young emperor. " Happy is the man," he exclaimed, " who has nothing to do with courts !" The disagreement between himself and his nearest neighbour and cousin, the turbulent Duke George, became more and more serious and evident. " Ah, my cousin George !" said he,—" truly I have no friend left but my brother ;" —and to him he gradually confided the greater share of the government. The protection he afforded to Luther had arisen naturally out of the course of events ; at first, partly from political motives, then from a feeling of duty and justice.[4] Nor was this all ; he conscientiously shared the profound, unquestioning veneration for the Scriptures inculcated by Luther. He thought that everything else, however ingenious and plausible, might be confuted ; the word of God alone was holy, majestic,

[1] *E.g.*, Martin Borrhaus (Cellarius) of Stuttgart had set on foot a private school for Melanchthon. Adam, Vitæ Theolog., p. 191.

[2] Luther to John Frederick and Moritz, 1542.

[3] Epistola Carlstadii ad Spalatinum in Gerdes Scrinium, vii. ii. 345.

[4] His counsellors in Wittenberg declared, on the 2d Jan., 1522, " S. Ch. G. hatt sich Doctor Martinus Sachen bisher nicht anders—angenommen, denn allein weil er sich zu Recht erboten, dass er nicht bewältigt würde."—" His Christian grace, the elector, had as yet taken up Dr. Martinus's cause in no other way beyond offering to see that he had justice, and was not overpowered by force."— Corp. Ref., p. 537.

and truth itself : he said that this word should be " pure as an eye." He had a deep reverential fear of opposing or disobeying it. The basis of all religion is this sense of what is sacred—of the moral mystery of the universe ; this awe of offending against it under the momentary influence of impurer motives. Such was eminently the religion of Frederick the Wise, and it had withheld him from interfering decidedly and arbitrarily in Luther's behalf ; but it also hindered him from exerting his power to put down these new sectarians in Wittenberg, displeasing as they were to him. He did not venture, any more than Melanchthon, to pronounce an absolute condemnation of them. After listening to the doubts and scruples of his counsellors and learned men at Prettin on this subject, he appeared perplexed and overpowered at the idea that these people might possibly be in the right. He said that as a layman he could not understand the question ; but that, rather than resist the will of God, he would take his staff in his hand and leave his country.[1]

It certainly might have come to this. The movement that had begun could lead to nothing short of open rebellion,—to the overthrow of civil government in order to make room for a new Christian republic ; violence would then certainly have called forth violence, and good and evil would have perished together.

How much now depended on Luther ! Even these disturbances were the offspring or the consequence of ideas that he had set afloat, or were closely connected with them : if he sanctioned them, who would be able to stem the torrent ? if he opposed them, it seemed doubtful whether his opposition would have any effect, or whether he himself would not be overwhelmed in the common ruin.

During the whole of this time he was in the Wartburg, at first keeping closely within the walls, then venturing out timidly to gather strawberries on the castle hill, and afterwards, grown bolder, riding about as Junker George, accompanied by a groom. He once even ventured into Wittenberg, trusting to the disguise of his long hair and beard, and completely cased in armour. But though his mode of life and his accoutrements were those of a Reiter, his soul was ever in the heat of ecclesiastical warfare. " When hunting," says he, " I theologized :" the dogs and nets of the hunters represented to him the bishops and stewards of antichrist seeking to entrap and devour unhappy souls.[2] In the solitude of the castle he was again visited by some of the struggles and temptations which had assailed him in the convent. His chief occupation was a translation of the New Testament, and he likewise formed the project of giving to the German nation a more correct translation of the Bible than the Latin church possesses in the Vulgate.[3] Whilst endeavouring to fortify his resolution for the accomplishment of this work, and only wishing to be in Wittenberg that he might have the assistance of his friends, he heard of the excitement and disorder prevailing there. He was not for a moment in doubt as to their nature. He said that nothing in the whole course of his life had given him greater pain ; all that had been done to injure himself was nothing in the comparison. The pretensions of these

[1] Spalatin, Leben Friedrichs des Weisen. Vermischte Abhandlungen zur sächsischen Gesch. B. v.
[2] To Spalatin, 15th Aug., D. W., ii. 43.
[3] To Amsdorf, 13th Jan., p. 123.

men to the character of divinely inspired prophets and to immediate
communion with God, did not impose on him ; for he too had fathomed
the mysterious depths of the spiritual world, and had gained a far deeper
insight into it, and a far too exalted conception of the divine nature,
to allow himself to be persuaded that God would appear visibly to his
creatures, converse with them, or throw them into ecstasies.   " If you
want to know the time and place and nature of the divine communications,"
writes he to Melanchthon,[1] " hear ; ' Like as a lion he hath crushed my
bones ;' and, ' I am cast out from before thy countenance, my soul is
filled with heaviness, and the fear of hell is upon me.'   God spake by
the mouths of his prophets, because if he spoke himself we could not
endure it."   He wishes his prince joy of the cross which God has laid
upon him, and says that the Gospel was not only persecuted by Annas
and Caiaphas, but that there must be a Judas even among the apostles ;
he also announces his intention of going to Wittenberg himself.   The
elector entreated him not to leave his retreat so soon, saying that as
yet he could do no good, that he had better prepare his defence for the
next diet, at which it was to be hoped he would obtain a regular hearing.[2]
But Luther was no longer to be restrained by these arguments ; never
had he been more firmly convinced that he was the interpreter of the
divine word and that his faith would be a sufficient protection ; the
occurrences in Wittenberg seemed to him a disgrace to himself and to
the Gospel.[3]   He accordingly set out on his way, regardless of the pope's
excommunication or the emperor's ban, bidding his prince have no care
about him.   He was in a truly heroic state of mind.

A party of young Swiss who were on their way to the University of
Wittenberg stopped to dine at the sign of the Black Bear at Jena.   On
entering they saw a horseman who sat at the table resting his right hand
on the hilt of his sword, with a Hebrew psalter before him ; this horseman,
as they afterwards discovered, was Luther, and we read in the notes of
one of them, how he invited them to dine with him, and how gentle and
dignified was his deportment.[4]   On Friday 7th of March he arrived at
Wittenberg ; on the Saturday the same Swiss found him surrounded by
his friends, inquiring minutely into all that had occurred during his
absence.   On Sunday he began to preach, in order immediately to ascertain whether his popularity and influence were still sufficient to enable
him to allay the disturbance.   Small and obscure as was the scene to
which he returned, his success or failure was an event pregnant with
important results to the whole world ; for it involved the question, whether
the doctrine which had forced itself on his conviction from its own inherent
weight, and which was destined to give such an impulse to the progress
of mankind, had also power to subdue the elements of destruction fermenting in the public mind, that had already undermined the foundations of
society and now threatened it with total ruin.   It had now to be tried
whether it were possible to reform without destroying ; to open a fresh
career to mental activity, without annihilating the results of the labours
of former generations.   Luther's view of the question was that of a

[1] 13 Jan., 1522, to Amsdorf, p. 125.
[2] Instructions to Oswald, Corp. Ref., i. 561.
[3] To the elector, 5th March, ii. 137.
[4] From the Chronicle of Kessler, in Bernet, Leben Kesslers, p. 27.

preacher and pastor of souls ; he did not denounce the changes that had been made as utterly pernicious, nor the doctrines from which they had sprung as fundamentally bad, and he carefully refrained from any personal attacks on the leaders of the new sect.   He merely said that they had acted with precipitation, and had thus laid a stumbling-block in the way of the weak and transgressed the commandment of charity.   He allowed that there were practices which undoubtedly ought to be abolished ; such, for instance, as private masses ; but that these reforms ought to be effected without violence or scandal.   As to a number of other usages, he thought it indifferent whether a Christian observed them or not.   That it was a matter of very small importance whether a man received the Lord's Supper in one kind or in both, or whether he preferred a private confession to the general one, or chose rather to remain in his convent or to leave it, to have pictures in the churches, and to keep fasts, or not ; but that to lay down strict rules concerning these things, to raise violent disputes, and to give offence to weaker brethren, did more harm than good, and was a trangression of the commandment of charity.

The danger of the anarchical doctrines now broached, lay in the assumption that they were an indispensable part of true Christianity ; an assumption maintained with the same vehemence and confidence on the side of the anabaptists, as the divine and thence infallible origin of every decree of the church was on that of the papists.

These doctrines, therefore, like those of the papacy, were intimately bound up with the whole system of morals, and the whole fabric of civil life.   It was therefore most important to show that religion recognised a neutral and independent province, over which she was not required to exercise a direct sway, and where she needed not to interfere in the guidance of every individual thought.   This Luther did with the mildness and forbearance of a father and a guide, and with the authority of a profound and comprehensive mind.   These sermons are certainly among the most remarkable that he ever preached ; they are, like those of Savonarola, popular harangues, not spoken to excite and carry away his hearers, but to arrest them in a destructive course, and to assuage and calm their passions.[1]   How could his flock resist the well-known voice, the eloquence which carried the conviction it expressed, and which had first led them into the way of inquiry ?   The construction commonly put upon moderate councils, namely, that they arise from fear of consequences, could have no place here.   Never had Luther appeared in a more heroic light ; he bid defiance to the excommunication of the pope and the ban of the emperor, in order to return to his flock ; not only had his sovereign warned him that he was unable to protect him, but he had himself expressly renounced his claim to that protection ; he exposed himself to the greatest personal danger, and that not (as many others have done) to place himself at the head of a movement, but to check it ; not to destroy, but to preserve.   At his presence the tumult was hushed, the revolt quelled, and order restored ; a few even of the most violent party

---

[1] " Sieben Predigten D. M. L. so er von dem Sontage Invocavit bis auf den andern Sontag gethan, als er aus seiner Pathmos zu Wittenberg wieder ankommen."   (" Seven sermons of Doctor Martin Luther, delivered by him during the week between the Sunday Invocavit and the following Sunday, when he returned from his Patmos to Wittenberg.")—Alt., ii. 99.

leaders were converted to his opinions and joined him. Carlstadt, who could not be brought to confess his error, was condemned to silence.   He was reproached with having intruded himself uncalled into the ministry, and was forbidden to enter the pulpit again.   Some approximation took place between the moderated opinions now maintained by Luther, and those of the civil authorities, who were delivered from the danger that had threatened the state. A treatise of Carlstadt's, written in the same spirit as heretofore, part of which was already printed, was suppressed by the university, and a report of it sent to the elector.   The Zwickauers once more sought an interview with Luther ; he exhorted them not to suffer themselves to be deceived by the illusions of the devil ; they answered, that as a proof of their divine mission, they would tell him what were his thoughts at that instant ; to this he agreed, upon which they said that he felt a secret inclination towards themselves.   " God rebuke thee, Satan !" exclaimed Luther.   He afterwards acknowledged that he had, indeed, been conscious of such a leaning ; but their guessing it, he held to be a sign of powers derived from Satan rather than from God ;[1] he accordingly dismissed them with a sort of challenge to their demon to resist his God. If we soften the coarseness of his language, this struggle between two antagonist spirits, the one destructive, the other tutelary, is the expression of a mighty and profound truth.

Wittenberg was now once more quiet ; the mass was as far as possible restored, preceded by confession, and the host was received as before with the lips.   It was celebrated in hallowed garments, with music and all the customary ceremonies, and even in Latin ; nothing was omitted but the words of the canon which expressly denote the idea of a sacrifice.[2]   In every other respect there was perfect freedom of opinion on these points, and latitude as to forms.   Luther himself remained in the convent and wore the Augustine dress, but he offered no opposition to others who chose to return to the world.   The Lord's Supper was administered in one kind or in both ; those who were not satisfied with the general absolution, were at full liberty to require a special one.   Questions were continually raised as to the precise limits of what was absolutely forbidden, and what might still be permitted.   The maxim of Luther and Melanchthon was, to condemn nothing that had not some authentic passage in the Bible,— " clear and undoubted Scripture," as the phrase was,—against it.   This was not the result of indifference ; religion withdrew within the bounds of her own proper province, and the sanctuary of her pure and genuine influences.   It thus became possible to develop and extend the new system of faith, without waging open warfare with that already established, or, by the sudden subversion of existing authorities, rousing those destructive tendencies, the slightest agitation of which had just threatened such danger to society.   Even in the theological exposition of these doctrines, it was necessary to keep in view the perils arising from opinions subversive of all sound morality.   Luther already began to perceive the danger of insisting on the saving power of faith alone ; already he taught

[1] Camerarius, Vita Melanchthonis, cap. xv.
[2] " Luther von beider Gestalt des Sacraments zu nehmen."—Altenb., ii., p. 126.

that faith should show itself in good conduct, brotherly love, soberness and quiet.[1]

The new religious opinions, in assuming the character of a distinct creed, threw off from themselves all that was incongruous, and assumed a more individual, and at the same time a more universal character,—the character inseparable from its origin and tendency. As early as December, 1821, in the heat of the disturbances, appeared the first elementary work on theology, founded on the new principles of faith—Melanchthon's ' Loci Communes.' This was far from being a complete work ; indeed it was originally a mere collection of the opinions of the apostle Paul concerning sin, the law, and grace, made strictly in accordance with those severe views to which Luther had owed his conversion, but remarkable on account of its entire deviation from all existing scholastic theology, and from being the first book which had appeared for several centuries in the Latin church containing a system constructed out of the Bible only. Sanctioned by Luther's approbation, it had great success, and in the course of repeated editions it was recast and perfected.[2] The translation of the New Testament by Luther, which he corrected with Melanchthon's assistance on his return to Wittenberg, and published in September, 1522, had a still more extensive effect, and acted immediately on the people. Whilst with one hand he emancipated them from the forms imposed on religion by the schools and the hierarchy, with the other he gave to the nation a faithful, intelligent and intelligible translation of the earliest records of Christianity. The national mind had just acquired sufficient ripeness to enable it to apprehend the meaning and value of the gift : in the most momentous stage of its development it was touched and penetrated to its very depths by the genuine expression of unveiled and unadulterated religion. From such influences everything was to be expected. Luther cherished the noble and confident hope that the doctrine alone would accomplish the desired end ; that wherever it made its way, a change in the outward condition of society must necessarily follow.

---

[1] Eberlin of Günzberg quotes a remarkable passage from one of his sermons : " Vermanung an alle frumen Christen zu Augsburg am Lech :"—" Ich hab gehort," says he, " von D. Martin Luther in ainer Predig ain gross war wort, das er sagt : wie man die sach anfacht, so felt unrat darauf : predigt man den glauben allein, als man thon sol, so unterlesst man alle zucht und ordnung, predigt man zucht und ordnung so felt man so gantz darauff das man alle selickait darein setzt und vergisst des glauben ; das mittel aber were gut, das man also den glauben yebte das er ausbreche in zucht und ordnung, und also übte sich in guten siten und in briederlicher liebe das man doch selickait allein durch den glauben gewertig were."—" An Exhortation to all pious Christians at Augsburg on the Lech :"—" I have heard in one of Luther's sermons a great and true saying : that as you stir up the matter, some mischief arises ; if a man preach faith alone, as he should do, he omits all soberness and order ; if he preach soberness and order, he insists upon them alone, and places all salvation therein, forgetting faith ; the middle course, however, would be the best, that man should so use faith that it should break out in soberness and order, and that they should so exercise themselves in good habits and in brotherly love, as to look for salvation only through faith."

[2] The original composition of this book is to be seen by a comparison of the first sketch of it in 1520 (which appears written by many different hands, in Strobel's Neuen Beiträgen, v. 323) with the first edition of 1521, printed in V. D. Hardt's Hist. Lit. Ref., iv.

The course pursued by the authorities of the empire, in the altered form they had meanwhile acquired, not only justified this hope, but led to results calculated to give it still greater assurance.

CHAPTER II.

TEMPORAL AND SPIRITUAL TENDENCIES OF THE COUNCIL OF REGENCY.

1521—1523.

IT is a remarkable and striking coincidence, that the mighty national movement we have just been considering was exactly coeval with the institution of that representative (*ständisch*) form of government which had been the object of such various and persevering exertions.

The Emperor, powerful as he was, had been forced to grant it as the condition of his election ; the plan was agreed upon at Worms, and was carried into execution in the autumn of 1521. The electors and the circles severally elected deputies, who, as we find, were freed from their feudal obligations, and exhorted to attend only to the general welfare of the empire. The old acts of the Imperial Chamber, weighing many hundred weight, and containing the pleadings in about 3500 long pending and yet undecided suits, and a vast number of fresh plaints on which no proceedings had yet been taken, were transported to Nürnberg.[1] One by one the deputies arrived ; those from the emperor, the last of all. During the course of the month of November they got so far as to open first the Council of Regency, and then the Imperial Chamber.

At first they had to endure a great deal from the interference of the imperial councillors ;[2] the same, for the most part, with whom the states had had such frequent disputes under Maximilian, and who were still unwilling to give up any of their lucrative privileges, and still, as formerly, accused of taking bribes. Very strange things occurred ; among others, the Bishop of Würzburg had seized the person of a certain Raminger, who was furnished with a safe conduct from the emperor, and kept him prisoner. The Council of Regency very properly took the injured man

---

[1] Hans v. d. Planitz to Friederich v. Sacksen, 18 Oct., 1521, according to communication made by Adam v. Beichlingen. The correspondence of Planitz, in two volumes, and a smaller pamphlet in the Archives of Weimar, are the authorities for the following. Harpprecht and Müller (Staats Cabinet, i.), give very superficial information.

[2] Planitz says, as early as the 18th October, " Churfürsten Fürsten und Andre so itzund allhie vorhanden haben Beisorge, es werde bei etzlichen Kaiserischen gefleissigt, ob sülch Vornemen des Regiments in Verhinderung oder Aënderung gestellt werden mecht."—" The electors, princes, and others, at this present here assembled, have a fear that some of the imperial court are busied in endeavours to hinder, or at least to alter, this project of the Council of Regency." On the 14th of May he mentions a certain Rem, who after long imprisonment succeeded in obtaining an imperial absolution. " Ist vermutlich, weil das Regiment die Sach zu sich forderet und die Sach den Hofretten nicht gestatten wollte, hierin zu handeln, das sie die Absolution gefürdert, damit das Regiment auch nichts daran haben solt."—" It is probable, since the Regency brought the matter within its own jurisdiction, and did not allow the imperial councillors to act in it at all, that the latter furthered the absolution, in order to take it out of the hands of the Regency." The letters are full of similar expressions.

under their protection.   Their surprise may be conceived when a declaration arrived from the emperor, that he had given the safe conduct without
reflection, and that it could not be supposed that the Bishop of Würzburg
had violated a real imperial safe conduct.   It made no difference whether
the States supported the Regency or not.   The states met in March, 1522,
and both bodies jointly interceded for the Bishop of Hildesheim, who
complained of the ban which had been pronounced against him and his
friends, without any previous summons and trial.   But the emperor would
not endure any interference with "his affairs," and rejected the intercession with some short unmeaning answer.

Towards the end of May the emperor quitted the Netherlands.   His
presence was required in Spain to quiet the disturbances of the Comuni-
dades,[1] and his mind fully occupied with the perplexities of the war he
had begun in Italy, and with the extraordinary conquests and discoveries[2]
made on a distant continent by a handful of fortunate and intelligent
Castilian adventurers serving under his banner.   Even the German
councillors who accompanied him could not possibly influence the details
of the administration of Germany from so distant a country as Spain.
At this time, therefore, the Council of Regency first acquired complete
independence.   The young emperor's presence had been needed to confer
upon it the authority which his absence now left it at liberty to exercise.

Let us first consider the temporal part of its administration.

Several very important matters had come under consideration ; above
all, the executive ordinance, on the plan proposed in the year 1512, and,
then so violently resisted by Maximilian, was determined upon ; namely,
that the circles should elect their own captains or governors.   The affairs
of Turkey and Hungary also urgently demanded attention.   Whilst the
two principal rulers of Christendom inflamed their natural jealousy into
bitterer antipathy in the Italian wars, the potentate of the Osman empire
led out his armies, fired by hatred of the Christians and love of conquest,
and took possession of Belgrade, the ancient bulwark of Christendom
which was but feebly defended on that frontier.   Germany was not
insensible to the danger : the States met expressly on this account in
the spring of 1522,[3] and again in the autumn ; a part of the supplies

[1] The revolt of the cities in Castile, which broke out in 1521.   *Cf.* Armstrong,
Charles V., Chap. V.

[2] Conquest of Mexico completed 1522 ; conquest of Peru, 1532.   For a succinct
account of the Spanish conquests in the New World, *cf.* Cambridge Modern
History, vol. i., Chapters I. and II., esp. p. 40 *ff.*

[3] The summons is dated Feb. 12 : for the Sunday Oculi (March 23, 1522), so
as to allow time to arm.   On March 28, a number of the States were present, and
processions and prayers were ordered : " Damit S. göttlich Barmherzigkeit den
Zorn, ob und wie wir den durch unsre Schuld und Missethat verschuldet hätten,
von uns wende."—" In order that the Almighty mercy may turn from us the
wrath which we have brought upon ourselves by our guilt and misdeeds."   The
Proposition was made on the 7th of April : the emperor therein declared that
he gave up the supplies voted for his expedition to Rome to be applied to the
war against the Turks.   The States determined to vote three-eighths thereof to
the war,—not, however, in men, but in money ; every thing was done in haste,
as a better method of equipment was to be arranged in a conference with the
Hungarian commissioners.   The Frankfurt deputy thought that little would
be effected, but " aufs fürderlichste wieder zum Thor hinaus."—" That they
would be out of the gate again as fast as possible."   The chief delay was caused

which had been granted to the emperor for his expedition to Rome were, with his permission, appropriated to the succour of the Hungarians. Schemes for the complete equipment of an army, to be kept always in readiness for the same purpose, were proposed and discussed. The main point, however, on which every thing else depended, was the secure establishment of the form of government itself. Every day showed the inconveniences of allowing the salaries of the members of the Imperial Chamber and the Regency to be dependent on the matricular taxes, which were granted from year to year, and were always difficult to collect ; neither would it do to leave these salaries to be paid by the emperor, as it was justly feared he would then raise a claim to appoint the members himself. Many other expedients were proposed, such as the application of the annates to this purpose ; a tax upon the Jews ; or finally, the reimposition of the Common Penny, in connection with a permanent war establishment. But all were alike impracticable. For the annates, a previous agreement with the see of Rome was necessary, and that was not so easily made. The towns which had obtained from earlier emperors the right of taxing their own Jews (a right which they had lately maintained in opposition to the imperial fiscal) absolutely refused to surrender it. As to a return to the Common Penny, it did not get beyond a mere project, and was not even seriously debated. Under these circumstances, the Council of Regency adopted a plan which had formerly been entertained, and which, in itself, must have been productive of very important national consequences, besides being connected with other views of the administration of the empire well worthy of our attention.

Among the charges and complaints which the several classes of the community made against each other in those times, one which was urged with the greatest frequency and vehemence was directed against the merchants.

Commerce still travelled along its accustomed roads ; the Hanse Towns[1] still enjoyed most of their privileges in foreign countries ; peace had restored the markets of Venice ; but the splendour and importance of this traffic was eclipsed by the brilliant and adventurous commerce across the seas, to which the discovery of both the Indies had given rise. Some of the great commercial houses of Upper Germany placed themselves in immediate communication with Lisbon, or shared in the West Indian enterprises of the Spaniards. Antwerp owed its prosperity chiefly to being the emporium of German maritime trade.

In Germany, however, no one was satisfied ; the stricter part of the community disapproved the importation of new luxuries and wants ; others complained of the quantity of money sent out of the country, and almost all were discontented at the high prices of the wares. During the years 1516 to 1522, especially, a general rise in prices was observed. Cinnamon cost upwards of a gulden the pound, sugar from twelve to twenty

---

by the disputes in the sessions of the colleges. " Der Sachen halber bleiben andre Händel unausgerichtet und wir verzehren das Unsre ohne Nutzen."— " For the sake of these, other affairs remained undetermined, and we eat up our susbtance without profit." The order is dated May 7 (Frank. A.). At the following diet, in Dec., 1522, two-fourths more of the money intended for the expedition to Rome were voted for this service.

[1] The Hanse Towns, so called from Hansa=a guild. *Cf.* article on the Hanse Towns in Encyclopædia Britannica, and Zimmern's The Hanse Towns.

gulden the cwt., and some of the East Indian spices had risen to four times their former price.[1] Several causes might conduce to this effect ; such as increased luxury and consequent demand ; the Venetian war, which had interrupted the course of trade, and a diminution of the value of money, arising from the importation of precious metals from America, which began to be felt, though far from what it afterwards became. At that period, however, the cause was chiefly sought, and perhaps not without justice, in the system of monopoly arising from the combination of the great commercial houses ; a practice which had continued to increase, in spite of the repeated enactments of the diets. They were already, it was alleged, possessed of such an amount of capital and such numerous and extensive factories, that no one could possibly compete with them. They were willing to give the King of Portugal higher prices even than he had previously asked, only on condition that he would demand still higher from those who came after them. It was calculated that every year 30,000 cwt. of pepper and 2,000 cwt. of ginger were imported into Germany, and that within a few years, the first had risen in price from 18 to 32 kreutzers per lb., and the second from 21 kreutzers to 1 gulden, 3 kreutzers ; this must, of course, have afforded an enormous profit.

As Rome was constantly assailed for her sale of indulgences, and the knights for their robberies, so the merchants and commercial towns were now incessantly inveighed against for their extortions. At all events, the Frankfurters attributed the disfavour shown them for some time past in their transactions with the Estates of the empire, almost exclusively to the unpopularity of monopolists.

At the diet of 1522–23, the resolution was taken to interdict all companies possessing a capital of more than 50,000 gulden : they were to be allowed a year and a half to dissolve their partnership. It was hoped that this would enable the smaller commercial houses to enter into competition with the great ones, and would also have the effect of preventing the accumulation of money and merchandise in few hands.

Overlooking the enormous advantages afforded by foreign commerce, however carried on, the diet conceived the idea of covering the general deficiencies of the state by a tax upon trade. It was notorious that each individual prince drew the greater part of his revenues from the

---

[1] I have extracted the following tables from a decree of the Select Committee on Monopolies in 1523 (Frank. A.) :—

The best saffron from Catalonia, which	} in 1516 cost	3 g. 6 kr.,	cost in 1522	4 g. 15 kr.	
Second rate do.	,, 1519 ,,	2 g. 21 to 27 kr.	,,	4 g.	
Cloves	,, 1512 ,,	19 schill.	cost in ,,	2 g.	
Stick cinnamon	,, 1516 ,,	1 g. 18 kr.	,, 1518	2 g. 3 ort.	
Short do.	,, 1515 ,,	3 ort.	,, 1519	1 g. 21 kr.	
Nutmeg	,, 1519 ,,	27 kr.	,, 1522	3 g. 28 kr.	
Mace	,, 1518 ,,	1 g. 6 kr.	,, ,,	4 g. 6 kr.	
Best pepper in the husk	,, 1518 ,,	18 kr.	,, ,,	32 kr.	
Ginger, formerly from 21 to 24 kr.			,, 1516	1 g. 3 kr.	
Galingal ,, ,, 1 g. 36 kr.			,, ,,	1 g. 39 kr.	
Sugar, the hundred weight in 1516	,,	11 to 12 g.	,, 1518	20 g.	
Sugar candy	,, 1516 ,,	16 to 17 g.	,, 1522	20 to 21 g.	
Venetian almonds the cwt.	,, 1518 ,,	8 g.	,, ,,	12 g.	
Do. raisins	,, 1518 ,,	5 g.	,, ,,	9 g.	
Do. figs	,, 1518 ,,	3 g. 2 sch.	,, ,,	4 g. 1 ort.	

tolls, the right of levying which had been granted to him by former emperors ; and as it was evident that no direct tax could be collected, a plan was adopted for an indirect one, in the form of a general system of import duties to be levied for the use of the empire.

This project is worthy of a moment's attention ; if carried into execution it must have produced incalculable results ; but it is remarkable that it could even be entertained. So early as the year 1521 it was discussed : the Elector Joachim I. of Brandenburg adopted it with great eagerness and continually recommended it.

In the spring of 1522 the States were really resolved to accede to it, principally because it did not appear burdensome to the common people ; but in order to make sure of carrying it into effect, they determined to ask the previous consent of the emperor, before taking any further step.

This consent having been received from Spain, accompanied, however, with the condition that the further provisions should be again submitted to him for approbation, a commission was appointed at the diet of 1522–23, by the general vote of the States, to work out the plan in detail.[1]

The commission went on the principle of leaving all the necessaries of life duty-free. Under this head were classed corn, wine, beer, cattle for draught and slaughter, and leather. All other articles were to pay both an import and export duty, not to be regulated either by weight or by a tariff, which would have occasioned a great deal of troublesome investigation, but by the price at which the article was bought, to be stated by the purchaser ; upon this, the duty was to be four per cent.

The whole extent of the Roman empire inhabited by the German race was to be surrounded by a line of custom-houses, which was to begin at Nikolsburg in Moravia, and thence pass towards Hungary through Vienna and Grätz to Villach or Tarvis ; thence to extend along the Alps towards Venice and Milan. Custom-house stations were to be erected in Trent, Brunegg, Insbruck, and Feldkirchen. The frontier of Switzerland, which refused to submit to the imposition of the duty, was to be guarded by custom-houses ; the line was then to cross the Rhine and run through Strasburg, Metz, Luxemburg, and Treves, to Aix-la-chapelle ; which would bring it near the coast and within the region of maritime commerce. The Netherlands were without hesitation considered as part of the empire ; Utrecht and Dordrecht, as well as Cologne and Wesel, were proposed as custom-house stations for inland trade ; Antwerp, Bruges and Bergen-op-zoom, for maritime trade, especially that with England and Portugal. The line was thence to follow the coast northward and eastward. Towards Denmark, which according to public law was still regarded as a permanent confederate of the empire, the Hanse towns, from Hamburg to Danzig inclusive, were to be the custom-house ports ; towards Poland, Königsberg in the Newmark and Frankfurt on the Oder, besides a few other towns in Silesia and Lusatia.[2]

Much was still left undetermined in this project ; for instance, it was immediately proposed that the frontiers should be surveyed, in order

[1] " Ordnung ains gemainen Reichs Zolls in Ratschlag verfast."—Fr. Ar., vol. xxxviii. " Ordinance for customs' duties for the whole empire."

[2] This anticipation of a Zollverein, which has only been accomplished in our own day, and was the precursor of the foundation of a new German Empire on an enduring basis, is very remarkable.

to ascertain whether better places could not be found for the prevention of smuggling, than those already named : it was still a matter of doubt whether Bohemia could be included, and neither Prussia nor Livonia had yet been taken into consideration ; but all these were mere details which could easily be determined when the project was carried into execution ;—the main point was seriously resolved upon.

As might have been expected, the whole commercial body thought it would be injured by this measure, which it attributed merely to the hostility generally shown towards itself, and accordingly raised numerous objections to it, more or less well founded.   An attempt was made to answer all these objections at length.   The example of neighbouring kingdoms was cited, where much heavier restrictions existed, and where, nevertheless, trade was most flourishing.   It was argued that the duty by no means fell on the merchant, but on the consumer ; and that it would be a prodigious advantage to commerce if, by means of this tax, the disturbances in the empire could be put down, and general security restored.

At all events, it cannot be denied that this project might have been the means of producing the most important results for the future fate of Germany.   The establishment of accurately defined and well guarded frontiers, the entire circumference of which were closely bound to a common active centre, would in itself have been a great advantage ; this alone would have at once awakened a universal feeling of the unity of the empire.   Besides the whole administration would have assumed a different character.   The most important national institution, the Council of Regency, the formation of which had cost so much labour, would by this means have acquired a natural and firm basis, and sufficient power for the maintenance of order.   As yet there was no peace throughout the country ; all the roads were unsafe ; it was impossible to reckon on the execution of any sentence or decree.   But had this ordinance been vigorously carried into effect, the Regency would have had the means of paying the governors and councillors in the circles, so often discussed, and of maintaining a certain number of troops under their own orders and those of the subordinate authorities.

In the spring of 1523 it seemed as if this point would certainly be achieved : the plan was again sent for final confirmation to the emperor who was already bound by his former consent.

It is evident that the Council of Regency entertained the project of constituting itself a powerful central government, and, in conjunction with the States, resorted to every possible expedient to accomplish this end, in spite of all opposition.

Hence the question, what course this rising power would take with respect to the religious movement, acquired additional importance.

At the beginning of the year 1522 the feelings of the Council of Regency were much opposed to the innovation.   Duke George of Saxony was present, in whom a natural attachment to traditional opinions,[1] the

---

[1] Duke George said to our informant Planitz : " Wenn S. F. Gn. nicht mit der Tatt und Gewalt dazu thät, würd S. Gn. Land schyr gar ketzerisch : wollten alle die behemische Weis an sich nemen, und sub utraque communiciren : *er gedächt es aber mit Gewalt zu weren.*"—" If his princely grace did not interfere with might and deed, his grace's subjects would soon become sheer heretics, for they all wanted to follow the Bohemian fashion, and to communicate sub utraque ; *but that he intended to prevent it by force.*"—Letter of the 2nd Jan., 1522.

various old quarrels with his cousins of the Ernestine line, and a personal
dislike to the bold and reckless monk, combined to raise a violent and
active hostility to the new doctrines. The disturbances in Wittenberg
happened opportunely to give more weight to his accusations ; and he
actually obtained an edict in which the Regency exhorted the neighbouring
bishoprics of Naumburg, Meissen, and Merseburg not to allow the innovations to be forced upon them, but to maintain the customary rites and
practices of the church.[1]

But in the course of the next three months, when news arrived that the
disturbances had ceased, the feelings of the Council of Regency underwent
a total change. One subject of discussion, of course, was Luther's return
to Wittenberg, by which he had openly bidden defiance to the imperial
ban, and Duke George even proposed an appeal to the immediate intervention of the emperor ; this, however, merely wounded the self-love of
the Council of Regency. John of Planitz, the envoy of Elector Frederick,
would not hear his master blamed for permitting Luther to remain in
Wittenberg ; nor would he allow it to be said that the monk's doctrine was
heresy. " The receiving the sacrament in both kinds, the marriage of a
few priests, and the desertion of the convent by a few monks, could not,"
he said, " be called heresies ; these acts were merely opposed to regulations established not long since by popes and councils, and which would
perhaps be eventually abolished. If, on the other hand, Luther were
banished, imitators of him would arise, but animated with a different
spirit ; who, instead of preaching only against the dogmas of the church,
might declaim against Christianity and God himself ; and not only a
rebellion, but complete unbelief might be the result." This envoy was
a man of talent, equally resolute and dexterous : he was strongly in favour
of Luther, less indeed from religious belief, although in the main their
opinions were the same, than from the conviction that Luther's cause was
equally the cause of his prince, of the Council of Regency, and of the empire.

In the summer of 1522 it was the turn of the Elector Frederick to attend
the Council of Regency in person. He was one of the few who remained
of the old school of princes, to whom that body owed its establishment,
and he had lately taken the most active part in the firm settlement of its
constitution. He had already been frequently consulted concerning
questions of form. His calm judgment, his well-known experience,
and the universal respect paid to his acknowledged integrity and talents
for business, invested him with singular authority.[2] He might indeed

---

[1] Resolution und Decisum, &c., 20th Jan., 1522. Walch xv. 2616. The
Appendix No. 10 is remarkable : " Bis so lang durch Versehung der gemeinen
Reichsstände, christliche Versammlung oder Concilia solcher Sachen halben,
eine bedächtliche wohlerwogene gegründete gewisse Erklärung—vorgenommen
werde."—" Until such time as, by the care of the general Estates of the empire,
a christian assembly, or council for such matters, shall have made a prudent,
deliberate, well grounded, and certain declaration of faith." From this passage
we may perceive the existence of another tendency, although as yet vague.

[2] The Elector of Treves hearing that Frederick was ill, sent him word through
his minister, " E. Ch. Gn. solten vest halten, nicht krank werden noch abgehen,
denn man hett im Reich E. Ch. Gn. nye als wol bedurft als itzund, nachdem
E. Ch. Gn. wusste, wye es allenthalben im Reiche stünde."—" Your Electoral
Grace must stand firm, and not fall sick nor die, for your Electoral Grace was
never so greatly needed by the empire as now, for your Electoral Grace knows
how matters stand in the empire."—Planitz, 1st Nov., 1521.

at this time be said to govern the empire, in as far as it could be governed at all.

Under these circumstances, it is evident that Luther, who enjoyed so fully the favour of this prince, had nothing to fear from the Council of Regency. Duke George continued to attack him before that assembly : he repeatedly complained of the monk's violence, and of the abuse which he poured forth against the princes of the empire, the emperor and the pope. Never perhaps was a more evasive answer given than that which he received from the Council of Regency, to one of these accusations. " We perceive," they write on the 16th of August, " that your grace feels displeasure at insults to the pope's holiness and the emperor's majesty, and we thereupon make known to your grace, that we would not patiently endure insult or injury to the emperor's majesty, wherever we should see or hear of it."[1] No wonder that, when the duke afterwards complained of this answer to the lieutenant of the empire, Count Palatine Frederick, he replied that at that time there was nothing to be done in matters of this kind.

An independent party favourable to Luther was now forming in the Council of Regency. It was, it is true, subject to fluctuations from the entrance of new members every quarter of a year ; but from the permanent operation of principles once imbibed, it always regained the upper hand, and, in fact, constituted a majority. Here was, indeed, a wonderful change in the aspect of affairs !—In 1521 the emperor published sentence of ban against Luther, and in 1522-23, the body which represented the imperial power, took him, though still under ban, under its protection, and even approximated to his opinions. That body was, of course, not affected by the political combinations which had influenced the emperor.

The bias it had received was all the more important, since the States had assembled during the last months of the one year and the first of the ensuing ; and at the instigation of the new pope, Adrian VI., were to come to a decision concerning the Lutheran affairs.

Adrian VI. was undoubtedly an extremely well-intentioned man. He had formerly been professor at Louvain, and had even then zealously reproved the arrogance of the priesthood, and the waste and misapplication of church property.[2] He subsequently became tutor to Charles V., and took part in the administration of the affairs of Spain, there he imbibed a thorough disgust of the worldly tendencies of the papacy. He was therefore strongly disposed to attempt some reform. He declared that he had only bent his neck under the yoke of the papal dignity, in order to restore the defiled bride of Christ to her original purity. At the same time he was a decided opponent of Luther, and belonged to those ' Magistri nostri ' of Louvain, who had so long waged war against the innovating literature and theology ; he had expressed unqualified approbation of the opinions professed by that university. The orthodox dominican tendency, which, as early as 1520, had once more formed a close alliance

---

[1] Instruction to the Regency at Nürnberg. Answer to the same ; letter from Duke George, dated the Tuesday after the Nativity of the Virgin (9th Sept.), and from Otto Pack to the duke, the Monday before the XImille Virginum (20th Oct.).—Dresden Archives.

[2] Extracts from his " Commentary in Quartum Sententiarum," in the letter of Joh. Lanoy to Henr. Barillon ; Burnam's Vita Adriani, p. 360.

with the court of Rome, had now obtained a temporary sovereignty in his person.

In conformity with these sentiments were the instructions which Adrian gave to his nuncio Chieregati, whom he sent to the German diet. He looked upon the spread of Lutheran doctrines as a punishment for the sins of the prelates. " We are aware," said he, " that, some years ago, many abominations took place in this chair : every thing was turned to evil, and the corruption spread from the head to the members, from the pope to the prelates." Whilst he now declared himself willing to reform the existing abuses, he at the same time exhorted the States of Germany to offer a determined resistance to the diffusion of Luther's opinions ;[1] and brought forward eight arguments in favour of that course,which he thought of irresistible cogency.

An answer to these propositions of the pope had now to be given, and a resolution to be formed upon them. This duty devolved on the Council of Regency.

At the first appearance of the nuncio, a trial of strength ensued between the two parties in that body. The orthodox minority brought forward a complaint from the nuncio, concerning two or three preachers who proclaimed the Lutheran tenets under the very eyes of the Regency, to their and his serious offence. Archduke Ferdinand, who then filled the office of lieutenant of the empire, and the Elector of Brandenburg, who was the next in succession for the ensuing quarter, declared themselves in favour of the nuncio. The majority however, led by Planitz, resolutely opposed them. This gave rise to several violent discussions. Ferdinand exclaimed, " I am here in the place of the emperor."—" Yes, certainly," rejoined Planitz, " but in conjunction with the Council of Regency, and subject to the laws of the empire " ;—and, in accordance with his suggestion, the affair was referred to the States ;[2] *i.e.* indefinitely adjourned. It is easy to imagine that this increased the boldness and vehemence of the Lutheran preachers. " Even if the pope," exclaimed one of them in the church of St. Lawrence, " had a fourth crown added to the three he already wears, he should not make me forsake the word of God." Thus was defiance hurled from the pulpit against the pope, before the very eyes of his nuncio.

Under these circumstances the Council of Regency appointed a committee to draw up the answer which the States should give to the nuncio. This committee, like the Regency itself, contained representatives of both parties ; some of its members belonging to the clergy, and others to the laity, and for a time it was doubtful which side had the majority. This was however very soon decided.

The most influential member was undoubtedly Johann von Schwar-

[1] " Expergiscantur, excitentur—et ad executionem sententiæ apostolicæ ac imperialis edicti præfati omnino procedant. Detur venia iis qui errores suos abjurare voluerint."—*Instructio pro Cheregato.*

[2] Planitz relates this himself, on the 4th Jan., 1523. The States answered, that it was a grave matter which required much consideration : they asked for copies of the brief and of the instruction, and wished " etzliche darüber verordnen, die die Sach mit Fleiss bewegen." " In der Stadt ist gross Murmeln, will nicht rathen, das man einen gefangen annehme."—" To appoint certain people who should manage the matter with diligence." " In the town is much murmuring. I cannot advise that any person should be imprisoned."

zenberg, the Hofmeister[1] of Bamberg, who was now advanced in life. In his early youth he had quitted the dissipation of a court which had threatened to hurry him along in its vortex, and, in consequence of his father's admonition, had formed earnest and effectual resolutions of a virtuous life ; from that time he had devoted himself with untiring perseverance to study and to the service of the state. We have translations of some of Cicero's works, bearing his name, in which he has carefully adopted the purest and most intelligible forms of the language of his age.[2] The first criminal code for Bamberg, if not entirely his work, was at least in great measure constructed by him. In this he evinces as much capacity for appreciating the value of traditional and local usages, (for he adheres in the main to the old customary law of the city of Bamberg,) as the scientific merits of the Roman law. Wherever he applies the principles of the latter to supply some deficiency, he does it in a manner corresponding with existing maxims.[3] He was, as we see, a man of original and productive talent, both in literature and in politics : he expressed his wonder how any one could find the time too long. He eagerly embraced the Lutheran cause at its very first appearance, finding in it the scientific and practical tendencies of his own mind exalted by an alliance with religious sentiments and aims. He accordingly exchanged several very serious letters on the subject with one of his sons, and removed one of his daughters from her convent ; indeed his mind was entirely engrossed by the new opinions.[4] With all the force of a full and well-grounded conviction, armed against every objection, he adopted them, and, partly perhaps owing to the high and important station he filled, he carried with him the minds of his colleagues ; some because they already inclined to those opinions—like Sebastian von Rotenhan and Dr. Zoch, and others, like the Bishop of Augsburg, because they knew not, just then at least, what resistance to offer. Those who did not share these opinions, such as Dr. v. Werthern, the envoy from Duke George, and the Archbishop of Salzburg, found it better to stay away from the assembly. Thus, with very slight opposition, this committee, which now represented the central government of the empire, agreed upon a report in a spirit of decided opposition to the papacy, and of the greatest importance to the whole future progress of the new doctrines.

This report was based on the admissions and promises of reform made by the pope, which the committee accepted, but without giving in return the promise which the pope demanded,—to unite with him in the endeavour to crush the Lutheran doctrines. On the contrary, it declared that these

---

[1] Title applicable to the Governor of Bamberg only.

[2] *E.g.*, De Senectute. Neuber's was revised and collated with the text by Hutten, and put into Hoffränkisch Deutsch by Schwarzenberg. Neuber's translation of the De Officiis was put into " zierlicher Hochteutsch,"—" elegant High German,"—by Schwarzenberg, and then revised by a third person to see " obs dem Lateyn gemess sey,"—" whether it were according to the Latin." Christ praises it for the " emergens e stilo nativa et vere Germanica simplicitas." De Amicitia was translated " von Synnen zu Synnen, nicht von Worten zu Worten,"—" from sense to sense, not from words to words."—*Cf.* Degen, Literatur der Übersetzungen, i. 55.

[3] Zöpfl das alte Bamberger Recht als Quelle der Carolina, pp. 166, 170.

[4] There is a notice of him in Strobel Vermischte Beiträge, 1775, No. 1. Heller, Reformationsgeschichte von Bamberg, p. 45.

admitted abuses rendered it impossible to carry into execution the bull of Leo X. and the edict of Worms, for that Luther had been the first to expose these abuses, and any display of rigour towards him would make everyone believe that it was the object of the government " to suppress the truth of the Gospel by tyranny, and to maintain unchristian abuses, wherefrom nothing could arise but resistance to authority, sedition and heresy."   The pope was exhorted to adhere to the concordats, to redress the grievances of the German nation, and above all, to abolish annates : it was not indeed pretended that these reforms would now suffice to put an end to the schism ; that, it was said, could only be effected by a council. The convocation of a council, which would occupy men's minds for half a century, had already been the subject of a serious conversation between the nuncio and Planitz, and was now officially agitated by the committee of the Council of Regency.   Some of the conditions were at once stated by it : they were as follows :—The council to be convoked by the pope's holiness, with the assent of the emperor's majesty, as befitted the respective privileges of the two sovereigns ; to be held at a convenient neutral town without delay ; to begin within a year, and under a form materially differing from any previous council.   One important innovation was, that the laity were to be allowed a seat and a voice in it, and all present were to be absolved from every obligation which might restrain them from bringing forward whatever might be of service in " godly, evangelical, and other generally profitable affairs."   An assembly thus constituted would have answered to the Lutheran ideas respecting the Church, and would have been totally different from what the Council of Trent afterwards was. In answer to the inquiry, what course would be pursued till the council had given its decision, the committee answered, that they should hope, in case the pope agreed to their proposals, to prevail on the Elector Frederick and on Luther, that neither the latter nor his followers should write or preach any thing which might occasion irritation and disorder ; they should only teach the Holy Gospel and the authentic Scriptures according to the true Christian sense.   These last conditions were of course the most important ; all the rest was vague and remote, but these would serve as a rule of conduct for the present moment.   They were, as may be easily perceived, entirely in accordance with the opinions which prevailed at Wittenberg and at the court of Saxony, and were evidently proposed with the intention of promoting the free development of the doctrine embraced there.   The 13th January, 1523, was the day on which this ever-memorable decision of the States was announced for further discussion.   Hans von Planitz joyfully sent it to his master on the very same day.[1]

A great fermentation, and sharp collisions between the clerical and lay members began moreover to be observable in the States.   It had indeed at first appeared as if both intended to make common cause against Rome, and at Worms the bishops had stated their own peculiar grievances in addition to those of the German nation ; yet it was there that the division began ; the clergy found that their interests were touched by

[1] " Wess der Ausschuss zu pepstlicher Heiligkeit Antwurdt den lutherischen Handell betreffen verordnet derhalb gerathschlagt hat."—" What the committee argued and decided with respect to his papal holiness's answer concerning the Lutheran affairs."—Frankf. R. A. A., tom. xxxviii., f. 99.

the complaints of the laity, and resolved to defend their prescriptive rights. Several outbreaks of this animosity had already taken place in that assembly. A memorial from the cities, full of the most violent invective, was read, and the head of the German clergy, the elector of Mainz, warmly expressed his displeasure at it. It appeared, he said, as if the clergy were to be treated like criminals, and not to be secure from personal violence. But even the most zealously catholic lay princes demanded reforms ; and if a prince had given no instructions on the subject himself, his councillors of their own accord inclined to that side. The grievances of the nation were again recapitulated ;—this time indeed without the participation of the clergy, but with much more vehemence, and with many additions, chiefly directed against the clergy themselves ; for the thousandfold abuses enumerated, no reform was more strongly urged than the separation of the spiritual from the temporal jurisdiction.

Nothing could be more calculated to drive these two hostile parties into open warfare than the report which the committee of the Council of Regency had sent in to the States.

The clergy did, however, succeed in introducing some modifications into it.

First of all, the admissions quoted from the papal brief were only allowed to stand as far as they regarded the pope himself : the words relating to priests and prelates were struck out.[1] Then no mention was made of the claims of the laity to a seat and voice in the council. A single phrase was frequently the cause of violent disputes ; for instance, the clergy would not admit the word " evangelical " into the article concerning obligations ; whereupon such offensive expressions were used by the lay party, that the elector of Mainz left the assembly and rode home to his lodging. In the end however the majority decided in his favour, and the word was omitted.

Whatever were the changes made in particular expressions, the main point was left unaltered ; the States declined to carry into execution the edict of Worms ;[2] a council was demanded, which was to begin, if possible, within a year, in a German town, and with the co-operation of the emperor : a suggestion was even made to alter the form of such an assembly,

---

[1] In the rough draft it is stated : " Ist von Ppl. Heiligkeit . . . woll angezeigt dass solches von wegen der Sund beschee und dass die Sund des Volks von den Sunden der Priester und Prälaten herfliessen, und dass darum dieselben zuförderst und am ersten als die endlich Ursach solcher Krankheit von der Wurzel geheilt gestraft und abgewendet werden soll."—" It is well shown by his holiness the pope that such things happen on account of sin, and that the sinfulness of the people flows from the sins of the priests and prelates ; that these therefore should, first and foremost, as the ultimate cause of such evil, be cured from the root upwards, and should be cured, punished and turned from their evil ways." This passage is wanting in the answer which was really sent to the papal nuncio.—*See the reprint in Walch*, xv., p. 2551, No. 8.

[2] This was expressed in the following manner in the answer given to the nuncio : " Majori namque populi parti jam pridem persuasum est . . . nationi Germanicæ a curia Romana per certos abusus multa et magna gravamina et incommoda illata esse : ob id, si pro executione apostolicæ sedis sententiæ vel imperatoriæ majestatis edicti quippiam acerbius attemptatum esset, mox popularis multitudo sibi hanc opinionem animo concepisset ac si talia facerent pro evertenda evangelica vertitate et sustinendis manutenendisque malis abusibus, unde nihil aliud quam gravissimi tumultus populares intestinaque bella speranda essent."—*Fr. A.*

and the participation of the temporal states in it was tacitly assumed ; both clergy and laity were to be relieved from all obligations restrictive of the free utterance of opinion.   In short, the party which strove to alter the entire constitution of the Church had now decidedly the upper hand in both estates of the empire.   The clergy were aware of the necessity of a change, and the laity eagerly pressed for it ;—it is said that even Duke Louis of Bavaria insisted upon it, in spite of the opposition of the adherents of Rome.[1]

The only points that now remained to be discussed—and for the present the most important—were, the conduct of affairs in the interval before the convocation of the council, and the degree of liberty of speech and action which was to be allowed to writers and preachers.

On this question the clergy succeeded in introducing still further restrictions.   They insisted that the elector should be requested not alone to prohibit whatever might lead to disorder, but to allow nothing whatever to be written, printed or done by Luther or his followers ; and also that the request should be made immediately without waiting for the pope's consent to the council.   The Saxon envoy to the diet, Philip von Feilitzsch, endeavoured to maintain the terms proposed by the Council of Regency, and failing in this, protested that " his prince could not consider himself bound by this resolution, and would always know how to act in a christian, praiseworthy and irreproachable manner."

Thus we see that in this contest the victory inclined first to one side and then to the other.   The two parties collected all their forces for the last point at issue, which was, perhaps, still more important than the preceding one, as it was to decide the latitude to be allowed to preaching ; a matter which immediately concerned the mass of the people.   The clergy were not satisfied with merely directing the preachers to confine themselves to the Gospel and to writers approved by the Church, but required a more accurate specification of what was meant by the latter, and wished to include the four great Latin fathers, Jerome, Augustin, Ambrose and Gregory, to whom they ascribed canonical authority.   This is the more remarkable, since a century earlier the more explicit of the Hussite doctrines had been regarded mainly as a departure from these four founders of the Latin church.   But the nation was now so deeply imbued with the spirit of Luther's teaching, that it would no longer be bound by the particular form and character assumed by the Latin church ; the common-sense of the people revolted against the imputing to St. Paul less authority than to Ambrose.   The time was past in which the clergy could carry their point.   After a great deal of debating a resolution was passed, which was in reality only a more complete expression of the meaning of the original proposition.   It was decreed, that nothing should be taught but the pure, true and holy Gospel ; mildly, piously and in a Christian spirit, according to the doctrine and interpretation of writings approved and accepted by the Christian church.[2]   Perhaps the adherents

---

[1] Planitz names him as early as on the 18th Jan. with Schwarzenberg and Feilitzsch.

[2] " Quod nihil præter verum purum sincerum et sanctum evangelium et approbatam scripturam pie mansuete christiane juxta doctrinam et expositionem approbatæ et ab ecclesia christiana receptæ scripturæ doceant."   This is the passage in the answer given to the papal nuncio.

of the established faith were satisfied by the decision, because it recognised the authority of the expositions of the Latin fathers ; but this recommendation was couched in vague, general and uncertain language ; whereas that of the evangelical doctrine was precise, decided and emphatic, and therefore was alone likely to make an impression.

Thus, after all, the answer went back to the Council of Regency, having undergone a few partial changes, but agreeing in the main with the spirit of the original plan. Contrary to all expectation, it caused another very stormy debate in that assembly. Some of the members (among whom was the Bishop of Augsburg) who had repented of the part they had taken in the original scheme, made another attempt to retain the express mention of the four fathers of the Church. Planitz reports that he had to endure many proud and wicked words, and to resist a violent storm on this question. He expresses the greatest indignation at the apostasy of the bishop, whom, he says, God had raised out of the dust and made a ruler over his people, and who in return persecuted the Gospel.[1] However, with resolution and patience, and the assistance of Schwarzenberg, he succeeded in maintaining the form which had at last been decided upon, and the answer was delivered to the nuncio as it had been returned from the assembly of the States.[2]

The nuncio did not attempt to conceal his astonishment and vexation. Neither the pope nor the emperor, nor any other sovereign, he said, had expected such a decision from them. He renewed his request for the execution of the edict of Worms and the establishment of an episcopal censorship ; but it was impossible to persuade a body which moved so slowly and with so much difficulty, to think of retracting a resolution once formed, and all his endeavours were fruitless.

The substance of the answer was published in an imperial edict. The Elector of Saxony and Luther himself were highly pleased with it ; Luther, indeed, thought that the ban and excommunication which had been proclaimed against him were virtually revoked by it.

It is indisputably true that these decisions of the diet of Nürnberg were exactly the contrary of those passed at Worms. The important step which had been expected of Charles V., namely, that he would place himself at the head of the national movement, was now actually taken by the Council of Regency. The political opposition which had so long been

---

[1] Planitz, 4th Feb. : " Ich will aber Patienz und Geduld tragen. Es haben die Stände obangezeigte Wort (he has inserted them in his letter) haben wollen und nit die vier Doctores zu benennen und sulchs dem Regiment anzeigen lassen, dabei es blieben."—" I will, however, have patience and temper. The States would have the words I have before mentioned, and would not allow the four doctors to be named or specified to the Council of Regency, so it remained as it was."

[2] Planitz, 9th Feb. : " Die Schrift ist dem päpstl. Nuntius auf die Mass übergeben wie ich E. Chf. G. zugeschickt. Der ist der nicht zu frieden und hat darauf replicirt. . . . Er will den Kayser dabei nit haben, so gefällt ihm auch nit dass es so gar frei seyn soll wie begehrt."—" The paper is handed over to the papal nuncio, on the whole much as I have sent it to your electoral grace. The nuncio is not satisfied with it, and has replied, he will not allow the emperor to be mentioned in it, nor does he like that there should be so much freedom as is demanded."

gathering its forces, offered a more vigorous resistance than ever to the pope : allied with it, and protected by the representatives of the imperial power, religious discussion was now left to its free and unfettered course.

CHAPTER III.

DIFFUSION OF THE NEW DOCTRINES.

1522—1524.

No new arrangement needed to be made, no plan to be concerted, no mission to be sent : like the seed which shoots up on the ploughed field at the first genial rays of the sun in spring, the new opinions, the way for which had been prepared by all the events and discussions we have endeavoured to trace, now spread abroad through the whole land where the German language was spoken.

A religious order was destined to afford the first common centre to the various elements of opposition.

The Augustines of Meissen, and of Thuringia generally, had made the first step towards emancipation, by a formal resolution. Among them were old friends of Luther's, who had followed the same career of studies and of opinions as he had : even among the more distant Augustine convents, there were few in which similar questions had not been agitated, and similar changes of opinion manifested ; indeed, a list is still extant, of those who took part in the movement at Magdeburg, Osnabrück, Lippe, Antwerp, Regensburg, Dillingen, Nürnberg and Strasburg,[1] and in the territories of Hessen and Würtemberg. Many of these reformers were men advanced in life, who had held these doctrines ever since the time of Johann Proles, and who now exulted to see them attain a fuller development and greater power : others again, were youthful and fiery spirits, inspired with admiration for their victorious brother of Wittenberg. Johann Stiefel of Esslingen beheld in him the angel of the Apocalypse flying through the heavens, and holding in his hand the everlasting Gospel ; he composed a mystical and heroic poem in his praise.[2] This body, moreover, had the glory of being the first to draw down persecution on itself. Two or three

[1] According to Eberlin's, "Syben frumme aber trostlose Pfaffen," "Seven devout but comfortless Priests," Dr. Caspar Amon, " ain erwirdig Man," " a reverend man," taught at Dillingen. This is doubtless the same person who in 1523 published a Psalter done into German from the genuine text in the Hebrew tongue,—" geteutscht nach warhaftigem text der hebreischen zungen." The dedication of this book is dated Lauingen. Panzer, ii., p. 131.

[2] Von der christförmigen rechtgegründeten Lehre Doctoris Martini Luthers :
" Er thut sich worlich fyegen zu Got in rechten mut,
    Gwalt mag ihn auch nit biegen : er geb er drum sein blut.
    Zu Worms er sich erzeyget : er trat keck auf den plan.
    Sein feynd hat er geschweyget : keiner dorft ihn wenden an."
" Concerning the Christian-like well-grounded doctrine of Doctor Martin Luther :
" He trusted truly in God with a good courage,
    Force could not bend him : for it (the cause) he would have spilled his blood.
    He proved himself at Worms ; stepping boldly into the field.
    He silenced his enemies : none could answer him."
See Strobel's Neue Beiträge, i., p. 10.

Augustine friars at Antwerp were the first martyrs of the new faith.   Jean
Chatelain of Metz was soon afterwards condemned to the flames for the
attacks he had made on the prerogatives of the clergy in the Advent of
1523, and the Lent of 1524.

A number of Franciscans, not, like the Augustines,[1] supported by their
order, but separating themselves entirely from it, and, as we may infer
from that act, men of more energetic temper, were the next to join the
new sect.   Some of these were learned men, like Johann Brismann of Cott-
bus, who had been for many years devoted to the study of the schoolmen
and had become doctor of theology, but who now, like Luther, drew from
their works entirely opposite opinions.[2]   Others were spirits full of deep
religious yearnings, which the conventual rule and discipline failed to
satisfy ; such was Friedrich Myconius.   It is related that on the night
following his investiture, he dreamed that whilst wandering in steep and
tortuous paths, he was met by a holy man, baldheaded, and clothed in an
antique dress, as St. Paul is painted, who led him first to a fountain whose
waters flowed from a crucified body, whereat he slaked his thirst, and then
through endless fields of thick standing corn, in which the reapers were
making ready for the harvest.[3]   This vision is sufficient to show the turn
of his mind ; and we may easily infer from it the impression which must
have been produced on him by the revival of the apostolical doctrine, and
the prospect of an active co-operation in its diffusion.   Others again were
men who in the various intercourse with the lower classes, to which the
duties of a Franciscan convent leads, had perceived the pernicious effects of
the doctrine of justification by works, and now attacked it with all their
might : among these were Eberlin of Günzburg, and Heinrich of Kettenbach, who came out of the same convent at Ulm, and who both possessed
in an extraordinary degree, the gift of popular oratory.   Eberlin's opponents said of him, that he alone had power to mislead a whole province ;
so great was the effect of his eloquence on the common people.   Among
them were found the most steadfast champions, like Stephen Kempen,
whose brave and warlike bearing was worthy of his name.   The Franciscans were almost everywhere among the first reformers : Kempen was the
founder of the new doctrines in Hamburg, where he defended them nearly
single-handed for three years against all opponents.

But there was not, perhaps, a single religious order which did not furnish
partisans to the new opinions, many of whom were among its most celebrated champions.   Martin Butzer had been appointed professor of the

[1] The Reimchronik of Metz speaks very favourably of this Augustine monk.

> " A Metz prescha ung caresme,
>   devant grand peuple homme et femme,
>   qui en sa predication
>   avoient grande devotion."

His persecutor says to him,—

> " Tu as presché de nostre estat,
>   je te hai plus qu'un apostat :
>   as tousché sur le gens d'eglise :
>   maintenant te tiens a ma guise."
>   *Calmet*, Histoire de Lorraine, ii., Preuves cxix.

[2] Extract from his sermons in Seckendorf, Historia Lutheranismi, i., p. 272.
[3] Adami Vitæ Theologorum, edition of 1705, p. 83.

Thomist doctrines by the Dominicans ; but he dissolved his connection
with that order by a kind of lawsuit, and from that time forward took a
most active and successful part in the establishment of the new system of
faith.   Otto Brunnfels came out of the Carthusian convent at Mainz and
became the follower of Hutten, whose labours he shared with rival ardour.
The young reading-master of the Benedictine abbey of Alperspach,
P. Ambrosius Blaurer, was incited by the general ferment to the study of
the sacred writings, and formed opinions which soon rendered a longer
residence in the convent impossible to him.   Œcolampadius, who had but
lately taken the vows in the convent of St. Bridget at Altomünster, raised
his voice in favour of the new views : he had hoped to find in the convent
undisturbed leisure for the learned works he purposed to write ; but the
conviction which soon forced itself on his mind hurried him into an eager
participation in all the mental conflicts of the times.   The brothers of Our
Lady of Mount Carmel at Augsburg declared themselves for Luther from
the very first, with the prior at their head ; and to them belonged, for a
time, at least, Urban Regius,[1] one of the most devoted and favourite
disciples of Johann Eck, whom he now, however, deserted for the new
cause :[2] he supported it with great effect, first in Upper, and afterwards
still more successfully in Lower, Germany.   Here he was, after a while,
assisted by Johann Bugenhagen, who had also for a long time followed a
very different course of studies and opinions, in a convent of Præmonstra-
tenses[3] at Belbuck in Pomerania.   Bugenhagen, as his history of Pomerania,
written in 1518, and vigorously attacking the abuses prevailing in the
Church, shows, was even then convinced of the necessity of a complete
change in the body of the clergy ;[4] but he was no less strongly opposed to
Luther ; and when Luther's book on the Babylonish captivity was brought
to him one day as he sat at dinner, he exclaimed, that since the Passion of
Christ a more pernicious heretic had never existed.   But this very book
wrought a complete revolution in his mind : he took it home with him
read it, studied it, and became convinced that the whole world was in error
and that Luther alone saw the truth.   Of this change of sentiments he
informed his colleagues at the conventual school over which he presided,
his abbot, and all his friends.[5]   Similar conversions took place in all the
religious orders.   The superiors were often the most strongly impressed,
like the priors of the Augustine and Carmelite convents, of whom we have
spoken : among others were Eberhard Widensee, provost of the convent
of St. John at Halberstadt, and by his influence, Gottes-Gnaden and St.
Moritz, provosts of Neuenwerk and Halle, and Paul Lemberg, abbot of
Sagan, who openly declared that if any one of his monks felt his
conscience burdened by remaining in the convent, so far from attempting

[1] Braun, Geschichte der Bischöfe von Augsburg, iii. 239.   He is also called
a Carmelite in Welser's Augsburger Chronik.
[2] There are a few letters which passed between them in Adami, p. 35.   Eck
is violent and bitter.   Regius (König), in spite of the firmness of his opposition,
never forgets the accustomed reverence towards his master.
[3] One of the monastic orders—a branch of the Augustinian Canons.   So called
because founded at Prémontré, near Lâon.   *Cf.* Gasquet, English Monastic
Life p. 226.
[4] J. H. Balthasar, Præfatio in Bugenhagii Pomeraniam, p. 5.
[5] Chytræi Saxonia, p. 287.   Lange, Leben Bugenhagens, 1731, contains
nothing of importance.

to keep him there, he would rather carry him out of it on his own shoulders.[1]

On a careful examination, I do not find, however, that love of the world, or any licentious desire to be freed from the restraints of the convent, had much effect in producing these resolutions ; at all events, in the most conspicuous cases, where motives have been recorded by contemporaries, they were always the result of a profound conviction ; in some, gradually developed, in others, suddenly forced on the mind, sometimes by a striking passage in the Bible : many did not leave the convent of their own accord, but were driven out of it ; others, though of a most peaceful nature themselves, found their abode between the narrow walls embittered by the frequent disputes which arose out of the state of men's minds. The mendicant friars felt disgust at their own trade : one of them, a Franciscan, entered a smithy at Nürnberg with his alms-box in his hand, and was asked by the master why he did not rather earn his bread by the work of his hands : the robust monk immediately threw off his habit and became a journeyman smith, sending back his cowl and box to the convent.

There is no doubt that the monastic institutions of the West were originally founded in imitation of the Hindu penitents, who live in lonely forests, clothed in the bark of trees, eating only herbs and drinking only water, free from desires, masters of their passions, beatified even in this life, and a sure refuge to the afflicted.[2] But how widely had the recluses of Europe departed from their model ! They took part in all the pursuits, dissensions and troubles of the world, and their main object was the maintenance of a dominion at once temporal and spiritual, aided by masses actuated by the same sentiments and working to the same ends ; they were held together by servile vows, frequently taken from interested motives, and, as much as possible, disregarded. No sooner, therefore, had the validity of these vows, and their religious efficacy to the soul, become doubtful, than the whole structure fell in pieces ; nay more, the institution on which the Western Church mainly rested, sent forth the most sturdy antagonists to its further hierarchical development.

This general movement among the regular[3] clergy was now seconded by all ranks of the secular priesthood.

There was one even among the bishops, Polenz of Samland, who openly declared himself for Luther, occasionally preached his doctrines from the pulpit at Königsberg, and took care to appoint preachers of his own way of thinking to a number of places in his diocese. Luther was overjoyed at this ; such a peaceable and lawful change was exactly what he desired.[4]

A few other bishops were also supposed to be favourably inclined to the new doctrine. Johann Eberlin of Günzburg mentions the Bishop of

---

[1] Catalogus Abbatum Saganensium, in Stenzel's Scriptt. Rer. Siles., i., p. 457.

[2] Nalas, twelfth song.

[3] The regular clergy as opposed to the secular are the members of the monastic orders, who live under strict rule, although all monks are not ordained.

[4] " Lutheri Dedicatio in Deuteronomium : Reverendo . . . Georgio de Polentis vere episcopo. Tibi gratia donata est, ut non modo verbum susciperes et crederes, sed pro episcopali autoritate etiam palam et publice confessus doceres docerique per tuam diocesim curares, liberaliter his qui in verbo laborant provisis."—*Opp.*, iii., p. 75. Hartknoch's Preussische Kirchengeschichte, i., p. 273.

Augsburg, who did not conceal that " the life and conversation of the Lutherans were less sinful than those of their adversaries ;" the Bishop of Basle, who was pleased when Lutheran books were brought to him, and always read them diligently ; the Bishop of Bamberg, who no longer opposed the preaching of Lutheran doctrines in his city, and the Bishop of Merseburg, who sent for the writer to consult him concerning the reforms which were wanted.   He assures us that several others sent their canons to study at Wittenberg.   Most of the names which we find in the list of Reuchlin's patrons appear among those who took part in the religious innovation.

They were also joined by the patrician provosts of the great towns, such as a Wattenwyl in Berne, and a Besler and Bömer in Nürnberg, under whose protection the evangelical preachers were established in the churches of their respective cities.

Even without this encouragement, a great number of the officiating priests and preachers in Lower, and still more in Upper, Germany, declared themselves converts to Luther's opinions.   The name of Hermann Tast, one of the twenty-four papal vicars in Schleswig, is well known.   In the churchyard at Husum stood two lime-trees, which were called the Mother and the Daughter ; under the largest of the two, the Mother, Tast used to preach, escorted to and from the place of meeting by his hearers, who went armed to fetch him and conduct him home.   At Emden, in East Friesland, Georg von der Dare was driven out of the great church when he began to preach Luther's doctrines ; but the people, after flocking to hear him for some time in the open air, at length obtained re-admittance for him into the church.   Johann Schwanhäuser, custos of St. Gangolph in Bamberg, declaimed, in the language of a Carlstadt, against the adoration of the saints.[1]   The parish priest of Cronach was one of the first who married.   At Mainz, it was the preacher in the cathedral, Wolfgang Köpfl (for a long time the confidential adviser of the elector) ; at Frankfurt, the preacher in the church of St. Catharine, Hartmann Ibach ; at Strasburg, the parish priest of St. Laurence, Matthew Zell ; at Memmingen, the preacher of St. Martin's, Schappeler, who were the first to propagate the new doctrines.   In the imperial city of Hall, Johann Brenz, a mere youth, but deeply impressed with the doctrines of St. Paul, and an imitator of the apostle's style of speaking, pronounced his sermon of trial in September, 1522, and drove his antagonists, the guardian and the reader of the Minorite convent, out of the field without further contest, by the doctrine of the sole merit of Christ.[2]   In the Kreichgau, a band of village priests, united by similarity of opinion, collected around Erhard Schnepf, under the protection of the Gemmingen.   In Basle, at the procession of the Corpus Christi, Röubli, the priest of St. Alban's, carried a splendidly-bound Bible instead of the host, declaring that he alone bore the true Holy of holies.   Next followed, at the minster of Zürich, the great secular priest, Ulrich Zwingli, equally courageous and influential in politics and in religion, and in whom the Vicar of Constance soon thought he beheld a second Luther.   We may follow these movements even into the lofty regions of the Alps.   The leading men of Schwytz often timed their rides so as to arrive at Freienbach, where a friend of Zwingli's preached, at the time of divine service, after which they

[1] Extracts from his sermons in Heller, p. 62.
[2] Hartmann and Jäger, Johann Brenz, i. 43, 59.

stayed and dined with him.[1]   It made no difference that they were Swiss, for in those days the feeling of nationality had not yet separated them from Germany ; indeed the people of the Valais called the territory of the confederate cities, Germany.   The new doctrines then followed the course of the mountains as far as the valley of the Inn, where Jacob Strauss first expounded them to many thousand converts ; then to Salzburg, where Paul von Spretten made the cathedral resound with them, and finally into Austria and Bavaria.   At Altenöttingen, where there was one of the most popular miraculous pictures, the regular priest, Wolfgang Russ, had the courage to declaim against pilgrimages.

It may be concluded that all these changes were not brought about without stout resistance and a hard struggle.   Many were compelled to yield, but some persevered, and at all events the persecution did no harm to the cause.   When that zealous Catholic, Bogislas X. of Pomerania, destroyed the protestant society at Belbuck, and confiscated the property —for the seizure of church lands began on that side—the only result was, that one of their teachers accompanied some young Livonians, who had been studying there, to Riga, and thus scattered the seed of the Word over the most remote parts of Germany.[2]

Paul von Spretten was expelled from Salzburg, after which we find him preaching in St. Stephen's church at Vienna, and when driven thence, at Iglau in Moravia : there also he was in imminent danger, and at last found a safe asylum in Prussia.   With this scene of action, the ardent Amandus was not content ; he soon left it and went to Stolpe, where he challenged the monks to a disputation on the truth of the old or the new system : he told them they might prepare a stake and faggots, and burn him if he was overcome in argument ; and that if he obtained the victory, the sole punishment of his opponents should be conversion.

As yet no attention was paid to the place where the Gospel was preached. It is almost symbolic of the ecclesiastic opposition, that at Bremen it was a church standing under an interdict, in which two or three Augustine friars who had escaped the stake in Antwerp, first assembled a congregation.   At Goslar the new doctrine was first preached in a church in the suburbs ; and when that was closed, a native of the town who had studied at Wittenberg proclaimed it on a plain covered with lime-trees (the Lindenplan), whence its adherents were there called Lindenbrüder (brothers of the lime-tree).[3]   In Worms a moveable pulpit was put up against the outer walls of the church.   The Augustine monk, Caspar Güttel of Eisleben, at the request of the inhabitants of Arnstadt, preached seven sermons in the market-place there, according to ancient custom.   At Dantzig the people assembled on a height outside the town, to hear a preacher who had been driven from within its walls.

But even if none of the clergy had embraced the new faith, it would have found many proclaimers and defenders among the laity.   At Ingolstadt,

---

[1] Hottinger, Geschichte der Eidgenossen.

[2] Andreas Cnoph von Cüstrin.   " Er hat viel herrlicher und geistreicher Lieder, darin die Summa von der Lehre von der Gerechtigkeit, dem Glauben und desselbigen Fruchten . . . verfasset."—" He has composed many most beautiful and ingenious songs, wherein is contained the essence of the doctrine of righteousness—faith and its fruits."—Hiarn, Liefländische Gesch., book v., p. 193.

[3] Hamelmann, Historia renati Evangelii.   Opp. Hist. Gen., p. 869.

under the very eyes of Dr. Eck, an enthusiastic journeyman weaver read aloud Luther's writings to assembled crowds ; and when, in the same town, a young Master of Arts, called Seehofer, who had begun to teach from Melanchthon's pamphlets, was forced to recant, his defence was undertaken by a lady, Argula von Staufen, whose attention having been directed by her father to Luther's books, had, in conformity with their precepts, devoted herself exclusively to the study of the Scriptures. Believing herself fully able to compete with them in knowledge of the Bible, she now challenged all the members of the university to a disputation, and hoped to maintain the superiority of her own faith in the presence of the prince and the whole community.[1] It was in this intimate acquaintance with Scripture that the leaders of the religious movement trusted. Heinrich von Kettenbach exultingly enumerates countries and cities—Nürnberg, Augsburg, Ulm, the Rhenish provinces, Switzerland and Saxony—where women and maidens, serving men and artisans, knights and nobles, were more learned in the Bible than the high schools.[2]

There was indeed something very extraordinary in this simultaneous and universal conviction, unquestionably religious in its origin, rising up in opposition to forms of ecclesiastical and political life which had been revered for centuries, though now men could see in them only their wide departure from true primitive Christianity, and their subservience to an oppressive and odious power.

As every effort on the one side was followed by a reaction, and every attack by persecution, it was of great importance that there should be one spot in Germany where such was not the case : this spot was the electorate of Saxony.

In the year 1522 the neighbouring bishops made another attempt to re-establish their power here also, in consequence of the favourable tone of the first proclamation of the imperial government ; and the Elector Frederick offered no opposition to them so long as they promised to send preachers who should combat the Word with the Word.[3] When, however, not content with this, they demanded that the priests who had married or dared to administer the Lord's Supper in both kinds, and the monks who had quitted their convents, should be given up to them, he declared, after brief consideration, that the imperial edict did not oblige him to this.[4] By withdrawing his countenance from them, he of course annihilated their influence.

This naturally induced all those who were forced to fly from other places, to take refuge in his dominions, where no spiritual authorities could reach them. Eberlin, Stiefel, Strauss, Seehofer, Ibach from Frankfurt, Bugenhagen from Pomerania, Kauxdorf from Magdeburg, Mustæus from Halber-

[1] Winter, Gesch. der evang. Lehre in Baiern, i. 120 f.

[2] " Ein new Apologia vnnd Verantwortung Martini Luthers wyder der Papisten Mortgeschrey, die zehen klagen wyder jn ussblasiniren so wyt die Christenheyt ist, 1523."—" A new Apology and Answer of Martin Luther against the Papist's Cry of Murder, who trumpet forth Ten Complaints against him throughout Christendom."

[3] Frederick instructs his officers, " An Verkündigung des Wortes Gottes nicht zu hindern."—" Not to hinder the preaching of the Word of God." He takes for granted, " sie würden die Ehre Gottes und die Liebe des Nächsten suchen " —" that they would seek the honour of God and the love of their neighbour."

[4] Geuterbock, St. Lucastag. The very remarkable correspondence in the Sammlung vermischter Nachrichten zur sächsischen Geschichte, iv. 282.

stadt, where he had been barbarously mutilated,[1] and numbers more, flocked together from all parts of Germany ; they found a safe asylum, and in many cases temporary employment, and then went forth again confirmed in their faith by intercourse with Luther and Melanchthon. Wittenberg was the centre of the whole movement ; without the existence of such a centre, the unity of direction, the common progress, which we observe, would have been impossible ; we may add, that the admixture of foreign elements was of great importance to the development of the public mind of Saxony. The university especially thus acquired the character of a national body,—incontestably the true character of a great German high school. Both teachers and hearers resorted from all parts of Germany, and went forth again in all directions.

Wittenberg became equally important as a metropolis of literature.

It was the agitation of these important questions which first obtained for the German popular literature general circulation and influence. Up to the year 1518 its productions were far from numerous, and the range of its subjects very narrow. During the last twenty years of the fifteenth century there appeared about 40 German works ; in 1513 about 35 ; in 1514, 47 ; in 1515, 46 ; in 1516, 55 ; in 1517, 37 : these were chiefly mirrors for the laity, little works on medicine, books on herbs, religious tracts, newspapers, official announcements, and travels,—in short, the books fitted to the comprehension of the many. The most original productions were always those of the poetical opposition—the satires which we have already noticed. The increase in the number of German publications which followed Luther's appearance before the public was prodigious. In the year 1518 we find 71 enumerated ; in 1519, 111 ; in 1520, 208 ; in 1521, 211 ; in 1522, 347 ; in 1523, 498. If we inquire whence this wonderful increase emanated, we shall find it was from Wittenberg, and the chief author, Luther himself. In the year 1518 we find 20 books published with his name ; in 1519, 50 ; in 1520, 133 ; in 1521, when he was interrupted by his journey to Worms, and hindered by a forced seclusion, about 40 ; in 1522, again 130 ; and in 1523, 183.[2] In no nation or age has a more autocratic and powerful writer appeared ; and it would be difficult to find any other who has united so perfectly popular and intelligible a style, and such downright homely good sense, to so much originality, power and genius ; he gave to German literature the character by which it has been ever since distinguished, of investigation, depth of thought, and strenuous conflict of opinions. He began the great discussion which has been carried on in Germany through all the subsequent centuries ; though often griev-

---

[1] What cruelties then took place ! " Aliquot ministri canonicorum capiunt D. Valentinum Mustæum,"—" with the sanction of the burgher-master he had preached the Gospel in Neustadt," " et vinctum manibus pedibusque, injecto in ejus os freno, deferunt per trabes in inferiores cœnobii partes ibique in cella cerevisiaria eum castrant."—Hamelmann, l. c., p. 880.

[2] I rely upon Panzer's Annalen der ältern Deutschen Literatur, 1788-1802. That the information, useful as it is, is not quite complete, is a defect this has in common with most statistical works. We can, however, gather from them the general facts, which is all we here have to do with. According to Adam, Vitæ Jurisconsult., p. 62, it was Schneidewin's father-in-law—ex honorata familia, quæ nomen gentilitium Turingorum habuit, agnomen vero Aurifabrorum—who established the first printing-press at Wittenberg, socio Luca pictore seniore. This is another of Lucas Cranach's merits.

ously interrupted by acts of violence and by the influences of foreign policy. In the beginning he stood quite alone, but by degrees, especially after the year 1521, disciples, friends, and rivals began to appear in the field.   In the year 1523, besides his own works, there were published 215 by others, in favour of the new opinions ; that is, more than four fifths of all that appeared, while we do not find above 20 decidedly catholic publications. It was the first time that the national mind, uninfluenced by foreign models, and manifesting itself purely in the form impressed on it by the great events of the times, and the high destinies to which Germany was called, found a general expression ; moreover this expression regarded the most important interests that can occupy the attention of man, and its very first utterance was prompted by ideas of religious freedom.

It was a singular felicity, that at the very instant of full intellectual awakening, the Holy Scriptures, both of the New and Old Testament, were laid open to the nation.   It is true that the Bible had long been known in translations ; but it is impossible to conceive, without reading them, how full of errors, how rude in style, and how unintelligible these versions are.   Luther, on the contrary, spared no labour to obtain an accurate knowledge of the meaning of the original, and gave it utterance in German, with all the clearness and energy of which that language is capable.   The imperishable records of the earliest ages of the world, characterised by the freshness of the youth of mankind, and the sacred writings of later date, in which true religion appears in all its childlike candour, were now put into the hands of the German people in their own vernacular tongue, piece by piece, like a periodical work which relates to the immediate interests of the day, and were devoured with equal avidity.

There is one production of the German mind which owes its origin directly to this concurrence of circumstances.   In translating the Psalms, Luther conceived the project of making a paraphrase of them for the purpose of congregational singing ;[1] for the idea of a Church, such as he had described and begun to call into existence, supposed that the congregation should take a far more considerable part in the service than it had ever done before.   In this case, however, as in some others, a mere paraphrase did not suffice.   The devout spirit, tranquil in the conviction of possessing the revealed Word of God ; elevated by the strife and danger in which it was placed, and inspired by the poetical genius of the Old Testament, poured forth lyrical compositions, at once poetry and music ; words alone would have been insufficient to express the emotions of the soul in all their fulness, or to excite and sustain the feelings of a congregation.   This could only be done by the melody which breathed in the solemn old church music, and the touching airs of popular songs.   Such was the origin of the evangelical hymns, which we may date from the year 1523.[2]   Detached hymns by

[1] Luther's preface to Johann Walter's Hymns recalls " das Exempel der Propheten und Könige im alten Testament, die mit singen und klingen, mit dichten und allerlei Seitenspiel Gott gelobet haben,"—" the example of the prophets and kings in the Old Testament, who, with songs and music, with verses and all manner of stringed instruments, praised God."—Altenb. A., ii., p. 751.

[2] Riederer, " von Einführung des deutschen Gesanges " p. 95.   The remarkable letter to Spalatin concerning the translation of the Psalms into German verse, in De Wette, ii., p. 490, is doubtless earlier than that dated 14th Jan., 1524, ibid., p. 461.   In it we see what the Musæ Germanicæ, about which De

Luther and Spretten acquired immediate popularity, and lent their aid
to the earliest struggles of the reforming spirit ; but it was many years
later that the German mind displayed its whole wealth of poetical, and still
more of musical, productions of this kind.

The popular poetry also devoted itself in other ways to the new ideas
with that spirit of teachableness, and at the same time resistance to
arbitrary power, which characterised it. Hutten published his bitterest
invectives in verse ; Murner depicted the corruption of the clergy in long
and vivid descriptions : to this feeling of censure and reprobation was now
added, if not in Murner himself, at any rate in most others, a positive conviction of the truth of the new doctrine, and a profound admiration of its
champion ; the man who maintained the righteous cause among crimson
barrets and velvet caps was celebrated in verse.   The pope was brought on
the stage in carnival farces ; he congratulates himself that, in spite of his
knavery, men continue to ascribe to him the power of admitting them into
heaven or binding them in hell, which brings many birds to his net to be
plucked ; that he reaps the fruits of the sweat of the poor man's brow,
and can ride with a retinue of a thousand horses—his name is Entchristelo ;
there also appear, uttering like sentiments, Cardinal Highmind (*Hochmuth*),
Bishop Goldmouth Wolfsmaw (*Goldmund Wolfsmagen*), Vicar Fabler
(*Fabeler*), and a long list of personages held up to ridicule and contempt
under such names : the last who enters is the Doctor, who expounds the
true doctrine very much in the tone of a sermon.[1]   Under the influence of
these impressions was educated Burckhardt Waldis, who afterwards made
such a happy application[2] of the old fable of the beasts to religious controversies.   The greatest German poet of that day warmly embraced
Luther's cause.   Hans Sachs's poem, the Nightingale of Wittenberg,
appeared in 1523 ; he compares the faith which had prevailed for four
hundred years, to the moonlight which had led men astray in the wilderness ; now, however, the nightingale announces the rising sun and the light
of day, while she herself soars above the dark clouds.   Thoughts emanating
from a sound understanding, instructed by the infallible Word, and confident of its own cause, form the basis of the many ingenious, gay, and
graceful poems—not the less attractive for a slight smack of the workshop—
with which the honest master delighted all classes of the nation.

In Germany, the proper aim of art—to teach by giving a sensible form
to ideas—had never been lost sight of.   Hence, there is no less fancy displayed in her symbols, than earnestness in her character.   It so happened
that one of the great masters of the time, Lucas Kranach,[3] went to live at

---

Wette seems to be in doubt, really meant.   It appears from the letters to Haus-
mann, that Luther was employed in November and December, 1523, in the
composition of the liturgy.

[1] " Ein Fassnachtspyl, so zu Bern uf der Hern Fassnacht in dem MDXXII.
Jare von Burgerssonen offentlich gemacht ist, darnin die warheit in Schimpffs-
wyss vom Pabst und siner Priesterschaft gemeldet würt."—" A Carnival Play,
the which was publicly enacted in the Lord's carnival of the year 1522, at Bern,
by the sons of burghers, wherein the truth is satirically told of the pope and of
his priesthood."   Newly printed by Grüneisen.—Nicl. Manuel, p. 339.

[2] An adoption of Æsop's Fables.   For Burckhardt Waldis.   *Cf.* Bibliographie
Universelle.

[3] Lucus Kranach.   1472-1553.   *Cf.* Schuchard's Lukus Kranach.

Wittenberg, and, in a constant familiar intercourse with Luther, became
thoroughly imbued with the modes of thinking of the reformers, and consecrated his talents to embodying them.   He sometimes entered the ranks
as a combatant.   Some of his smaller pictures, such as the Passion of Christ
and Antichrist, in which the lowliness and humility of the Founder, and the
pride and pomp of his vicegerent, are contrasted, are protests against
Catholicism ; and accordingly woodcuts of them were inserted into
Luther's writings.   It may be imagined that his chaste pencil was employed
in no works but such as harmonised with the evangelical faith.   The grace
and loveliness with which he had formerly adorned groups of beatified
female saints, he now shed over the little children receiving the blessing of
our Saviour.   The mysteries shadowed forth in early art, were now expressed in representations of the Sacraments retained by Luther, which
were sometimes painted on one canvas, and of the sublime work of Redemption.   The eminent statesmen and divines by whom he was surrounded, presented forms and features so remarkable and characteristic,
that he had no temptation, except in the cause of religion, to strive after
the ideal.   Albert Dürer, though his genius had already reached maturity,
was powerfully affected by the prevailing spirit : the most perfect, perhaps,
of all his works,—the evangelists Mark and John, and the apostles Peter
and Paul,—were produced under the impressions of these times.   There
exist studies for these pictures with the date 1523 : they reflect the image
suggested by Scripture (now rendered accessible to new views), of the
wisdom, devotion and energy of these first witnesses of the Christian
church.   Vigour and grandeur of conception manifest themselves in every
feature.[1]

The general development of the German mind was closely connected
with the new ideas ; the same spirit was stirring in the learned, as in the
popular branches of mental activity.

Wittenberg was far from being the only university in which the course
of studies was changed.   At Freiburg, where Luther was detested, the
Aristotelian philosophy ceased to be studied and inculcated as hitherto.
" Petrus Hispanus," says Ulrich Zasius, " has had his day; the books of
Sentences are laid aside ; our theologians are some of them reading
Matthew and others Paul ; nay, even the very beginners, those who are
but just arrived, crowd to these lectures."[2]   Even Zasius himself, one
of the most distinguished German jurists of that time, gives a remarkable
testimony to the universal diffusion of the reforming spirit.   He complains
that his lecture-room is deserted ; that he has barely half a dozen hearers,
and they, all Frenchmen ; and at the same time he can find no better
mode of recommending his own exertions in the cause of learning, than
by comparing them to the labours of Luther.   The glossators of the genuine
texts whom he was engaged in combating, appeared to him in the same
light as the schoolmen on whom Luther was waging war ; he laboured to
restore the Roman law to its original purity, just as Luther strove to revive
the theology of the Bible.

Of all departments of learning none, however, stood more in need of a

---

[1] How Pirkheimer and Dürer disputed about the question of the Lord's Supper
in Melanchthon's presence : related by Peucer in Strobel's " Nachricht von
Melanchthons Aufenthalt in Nürnberg," p. 27.

[2] Zazii Epistolæ, i. 63.

similar reform than history. There existed an immense accumulation of materials ; but the earlier periods were obscured by the learned fables which were continually receiving fresh and more circumstantial additions ; while the later were known only in fragments dressed up to suit the interests of the dominant party : the most important parts had been intentionally falsified, in consequence of their necessary connection with the great ecclesiastical fiction. It was impossible to arrive at a true, lively and connected view of history ; even minds thirsting for real information shrank from such insuperable masses of reading. An attempt to penetrate them was, however, made just about this time by Johann Aventin, who, at an earlier period, had sympathised in the literary tendencies of the new school of thinkers, and now followed its religious direction with the liveliest zeal. In writing his Bavarian chronicle, the contents of which are interesting to Germany generally, and even to the world, he spared no pains in searching libraries and archives in order to substitute genuine records for the shallow and improbable traditions hitherto current. He puts the reader on his guard against the representations of the ignorant ; especially " people who have seen nothing of mankind, who know nothing of cities and countries, have no experience of earthly or heavenly matters, and yet pretend to judge of every thing." His endeavour is to understand history in its true and necessary aspect, " such as it should be." The spirit of the national opposition to the papacy is powerfully at work within him : whenever he strives to depict the simplicity of the Christian doctrine, or alludes to its origin, he never fails to contrast with it the spiritual power in its rise, progress, and operation. His history of Gregory VII. is even now the best extant : he takes a very comprehensive view of the results arising from the dominion of the hierarchical principle, though he had not the peculiar talent requisite to place them distinctly before the reader. His works are indeed generally unfinished ; but he was the first labourer in that field of profound and penetrating research into universal history, which in our day occupies so many minds.

For a time, it seemed as if the interest in theological questions would absorb all others. Erasmus complains that nothing was read or bought but publications for or against Luther ; he fears that the study of the humanities, which was but just established, would be stifled under a new system of school learning. The chronicles of the time describe how the contempt into which the clergy had fallen reacted on learning : the proverb, " Die Gelehrten, die Verkehrten," (the more learned, the more wrongheaded), was in everybody's mouth, and parents hesitated to devote their children to studies which offered so doubtful a prospect. This, however, was only a momentary aberration ; the mind, roused to a desire for authentic knowledge, could not reject the very instrument which had awakened it. In the year 1524 Luther published a letter to the " burghermasters and councillors of all the towns on German ground," exhorting them " to establish Christian schools."[1] He means by this, especially for the training of priests ; for, he says, it is only by the study of languages that the Gospel can be preserved in its purity, to which end it was delivered

---

[1] Altenb. edition, ii., p. 804. Eoban Hess caused the letters which he had received on this subject from Luther, Melanchthon, Jonas, Draco and others, to be printed collectively in 1523, in the pamphlet, " De non contemnendis Studiis humanioribus."

down to us in writing ; otherwise there would be nothing but wild and
perilous disorder, and an utter confusion of opinions. Yet he does not
by any means confine his recommendation to ecclesiastical schools ; far
from it : he deplores that schools have been so exclusively calculated for
the education of the clergy, and his chief object is to free them from this
narrow destination, and to found a learned class among the laity. He
holds out the education of the ancient Romans as an example to Germany ;
and says that instructed men well versed in history are absolutely necessary
for the government of the state ; he also insists upon the establishment
of public libraries, not only to contain editions and expositions of the
sacred writings, but also orators and poets, whether heathen or not ;
besides books on the fine arts, law and medicine, chronicles and histories ;
" for they be profitable for the learning of the wonders and works of
God." This letter had as great an effect on secular learning, as his book
addressed to the German nobility had on the general condition of the
laity. Luther first conceived the idea of that learned body of official
laymen which has exercised such an incalculable influence over the social
and political condition of Germany ; he advocated the popular cultivation
of knowledge for her own sake, apart from the church ; it was he who
laid the first stone of that edifice of learning in northern Germany, which
succeeding labourers have reared to such a height. In this he was vigorously seconded by the indefatigable Melanchthon, who was the author
of the Latin grammar used in the schools throughout the North of Germany,
till the beginning of the eighteenth century.[1] He completed it in the
year 1524, beginning from some notes made for the private instruction
of a young Nürnberger ; at the same time, the Greek grammar, of which
he had previously drawn up the plan, received the form in which it was
taught for centuries afterwards. Teachers were formed under Melanchthon's discipline, who adopted all his ideas, and became the founders of
the German school-training. The most remarkable of these was Valentine
Trotzendorf, who was called from Wittenberg to Goldberg in Silesia,
in the year 1523, and who was said to be born a schoolmaster as much as
Cæsar was born a general, or Cicero an orator. Innumerable German
schoolmasters were formed by him.

A large and coherent survey of all these facts suffices to convince us
that the Reformation was by no means confined to theological dogmas ;
a whole circle of aspirations and thoughts of a peculiar character, and
pregnant with a new order of things, had arisen ; closely connected, it is
true, with the theological opposition, and partly developed under that form,
but the existence of which is neither to be ascribed to, nor confounded
with, that phenomenon. The opposition was itself merely one manifestation of this spirit, the future workings of which were entirely independent
of it.

The first object of the awakened mind undoubtedly was, deliverance
from that mighty power which claimed the right of retaining it
captive.

In examining more closely the course of this struggle, as it displayed
itself in all parts of Germany, we shall fall into error if we expect to find

---

[1] The editions most worthy of note till 1737 are enumerated in Strobel, Von
den Verdiensten Melanchthons, um die Grammatik . . ., neue Beiträge, ii., iii.,
p. 43.

the same points of variance which exist between the later Protestant and the revived Catholic systems. The ideas and intellectual powers which were then arrayed against each other, stood in a far more distinct, broad and intelligible opposition.

One of the most violent conflicts was that concerning faith and good works. We must not understand by this the more deep and abstruse controversy which has since arisen out of the subtilty or the obstinacy of the schools. At that time the question was very simple : on the one side, by good works were meant those ritual observances through which men then really hoped to merit reward, both in this world and the next— such as pilgrimages, fasting, the foundation of masses for the souls of the dead, the recital of particular prayers, the reverence paid to certain saints, and the gifts to the churches and the clergy which formed so important a part of the piety of the middle ages. To this perversion of the idea of moral obligation, which had been so culpably allowed to gain currency and strength, the other party opposed the doctrine of the efficacy of faith without works. But—especially after the troubles in Wittenberg —no one now ventured to inculcate an ideal, abstract, inactive faith. We still possess many of the sermons of that period, and it would be difficult to find one in which faith and charity are not spoken of as indissolubly united. Caspar Güttel earnestly inculcates the doctrine, that the conduct which a man pursues towards his neighbour for the love of God is the one essential thing.[1] The preacher blamed those who spent their substance in enriching the clergy, decorating the image of a saint, or going on distant pilgrimages, and at the same time forgot the poor.

The same thing took place with respect to the opinions concerning the church. The reformers entirely refused to recognise the holy church of Christ, out of whose pale there is no salvation, in the persons of the pope, his prelates and priests ; they considered it profane to say that the Church commands or possesses any thing ; they distinguished that ecclesiastical institution, which, by its scandalous government, gave the lie to the principles on which it was founded, from the mysterious existence of that holy fellowship which appears not outwardly, which, according to the words of the Symbol, is a pure object of faith, and which unites heaven and earth indeed, but without the intervention of the pope.[2] " Far be

[1] Schutzrede wider etzlich ungezemte Clamanten. The very sermons preached at Arnstadt : printed in Olearii Syntagma Rerum Thuringicarum, ii. 274 ; an edition which Panzer does not mention in his Annals, ii., p. 93.

[2] Ain Sermon oder Predig von der christlichen Kirchen welches doch sey die hailig christlich Kirche, davon unser Glaub sagt, geprediget zu Ulm von Bruder Heinrich von Kettenbach, 1522.—" A Sermon or Preaching touching the Christian Church—which is the holy Christian Church of which our belief speaketh ? Preached at Ulm by Brother Henry of Kettenbach." Johann Brenz took up this doctrine very vehemently. He will not allow that the church is to be believed because it received Christ. " Juden und Heiden die haben Christum angenommen—und sind nachfolgends die äusserliche christliche Kirche geworden, und hat die Kirche ihren Ursprung von den frommen Christenmenschen und ist nachfolgends die äusserliche christliche Kirche worden, doch nit dass die Menschen ihre Seligkeit haben von der äusserlichen Kirche. . . . Dieweil die Kirche ein geistlicher verborgener Leib ist und nit von dieser Welt, so folgt, dass in diesem Leib kein weltlich äusserlich noch sichtbar haupt ist."—" Jews and Pagans received Christ, and thereupon became the outward Christian church, and the church has its origin from pious Christians, and is thereafter become the outward

it from us to suppose," said Pastor Schmidt, in a sermon he preached with great effect at Küssnacht, " that the Christian church can acknowledge a head so spotted with sin as the pope ; and thus forsake Christ, whom St. Paul so often calls ' the head of the church.' "[1]

In like manner the institution of the Lord's Supper, freed from all priestly intervention, was contrasted with the compulsory obligation of confessing every individual sin,—an obligation which led and still leads to all the odious abuses of the confessional, and to the despotism of a stern and tyrannical orthodoxy.   The discretionary power of the priest to grant absolution was denied, together with the doctrine of the actual presence ; and people were even dissuaded from too nice a pondering over particular sins, as tending to stimulate the desires anew, or to produce despair : nothing was required but an undoubting, cheerful, steadfast reliance on the mercy of God, and faith in His present favour.[2]

But perhaps the most strongly and totally opposed were the opinions as to creeds of human origin and the pure word of God.   Here again the dispute was not concerning tradition, as it has been defined by the more ingenious and enlightened controversialists of modern times ; that is to say, little more than the Christian spirit propagating itself from generation to generation,—the Word living in the hearts of the faithful.[3]   What the reformers combated, was the entire system of the Latin church, developed in the course of centuries by hierarchical power and school learning, and claiming absolute authority.   They remarked that the fathers of the church had erred, Jerome often, and even Augustin occasionally ; that those holy men had themselves been well aware of it ; and that nevertheless a system from which no deviation was allowed, had been based on their decisions, and spun out with the aid of heathen philosophy.   Thus it came to pass that they had given themselves up to human devices, and that there was not a teacher among them who led his hearers to the true understanding of the Gospel.   And to this human doctrine, which neither satisfied the reason nor consoled the heart—which was connected with all sorts of abuses—they now opposed the eternal word of God, " which is noble, pure, cordial, steadfast and comfortable, and should therefore be kept unadulterated and undefiled."[4]   They exhorted the laity to work out their own salvation ; to gain possession of the word of God, which

---

Christian church, not that men receive salvation from the outward church. . . . For since the church is a spiritual hidden body, and not of this world, it follows that this body cannot have a worldly, outward and visible head."

[1] Myconius ad Zwinglium.   Epp. Zw., p. 195.

[2] " Eyn verstendig trostlich Leer über das Wort St. Paulus : Der Mensch sol sich selbst probieren und alsso von dem Brott essen und von dem Kelch trinken : zu Hall in Innthal von D. Jacob Strauss geprediget, MDXXII."—" A reasonable and comfortable Doctrine concerning the Word of St. Paul : ' But let a man examine himself, and so let him eat of that bread, and drink of that cup.' Preached by D. Jacob Strauss, 1522, at Hall, in the valley of the Inn."   The body and blood of Christ are taken as the surest sign of His merciful promises to forgive us our sins, if we have faith.   This contradiction appears in some later writings of this author.

[3] Möhler Symbolik, p. 361.

[4] Das hailig ewig Wort Gots was das in im kraft, sterke, frid, fred, erleuchtung und leben in aym rechten Christen zu erwecken vermag—zugestelt dem edlen Ritter—Hern Jörgen von Fronsperg ; von Haug Marschalk der genennt wirt

had now come forth in full splendour from its long concealment, to take
it as a sword in their hands, and to defend themselves with it against the
preachers of the contrary faith.[1]

Such were the questions concerning which the warfare of popular literature—preaching, was mainly carried on.   On the one side, certain external
ecclesiastical observances were deemed meritorious ; the idea of a Church
was identified with the existing hierarchy ; the mystery of the individual
relation to God, which is expressed in absolution, was made dependent on
absolute obedience to the clergy.   These opinions belonged to the system
of faith which defended its authority with fire and sword.   On the other
side, was the obligation of faith and love ; the idea of the unity of an invisible Church consisting in a community of souls ; the forgiveness of sins
through faith in the redemption, and reception of the sacrament without
the necessity of confession ; and, finally, belief in the Bible alone as a rule
of faith and doctrine.   We are not now treating of the modifications given
to their opinions by individual theologians, but simply of the prevalent
trains of ideas which were at war in every part of Germany.

So early as the year 1521, a little work was published, containing the
allegory of this contest, under the name of " The old and the new Gods."
On the title-page we see, as representatives of the new God, the pope,
some of the fathers of the church, Aristotle, and, at the bottom of the leaf,
Cajetan, Silvester, Eck and Faber ; on the opposite page, the true and
ancient God in his triune form, the four evangelists, St. Paul grasping a
sword, and lastly, Luther.   The contents of the book were quite in character with the frontispiece.[2]   With the ceremonies, rites, and articles of
faith which had grown up under the protection of the rising hierarchy and
its bloody sword, and turned Christianity into a kind of Judaism, is contrasted the old God, with his authentic word, and the simple doctrine of the
redemption, of hope, faith, and love.[3]

Zoller zu Augsburg, 1523.—" The holy eternal word of God, what strength,
power, peace and joy, light and life it is able to awaken in a true Christian.   Addressed to the noble Knight George von Fronsperg, by Haug Marshalk, who was
named tax-master at Augsburg in 1523."   In his preface he praises the knight,
" dass Eur Gestreng yetzumal so hoch benennt und gepreist wird, dass das edel
rain lauter und unvermischt Wort Gottes, das heilig evangelium bey eur gestreng
statt hat, und in eur ritterlich gemüt und herz eingemaurt und befestiget," &c.—
" that your worship is now so highly famed and praised, for that the noble, clear,
plain and pure word of God, the holy Gospel, has an asylum with your worship,
and is enclosed and made fast in your knightly spirit and heart," &c.

[1] Cunrad Distelmair von Arberg : ain trewe Ermanung, &c., 1523.
[2] Panzer, ii., p. 20.
[3] See the preface by Hartmann Dulich, printed in Veesenmeier's Sammlung
von Aufsätzen, p. 135.   The following passage in Eberlin of Günzburg's Fraind-
licher Vermanung, p. iii., shows how much the purpose of the whole movement
was recognised in these its most prominent tendencies : " Ich halt, Luther sey
von Gott gesandt zu seubern die Biblia von der lerer auslegung vnd zwang, die
gewissen zu erlösen von banden der menschlichen gebot od' bapstgesetzen, und
den gaistlichen abziehen den titel Christi uñ seiner kirchen, dz fürohyn nit mer
sollich gross büberey—strafflos sey und' dem heyligen namen Gottes . . . auch
ist der Luther gesant dz er lere das creutz vnd glauben, welche schier durch alle
doctores vergessen seindt ; darzu ist Luther beruft von Got vnd Got gibt im
weysshait, kunst, vernunft, sterke, vnd herz dazu."—" I hold that Luther was
sent by God to free the Bible from the empty expositions and restrictions of the

These coarse and naked expressions suffice to show that the nation felt what were the real points in debate. The German mind became conscious that the hour of its maturity was come ; boldly resisted the tyranny of those accidental forms which had governed the world, and returned to the only true source of religious instruction.[1]

Considering the vast agitation, the strong feeling of conflict, which prevailed, it is doubly remarkable how much control men had over themselves, and with how much caution they often acted.

Heinrich of Kettenbach continued to assume that the Church—by which however he understands an invisible community—possessed the treasure of the merits of Christ, of the Virgin Mary, and of all the elect.

Eberlin of Günzburg, whilst writing from Wittenberg to exhort his friends in Augsburg to procure for themselves each a copy of the New Testament, even if they had to save the price of it out of their food or raiment, admonishes them at the same time not to be too hasty in condemning the opinions of their fathers. There were many things, he said, which God in his wisdom had kept secret, and which they needed not to inquire about ; such as purgatory, and the intercession of saints. He adds, that even Luther condemned nothing that had not some distinct passage of Scripture against it.

A young Bohemian critic brought forward a whole train of arguments to prove that it was very doubtful whether St. Peter had ever been in Rome ; and the Catholic party clearly perceived that if this question was decided in the negative, the whole doctrine of the primacy would be overthrown. But the theologians of Wittenberg did not allow themselves to be dazzled by the brilliant results to which this line of argument would lead ; they pronounced it to be of no avail[2] towards furthering faith and piety ; and, indeed, in a work wherein this question is treated at length, and the ill effects of the abuse of the doctrine of primacy set forth with great earnestness, a hope is expressed that the new Pope, Adrian VI., would renounce all existing errors, and confine himself entirely to the precepts of the Bible —which some passages in his writings seemed to promise ; and that then not only the present differences would be healed, but also the old schism ended, and that even Greeks and Bohemians would return to the bosom of the Church.[3]

---

teachers, to release the conscience from the bondage of human commands or popish laws, and to strip ecclesiastics of the title of Christ and of his church, so that in future such great knavery should no longer remain unpunished in the holy name of God. Luther is likewise sent to teach the cross and the faith, which are clean forgotten by all the doctors. Hereunto was Luther called by God, and to this end has God given him wisdom, knowledge, prudence, strength and courage."

[1] Sermon von der Kirche, at the very beginning.

[2] Luther to Spalatin, 17th Feb., 1520, in De W., i. 559.

[3] Apologia Simonis Hessi adv. dominum Roffensem Episc. Anglicanum super concertatione ejus cum Vlrico Veleno. Julio mense, 1523. The author maintains chiefly, " quod gentiliter et ambitiose pro Petri primatu a multis pugnetur, cum hinc nihil lucri accedat pietati : quod impie abusi sint potestate sua Romani pontifices in statuendis quibusdam articulis seditiosis magis quam piis." The passage of Adrian, in titulo de Sacram. baptismi, is : " Noverit ecclesia se non esse dominam sacramentorum sed ministram, nec posse magis formam sacramentalem destituere aut novam instituere quam legem aliquam divinam abolere vel novum aliquem fidei articulum instituere. Spero fore," he then proceeds, " si

Others who were less sanguine, were yet of opinion that all violent measures were to be avoided, and that the abolition of abuses should be left to the government. Some, indeed, exhorted their followers to free themselves from the dominion of the priesthood, as the Israelites did from that of Pharaoh. But even such men as the vehement Otho Brunfels opposed them, saying, that " the Word had power to improve the state of the world without trouble or the sword ; and that things rashly and inconsiderately begun never ended well."[1]

This was Luther's opinion also ; and for a long time it was acted on throughout the whole empire.

Everything might yet be hoped from the guidance of the Council of Regency ; for in directing that the pure word of God should be preached, and in avoiding all reference by name to the fathers of the Church, who were looked upon as the corner-stones of modern Romanism, the Council of Regency had adopted the most important ideas of the reformers.

In the year 1523 it took the cause of reform more expressly under its protection.

When Faber, the vicar of Constance, received a commission from Rome to preach against Luther, and applied to the Council of Regency for protection and safe conduct, they gave him a letter purporting, indeed, to have that effect, but conceived in such terms that, as Planitz says, he would gladly have had a better.

Duke George made fresh complaints to the Regency of Luther's violent attacks, and several members of that body were of opinion that the elector should be admonished to punish him. This, however, was opposed by the majority. Count Palatine Frederick, the emperor's lieutenant, proposed that the duke's letters should, at any rate, be sent to the elector. " Sir," said Planitz, " the voice of the majority decides that my gracious master shall not be written to ;" and the duke was told that he might make the application to the elector himself.

In the convocation of a fresh diet, care was taken to make no allusion to the religious troubles.[2]

The main point, however, was that no step whatever was taken towards the execution of the edict of Worms ; but the new doctrines were allowed freely to take their course, in expectation of the ecclesiastical council which had been demanded.

It is evident of what importance to the State as well as to the Church was the question,—whether a government in which sentiments of this kind predominated, would be able to maintain itself or not.

---

ille perstat in sua sententia, ut tota catholica ecclesia, quæ nunc in sectas videtur divisa, in unam fidei unitatem aggregetur, adeo ut et Bohemos et Græcos dexteras daturos confidam bene præsidenti Romano pontifici."

[1] Vom evangelischen Anstoss, Neuenburg in Breisgau Simonis und Judä, 1523.

[2] Letter from Planitz, dated 28th Feb., 3d March, and 18th August, 1523.

CHAPTER IV.

OPPOSITION TO THE COUNCIL OF REGENCY.—DIET OF 1523-24.

Two great ideas occupied the mind of the whole German nation ; that of a national, representative, and at the same time, powerful government, and that of a complete renovation of the religious condition of the country : both these ideas were now, to a considerable extent, represented ; each received support from the other ; and, united, they seemed to promise a future equally important from a political and intellectual point of view.

All endeavours, however, which are directed towards ends so vast and comprehensive inevitably provoke strong and various opposition from many quarters.

Not that the connection between these two important objects was so close as to be evident to all minds, or that the antagonists of the opposition were fully aware of both its bearings ; but each of them roused the peculiar antipathies of a class.   It by no means followed that those who opposed the Council of Regency were hostile to the reformation of the Church.

We are generally inclined, in our views of the past, to fall into the error of ascribing too soon an exaggerated influence to a new element of social and political life.   However powerful it may be, there are other influences at work which it cannot immediately overcome, and which continue to exercise their own independent action.

The hostility to the Council of Regency arose from two causes fundamentally opposed.   In the first place, that body seemed destined to become a powerful and efficient government,—a prospect which was far from welcome to everyone.   In the second, it was at present very feeble ; it possessed no executive power.   Hence the first obstacle it encountered was disobedience.

SICKINGEN AND HIS ADVERSARIES.

It was not to be expected that the Public Peace proclaimed by Charles V. would be better observed than those of former reigns.   Two imperial councillors, Gregory Lamparter and Johann Lucas, the master of the treasury, were attacked and taken prisoners on their way to Augsburg from Worms, where they had assisted at the closing of the diet.   Nürnberg, the seat of government and of the courts of law, and at this time in a certain sense the capital city of the empire, was surrounded on all sides by the wildest private wars.   Hans Thomas of Absberg, doubly irritated by the resolutions taken against him by the Swabian League, assembled again, in 1522, the most daring and reckless reiters from all the surrounding districts : fresh letters of challenge were brought to Nürnberg every day, or were found stuck on the whipping-post in the neighbouring villages ; the roads east and west became unsafe.   There was a lonely chapel at Krügelstein, in the territory of Bamberg, where mass was said three times a week. Here, under colour of hearing it, all the bands of robbers and their scouts met together.   Woe to the company of merchants that fell in their way, for they not only plundered them of all their wares, but had now adopted the barbarous practice of cutting off the right hands of their prisoners : it was in vain that the wretched sufferers implored them at least to cut off

the left and leave the right.   Hans Thomas of Absberg thrust the right
hand of a shopkeeper, which he had chopped off, into the bosom of the unfortunate man, and told him that when he got to Nürnberg he might give
it to the bürgermeister in his name.[1]

The Frankfurt Acts of 1522 present a very striking example of the
general insecurity.   Philip Fürstenberg, who was sent by the town of
Frankfurt to the Council of Regency to take part in the government of the
empire, found the road he had to travel from Miltenberg to Wertheim
so unsafe, that he quitted his carriage, and joining a party of some 'prentice
tailors whom he met, assumed their garb, and took a by-road on foot.   The
carriage was attacked by several horsemen with bent cross-bows.   In order
to reach Wertheim he was forced to take an escort of five or six men armed
with fire-locks or cross-bows.[2]   " The Reiters are angry," says he : " what
they are about I know not."

In this state of things, when the Council of Regency could not even protect its own members, there broke out a private war, more violent than any
that had disturbed the peace of the empire during Maximilian's reign.
In August, 1522, Franz von Sickingen, with a well-armed force of infantry,
cavalry and artillery, ventured to attack an elector of the empire, the
Archbishop of Treves, in his own country and strongly fortified capital.

In the main this was merely a private war (*Fehde*) like many others,
originating in a personal quarrel (this same elector having once earnestly
entreated the assistance of the empire against Sickingen's outrages in
Hessen) ; the pretext for which was some doubtful legal claims,—especially
concerning a fine which had been transferred from the archbishop to
Sickingen ; and the real object, the plunder and, if possible, the conquest
of the fortified towns.   There exists a most interesting letter from an old
confidential friend of Sickingen's, in which the writer dissuades him from
the enterprise, and lays before him all the chances of success or failure.[3]

Other motives were also at work, which gave public importance to this
undertaking : success in a hostile enterprise was no longer Sickingen's
ultimate aim ; he had an eye to interests of far greater moment.

First of all, to those of the whole body of the Knights of the Empire.
We have seen how great was their discontent at the state of public affairs
at that time : at the Swabian League, which took upon itself to be at once

---

[1] Müllner's Nürnberger Annalen for the years 1522 and 1523 contain this and
many other details ; for example, Rüdigkheim und Reuschlein " haben im Junio 2
Wägen mit Kupfer beladen zwo Meil von Frankfurt angenommen und die Fuhr-
leut ungescheut benöthiget, dass sie das Kupfer in das Schloss Rücking, dem von
Rüdigkheim zugehörig, führen müssen."—" Rüdigkheim and Reuschlin did in
June take, two miles from Frankfurt, two waggons loaded with copper, and in
the most shameless manner constrained the drivers to convey the copper to the
castle Rücking, which belonged to Rüdigkheim."   Rüdigkheim wrote to the
burgher of Nürnberg, to whom the copper belonged, that if he wished to have it
back, he might come and buy it of him.   They were exasperated because the
citizens of Nürnberg had complained to the emperor.

[2] Fürstenberg writes from Wertheim on St. Peter's and Paul's day, 1522 :
" also hab ich meyn gnedigen Herrn gebeten, uns gen Wirtzburg zu verhelfen :
ist er willig, Gott helf uns furter."—" I have then besought my gracious Lord to
assist us in our journey to Würzburg : if he be willing, God help us further."

[3] Balthazar Schlör's letter to Sickingen, without date, but immediately before
the outbreak of hostilities, in Günther's Codex Diplomaticus Rheno-Mosellanus,
v., p. 202.

accuser, judge and executor of its own sentences ; at the Imperial Chamber, whose proceedings were only directed against the weak, and left the strong to their own guidance ; at the encroachments of the princes, their courts of law, taxes and feudal privileges.   In the spring of 1522 the nobility of the Upper Rhine met at Landau, and resolved that they would only allow their feudal affairs to be judged before feudal judges and vassals, according to old custom ; and their differences with those of other classes, before tribunals composed of impartial judges, of knightly rank ;[1] and that they would come to the assistance of every man to whom this was refused. They elected Franz von Sickingen their leader in this matter.   An address to the imperial towns, written by Hutten and dated 1522,[2] is the manifesto of the opinions entertained by Sickingen and his followers.   Never were the sovereign princes more vehemently accused of violence and injustice ; the towns were invited to accept the friendship and alliance of the nobility, and above all, to destroy the Council of Regency, which Hutten looked upon as the representative of the princely power.

The religious dissensions gave, of course, a strong additional impulse to hostilities undertaken against one of the most powerful of the spiritual princes.   The Ebernburg was, in fact, the first place in which the evangelical service was regularly celebrated in its new form.   Sickingen's followers went further than the school of Wittenberg.   They considered the administration of the Lord's Supper in both kinds not alone lawful, but absolutely necessary.   John Œcolampadius was the first who condemned as pernicious, the spiritual satisfaction which the people felt at listening every day to the unintelligible muttering of the mass, being present at the ceremony of benediction, and commending themselves to God without much expenditure of time or attention ; and he accordingly read the mass only on Sundays, omitting the elevation of the host, and using none but the German language.[3]   There is a letter extant written by Sickingen himself, in which he inveighs against the use of pictures in churches, and pronounces them better fitted for the decoration of stately halls ; he also declaims against the invocation of saints.   The marriage of Johann Schwebel, one of his preachers, was arranged by him.   One of his friends was Hartmuth von Kronenberg, who may be considered as the earliest

---

[1] ". . . wo der Kleger den Antwurter erfordert vor sein des Antwurters Genoss, oder ungefehrlich dem etwas gemess oder darüber, unparteilichs Rechten oder Austrags, vor die, so inlendisch der Sachen gesessen oder gelegen seyn."— "where the plaintiff cites the defendant before a tribunal composed of his own and the defendant's peers (or nearly so), and having jurisdiction over affairs occurring in the country."

[2] "Beklagunge der Freistette deutscher nation."—"Complaints of the free cities of the German nation."—The date is ascertained by these words :—

> " Der (Kaiser) zeucht nun von unst wider Mher ;
>   Sie wollen nit, dass er widerkheer."

> " The emperor now leaves us again ;
>   They wish he may not come back."

These ideas prevailed in the following year also, as we learn from a writing by Kettenbach : " Practica practicirt," &c. (*Panzer*, ii. 190), wherein the cities are exhorted not to involve themselves in the disputes between the nobles and the princes.

[3] Œcolampadii Epistola ad Hedionem in Gerdesius Historia Evangelii, tom. i., Monumenta, p. 166.

specimen of a pious and earnest Lutheran in the style of more modern times.[1]

The connexion with these mighty elements gave unwonted importance to Sickingen's enterprises. The majority of the whole knighthood of the empire was on his side, and exerted itself in his favour ; he also called on Luther, to whom he had formerly offered protection, for his support. And assuredly it would have been no mean alliance, had the monk, whom the nation honoured as a prophet, taken up his abode with the brave and puissant knight, and lent to the formidable bands of the Ebernburg the powerful aid of his word. But Luther had the great good sense to avoid all political connections, to attempt no violence, and to trust solely and entirely to the might of his doctrines. Sickingen received nothing from Saxony but dissuasions. Nevertheless, his manifesto to the inhabitants of Treves shows how much he reckoned on the prevailing national inclinations ; for he promises that " he will deliver them from the heavy antichristian yoke of the priesthood and lead them to evangelical freedom."[2] The ideas and sentiments of a warlike noble, who feels himself a match even for a powerful prince ; of the head of the whole order of knighthood ; and of a champion of the new religious opinions, were all blended in his mind. It is a significant fact that Hutten, in one of his dialogues, puts into the mouth of Sickingen an ardent panegyric on Ziska, the invincible hero who cleared his country of monks and idle priests, employed their property for the general good, and put a stop to the depredations of Rome.[3]

On the 27th of August, 1522, Sickingen declared war against the archbishop, chiefly for those things " wherein he had acted against God and the emperor's majesty." Secretly assisted, rather than hindered, by the Elector of Mainz, he arrived before Treves on the 7th of September, having taken St. Wendel. He crossed the Marsberg with 1,500 horse, 5,000 foot, and a considerable body of artillery ;[4] and we have reason to believe that he expected to be joined at this point by his friends, Rennenberg, who was recruiting for him in Cleves and Julich ; the bastard of Sombreff, who was doing the same in the archbishopric of Cologne ; and Hanz Voss, who was arming in the territory of Limburg ; Nickel Minkwitz, too, was to join him with 1,500 men out of Brunswick. In Sickingen's camp, it was rumoured that he would soon be elector ; nay, perhaps something even greater still. The eyes of the whole empire were turned upon his movements ; the delegate of Duke George of Saxony wrote to his master that nothing so dangerous to the princes of the empire had been attempted for centuries.[5] Others affirmed that affairs were in such a state, that before long it would be impossible to know who was king or emperor, prince or lord.

The turbulent and anarchical power of the knights thus once more threatened the peace and security of the whole empire. It is not easy to imagine what would have been the result had they been successful.

---

[1] Letters from Kronenberg to the four mendicant orders, 25th June, 1522, and to the inhabitants of Kronenberg ; Münch's Sickingen, ii., pp. 145 and 153.

[2] Extracts from the manifestoes in Meiner's Leben Huttens, p. 317.

[3] Monitor Secundus Opp., iv., p. 144.

[4] This number, smaller than that which is usually given, is taken from the Flersheimer Chronik, in Münch's Sickingen, iii., p. 215.

[5] Letter in the Royal Saxon Archives.

It is scarcely credible that a tolerably well organised government could have been formed out of the several knightships which were now become absolute and independent sovereignties ; or that the wild and arbitrary courses of men who were accustomed to look to their swords for right and security, could easily have been restrained by the sermons of the reformers : it is at least certain that Œcolampadius found a hard and un-grateful soil on Sickingen's mountain fortress.   Moreover, the elements of which this body were composed were of the most heterogeneous natures : the knighthood—one of the most peculiar products of the middle ages— arose out of, and existed in, the disorganisation of the powers of the state : whereas the declared tendency of the new religious system was to renovate and confirm those powers.   The position of Sickingen himself was anom-alous : the forces which he led were by no means of a chivalrous kind ; he was at the head of a hired army which could only be held together by money, and furnished with the apparatus for a kind of warfare essentially opposed to all knightly modes of combat.   Strange spectacle !—the forces which decided the fate of the world in two different ages were here in contact, and it was imagined that they could be brought to unite and co-operate !   We, in our days, can see how impossible was such a union ; for it is only by keeping pace, sincerely and energetically, with the progress of society, that any thing permanent can be effected.   Even at that time, however, it was perceived, that if the power of the princes were overthrown, and the constitution of the empire (which was as yet by no means firmly established) broken up, nothing was to be expected but an exclusive, violent, and at the same time self-conflicting rule of the nobles.

The question then was, who should undertake the defence of public order, thus fearfully menaced.

The Council of Regency did all that was in its power.   Remonstrances were sent to Sickingen, and mandates to all the neighbouring princes, enjoining them to resist his attempts.   On Sickingen, the warnings from the Regency made little impression : he replied, that he himself intended to introduce a new order of things into the empire.[1]   He utterly refused to submit to a decision of the Imperial Chamber, and said that he had a court of justice of his own, composed of soldiers who argued with muskets and carronades.   It is very probable that his whole army did not think as he did ; at any rate, the Council of Regency asserted that Franz's following and power were greatly diminished in consequence of their efforts.   But a far weightier authority was required to force him to submission, and every-thing depended on the resistance he would find from the olector and his allies.

Richard von Greiffenklau, Archbishop of Treves, had made the best

[1] Planitz to the Elector Frederick, 13th Sept. : " Sickingen habe gesagt, er wolle sich eines Thuns unterstehn, dessen sich kein römischer Kaiser unterstanden. 28th Sept. er habe den Boten des Regiments gesagt : er wisst vorwar, sein Herr der Kaiser werde nicht zürnen, ob er den Pfaffen ein wenig strafet und ihm die Kronen eintränkt, die er genommen hätte."—" Sickingen had said that he would dare to do a deed which no Roman emperor had yet dared.   28th Sept. he said to the messenger of the Regency, he knew for certain that his lord the emperor would not be angry because he punished the priest a little, and paid him off for the crowns he had taken."   People really began to believe that the emperor might have some understanding with him.   The emperor afterwards said, Franz had not served him well enough to induce him to connive at matters of this sort.

possible preparations.   He had burned down the convent of St. Maximin, on which the enemy reckoned for stores, bringing in his own hand the first torch that fired it : in the town his presence kept down the disturbances which certainly had begun.   The clergy mounted guard round the cathedral, the citizens in the market-place, the mercenaries on the walls and in the towers ; and the conduct of the war was entrusted to the native nobles who had not deserted the cause of the see.

While Sickingen, who had calculated on making a *coup-de-main*, now met with an unexpected and determined resistance, it so happened that all his friends and allies, whose arrival was necessary to the completion of his force, were either detained or beaten.   The Duke of Cleves and the Elector of Cologne ordered all the horsemen who had been recruited in their territories, to stay at home, under pain of forfeiture of their fiefs, and even of their lives.   The young Landgrave of Hessen succeeded in defeating Minkwitz's troops as they were marching from Brunswick ; taking their leader, with all his papers, prisoner, and finally inducing the soldiers to enter his own service.[1]   All these reverses deterred the Lüneburg and Westphalian troops from taking the field at all.

On the other side, the Elector Palatine, Sickingen's former patron, as well as his old and bitter enemy the Landgrave of Hessen, took arms and hastened to the assistance of their neighbour and ally, the Elector of Treves.

Sickingen, deprived of the support he had expected, and encamped before a bravely-defended town, in an open country, among a people exasperated by his devastations, did not dare to await the conjunction of forces so superior to his own ; besides this, he himself did not evince that energy and those resources of talent and bravery, without which no one can venture with impunity on such hazardous enterprises.   On the 14th of September he was compelled to abandon Treves.[2]

That one week sufficed to give a turn to the whole destiny of Germany.

The three sovereigns who represented the threatened princely power, were thus triumphant over the rebellious knights and their leaders.   They were not content with clearing the archbishopric of its enemies ; and though, strange to say, they did not pursue Sickingen, they immediately attacked his allies.

The Elector of Mainz, who was accused of allowing a detachment of Sickingen's horse to pass the Rhine unmolested, was forced to buy his peace at the cost of 25,000 gulden.[3]

Hartmuth von Kronenberg, whom the landgrave wanted above all to punish for the share he had taken in Sickingen's foray on Darmstadt, was beleaguered in his castle near Frankfurt.   The landgrave would not hear of pardon or conditions ; he helped to point the cannon with his own hand.   The knight escaped but just in time, for his fortress was forced to surrender on the 16th of October.   The three princes received in person

---

[1] Letter from Landgrave Philip to the Elector of Treves, 5th Sept., 1522, in Rommel's Geschichte von Hessen, vol. v., p. 858.

[2] These events at Treves are described by Latomus and Browerus, Annal. Trev., ii. 340, who has also quoted Latomus Gesta Trevirorum in Hontheim's Prodromus, p. 858, Chronicon S. Maximini, ibid., p. 1035.

[3] The delegate of Duke George says that this is one of the reasons : " Die andern stecken in der Feder."—" The others stick in the pen."

the oaths of allegiance from the inhabitants, and the town was for a long time treated as Hessian.[1]

They next marched against Frowen von Hutten, " because he had taken part in the rebellion, and received proclaimed outlaws in his house : " his castle of Saalmünster was taken.

The same fate was shared by Philip Waiss of Haussen in the Mark of Fulda, and by Rudeken in Rukingen ; others endeavoured to save themselves by negotiation.

A similar storm threatened Sickingen's allies in distant parts of the country. The Franconian nobles had not, it is true, directly assisted him, but they had encouraged him in his project, and had generally adhered to his faction : the Swabian League, on the contrary, had made common cause with the princes, especially with the Elector Palatine, and now summoned the Franconian knights before its tribunal, to stand their trial for certain breaches of the Public Peace. The knights did not consider themselves bound to obey this citation, and, accordingly, met at Schweinfurt to protest against it : they were still determined to defend themselves. The vassals of the Bishop of Würzburg, who had been the last to join the League, were so exasperated at his tardiness, that, in the beginning of the year 1523, they deprived him of all his offices. This threw all Swabia and Franconia into confusion. From the very superior strength of the League, the result of the struggle was easily foreseen, unless the Council of Regency had power to prevent it.

Events indeed now acquired a totally different character and importance, from their effect on this supreme administrative body of the empire. Its authority was formerly resisted and contemned by Sickingen and his friends, for which, on the accusation of the procurator of Treves, Sickingen had been outlawed on the 8th of October, contrary to the laws of the empire, without summons or trial. Now, however, his enemies placed themselves in an attitude of equal defiance, and of equal peril to the Council of Regency : instead of pursuing the outlaw himself, they attacked his supposed allies, frequently without proof of their guilt, and took their fortified dwellings. The Swabian League, which already declared that it had only acquiesced in the creation of the Council of Regency on the supposition of its union, now openly usurped part of the functions of the Imperial Chamber by the citations before its own tribunal to which we have alluded ; and it did not deign even to return an answer to an admonition, not to molest people about the Public Peace.

Men's pretensions naturally rise with their power. As the attempts of Sickingen, and the insubordinate spirit of the Franconian nobility had not been put down by the Council of Regency, but by the superior force and the arms of their neighbours, it was natural that the latter should now continue the struggle with a view to their own interests, without much regard to the supreme authority of the empire.[2]

Hence it happened that the Council of Regency soon took under its protection the very men it had but just before treated as its enemies. Frowen von Hutten, after the opinions of the most considerable members of the Imperial Chamber had been heard, obtained without much trouble

[1] Tendel : " Beschreibung der Belagerung von Kronenberg."—Munich, iii., p. 28.
[2] See the letter from the Elector of Treves, 2d Nov., 1522, in Münich, iii. 33.

a mandate wherein the princes were required to restore all his castles to him ; and shortly after a formal judgment was given in his favour. At the same time, the Council of Regency pressed the princes to release the Elector of Mainz from the conditions so arbitrarily imposed on him.[1] These princes had wished for the aid of the empire to put down the outlawed Sickingen ; but this they found it impossible to obtain, either from the Regency or from the Estates assembled in the beginning of the year 1523 ; if the sentence of outlawry had not already been pronounced, we may safely assume that it would not have been pronounced at all.[2] Some members of the Swabian League proposed that all meetings and associations among the order of knights should be forbidden, but to this the Regency could not now be brought to consent ; on the contrary, it proclaimed its intention of protecting all the knights, except those who had committed any offence against the Public Peace.

It appears to me that the knights as a body now first became of real importance to the organisation and progress of the empire. Their wild project of founding an independent power was at an end. The Council of Regency was their sole support, and they found themselves under the necessity of making common cause with it. The union of these two bodies, essentially distinct, was rendered more strict by the circumstance that the knights and the Regency had both embraced the evangelical doctrines. For the same reason, the Elector of Saxony, who was the main prop of the Regency, entered into a kind of alliance with the knights. In the second quarter of the year 1523, when the duty of personal attendance at the Council of Regency fell upon the Elector of Mainz, his place was filled by his cousin, the grand master, Albert of Prussia, whose sole purpose was to maintain the dominion of his order, *i.e.*, the Teutonic knights, and especially those of Swabia and Franconia, in their own country, and to set the whole powers of the empire in motion to that effect.

Little as it had been to be desired a year ago, that Sickingen should conquer Treves, it was of great importance that he should be able to defend himself against the attacks which were preparing against him in the spring of 1523.

Thus, by a strange turn of fate, the safety of the knight who had so often disturbed the Public Peace, and committed so many deeds of violence, became now, after he was outlawed, inextricably bound up with the interests of order in the empire.

Nor did he by any means give up his cause : he expected to receive assistance from Lower Germany, and from the Upper Rhine ; to be joined by the Bohemian and Franconian knights, and to be supported by the Lutherans. From his fortress of Landstuhl, where he was then living, he one day descried horsemen among the distant underwood ; he flattered himself that they were Lutherans who were coming to see what he was about, but they came no nearer, and tied their horses to the bushes.[3] What

---

[1] Planitz, 4th Feb., 1523, says, they should release him from his obligations, and give Sickingen an amicable hearing.

[2] Planitz thought on the 24th Nov. that sentence of outlawry would not be pronounced against Sickingen, " man hätte ihn denn citiert ; aber geschehn ist geschehn "—" without citing him to appear ; but what is done is done."

[3] Hubert Th. Leodius, Acta et Gesta Francisci de Sickingen in Freher Script. Rer. Germ., iii., p. 305.

he saw was the advanced guard of the enemy who were approaching to besiege him.

Meanwhile he had no apprehension. He had just repaired his fortress ; and had no doubt that he would be able to stand a siege of three months at least, in which time his allies would come up and relieve him.

But the·event proved that he had not rightly calculated the improvement that had taken place in the engines of war during the preceding century. He had no other means of defence than those used by the knights of old : it remained to be seen whether the lofty situation, the vaulted towers—solid as the rocks they stood on—and the massive walls, could afford protection against artillery. It was soon evident that the old defences were far too weak for the modern arts of war. On the 30th of April, 1523, the princes began to bombard the castle with carronades and culverins, well supplied with ammunition and well served. The young landgrave, who appeared in the dress of a landsknecht, showed courage and skill :[1] the great tower, which commanded and threatened their camp, fell the same day : the newness of its walls made them less able to withstand the shock of the cannon-balls. Sickingen seeing this unexpected misfortune, went to a loophole, and leaning on a battering engine, sought to get a view of the state of things, and of what was to be done. A culverin happened at the moment to be pointed in that direction with but too sure an aim ; the implements of defence were scattered in all directions, and Sickingen himself was hurled against a sharp beam and mortally wounded in the side.

The whole fortress was a ruin: in the only vault which remained standing, lay the lord of the castle, bereft of all hope. No help appeared in sight. " Where now," said Sickingen, " are those gentlemen, my friends, who promised me so much ? Where is Fürstenberg ? where are the Swiss and the Strasburgers ?" He was at last forced to capitulate.[2]

The princes having refused to allow him liberty to evacuate the castle, as, according to custom, he proposed, he said, " I will not be their prisoner long." He had scarcely strength enough left to sign the conditions, and lay dying when the princes entered the donjon.

The Elector of Treves said, " What charge had you to bring against me, Franz, that you attacked me and my poor subjects in my see ?" " And what against me," said the landgrave, " that you invaded my land in my nonage ?" Sickingen replied, " I have now to render an account to a greater sovereign."

His chaplain Nicolas asked him whether he wished to confess, but he answered, " I have already confessed to God in my heart."

The chaplain addressed to him some last words of consolation, and held up the host ; the princes bared their heads and knelt down : at that moment Sickingen expired, and the princes said a paternoster for his soul.[3]

---

[1] Lettera da Ispruch a dì 12 Mazo, 1523, al Sr Mch. di Mantoa. " Il Landgrafio si è portato magnanimamente, essendo sempre stato de li primi, in zuppone con le calze tagliate et in corsaletto da Lanzichenech, et è giovane di 18 anni."— Sanuto's *Cron. Ven.*, vol. xxxiv.

[2] Account of what occurred in the wars of Franz Sickingen ; Spalatin, Sammlung zu Sächs. Gesch., v., p. 148.

[3] The Flersheimer Chronik contains the most authentic account. Münch, iii. 222.

Sickingen's memory will live for ever ; not on account of any great achievements productive of lasting results, nor even on account of his extraordinary bravery, or of any eminent moral qualities he evinced, but for the novelty and importance of the position to which he gradually attained. The first step in his rise was his connexion with the Elector Palatine, who employed him against his enemies, opened a career to him, and afforded him support and assistance both publicly and in secret. Thus in a short time, from an inconsiderable knight, possessor only of two or three mountain castles, he became a powerful Condottiere who could bring a small army into the field at his own charges. The more considerable he became, the more he felt tempted to pursue his own line of policy, and justified in doing so. The Würtemberg war was the first occasion on which he separated himself from the elector, who did not cordially approve that enterprise. He did not, however, on that account join the Swabian League ; on the contrary, he soon entered into the closest alliance with the Franconian knights, with whom that body was at enmity. This it was that rendered his position so imposing. We have seen how a few years before, Würtemberg, the Palatinate, and Würzburg opposed the Swabian League with the aid of the knights. Now, however, the princes had been forced to join the League, and Würtemberg had been subdued ; so that Sickingen and the knights maintained the opposition single-handed. Visions of reviving the ancient independence of the nobility ; of freeing themselves from the territorial jurisdiction of the temporal and spiritual princes, and of opening the way for the spread of the new religious convictions, floated before their minds. Never was there a more singular combination : in the midst of the deeds of violence that were committed, there was a lively and ready apprehension of great ideas : it is this strange union which characterises the nobility of that time. Meanwhile they had neither the intellectual power nor the political influence necessary to carry out projects of such a nature. When Sickingen at last decidedly attacked the princely authority, mightier powers took the field against him ; the Palatinate not only abandoned him, but combined with his enemies for his destruction.[1] He then discovered that he was not so strong as he believed himself to be, that he did not owe his elevation to his own powers alone, and that those which had helped to raise, were now turned against him. In this conflict he perished.

The taking of Landstuhl was a victory of the order of princes (*Fürstenthum*) over that of knights (*Ritterthum*) ; of the cannon over the stronghold, and in so far, of the new order of things over the old ; it fortified the newly-arisen independent powers of the empire.

All the castles belonging to Sickingen and his friends now fell into the hands of the princes. They were twenty-seven in all, including those taken in the course of the autumn. Those on the right bank of the Rhine fell to the share of the landgrave, those on the left, were divided between

---

[1] Contemporaries saw it in this light, as is shown by the dialogue between the Fox and the Wolf : " Wolf : Wie mainstu hat der Pfalzgraff gethon, wir wolten gut feiste Bölz erlangt han ? Fuchs : es ist bei Got war, derselb hat uns allein den Schaden thon des wir uns nit versehen."—" The Wolf : How thinkest thou, has the elector palatine done—should we have received good large cross-bow bolts ? The Fox : It is true, by God ; he alone has done us the mischief against which we had not guarded."

the elector palatine and the archbishop.   In the Ebernburg, the only castle that defended itself for any time, rich booty was taken,—splendid jewels and plate, both for worldly and religious purposes ; but above all, thirty-six pieces of artillery, the finest of which—the Nightingale, cast by Master Stephen of Frankfurt—measured thirteen feet and a half, weighed seventy hundred weight, and was decorated with the figures of the knight and his lady, their respective ancestors, and the saint for whom they had formerly had a peculiar devotion—St. Francis.[1]   This was part of the landgrave's share.   The princes bound themselves to aid each other to keep what they had won in common, after which, on the 6th of June, they separated.

At the same moment the Swabian League held a meeting at Nördlingen, to which all the Franconian knights accused of a breach of the Public Peace were summoned for trial.   Some of them succeeded in clearing themselves from suspicion ; others appeared, but failing to prove their innocence, they were not admitted to their oath.   Many altogether disdained to present themselves before the councillors of the league.[2]   Against the two last classes, an army of 1,500 horse and 15,000 foot assembled on the 15th June, at Dünkelspiel, under the command of George Truchsess : the cities of Augsburg, Ulm, and Nürnberg provided the artillery.[3]   Such an army as this was far too powerful to be resisted by the Franconian nobles. Bocksberg, near Mergentheim, was considered the strongest castle in Franconia, and upon it, on the advice of the Nürnbergers, the march was first directed.   The Rosenbergs, to whom it belonged, had originally meant to defend themselves, and had hired a troop of Landsknechts and musketeers to serve their guns ; but when they saw such an overpowering force, they gave up all idea of defence, and surrendered their castle with its stores. This example put an end to all resistance.   The castle of Absberg was burnt, and nothing left standing but the bare walls.   In the Krügelstein there stood a tower, the walls of which were eight feet thick, even at the top ; this was blown up with gunpowder.   Waldstein, in the midst of its wilderness, whither many a prisoner had been dragged, was blown up and destroyed by Wolf von Freiberg, the captain of the city of Augsburg : twenty-six castles are enumerated, all of which were seized, and most destroyed.   Some of these were Bohemian fiefs ; and at first the Bohemians had made a show of resistance in the neighbourhood of the mountains ; but the League ordered its commander to act up to his instructions, without regard to the Bohemians, who accordingly retreated, leaving him to fulfil his terrible commission.

The independent knights were utterly crushed.   Just as they had caught the inspiration of religion, and had hoped by its influence to open a new career for themselves, their power was broken for ever.   We must not fail to observe a fact intimately connected with this event.   The man who first brought the warlike spirit of knighthood into contact with the religious agitations of the times, Ulrich von Hutten, was involved in the common

---

[1] Report in Spalatin, p. 151.

[2] Letter from Nördlingen in the Dresden Archives, beginning of June, 1523, " der Bund geht teglich zwir in Rath."—" The league meets in council every day." Chiefly from Müllner's Annalen, which contains a journal of the whole expedition.

[3] Nürnberg gave 2 cannon, 2 carronades, 2 nightingales, 2 culverins, 6 rabinets, 6 mortars, 60 pole-axes.

catastrophe. He had given to Sickingen's enterprises the incalculable aid
of a zealous counsellor and encouraging friend : he was, therefore, naturally
struck with consternation at his fall.   He dared not endanger the safety
of his relations by his presence ; and in Upper Germany he was equally
obnoxious to the vengeance of the spiritual, and of the victorious temporal
authorities ; he took refuge in Switzerland, as others had done in Saxony.
There he fell again into the same bitter and desponding state of mind
which he had once laboured under in his youth.   Nor, even here, did he
always find a welcome ; he wandered from place to place, under the unhappy necessity of asking money and assistance of his literary friends,
many of whom shunned him as dangerous.   Erasmus, who carefully kept
up his connexions among the great, was frightened at the idea of receiving
a visit from him, and avoided and repulsed him.   In addition to this, his old
disease broke out again in a dreadful manner.   Yet the veteran combatant
did not lose his courage ; once more he poured forth all the vehemence
of his rhetoric against Erasmus, whom he looked upon as an apostate.
But he had now no longer strength to bear such violent emotions and exertions, and before he could receive the answer of Erasmus, disease put an
end to his life :—he died at Ufnau, on the lake of Zürich, where he had gone
at Zwingli's advice to consult a priest skilled in the healing art.[1]

It was fortunate for Luther that he had made no closer alliance with the
knights ; as both he and the doctrine he preached would have been involved in their evil destiny.

If we now return to the point whence we started, we shall clearly perceive, that the whole turn of affairs was unpropitious, and even dangerous,
to the Council of Regency.   It would indeed have been unable to do any
thing for Şickingen, having tied its own hands by declaring him an outlaw ;
it would however gladly have afforded protection to the knightly order ;
but what resistance could it possibly make to two such powerful armies as
those of the League and of the princes ?   Moreover these two powers,
emboldened by conquests, assumed an attitude of still greater defiance,
and even hostility.   The princes declared the judgment in favour of
Frowen von Hutten invalid and illegal,[2] and rejected the proceedings of the
Regency in that and all other cases.

To this dangerous hostility another no less formidable was soon added.

THE CITIES AND THE IMPERIAL COURT.

Under the circumstances we have been describing, the establishment of
the proposed import duties, by which the power of the Council of Regency
must have been materially increased, could not have failed to produce
important results.   There ought to have been no hesitation on the subject ;
the States had resolved on it ; the emperor had given his consent beforehand.   A messenger from the lieutenant of the Empire had already carried
the acts and the Recess of the diet to Spain.

---

[1] Zwinglius to Wolfhardt, 11th Oct., " libros nullos habuit, supellectilem
nullam præter calamum."—*Epp.*, p. 313.
[2] Planitz, 22d July.   He thinks that, under such circumstances, the Council
of Regency could not last long : " Denn der dreier Fürsten und des Bunds Vor-
nehmen will sich mit unsern gethanen Pflichten gar nicht leiden."—" The intentions of the three princes and of the league will not square with our duties."

But we have already remarked how much the cities thought themselves injured and endangered by such an interference with commerce : they were determined not to submit to it without resistance.

They had also many other grievances to allege.

In the year 1521, the decree concerning the levies for the expedition to Rome had been passed without summoning the cities, according to ancient usage, to the deliberation. The cities immediately complained, whereupon an explanation was given which satisfied them for the moment.

Since then, however, the attempts made to meet the exigencies of the empire by taxes which would have fallen most heavily on the cities ; their determined resistance ; the attacks on the monopolies on the one side, and the obstinate maintenance of them on the other, had been continually augmenting the ill-will between the cities and the higher classes ; and at the diet of 1522-3 it openly burst forth.

A general meeting of the States was announced for the 11th of December, 1522, in order to hear and discuss the proposals to be made by the Council of Regency and the committee, for succours to be granted to the Hungarians. It had formerly been customary for the Council of Regency, after submitting a proposition, to retire and leave the three colleges to deliberate thereupon. On this occasion, however, the Regency did not retire : the electors and princes assented to its proposal without separating, and it was then laid before the cities. The cities, which were peculiarly interested in questions of this kind, and always rather hard to satisfy, asked time for consideration—only till the afternoon. Hereupon they received an answer which they little expected : they were told, that " the usage in the empire was, that when a thing was determined on by the electors, princes and other Estates, the cities should be content to abide by it." The citizens, on their side, contended, that if they were to share weal and woe with the other States they ought also to have a voice in the deliberations ; in short, that those who took their purses must be fain to take their counsel. The subsidies in money were what they particularly objected to ; like the other States, they would only furnish men. But no attention was paid by the assembly to a resolution they drew up to this effect. A mandate was issued, requiring them to furnish contributions which they had never voted : they asked fresh time for deliberation, but were again told that it was not the practice : they were preparing to reply when it struck eleven, and the sitting was dissolved.[1]

The cities were the more confounded at this proceeding, on being told that it was by special favour that two of their deputies were received into the committee, whereas the counts had only one : they thought this betrayed an intention of excluding them from the committees altogether. In the year 1487, they had given up the opposition which, as a body, they had long maintained, because the Elector Berthold of Mainz had, as we saw, obtained for them a practical share in the deliberations ; and we know how powerfully this was sometimes exercised : they now supposed that the intention was to strip them of all their rights, at the same time that the fulfilment of their obligations was strictly enforced.

As measures which threatened to be extremely injurious to their trade and manufactures were now resolved on with reference to monopolies and

[1] Letter from Holzhausen to Frankfort, Dec., 1522. Frankf. Arch., vol. xxxvi., particularly f. 110, Die Supplik der Städte.

import duties, and as a fresh petition, in which all their grievances, past and present, were set forth, had proved as ineffectual as the preceding ones, they determined to resist with all their might.

They steadily withheld their assent to the decisions of the diet, and obstinately refused to grant a loan which they were called upon to advance, and which was to be repaid out of the proceeds of the tax for the Turkish war. Hereupon the princes took care to let them feel their displeasure. " The imperial towns," writes the deputy from Frankfurt,[1] " are departing under heavy disgrace : time alone can show what will be the result ; but my journey home is a sad one."

It was fortunate for the cities that the decisions of the States did not immediately acquire the force of law, but had first to be sent to Spain to receive the emperor's ratification. Their only hope lay in this. In March, 1523, the cities assembled in Spire, and resolved to send an embassy of their own to Spain, to represent to the emperor the injury they apprehended from the proposed duties, as well as their other grievances.

The report of this mission is fortunately still extant, and we will pause over it for a moment, as it affords us a curious specimen of the manner in which the affairs of Germany were conducted at the imperial court in Spain.

The journey was extremely long and fatiguing. On the 15th of June, the delegates met at Lyons, and it was not till the 6th of August that they reached Valladolid : the chief cause of delay was the oppressive heat, which even caused some of the party to fall sick.

They began by visiting Markgrave Johann of Brandenburg, the high chancellor, and above all the councillors to whom the affairs of Germany were referred ; Herr von Rösch, Hannart, Provost Märklin of Waldkirchen, and Maximilian von Zevenberghen.

Hereupon, on the 9th of August, the emperor gave them a formal audience in the presence of a brilliant assembly of grandees, bishops, and ambassadors : they addressed him in Latin, and were answered in the same language by the chancellor, in the emperor's name.

A commission was then appointed to discuss affairs with them, consisting only of the four German councillors we have named above : the proceedings commenced on the 11th of August.

The delegates had drawn up a statement of their grievances under six heads ;—administration of justice, tolls, subsidies, Public Peace, monopolies, and other things of less importance. These they laid before the commissioners in German and Latin, and then went through them together, which gave them an opportunity of expressing their wishes orally.

The councillors at first appeared unfavourably inclined. They thought it unjust that the question of the jurisdictions should not have been brought forward till now, when a young emperor had just ascended the throne : they complained that no class in the empire would do its part, although neither the Council of Regency nor the courts of justice could be maintained without supplies from the several Estates : they exhorted the cities to submit for a short time longer, and not to refuse their share of the contributions voted by the diet on the part of the whole empire, in aid of the Hungarians. A draft of a ratification of the decree of the diet had actually

[1] Holzhausen, 25th, 26th, 29th Jan., 1523. Vol. xxxvii. of the Frankf. Archives is here my chief authority.

been prepared at the instigation of another imperial councillor, Doctor Lamparter. But the delegates were not so easily put off : they declared that the cities were ready to contribute their share ; for example, to pay two members of the Imperial Chamber, and even to pay the contributions, at the rate determined at the diet of Constance ; but that they had no intention of submitting to the unjust demands attempted to be enforced against them. They supported their declarations with a few very acute and stringent remarks. " Who can foretell," said they, " what will become of the revenues raised from these import duties ? It is reported that a scheme has already been proposed by the princes for sharing the proceeds amongst themselves ; and even if this be not true, there is a project of electing a king of the Romans, who would be able to maintain his power out of the revenue thus raised." In short, they made it appear that the duty would be dangerous to the emperor himself ; remarking, at the same time, that the Council of Regency was not composed in the manner most favourable to the interests of the emperor. They also promised the councillors, personally, " to make a grateful return to them for their trouble."

The cities had thus hit upon the means by which any thing was to be accomplished at the imperial court.

At the next meeting the Provost of Waldkirchen gave them to understand, that the emperor, finding how unpopular it was, was not inclined to impose the duty in question ; neither was it his intention to continue the Council of Regency ; but he must then ask, what the cities were prepared to do for his imperial majesty, if he took the government into his own hands ? The delegates replied, that if the emperor granted their petition, and then made any reasonable suggestion to them, they would show themselves grateful and obedient subjects. Waldkirchen reminded them that it appeared from the old registers, that the last emperors on their accession had received a gift of honour from the cities ; and asked, why this had been omitted for the first time with the young emperor, who, he said, placed his whole confidence in the cities, and, were it not for the wars, would take a straightforward and royal course with regard to them.

Another matter next fell under discussion. The pope's nuncio had complained that in Augsburg, Strasburg, and Nürnberg, Luther's doctrines were received, and his works printed. The delegates, on being called to account for this, denied the fact. They declared that not a syllable of Luther's writings had been printed in their towns for several years : nay more, that foreign itinerant vendors of his books had been punished ; and that, however much the common people might thirst after the Gospel and reject human doctrines, it was not from the towns that Luther found protection : it was well known who his defenders were ; the cities, for their part, were resolved, hereafter as heretofore, to remain Christian members of the Christian church.

Hereupon the two parties came to an agreement on the most important points. Another conference between the whole commission and the delegates was held on the 19th of August, and attended also by the Count of Nassau. The doors having been carefully closed, the delegates were informed, that the emperor intended to take the government into his own hands, to appoint a valiant lieutenant, and a noble and dignified Imperial Chamber, and not to allow the imposition of the import duties. The amount of the sum to be offered to him was left to the discretion of the delegates ; but they promised to come to an agreement on the subject with Hannart, who was to go to Germany as the imperial commissioner.

The delegates were also to treat concerning the monopolies ; not exactly on the part of the cities as a body, but in the name of the great mercantile companies. The omnipotence of money and its possessors soon helped them to the attainment of their object. It was settled that the Council of Regency was to be directed to pass no resolution with regard to the monopolies, without again asking the consent of his imperial majesty.[1]

Their commission being thus satisfactorily executed, the delegates quitted Spain. At Lyons they had an audience of Francis I., who vented upon them his anger against the emperor. In December they reached Nürnberg, where a fresh diet had just assembled.

The final result then was, that the imperial court had entered into a combination with the cities, against the existing form of government in the empire, and especially against the Council of Regency.

And, indeed, it was only natural that the imperial councillors, who had always been in competition with this administrative body, should take advantage of any internal dispute to rid themselves of it.

Another and a still stronger motive existed. The idea had really arisen in Germany, as the towns had hinted, of electing a king of the Romans. Ferdinand of Austria, the emperor's own brother, was the man pointed out by the public voice. It was believed, as far as I can discover,[2] that he would govern in concert with the Council of Regency, according to the forms of the constitution which had just been established ; and it is manifest that this could only have attained its completion, had Germany possessed a sovereign of limited power, and dependent on constitutional forms. No wonder that the mere suggestion should be very ill received in Spain ; in fact, it almost implied an abdication on the part of the emperor.

Moreover, Ferdinand was very unpopular there. He was constantly making fresh demands, while frequent complaints were preferred against him ; besides the Spaniards believed his most confidential adviser, Salamanca, to be equally ambitious and selfish. When Hannart went to Germany, he was commissioned, if possible, to effect Salamanca's dismissal, and to counteract all his ambitious schemes.

DIET OF 1524.

If in a former chapter we have endeavoured to show what weighty interests of church and state were involved in the existence of the Council of Regency, we must now turn our attention to the mighty and determined opposition arrayed against it.

Three warlike and victorious princes ; the Swabian League, which wielded such formidable forces ; wealthy cities ; and finally, though as

[1] " Der gemeynen Frey und Reichs Städt Potschafften Handlung bei Romisch Kayserl. Majestadt zu Valedolid in Castilia."—" The Negotiation of the Embassy of the united, free, and imperial Cities, with his Roman Imperial Majesty at Valladolid in Castile." In the month of August, anno 1523. In the Frankf. Arch., tom. xxxix., fol. 39-56.

[2] I extract from a roll of the Weimar Archives, which contains a number of scattered papers written by the chief councillors of the archduke to Elector Frederick.

yet in secret, the Emperor, whose whole hope of regaining unlimited authority rested on the overthrow of this representative body.

The Council of Regency was not, however, destitute of support. Archduke Ferdinand promised not to consent to its overthrow, and some of his councillors were its decided adherents, as might be expected, from the prospects it held out to him and to them. The Elector of Saxony, to whom it chiefly owed its existence, attended the diet in person in order to defend it. The Elector of Mainz, who had suffered from the oppression of the three princes alluded to, together with the whole house of Brandenburg, were among its champions. The Regency also enjoyed the whole sympathy of the knightly order (whose only hopes were founded upon it), and of the partisans of the religious innovations.

Thus it still stood on firm ground : in spite of all the changes of individual members, the majority once established, remained : those who did not belong to it, like the Chancellor of Treves, Otto Hundt of Hessen, stayed away.[1] The imperial fiscal commenced the proceedings against the great mercantile companies, and a judgment against the three princes was prepared. Several most important questions were laid before the diet, which opened on the 14th of January, 1524, concerning the means of maintaining the government and the administration of justice ; the execution of decrees of the diet, the code of criminal procedure,[2] &c.

It is a calamity for any power to have produced no great results ; and under this disadvantage the Council of Regency laboured. It had been unable to maintain the Public Peace, or to control either Sickingen or his adversaries. The great scheme of customs duties, on which all the resources for carrying on the government depended, had come to nothing. It was now assailed by blow upon blow.

On the 1st of February the attorney of the three princes, Dr. Venningen, appeared before the general assembly of the States, and made a long, bitter, and insulting speech against the proceedings of the Council of Regency.

A mandate from the emperor was produced, by which the proceedings already commenced against the commercial companies were stayed. The court of Spain demanded to have the documents relating to the case laid before it.

Hannart next arrived, and from the first took part with the opponents of the Regency—the Elector of Treves, in whose company he came, and the cities, from whom he had received a present of 500 gulden.[3] At his first interview with the archduke he did not pay him the respect which that prince expected, nor did he attempt to conceal that the emperor wished for the dissolution of the existing form of government.

Such were the circumstances under which the assembly of the states began their deliberations : the debate on the grant necessary to the

[1] Otto von Pack to Duke George of Saxony, the Friday after St. Lucia (Dresden Arch.), thinks that they were driven out. " Darnach wissen E. F. Gn. wer die andern seint, welche alle E. F. Gn. Abwesen wol erdulden können."—" Your princely grace will by this know who the others are, that can all well bear your grace's absence."

[2] Frankfurter Acten, vol. xxxix., in which are these documents, and vol. xl., containing the letters of Holzhausen concerning this diet.

[3] Letter of Ferdinand's in Bucholtz, ii., p. 46.

maintenance of the Council of Regency must, of course, bring the matter to a decision.

The Regency was, after all, the expression of the power of the several states of the empire ; was it then credible that the States would themselves assist in its dissolution ?

We have seen that the Regency obtained a majority in the former diets of the empire ; though after laborious efforts and with precarious results. A host of new antipathies were now added, arising out of the interests of the sovereign princes and the free cities ; of money and of religion. The influence of the great capitalists was enormous even in those times. The Fuggers were instrumental in the election of Charles V. ; and, in all probability, in the publication of the bull of Leo X. against Luther. They brought about the alliance between the court and the discontented towns ; and it was mainly by their influence that the projected system of duties was abandoned ; and now they had the audacity to turn the affair of the monopolies, which had called forth so many decrees of the diet against themselves, into a subject of accusation against the Council of Regency ; alleging that that body had assumed judicial powers which properly belonged to the Imperial Chamber alone.[1] The Bishop of Würzburg accused the Council of Regency of openly favouring the new creed : he said that it had set at liberty two members of his chapter whom he had brought before the ecclesiastical court on the charge of contracting marriage, and that it had given a safe-conduct to a canon whom he had banished for Lutheran opinions. The imperial commissioner was informed that most of the members of the Council of Regency were zealous Lutherans.[2] The majority which had hitherto been in favour of that body was not compact enough to resist such a multitude of hostile influences, and after some debate and vacillation, turned against it. The States did not, indeed, go so far as to propose its total abolition, but resolved not to meet on the 20th of February to consider the means for its maintenance, unless its members were previously changed ; and declared they could by no means consent to its continuance, composed as it then was.

This was, however, decisive. The important point was, the establishment of a vigorous government, chosen out of the body of the States ; but what could be expected for the future, if the present members, who had been really earnest in the performance of their duties, and had actually begun to govern, were to be deprived of office, without any charge worthy of a moment's discussion being brought against them ? Was it likely that their successors would show any courage or independence ?

It was once more rendered evident, that the powerful separate elements, of which the empire was compounded, could never be controlled by one central government.

Frederick the Wise of Saxony felt the whole significance of this decision.

---

[1] Holzhausen, 12th Feb., 1524. It appears from this that only Augsburg offered any resistance to the imperial edicts in the matter of the monopolies. All the other towns were in favour of their abolition. Dr. Rolinger had inserted the article touching monopolies of his own accord in the instruction given to the delegates sent to Spain.

[2] Hannart to the emperor, 14th March :—" Et certes je me suis pour vray averty, la pluspart du régiment sont grands Luthériens : car en beaucoup de choses et provisions qu'ils ont fait, ils eussent bien peu user de plus grande discretion et moderation qu'ils n'ont (usées)."

He now, at the close of his life, saw the idea of a representative government, which had been the object of his whole existence, completely wrecked. He said, that he had never witnessed such a diet :[1] he left it on the 24th of February, and never appeared at one again.

Archduke Ferdinand, it is true, still refused his assent to the decision ; he even used his personal influence to win over the cities to the side of the Council of Regency ; but in the course of a short time, observes the Saxon ambassador, his councillors were no longer of the same opinion : it seemed as if Hannart, instead of destroying Salamanca's power, had gained him over ; at all events, he never delivered the letter in which the emperor desired the Elector of Saxony to assist in getting rid of Salamanca. These causes at length produced their effect on Ferdinand : " after holding out resolutely for nine weeks," writes the Saxon ambassador, on the 1st of March, " he has suddenly fallen away." He consented that not a single member of the old Council of Regency should be admitted into the new.[2]

The Imperial Chamber underwent the same sort of purification. No inquiry was made as to whether the members had been attentive or negligent, capable or incapable ; but merely whether they had supported the nobles against the princes, or aided the fiscal in the prosecution of monopolists. Their conduct as to religious matters was also taken into consideration. Dr. Kreutner, the assessor[3] for the circle of Franconia, was dismissed for having eaten meat on a fast-day, without considering that he had a claim for upwards of 1000 gulden, arrears.

This brings us to the main question,—how far these great changes re-acted on the conduct of spiritual affairs. The cause of the Council of Regency and that of the religious reformation were, as we see at every step, connected, though not indissolubly : the question now was, whether the States, which had abandoned the Regency to its fate, would be equally unfavourable to the new faith.

After the early and unexpected death of Adrian VI., the purer and severer spirit which he had introduced and exemplified, disappeared. Clement VII., who next ascended the papal chair, was, like his predecessors, exclusively bent on maintaining the papal privileges ; and on applying the temporal forces of the states of the church to personal or political ends, without troubling himself seriously about the necessity of reform. He sent to the German diet a man of his own way of thinking,—Lorenzo Campeggio.

Campeggio found Germany, which a few years before he had traversed,

[1] At all events the provost of the cathedral of Vienna excused him with these words, to Campeggi, who asked the cause of his absence. Letter from Wolfstal, 14th March, Weimar Arch. The Italians thought he had gone away because the legate had come. " Assai sdegnato," as the Venetian Ziani expresses himself, Disp. 29 Martio. The same person remarks that Nürnberg had already entirely fallen away from Catholicism : " Di qui è totalmente scancellata la sincera fede."

[2] According to a letter of Wolf von Wolfstal, Ferdinand, even on the 17th of April, said, " Dass Hannart ihn sampt ihm selbst verführt, wie wenn ein Blinder den andern führt."—" That Hannart had deceived him, as well as himself, like as when the blind lead the blind."

[3] Assessor = judge. For the constitution of the Imperial Chamber, which was first organized in 1495, see Cambridge Modern History, vol. i., p. 304.

surrounded with the halo of an unshaken and sacred authority, in a state
of complete apostasy. In Augsburg he was assailed with derision and
mockery when, at his entrance into the town, he raised his hand to give
the customary benediction. After this he was advised by others, and
thought it most prudent himself, to enter Nürnberg without any ceremony
whatever. He did not wear his cardinal's hat, and made no sign of
benediction, or of the cross ; and instead of riding to the church of St.
Sebaldus, where the clergy were assembled to receive him, he rode straight
to his lodging.[1]

His presence, instead of damping the zeal of the reforming preachers,
seemed to inflame it to the utmost. The pope was characterised as antichrist, before the face of his legate. On Palm-Sunday no palms were
strewed ; and in Passion-Week the ceremony of laying down the cross and
raising it again, was omitted : thousands received the sacrament in both
kinds,[2] and not only among the common people ; several members of the
Council of Regency were among the communicants, and even the sister
of the archduke, Queen Isabella of Sweden, partook of the cup at the
castle of Nürnberg.

It is very possible that these public demonstrations produced in the
mind of Ferdinand, on whom the new doctrines had made no impression,
and who had been brought up in all the rigour of Spanish catholicism,
the determination to abandon the Council of Regency ; and it is also
likely enough that the pope's legate had some influence in the same direction. At all events, the fall of the Council of Regency, which had taken
the new doctrines under its protection, would necessarily be very favourable to the maintenance of catholicism.

Perhaps the legate founded on this a hope of obtaining from the States
a decision agreeable to his wishes on religious affairs generally. He complained of the innovations which were made before his eyes. He reminded
the States of the edict published at Worms, and expressed his astonishment
that ordinances of this kind were so imperfectly enforced in the empire.
Hannart also demanded the execution of the edict in the emperor's name.

On this occasion, however, it became manifest that religion had by no
means decided the course of affairs, however it might have influenced
the conduct of some individuals. Had no political motives existed, the
councillors of the Regency would never have been dismissed on account
of their religious inclinations. The complaints of the legate made no
impression. " Some," writes Planitz, " are indignant, but most only
laugh." The cities, which had contributed so greatly to the overthrow
of the Council of Regency, were furious at the mention of the edict. They
declared that the common people were so eager for the word of God,
that to deprive them of it would cause rebellion, bloodshed and general

[1] The Regency recommended him " dass er seinen Segen und Kreuz zu thun
vermeyd, angesehen wie es deshalb jetzund stee."—" To avoid making the sign
of the cross or the benediction, seeing how matters then stood."—Feilitzsch to
Frederick of Saxony, 11*th March*."
[2] Planitz (28th March) reckons 4000. " Ist deshalb Mühe und Erbett, und
sunderlich, dass es des Regiments Personen eines Theyls also genommen."—
" On this account is trouble and labour, and especially as the persons of the
Regency have in part received it thus." He remarks that Ferdinand was very
angry at such a manifestation of his sister's opinions. " Nicht weiss ich wie es
gehn will."—" I know not how it will end."

ruin ; and that the resolutions of the preceding year must be absolutely adhered to.   In short, with regard to religious affairs, those who were hostile to Rome still constituted the majority in the States.   The legate was reminded soon after his arrival of the hundred grievances of the nation which had been sent to Rome by his predecessor.   This had been foreseen in Rome ; and the legate had been instructed to feign that the memorial containing these complaints had not been delivered in the names of the princes.[1]   Accordingly Campeggio answered with a perfectly untroubled countenance, " that no official announcement of those grievances had reached Rome ; that three printed copies had been sent thither, it was true, one of which he had seen himself, but that he could not bring himself to believe that anything so beyond measure ill-written could be produced by the diet."   This was certainly not at all calculated to satisfy the temporal Estates, who had been extremely in earnest with regard to the grievances, the statement of which had cost so much trouble and deliberation.

Moreover, the personal behaviour of the legate, who was accused of sordid avarice, and of revolting oppression towards the poorer sort of German priests, was far from favourable to the success of his negotiations.[2]

When the decisive discussion on religious affairs arrived, the order necessary to the transaction of public business and the presence of the imperial commissioner so far influenced the States, that they did not deny the obligation they lay under to carry the edict of Worms into execution ; but to this admission they added a clause to a directly contrary effect ; namely, that they would execute it " as far as was possible,"—a modification of so vague a nature that it was left to the discretion of each individual to do what he pleased.   The cities had already represented at length that it was not possible.   At the same time the demand was renewed, that the pope should convene a council in the German dominions, with the emperor's consent.   This the legate undertook to advocate faithfully to his holiness.

It was, however, questionable whether this was sufficient to tranquillise men's minds ; or whether, in such a state of fermentation, they would wait patiently for so remote an event as the convocation and decision of an ecclesiastical assembly : lastly, whether the German nation would so far renounce the unity of its anti-Romish tendencies, which had taken so deep a root, as to consent to abide by the results of a council composed of all nations.

No sooner were the representatives of the reforming principles dismissed from the Council of Regency, than the necessity of supplying the place of their labours in some other manner was doubly felt.   This aroused the champions of the new doctrines to unite in forming a most remarkable determination.

The question which had once before been so important was still unanswered ; namely, what was to be done in Germany in the interval till the council met.   In spite of all opposition, a resolution still more extra-

[1] Pallavicini, i., p. 222 : " che dissimulasse che la scrittura si fosse ricevuta per nome dei principi."

[2] A detailed contemporary account of the manner in which the legate induced the learned but poor Schoner to present to him his mathematical instruments, on the promise of a benefice, and then neither procured him the benefice nor paid him for his instruments.   Strobel, Nachricht vom Aufenthalt Melanchthons, in Nürnberg, p. 18.

ordinary, and of which the results were still more incalculable than that of the former year, was adopted on this point. It was determined that, in the month of November of the current year, a meeting of the States should be convened at Spire, and should there hold a definitive deliberation. To this end, the sovereign princes were to direct their councillors and learned clerks to draw up a list of all the disputed points which were to be discussed and decided. Besides this, the grievances of the nation and means for their redress were to be considered anew. Meanwhile it was resolved, as the year before, that the holy Gospel and God's word should be preached.[1]

It is indeed true that the party favourable to Rome, emboldened by the overthrow of the Council of Regency, had regained somewhat of its influence at this diet, but still it was kept in check by a large majority : the German nation asserted its claim more strenuously than ever, to complete independence in ecclesiastical affairs, as against the pope and the unity of the Latin church.

CHAPTER V.

ORIGIN OF THE DIVISION IN THE NATION.

THERE are probably few reflecting men, however well-disposed on other grounds to the cause of ecclesiastical reform, who have not occasionally felt inclined to join in the usual condemnation of it, as the cause of the separation of Germany into two parts,—often at open war and never thoroughly reconciled ;—to impute to the adherents of the new opinions all the blame of having broken up the unity, not only of the church but of the empire.

So long as we regard the facts from a distance they doubtless wear this aspect ; but if we approach nearer to them and contemplate the events which brought about this division, the result we shall arrive at will, if I mistake not, be far different.

No man, to whatever confession he may belong, can deny, what was admitted even by the most zealous Catholics of that day ; viz., that the Latin church stood in need of reform. Its thorough worldliness, and the ever-increasing rigidity and unintelligible formalism of its dogmas and observances, rendered this necessary in a religious view ; while the inter-

---

[1] Decree of the Diet of Nürnberg, 18th April, 1524. When, after this decree, we read Luther's paper,—" Zwei kaiserliche uneinige und widerwärtige Gebote " (Altenb., ii. 762), " Two imperial contradictory and incompatible Orders,"— we are astonished that he was so ill satisfied. The cause of this, however, is, that in the mandate founded on the Recess, the article prescribing the teaching of the holy Gospel was omitted, while, on the other hand, great stress was laid on the observance of the edict of Worms. The clause " so viel möglich," indeed, is there ; but almost disappears under the constant reiterations of the edict of Worms ; hence we perceive the influence which the imperial chancery obtained after the abolition of the old Council of Regency. Luther does not appear to have been aware of the Recess, and still less of the preceding negotiations. The imperial delegate, Hannart, and the papal legate, took a far more complete view of the matter. They thought it a great gain that at any rate the name of national council had been avoided. Nevertheless, Hannart concludes his letter of the 16th April with the words, " que cependant se fera ung concil national d'Allemagne."

ference of the papal court, which was not only oppressive in a pecuniary sense, by consuming all the surplus revenue, but destructive of the unity and independence of the nation, made it not less essential to the national interests.

Nor can it be alleged, either on religious or national grounds, that any unjustifiable measures were resorted to to effect this change.

Independently of all the more precise articles of the protestant creed, which were gradually constructed and accepted, the essence of the religious movement lay in this,—that the spirit of Christianity, so deeply implanted in the German mind, had been, by degrees, ripened to a consciousness of its own independence of all accidental forms ; had gone back to its original source,—to those records which directly proclaim the eternal covenant of the Godhead with the human race,—and had there become confident in its own truth, and resolute to reject all untenable theories and subjugating claims.

No one could shut his eyes to the peril impending over the whole existing order of things in the nation, from a departure from those established ecclesiastical forms which had such mighty influence over domestic as well as public life. We have, however, seen with what care all destructive elements were rejected, with how much self-control every violent change was avoided, and how patiently every question was still left to the decision of the empire.

Let it not be objected that discord had already arisen, and that, as we have remarked, action was encountered by re-action ; no momentous crisis in the life of a great nation was ever unaccompanied by this stormy shock of conflicting opinions. The important point is, that the divisions should not have sufficient power to overthrow the paramount and acknowledged supremacy of the principle of unity.

Such was the tendency of affairs in Germany in the year 1524.

The adherents of the new faith had hitherto always submitted to the constitutional government of the empire ; in the hope of obtaining from its proceedings and favour a reconstruction of the ecclesiastical institutions, in accordance both with the wants of the nation and the commands of the Gospel.

The majority in the Council of Regency, as we have seen, influenced the States in this spirit. In spite of all the efforts of opponents, and of the various external difficulties, a majority was formed in the diet, favourable to the reformation. Two Recesses were drawn up and agreed to in its favour. Even after the fall of the Regency, this majority maintained itself, and resolved that a national assembly should be convened at an early date, and should occupy itself exclusively with the endeavour to bring the religious affairs of the empire to a definitive conclusion.

A nobler prospect for the unity of the nation, and for the further progress of the German people in the career they had already entered upon, certainly never presented itself.

To form some notion of the degree to which it occupied the minds of men, we have only to examine the state of Franconia, where, during the summer of 1524, six opinions or reports, destined to be laid before this assembly, appeared, all conceived in the spirit of the evangelical party. Luther felt contented and happy when he saw the judgment of the learned men of Brandenburg ; he said that this was coin of the right stamp, such as he and his friends at Wittenberg had long dealt withal. That of Henneberg was not so completely in accordance with his opinions. Luther's doctrine concerning free will was combated in it ; but in all other respects it was soundly evangelical, and condemned the invocation of saints, the seven sacraments, and the abuses of the mass. The reports of Windsheim and Wertheim were particularly violent against the saints ; that of Nürnberg, against the pope. One of the two parties which divided Rothenburg sent in an opinion favourable to the evangelical side.[1] The other party, however, which was more faithful to the ancient doctrine, was no less active. Ferdinand required his universities of Vienna and Freiburg to send in full and minute explanations of the disputed points. At the former university, the faculties immediately prepared to draw up their report, and that of theology exhorted the others to abstain from all mutual offence.[2] It is evident that the most various modifications of opinion must have been in agitation and in conflict at Spire. What results might not have been anticipated, had it been possible to execute the project of holding a peaceful and moderate discussion,—of endeavouring to sever the good from the bad !

It is true that another evangelical majority, like that with which the proposal originated, was fully to be expected ; but this was the inevitable consequence of the present state of things : the nation had no alternative ; it must resist the encroachments of Rome, or fall ; the religious movement could no longer be suppressed, it could only be guided. This was the part assigned to the national assembly ; nor can it be said that the unity of the nation was thus endangered ; on the contrary, had it attained its object, it would have given to that unity a much more solid foundation.

In order to discover who it was that, at this decisive juncture, broke the bond of the national unity, we must examine how it happened that an assembly for which such solemn preparation had been made, never took place.

The See of Rome naturally opposed it ; for in proportion as the prospect it afforded was full of hope and promise to the German nation, it was threatening and disastrous to the court of Rome.

We have the report of a congregation held at this crisis by Pope Clement VII., at which means were discussed for carrying into effect the bull against Luther, and the edict of Worms, in spite of the Recesses by which they were counteracted. A vast variety of schemes were suggested ; such as, that Frederick of Saxony should be deprived of his electorate,—a measure proposed by Aleander ; or that the kings of England and Spain should be prevailed on to threaten to put a stop to all commerce with the German towns, from which the pope anticipated great results. The only conclusion they came to, however, was to oppose the meeting at Spire, both to the emperor and the States, whom the legate was instructed to use every means to prejudice against that assembly.[3]

The question for immediate decision—a question which we must here

---

[1] Extracts from v. d. Lith Erläuterung der Fränk. Reformationshist : p. 41.

[2] Raupach Evangel. Oestreich, ii., p. 29. Struve mentions a similar exhortation from the elector palatine to the University of Heidelberg in his Pfälzische Kirchenhistorie, p. 19.

[3] Pallavicini, lib. ii., c. x., p. 227.

examine—was, whether there could be found estates in Germany who would prefer joining with the pope to awaiting the decisions of a general assembly.

The papal court had already found means to secure to itself allies in Germany : it had won over one of the most powerful of the sovereign houses—that of the dukes of Bavaria.

The government as well as the people of Bavaria had formerly shared the common aversion of the German nation to the ascendency of Rome ; neither the bull of Leo X. had been carried into effect, nor the edict of Worms observed.[1] The dukes had been as much displeased at the encroachments made by the spiritual on the temporal jurisdiction, as any other princes; and Luther's doctrines spread among the learned, the clergy, and the commons, as rapidly and as widely as in other parts of the empire.

But as early as the end of the year 1521 the dukes began to incline towards Rome, and had ever since been becoming more and more decided partisans of the old faith.

Contemporary writers ascribed this to the great power and extensive possessions of the regular clergy in Bavaria ;[2] and certainly this had an influence, though rather of a different kind from that supposed.

The first symptom of an intimate connection between Rome and Bavaria was a draft of a bull which Leo X. caused to be prepared on the 14th Nov., 1521, wherein he authorises a commission of prelates, before proposed by the dukes, to visit the convents and restore order and discipline in them.[3] He died before this bull was finished ; but not before he had thus pointed out to the Bavarian Government what might be done in this direction. A standing commission, independent of the bishopric, and under the influence of the sovereign, was charged with the superintendence of spiritual affairs.

About this time the university of Ingolstadt was almost broken up by a pestilential disease. When the contagion had ceased, and the professors reassembled, they found that it would be impossible to maintain their strict catholic discipline without other support than that of the spiritual jurisdiction ; and that a ducal mandate would be necessary to help them to withstand the innovations which threatened to invade even their own body. The three most resolute champions of the old system, Franz Burckhard, Georg Hauer, and Johann Eck, who had again been at Rome in the autumn, joined in urgent representations of the necessity for such a measure ;[4] of which Duke William's chancellor, Leonhard von

---

[1] Winter, Geschichte der Schicksale der evangelischen Lehre in und durch Baiern, i., pp. 62, 76.

[2] Pamphlet of Reckenhofer touching the affairs of Seehofer : " Denn sobald du für München herauskömpst auf drey Meyl gegen Burg, und fragst wes ist der Grund, Antwort : ist meines gnedigen Herrn von Degernsee, Chiemsee, Sauner see, also dass mer denn der halb Teyl des Bayrlandes der Geistlichen ist."— " For as soon as you leave Munich, about three miles toward Burg, and ask whose is the land ? the answer is, It belongs to my Lord of Degernsee, Chiemsee, Saunersee, so that more than half of Bavaria belongs to the clergy."—Panzer, No 2462.

[3] Winter, ii., p. 325.

[4] He could not have gone thither before October, as he was still at Polling during the months of August and September. Leben des berühmten Joh. Eckii in the Parnassus Boicus, i., ii., p. 521.

Eck, one of the most active and influential statesmen of that time, was fully convinced.[1]

The dukes were soon won over to the same opinion ; probably the report of the riots which had just then broken out at Wittenberg (but which Luther so quickly tranquillised) made them anxious to prevent similar disturbances in their own territories.

On Ash Wednesday, 5th of March, 1522, the dukes issued a mandate,[2] wherein they commanded their subjects, under heavy penalties, to adhere to the faith of their forefathers.   That which had been considered necessary for the university, was thus extended to the whole nation.   The dukes' officers were directed to arrest all refractory persons, ecclesiastics as well as laymen, and to report upon their offences.

In spite of the rigour which was used, these measures had not, at first, the anticipated effect.   In Saxony the temporal power refused to lend its arm to support the episcopal authority ; in Bavaria, on the contrary, the bishops, who had a vague perception of the danger which must accrue to their independent authority from such an alliance, did not second the efforts of the temporal power with much zeal.   The followers of Luther, arrested by the civil officers, often escaped free and unpunished, from the ecclesiastical court which had jurisdiction over them.

When Dr. Johann Eck returned to Rome in the summer of 1523, at the invitation of Pope Adrian,[3] he was commissioned by the dukes to make a formal complaint against the bishops on this head, and to request an extension of the ducal authority in the proceedings against heretics.[4] It was impossible to refuse the demand of the orthodox doctor, who took part in the most secret consultations on religious affairs.   Pope Adrian therefore published a bull empowering a spiritual commission to degrade ecclesiastics who should be convicted of heresy, and to deliver them over to the temporal criminal tribunals, even without the concurrence of the bishops.   Adrian added only the limitation, that the bishops were to be once more admonished to perform their duties within a given term ; but this was subsequently disregarded.

Thus we see that it was not the independent authority of the great institutions of the church, that the dukes took under their protection : they raised up a collateral authority, standing under their own immediate influence, and empowered to intervene in the most peculiar sphere of ecclesiastical rights and duties.

Dr. Eck is not to be regarded only as one of Luther's theological opponents.   He exercised an extraordinary influence on the state, as well as the church in Bavaria ; and to him principally is to be attributed that alliance between the ducal power, the university of Ingolstadt, and the

---

[1] Winter, passim, p. 81.

[2] " Erstes baierisches Religionsmandat, München am Eschermittiche angeender Vassten."—*Ibid.*, p. 310.

[3] " Er entbot denselben durch zwei Brevia nach Rom."—" He summoned him by two briefs to Rome."—Parnassus Boicus, i. ii., p. 206.

[4] " Fragmentum libelli supplicis, quem Bavariæ Ducis oratores, quorum caput celebris ille Eckius, Adriano VI. Romæ obtulerunt anno 1521," ap. Œfele, ii. 274.   The date is wrong, as Adrian was not pope in 1521.   The bull, which was prepared according to the words of the petition, is dated June, 1523.   The Bavarian bishops first appealed against it in December, 1523, so that there can be no doubt that that is the proper date.

papal authority, which checked the progress of the national movement in that country.

Nor was it the authority alone of the church that was assailed ; claims were soon advanced to her possessions.

Pope Adrian granted to the dukes one fifth of all the revenues of the church throughout their territories ; " for," said he, " the dukes have declared their readiness to take arms against the enemies of the true faith."[1] When Pope Clement VII. came to the tiara, he revoked all grants of this nature ; nevertheless he saw reason to confirm this one for the three following years : since then, it has been renewed from time to time, and has always remained one of the chief foundations of the Bavarian financial system.[2]

On this occasion the university was not forgotten. Adrian consented that in every chapter in Bavaria, at least one prebend might be conferred on a professor of theology, " for the improvement of that faculty, and for the better extirpation of the heresies that had arisen in that, as well as in other German countries."[3]

Thus, before any form of government constituted according to evangelical views, could be thought of, we find an opposing body organised expressly for the purpose of supporting catholic principles, which gradually became of immense importance to the destinies of Germany.

We have already shown that the disturbances of those times mainly arose out of the struggle between the spiritual and temporal power. The rising temporal sovereignties naturally sought to defend themselves against the encroachments of their ecclesiastical neighbours. With this tendency, Luther's views of government exactly coincided ; he advocated a total separation of the two powers. The dukes of Bavaria, however, found that such a separation was not the only way to attain the desired end ; they took a directly opposite course, which was both shorter and more secure. What others were striving to wrest from the pope by hostile measures, they contrived to obtain with his concurrence. By this means they at once gained possession of a large share of the ecclesiastical revenues, and an authority, sanctioned by the papal see, over the surrounding bishops, even in the most important branch of the spiritual jurisdiction ;

---

[1] Bull of the 1st of June. It is there said of the dukes, " Ad arma contra perfidos orthodoxæ fidei hostes sumenda sese obtulerunt."—*Ibid.*, 279. The Turks were also included in this.

[2] See Winter, ii., p. 321.

[3] 30th of August, Œfele, p. 277. In Mederer, Annales, Acad. Ingolstadt, iv. 234, is to be found the bull of Clement VII. concerning this matter ; by this bull the dukes of Bavaria are entitled always to promote one of their professors of theology at Ingolstadt to a prebendal stall in the chapters of Augsburg, Freisingen, Passau, Regensburg, or Salzburg. They gave out : " quod ecclesie predicte a Ducibus Bavarie fundate vel donationibus aucte fuerunt." The reason assigned was, that they wished to have theologians " hoc tempore periculoso, quo Lutheriana et alie plurime hereses contra sedem apostolicam . . . propagantur, qui se murum pro Israel exponent et contra hereses predictas legendo predicando docendo et scribendo eas confutent dejiciant et exterminent." This is the more important, because in the years immediately after the plague, the university, as is mentioned by the statutes of the faculty of jurists, was almost entirely reconstituted.

an authority which was very soon manifested in the proceedings of the Bavarian council for religious affairs. These were advantages which the adherents of the new faith could not yet so much as contemplate.

There was still, however, this immense distinction ;—that, while the latter were the representatives of the tendency of the nation to emancipate itself from Rome, Bavaria fell into much more absolute subjection to that power, from whom she held all the privileges she now enjoyed.

Under any circumstances, however, so decisive a step, taken by one of the most powerful houses of Germany, and the example of the advantages resulting from a renewed connection with Rome, could not fail to have a great effect on all its neighbours.

We find from a very authentic source, the transactions of the Archbishop of Salzburg with his states, that a compact had already been entered into between Bavaria and Austria, " against the Lutheran sect."[1]

It is certain that Archduke Ferdinand had likewise formed a closer connection with the see of Rome, and had obtained thence, in behalf of his defence against the Turks, the enormous grant of a full third of all the ecclesiastical revenues.

Rome did not neglect to conciliate the more influential spiritual, as well as temporal, princes. The long contested appointments to the bishoprics of Gurk, Chiemsee, Seckau, and Lavant, were granted to the Archbishop of Salzburg, even during the disputed months.

By these means the papal see succeeded in regaining a party in the States : no doubt it is to be attributed to these and similar causes, that catholic opinions were more strongly represented at the diet of 1524 than they had been the year before.

Still, as we have already seen, they were not triumphant at that diet. A number of bishops even, offended by the support given by the pope to the claims of the temporal sovereigns, offered a determined resistance to every suggestion emanating from Rome.

The legate Campeggio plainly saw that nothing could be gained from a general assembly in which Lutheran sympathies so greatly predominated. He complained that he could not here venture to speak freely.[2]

On the other hand, as he saw around him a number of friends holding the same opinions, he hoped that he should be able to effect more completely all he wanted at a provincial meeting, where only these partisans would be present.

Accordingly, even at Nürnberg, where the national assembly at Spire was resolved on, he proposed another which, in spirit, was directly at variance with it. He made no secret that his object was to obviate the danger which must ensue from an assembly convoked with the avowed intention of listening to the voice of the people.[3]

This proposal was first agreed to by Archduke Ferdinand and a few bishops, and then by the dukes of Bavaria. At the end of June, 1524, the meeting was held at Ratisbon. The dukes, the archduke, the legate, the Archbishop of Salzburg, the Bishop of Trent, who came in the retinue of the archduke, and the administrator of Ratisbon, were

---

[1] Zauner, Salzburger Chronik, iv. 359.

[2] From a letter of Ferdinand's, dated Stuttgard, 19th May, in Gemeiners Regensburger Chronik, iv., vi., p. 514.

[3] From the letter of the legate, dated 8th May. Winter, i., p. 156.

present.   Delegates appeared for the bishops of Bamberg, Augsburg, Spire, Strasburg, Constance, Basle, Freising, Passau, and Brixen : thus not only Bavaria and Austria, but the Upper Rhine and a considerable portion of Swabia and Franconia, took part in it.

The legate opened the meeting with a discourse on the perils with which the religious troubles threatened both estates : he exhorted them to abandon their disputes, and to unite in measures " for extirpating the heretical doctrines, and making men live after the ordinances of the Christian church." Archduke Ferdinand supported the proposal, and strongly insisted to the assembly on the pecuniary grants he had obtained.

The prelates then divided into three commissions : the first of which was to consider the disputes between the clergy and laity ; the second, the reforms to be immediately undertaken, and the third, the measures to be taken with respect to doctrine.[1]

The conference lasted for sixteen days in the town hall at Ratisbon, and sittings were held before and after noon.   The grave course of affairs was on one occasion interrupted by a festive dance.

The affair of the pecuniary grant was the first settled.

The bishops plainly perceived that the popular ferment, which, from its first origin, had been constantly increasing in strength and impetuosity, must be far more dangerous to them, than any supremacy of the temporal sovereign.   There were few among those we have named who had not had to struggle with a growing opposition in their own capitals.   A year before, Cardinal Lang had found it necessary to bring six troops of veteran soldiers into Salzburg.   He himself rode at their head habited in a red slashed surcoat, under which glittered a polished cuirass, and grasping his marshal's baton ; and thus compelled the corporation to sign fresh declarations of submission.   Perhaps, too, a few such prelates may have been favoured with fresh concessions from the pope ; we find many decided partisans of Rome among their delegates, for example, Andreas Hanlin of Bamberg, who was once himself vicerector at Ingolstadt ;[2] Eck and Faber also were present.   The spiritual lords ended by making a virtue of necessity ; those of Bavaria consented to pay to the temporal power (as near as I can discover) a fifth part of their revenues, and those of Austria a fourth.[3]

[1] Letter from Ebner and Nützel to the Elector Frederick, wherein they inform him, " was eine Schrift enthält, die ihnen vom Hofe fürstlicher Durchleuchtigkeit (Ferdinands) zugekommen ist,"—" of the contents of a letter which had reached them from the court of his Royal Highness (Ferdinand)," 8th July, 1524.— *Weimar. A.*

[2] Heller, Reformationsgesch. von Bamberg, p. 70.

[3] Planitz, who had been at Esslingen, writes to the Elector Frederick, Nürnberg, 26th July : " Die Geistlichen in des Erzherzogs Landen haben bewilligt, ihm den vierten Pfennig zu geben, 5 Jahr lang, und die Geistlichen unter den Herrn von Baiern geben ihren Fürsten den 5ten Pfennig 5 Jahr, allein dass sie in ihren Fürstenthumen die lutherische Lehr nicht zulassen und vest über ihnen halten wollen."—" The ecclesiastics in the archduke's dominions have agreed to give him the fourth penny for 5 years, and the ecclesiastics under the lords of Bavaria will give to their princes the fifth penny for 5 years, but on condition that they shall not suffer the Lutheran doctrines in their dominions, and that they will keep them down with a strong hand."   I have not been able to discover whether Planitz was rightly informed as to the duration of this impost. According to Winter, ii., p. 322, it was continued for several years longer.

They next proceeded to consider the points of doctrine and life.

The most important result of this consultation was a decision which it had been found impossible to carry at the meeting of the States of 1523. The preachers were directed to refer principally to the Latin fathers of the church for the interpretation of difficult passages in Scripture ; and (what could not be accomplished on a former occasion) Ambrose, Jerome, Gregory and Augustin were specified as the patterns of faith.   In former days, this might have been looked upon as a concession to the literary tendencies of the time, since it relaxed the fetters of the scholastic system ; but now, it mainly betokened opposition to Luther and to the majority of the States of the empire, by sanctioning, at any rate, the authorities on which rested the later systems of the Latin church.   It was resolved that divine service should be preserved unaltered according to the usages of former generations, and an attempt was made to put an end to Luther's influence.   His books were once more forbidden, and all subjects of the allied princes were interdicted, under pain of forfeiture of their patrimonies, from studying at the university of Wittenberg.

At the same time, steps were taken towards the removal of those abuses which had occasioned such a general ferment.   All the extortions of the inferior clergy which raised so much discontent among the common people, the enforcement of expensive ceremonies, the burdensome fees, the refusal of absolution on account of debts, were abolished.   The relation of the clergy to their flocks was to be put on a fresh footing, by a commission composed of clerical and lay members.   The reserved presentations were diminished, the number of holydays materially lessened, the practice of stations abolished.   The assembly pledged itself for the future to a more careful consideration of personal merit in the appointment of ecclesiastics. The preachers were admonished to show greater earnestness, and to avoid all fables and untenable assertions ; and the priests, to follow a chaste and irreproachable course of life.[1]

We are, I believe, warranted in looking on these resolutions as the first effects of the principles of the reformation in reviving the profounder spirit of catholicism.   As the alliance of the sovereign princes with the papal see fulfilled the political demands, so this attempt supplied (at first indeed very inadequately) the religious wants, which had given birth to the reforming spirit.   These attempts at regeneration were unquestionably more important and effective than has been supposed, even by the catholic party itself ; and, indeed, modern catholicism is in great measure based upon them ; but neither in depth of religious intuition, in the genius which produces a permanent impression on remote nations and ages, or in force and intensity of enthusiasm, could they be compared to those movements which took their name from Luther, and of which he was the centre.   His opponents offered nothing original ; the means they adopted, and by which they thought to keep their ground, were mere analogical imitations

---

[1] " Constitutio ad removendos abuses et ordinatio ad vitam Cleri reformandam per Rev^{dum} D^m Laurentium," &c.—Ratisponæ Nonis Julii, in Goldast, Constitutt. Impp., iii., p. 487.   What is given by Strobel (Miscel., ii., p. 109, &c.), from an old printed book, which is also before me, by no means embraces the whole contents of the Constitution.   The abolition of a great number of holydays in the 21st article, which differs but little from the later protestant regulations, is very remarkable.

of what he had already done. Thus, at Campeggio's suggestion, Dr. Eck published, as a corrective to Melanchthon's "Loci communes," a hand-book of the same kind,[1] and Emser made a translation of the Bible, as a rival to that of Luther. The works of the Wittenberg teachers had issued forth in the natural course of their own internal development : they were the product of minds goaded by a resistless impulse, pressing forward in their own peculiar path, and were filled with the vigour and originality that forces conviction : the catholic books, on the contrary, owed their existence to external motives ;—to the calculations of a system which looked about for any means of defence against the danger pressing upon it from every side.

But those who adopted such a line of conduct, thus cut themselves off from the great and vigorous expansion which the mind of the German nation was now undergoing. The questions which ought to have been discussed and determined at Spire, with a view to the unity and the wants of the nation, were disposed of by the allied powers in a narrow and one-sided manner. It was said that a single nation had no right to decide on the affairs of religion, and of Christendom generally : this was easily asserted ; but what was the nation to do, if, from the peculiarities of its constitution and character, it was the only one that had fallen into this state of ferment ? At first it had petitioned for the immediate convocation of a council ; but as the hope of this grew fainter and more remote, it felt the necessity of taking the matter into its own hands. This is suf-ficiently proved by the ordinances issued at Ratisbon. The difference was this—at Spire, in all probability, resolutions would have been taken in opposition to the Pope of Rome ; whereas at Ratisbon it was thought expedient, from a thousand considerations, to form a fresh alliance with him. This was the origin of the divisions in the nation. The national duty of awaiting the decisions of a general assembly which was already fixed ; of taking part in its deliberations ; and, let us add, of influencing them to wise ends, was sacrificed to the narrow and partial expediency of an alliance with Rome.

One part of the projects of the congregation at Rome being thus executed with unhoped-for success, Campeggio next pointed out the necessity of endeavouring to accomplish the other ; which was, to induce the emperor to give the cause his cordial support.[2]

Not a moment was lost at Rome in gaining over Charles V. Whilst the official proclamations from Ratisbon dwelt only upon such points in the Recesses as were favourable to the papacy, and affected to consider them as mere confirmations of the edict of Worms, it was at the same time represented to the emperor in Spain how greatly his authority must suffer by his edict being limited by two following Recesses ; nay, by an attempt having actually been made to revoke it,—a measure which he himself could not have ventured upon : it was evident, they said, that the people

---

[1] "Enchiridion, seu Loci Communes contra Hæreticos :" printed in 1525, and, according to Eck, composed ,"Hortatu Cardinalis de Campegiis, ut sim-pliciores, quibus cortice natare opus est, summarium haberent credendorum, ne a pseudoprophetis subverterentur."

[2] He complained : " non haver quella causa (Luterana) di costà (della Spagna) il caldo che bisogneria, fa che d'ogni provisione che si faccia si trahe poco frutto." —Giberto Datari agli Oratori Fiorentini in Spagna, Lettere di Principi, i., f. 133.

of Germany were preparing to throw off all obedience, both to temporal and spiritual authority. And what insupportable insolence was there in fixing a meeting in that country, to decide on matters of faith, and the affairs of Christianity at large ; as if the Germans had a right to prescribe laws to his imperial majesty and to the whole world !¹

Similar arguments were vehemently pressed upon Charles's ally, Henry VIII., who had entered into a literary warfare with Luther, to induce him to use all his credit with Charles V. in support of the pope's exhortations.

The state of political affairs generally was highly favourable for promoting the influence of the papal power over the emperor. War had been formally declared against Francis I., in May, 1524, and was now raging with the utmost violence. The emperor attacked the king in his own territory, from the side of Italy. It would therefore have been extremely dangerous to offend the pope, who was in his rear, and who did not quite approve the invasion ; or to refuse him a request which, moreover, was consonant to the catholic education he had himself received in his youth.

Charles V. did not hesitate a single moment. On the 27th of July, he despatched a proclamation to the empire entirely in favour of the pope, and expressed with unwonted vehemence. He complained that his mandate from Worms was disregarded, and that a general council had been demanded, without even the due decorum of consulting him. He declared, that he neither could nor would allow the intended assembly to take place ; that the German nation assumed to do what would be permitted to no other, even in conjunction with the pope,—to alter ordinances which had been so long held sacred. He pronounced Luther's doctrines to be inhuman, and, like his master, Adrian, he compared him to Mahomet. In short, he forbade the assembly, on pain of being found guilty of high treason, and incurring sentence of ban and reban.²

Thus did the court of Rome succeed in gaining over to its cause not only several powerful members of the empire in Germany, but even its supreme head in Spain, and by their means, in putting a stop to the dangerous

---

¹ We have not indeed the very letter from the pope to the emperor, but there is a sufficient account of it in the despatch from the papal datarius to the nuncio in England, Marchionne Lango, Lettere di Principi, i. 124. " N. S^{re} ha di ciò scritto efficacemente alla M^{tà} Ces, accioche la consideri, che facendo quei popoli poco conto di dio tanto meno ne faranno alla giornata della M^{tà} S. e degli altri Signori temporali : . . . l'absenza della M^{tà} Cesarea ha accresciuta l' audacia loro tanto che ardiscono di ritrattar quell' editto, cosa che Cesare proprio non faria." On the other hand, in the edict given at Ratisbon, it is stated, " Darumb so haben wir auf des hochwürdigsten Herrn Lorenzen, etc. Ersuchen uns vergleycht, dass wir und unser Principal obgemelt Kaiserlich Edict zu Worms, auch die Abschied auf beyden Reichstägen zu Nürnberg deshalb beschlossen . . . vollziehen."—" Wherefore we have, at the request of the most worshipful master Lorenzo, &c., agreed, that we and our principal should execute the above-named imperial edict of Worms, and the recesses of both diets at Nürnberg confirming the same."

² Frankf. Arch.   It appears from a letter from the Elector of Saxony to Ebner, dated Oct., 1524, Walch, xv. 2711, that, in the letter which had been sent to him, the expression, " bei Vermeidung criminis lese majestatis, unser und des Reicht Acht," &c.—" on pain of being found guilty of high treason, and of our ban and that of the empire," &c., had been omitted.

resolutions of the diet : this was its first energetic interference with the ecclesiastical affairs of Germany.

The main cause of this was, that the emperor, residing in Spain, followed a line of policy, on which the character and the opinions of Germany had not the slightest effect, and suggested solely by his relations with other countries. His government during the first years of his reign exercised merely a negative, decomposing influence. Without taking any serious steps for the redress of the grievances charged upon Rome, he allowed himself to be induced by his political position to issue the edict of Worms, which, after all, could not be carried into effect ; while on the one hand, it inflamed the antipathy of the nation to the utmost, and, on the other, put fresh arms into the hands of the adherents of the Curia. He first checked the growing consolidation of the Council of Regency, by rejecting the system of import duties to which he had at first consented, and then thought it advisable to overthrow that body entirely. Another Council of Regency was, it is true, formed at Esslingen ; but it took warning from the fate of the former, and neither enjoyed authority, nor even made the least attempt to acquire any ;—it was the mere shadow of a government. We have already shown what prospects in favour of religion and of national unity were connected with the projected assembly at Spire. This assembly was forbidden by the court of Spain, as if it were criminal.

The unity of Germany has ever depended, not so much on forms of government, or decisions of the diet, as on an intimate understanding among the more powerful sovereigns. Maximilian had found, during the latter half of his reign, what it was to have offended and alienated the Elector of Saxony ; and it was only by healing this breach and entering into a close alliance with the Ernestine line of Saxony, that the election of Charles V. could be secured ; from that time the Elector Frederick had always been treated, in externals at least, with the confidence and consideration due to a powerful and undoubted ally. This intimate connexion the emperor now broke off. He thought it more advantageous, and more suitable to his own station amongst the powers of Europe, to marry his sister Catharine to John III. of Portugal, than to the nephew of the Elector of Saxony, to whom he had betrothed her. Hannart was commissioned to communicate this resolution to the court of Saxony.[1] We may remember how flattering the proposal had been to Duke John, Frederick's brother; the objections which he raised from mere modesty, and his ultimate joyful acquiescence. Hannart's communication was proportionately mortifying to him. The Saxon court was deeply offended. Such of the elector's friends as were about the archduke wanted him to use his influence to prevent so offensive a proceeding ;[2] but as he had at

[1] Müller, Geschichte der Protestation, gives the particulars of this event. Hannart's letter to the emperor, dated 14th March, shows that the affair was to have come before the diet, which Ferdinand now purposely avoided. "Il a semblé à mon dit S^r par plusieurs raisons que ne debvai parler à Mr de Saxen de la matière secrète, que savez, que jusque après la fin de cette journée impériale." These letters altogether show a better understanding between Hannart and the archduke than the Saxon documents would lead one to imagine.

[2] Among the secret correspondence between Frederick's and Ferdinand's councillors, there is a note in which one of them says, " S. Fürstl. Durchlaucht begeren sonderlich, das der Heirath vollzogen werd, damit S. F. Gn. desto mer Fug und Statt hab, S. Chf. Gn. als irn angenommenen Vatern um Rath teglich

first taken no personal share in the negotiation, neither did he now say one word, but suppressed his vexation. Duke John was less reserved. With wounded pride he rejected every communication, every offer, tendered to him on the subject : he expressed to those about him that nothing during the whole course of his life had ever hurt his feelings so deeply.

With the other sovereign princes, too, Austria stood but ill. The house of Brandenburg, which had supported the first council of Regency for the sake of the interests both of Prussia and Mainz, was much disgusted by its overthrow, and concealed that feeling so little, that overtures were made to the Grand Master, Albert, by France, though indeed he did not accept them. In the month of August, the Rhenish electors held a congress, from which Archduke Ferdinand said he expected no good either to himself or his brother.[1] The electoral councillors did not attempt to disguise from the imperial commissioner that people were extremely discontented with the emperor ; that his capitulation would be laid before the meeting ; and as he had not fulfilled the conditions contained in it, they would proceed to the establishment of a new form of government, either under a lieutenant, the vicars of the empire, or a king of Rome, whom it was intended to elect.[2] This project was discussed at a great cross-bow match at Heidelberg, where several princes were met together, and the palatine house of Bavaria was particularly busied with negotiations to that effect. The bond of catholicism between Bavaria and Austria was not strong enough to prevent Duke William of Bavaria from conceiving the idea of obtaining the crown for himself.

Thus the unity of the government of the empire was again dissolved, almost before it had felt its own purposes or destinies. At a crisis so immeasurably eventful, in which all the energies of the nation were rushing with boundless activity into untried regions, and eager for a new state of things, all directing power was wanting.

Hence it happened that the local powers proceeded to act upon the principles which severally predominated in them.

Persecution began in those countries which had combined to pass the resolutions of Ratisbon.

In Bavaria we find priests ejected or banished, and nobles driven from their estates, till they consented to recant. The tempestuous, oppressive atmosphere of the times is most strikingly exemplified in the fate of an officer of the duke, Bernhard Tichtel von Tutzing. He was travelling towards Nürnburg on the duke's business, when he was joined on the road by Franz Burkhard, one of the orthodox professors of Ingolstadt : they put up together at Pfaffenhofen, and after supper, the conversation turned on religious matters. Tichtel perhaps knew who his companion was ; he reminded him that conversations of this kind were forbidden by the new edict, to which Burkhard answered that that did not signify between them. Hereupon Tichtel did not conceal his opinion that the edict could not be carried into effect, and would merely be a disgrace to

---

anzusuchen."—" His princely highness greatly desires the consummation of the marriage, so that his princely highness may have more excuse and reason for daily asking counsel of his electoral grace as his adopted father,"—a wish which could scarcely have been shared by the whole court.

[1] Letter from Ferdinand, Bucholtz, ii., p. 68.
[2] Letter from Hannart, ib., p. 70.

the dukes ; he even went so far as to speak somewhat equivocally of purgatory and of the obligation to fast ; sanguinary punishments for differences of opinion he condemned altogether.   On hearing these sentiments, Burkhard, who had advised the dukes to all the most odious measures, was seized with the savage fury of a persecutor : he said, in so many words, that decapitation was the proper punishment for Lutheran villains, and at the same time called Tichtel himself a Lutheran.   At parting he affected to be reconciled to him, but he hurried to denounce the crime he had detected.   Tichtel was arrested and confined in the Falkenthurm, subjected to an inquisition, and compelled to recant : it was only by dint of great exertions and powerful intercession, that he escaped a most degrading punishment which had been suggested to the duke.[1]

In the territory of Salzburg a priest arrested for Lutheranism was on his way under guard to Mittersill, where he was to remain imprisoned for life, and while the constables were carousing, was set free by two peasants' sons.   For this offence the poor youths were, by order of the archbishop, secretly beheaded without public trial, early in the morning, in a meadow in the Nonnthal outside the town—a place never used for execution. Even the executioner had scruples, because the condemned prisoners had not had lawful trial ; but the bishop's officer said, " Do what I command you, and let the princes answer for it."[2]

A citizen of Vienna, one Caspar Tauber, who had expressed anti-catholic opinions respecting the intercession of saints, purgatory, confession and the mystery of the communion, was condemned to make a recantation.   On a great holyday—the Nativity of the Virgin Mary— two pulpits were erected for this purpose in the churchyard of St. Stephen's ; one of these was for the precentor, the other for Tauber, to whom the form of recantation which he was to read was given.   But whether it was that he had never promised this, or that an opposite conviction suddenly forced itself more strongly than ever on his mind, he declared from the pulpit whence the assembled multitude was expecting to hear his recantation, that he did not consider himself to have been refuted, and that he appealed to the Holy Roman Empire.   He must have been well aware that this would not save him : he was beheaded shortly after, and his body burnt ; but his courage and firmness left a lasting impression on the people.[3]

There were some other people arrested with Tauber, who, terrified by his fate, made the recantation demanded of them, and escaped with banishment.[4]

---

[1] Another of the same party, the Chancellor Leonhard v. Eck, had proposed that the duke should follow the merciful course " (den barmherzigen Weg "), viz., that Tichtel should only be placed in the pillory, his crimes be there read aloud, and then by him be orally confessed and renounced : he should then, as a mark of his heretical backsliding, be branded on both cheeks ; after this he was to be conveyed back again to the Falkenthurm, and kept there until further orders from the duke.   See the Extracts from the Acts, Winter, i., pp. 182-199.

[2] Zauner, iv., p. 381.

[3] Ein warhafftig Geschicht, wie Caspar Tawber, Burger zu Wien in Osterreich für ein Ketzer und zu dem Todt verurtaylt und aussgefürt worden ist," 1524.— " The true History how Caspar Tawber, a burgher of Vienna in Austria, was condemned and executed as a heretic."   The execution took place on 17th Sept.

[4] Sententia contra Joannem Væsel—one of the condemned—ult. Septembr, 1524.   Raupach Evangel. Oestreich. Erste Fortsetzung ; Beilage, No. V.

The same severity was practised throughout the Austrian dominions. The three governments of Innsbruck, Stuttgart, and Ensisheim appointed a commission at Engen, whose especial business it was to suppress the movement in their provinces. The people of Waldshut gained nothing by dismissing their preacher, Balthasar Hubmaier : the Engen commission declared that they should be punished, or, as it was coarsely expressed, " that the Gospel should be banged about their ears till they were fain to hold their hands over their heads." The weeds were to be pulled up by the roots ; and already the other towns had been summoned to furnish subsidies of artillery and infantry for the attack on Waldshut, when a body of Swiss volunteers, principally from Zürich, came to the assistance of the town, and caused the commission to pause awhile.[1]

Kenzingen did not escape so well ; the little town was actually taken and invested.

Similar disturbances were going on in all parts of the country, though sometimes the measures taken stopped short of bloodshed ; Luther's books were forbidden, and his adherents were not endured in the pulpit or the councils of the princes, but were exiled from their country. The government of Würtemberg wanted to break off all communication with Reutlingen, because it tolerated evangelical preachers. Neither were the most barbarous executions wanting. We read of preachers nailed to the pillory by the tongue, so that in order to get free they were forced to tear themselves away, and were thus mutilated for life. The fanaticism of monkish bigotry was awakened, and sought its victims in Lower as well as Upper Germany. The most awful example was made of the wretched Heinrich of Zütphen, at Meldorf in Ditmarsch. A small congregation had formed itself there, which had invited this Augustine monk from Bremen to join them for a time : they had obtained permission from the governors of the country, the Forty-eight, that until the meeting of the expected ecclesiastical assembly, the Gospel should be preached pure and unchanged. But their opponents, the prior of the Dominicans of Meldorf and the Minorites of Lunden, were far more powerful ; and in combination with the vicar of the bishop's official, they obtained a contrary sentence, which delivered the poor man into their hands, alleging that he had preached against the Mother of God.[2] A drunken mob, headed by monks bearing torches, went one night in January to the parsonage and dragged forth the preacher, whom they put to death by the most atrocious tortures, executed with equal cruelty and unskilfulness.

Meanwhile the other party was aroused to a sense of the necessity of taking more decisive measures.

Immediately after the congress at Ratisbon, the cities, seeing the danger that threatened them from the support which their bishops

---

[1] Letter from Balthasar Hubmaier in the Taschenbuch für Süddeutschland, 1839, p. 67, from the Archives of Switzerland and the Upper Rhine.

[2] Neocorus, edited by Dahlmann, ii., p. 24. The judgment of the magistrate runs thus : " Desse Bosewicht hefft gepredigt wedder de Moder Gadess und wedder den Christen Gloven, uth welkerer Orsake ick ehn verordele van wegen mines genedigen Herrn Bischops van Bremen thom Vuere."—" This miscreant hath preached against the mother of God and the Christian faith, for which reason I condemn him to the fire, in the name of my gracious Lord Bishop of Bremen."

appeared to receive from the princes, held a great town meeting at Spire, and resolved, in direct opposition to that adherence to the Latin fathers of the church which had been enjoined, that their preachers should confine themselves wholly to the Gospel and the prophetic and apostolic Scriptures.[1] At that time they still expected that the assembly would be held at Spire, and their intention was to propose some common resolution. When, however, this meeting was forbidden by the emperor, and it seemed as if another serious attempt would be made to carry into effect the edict of Worms, they assembled towards the end of the year at Ulm, in order to aid each other in resisting all measures proposed with that view. Weissenburg, Landau, and Kaufbeuren, which had already received some rebukes, were admonished as to their future conduct.

The towns were joined by a part of the nobility. Count Bernhard of Solms appeared at the meeting, in the name of the counts on the Rhine and the Eifel, of the Wetterau, the Westerwald, and the Niederland ; and asked the towns their opinion concerning a proposed levy and tax of the empire for an expedition against the Turks, and also concerning the Lutheran matter. The towns judged rightly that this combination with the nobles would be very advantageous to them ; and after interchanging a few letters, the affair was concluded, and a resolution was taken on the spot at Ulm, " not to act separately in affairs of such weight, and during such perilous times."[2]

The most important event of all was, that a considerable number of the princes declared their complete dissent from the compact of Ratisbon.

Markgrave Casimir of Brandenburg, who had certainly never shown any great religious enthusiasm, could no longer withstand the aroused and declared convictions of his whole country : he rejected the proposal of becoming a party to that compact, alleging the general expectation of the assembly at Spire. When this meeting was forbidden by the emperor, he passed a decree in concert with his estates, that, in his own territories at least, nothing should be preached but the Gospel and the word of God of the Old and New Testament, pure and undefiled, and according to the right and true interpretation. Such was the tenour of the recess of the Brandenburg diet of the 1st of October, 1524. His brother George, who lived at the Hungarian court at Ofen, was not satisfied even with this. He thought that the word of God ought not only to be preached, but to be implicitly obeyed, in defiance of all human ordinances.[3]

A most unlooked-for change now took place in Hessen. It was expected that the three warlike princes who had conquered Sickingen and overthrown the Council of Regency, would also combat the reforming ideas which their enemies had supported. The most energetic of the three, however, very soon followed an exactly contrary course.

In May, 1524, one day as Landgrave Philip of Hessen was riding to a cross-bow match at Heidelberg, he met, near Frankfurt, Melanchthon, whose fame was well known to him, and who was then returning from a

---

[1] Town meeting at Spire, St. Margaret's day, 1524.   Summary extract in Fels Zweiter Beitrag, p. 204.

[2] Fels Zweiter Beitrag, p. 206.   Nicolai, 1524.

[3] Von der Lith, pp. 61-65.

visit to his home in the Palatinate, accompanied by a couple of intimate friends who had been there with him.   The landgrave stopped him, made him ride some distance by his side, and asked him several questions which betrayed the deep interest he felt in the religious dissensions ; and, at last, he only dismissed the surprised and embarrassed professor, on condition that he should send him, in writing, his opinion on the most important points under discussion.[1]   Melanchthon executed this task with his usual mastery of his subject ; his letter was short, logical, and convincing, and produced a strong impression.   Not long after his return from the festivities, on the 18th of July, the landgrave issued a mandate (also in manifest contradiction to the resolutions of Ratisbon), wherein, among other things, he commanded that the Gospel should be preached pure and unadulterated.   From day to day he became more deeply imbued with the peculiar opinions of the new creed : at the beginning of the following year, he declared that he would sooner give up his body and life, his land and his people, than forsake the word of God.

It appears as if some general understanding had been come to at Heidelberg on the subject of religion ; for, at first, Philip of Hessen fully expected that the Elector Palatine would follow his example ; and although it was not in the nature of that prince to take so decided a part as the landgrave, at least he did not allow himself to be hurried into any acts of persecution.

The banished Duke of Würtemberg, too, might already be regarded as a convert to the cause.   Lutheran preachers resided with him at Mümpelgard, and in October, 1524, Zwingli expressed his wonder and joy that this Saul was become a Paul.[2]

Duke Ernest of Lüneburg, the nephew of Frederick of Saxony, who had studied at Wittenberg, showed a similar leaning to the doctrines of the reformers, and was strengthened in his opposition to Austria by the affair of Hildesheim.   The first beginnings of the reformation at Celle under his protection, date from the year 1524.[3]

He was joined by Frederick I. of Denmark, who, a year before, had become sole master of Silesia and Holstein.   His son Christian had attended the Diet at Worms, with his tutor Johann Ranzau : they both returned home filled with admiration of Luther, and deeply imbued with his doctrines.   They invited Peter Suave—the very man who had accompanied Luther on that journey— to Denmark ; by degrees the duke himself was won over to the same cause.   While bloody persecutions were set on foot in so many places, Frederick I. published an edict, dated the 7th August, 1524, wherein he made it a capital offence to molest or injure any one on account of his religion : every one, he declared, ought so to order his conduct in that behalf, as he could best answer it to Almighty God.[4]

A still more important circumstance for the prospects of Lutheranism was, the secession of a powerful spiritual prince, the Grand Master Albert of Prussia, from the doctrines of the papacy.   At the diet of Nürnberg he had been much impressed by Osiander's preaching ; and having examined the Scriptures himself, he felt convinced that the order to which

---

[1] Camerarius Vita Melanchthonis, cap. 26. Strobel's Neue Beiträge, iv. 2, p. 88.
[2] Zwinglius Œcolaompadio, Tiguri, 9th Oct.   Epp. Zwinglii, i., p. 163.
[3] Hüne, Geschichte von Hannover, i., p. 747.
[4] Münter, Kirchengeschichte von Dänemark, ii., p. 565.

he belonged was not in accordance with the word of God.[1] Another motive probably was, that the fall of the Council of Regency, and the depressed state of the nobility in general, deprived him of the last hope of obtaining assistance from the empire against Poland. What then must have been his feelings when no hope was left of successfully resisting his old enemies, while at the same time his mind was agitated by doubts of his own condition and calling ? He returned to Saxony in the company of Planitz, the Saxon assessor to the Regency, with whose sentiments we are well acquainted. Here he saw Luther. This intrepid and resolute man, who considered all things with relation to the intrinsic necessity, rather than the outward pressure which enforced them, advised him to forsake the rules of his order, to marry, and to convert Prussia into an hereditary principality. The Grand Master had too much of the discretion and reserve befitting a prince, to express his assent to this suggestion : but it was easy to read in his countenance how strongly he inclined towards it.[2] We shall see how, impelled by the situation of his country, and by the course which his negotiations took, he soon proceeded to the execution of this project.

Such were the results of the prohibition of the national council, the announcement of which had excited such ardent hopes.

It cannot be affirmed that violence was met by violence, or that the tenacity with which the old doctrines were maintained was opposed by an equally resolute adoption of the new.

How little such was the case, is shown by the example of the Elector of Saxony, who in spite of Luther's continual and violent expostulations, caused the mass to be celebrated throughout the whole of the year 1524, in his chapel of All-Saints, and continually reminded the chapter of their clerical duties.

The state of things may rather be summed up as follows. The empire had determined to hold a general deliberation on the important affair which occupied the whole mind of the nation. The pope succeeded in preventing the execution of this project, and in drawing a certain number of the German sovereigns into a partial combination in his own favour ; but the others still pursued the path they had entered upon conformably with the laws of the empire. They were indeed forced to renounce the general assembly, since the emperor so peremptorily forbade it ; but they were not so easily persuaded to relinquish the old decrees of the empire. They determined to abide by the provisions of the Recess of 1523, which, in spite of a few additions and amendments, had in the main been confirmed in 1524. Indeed all the various mandates of that year have fundamentally the same character and purport.

Such was the origin of a division which has never since been healed ; which has constantly been kept open by the same foreign influences that originally caused it. It is very remarkable that all the different party leanings which have lasted through successive centuries, manifested themselves thus early. We have still to observe their establishment and further progress ; but the first moment of their existence revealed the incalculable amount of the danger with which they were pregnant.

---

[1] Memorandum of a conversation between Markgrave Albrecht and Achatius v. Zemen. Beiträge zur Kunde Preussens, vol. iv.

[2] Letter from Luther to Brismann in de W., ii. 526.

CHAPTER VI.

THE PEASANTS' WAR.

PUBLIC order rests on two foundations—first, the stability of the governing body; secondly, the consent and accordance of public opinion with the established government; not, indeed, in every particular, which is neither possible nor even desirable, but with its general tenour.

In every age and country there must be disputes concerning the administration of the government; but so long as the foundations of public confidence remain unshaken, the danger is not great. Opinions are in perpetual flux and perpetual progress; so long as a strong government is actuated by the same general spirit, and feels the necessity of moving in the same direction, no violent convulsion need be feared.

But when the constituted powers doubt, vacillate, and conflict with one another, whilst at the same moment opinions essentially hostile to the existing order of things become predominant, then, indeed, is the peril imminent.

The first glance will suffice to show us that such was now the state of Germany.

The government of the empire, which it had cost so much labour to constitute, and which certainly enjoyed the general confidence of the nation, was now broken up, and its place filled by the mere shadow of a name. The emperor was at a distance, and recently the authority he had exercised was merely negative; he had only prevented the execution of whatever was resolved on. The two hierarchies, the spiritual and the temporal, which had been the work of past centuries, were now separated by a deep and wide chasm. The good understanding of the more powerful sovereigns, on which the unity of the empire had always depended, was destroyed. On the most important affair that had ever presented itself, all hope of framing measures in concert was at an end.

This, of course, reacted very powerfully on the state of opinion. A sort of understanding, with regard to which it was unnecessary to fix any precise terms, had hitherto been evinced in the tendencies of the imperial government, and the moderated tone adopted by Luther; and this it was that had enabled them to crush the destructive opinions which arose in 1522. But now that all hope of further change being effected by a decree of the empire was over, Luther could no longer maintain the authoritative position he had assumed, and the anarchical theories he had helped to stifle broke out afresh: they had found an asylum in the territory of his own sovereign—in electoral Saxony.

In Orlamünde, one of the cures which had been incorporated with the endowments of Wittenberg for the benefit of that University, Carlstadt now preached. He had entered into possession of the cure in an irregular manner, in opposition to the proper patrons of it, partly by means of a certain claim which he raised as belonging to the chapter, but mainly, by the election of the parishioners. He now removed the pictures, performed divine service after his own fashion, and promulgated the most extraordinary opinions concerning the doctrines of the church, and especially the obligations of the Mosaic law. We find mention of a man who, by

Carlstadt's advice, wanted to marry two wives.[1] His rash and confused mind led him entirely to confound the national with the religious element of the Old Testament. Luther expected that before long circumcision would be introduced at Orlamünde, and thought it necessary seriously to warn the elector against attempts of this nature.

At Eisenach, Johann Strauss had already struck into a like crooked path. He was particularly violent against the practice of receiving interest on a loan. He declared that the heathenish laws of the jurists were not binding, and that the Mosaic institution of the year of jubilee, " wherein every man shall return unto the inheritance he had sold," still continued to be a valid commandment from God ; thus calling all vested rights of property in question.[2]

Not far from thence, Thomas Münzer had founded a church on the doctrines which had been suppressed at Zwickau and Wittenberg. Like the former propagators of those doctrines, he assumed as its sole basis, those inward revelations to which alone he attached any importance ; and he far surpassed them in the vehemence with which he preached the Taborite doctrine, that unbelievers were to be exterminated with the sword, and that a kingdom should be established, composed of the faithful only.

These doctrines could not fail to find a welcome and an echo in all parts of Germany. In Würtemberg, too, the Israelitish year of jubilee was preached to the peasants. " Oh, beloved brethren !" said Dr. Mantel, " oh, ye poor Christian men, were these years of jubilee to arrive, they would indeed be blessed years !"[3] Otto Brunfels, who had previously been very moderate in his language, in 1524 published at Strasburg a series of essays on tithes, wherein he declared them to be an institution of the Old Testament, which was abrogated by the New, and entirely denied the right of the clergy to them.[4]

While new champions of these opinions started up in various parts of Germany, Nicolas Storch reappeared at Hof, where he found believers in his revelations, and gathered round him twelve apostles who were to disseminate his doctrine throughout the nation.[5]

The exile of Münzer and Carlstadt from Saxony, which was partly effected by Luther's influence,[6] greatly contributed to the spread and the

---

[1] Letter of Luther to Brück, 13th Jan., 1524. (De W., ii., No. 572.)

[2] " Dass wucher zn nemen und geben unserm christlichen Glauben entgegen ist, 1524."—" To give and take usurious interest is against our Christian faith." C. iii., it is said : " So dann in der Ordnung des Jubel Jars im Text offenbarlich aussgedruckt wirt das Gebot, das die notürfftig bruderlich Lieb fordert, muss alle Einrede still halten und allen Christen desgleychen zu thun gebotten ungezwey-ffelt seyn."—"Seeing, then, in the text, ordaining the year of jubilee,the command requiring brotherly love is clearly expressed, so all disputes must cease ; and there can be do doubt that all Christians are commanded to do likewise."

[3] Sattler, Würtenbergische Geschichte, Herz, ii., p. 105.

[4] " De Ratione Decimarum Ottonis Brunfelsii Propositiones." Among others, prop. 115 : " Proditores Christi sunt Juda pejores et sacerdotibus Baal, qui pro missis Papisticis et Canonicis preculis decimas recipiunt."

[5] Widemann, Chron. Curiense : Mencken, iii., p. 744.

[6] Who has not read the scenes in Jena, where Luther is said to have given Carlstadt a gulden to write against him, and to be his enemy ? Acta Jenensia, Walch, xv. 2422. Luther always complained of the malignity of these stories. That they are received in Luther's works does not prove their truth, as Fuessli

force of the agitation. They both went to the Upper Rhine, where
Carlstadt began by unreservedly proclaiming his doctrine of the Lord's
Supper ; and, however untenable was his own exposition of it, the excitement he thus occasioned was most violent, and productive of incalculable
results. Münzer proceeded through Nürnberg to Basle and the frontier
of Switzerland, where he was soon surrounded by fanatics who called themselves " the young Münzers," as Carlstadt was, by men of learning. He
confirmed them in the rejection of infant baptism, which by degrees was
become the watchword of the party that meditated a universal revolution.

Thus, to the disorganisation of the supreme authorities, was added the
general revolt of opinion against all existing institutions ; a state of the
public mind, which opened a boundless vista of possible changes in the
order of things.

The result was inevitable.

We have already seen in what a state of ferment the peasantry of all
parts of the empire had been for more than thirty years ; how many
attempts they had made to rise ; how violent was their hatred to all
constituted authorities. Long, however, before the Reformation had been
even thought of, their political schemes were tinged with a religious
character : this was shown in the case of the Capuchins at Eichstadt,
in that of Hans Behaim in the Würzburg dominions, and of the peasantry
in Untergrumbach. Joss Fritz, who in 1513 renewed the Bundschuh
at Lehen, in the Breisgau, was encouraged in his purpose by the parish
priest, " because justice would be furthered by it : God approved the
Bundschuh, as might be shown from the Scriptures ; it was, therefore, a
godly thing."[1] Poor Kunz of Würtemberg declared, in 1514, " that he
would stand up for righteousness and divine justice." It was immediately
after a sermon of a former very orthodox professor of catholic theology,
Dr. Gaislin, that the tumult first broke out on the banks of the Glems.[2]

It was the manifest and inevitable tendency of the reforming movement, which shook the authority of the clergy from its very foundations,
to foster ideas of this kind ; but it is not less clear that the evangelical
preaching, which was undertaken with far different views and aims, was
likely to be affected by an excitement already so powerful. The political
excitement was not produced by the preaching, but the religious enthusiasts
caught the political fever. For all had not the sound sense and the penetra-
tion of Luther. It was now taught that as all were the children of one
Father, and all equally redeemed by the blood of Christ, there should no
longer be any inequality of wealth or station.[3] To the complaints of the

---

says in his Life of Carlstadt, p. 65. Luther was placed in a false position by
hinting that Carlstadt's opinions were seditious, like those of Münzer, which could
not be clearly proved.

[1] Confession of Hans Hummel ; Schneider, Bundschuh zu Lehen, p. 99.

[2] Heyd Herzog Ulrich von Würtemberg, i., p. 243.

[3] " Kurz das es zugang auff Erden, wie mir Theutschen von Schlauraffenland,
die Poeten de Insulis fortunatis, und die Juden von ihres Messias Zeytten dichten,
also auch zum Tayl die Junger Christi gedachten vom Reych Christi."—" In
short, that it should be on earth, as we Germans romance of the Schlauraffenland
(a sort of pays de Cocaigne), poets, of the happy isles, and the Jews of the times
of their Messiah ; so some of the disciples of Christ thought about the kingdom of
Christ."—Eberlinvon Günzburg Ein Getrewe Warnung an die Christen in der
Burgau.

misconduct of the clergy, were added the old accusations against lords and rulers : their wars ; the harsh, and often unjust administration of their ministers and subordinates, and the oppressions under which the poor groaned ; in short, it was asserted that if the spiritual power was anti-christian, the temporal was no less so.　Both were accused of heathenism and tyranny.　" Things cannot go on as they have done," concludes one of these writings ; " the game has been carried on long enough, and both citizens and peasants are tired of it ; everything will alter—omnium rerum vicissitudo,"[1]

The first disturbances broke out in the same district in which most of the former commotions had begun,—in that part of the Schwarzwald which divides the sources of the Danube from the upper valley of the Rhine. Several causes concurred to render this the scene of peculiar discontent :— the vicinity of Switzerland, with which that part of Germany stood in various and close relations ; the peculiar severity with which the Austrian government at Ensisheim and the commission at Engen pursued even the most blameless preachers of the new doctrine ; the personal share taken in these measures by the Count of Sulz, governor of Innsbruck, and heredi-tary judge at Rothweil, who, as well as the Counts of Lupfen and Fürsten-berg, was distinguished for his hatred of Lutherans and peasants ; the presence of Duke Ulrich of Würtemberg at Hohentweil, who beheld his most formidable enemies in these noble partisans of Austria, and used every means to irritate the people against them ; lastly, perhaps, the consequences of a hailstorm which, in the summer of 1524, destroyed all hopes of the harvest in the Kletgau.　The insurrection broke out in the Stühlinger district, the domain of Count Sigismund of Lupfen.　If it be true, as the contemporary chronicles affirm, that the immediate cause of the revolt was a strange whim of the Countess of Lupfen, for winding yarn upon snail-shells which her subjects were forced to collect, it is certain that never did a more trifling and fantastic cause produce more serious and violent effects.[2]

On the 24th of August, 1524, Hans Müller of Bülgenbach, a Stühlinger peasant and soldier, went to the anniversary of the consecration of the church at Waldshut, followed by a considerable troop of insurgent peasants bearing a black, red and white flag : but resistance to a single count was

---

[1] Ein ungewonlicher und der ander Sendtbrieff dess Bauernfeyndts zu Karst-hannsen."—" An uncommon and another missive of the peasants' enemy to Karsthannsen," towards the end : printed by Johann Locher of Munich.　Panzer (ii., No. 2777.) mentions a previous letter of Karsthannsen, dated 1525.　In the second, I find no mention of the peasants' war, and it must have been written, at latest, during the latter half of the year 1524.

[2] Extract from the Villinger Chronik ; Walchner, Ratolphzell, p. 89.　Accord-ing to Anshelm, vi., p. 298, the subjects of the Counts Von Lupfen and Fürsten-berg complained, " Dass sie am Fyrtag müssten Schneggenhüssli suchen, Garn winden, Erdbeer, Kriesen, Schlehen gewinnen, und ander dergleichen thun, den Herren und Frouwen werken bei gutem Wetter, ihnen selbs im Ungewetter : das gejägd und d'hund lüffent ohne Achtung einigs Schadens."—" That on holydays they were obliged to hunt for snails, wind yarn, gather strawberries, cherries, and sloes, and do other such like things ; they had to work for their lords and ladies in fine weather, and for themselves in the rain.　Their huntsmen and hounds ran about without regarding the damage they did."　The matter was laid before the Kammergericht, but the people did not wait for the decision.

far too mean and trifling an object for him ; he announced his intention
of founding an evangelical brotherhood for the purpose of emancipating
the peasantry throughout the German empire.[1] A small contribution
levied on the members was destined to pay emissaries who were to extend
the confederation over all parts of Germany. This project did not originate
with himself. It was suggested by Thomas Münzer, who had long kept
up a correspondence with this district, and now arrived there in person.
He stayed a few weeks in Griesheim, and then traversed the Hegau and the
Kletgau,—for he could find no permanent resting-place,[2]—preaching
wherever he went the deliverance of Israel, and the establishment of a
heavenly kingdom upon earth. The subjects of the Counts of Werdenberg, Montfort, Lupfen, and Sulz, of the Abbot of Reichenau and the
Bishop of Constance, gradually joined the Stühlingers. Those of Sulz
previously consulted the inhabitants of Zürich, in which town their lord
possessed the rights of citizenship ; and although the latter did not, as
they assured the count, approve the insurrection, they did not hesitate
to make the toleration of evangelical preachers one of the conditions of
their obedience.[3] It would be well worth while to examine the course of
these movements more narrowly than has yet been done. The various
motives which concurred to produce the peasants' war were more distinguishable at this, than at any other period ; for this was the moment
at which they assumed the form of those general ideas, which from that
time to this have possessed such a singular power of inflaming and attaching
the minds of men.

The lords vainly called upon the Swabian League for aid in their peril.
Here and there a band of insurgents was induced by its persuasions and
promises to return home ; but wherever a serious engagement took place,
the peasants maintained their ground.

Hearing that a body of the infantry and cavalry of the League was
advancing against them under Jacob von Landau, they took up a strong
position, from which it was impossible to dislodge them.[4] Nor could the
most zealous efforts of well-intentioned mediators bring about any
reconciliation. The peasants drew up a statement of their grievances
in twelve articles, which they did not hesitate to lay before the Council
of Regency at Esslingen. If, however, the lords refused to enter on the
discussion of the whole of these collectively, the peasants were equally
determined not to concede any point : they had indeed far more extensive
schemes in reserve. At the end of the year 1524, and the beginning of
1525, the peasants were masters of the whole land.[5] The lords and their
ministers were at length compelled to seek safety behind the massive walls
of Ratolphzell, defended by its devoted townsmen.

Meanwhile, however, similar disturbances had broken out in larger
districts.

Nowhere were the complaints of the people better grounded than in the

---

[1] Schreiber, Taschenbuch für Süddeutschland, i., p. 72.

[2] "Certis de causis." Bullinger adversus Anabaptistas, and his Reformations-
geschichte, p. 224.

[3] Füesslins Beiträge zur Historie der Kirchenreformation, vol. ii., p. 68.

[4] Walchner, Geschichte von Ratolphzell, p. 92.

[5] The instruction given by Archduke Ferdinand to Veit Suiter (Walchner and
Bensen, p. 558) shows the state of lawless violence produced under these circumstances.

dominions of the Abbots of Kempten. These ecclesiastical rulers continually vexed their subjects with fresh taxes, which they spent in building or travelling. As long ago as the year 1492, riots had broken out in consequence, but had led to no redress of the people's wrongs. The free peasants, who were very numerous in the Abbacy, were continually ground down to the station of Zinsers,[1] and these again to that of villeins ;[2] while the latter were compelled to perform services that rendered their condition more intolerable. Free lands were taken possession of ; tithe-free estates subjected to tithes ; the money paid by the peasants for protection and defence was raised twentyfold ; the popular courts of justice held at markets or fairs were suppressed ; the revenues of the communes or villages were seized ; occasionally, even, the spiritual power was applied to carry through these oppressions. It was not surprising, therefore, that, in the year 1523, when a new Abbot, Sebastian von Breitenstein, entered on the government, the peasants refused to do homage, except on condition that he would redress their grievances. At first he held out the hope that he would comply with their demands ; thirteen sittings were held to consider them, but all in vain ; the Abbot at length exclaimed that he would leave things as he found them ; if his subjects would not obey him, George von Frundsberg should come and teach them. This was assuredly a most ill-timed stretch of the spiritual rights of supremacy, just when all men were refusing their belief in the basis on which those rights were founded—the divine authority of the clergy. As the Abbot made this appeal to force, his subjects thought it time to pepare for defence. On the 23d of January, 1525, the seceders (*Gotteshausleute*—God's house people) held a meeting at their old place on the Luibas. They determined to pursue the matter legally before the judges and councillors of the League, and if they could get no redress, to sound the tocsin, and repel force by force.

Already they beheld allies rising around them on every side. Similar, if not equal, wrongs ; the force of example, and the hope of success, set the peasantry all over Swabia in motion.

In February, the people of the Allgau, led by Dietrich Hurlewagen of Lindau, rose against the Bishop of Augsburg, and formed a strict alliance with the villages of Kempten. On the 27th of February, the two districts held a meeting on the Luibas. If any inhabitant of them refused to join the association, a stake was driven into the ground before his door, as a token that he was a public enemy. At their call, the peasants all along the Lake of Constance, and across the Alps to Pfullendorf, joined them, led by Eitelhans of Theuringen, whom his followers celebrate as " a good captain of the Lord, who kept a faithful hand over them." No bells could be tolled for divine service ; the sound of them instantly gave the alarm, and all the people rushed to the place of meeting at Bermatingen.[3] A third party, consisting of the subjects of the Abbot of Ochsenhausen, the

---

[1] The word " Zins " corresponds to the French " cens," and Zinsers to peasants with tenure " in censive," which is the English " copyhold."

[2] Haggenmüller, Geschichte der Stadt und Grafschaft Kempten, p. 505, says, that four hundred cases of this kind are recorded in the Rotula of the Provincial Acts.

[3] Salmansweiler's description in Oechsle, Beiträge zur Geschichte des Bauern-kriegs, p. 485.

Baron of Waldburg, and many other lords and cities, rose on the Ried. The villages that refused to join them were threatened with fire and sword;[1] the people on the Iller hastened to unite with them. Their centre of operations was at Baldringen.

Thus united, and grown to a formidable force, the peasantry now again laid their grievances before the Swabian League. In the course of March, negotiations were again set on foot in Ulm with the three insurgent bands. But it may be doubted whether it was not the character of the League itself which caused these discontents;—the incessant wars, the expenses of which were either thrown directly on the subjects, or raised by an increase of all the established burthens ; the support it gave to the several lords individually ; being itself composed of the very sovereigns against whom the complaints were made. It now clearly appeared how great a calamity it was for the country that the Council of Regency had recently lost so immensely in power and consideration. It sent, indeed, two of its members to command peace, and to try to bring about a reconciliation ; and they proposed to erect a court of arbitration,—each party to nominate one prince and three cities, who should hear the complaints and adjudge the remedy. But the Council of Regency was far too weak to obtain a hearing for even these moderate proposals. For a moment (in February and March) the invasion of his own land by the Duke of Würtemberg had occupied the attention of the League. It is difficult to say what would have happened if the Confederation, on whom this prince again relied, had adhered firmly to his cause, as it appeared its interest to do. For it seemed consistent enough that the Swiss, in opposition to whom the Swabian League was originally formed, should support the duke who attacked, and the peasants who revolted against it ; and it was this danger which had induced the councillors of the League to enter into negotiations. But on this occasion, as on former ones, other considerations preponderated with the Swiss diet ; and when the duke had already forced his way into the outskirts of Stuttgart, they recalled their troops from him with the greatest urgency,[2] and he was compelled to retreat without gaining any solid advantage.

[1] See the account of the treaty of Hegöwisch, Walchner, p. 298 : " Wie wol es den Frommen und Erbaren nit lieb, sonder ein gros beschwärd was. Nütt dester minder so was der Jungen und auch deren die niemen nutz ; so vil das die Allten und auch die Frommen mit innen müsten züchen, oder sy im der nit ziechen wöllt ein . Pfal für sin hus schlugent, und im darby tröwtend."—" Although, indeed, to the honest and godly it was not welcome, but rather a grievous burthen ; nevertheless, not only the young, and those who were of no use to any man, but also the old and godly men even were forced to go along with them. And if any man would not, they thrust a stake into the earth before his door, and threatened him thereat."

[2] Hans Stockar's Heimfahrt und Tagebuch, p. 131 : " und dye Botten, die miantend uns ab, das wier hiam zugend mit Mund und mit Brieffen, by Lib und by Leben, ain Eren und Gutt, by Verlürn unser Vatters-land, und ckemend wier, so wettind sy uns aller Straff ledyg lon, und erzalttend uns von dem Schaden, den wier zu Mialand und der Frantzoss Küng hatt aimpfangen. Und also warend wir unseren Heren und Oberen gehorsam, und brachen in der Nacht uff."—" And the messengers warned us to depart to our homes by word of mouth and by letter, as we loved our lives and limbs, our honour and goods, and feared to lose our country; and if we went there they would forgive us all punishment. And they told us of the losses we had suffered in Milan, and those of the French king. And accordingly we obeyed our lords and masters, and set out that same night."

The League was thus at liberty to act against the peasantry.   Without
further hesitation it required them first to lay down their arms, after which
it would treat with them.[1]   As the peasants had gone much too far to
agree to these conditions, the League, well prepared for war, determined
on an immediate resort to force.   But it was destined again to find a wholly
unexpected resistance.   Detached bands were easily routed and dispersed, and a few small places quickly reduced ; but this had no effect on
the main body.   The duke's enterprise had so far been of use to the
peasants, that it had given them time to assemble in masses which kept
even such a commander as George Truchsess in check.   Many of these
men had borne arms in the field.   While the League had excited the
insurrection by grinding taxes and religious persecutions, it had also made
the insurgents capable of self-defence, by its continual wars.   The feeling
of their own power of defending themselves was, indeed, one chief motive
to the revolt.   The foot-soldiers of the League, who had not unfrequently
served under the same banners with these peasants, had a natural fellow-
feeling with them.   And now, from the time that the last negotiations
had proved abortive, the disorder began to assume a really serious
character.

The twelve articles had appeared, and every one knew what he had
to expect, and why he had taken arms.   These articles contained three
different kinds of demands ; first of all, the liberty of the chase, of fishing,
and of hewing wood, and the prevention of or compensation for the damage
done by the game :—demands and complaints reiterated by the peasantry
of all countries ever since the rise of feudal societies : as early as the year
997, we find them urged in Normandy.[2]   Secondly, the peasants pressed
for relief from some newly-imposed burthens, new laws and penalties,
and for restoration of the property of the parishes which had been
abstracted, as we remarked in speaking of the usurpations of the lords.
Lastly, the desire for religious reform was mingled with these secular
motives.   The peasants were determined no longer to be serfs, for Christ
had redeemed them also with His precious blood ; they would no longer
pay the small tithe, but only the great one,[3] for God had ordained that
alone in the Old Testament.   Above all, they demanded the right to
choose their own preachers, in order to be instructed by them in the true

[1] Haggenmüller, Kempten, p. 522.   A book which I have constantly found
very useful.   I am surprised to find the movement at Kempten so falsely represented, even in contemporary works, and hence, of course, in all subsequent ones.
Cochläus seems to be the originator of the errors.

[2] Gulielmus Geneticensis, Hist. Norm., lib. v. 2 : " Juxta suos libitus vivere
decernebant, quatenus tam in sylvarum compendiis quam in aquarum commer-
ciis nullo obsistente ante statuti juris obice legibus uterentur suis."

[3] This is shown in the following passage from Müllner's Annals.   The council
at Nürnberg caused it to be proclaimed from all pulpits, " dass aller leben-
dige Zehent, als Füllen Kälber Lämmer, &c., desglaichen der kleine Zehent,
den man nennt dan todten Zehent, als Heidel Erbeiss Heu Hopfen, &c.,
ganz todt und abseyn solle, aber den grossen harten Zehenten von hernach
benanntem Getreide, so man die fünf Brand nennt, nemlich von Korn Dünkel
Waitzen Gerste habern, sollte man zu geben schuldig seyn."—" That all tithes
on living things, such as foals, calves, lambs, &c., likewise the small tithes called
the dead tithes, such as buck-wheat, pasture, hay, hops, &c., should be entirely
abolished ; but the people should be bound to pay the great hard tithes on the
following sorts of grain, viz., rye, spelt, wheat, barley, and oats." (According to
custom the fifteenth, twentieth, or thirtieth sheaf.)

faith, "without which they were mere flesh and blood, and good for
nothing." The characteristic feature of these articles is a mixture of
spiritual and temporal demands, a derivation of the latter from the former,
which is certainly at variance with the sentiments of Luther, and with
the pure and unmixed tendencies of the reformation ; but which is also
far removed from all schemes of general convulsion, and not at variance
with common sense and humanity. As to the political demands, the
local and particular interests are far less prominent than those of a general
or a universal character,—as was indispensable where various bands of
men were to combine : the author of them, be he who he may, gave evidence of sagacity and address. For thus alone could the articles obtain
general approbation, and be regarded as the manifesto of the whole body
of the peasantry.[1] But further demands were by no means withdrawn
in consequence.

All the people of the Black Forest, from Wutachthal to Dreisamthal,
now flocked together under Hans Müller of Bulgenbach. This leader
journeyed from place to place, brilliantly attired in a red cloak and cap,
at the head of his adherents ; the great standard and the battle flag
followed him in a cart decorated with leaves and ribbons—a sort of car-
roccio.[2] A herald, or messenger, summoned all the parishes, and read
the twelve articles aloud. Nor did their commander stop here ; he
declared them the symbol of the evangelical brotherhood, which he intended to found ; whoever refused to accept them should be put under
temporal ban by the union. Already had this been declared against the
lords of castles, the monks and priests in convents and chapters : though
even these men might be admitted into the association, if they chose to
enter it, and to live for the future in common houses like other people ;
everything should then be granted them which was their due according
to the laws of God. Müller's first vague idea of an evangelical brotherhood thus assumed a very distinct form. A radical change in political
and even in social relations was the object now clearly aimed at.

In the course of April, 1525, it really appeared likely to come to this.

It is a very remarkable circumstance that while Münzer was fomenting
the disorders in Upper Swabia, Dr. Carlstadt, a Franconian by birth, was
equally active in Franconia. Compelled to quit Strasburg and to return

[1] "Dye grunlichen und rechten Hauptartikel aller Bauerschafft und Hynder-
sessen :" printed among others in Ströbel's Beiträge, ii., p. 9. Among the editions,
one in Panzer, No. 2705, has this addition : " des monadts Martii." According
to Haggenmüller, p. 513, their first appearance in the form of a document was
during the negotiation between the three united bodies of peasants and the
Swabian League, in February and March, 1525, in which case they must have
been drawn up by a preacher who had joined the peasants. According to the
unanimous opinion of contemporaries, among whom was Melanchthon, Christopher
Schappeler was the author. Even in the Florentine History of Nardi (viii.,
p. 187), he is called, " uno scellerato rinnovatore della setta degli anabattisti
chiamato Scaflere." Schappeler, however, always denied this (Bullinger, p. 245) ;
and, indeed, it seems to have been an error. It was afterwards supposed, and
from his own confession (see Strobel, ib., p. 76), that Joh. Heughlin, of Lindau,
was the real author, yet his confession relates only to the articles which were
granted to the peasants of Sernatingen, to prevent their joining the other peasants:
the famous twelve articles would have been mentioned in another manner.

[2] Schreiber der Breisgau im Bauernkriege, Taschenb. für Süddeutschland,
i., p. 235.

home, but there subject to incessant persecution, and regarded with double horror in consequence of the notoriety of his doubts as to the sacrament, he at length found an asylum at Rothenburg on the Tauber, where his opinions were regarded with sympathy. The citizens of the guilds demanded that the church reform which had just been begun should be carried through, which the patrician families (*die Geschlechter*), whose domination was, moreover, not wholly legal, opposed. The guilds had a most powerful ally on their side, in the sturdy war-like peasants of the Landwehr, who were also vexed with exorbitant and illegal charges, and who claimed the liberty of the Gospel. We are too well acquainted with the character of Carlstadt not to know that he would approve all the objects of the people. Already banished by the council, but secretly protected by certain powerful members of it, he suddenly appeared near the crucifix in the great burial-ground, in his peasant's coat and hat of rough white felt, and exhorted the country people not to desist from their endeavours.[1] It may easily be imagined, however, that the movement was not confined to religious innovations. In the last week of March disturbances broke out, first in the country, and then in the town, in which a committee of the guilds seized on all the power ; while the rural communes formed themselves into a great association, set forth their grievances—which had indeed spiritual grounds, but were by no means of an exclusively spiritual nature—and took up arms to compel redress.

In Franconia the slumbering fires of discontent burst forth with still greater rapidity than in Swabia ; either in consequence of the combinations formed by the emissaries sent by Hans Müller, or by the excitement produced in the minds of the disaffected ringleaders by the example of their neighbours. A few thousand peasants, excited by the twelve articles which had fallen into their hands, assembled in a valley of the Odenwald, called the Schüpfergrund, and chose for their leader George Metzler, the inn-keeper at Ballenburg, in whose house the first arrangements had been made,—a bold man, whose life had been passed in the noisy revels of a frequented tavern.[2] Similar meetings were held at Böckingen, Mergentheim, and many other places. The first thing usually was to break the fasts ; a banquet was held at which the most eloquent and the most disaffected spoke ; the twelve articles were brought out, read, and approved ; a leader was chosen, and the alarm bell sounded. Such was the beginning of the riot, the first act of which, in almost every case, was to seize upon a flour store or a wine-cellar, or to drag a seigneurial fish-pond. The newly-chosen commanders might be seen riding about with an air of authority, mounted upon the priest's pony. But though these tumults seemed contemptible enough in their beginnings, they became more and more formidable as they advanced. On an appointed day the several bands repaired together from every side, not exactly at the customary meeting-place, but at some convent they had doomed to destruction, as for example, at Scheflersheim, where they swore to pay neither tax, rent,

---

[1] Bensen der Bauernkrieg in Ostfranken, p. 79. According to the sentence passed on Stephan von Menzingen, this leader of the town movements, an adherent of Duke Ulrich of Würtenberg, associated frequently with Carlstadt. See Anfang und Ende des Bauernkriegs zu Rothenburg, Walch, L. W., xvi. 180.

[2] According to Hubert Thomas Leodius, this occurred about the middle of Lent, at Lätare, 26th March.

nor tithe to any lord, temporal or spiritual, till they would come to some terms ; and in future, as they had only one God, to acknowledge only one master. It was as if the insurgents were led by some secret guidance to one predetermined end. Their object was in the first place to emancipate themselves from their lords, but then to unite with them and take measures in concert against the clergy, and, above all, against the spiritual princes.

To accomplish this work by forcible means, two troops marched into the field, one called the Black from Rothenburg, under Hans Kolbenschlag, the other, the White, from the Odenwald, under George Metzler. The lords were compelled to accept the twelve articles, of which the Odenwald band published a distinct declaration, wherein the abolition of the punishment of death, of the lesser tithes, and of villeinage were especially insisted on, without omitting such local modifications as should seem necessary, and holding out the prospect of further reforms.[1] This band had not, like the Swabian, the forces of the League to deal with ; there was nobody capable of resisting them. The Counts of Hohenlohe and Löwenstein, the commander of the Teutonic Order at Mergentheim, and the Junker of Rosenberg, were forced in succession to subscribe to the conditions laid before them by the peasants, and to submit beforehand to the reforms they purposed to introduce. The Counts George and Albert of Hohenlohe consented to appear before the peasants' army at Grünbühl. " Brother George and brother Albert," said a tinker of Ohringen to them, " come hither and swear to the peasants to be as brothers to them, for ye are now no longer lords but peasants."[2] Terrible, indeed, was the fate of those who ventured to resist, like Count Helfenstein at Weinsberg. The natural rudeness of peasants was inflamed by the first opposition into the wildest and most wanton bloodthirstiness : they swore that they would kill every man that wore spurs ; and when Helfenstein had fallen into their power, it was in vain that his wife, a natural daughter of Emperor Maximilian, threw herself at the feet of the leaders with her little son in her arms : a lane was formed, and the victim brought out, preceded by a peasant playing on a pipe ; Helfenstein was then driven onto the spears of his peasants amidst the sound of trumpets and horns. Hereupon everyone gave way : all the nobility, from the Odenwald to the Swabian frontier submitted to the laws of the peasants,— those of Winterstetten, Stettenfels, Zobel, Gemmingen, Frauenberg, and the Counts of Wertheim and Rheineck ; those of Hohenlohe (now) even gave up their artillery to the peasants.[3] In order to bring the matter to a conclusion, both bodies now marched against the most powerful lord in Franconia, who bore the title of duke there,—the Bishop of Würzburg. On their way, they had not alone enriched and strengthened themselves, but had also secured distinguished commanders of the knightly class. Götz von Berlichingen had undertaken the command of the Odenwald troop ; partly because it would have been dangerous to refuse ; partly attracted by the prospect of active war, which was the sole object and passion of his life, and in which he was the more ready to engage, as it was directed

---

[1] Explanation of the 12 articles. Ochsle, p. 572, and Bensen, p. 526.
[2] Letter from Count George to the city of Hall. Tuesday after Palm Sunday. Oechsle, p. 271.
[3] Chronik der Truchsessen, ii., p. 195.

against his old enemies of the Swabian League.[1] Florian Geier led the Rothenburgers. On the 6th and 7th of May these bands approached Würzburg in opposite directions, and were joyfully received by the inhabitants of the town, who hoped to gain the privileges of a free imperial city ;[2] the citizens and the peasants swore not to forsake each other till they had conquered the Frauenberg, in which the last remaining forces of the princes and knights of Franconia, who were now united, had assembled.

At the same moment (the end of April and beginning of May, 1525) a similar state of things began throughout Upper Germany. Disturbances broke out in all directions, and everywhere they were in effect successful.

The Bishop of Spire had been forced to submit to the conditions imposed by the peasants ;[3] the Elector Palatine had met them in an open field near the village of Horst, and promised to redress their grievances on the conditions laid down in the twelve articles.[4] In Alsace, Zabern, the residence of the bishop himself, had fallen into the hands of the insurgents ; the inhabitants of the small towns declared that they had no spears wherewith to pierce the peasants ; for a time their leaders, Schlemmerhans and Deckerhans,[5] were all-powerful. On Markgrave Ernest of Baden refusing to accept the terms offered by the peasants, his castle was taken and he was forced to fly. The knights of the Hegau were surrounded and besieged by them in the town of Zell on the Untersee. Even the powerful Truchsess, at the head of the forces of the Swabian League, was compelled to come to terms with the peasants of the Allgau, See and Ried, and, with the mediation of the cities, to promise them relief from their oppressions, before they would submit. It was unusual good fortune when they would thus consent to wait for future arrangements. In Würtemberg they would not hear of any more diets of the duchy (*Landtäge*), but insisted on instantly placing everything in the hands of their Christian brotherhood, which had already spread over the chief part of the country. Each place sent a certain number of people into the field.

The Bishop of Bamberg, the Abbot of Hersfeld, and the coadjutor of Fulda, had already made concessions of a spiritual, as well as temporal kind. The last-named of the three agreed to these changes with peculiar readiness, and immediately allowed himself to be saluted Prince von der Buchen ; his brother, the old Count William of Henneberg, also entered into the peasants' league, and promised to leave in freedom " all whom God Almighty

---

[1] Lebensbeschreibung des Götz, p. 201. See his Apology in the Materialien, p. 156.

[2] Johann Reinhards Würzburgische Chronik in Ludwig, Würzb. Geschichtschr., p. 886.

[3] Gnodalius, ii., p. 142.

[4] Letter from the Elector to Melanchthon: "Haben uns mit ihnen den 12 Artikel wegen eines Landtags vereinigt, dergestalt wes wir uns derselben mit ihnen vergleichen möchten, das hat seine wege, wes wir uns aber nicht vertragen können, das solt stehen zu Thürfursten Fürsten und Ständen des Reichs."— " We have agreed with them about a diet to consider the 12 articles ; in such wise that whatever we could arrange with them was to stand, but what we cannot settle was to be referred to the electors, princes, and states of the empire." This was the principle of most of the arrangements that were made (Mel. Epp., i., p. 743).

[5] Two names, equivalent to Jack the Guttler and Jack the Tiler.—TRANSL.

had made free in Christ his son."[1]   The boldest attempt at a complete
change in all the relations of life was perhaps that made by the inhabitants
of the Rheingau.   They once more assembled on the old traditional
meeting-place, the Lützelau, at Bartholomewtide,[2] and agreed to demand,
above all, the restoration of their ancient constitution, the Haingericht
(Bush Court)[3] subsisting under their old law, and the Gebick, which converted the country into a sort of fortress : besides this they insisted on the
participation of the lords, both spiritual and temporal, in the burthens
borne by the community at large, and the application of conventual
property to the use of the country.   They encamped on the Wachholder
at Erbach, and actually in open rebellion, compelled the governor, dean
and chapter to grant their demands.[4]   At Aschaffenburg too, the governor
for the Archbishop of Mainz was forced to submit to the conditions of the
peasants.

The whole Swabian and Franconian branch of the German nation was
thus in a state of agitation which seemed likely to end in a complete overthrow of all the existing relations of society ; a great number of towns
were already infected with the prevailing spirit.

The small towns were the first to join the cause of the peasantry,—
Kempten, Leipheim, and Günzburg on the Danube (which, indeed, soon
received severe chastisement) ; the nine Odenwald towns in the see of
Mainz, and the towns in the Breisgau, in some of which the town clerk himself opened the gates to the peasants ; none of these, indeed, were in a condition to resist, and most of them groaned under the same oppressions as
the peasantry.   The people of Bamberg conceived the bold project of com-
pelling the surrounding nobles to come and live within the walls of their
town and to become burghers ; nearly fifty castles were stormed in this
neighbourhood.[5]   The Abbot of Kempten being forced to surrender his
castle of Liebenthann to the peasants, and to seek refuge in the town, the
burghers took advantage of the favourable moment to bring him to an
agreement they had long desired, for the release of all his rights of sovereignty.   Some of the free imperial towns of the second and third classes
were next drawn into the league by persuasion or by force : these were
Heilbronn, Memmingen, Dünkelspiel, and Wimpfen ; Rothenburg entered
into an alliance with the peasantry for a hundred and one years, which was
ratified at a solemn assembly held in the parish church : Windsheim was

---

[1] The formula of the League.   Ludwig, p. 879.
[2] According to Bodmann's Rheingauischen Alterthümern, p. 461, Vogt's
assertion, that the juniper-tree was the ancient place of meeting, is erroneous.
[3] Grimm, in his Deutsche Rechtsalthümer, p. 793, says, " The ancient *Gericht*
was invariably held in the open air, in a wood, under shady trees, on a hillock,
or near a spring : the assembled multitude could not have been contained in any
moderate building, and pagan ideas required that the Gericht should be holden in
a holy spot, on which sacrifices were offered, and the judgment of heaven appealed
to.   Christianity abolished the sacrifices, but left the old *Gerichtstatten* undisturbed."   I have sought in vain for any explanation of the word *Gebick*.   It has
been suggested to me that it is something like a Mark (district), or rather the lines
by which each Mark was enclosed.   These were chiefly formed by forests, and
also by rivers, ditches, and other natural boundaries.   See Grimm's account of
the primitive territorial divisions of Germany (book iii., p. 491).—Transl.
[4] Artikel gemeiner Landschaft : Schunk, Beiträge zur Mainze Gesch., i., p. 191.
[5] Lang's Geschichte von Baireuth, i., p. 187.   Heller, p. 88.

only restrained from the same course by the dissuasions of Nürnberg. Even in the great cities a similar spirit manifested itself. Mainz claimed the restitution of its rights as an imperial city, of which it had been deprived since the last disturbances. The council of Trier not only demanded that the clergy should be called upon to bear their share in the burthens of the citizens, but even laid claim to a part of the spiritual revenues accruing from the relics in the cathedral.[1] The council of Frankfurt was forced to agree to the articles laid before it by the commonalty, word by word ;[2] alleging as an excuse that the same thing had happened in several other imperial cities. It was remarked that Strasburg received the insurgents as citizens, and that Ulm supplied them with arms, and Nürnberg with provisions. A learned writer of this period states it as his opinion, that the movement had originated even more with the towns than with the peasantry, and that the former had been originally stirred up by Jewish emissaries : he believes that the intention of the towns was to shake off the authority of the princes altogether, and to live like Venice, or the republics of antiquity.[3]

Unfounded as was this opinion—for we know how zealously many of the imperial towns, Nürnberg for example, strove to suppress the rising disorders in their own dominions, and we have seen that the disturbances in the towns which corresponded to those of the peasants were only called forth by circumstances,—yet we cannot but perceive what force and extension must have been given to the rebellion by the addition of this second element, and how wide and threatening the danger was become.

The ideas to which this crisis gave birth were most remarkable.

The Franconian peasants formed projects for the reform of the whole empire.

So deeply rooted was this purpose in the very heart of the nation. That which the princes had vainly endeavoured to accomplish at so many diets, —which Sickingen and his knights had attempted three years before to execute after their fashion,— the peasants now believed they could effect—of course in the manner most calculated to raise their own condition.

The first object was to give a general direction and guidance to the present tumultuous movement. A common office for the business of all the separate bands, in fact a sort of central government, was to be established at Heilbronn. The masses were to be ordered to return home to their daily work, leaving only a certain levy in the field, whose duty it would be to compel all who still remained unsubdued to accept the twelve articles.

In the further attempts to create some positive institutions, the predominant idea was that of freeing the peasantry from the burthen of all the oppressive privileges of the lords, both spiritual and temporal. To accomplish this, it was determined to proceed at once to a general secularisation of the ecclesiastical property. As this would involve the abolition of the spiritual principalities, means would thus be obtained for giving com-

[1] Scheckmann : Additamentum ad Gesta Trevirorum in Wyttenbach's Edition ôf the Gesta, ii., Animadv., p. 51.

[2] Lersner's Frankfurter Chronik.

[3] Conradi Mutiani Literæ ad Fridericum Electorem, 27th April, 1525, in Köhler's Beiträge, i. 270.

pensation to the temporal sovereigns for the loss of their rights, for which
some indemnity was thought due.   The amount of church property was so
enormous that the people hoped still to have enough left to satisfy all the
public exigencies of the empire.   All duties and tolls were to be taken off,
and all charges for safe conduct ; and only every tenth year a tax was to
be levied for the Roman emperor,[1] who was in future to be the sole protector and ruler of the country, and to whom alone the people were to owe
duty and allegiance.   The courts of law were to be remodelled and popular-
ised on one comprehensive principle.   There were to be sixty-four free
courts (*Freigerichte*[2]) in the empire, with assessors of all classes, even the
lowest ; besides these, sixteen district courts (*Landgerichte*), four courts of
appeal (*Hofgerichte*), and one supreme court (*Kammergericht*); all organised
in the same manner.   The members of the Kammergericht were to be as
follows :—two princes, two regining counts, two knights, three burghers
of the imperial towns, three from the princely residences, and four from all
the communes of the empire.   These were plans which had often been
suggested, and are, for instance, to be found in a work which appeared as
early as 1523, called " Need of the German Nation " (" *Nothdurft deutscher
Nation*")—they were now adopted and developed by two clever and daring
peasant leaders, Friedrich Weigant of Miltenberg, and Wendel Hipler,
formerly chancellor of Hohenlohe.[3]   The doctors of the Roman law were
especially hated by the peasantry ; they were not to be admitted into any
court of law, and only to be tolerated at the universities, in order that their
advice might be taken in urgent cases.   All classes, too, were to be made

---

[1] They refused to acknowledge Markgrave Ernest of Baden as their sovereign,
and were determined to be governed in future by the Emperor and his
deputy alone.   They also meant something similar by the divine right which
they conceded to the Duke of Würtemberg.   The chief ground of their recognition of the Emperor (*Kaiser—Cæsar*) was that he was named in the New
Testament.

[2] Grimm says, in his Deutsche Rechts Alterthümer (p. 829), " Originally almost
every *Gau* or *Merkgericht* might be called a *Freigericht*.   Later, however, when the
sovereignty of the princes gained force and consistency, this term acquired a
peculiar meaning.   Particular districts which maintained their independence,
and remained immediately subject to the empire, bore the name of *Freigerichte*,
just as immediate cities were called *Freistädte*."   Courts called *Freigerichte*, of
which the lord of the soil appoints the president, and the peasants the assessors,
exist, I am told, in the German provinces of Russia.—TRANSL.

[3] See the plans of the peasants in Ochsle, p. 163, and in the Appendix.   It has
already been remarked by Eichhorn (Deutsche Staats und Rechtsgesch., iii.,
p. 119, 4th ed.) that these designs throw a new light on the so-called Reformation
of Frederick III.   Goldast does not indeed deserve the blame which Eichhorn
attributes to him : he has not given this little work as a reformation of the Emperor's.   The old work he quotes bears the title " Teutscher Nation Notturft : die
Ordnung und Reformation aller Stend in Röm. Reych, durch Kayser Friedrich III.
Gott zu Lob, der ganzen Christenheit zu Nutz und Seligkait fürgenommen."
(Panzer, ii., p. 226.)—" The Needs of the German Nation : the ordering and reformation of all the classes of the Roman empire by the Emperor Frederick III.,
undertaken for the glory of God, and for the benefit and salvation of all Christendom."   But this, no doubt, is a mere author's fiction.   The paper breathes
throughout the spirit of the first years of the reformation.   The calamity at Erfurt,
which is there mentioned among those communes which owed their ruin to self-
interest, refers, no doubt, to the destructive riots of 1510, and not to any previous
and less remarkable events.

to return to their original vocation ; the clergy were to be only the shepherds of their flocks ; the princes and knights were to occupy themselves
in defending the weak, and to live in brotherly love one with another.   All
the commons were to undergo a reformation consonant to the laws of God
and of nature : only one sort of coin was to be current, and uniform weights
and measures were to be introduced.

Ideas more radically subversive than were ever again proclaimed till the
time of the French Revolution.

But bold and anarchical as they were, they were not without a considerable prospect of being realised.   The contagion spread every instant : it
had already seized on Hessen, whence it threatened to extend its conquests
over the Saxon race ; as from Upper Swabia over the Bavarian, and from
Alsatia over that of Lorraine.   Corresponding disturbances took place in
Westphalia ; for example, at Münster, where the town demanded the same
concessions from its chapter as at Trier, and the bishop already feared
that he should see the whole country hurried away by the storm.[1]   It also
broke out on the Austrian frontiers, where all that offered resistance were
put under ban by the peasantry ; all the Alpine districts were in the same
state : in Tyrol, Archduke Ferdinand found himself compelled, in manifest
contravention of the decrees of Ratisbon, to concede to the committees
of the states of Inn and Wippthal that the Gospel should in future be
preached " pure and plain, according to the sense borne by the text ;" [2]
in the see of Brixen, the bishop's secretary, Michael Geissmayr, headed the
insurgents ; at Salzburg, the miners flocked to the churches at the sound of
the alarm-bell ; even between Vienna and Neustadt the labourers in the
vineyards talked of a combination which would enable them to send about
ten thousand men into the field within a few hours.[3]

Meanwhile, the rebellion had broken out in Thuringia, and had there
assumed another character.

It appears probable that in Thuringia and the Harz, traditions of the
fanaticism of the flagellants, the effects of which may be traced down even
to the end of the 15th century,[4] had prepared the ground for the insurrec-

---

[1] " Alle und semptliche Artikel durch die van Munster by sick solvest up-
gericht."—" All and every article drawn up for themselves by those of Munster,"
and especially the letter of the Bishop Frederick, dated 8th of May, in Niesert,
" Beiträge zu einem Münsterschen Urkundenbuch," i., p. 113.   " So juw vor-
gekommen, was grotes uprores jtzont im hylligen Ryke und daitscher nation
weder alle Christliche Ordenunge Obericheit geistlich und weltlich vorhanden
is—werden wy berichtet—das sulchs allhier in unserm Gestichte unser Obericheit
und insonderheit dem geistlichen Stande zü gyner geringen Verhonynge Inbrock
und Besweringe im Deile och vorgenommen und betenget."—" And it has come
to our knowledge what great uproar there is now throughout the holy empire and
German nation, against all Christian order and all rulers, both spiritual and temporal ; and we are informed that, in our diocese, this has been the cause of no
little contempt, resistance, and complaining against our magistrates, and especially against those of the ecclesiastical order."

[2] Excerpts in Bucholtz, viii., p. 330.   Bucholtz shows a want of knowledge of
the language of this period in assuming that by these concessions the difficulties
were avoided.

[3] Schreiben von Hofrath und Renntkammer, Bucholtz, viii., p. 88.

[4] According to Johann Lindner's Onomasticon (Mencken, ii., p. 1521) this sect
prevailed chiefly in Aschersleben and Sangerhausen.   In a document which is
quoted by Forstemann in his Provincialblättern für Sachsen (1838, No. 232)

tion of the peasantry.   At all events motives arising out of religious
enthusiasm were much more powerful there than political causes.   The
opinions which Luther had overcome at Wittenberg, and which he had
warned his prince not to suffer to take root in Thuringia, were now eagerly
listened to by a numerous and excited population.   Münzer had returned
to Thuringia ; he had been received at Mühlhausen,[1] where, as at Rothenburg, a change of the constitution and of the council had been brought
about by the co-operation of the lower class of burghers with the country
people ; and from hence he soon spread the ferment far and wide around
him.   He scorned, as we are already aware, the " fabulous gospel " preached
by Luther, his " honeysweet Christ," and his doctrine that antichrist must
be destroyed by the Word alone, without violence : he maintained that the
tares must be rooted out at the time of harvest ; that the example of
Joshua, who smote the people of the promised land with the edge of the
sword, must be followed.[2]   He was moreover dissatisfied with the compacts
made by the peasants in Swabia and Franconia.   His views went much
farther ; he deemed it impossible to speak the truth to the people so long
as they were governed by princes.   He declared it intolerable that all
creatures had been converted into property,—the fish in the water, the
birds in the air, and the plants on the earth ; these creatures must be free
to all before the pure Word of God could be revealed.   He utterly rejected
all the principles on which the idea of the State rests, and acknowledged
nothing but revelation ; " but this," he said, " must be expounded by a
second Daniel, who will lead the people like Moses."   At Mühlhausen he
was regarded as a master and a prophet ; he had a seat in the council, and
gave judgment in the court of law according to revelation ; under his direc-

---

we find an inquisition at Castle Hoym against one of these flagellants, in the year
1481.   It was perhaps a point of union that they too looked upon their preacher
as a prophet, and thought that in him they beheld the judge at the day of judgment.   But, indeed, the whole is dressed up with metaphor.

[1] Not the more famous town in Alsace, but Mühlhausen in Thuringia.

[2] Auslegung des andern unterschyds Danielis dess propheten gepredigt aufm
Schloss zu Alstedt vor den tetigen thewren Herzogen und Vorstehern zu Sachsen
durch Thomas Münzer, 1524."—" Explanation of the other distinction of the
Prophet Daniel, preached at the Castle of Alsted, before the active and beloved
dukes and governors of Saxony, by Thomas Müntzer."   Certainly one of his most
remarkable productions.   He takes great pains to prove the difference between
genuine revelations and false visions, *e.g.*, that the former descends on a man in
a joyful amazement (" in eyner frohen Verwunderung ").   A man must be free
from all temporal comforts of the flesh (" abgeschieden sein von allem zeitlichen
Trost seines Fleisches ").   The work of visions should flow not from human
endeavours, but simply from the unchangeable will of God (" nit rausser quellen
durch menschliche anschlege, sondern einfaltig herfliessen nach Gottes un-
vorrucklichen Willen ").   It is clear that he does not go nearly so far as Ignatius
Loyola ; at the same time he combats Luther's more moderate theory, which he
ascribes to " imaginary goodness " (" einer getichten Güte ").   He says quite
openly, that the ungodly should not be suffered to live.   " I say with Christ
that ungodly rulers, more especially priests and monks, should be put to death "
(" Ich sage mit Christo, &c. das man die gotlosen regenten, sunderlich pfaffen
und mönche tödten sol ").   Princes are to exterminte the ungodly, or God will
take the sword from them.   " Oh, my dear masters, how finely will the Lord
smite the old pots with an iron rod ! "   (" Ah lieben Herren, wie hubsch wirt der
Herr unter die alten Topf schmeissen mit einer eysern Stangen.")

tion convents were suppressed, and their property confiscated ; cannon of prodigious calibre founded, and warlike enterprises executed. The priests' houses in the territory of Duke George were first attacked, and then the convents stormed, with the assistance of the enraged populace ; in the Harz and throughout the great plain of Thuringia, up to the edge of the forest. The monuments of the old Landgraves at Reinhardsbrunn were defaced, and the library destroyed.[1] The next step was to attack the castles and farms of the lords, both in Eichsfeld and in Thuringia. We no longer find any mention of conditions and treaties, or of a future reformation ; the object of these fanatics was a general and pitiless destruction. " Beloved brethren," writes Münzer to the miners at Mansfeld ; " do not relent if Esau gives you fair words ; give no heed to the wailings of the ungodly. Let not the blood cool on your swords ; lay Nimrod on the anvil, and let it ring lustily with your blows ; cast his strong tower to the earth while it is yet day." " Know then," he writes to Count Ernest of Heldrungen, " that God has commanded us to cast thee from thy seat with the might that is given to us."[2] When the country people of Schwarzburg, also in league with the small towns, rose against the count, and assembled in considerable force at Frankenhausen, Münzer feared nothing but the conclusion of a treaty ; " a fraud," he calls it, " under colour of justice " : he left his stronghold of Mühlhausen in order to prevent this and to attack " the eagle's nest " in person. He proved from the Apocalypse that the power was to be given to the common people. " Come and join in our measure," he writes to his friends at Erfurt, " it shall be right fairly trod ; we will pay the blasphemers back all that they have done to poor Christendom." He signed himself " Thomas Münzer, with the sword of Gideon."

Fanatic as he was, Münzer still occupied a most formidable position. In him the mystical notions of former ages were blended with the tendencies toward ecclesiastical and temporal reform which had just arisen. Out of this combination he formed a set of opinions which addressed themselves immediately to the common people ; incited them to rise and annihilate the whole existing order of things, and prepared the way to the absolute sway of a prophet. The people assembled in troops all around on the hills of Meissen and Thuringia,[3] awaiting the first decisive result of his enterprise, in order to join him immediately after it. The popular current would then have flowed in this direction from all parts of Germany.

At length, therefore, the results which might long have been anticipated, appeared. No sooner were the authorities which constituted the State in Germany at variance with themselves and each other, than the elementary forces on which it rested arose. The lightnings flashed from the ground, and the streams of public life left their accustomed channels : the storm which had so long been muttering underground now poured out all its fury on the upper regions, and everything seemed to threaten a complete convulsion.

If we examine more closely this great elemental strife of the German State in all its bearings, we shall be able to distinguish several different steps in its progress.

Its origin was, no doubt, to be found in the oppression of the peasantry,

[1] Thuringia Sacra, i., p. 173.
[2] Letter in Strobel : Leben, Schriften und Lehren Thomæ Münzer, p. 95.
[3] Pauli Langii Chronica Nurnburgensia, in Mencken, ii., p. 67.

which had been gradually increasing during the preceding years ; in the imposition of fresh taxes, and, at the same time, the persecution of the evangelical doctrines which had seized on the minds of the common people more strongly than any intellectual influence before or since, and had more effectually stimulated them to individual exertion. Had the peasants been content with resisting all arbitrary claims, and securing the liberty of hearing their own doctrine preached, they would have avoided calling up against them the whole strength of the existing order of things, and might have secured to themselves a long course of peaceful and lawful improvement.

Nay, even more might have been obtained ; in many places, treaties were concluded by which the lords gave up the most oppressive of the rights they had formerly acquired ; it was probable that these would be observed on both sides, and that a lawful and well-defined relation would thus be established between the classes.

But it is not in human nature to rest content with moderate success ; it is vain to expect reason or forbearance from a conquering multitude. Here and there a confused tradition of some ancient rights of the commons was revived, or the people found themselves a match for the knights in the field ;—indeed, the rebellion must be considered partly as a symptom of the revived importance of infantry ;—but for the most part, they were goaded by long-cherished hatred and lust of revenge, which now found vent. While some of their chiefs boasted that they would introduce a better order of government into the empire, the wildest destruction was carried from castle to castle, from convent to convent, and even threatened the towns which had refused to join the rebellion. The peasants thought they ought not to rest while a dwelling was left standing in Germany superior to a peasant's cottage.[1] Their fury was inflamed by the ravings of fanatical preachers, who justified the work of destruction, and thought it a duty to shed blood ; and, following the inspiration of the moment, which they called divine, to erect a new kingdom of heaven. Had this movement been successful there must of course have been an end of all peaceful progress, according to the laws which have ever governed the human race. Happily, it could not succeed ; Münzer was far indeed from being the prophet and hero required to execute so gigantic an enterprise ; besides which, the existing order of

---

[1] According to Müllner's Annalen, the peasants, in anger at receiving some refusal, declared to the council of Nürnberg, that the council might stand in greater need of the peasants than the peasants of the council : " darauf sind sie mit einem solchen Trutz und Hochmuth abgescheiden, als wann die Welt ihr eigen wäre ; haben sich auch ingeheim gegen etliche vernehmen lassen, sie gedenken kein Hauss in ganzen Land zu gedulden, das besser sey denn ein Bauernhaus :"—" thereupon they departed with such insolence and pride, as though the world were their own : they also in private gave many to understand that they were resolved to suffer no house to stand which was better than a peasant's hut." In the ordinance made by Michel Geismair in 1526 (" Lanndsordnung, so Michel Geismair gemacht hat, im 1526 Jar," Bucholz, ix. 651), the fifth article is, " alle Rinkmauern an den Stetten, dergl. alle Geschlösser und Bevestigung im Lannd niedergeprochen werden und hinfur nimmer Stätt sonnder Dörfer sein, damit Unterschied der Menschen (aufhöre), und ain gannze gleichait im Lannd sei "—" That all walls round towns, likewise all castles and fortified houses in the country, should be thrown down, and thenceforth there were to be villages but no towns, so that all distinction among men should cease, and a complete equality should prevail in the land."

things was too firm to be so completely overthrown. Moreover, the strongest and most genuine element of the reforming party was opposed to it.

Luther had not allowed himself to be hurried into any political enterprise by Sickingen and the knights ; nor had the insurrection of the peasantry any attractions for him. At the beginning, ere it assumed its more frightful form, he exhorted them to peace : while he rebuked the lords and princes for their acts of violence and oppression, he condemned the rebellion as contrary to divine and evangelical law, and as threatening destruction to both spiritual and temporal authorities, and hence to the German nation.[1] But when the danger so rapidly increased, when his old enemies, the " murder prophets and mob spirits," took so prominent a part in the tumult, and when he really began to fear lest the peasants should prove victorious (a state of things which he thought could only be the precursor of the day of judgment), the whole storm of his indignation burst forth. With the boundless influence which he possessed, what must have been the consequences had he taken part with the insurgents ! But he remained a staunch advocate for the separation between the spiritual and the temporal, which was one of the fundamental principles of his whole system ; and to the doctrine that the gospel gives freedom to the soul, but does not emancipate the body from restraint, or property from the control of the laws. The origin of the rebellion has been often ascribed to his preaching, but this is not confirmed by the facts. Luther now, as three years before, did not for one instant hesitate to brave the storm, and to do everything in his power to prevent the general destruction which he clearly foresaw. A pious Christian, said he, should rather die a hundred deaths than give way one hair's breadth to the peasants' demands. The government should have no mercy ; the day of wrath and of the sword was come, and their duty to God obliged them to strike hard as long as they could move a limb : whosoever perished in this service was a martyr of Christ. Thus he supported the temporal order of things with the same intrepidity that he had displayed in attacking the spiritual.[2]

The secular authorities, too, aroused themselves, and took courage in this, the greatest peril that had ever threatened them.

The first who rose was the same man who had done the best service against Sickingen,—the young Philip of Hessen : towards the end of April he assembled his knights and his most trusty subjects of the towns in

---

[1] " Ermanung zum Friede auf die 12 Artikel der Baurschaft in Schwaben."— Altenb., iii., p. 114.

[2] Wider die räubischen und mördischen Bauern.—Against the robbing and murderous peasants.—*Ibid.*, p. 124. See the letter to Rühel, ii., p. 886. Melanchthon came to his aid on this occasion with his convincing, dogmatical, and clear conclusions ; *e.g.*, to Spalatin, 10th April, 1525, chiefly to be understood as directed against the introduction of the Mosaic laws, but also to be understood generally : " Rationi humanæ commisit Christus ordinationes politicas : . . . debemus uti præsentibus legibus." (Corp. Ref., i. 733.) It is necessary to have a front of brass to persist in affirming, as Surius and Cochlæus have done, that Luther abandoned the peasants when he saw that they were beaten. I do not know whether the partial successes of George Truchsess, gained at a great distance, were really known to Luther ; it is, however, certain that they decided nothing : the revolt of the peasants had just taken full possession of Thuringia and Saxony, when Luther, at his own personal risk, opposed it.

Alsfeld ; he promised them that no new burthens should be laid on the peasants ;[1] while, on their part, in answer to his inquiry, they swore with outstretched hands to live and die with him. His first care was to defend his own frontiers ; he tranquillised Hersfeld and Fulda, not, indeed, without violence, though his cruelties have been fabulously exaggerated ; and then crossed the mountains and marched into Thuringia to the assistance of his Saxon cousins, with whom he stood in hereditary alliance.[2]

Just at the moment that these disorders reached their height in that district, the Elector Frederick died. How striking was the contrast between the fierce intestine discord which raged throughout Germany, and the quiet chamber at Lochau in which Frederick, calm and collected in the midst of agonizing pain, was awaiting the approach of death ! " You do well," said he to his preacher and secretary Spalatin, who after long hesitation had taken courage to demand an audience of him, "you do well to come to me, for it is right to visit the sick :" he then caused the low chair in which he reclined to be rolled to the table, and laying his hand in that of the intimate friend and adviser of his latter years, he once more talked of the things of this world, of the peasants' rebellion, of Dr. Luther, and of his own approaching death. He had ever been a gentle master to his poor people, and he now exhorted his brother to act prudently and leniently ;[3] he was not frightened at the danger of the peasants becoming masters, serious as he believed it to be ; for if it were not the will of God, it could not happen. This conviction, which had guided and supported him through the whole course of the Lutheran movement, was doubly strong in his last moments. None of his relations were with him ; he was surrounded only by servants. The spirit of opposition which everywhere else divided rulers and their subjects, had not yet reached them. " Dear children," said the prince, " if I have ever offended any of you, I pray you to forgive me for the love of God ; we princes do many things to the poor people that we ought not to do." He then spoke only of the merciful God who comforts the dying. For the last time Frederick strained his failing eyes to read one of his friend Spalatin's consolations ; he then received the sacrament in both kinds from the hands of a clergyman to whom he was attached. The new doctrine, which had flourished under his prudent and sheltering care, now no longer appeared to him in the light of a power of this world which had to fight for its existence, and the herald of a new order of things ;—he only saw in it the true Gospel, the true Christian faith, piety, and comfort to the soul. The dying man leaves the world to itself, and withdraws entirely within the circle of his own relations to the Infinite,—to God, and eternity. Thus he died on the 5th of May, 1525. " He was a child of peace," said his physician, " and in peace he hath departed."[4]

His successor, now the Elector John, ascended the throne in the midst of the wildest and most formidable confusion. Concessions were no longer to be thought of ; there existed the same difference between Frederick and John as between Luther's first and second book ; between doubt and

---

[1] This information is afforded by a declaration of Landgrave William at the Diet of 1576. Rommel, Neuere Geschichte von Hessen, p. 255, 848.

[2] Haarer, Warhafftige Beschreibung des Bauernkriegs, c. 49, in Göbel's Beiträgen, p. 139. Rommel, i. 108.

[3] His letters of the 14th of April, and 4th of May, in Walch, L. W., xvi., p. 140.

[4] Spalatin, Leben Friedrichs des Weisen, p. 60.

cautious counsel and downright hostility.   Philip of Hessen came to his
assistance at the right moment ; Duke George and Duke Henry took the
field about the same time, and four princes thus marched with their forces
to meet the peasants.

Münzer had taken up a position on the rising ground above Frankenhausen, which commands the whole length of the valley ; the spot was
well chosen for preaching to assembled multitudes, but offered no advantages whatever for defence.   He showed utter incapacity : he had not even
provided powder for his laboriously cast guns ; his followers were miserably
armed, and had only entrenched themselves behind a feeble barricade of
waggons.   The prophet who had said so much about the force of arms,
and who had threatened to destroy all the ungodly with the edge of the
sword, was now reduced to reckon on a miracle, which he saw announced
in the portent of a coloured circle round the sun at noon.   At the first
discharge of the enemy's artillery the peasants sang a hymn ; they were
totally routed, and the greater number killed.   Hereupon the panic
which accompanies a half accomplished crime seized the whole country.
All the troops of peasants dispersed, and all the towns surrendered ; even
Mühlhausen attempted hardly any resistance.[1]   Münzer was executed in
the camp before Mühlhausen, where for a time he had reigned.   He seemed
possessed by a savage demon up to his last hour.   When, under the pangs
of torture, he was reminded of the countless number he had led into
destruction, he burst into a loud laugh, and said it was their own desire.
When he was led out to death he could not remember the articles of faith.

At this conjuncture movements were made in all directions for attacking
the forces of the peasants.

Duke Antony of Lorraine came with the various garrisons from Champagne and Burgundy, and a few companies of German landsknechts and
reiters, to the assistance of the Landvogt of Mörsperg in Alsatia.   He cut
off some scattered troops in the open field, after which, those who had
assembled in Zabern capitulated ; they were, however, accused of having
made a subsequent attempt to gain over the landsknechts, and were
attacked and slaughtered to the number of seventeen thousand, as they
were leaving the fortress on the morning of the 17th of May.[2]

Thus Würtemberg once more fell into the hands of the Swabian League,
whose general, Truchsess, having in a great degree secured his rear by a
treaty with the peasantry around the lakes, marched upon the Würtemberg insurgents, whom he encountered at Sindelfingen, and having first
thrown them into disorder with his field artillery, he charged and cut them
down with his numerous and well-armed cavalry.   Having then taken
and garrisoned a succession of towns and cities, he marched on Franconia.
There he was joined by the other two princes who had fought against
Sickingen,—the Electors of Treves and the Palatinate, who marched to
meet him from Bruchsal, which had just fallen into their hands.   The
two armies united on the 29th of May, in the open field between Helspach
and Neckarsulm.   They made up together a force of two thousand five

---

[1] Die Histori Thomä Muntzers des Aufengers der Döringischen Urfur.''
Hagenau.—This book contains the well-known narrative of Melanchthon, also
to be found in Luther's works (Altenb., iii. 126).

[2] Bellay, No. III.   Account by Rappoltstein in Vogt's Rheinisch. Gesch.,
vol. iv., p. 49.

hundred horse, and eight thousand foot, and marched on into Franconia.[1]

It was a most important advantage to them that the castle of Würzburg still held out against two powerful bodies of Franconian peasants. At first, indeed, the garrison would have consented to accept the twelve articles, and had already received authority from the bishop to do so ; a part of the peasants were anxious to come to terms, which would enable them to go to the assistance of their allies, hard pressed on all sides. But the citizens of Würzburg, determined to get rid of the castle, which had always been a bridle in their jaws, contrived that the conditions offered to the garrison should be such as it was impossible it should accept. Hereupon the latter resolved to resist to the utmost. Sebastian von Rotenhan, who had so greatly promoted the interests of the Lutheran doctrines in the Council of Regency, had supplied the fortress with every requisite, even with powder mills ; erected chevaux-de-frise within the ditches, and palisades all round the castle, and had induced the garrison to swear with uplifted hands that they would stand the storming bravely and faithfully. On the 15th of May, the day of the battle of Frankenhausen, the peasants began the storm at nine o'clock at night, to the sound of trumpets and fifes, with loud shouts and flying colours. Pitch, brimstone, and other combustibles were thrown down on them from the castle, and incessant firing kept up from every loop-hole in the walls and tower. The lonely castle reared its head in haughty grandeur amid the many-coloured glare of the fire with which it kept off the wild hordes that had overrun Franconia, and now threatened all Germany. The artillery decided the victory here, as at Sindelfingen and Frankenhausen ; at two in the morning the peasants retreated.[2]

A second assault was entirely out of the question ; they received news of the defeat of their friends on all sides, and the storm impending over themselves became every moment more near and threatening.

They made one more effort to save themselves by negotiating ; they again offered the twelve articles to the acceptance of the garrison of Würzburg, and invited Truchsess, the general of the League, who was marching upon them, to appoint time and place for an interview for the purpose of negotiation. In a general address to the States of the empire, they endeavoured to set their views and objects in a favourable light ; and called upon the Franconian states especially to send delegates to Schweinfurt, that they might take counsel together with them, "for the establishment of the word of God, of peace and of justice."[3] But all this was now too late. They had never had confidence in their own strength, and now fortune had deserted them : they must either remain masters of the field or perish.

The united army advanced against them without delay ; all the places it passed in its march surrendered unconditionally. On the 2nd of June it fell in with the first troop of peasants at Königshofen : it was the band from the Odenwald which had had the courage to advance against the

---

[1] The autograph diary of the Count Palatine Otto Heinrich, in Freiberg's *Urkunden und Schriften*, iv., p. 367, gives these numbers.

[2] Johann Reinhard, in Ludwig, 889.

[3] Proclamation in Ochsle, of the 27th of May, p. 302. The meeting was fixed for the 31st day of May.

victorious enemy.   But it consisted of not more than four thousand men,[1] and all their measures were thoroughly ill-concerted.   The peasants had neglected to guard the fords of the Tauber, and had encamped round their baggage, within a barricade of waggons, on the Mühlberg ; and it would have been well for them if they had awaited the attack of the enemy even there ; but, terrified by the superior force which gradually presented itself, they endeavoured to reach a neighbouring forest, and thus invited an immediate assault.   The cavalry fell upon their exposed flank, the princes themselves helping to cut them down ; in the twinkling of an eye, before even the landsknechts could come up, the whole body of peasants was entirely broken and routed.[2]   A false rumour of victory induced the Rothenberg troop to quit its position near Würzburg, and on the 4th of June that also fell into the hands of the cavalry in an open field, between Sulzdorf and Ingolstadt, and was completely dispersed.   Both victories were accompanied by the most barbarous massacres.   Of six hundred peasants who attempted to defend themselves in a fortified house near Ingolstadt, all but seventeen were put to the sword.

A third band which was connected with the Thuringian insurgents was overthrown and routed, after a short conflict, on the Bildberg near Meiningen, where they had entrenched themselves behind waggons, by Elector John of Saxony.[3]   The mild and placable prince promised safety to all who would surrender themselves to his protection.

Thus the great Franconian bands, which had thought to reform the whole of Germany, were destroyed like those of Alsatia, Thuringia, and Würtemberg ; and, like those provinces, Franconia was now garrisoned and chastised by its former masters.

On the 7th of June, Würzburg was forced to surrender at discretion. The aged members of the town council assembled in the market-place and bared their grey heads to salute the leaders of the army of the League ; but they found no mercy from Truchsess, who declared that they were all perjured and dishonoured, and had forfeited their lives.   In Würzburg alone, sixty rebels from the town and country were hanged : the executions were equally frequent and terrible throughout the whole bishopric ; two hundred and eleven were put to death in different ways ; all arms delivered up, new services imposed, and heavy contributions extorted : the ancient ceremonies of the church were restored.   Meanwhile Markgrave Casimir of Brandenburg, having taken possession of all the rest of Franconia, of Bamberg, Schweinfurt, and Rothenburg, without encountering any serious resistance, proceeded to take vengeance on the insurgents in his own territories.

All that now remained was, to subdue the remnant of the insurgents who still kept their ground on the Upper and Middle Rhine.

The armies of Trier and the Palatinate, on their homeward march, fell

---

[1] I hold this to be the true number, as the report of Secretary Speiss, who accompanied the army (Ochsle, p. 197), and the Journal of the Elector, p. 368, agree on this point.   Others mention far greater numbers.

[2] Brower, Annales Trevirenses; lib. xx., p. 353.

[3] Spalatin, see Menken, ii. 1114.   The peasants had one carronade, sixteen cannons and mortars, four arquebusses, and matchlocks.   Their waggons were buried in the earth.

in with the insurgents of the Middle Rhine at Pfeddersheim,[1] and as on all former occasions the peasants were dispersed and cut down ; the warlike archbishop is said to have slain several with his own hand.   These districts hereupon submitted ; and even the people of the Rheingau had to give up their arms, and to pay contributions.   Mainz was forced to resign the liberties it had but just regained ; while the people of Trier, happy that they had not made any serious demonstration, readily dropped all the projects they had entertained.

The great army of the League on the Upper Rhine found a far more arduous task ; it was there that the rebellion had originated and taken the deepest root, and nothing decisive had yet been accomplished towards its suppression.   The men of the Allgau reappeared in the field ; they had occupied a very strong post on a steep hill, at the foot of which is the river Luidas, and on either side, large ponds : a considerable number of experienced landsknechts fought in their ranks.   They were able to keep their ground against even the artillery of Truchsess, and indeed had some intention of beginning the attack.   Fortunately for Truchsess, the veteran and successful leader, George Frundsberg, came to his assistance in time. It is highly probable [2] that he exercised a personal influence on many of the peasant chiefs, his old comrades and followers.   Contemporary writers positively affirm that he bought over Walter Bach, who treacherously persuaded the peasants to abandon their strong position.   Perhaps, however, their stores failed ; at all events they separated, and retreated towards the mountains.   Truchsess hastened in pursuit of them, and began to burn their farms and villages.   This was in direct violation of the orders of the League, at which he only laughed ; he, he said, a peasant himself, understood his business better ; he knew that this was the way to make every man think of his own home.   He kept his troops together and thus easily beat the separate bands of peasants whenever he met with them.   He was not, however, so absolutely master as at Würzburg.   George Truchsess was at last obliged to enter into a compact with the large body of rebels who held together on the Kolenberg, by which redress of the local grievances of their several villages was promised them.   Not till then did they lay down their arms and give up their ringleaders.[3]

At the same moment, Count Felix of Werdenberg put to the rout the peasants of the Hegau, Kletgau, and all that remained in the Schwarzwald —for many were gone home to their harvest—and compelled them to lay down their arms.[4]

Thus was arrested the great movement which threatened the total subversion of the whole existing order of things in Germany : all the schemes for reconstituting the empire from the groundwork of society upwards, or still more, for visionary changes in the order of the world under the guidance of a fanatical prophet, were now for ever at an end.

Wherever the matter had been decided by arms, the laws of war were enforced.   The most barbarous executions took place ; the severest contributions were exacted ; and in some places, laws more oppressive than ever were imposed.

[1] Haarer, c. 84-89.
[2] Reisner, Kriegsthaten der Frundsberge.
[3] Haggenmüller Kempten, p. 540.
[4] Walchner Ratolphzell, p. 109.

It was only in districts where the peasants had not sustained a total defeat, that, after all their former vague and ambitious projects had spontaneously died away, some alleviation of their burthens and sufferings was granted them.

The Count of Sulz and his subjects agreed to refer their differences to arbitrators chosen in common, and Archduke Ferdinand consented to appoint a chief umpire.[1]

To the people of the Breisgau, Ferdinand promised in his own name that due regard should be paid by magistrates and government officers to the complaints of the subjects.[2] The states of Upper Austria would not allow contributions to be levied upon the people.[3]

In Tyrol, steps were taken under the influence of the disturbances, towards drawing up a code of laws, whereby the subjects were relieved from all taxes that could not be proved by authentic documents, to have existed for more than fifty years; likewise from the lesser tithes in kind, and a variety of other dues and services; and the right of fishing, and even of shooting and hunting, granted them. Archduke Ferdinand also made concessions as to religion. Towns and councils were empowered to appoint their own clergy, and the Gospel was to be preached according to the letter.[4]

Salzburg was the only country in which the peasants kept the field against the advance of a regular army; and even when they were forced to bend before the might of the Swabian League, they began by making singularly advantageous terms.[5]

These events belong, however, to another state of things, which immediately followed the disturbances, and to which we will now turn our attention.

CHAPTER VII.

FORMATION OF THE ADVERSE RELIGIOSU LEAGUES—DIET OF AUGSBURG, DECEMBER, 1525.

THE conflict between the elements of German society was now at an end; the rebellious peasantry, and that portion of the population of the towns which took part with them, were subdued, as the knights had been before them. The local powers which had arisen during the course of ages had again withstood all the storms by which they were assailed: aided by the emperor or the Council of Regency, they had stood fast amidst the ruin of all central authority.

Nevertheless, peace was by no means restored, nor was one of those great questions which had so long occupied public attention decided.

The rebellion had been put down without any reference to religious creed; friends and foes of the new doctrines had taken up arms with equal eagerness against the common enemy; but as soon as that enemy was subdued, the old antipathies broke out with fresh violence.

---

[1] The treaty which the people of Zurich helped to negotiate is to be found in Bullinger's Reformations-geschichte, i., p. 249.

[2] The treaty of Offenburg: extract in Schreiber's Taschenbuch, p. 302.

[3] Declaration of the Stände, Bucholtz, viii., p. 104.

[4] Excerpts from the proceedings of the diet, Bucholtz, viii., p. 337.

[5] Zauner, Chronik von Salzburg, iv., p. 429.

The Ratisbon members of the Swabian League, who at this time exercised the chief influence in that body, seized upon this opportunity of carrying into execution by main force the measures which had been concerted at that city. The victories of the League were everywhere followed by religious persecutions. Among those who were beheaded at Würzburg, many were condemned, not for the rebellion, in which they had taken no part, but for the crime of professing the evangelical faith. Nine of the most wealthy burghers were executed at Bamberg, and it is asserted that some of them were remarkable for their peaceable conduct, and had rather tried to prevent than to encourage the attack of the country people on the bishop's palace ; they were punished, as was openly proclaimed, for their adherence to the evangelical party.[1] Their possessions were, by an unexampled exercise of arbitrary power, given to certain individuals, among whom was a secretary of Truchsess. All who professed the evangelical doctrines immediately fled out of both bishoprics. But even in all other territories, spiritual as well as temporal obedience was enforced on the peasantry ; the Lutherans stood—under that title—first on the list of those excluded from pardon. The bitterest persecution was directed against the preachers. A provost-marshal of the name of Aichili traversed Swabia and Franconia in all directions at the head of a band of reiters, in order to carry into effect the executions that had been decreed ; it is calculated that within a small district, he hung forty evangelical preachers on trees by the roadside.[2] This was the first restoration of Catholicism by violence in Upper Germany.

Similar attempts were now made also in the north.

After the taking of Mühlhausen, the allied princes had agreed on common measures against the peasants. Duke George relates, that one morning, as his son-in-law Philip was just setting off on a journey, he (Duke George) went to him once more, and entreated him not to attach himself to Luther's cause, "in consideration of the evil which had flowed therefrom;" that he repeated this warning to the Elector of Saxony within the same hour, and that it was kindly received by both of them. Duke George hoped to exercise great authority over his cousin John after Frederick's death, as well as over Landgrave Philip, to whom he stood in the relation of an affectionate father-in-law.

These three princes had agreed at Mühlhausen to communicate their resolutions to their neighbours ; and Duke George had an interview as early as in July with the electors of Mainz and Brandenburg and the Duke of Brunswick, at Dessau. These princes still adhered to the Catholic faith, and they allowed their belief, that the insurrection owed its existence to the new doctrines that had been preached, to influence their resolutions. Though we have no authentic document as to the nature of these resolutions, there is sufficient evidence that they were in the highest degree unfavourable to the religious changes. Duke George communicated them to his cousin and his son-in-law, expressing at the same time his persuasion

---

[1] Detailed account in Müllner's Annalen.

[2] Bullinger's 140th cap. treats of Provost Aichili (" von Profossen Aichili "). Anshelm also mentions him (vi., p. 291) as being peculiarly active against the Lutheran parsons : he seized, plundered, mulcted, and hanged them. " Er war sunderlich gflissen, uf die lutherischen Pfaffen, fiengs' beroubts' schatzts' und henkts'."

that they had ceased to entertain any Lutheran ideas.[1]   At all events he
did not suffer himself to be deterred by any consideration for them, from
condemning his own subjects to the severest punishments.   At Leipzig
two citizens were beheaded for no other reason than that some Lutheran
books had been found in their possession.[2]

It appeared probable that the Lutheran movement, from the time it
was associated with an insurrection of the peasantry, would, like that of
Wicklyffe, be encountered by a reaction which would end in its entire
suppression.

But the reform set on foot by Luther stood on a far wider and firmer
basis than that of Wicklyffe, and had already found resolute and powerful
supporters both in North and South Germany.

Landgrave Philip even brought an evangelical preacher with him to
Mühlhausen ; and Duke George, while in the act of expressing his conviction of his son-in-law's altered sentiments, was struck with surprise at
the appearance of this man.   From that time Philip had become more and
more deeply imbued with Lutheran opinions.   We have only to read the
letters he wrote to Duke George during this year,—in which he controverts
the doctrine of the canon and the mass, the received idea of the Church,
and the obligation of vows,—in order to see with what lively and yet
earnest zeal he adopted the new doctrines, and what accurate and extensive
knowledge he had acquired of the scriptural grounds on which they rested.[3]

The same state of things existed in Saxony.   Far from forsaking the
path trodden by his predecessor, the new elector advanced in it with far
more decided steps than Frederick had done.   On leaving Weimar in
August, 1525, he once more assembled the priesthood of that district—on
the 16th of that month—and, after causing their minds to be prepared by
two sermons, he announced to them that in future they were to preach the
pure word of God, without any human additions.[4]   Some old priests who

---

[1] The only authentic notice of these meetings is to be found in a letter from
Duke George in the Dresden Archives.   According to that, the determination
was " to stand by each other in case the Lutherans attacked any one of them,
in order to remain at peace from such rebellion."—" sich bei einander finden zu
lassen, wenn die Lutherischen einen von ihnen angreifen würden, um solches
Aufruhrs vertragen zu bleiben."   It is not, however, easy to perceive from
whom they expected an attack, if they really believed Philip and the Elector
John to have been reconverted ; and, indeed, Duke George says, " otherwise
he would not have made them a party to the treaty, for he well knew that one
could not beat Swiss with Swiss."—" denn sonst würde er ihnen den Vertrag
nicht mitgetheilt haben, er wisse wohl, dass man Schweizer mit Schweizern nich
schlage."   The explanation is, that in those times a defensive form was given
to all alliances, even when there was no intention of abiding by mere defence.
Duke Henry said to the emperor, that he had signed a treaty with his friends,
" against the Lutherans, in case they should attempt by force or cunning to
gain them over to their unbelief,"—" wider die Lutherischen, ob sie sich unter-
stünden, sie mit List oder Gewalt in ihren Unglauben zu bringen."

[2] Gretschel : Leipzigs kirchliche Zustände, p. 218.

[3] Rommel's Urkundenbuch, p. 2.

[4] " Das man das lauter rayn evangelion on menschliche Zusatzung predigen
soll, fürstlicher Befelch zu Weymar beschehen."—" That the pure Gospel should
be preached without any human additions.   Sovereign command issued at
Weimar."—Circular from the minister Kisswetter at Erfurt to Master Hainrich
at Elxleben, a.d. Gera, 1525.

were present having expressed the opinion that this would not be inconsistent with their saying masses for the dead and consecrating salt and water, they were told that the same rule applied to ceremonies as to doctrines.

In consequence of the recess of Mühlhausen, the elector had an interview with Markgrave Casimir of Brandenburg at Saalfeld, at which the evangelical tendencies predominated as much as the catholic had done at Dessau. These princes did not indeed form a regular alliance, but Markgrave Casimir declared that he would hold fast by the word of God.[1]

At the very time when the military force of the Swabian League was employed in checking the progress of the reformation, some of its most powerful members, the very towns in which it had originated,—Augsburg and above all, Nürnberg—organised their churches according to evangelical principles.   We shall return to this subject in another place.

The territory of Würtemberg, which had been conquered by the League, and could hardly have been imagined capable of taking any resolutions of its own, now declared itself on the same side ; the Estates expressed their conviction that the tranquillity of the country could only be maintained by preaching to the people the pure word of God, unalloyed by the selfishness and vain conceits of men.

Already the evangelical preachers began formally to emancipate themselves from the authority of the bishops.   At Wittenberg, in May 1525, they determined to give ordination themselves.   Melanchthon justifies this on the ground that the bishops neglected their duties.[2]   The preachers now asserted their underived vocation as against the bishops, in the same manner as those had done against the pope.   Melanchthon says that the princes could not be called upon to support a jurisdiction of whose abusive and corrupt nature they were convinced.   In Hessen and Brandenburg too, even in the towns, the clergy began to emancipate themselves from the episcopal jurisdiction.

We perceive that the two opposite tendencies came out of the conflict with the peasants, exactly in the same state in which they entered into it ; only with increased activity on either side.

The papal party had the advantage, in so far as in a great part of the empire, the penal power, of which it made such fearful use, was in its hands ; but on the whole, the evangelical party had gained still more in the struggle.

Never had the aversion to the spiritual part of the constitution of Germany been so general and so avowed.   The clergy were accused of those acts of grinding oppression which had mainly caused the revolt.   The hostility of the people was specially directed against them ; the peasants of the Allgau, for example, who were besieging Füssen, raised the siege as soon as that town threw off its allegiance to its lord, the Bishop of Augsburg, and hoisted the banner of Austria.   On the other hand, though the ecclesiastical princes had contributed very little to extinguish the flame of rebellion, they now made the most tyrannical and merciless use of the victory won by others.

[1] According to a description by Casimir himself in a letter from Schrauttenbach to the Landgrave Philip, dated 27th Dec., 1525, in Neudeckers Urkunden, p. 16.
[2] De Jure Reformandi.   Corp. Reform., i., p. 765.

Hence it happened that the evangelical party found it so easy to shake off the episcopal authority ; it is, however, more remarkable that an analogous effect was produced in the catholic party. If the one side questioned the spiritual, the other no less vigorously attacked the temporal jurisdiction.

We must here again recur to the events of Tyrol and Salzburg. Archduke Ferdinand had taken up the most remarkable position in the world.

At the diet of Tyrol, which we have already mentioned, there were assembled only the nobles, the cities, and rural districts (*Gerichte*) ;[1] the ecclesiastical body did not appear. The anti-ecclesiastical temper which this produced was very strongly expressed in the resolutions that were passed. In the recess of this diet it was proclaimed, that the appointment to the inferior situations in the church should be rendered totally independent of the bishops ; in future, cities and rural districts (*Gerichte*) should have the right of presentation, which the sovereign of the country should confirm, and all complaints of the clergy should be addressed by the former to the latter.[2] The petition of the Bishop of Trent for leave to call in foreign troops to punish the insurgents within his see, was refused ; for the common people were of opinion, says Ferdinand, that the clergy ought to have no jurisdiction whatever in temporal affairs ; were such a permission granted to the bishop, the nobles would complain that he was goading the people to a fresh revolt, which would bring trouble and ruin upon them also.[3] This was even carried much further. The Bishop of Brixen proving himself incapable of restoring order in his see, where one of his secretaries and toll collectors was the leader of the revolt, the Tyrolese determined not to afford him the least assistance, but at once to secularise the see. Archduke Ferdinand took possession of it, and committed the government to one of his council, "till some future council, or the reformation of the empire ;" he received the homage from all the vassals and the official persons of the see.[4] The captain of Ehrenberg, which was garrisoned by Tyrolese, would not go to the succour of the town of Füssen till it surrendered itself as an hereditary fief to the house of Austria, and did

[1] *Gericht* here means a certain community. Grimm (Deutsche Rechts Alterthümer, p. 755) says, " By *Gericht* we now understand a tribunal for the decision of litigated matters, or the punishment of offences. Originally, however, the predominant idea was that of a popular assembly (concilium), in which all the public business of the Mark, the commune, or the district was discussed, disputes settled, and fines adjudged. The main element of the *Gericht* is now the judges ; but then, it was the congregated free men. . . . All judicial power was exercised by the community of free men under the presidency of an elected or hereditary head."—TRANSL.

[2] Bucholtz, viii., p. 338.

[3] Ferdinand to Bishop Bernhard of Trent, Inspruck, 9th July, 1525 Bucholtz, ix., p. 640.

[4] Patent of occupation, 21st July. " Auf Beger und mit Rat ainer ersamen Landschaft dieser unsrer f. G. Tirol,—zu furkumung nachtail schadens und geferlichait, so dieselben unser Grafschaft und dem Stift zu Brichsen, des Vogt Schirm und Schutzherr wir dann sein, enstehen mechten."—" At the request and with the advice of the honourable province of this our free country of Tirol —for the prevention of loss, damage, and danger, which might accrue to our country and the see of Brichsen, whereof we are bailiff, lord, and protector."

homage to the Archduke.[1]   The Zillerthalers were thus enabled to throw
off their allegiance to Salzburg, to attach themselves to Tyrol, and to accept
the Archduke, who had already high authority over them, as their lord
and sovereign.[2]   Nay, even in Bavaria, similar notions prevailed.   When
Matthew, Archbishop of Salzburg, was besieged in his citadel by the
peasants, and reduced to the greatest extremity, Doctor Lesch, a Bavarian
chancellor, presented himself before the archduke and proposed to him to
sequester the archbishopric in common ; so that the part lying on the con-
fines of Bavaria should be taken possession of by the dukes, and that bordering on Austria by the archduke.   Ferdinand joyfully acceded to the
proposal ; he authorised the commissioners he had sent to the peasants
to use all their endeavours (but with the knowledge of the archbishop)
that the see might be given up to Austria and Bavaria.[3]   In Bavaria,
however, this was only a transient thought ; the plan here pursued was
that of an unconditional restoration, from the accomplishment of which
the dukes might justly expect a still greater degree of authority than they
had already acquired, over the neighbouring bishoprics.   They therefore
furnished aid in every direction.   In Tyrol, on the other hand, the province
had agreed with the prince on the concessions to be made to the rebels ;
by a resolute postponement of spiritual interests, they thought they should
at once allay the tumults and enhance their own liberty and power.   The
Bavarians, consequently, soon abandoned the plans above mentioned,
and resolved to come to the assistance of the archbishop in this exigency
with the forces of the Swabian League.   The motives which determined
the dukes were not, however, of a very disinterested nature ; they calculated on this opportunity of securing the succession to the archbishopric
for their brother, Ernest of Passau ; which they preferred to contributing
to place the greater part of it in the hands of Austria, and thence in a hostile
relation to themselves.   In vain the states of Tyrol made an attempt to
restrain the Swabian League from its intended campaign, by representations of the ancient privileges and alliances of Salzburg.[4]   At Innsbruck a
strong desire prevailed to secure the succession to Don George of Austria,
natural son of Emperor Maximilian, and a disposition to afford protection
to the peasantry.[5]   But the dukes had already the advantage.   Duke
Louis of Bavaria, the general in chief of the Swabian League, led its armies

---

[1] Martin Furtenbach, the town notary at Füssen : report on the insurrection
of the peasants, in Ochsle's Beiträge, p. 478.   " Das Volk schrie Hei Oestreich
damit wir nicht gar verderbt werden, der Hauptmann nahm die Erbhuldigung
auf ein Hintersichbringen an."—" The people cried, ' Hey Austria,' so that we
might not be entirely ruined : the governor received our hereditary homage on
a hint given him."   The delegates of the town went to Innsbruck, and were
there well greeted (wohl begrüsst).   Ferdinand declared that he would soon go
there himself and receive the homage in person.

[2] Instruction to Liechtenstein and Stöckel, " was sy mit dem Pfleger zu
Kropfsberg, mit der Nachparschaft im Zillerthal reden sollen."—" what they
should say to the parish priest at Kropfsberg, and to the neighbourhood in Zillerthal."—Bucholtz, ix., p. 630.

[3] Instruction of Ferdinand to the mediating commissioners, Bucholtz, p. 621.

[4] " Die vom Ausschuss der drei Stände—an Hauptleute und Räthedes
Pundts zu Schwaben 31 Juli."—*Ib.*, ix., pi 624.—" The committee of the three
estates to the governors and councillors of the Swabian League."

[5] Excerpts from a rescript of Ferdinand, *ib.*, viii., p. 109.

against Salzburg at the end of August.   He too deemed it expedient, and strongly urged George Frundsberg, who was general of the county of Tyrol, at first to grant the peasants a favourable treaty—afterwards, indeed, they were as severely dealt with here as elsewhere—as a means of attaining all their other objects.   The chapter of the cathedral promised the succession to the bishopric of Salzburg to the Bavarian prince Ernest, to whom the archbishop also made some concessions; the lordships of Laufen, Geisfelden, Titmanning, and Mattsee were mortgaged to the dukes for the expenses of the war.   In short, they obtained a general ascendancy in Salzburg ; nor was it till some time afterwards that the archbishop took courage timidly to admonish them to demand nothing of him at variance with the rights and dignities of his see.[1]

Thus, as we see, the plans of the League triumphed over the inclinations of the people of Tyrol.   The archduke was also forced to cede Füssen again to Augsburg, and the Zillerthal to Salzburg.

Notwithstanding this, Ferdinand did not relinquish the ideas he had once conceived.   When the Würtemberg territory made the demands we have mentioned, and pointed very unequivocally to a secularisation of the church lands, as a means of meeting the exigencies of the country, Ferdinand showed not the smallest displeasure : he permitted that country to send deputies to the approaching diet at Augsburg, and promised that whatever should there be determined in regard to a reformation of the clergy, should be carried into effect, as well in Würtemberg as in his other dominions.[2] The views entertained on these points by Archduke Ferdinand entirely coincided with those of the evangelical party, who, with perfect justice, regarded the revocation of the summons for the meeting at Spire as the immediate cause of the recent tumults.   In the autumn of 1525 the project of settling the religious differences at an assembly of the empire and of there proceeding to a thorough reformation, was once more universally stirred.

In addition to the meetings in Dessau and Saalfeld, there was a third and corresponding one between the Landgrave Philip and the Elector Palatine, at Alzey.   They agreed " that things must be put on an equitable footing :" every means must be employed to bring about union among the States.[3]

Markgrave Casimir proceeded from Saalfeld to Auerbach, to a conference with the Count Palatine Frederick, who governed the Upper Palatinate in the name of his nephew.   They determined, in the first place, to lighten the burthens of the common people as much as possible ; and in the next, again to petition the emperor to hold an ecclesiastical council in the German nation, " in order to come to some common understanding as to the exposition of the divine word."

In September the cities held a meeting, and Ferdinand thought he had reason to fear very hostile and objectionable resolutions on their part ;

[1] Zauner, Salzburger Chronik, v., pp. 225, 133.
[2] Extractus landschaftlicher Schlusserklärung bei Sattler, Herzoge, Beilagen zum zweiten Theil nr. 124, and Landtagsabschied, 30th Oct., 1525, nr. 125 (iii. i. 4).
[3] Letter from the Elector Louis of the Palatinate, in Neudeckers Actenstücken, i., p. 16.   From the words, " von E. L. und unserm Freund, von ir und uns,"— from E. L. and our friend, from him and from us " we may conclude that the Elector of Trier was also there present.

but their decision only amounted to this : to urge anew upon himself and the emperor the necessity of introducing a clear and uniform order into the whole empire, with respect to the ceremonies of the church.

In the universal discussion of these subjects, every possible change was suggested, and thus ideas and plans of the most extraordinary nature became current.

In a project drawn up towards the end of the year 1525, and discussed at one or two meetings of the empire, it is assumed in the outset, that the property of the church is no longer of any use or benefit either to religion or to the empire : that some change in the disposition of it is therefore indispensable ; that this must not, however, be left to the common people, but must be undertaken by the supreme authorities ; *i.e.* by the emperor and the temporal Estates.

People no longer scrupled to propose the secularisation of all ecclesiastical property.

So much might, they said, be assigned to the spiritual princes and prelates as was necessary for the maintenance of a suitable mode of living ; nor should anything, for the present, be taken from the canons, but both they and their superiors should be allowed gradually to die out. Of the convents, a few might be retained for young women of noble birth, but with full right and liberty to quit them.

With the funds thus obtained, the first care must be to supply the new spiritual wants ; to appoint pastors and preachers ; to nominate in every circle a pious and learned man as bishop, with a fixed salary, but wholly wihout temporal functions, and solely a superintendent of the other ministers of the church ; and, lastly, to establish a high school in every circle, in which the languages and the exposition of the Holy Scriptures according to their true sense, should be taught.

But the party which suggested these reforms also entertained the hope that they should thus acquire strength to give a new form to the whole secular constitution of the country.

The proposal to that effect contained in this project is, to establish a particular Council of Regency, or administrative body, in each circle ; consisting of twelve councillors, three from each of the four estates, sovereigns, princes,—counts and lords (nobles),—and imperial cities ; and a chief or president, chosen from the states of the circle, but approved by the emperor, with nearly the same powers as the governors and the councillors of the Swabian League. This body was to put in execution all the plans determined on by the States ; to form a supreme court of judicature, and, above all, to maintain the public peace, and for that purpose to keep a standing force of horse and foot always in the field. The young nobility were to serve in the army, instead of occupying the posts in the chapters. With these troops any succours granted by the emperor and the empire could then be rendered effective, without imposing burdens on anybody. They would constitute so great a permanent force as no emperor had had at his command since the birth of Christ.[1]

[1] " Ràthschlag was man mit geistlichen Gütern zu gemeinem und des Reichs Nutz furnemen und handeln soll."—" Opinion as to what should be done with ecclesiastical property for the common good and that of the empire." In the Weimar Records. It is indeed true that this is among the acts of 1526, but as the diet of Augsburg is mentioned in it, it was doubtless originally intended for that.

The particular provisions of this project are far less important and interesting than the general ideas upon which it is founded :—the secularisation of ecclesiastical property ; the empire represented exclusively by temporal estates (the constitution of which was mainly based upon the extension of the functions of the circles) ; a standing army specially for the advantage of the young nobles :—all things which, in their mature and finished form, gave their character to the succeeding centuries, and constituted modern Germany.   The most distant results were boldly contemplated, but the way that led to them was long and arduous.

The ecclesiastical princes were yet far too strong : and it may easily be imagined that plans of the kind above mentioned, which could not remain concealed from them, would make them feel the necessity of collecting all their strength.   The clergy already complained that they were kept out of possession of many things, of which they had been robbed during the late commotions ; and even that their enemies proceeded in depriving them of their accustomed jurisdiction ; they showed a determination not to await the attack at the next diet, but to press for a complete restitution of their rights and possessions.   To this course they were emboldened by a rescript of the emperor, in which mention was made of the suppression of all things that threatened the destruction of our holy faith, and in such severe terms as seemed to imply that an entire restoration of the old order of things was contemplated.[1]   The Council of Regency which was sitting in Esslingen, and of which we now hear once more, prepared to propose measures in the same spirit.[2]   The course taken by the Swabian League was nearly the same.   At a meeting held by that body in November, it received a letter from Pope Clement, exhorting it to show the same zeal in the completion of the work, that had inspired the first undertaking of it, and to finish the most glorious deed that had been done for centuries.[3]   The sovereigns of eastern Germany felt in the same manner ; the instruction given by Duke George to his delegate at the diet is still extant.   After vehement complaints of the enormous mischief done by the Lutheran Gospel, he demands that no change shall be made in the traditional ordinances without the sanction of a general council ; adding, that even if an angel should come down from heaven he was not to be obeyed, unless in a full Christian assembly.[4]   Moreover a papal nuncio was sent to attend the diet.

The idea of a change was, it is true, as widely diffused as it was comprehensive ; but the opposite tendency, towards the maintenance of the

---

[1] Tolleten in Castilien, 24th May, 1525 (W. A.).

[2] Feilitsch, Esslingen, Monday after St. Martin's day : " Er hält genzlichen dafür, dass von denen die sich der Aufruhr theilhaftig gemacht, auch denen die Kirchen und Klöster gewaltig zerstört, denselbigen Güter eingenommen und davon wieder geben was ihnen gefällig, dass wider diese auf dem Reichstag gehandelt werden soll."—" He was entirely of opinion that the property should be taken from those who had been parties to the seditious movements, and who had violently destroyed churches and convents, and that such of it should be restored as they thought fit.   Proceedings against these persons should be taken at the diet."

[3] Papal Brief, delivered in November.   Ochsle, p. 305.

[4] Instruction to Otto v. Pack in the Dresden Archives.   It also contains some censure of Luther's marriage ;—" that he and his Kate wanted as much for themselves alone as the whole Augustine convent had formerly required."

existing ecclesiastical institutions, or rather towards their restoration in their complete integrity, was still exceedingly powerful.   Even while the partisans of the new faith cherished the most sweeping schemes, they could not disguise from themselves that the diet might very possibly take a turn highly unfavourable to their wishes.   Some believed that the good and the bad would be destroyed together ; that truth would be suppressed together with falsehood ; that a rule of faith and life would be estab-lished in accordance with the old law, and that those who did not receive it willingly would be compelled by violence to conform to it.

As Elector John and Landgrave Philip had declared themselves most openly for the new doctrines, they had the greatest reason for fear.   The landgrave, because his territory was surrounded on all sides by puissant ecclesiastical princes ; the elector, because already there was an idea of depriving him of his electorate as a seceder from the Church of Rome ; he was advised to place himself on a better footing with his neighbours—doubtless especially with Duke George,—for that many intrigues were on foot against him in that direction.

It was less the view of effecting any change than the dread of danger to themselves, and the necessity of maintaining the position which they had taken up, that determined these two princes to enter into a closer alliance with each other.

Landgrave Philip made the first advances in this matter by sending his chamberlain, Rudolf of Waiblingen to Torgau, where Elector John was holding his court, charged with the proposal to combine with him in making a common resistance at the next diet, to any measures that might be attempted in support of abuses, or for the suppression of truth ; to accede to no ordinance at variance with the word of God, and to unite steadfastly to that end with all who held the same opinions.   This com-mission was received with great joy by the elector, with whose sentiments and convictions it so fully harmonised.   At the beginning of November his son John Frederick, set out to hold a conference with the landgrave, and to concert the course they were to pursue.[1]

The interview took place at the strongly defended hunting-seat of Friedewalt, in the Sullinger forest.   The two young princes perfectly understood each other.   There is in the Weimar archives a note of an opinion " of our dear cousin and brother the landgrave," in the hand-writing of John Frederick himself, which is, without doubt, the result of this conversation.   Its contents do not show that any actual treaty as yet existed ; the resolutions were such as the circumstances of the moment called forth : such as, that the contracting parties should come to a fuller understanding as to the evangelical cause, and should induce as many princes, counts, and cities of similar views as possible to join them (they had even the hope of gaining over the Elector of Trier) ; and should then enter a common protest against the expressions contained in the rescript, which were favourable to old usages, but pernicious to the word of God ; and that they should stand as one man for the evangelical cause.   The electoral court did not only approve these conditions, but

---

[1] Instruction in Rommel's Urkundenbuch, p. 10.   Credentials of the same date (5th Oct.) in the Weimar Records.   There is also a note of the answer that Waiblingen was to deliver to Torgau, 13th Oct.

thought it good to extend the agreement to other things, " in which one might be worse treated than the other."[1]

In the beginning of December the hostile parties thus met at Augsburg furnished with directly contrary instructions.

The same disagreement which prevailed among the deputies, manifested itself in the imperial commission.   This consisted (independently of Archduke Ferdinand, whose behaviour was necessarily ambiguous) of Duke William of Bavaria, the leader and champion of the papists, and Markgrave Casimir of Brandenburg, who had so long been attached to the evangelical party.   Casimir declined indeed to enter into the compact proposed to him by the envoys of Hessen and Saxony ; but he declared that he would advocate his own convictions in the commission, and thus, he urged, do more service to the cause than he could by joining a formal alliance.

Had the princes been present in person, the struggle must now have become vehement, earnest, and decisive ; it would soon have been clearly seen to which side the majority inclined.

But neither party was at bottom sincerely resolved on bringing matters to an issue.   Each saw too clearly what might be the consequences of such a decision : they wished to assemble all their forces, and to secure to themselves every kind of support.   The princes at Friedewalt thought it expedient to remove the diet of the empire immediately to Spire or to Worms. On the other side, the arrival of the Mainz deputy, without whom no step could be taken, inasmuch as he brought with him the imperial chancery, was unduly delayed.   No prince as yet appeared in person ; even the commission was not complete, and a great number of the deputies were still missing.

The first preliminary meeting was held on the eleventh of December. Archduke Ferdinand besought those who were assembled to have patience awhile, till a larger number arrived, and promised to report to the emperor the good dispositions of those present.[2]

But some weeks elapsed, and their numbers were little augmented : on the renewed application of the States, the commissioners at length held a definitive meeting on the 30th of December.[3]

It was evident to everybody that, considering the incompleteness of the assembly of the States, and the importance of the questions at issue, no permanent result could be obtained.   Duke William suggested whether it would not be better to adjourn the diet.   The three colleges separated, and were unanimously of that opinion.   They adjourned the diet to Spire,

[1] " Verzaichniss des Bedenkens unsres lieben Vetters und Bruders auf die vertreuliche Unterrede, so wir mit S. L. jetzo allhie gehabt, so vil das h. göttl. Wort belangen thut.   Friedewalt Mitw. nach Bernardi."—" Note of the opinion of our dear cousin and brother, expressed at our confidential meeting held here, so far as they concern the holy word of God.   Friedewalt, Wednesday after St. Bernard's day." (8th Nov.) The copy which was made in Torgau differs from the paper written in the prince's own hand in this respect :—the prince had only written that they would make an alliance together for the sake of the Gospel ; but in the copy the words above quoted are added :—" Auch sunsten in andern Sachen, do eyner vor dem andern Recht leyden kunt, ausgeschlossen gegen den, so in der Erbeynung sind."

[2] Letter from Feilitsch to the Elector John, 24th December.   Weimar Records.

[3] Feilitsch und Minkwitz to the Elector John, 2d Jan., 1526.

on the first of May ; there, however, they said, every prince must appear
in person ; " there they would with greater dignity treat of the holy faith,
of peace and justice."

In order, however, to have done at least something, and in consideration of the continued ferment among the people, a committee was appointed
to draw up a Recess.

The only remarkable circumstance as to this is, that the ordinances of
the foregoing diets of 1523 and 1524—that the Gospel should be preached
pure and intelligible, according to the interpretations of the received ex-
positors—was repeated, without any mention of the Fathers of the Latin
Church, or of the edict of Worms.   The States mutually agreed to hold
themselves prepared to put down instantly every attempt at insurrection ;
and so far restored to their rights and station those who had been declared
infamous on account of their participation in the disturbances, that the
latter were allowed to take part in the sittings of the courts of justice.[1]
They were so numerous that the village tribunals would otherwise have
been entirely at a stand.

The whole attention of the public, as well as its active measures of preparation, were now directed towards the approaching meeting, which,
indeed, proved to be decisive.

Saxony and Hessen had not as yet found the sympathy they expected
in their scheme of an evangelical league ; in fact, the Nürnberg deputies
alone had really shown an earnest inclination towards it : but this dis-
couragement did not induce those princes to abandon the idea: the two
ambassadors were of opinion that the affair must be undertaken with
redoubled vigour, in a personal interview between their respective
masters.

Meanwhile the other party also concentrated its forces.   The chapter of
the cathedral of Mainz brought forward its long-forgotten metropolitan
powers, and summoned the chapters of its suffragans to an assembly at the
mother-church.   The attention of this meeting was called to the danger
which threatened the clergy generally ; and the resolution was passed, to
send a deputation who should lay before the emperor and the pope a complaint that the spiritual jurisdiction was invaded by the temporal authorities ; to remind them of the services which the spiritual princes had, from
the earliest times, rendered to the empire and the church ; and to declare
that they were ready to perform similar and yet greater services in future,
but that, in return, they should expect their ancient privileges to be protected.   They thought it most expedient to entrust this protection to
certain princes who had not fallen off from the faith, whom they specified.[2]

The wishes of these princes seemed to tend to the same point.   Duke
George of Saxony and Duke Henry of Brunswick met at the residence of
the Elector of Mainz at Halle.   A few days after, we find them again at
Leipzig, together with the Bishop of Strasburg ; they too determined to

---

[1] Recess (Neue Samml.), ii. 271, §§ 1, 4. This was then looked upon as a
victory obtained by the Protestants.   Letters from the Nürnbergers, quoted by
Hortleder, i. viii. 1.   Spalatin Annales in Mencken, ii. 652 : " Concidit spes
sperantium, eo conventu totum Baalem restitutum, iri."

[2] Letter from Count Albert of Mansfeld, sent with a copy of the treaty, to
the Elector of Saxony, in the Weimar Records.   Letter from Waldenfels to
Vogler in v. d. Lith, p. 160.

address themselves to the emperor. They represented to him that, seeing the uninterrupted progress of the " damnable Lutheran doctrine," nothing could be expected but a repetition of the rebellion ; nay, even an open war, between the princes and lords themselves ; that attempts were daily made to draw them too over to the Lutheran party ; and, since these were not likely to succeed by amicable means, it seemed as if it were the design of the Lutherans to force them into it, by instigating their subjects to revolt. Against these attempts they now called upon the emperor for support.[1] Immediately after the meeting, Duke Henry of Brunswick went to Spain, thus throwing the weight of his personal solicitations into the balance.

Everything was thus prepared for the decisive battle. If the adherents of innovation found their strongest support in the sympathy of the nation, and in the mighty movement of the public mind generally ; on the other hand, the champions of the papacy were sustained by the natural strength of established institutions, and the resolute aversion of some powerful princes to all change.

But they now likewise sought to engage in their behalf the active interference of the two supreme authorities whose dignity was so intimately bound up with the spiritual constitution of the empire. They did not doubt that these potentates would bring all their influence to their aid.

But they thus came into contact with two great political powers which stood in very different relations to each other, from that which subsisted between them in Germany ;—a relation subject at every moment to be changed by the great events of Italy, and the course of European policy.

We shall be unable to understand the affairs of Germany, if we do not first devote our attention to these events : they are also important, as exhibiting another phase of the character and condition of the German people.

---

[1] Excerpt from a judgment given at Leipzig, quoted by Schmidt in his Deutsche Geschichte, viii., p. 202. Yet I know not whether this meeting took place a Leipzig or at Halle.